COGNITIVE PSYCHOLOGY

COGNITIVE PSYCHOLOGY

Douglas L. Medin

University of Michigan

Brian H. Ross

University of Illinois

Harcourt Brace Jovanovich College Publishers
Fort Worth   Philadelphia   San Diego   New York   Orlando   Austin   San Antonio
Toronto   Montreal   London   Sydney   Tokyo

For B.R.: To Cheri, Jocelyn, and Valerie
For D.M.: To a properly constrained "L"

PREFACE

For most of us, our everyday experience seems quite unremarkable. We move about pursuing goals, interacting with others, and responding to objects and events in our environment. Sometimes we are surprised but for the most part we have no difficulty making sense of the world. When we look beneath the surface of everyday experience, however, we see that what our cognitive system accomplishes is nothing short of amazing. In this book we will examine the what, why, and how of these accomplishments. Cognitive psychology is the study of the human mind; its domain includes questions concerning how people perceive the world, remember information, use knowledge, understand language, learn, reason, and solve problems. In each area one can show that an intelligent organism that objectively considers all possibilities is doomed to failure. It will not be able to learn a language, solve complex problems or understand events in the world as meaningful. For example, many readers may have looked at the cover of this book and wondered exactly what was being depicted. As we shall see in the chapter on perception, *any* visual input is consistent with an unlimited number of interpretations. The challenging question is how the perceptual system functions such that we are normally unaware of any ambiguity. Indeed our guesses about the world are so accurate that our experience is of simply seeing the world as it is, more or less directly.

Ambiguity is actually a quite general problem in cognition. In a sense we have organized this entire book around challenges posed by ambiguity. The world continually confronts us with situations that offer too little information about what is going on and too many possibilities about what to do. Rather than try to consider all the possibilities, we come prepared with certain biases or expectations that greatly influence what we consider and how we act. We may not experience ambiguity because we do not consider alternative possibilities. These "constraints" occur in all facets of cognition and, we believe, are responsible for the successful performance of the cognitive system. Finally, one should note that constraints represent an adaptation to our world and, therefore, should be thought of more as "guiding principles" rather than limitations. Although we often compare minds to computers, it is critically important to realize that our cognitive system is *not* a general-purpose computing device. Instead, our cognitive resources are exquisitely "tuned" to the demands of our unique environment.

We believe that ambiguity and responses to it provide some broad organizing themes. We hope that the framework we describe will allow the student to better appreciate not just each individual accomplishment of the mind (perception, language, and so on), but some basic commonalities that cut across these accomplishments.

In elaborating these themes, we bring in evidence from a variety of areas of psychology, as well as from other cognitive sciences. The book contains many sections explaining research on artificial intelligence (AI), connectionist or parallel distributed processing (PDP) models, and cognitive neuroscience. We believe that our unifying themes grow in part out of developments in other cognitive science disciplines and that cognitive science students from outside psychology will be able to learn about cognitive psychology from this book. We have not shied away from presenting technical details in many sections. Some discussions are complex, but we believe that current work in cognitive psychology requires detailed analysis. At the same time, we have tried to be careful about allowing the reader to understand the issues and their implications even without a grasp of the technical details.

To further help in giving some structure to the research areas, the book is organized into five large sections. The first section (Chapters 1 and 2) provides an overview of the themes and the approaches to studying the mind. The second section (Chapters 3, 4, and 5) examines how information is acquired, including basic learning processes, attention, and perception. The third section (Chapters 6, 7, and 8) addresses fundamental issues of representation of knowledge and its use, with investigation of imagery and memory. The fourth section (Chapters 9, 10, 11, and 12) provides information about language and understanding, including language comprehension, acquisition, and production, as well as chapters on inference and concepts. The final section (Chapters 13, 14, 15, and 16) addresses thinking, with information on decision making, reasoning, problem solving, expertise, and creativity.

This book is intended for a one-semester course in cognitive psychology. Although we have attempted to place the chapters in logical sequence, other orderings are possible. It is probably important that the introductory chapter outlining the themes be read first. Other than that, it would probably be best to read Chapter 7 before Chapter 8, Chapter 9 before Chapter 10, and Chapter 15 before Chapter 16. It is also possible to have the students focus more on "higher-level" cognition by omitting some of the earlier chapters. In addition, non–psychology students interested in cognitive science may get an overview of cognitive psychology by reading selected chapters related to their interests.

We have received much help throughout the writing of this book. We thank Marcus Boggs, the editor who expressed confidence through the early drafts and gave us much freedom in letting the book evolve. When he became President of Academic Press, he was succeeded at Harcourt Brace Jovanovich by Phil Curson and then Tina Oldham. Ruth Cottrell has combined patience with wisdom on the production side of things. A number of colleagues and external reviewers have left their mark on the book. We thank Ed Smith, Harold Pashler, David Swinney, Phillip Johnson-Laird, Evan Heit, Javier Sainz, Woo-Kyoung Ahn, Gordon Logan, Neal Cohen, and Gary Dell for thoughtful advice on what we wrote. In addition, we received much help with how the material was presented from Ed Smith, Joshua Medin, Rebecca Medin, Linda Powers, Cheri Sullivan, Tom Spalding, Keith Magnus, and Leigh Elkins. Many thanks are due to those who did the typing: Ruth Colwell at Illinois and Lisa Jones, Karen Rodwan, Leigh Elkins, and Ulyses Grant at Michigan.

We have noticed that it is traditional to thank significant others for their patience and support throughout a project of this sort. Now we know why. Linda and Cheri, thanks for your endurance.

Douglas Medin and Brian Ross

CONTENTS

12 Concepts and Categories: Representation and Use   361

OVERVIEW

1

POSSIBILITIES, INFORMATION, AND EXPERIENCE

All nature is but Art, unknown

to thee; all chance, direction, which

thou canst not see.

Alexander Pope

Introduction

Puzzles

This book is about the obvious and the nonobvious. Hidden under the cognitive tasks that people find natural and easy are some of the most challenging and mysterious puzzles concerning human intelligence. Most people do not spend a lot of time thinking about how we perceive objects and events in our environment. Our experience is of seeing the world more or less directly. We see what we see because the world is the way it is.

But there is a great deal more to perception than meets the eye. So much information is lost during the imaging process that projects the three-dimensional world into two-dimensional images that any perceptual experience has an unlimited set of possible interpretations. So how do we see the world accurately? To deal with ambiguity, the perceptual system appears to make assumptions about the nature of the world (see, for example, Poggio, Torre, & Koch, 1985). These assumptions are accurate enough that we can successfully get along in our environment but they are not infallible. Our visual system is structured so that the apparent shape of objects does not change across a variety of viewing conditions. The assumptions that allow for "shape constancy" lead us to systematically misperceive the parallelograms in Figure 1.1. This is a powerful visual illusion that does not disappear when we realize that it is an illusion.

Similarly, language learning may seem no more complicated than the obvious observation that children learn language from their parents. A closer look, however, reveals the deeper nature of the task. For example, any linguistic input has to be consistent with the correct grammar (for the moment we'll ignore the fact that speech is not always grammatical), but it

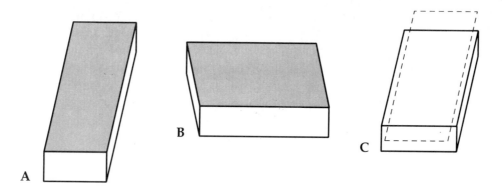

Figure 1.1   **A Shape Constancy Illusion.**
The shaded parallelogram in part B is congruent with the one in A and with the dashed outline in C (that is, if you cut out the shaded area in A it would fit exactly on the shaded area in B). If you are skeptical, try tracing the outlines of these parallelograms on thin paper and placing them on top of one another. *Source*: Shepard, 1981.

will also necessarily be consistent with an infinite set of alternative grammars. In Chapter 10 on language acquisition we will note that children are even capable of learning (maybe we should say constructing) a grammar when their language input is an inadequate or noisy version of the grammar. Many incorrect grammars will be ruled out by further sentences but there will always be an unlimited number of grammars that are consistent with any finite set of sentences. As a matter of fact, formal proofs have demonstrated (e.g., Gold, 1967; Pinker, 1984; Wexler & Culicover, 1980) that in its general form the language learning problem is impossible! So we are faced with the following paradox: Language learning is impossible and yet it's so simple that every child can do it.

As a general rule, tasks that seem natural and easy to us have proven to be among the most difficult to understand and implement in a machine. Although we may be impressed by computers that perform complex calculations at great speed, it is far more challenging to program common sense into a computer. The sort of plausible inferences that we take so much for granted are notoriously difficult to build into artificial intelligence programs. Consider the question, "Why did John roller-skate to McDonald's last night?" People have no difficulty realizing that the topic of the question is probably the roller skating and that "because he was hungry" and "because he was busy during the day" are not relevant answers. But if the question is changed to "Why did John drive to McDonald's last night?" people understand that the topic is not driving. Furthermore, an intelligent system would have to realize that John drove some vehicle and that vehicle was probably a car, possibly a truck, certainly not a tank or a sled pulled by a team of huskies. We make such inferences so naturally that we are scarcely aware of them.

Possibilities

Life is full of possibilities. In fact, the richness of life's possibilities places limitations on the ability of an organism to reason and act intelligently. Intelligent actions require information, and organisms are faced with a chronic shortage of information concerning the past, present, and future.

Suppose you are considering buying a car. Some of the information needed to make an intelligent decision is straightforward: how much the car will cost, how much money you have to purchase the car, how the car performs, what kind of mileage it gets, the likelihood that expensive repairs will be needed, and so on. But other potentially relevant information is not so obvious. For example, the future health of your grandmother might be important, because you might need to drive a long distance to visit her and the best car to buy might depend on the relative amount of city versus country driving that you anticipate. A sudden interest in anthropology could lead you to long for a station wagon to take on field trips. A chance to work in New York City could obviate the need for a car altogether. If you postponed the decision until *all* potential relevant information was examined and evaluated, the decision would never be made. The point is that you *cannot* anticipate all possibilities so as to guarantee that you will purchase the "best" car.

Even when the possibilities can be systematically enumerated there may simply be too many to allow an exhaustive search. Consider the game of chess. The number of ways in which the first 10 moves can be played is on the order of billions, and there are more possible sequences for the game than there are atoms in the universe! Obviously neither humans nor machines can determine the best moves by considering all the possibilities. In fact, grandmaster chess players typically report that they consider only a few branches or alternatives for at best a handful of moves ahead. The amazing thing is that grandmasters (as of this writing) can still defeat the best computers. The world champion, Gary Kasparov, recently defeated the best chess-playing computer, Deep Thought, in a highly publicized two-game match (Kasparov won both games). Deep Thought is able to examine 270,000 positions per second and search quite a few moves ahead. The next generation of chess-playing computers will be an order of magnitude faster, will be able to search further, and may well surpass the best chess player, but just how grandmasters select the best lines of play after very limited search remains a mystery.

Human experience is an infinitely more complex challenge than a game of chess. Grandmasters base their expertise on thousands and thousands of games in which their favorite variations can be tested and retested, and for every game the pieces are reset to common beginning positions. Not so in life. There is no resetting and no chance to systematically explore alternatives. Although in principle one could pursue a career as a psychologist and then take up law, any comparisons of psychology and law would be contaminated by factors such as difference in age, the fact that psychology was studied first, and so on. Many of these differences probably would not be important, but a fundamental puzzle is how organisms ever learn which differences make a difference in the face of a multitude of correlated possibilities. In some cases coming up with any possibilities at all is challenging (Kotovsky & Simon, 1990).

This book is organized around the idea that much of intelligent behavior can be understood in terms of strategies for coping with too little information and too many possibilities. As we shall see, problems of **computational complexity** arise in all the major domains of cognitive psychology: learning, perception, memory, concept formation, decision making, and problem solving. A fundamental goal in each of these areas is to identify guiding principles or **constraints** that allow organisms to explore the better (or at least satisfactory) possibilities.

A Closer Look

The examples we have considered so far are typical rather than exceptional. "So little time, so much to do" is literally true.

Learning.   Consider the problem of learning names for things. It may seem obvious that when a parent points to a rabbit and says "rabbit" a child ought to be able to associate the sound with the object. But the situation is far more ambiguous. The word could refer to "small" or "white" or "furry" or "pink-eyed" or "baby" or "hopping." Or the word could be a proper name, refer to a role (as in "pet") or a superordinate (as in "animal"), or even be some combination of the rabbit and other properties in the scene. It would take many, many examples to disentangle these possibilities. Even then, as Quine points out in his discussion of translation, not all meanings would be ruled out: "Point to a rabbit and you have pointed to a stage of a rabbit, to an integral part of a rabbit, to the rabbit fusion, and to where rabbithood is manifested" (Quine, 1960, p. 52).

To cope with the possibilities or ambiguities, organisms seem to come prepared with certain biases or expectations. Consider a rat that eats some contaminated food in the morning, wanders around its environment, sees a cat, hears thousands of sounds, scratches its fleas, and then gets sick late in the day. To what should the rat attribute its illness? Seeing the cat? Hearing rattling garbage can lids? Drinking water in the early afternoon? There are limitless possibilities, but laboratory research suggests that the rat would associate illness with the smell and taste of the food eaten in the morning and acquire an aversion to it. And of course, in this case the bias toward associating tastes and smells with illness serves the rat quite well. Pigeons, in contrast, readily link visual cues with food (Shapiro, Jacobs, & LoLordo, 1980). The cost of this bias or preference is that when the true association conflicts with a bias, learning may be difficult. This potential cost holds for all organisms, including humans, who have preferences that make some things easier and other things harder to learn. Ideally, we are biased to learn the things that we should learn. For example, young children who are learning words appear to have a bias for assuming that novel labels refer to names for whole objects rather than individual parts or complex scenes (Markman, 1989) and generally this is the correct inference to make. In order to understand learning, we need to identify the natural biases or guiding principles that predispose organisms for making some associations rather than others.

Memory.   There is scarcely anything that people do without relying on their past experience which, by definition, involves memory. Not simply memory, but accessing relevant memories. How do people access and use knowledge efficiently, and how do they determine relevance? The set of things that are potentially relevant in a given situation is so large that there is danger of getting lost in thought. One attempt to address relevance in artificial intelligence research is to use organized packets of knowledge (variously referred to as frames, schemas, or scripts) that are "triggered" by events (e.g., going out to eat triggers a restaurant script). Although these approaches have led to some progress, they have proven to be too rigid to capture the flexible use of knowledge that characterizes human cognition. Sometimes, of course, people do not transfer their prior relevant experience to a new task. This failure, however, should be viewed with the understanding that the general problem of relevant access is overwhelmingly complex. A central problem in memory research is to discover just how memory is organized so as to provide relevant knowledge when it is needed.

Problem Solving and Reasoning. **Artificial intelligence** is the science of writing computer programs to do intelligent things. Yet problem-solving and reasoning tasks often are unmanageably large. They cannot be analyzed exhaustively in real time. Procedures that are plausible and effective in their miniature versions simply do not "scale up" because of the exponentially increasing number of possibilities to be explored.

The computational complexity problem can be nicely illustrated by an example taken from Christopher Cherniak's (1986) book, *Minimal Rationality*. Suppose that we have a computer that can evaluate the consistency of an assertion in the time it takes a light ray to traverse the diameter of a proton, and suppose that the computer ran for 20 billion years. Even if we had a procedure for doing this, it would involve so many checks that there still would not be sufficient time to evaluate the internal consistency of a belief system containing only 138 logically independent propositions! Examples such as this underline the need for guiding principles and a variety of other strategies for coping with complexity.

Themes and Implications

Obviously, people cannot consider all the possibilities in a given situation. Therefore, it should not be surprising that human cognition is riddled with, if not organized around, heuristics (general guidelines or shortcuts) and strategies for simplifying situations. Rather than striving for the "best" decisions, people are more pragmatic and settle for the "pretty good." In Herbert Simon's terms, they **satisfice** (Simon, 1959). Measured against the standard of optimality, human cognition falls short, oversimplifies, and leads to systematic misperception. Measured against the problems of computational complexity, controlling relevance, and inadequate information, however, human cognition can achieve marvels.

It should be equally clear that passive organization of information is an inadequate solution to the complexity problems we have been discussing. In many cases people actively construct explanations, theories, or mental models as they attempt to organize and understand their experience. Most of the time people are forced to construct these explanations based on limited facts and, therefore, in some cases these explanations will be wrong. For example, although high blood pressure has no symptoms many people seem to equate high blood pressure with heart rate. They reason that high blood pressure means that the heart has to work harder and that it works harder by beating faster. Imagine that a person who equates blood pressure with heart rate is given a medication to control blood pressure and the medication has the side effect of slightly increasing heart rate. The person may discard the medication as ineffective. Although this behavior is inappropriate, it is consistent with the person's understanding of blood pressure. People are not passive processors of information. It is important to understand how people organize and theorize about their experience.

Experience and Learning

Experience and Explanations

Everyone knows that we learn from experience. We would rather be operated on by a brain surgeon who has performed a thousand similar prior operations than by a surgeon doing his or her first operation. Experience is the best teacher, but what exactly does experience teach us? As we shall see, ambiguity and shortage of information pose major obstacles to profiting from experience.

In some cases our experience systematically misleads us. Consider the practice of bloodletting, a common nineteenth-century treatment involving drawing blood from patients, typically by applying leeches. Bloodletting was employed for a variety of ailments. Claude Bernard, one of the strongest advocates of this practice, nearly died from it but he nonetheless took his recovery as additional evidence for its efficacy. As we discuss later in this chapter, one reason why bloodletting was so popular for so long is that no one bothered to run a comparison study in which the treatment was withheld. When this was done researchers observed that patients treated by bloodletting did not survive as well as patients who were not subjected to bloodletting. The fact that life does not come equipped with proper control groups is a major limitation on learning from experience.

Ordinary experience is extraordinarily challenging with respect to learning. Consider a simple social interaction. John greets Mary warmly and she replies in kind. Why is Mary friendly? One possibility is that she is friendly to everyone by virtue of her occupation or social role or because her natural disposition is to be friendly. Another possibility is that whether or not Mary is friendly depends on her mood and she happens to be in a good mood. Yet another explanation is that Mary's reaction is a response to John's warmth. Or Mary could be feigning friendliness to conceal underlying anger or resentment. The possibilities go on.

Which of the above explanations of Mary's behavior is the correct one? We don't know and the point is that John does not know either. John cannot recreate exactly the same situation and systematically vary his behavior to evaluate his role in Mary's response. Of course, psychologists can study the types of assumptions or guesses people make in explaining behavior. An important theoretical challenge in social psychology is to provide a description of the characteristic attributions that people make about themselves and others (see, e.g., Heider, 1958; Jones & Nisbett, 1972; Hilton & Slugoski, 1986). A particularly salient result is the finding that people tend to underestimate the role of situations and overestimate the role of traits or dispositional factors in making attributions about behavior (Kelly & Michela, 1980). For example, a person would be surprised to find that Judge Williams, who is the picture of sternness in the courtroom, is funny in private life.

People do not, in general, have sufficient information to choose between competing explanations. Therefore, people must adopt certain strategies in order to make attributions about other people's beliefs and behaviors. One idea is that people attempt to identify what is unusual in a situation and bias their causal attributions toward these abnormal conditions (see, e.g., Hilton & Slugoski, 1986). For example, if John has a car accident while driving home on a rainy evening, we might believe that the unusual rainy conditions were at least partly responsible for the accident. But if John lives in a climate where it rains every evening, we would be much less likely to assume that rain was the cause. In the absence of definitive information, we cannot ask whether these attributions are logically justified (they are not, in almost all cases) but rather whether they are accurate often enough to prove useful. This section provides an analysis of everyday learning by means of contrasting experience with experiments. By analyzing ordinary experience in terms of principles of experimental design, one may readily see that experience might fail to provide relevant information or even provide misinformation. Before turning to empirical or experience-based knowledge, we first consider the general issue of how we know (or think we know) anything.

Ways of Knowing

Nonempirical.   Not all knowledge is gained through observation and experience. Much of what we believe to be true we derive from logic, judgments of reasonableness, other authorities, or faith.

Deductive Logic.   We use logic when we use a set of facts to derive other facts that are logical consequences. For example, given the premise "if it rains there will be no baseball game" and the premise that "it is raining," we can conclude that (it follows that) there will be no baseball game. Of course, logic can be misused. For example, it is tempting to take the observation that there was no baseball game as proving that it rained when, in fact, no baseball game was scheduled. Furthermore, observations that are logically correct may not be sensible in normal discourse. The statement "if two plus two equals five, then the president of the United States is a Martian" is logically correct but has no useful content.

Reasonableness.   A major way in which we know or accept something to be true is by evaluating the plausibility of what is true. If it sounds reasonable, it is probably true. For example, someone might accept the statement that "the threat of punishment deters crime" as being true because it seems reasonable that people would want to avoid being punished. Although whether punishment really does reduce crime would seem to be an empirical issue, people may find the statement to be so transparently correct that it is treated as an *a priori* or self-evident truth.

Very often results from psychological experiments make intuitive sense, so much so that one is tempted to dismiss psychology as nothing more than common sense. But intuition is not an infallible guide. For example, in our culture there is a widespread belief that hypnotism can be used to improve eyewitness accuracy. The evidence from laboratory research, however, is that eyewitness accuracy is considerably worse when hypnotism is employed (Sanders & Simmons, 1983).

Probably the safest conclusion about reasonableness judgments is that they are close enough to the truth to be correct much of the time but that occasionally reasonableness is very misleading. For example, in earlier centuries when people drew an even sharper distinction between body and mind, explanations of mental disorders were stated in terms of possession by demons. The idea that unusual behavior might be caused by a brain tumor or a biochemical imbalance would have been dismissed as wildly implausible.

Authority.   Establishing knowledge by appeal to authority amounts to taking someone else's word for the truth. The dictionary is commonly used as the authority for how words are to be spelled. Children (for a short time, at least) usually assume that whatever their parents tell them is true and as adults, we usually accept the word of experts as correct. We could not get along without authorities, even if experts are not infallible.

Faith.   By definition, faith is a firm belief in something for which there is no proof. Religious beliefs are the most common example of faith. Faith in something is not an empirical issue, even if it is based on experience. For example, someone who believes that prayer heals the sick probably would not want to fund research that would compare the recovery rates for people who were or were not prayed for. One suggestion is that public figures ought to have a better prognosis than less well-known people because public figures have more people praying for them (a cynic might note that they also have more people praying against them!). Whatever sense this might make, it is not a good experimental design because the two groups would differ in quite a few ways other than the number of prayers said for them.

Empirical.   In the present age of modern science we take observation and experimentation as a natural road to truth. This attitude toward **empiricism** has not always been held. Francis Bacon, one of the founders of British empiricism in the sixteenth century, was severely chastised by fellow debaters for suggesting that the answer to the question of how many teeth a horse has might be best obtained by looking into the mouth of a horse. (This story may be apocryphal.)

Experience.   Much of our knowledge comes from inductive generalizations derived from experience. For example, based on their interactions with people someone might come to the conclusion that people who are polite and friendly are also honest. Some of these generalizations are based on limited experience. If the first three people from Bolivia that we meet are musically talented, we may be ready to conclude that most or all Bolivians are musically talented.

If our initial impressions are not representative or accurate, they should be corrected. A serious problem with taking experience as a guide is the *tenacity* of our beliefs, which may lead us to search for information in a biased manner. Once a person thinks Bolivians are musical, he or she may find it natural to elicit information that will reinforce that belief. This tenacity is particularly evident when people have conflicting beliefs or attitudes. Consider the following study conducted by psychologist Lee Ross and his colleagues (Ross, Lepper, & Hubbard, 1975; Ross, 1977). They identified people who had different beliefs about some controversial issue. In one study people were selected who either believed that marijuana had no harmful effects or thought it was very unhealthy. Both groups were then presented with the same set of information that consisted of descriptions of research studies showing a somewhat mixed picture. Their beliefs were measured again after they had read the material. One might expect the attitudes of the two groups to tend to converge on a moderate position, but surprisingly the beliefs became still more extreme! Apparently, people tended to see flaws in the studies whose results did not fit their views and did not see any problems with the studies that supported their views. A biased search for information can lead to a distorted view of the evidence.

A second factor that serves to increase tenacity is the phenomenon of **self-fulfilling prophecy.** That is, people may act on their beliefs in such a way that they bring about the expected state of affairs. For example, a person who thinks that someone is going to be hostile may act toward that person in a guarded manner, which may indeed be met with coolness. A striking demonstration of this phenomenon comes from an experiment by social psychologist Mark Snyder and his colleagues (Snyder, Tanke, & Berscheid, 1977). The experiment involved men and women talking on the phone, ostensibly to evaluate whether they might wish to date each other. The men were shown a picture of the woman they were conversing with. Two different men talked with each woman (at different times). Although the pair of men conversed with the same woman, they were shown different photographs—one photograph showed a woman of average appearance and the other showed a woman who was quite attractive. The photographs might well influence how much the men wanted to date the woman but in this study the focus was on how the men's expectations influenced the conversations. An independent set of raters did not see any photographs but simply judged the woman's attractiveness based on hearing her half of the telephone conversation. The results indicated that the woman was rated to be more attractive when engaged in a conversation with a man who had been shown an attractive photograph than with the man who had been shown the less attractive photograph. Apparently, the photographs changed the manner in which the men interacted over the phone and, as a consequence, also affected the way in which the woman interacted over the phone. Expectations are not just predictions; they also influence our behavior in such a way as to confirm them.

Personal experience is often accurate, provides lots of ideas or hypotheses to be more systematically explored, and provides a proof that often refutes generalizations or stereotypes. For example, if one has read or been told that New Yorkers are unfriendly, then a personal encounter with a helpful, friendly New Yorker may be valuable in correcting one's beliefs about people who live in New York. On the other hand, people often are willing to let specific experiences override massive amounts of statistical information. One may read about a survey of 10,000 automobile owners indicating that some make of car has low repair costs, only to disregard this information when a friend says "I bought one of them and I've had nothing but problems."

Whether or not you have read Robert Frost's poem "The Road Not Taken," it is likely to have occurred to you at one time or another that life does not allow us the luxury of certain comparison conditions. We can only speculate about what might have happened if we had been more frank or more friendly with someone in some situation, or chosen a different career, or decided to live somewhere else. Even though one can learn from experience, one may not be able to learn as much as one would like.

Systematic Observations in Natural Settings.   All good science begins with observation. In many cases these observations take the form of **correlations.** For example, we might note that there is a correlation between how much people smoke and how long they live. It is important to realize that correlation cannot be equated with causation. There is a positive correlation between ill people going to a hospital and their dying, but this does not mean that going to the hospital causes them to die. At the same time, one cannot simply rely on plausibility as a guide for interpreting correlations. For example, prior to the germ theory of disease it did not occur to people that there would be a correlation between operating room cleanliness and surgical survival.

Scientific Observation.   Just because we call an observation *scientific* does not mean we are immune from bias, but it does involve a commitment to a set of principles for evaluating observations. First, scientific observation is *public*. By public we mean that in principle different people could make the same observation under the same conditions. That is, observations should be repeatable. Observations that are not public have far less credibility, according to scientific standards. Consider, for example, certain paranormal phenomena such as levitation or telekinesis (e.g., lifting a book by thinking about it). Sometimes it is claimed that these phenomena are real but that they will not occur if any "nonbelievers" are present. If nonbelievers cannot observe telekinesis, then it is no longer a public, reliable event. It is conceivable that there are such paranormal phenomena and that they truly do not appear when nonbelievers are present, but an alternative view is that believers simply are not evaluating their observations carefully. The latter view is reinforced by the fact that professional magicians can produce many if not all of these phenomena by methods that are anything but paranormal. (Suspiciously, one noted psychic, Yuri Geller, was a professional magician earlier in his career.)

A second major feature of scientific observation is that it is, in principle, *self-correcting*. That is, we require that observations and theories be testable. The initial observation that the earth is apparently flat has been replaced by the idea that the earth is a sphere. The flat-earth theory was falsifiable. One criticism of Freud's description of personality in terms of id, ego, and superego is that it can explain any observation *after the fact* (e.g., "he cheated because his superego was weak" versus "he did not cheat because his superego was strong") but that, since it can predict anything, it explains nothing. Common-sense aphorisms tend to cover all bases and not be testable. For example, we are told that "haste makes waste" and "a stitch in time saves nine" as well as "absence makes the heart grow fonder" and "out of sight, out of mind." All of these aphorisms are true some of the time, but just exactly when? A person committed to scientific observation must be prepared for the possibility that what seems intuitively obvious may not be true. For example, the threat of punishment may not deter crime at all.

A third feature of scientific observation is that one systematically develops and evaluates alternative possibilities or theories. Consider the treatment of bloodletting. If it seems to be a good treatment for some illness, then patients who receive the treatment should fare better than those who do not. The people who do not receive the treatment constitute a *control group*. To ensure that the groups are comparable, patients should be randomly assigned to either the treatment group or the control group. If the treatment group survives better than the control group, we conclude that bloodletting is an effective treatment. If people were allowed to choose which group to be in, any differences between the groups might have to do not with the treatment but with whatever it is that leads people to select one group or the other. For example, the sickest people might elect to be in the treatment group and the groups would differ in severity of illness. Even if a well-designed experiment suggests that a treatment is effective, our inquiry need not stop there. It may be that any treatment would help or that a physician's attitude about the effectiveness of some treatment may affect results. For these reasons the control group may be given a **placebo** (a pill or drug that has no direct physiological effect) to separate the effects of giving a specific treatment from the effects of being treated per se. Although it may be reassuring to think of the practice of bloodletting as a treatment of less advanced times, remember that the practice of routinely performing tonsillectomies and adenoidectomies was common until 10 to 15 years ago even though there was no evidence from controlled clinical trials to suggest that the benefits outweighed the risks (and apparently, with some exceptions, they do not).

Psychotherapy as an Experimental Design

As one example of learning from experience consider a clinical psychologist in practice. Psychotherapy is far from an ideal experimental design.

Clinical psychologists are expected to help people so it is not very natural to include a control group. Instead, a sample of the people in some area decide they have a problem that is serious enough to require them to see a psychologist. The clinician makes some diagnosis and develops some treatment plan. The client may or may not improve and the problems may or may not recur after therapy has ended. The clinician may or may not hear about whether the treatment was successful or whether or not the client turned to another therapist. And of course, clients might have improved even if they had not sought treatment. Furthermore, the clients are not a random sample. For example, a psychologist cannot develop a good appreciation of how likely homosexuals are to be happy and well-adjusted because happy, well-adjusted people presumably would not seek treatment. In certain respects it is surprising that clinicians can learn anything at all from their practice. Indeed, one of the reasons for conducting psychological research is to try to disentangle some of the correlations and **confounding factors** that characterize our personal experience.

Clinical psychologists do have the opportunity to study a few people in great depth, but even that has its problems. For example, a person who wanted to understand the psychology of mass murderers might collect as much information as possible about a few mass murderers and try to find common threads in their lives. Case studies can often provide ideas for theories (this was certainly true for Sigmund Freud) and hints about underlying causes. The observation that each of five child abusers were themselves abused as children may tell us something about the underlying causes of child abuse.

Case studies also have their limitations. Often there is no control group as a basis for comparison. Some of the properties that mass murderers or child abusers have in common may be properties that people share in general. In fact, one might wish to have specially selected control groups. For example, in studying child abuse one might want a control group consisting of people who had been abused as children but who do *not* abuse their children. The biggest problem with case studies is that with small samples and large numbers of observations it is likely that the cases will have many things in common that have nothing to do with, for example, child abuse or psychopathology. This problem is known as **overdetermination of small samples**. A more down-to-earth example concerns predicting which horses will win races by studying racing forms. There is so much data that one can very likely find variables to predict yesterday's winners perfectly, but unfortunately the same variables may not work for today's horses. The more data obtained, the bigger the sample has to be to separate real factors from chance factors.

Experimentation

Experimentation can be distinguished from observation by the fact that some factor or factors are explicitly varied while some other factor or factors are measured. The factors that are varied by the experiments are known as **independent variables** and the factors measured are the **dependent variables**. For example, in a study examining how the dose of a drug affects blood pressure, the dosage would be the independent variable and would be varied; blood pressure would be the dependent variable and would be measured.

Experiments are an excellent tool for interpreting naturalistic observations. Suppose one observes the amount of time students spend studying and correlates study time with test performance. If the better students study more efficiently and need less time to prepare, one might find either zero correlation or even a negative correlation between time spent studying and test performance. Does this mean that students should study less? Obviously not, but one way to demonstrate this unequivocally would be to run an experiment in which different groups of students would be allowed to study for different amounts of time. Under these conditions one would almost surely find a positive correlation between study time and test performance. The problem with the naturalistic observation is that study time might have been confounded with ability if the better students studied less. Similarly, the positive correlation between being admitted to a hospital and dying involves a confounding factor in that people who are admitted to a hospital are on the average less healthy than people not admitted. To demonstrate this, one would need to admit a random sample of those who wished to enter the hospital, have those not admitted treated as a control group, and compare survival rates.

Summary

This chapter has laid the foundations for the themes we will carry through this book. As we have seen, organisms are constantly confronted with ambiguity and a shortage of information. Human cognition can be seen as organized around this challenge. People do not simply accumulate information—they also actively organize it and theorize about it. Furthermore, with rare exceptions we do not consider all the logical possibilities in a particular situation because there simply are too many of them. Instead, we use strategies or are otherwise biased to favor some possibilities over others. These guesses about which possibilities will prove to be most promising are often quite successful in the sense that they help us get along in our world. In short, the human mind is *not* a general-purpose information processing device but rather a special-purpose device, where the special purpose is adaptation to the environment.

As we have seen, there are major obstacles to learning from experience. Appropriate control or comparison conditions are almost always lacking. If our inferences are based only on outcomes or feedback, the information we receive may be systematically misleading (e.g., self-fulfilling prophecy). There are at least two morals to be drawn from these observations. One is that well-controlled experiments are critically important for understanding human thought and behavior. Intuitive judgments of reasonableness and informal observation are fallible guides. The other is that, in the face of inadequate information, the cognitive system must make some guesses about what inferences or attributions are likely to be correct.

Furthermore, random guesses about relevance or appropriate actions are too costly and too slow to allow organisms to learn which differences make a difference. To address this challenge, organisms have evolved in such a way that they favor some possibilities over others; that is, their learning is constrained. Although one might conclude that this paints a pessimistic picture of what people can hope to know or learn, we take a much more positive view. We have focused on fallibility to underline the inadequacy of experience but, in general, our guesses or biases appear to be nicely tied to the contingencies we face in the world. The quote from Alexander Pope at the beginning of this chapter sounds a theme that carries throughout this book. The next chapter provides an overview of different approaches to the study of the mind. How exactly can one use experiments to learn about human cognition?

Key Terms

artificial intelligence
computational complexity
confounding factors
constraints
correlations
dependent variables

empiricism
independent variables
overdetermination of small samples
placebo
satisfice
self-fulfilling prophecy

Recommended Readings

Cherniak's book *Minimal Rationality* (1986) does a nice job of analyzing the implications of computational complexity for what it means to be rational. For an overview of research on causal reasoning in the social domain consult Kelly and Michela (1980). Finally, Rosenthal's (1967) review of experimenter expectancy effects provides a sobering reminder that the experimenter is not necessarily a neutral figure.

2

APPROACHES TO THE STUDY
OF THE MIND

Chapter Outline

I have measured out my life with coffee spoons.

T. S. Eliot, "The Love Song of J. Alfred Prufrock"

Introduction

It is one thing to be interested in studying how the mind works but quite another problem to figure out exactly how to go about it. Suppose you were going to study the mind—what questions would you aim to answer? Some people balk at the very idea of trying to understand human beings—the complexity and uniqueness of individuals seem to defy analysis. Indeed, it was not until the latter half of the nineteenth century that people began to apply the scientific method to human thought and behavior. Wilhelm Wundt is credited with founding the first laboratory for psychological research at Leipzig, Germany in 1879.

Suppose that, like Wundt, you decided that the study of the human mind should be attempted. You might begin by wondering why people behave the way they do. Suppose you wanted to know why some people smoke whereas others do not. The most straightforward procedure might be to ask people why they do or do not smoke. You might hear some interesting explanations and they would likely differ for the two groups. However, we think it is highly unlikely that this sort of survey would provide deep insights into smoking behavior. Alternatively, you might study why some people have difficulty making decisions. The questions about smoking and about decision making are concerned with individual differences. Although cognitive psychologists are interested in individual differences, they usually believe that it is at least as important to study characteristics that people tend to share, since we cannot understand differences without first understanding similarities. That is, psychologists try to learn the principles underlying human thought and behavior that might give rise to these individual differences. As we shall see, in many cases individual differences can help researchers to formulate more accurate general theories. Just as genetic abnormalities such as Down's syndrome are best understood against the background of the science of genetics, we believe that individual differences in thought and behavior are best understood from the perspective of cognitive psychology.

In this chapter we will review several approaches to the study of the mind. Some of the methods seem straightforward; others are quite subtle. Some appreciation of the history of psychology is necessary to understand contemporary cognitive psychology (and to avoid repeating mistakes). There has been a diversity of approaches and this lack of uniformity is probably a good thing, because there are different levels at which one may understand cognition. But we are getting ahead of ourselves. Let us first turn to a little history.

Roots of Cognitive Psychology

Introspectionism.   It would seem that we are all potential experts on how the mind works because we have a lot of firsthand experience with our own thoughts and other people's behavior. We often make inferences about other people's beliefs, desires, and intentions and we seem to have privileged, direct access to our own thoughts. Therefore, what better source of information about the mind than introspection?

Introspection was one of the first methodologies adopted about a century ago when experimental psychology was getting its start in Germany. Wilhelm Wundt believed that just as physical things can be analyzed into their parts and elements, so too could thought be analyzed into its substructures or elements. Early research and debate included such issues as whether thoughts necessarily were or were not accompanied by images (see Boring's [1950] discussion of the Würzburg school). In the United States Cornell Titchener attempted to establish rigorous procedures for introspection that focused on separating direct sensations from inferences drawn from them.

Introspectionism was quickly buffeted with severe challenges. Hermann Helmholtz argued that perceptual processes involve unconscious inferences and Sigmund Freud emphasized the pervasiveness of unconscious influences on behavior. Even within the school of introspectionism there were problems. Observations by Marbe at Würzburg suggested that there were severe limitations on the data that could be obtained from introspection (again see Boring, 1950). Marbe asked people to lift two weights and judge which was the heavier. The participants noted numerous sensations and images but were not able to report any of the processes that actually generated or justified their judgments. In other words, the judgments came to mind but the participants could not say how they got there. An equally serious problem was that results from different laboratories often disagreed. These difficulties paved the way for a reaction against using introspection—behaviorism.

Behaviorism. **Behaviorism**, true to its name, takes psychology to be the study of *behavior*. John B. Watson, its founder, argued that behavior is objective and observable and that the agenda for psychology consists of formulating laws relating stimulus conditions to behavior. Consciousness, introspection, and the mind were to play no role in this science of behavior. His views were reinforced by the logical positivist movement in philosophy. Logical positivism emphasized operational definitions tied to specific operations or observations.

B. F. Skinner, another prominent behaviorist, helped promote behaviorism both by argument (his debates with Carl Rogers in the 1960s concerning free will received wide attention) and by the development of procedures for studying behavior. Skinner maintained that behavior is determined by reinforcements or rewards, not by free will. One of his notable findings was that, under tightly controlled learning conditions (taking place in what is known as the Skinner box, which we will describe and discuss in detail in Chapter 3), rats, pigeons, and monkeys displayed very similar learning curves. Skinner's brand of behaviorism had no place for theories (Skinner, 1950). He argued that the science of behavior consists of describing relationships between patterns of reinforcement and behavior. Skinner collaborated with Charles Ferster on a book that consists of nothing but hundreds of graphs of behavior under different schedules of reinforcement (Ferster & Skinner, 1957). No reference to internal processes of organisms was permitted.

As one example of the influence of behaviorism, there is the story of the distress suffered by a graduate student whose dissertation was on memory in animals. At least one member of his examination committee refused to participate because "memory" was considered an unscientific term referring to processes that could not be studied. According to the story, the committee member returned when the student agreed to use the word "retention" rather than memory.

Although behaviorism did help to promote psychology as a science, its strictures on what could and could not be studied were too severe. There were always pockets of resistance to behaviorism and, as attention shifted from studying simple learning in tightly controlled (and impoverished) situations to more complex learning, the inadequacies of behaviorism became increasingly apparent.

Critique of Behaviorism.   Although people talk about the replacement of behaviorism by the "cognitive revolution," it is probably more accurate to say that behaviorism gradually declined because of a series of related inadequacies. Skinner's demonstration that rats, pigeons, and monkeys showed similar behavior in the Skinner box may tell us more about the limitations of Skinner boxes than the generality of animal learning. One serious problem with behaviorism is its failure to distinguish between performance and learning. Memory (retention?) was assumed to be simply the performance of a learned act. This view is inadequate. An early demonstration of the need to distinguish between memory and performance comes from studies by Tinklepaugh (1928, 1932) using chimpanzees and monkeys as subjects. Tinklepaugh studied what is known as a "delayed response." An animal would be shown where either lettuce or a banana was hidden and then, after a delay, be allowed to choose among several response sites (including the correct one). If the chimpanzee found the reward, it was allowed to eat it. Everything proceeded normally in trials in which lettuce was hidden and was the reward and when a banana was hidden and was the reward. But Tinklepaugh also ran trials in which a banana was hidden but then lettuce was surreptitiously substituted as the reward. In these trials the chimpanzees would select the correct location, but then with an expression that can only be described as puzzlement they would ignore the lettuce and search for the bananas that should have been there! The chimpanzees were not just learning and remembering what to do, but also what the reward was. It is not clear how a behaviorist could account for these observations (other problems with equating learning with performance are described in Chapter 3).

Behaviorism also never got very far in accounting for complex learning. Skinner did attempt to describe language learning in terms of reinforcement principles. For example, some speech utterances, referred to by Skinner as *Mands*, make requests or demands that are rewarded when the hearer complies. Thus, a child who says "I wanna cookie!" is reinforced when the parent gives him or her a cookie. Another use of speech involves naming different objects (Skinner calls this the tact function). A child who hears what different things are called (often in response to the question "What's that?") can learn the meaning of words by abstracting the relevant properties. Thus a child knows that "dog" cannot refer to color because animals with very different colors are called dogs.

Skinner also described the acquisition of syntax or grammar. He proposed that learners abstract certain word-position frames to generalize to new utterances. For example, after hearing "the woman's dog," "the man's desk," and "the child's desk" the learner would begin to form the possessive frame and would generalize to a novel combination such as "the man's dog" or "the woman's desk."

Although Skinner's analysis seems to provide a reasonable beginning, it never proved influential. Quite early Skinner's *Verbal Behavior* was subjected to an extremely effective critique by the linguist Noam Chomsky (1959). Chomsky's most telling arguments concern the problems with mapping or determining "objective description" of stimulus and response in discussing language behavior. As one example, Skinner said that the past tense suffix *-ed* is controlled "by that subtle property of stimuli that we speak of as action-in-the-past" (Skinner, 1957, p. 121). But "action-in-the-past" is not some objective stimulus such as a red light turning on in a Skinner box. By directly postulating some "action-in-the-past" stimulus, Skinner was abandoning the behaviorist principle of describing learning in terms of objective, external stimuli. In short, the stimulus-response account was empty and circular.

Skinner's analysis also failed to take into account the role of the organism in organizing and theorizing about its experience. This neglect of internal processes mediating between stimulus and response eventually led experimental psychologists to move away from behaviorism. It soon became clear that one could analyze internal processes without running into the difficulties that plagued the early introspectionists.

Cognitive Psychology.   The decline of behaviorism began around the time of World War II. Psychologists such as Donald Broadbent in England were called on to improve human skills and performance in complex tasks such as piloting an airplane. Early observations made it clear that pilots were incapable of picking up all the information on the various dials and gauges of an airplane's instrument panel. One task for the psychologists was to suggest how instrument panels might be redesigned to improve performance; another was to better understand the human side of human performance. And a key factor in this understanding was the notion of information and information transmission.

The term *information* was also being formalized by Shannon and others who were developing mathematical theories of communication at about this time. Communication was viewed in terms of sending information over potentially "noisy" channels. These channels might be physical devices such as radio transmitters or radar screens but human beings could also be viewed in terms of channels for receiving and transmitting information. Broadbent and others began to develop and test theories of attention in terms of channels and information. It proved to be very useful to think of human performance as **information processing**.

The information processing metaphor served as a rallying point in the development of cognitive psychology. The initial inspiration from communication theory was strongly reinforced by the development of computers and the corresponding theory of computation. Computers also provided a rich set of analogies for theorizing about human cognition. One could talk about buffers (locations where temporary results were kept and integrated), information storage, and information retrieval in describing the function of both machines and human beings. In short, one could theorize about internal processes without retreating into subjectivism. Terms like storage and retrieval became essential ingredients in theories of memory, and psychologists began to ask questions about information processing capacity. In a classic paper George Miller (1956) noted that human short-term memory capacity seemed to conform to "the magical number seven, plus or minus two" *chunks of information*. He was referring to the finding that people can remember a series of seven words as well as a series of seven letters even though those words are comprised of many more than seven letters. Miller's paper showed that generalizations about capacity must take into account how the learner organizes that information into **chunks** or units. His paper also underlined the role of the information processor in organizing its experience.

Cognitive psychology became predominant in the late 1960s. One touchstone was Ulric Neisser's (1967) book, *Cognitive Psychology*, which summarized a body of work within what is known as an information processing framework. A central factor was the development of techniques that allowed researchers to use indirect measures such as response times to reveal the workings of the mind. For example, Neisser's early research involved asking people to search through lists of letters to detect particular letters. He reasoned that if people can search for any one of five letters (for example) as rapidly as they can for a single letter then people must be able to make comparisons in parallel rather than serially.

The rationale for using reaction time to study how the mind works comes naturally from an information processing framework. Information processing models conceive of cognitive activities as involving a series of steps, procedures, or processes that take time. Frequently, one is able to decide between competing theories only on the basis of what they predict about reaction time.

In some cases experiments interrupt processing in order to see what information is available at different points in time. A nice example of this approach comes from a recent paper by Ratcliff and McKoon (1989). Participants learned lists of active and passive sentences such as "John hit Bill" or "Jeff was attracted by Helen" and then had to discriminate those sentences from new sentences like "Bill hit John." They were allowed varying amounts of time to decide if a sentence was old or new. Ratcliff and McKoon measured accuracy for discriminating different types of information as a function of time. They found that early in processing (responses between three- and seven-tenths of a second) people could discriminate previously studied sentences from sentences containing all new words. However, people were completely unable to discriminate between a new sentence like "Bill hit John" and an old sentence like "John hit Bill." Ability to discriminate on the basis of relational information (e.g., who hit whom) began after about seven-tenths of a second and then increased systematically. In short, Ratcliff and McKoon found that different *kinds* of information became available at different times during the retrieval. The observation is important because it is inconsistent with numerous models or theories that do not distinguish between item information and relational information or assume that they become available in a unitary manner. An excellent overview of research using time to understand cognitive processes is provided by Meyer, Osman, Irwin, and Yantis (1988).

Another way to understand cognitive processes is to look at the pattern of errors that are made. For example, suppose a person is shown the letter string X, R, B, T and later on recalls X, R, V, C. V and C do not seem visually similar to B and T so this pattern of errors may seem puzzling. Note, however, that V and C are acoustically similar to B and T. This observation led psychologists to postulate an information processing step in which the initial visual code becomes converted into an acoustic code (see, e.g., Conrad, 1964).

In short, the information processing framework offered a host of exciting questions to be asked and a sound experimental methodology for answering them. Early successes, coupled with the handy computer metaphor, prompted researchers to explore a greater variety of paradigms and to be willing to tackle more complex cognitive tasks. In doing so, cognitive psychologists laid the groundwork for their role in the emergence of cognitive science, a topic to which we now turn.

The Emergence of Cognitive Science

Background. We have already alluded to the development of computers and their influence on cognitive psychology. In addition to providing a technological tool and descriptive language for formulating information processing theories, the underlying theory of computation, notably the work of Alan Turing, had an enormous influence on how people thought about the mind. If computers are capable of true intelligence, then intelligence can be understood in terms of computations and symbol manipulation, because that is what computers do. Alan Turing is known for two observations that support this view.

Turing Machines.   A **Turing machine** is very simple. It can be described as consisting of a tape of any length divided into cells in which a symbol (usually 1 or 0) can be written, and a device that can read the contents of a cell and then carry out some actions. The actions consist of replacing the current symbol with another symbol and then moving the tape one cell to the left or right. In addition, the machine has a finite list of states or conditions it can be in and a table that describes what action should take place for each of these states and what state should be entered after the action is completed. Turing (1936) showed that this simple device can do any computation that can be performed by a digital computer (as long as it has enough tape and enough time) and he further conjectured that anything that can be computed at all can be computed on a Turing machine. Given that the Turing machine is both a physical system and an abstract computing device, it is tempting to assert that the same principle holds for human beings. The suggestion is that the nervous system is a physical system that performs abstract computations and these computations are the cornerstone of intelligence. These observations encourage a computational approach to understanding the mind in which the focus is more on the functional characteristics of intelligence than on its physical realization. This lays the groundwork for the belief that one may learn something about human intelligence from seeing how a computer does something intelligent and vice versa.

The Turing Test.   Turing is also well known for his proposal for answering the question of whether or not machines can think. The idea is to have a person communicate over a teletype with either another person or a computer. Turing suggested that if the person was unable to tell which was which, one ought to concede that the machine could think. The **Turing test** cuts through a lot of vagueness concerning what we mean by thought and again encourages us to view intelligence in terms of functional rather than physical characteristics.

When computers began to be available in the 1950s they were quickly put to use to do some fairly intelligent things. Herbert Simon and Allan Newell developed a program known as the Logic Theorist that could prove logical theorems and, furthermore, prove them in a way that resembled human performance. This work encouraged both the development of artificial intelligence (AI) and an interaction between cognitive psychology and artificial intelligence. And, of course, questions about whether computers can think are relevant to and informed by work on the philosophy of mind (see, e.g., Putnam, 1960; Fodor, 1981).

At roughly the same time, there were developments that led to increasing interaction between psychologists and linguists. Psychologists began to shift from an interest in memory for nonsense syllables and single words to memory for sentences, paragraphs, and stories. In addition, Chomsky's transformational grammar provided a rich source of ideas. Psychologists began to evaluate the psychological reality of some of the insights provided by linguists (see, e.g., Miller, 1962; Fodor, Bever, & Garrett, 1974).

The net effect of these developments was that some of the traditional distinctions among disciplines began to break down. A computer scientist, a philosopher, a linguist, and a psychologist might all be interested in concept formation and might bring insights from their disciplines to bear on the problem. Philosophy, linguistics, AI, cognitive psychology, along with anthropology and neuroscience, have begun to formalize their similar interests under the banner of cognitive science.

Cognitive Science.   **Cognitive science** is an interdisciplinary approach to the study of the mind. Each constituent discipline is distinct in its methods, theories, and observations but they are united by their shared interest in the nature of intelligence. Clearly, cognitive psychology is not an isolated discipline. Although our focus here is on cognitive psychology and the state of its art, part of this art reflects the influence of AI, philosophy, anthropology, and linguistics.

Diversity of Approaches

So far we have considered information processing from a fairly abstract level. When we look closer we will see a wide range of styles of research and theorizing within this general framework.

Although most researchers subscribe to the information processing framework, that framework does not dictate exactly how research should be done. No single approach dominates cognitive psychology. In this section we offer an organizational scheme for understanding some of these different perspectives. Approaches differ along three major dimensions:

degree of formalism, simplicity versus sufficiency, and explicit versus implicit structure.

Degree of Formalism—From Frameworks to Mathematical Models.

Cognitive psychologists perform experiments to answer questions but the questions being asked vary enormously in terms of their formalism. At one end of the continuum are frameworks that attempt to describe general principles to organize research findings. No particular experiment really tests the framework and the framework is not falsifiable in any formal sense. Rather, frameworks either are or are not useful in organizing research. An example of a useful framework is Tulving's *encoding specificity* principle (Tulving & Thomson, 1973).

The encoding specificity principle states that a retrieval cue will help memory only to the extent that it overlaps with the ways in which the material to be remembered was originally coded. Tulving, Thomson, and others produced a variety of observations that are consistent with this principle. For example, suppose that one studies the word *iron* in the context of steam and encodes iron as an appliance rather than as a type of metal. Then recall of iron ought to be prompted by a context created by presenting *laundry* as a hint or cue but not prompted by hints such as *ore*. And that is what happens. Frameworks are not directly refutable but they do provide general principles that can guide the development of testable theories.

Testability is one of the more salient characteristics of mathematical models of cognitive processes. **Mathematical models** can vary considerably in their complexity but they have in common the goal of predicting or "fitting" data. For example, Bower's (1961) one-element model for paired-associate learning (people have to learn to associate two things, one known as the stimulus, the other as the response, and to produce the response when given the stimulus) consisted of the idea that whenever a pair was presented, there was some certain probability that complete learning would take place. This all-or-none learning idea contained just one parameter or unknown (namely, the value of this probability), but Bower was able to predict a wide variety of statistics associated with learning. For example, his model correctly predicted the distribution of errors across trials, the average trial of last error, total runs of errors, and so on.

Mathematical models also serve to organize data. No one had thought to calculate the probability that two errors would fall three trials apart until Bower's model made predictions about it. That might not seem like a very important thing to do but it helped to distinguish the idea that learning takes place in an all-or-none manner from the idea that learning is gradual. In some research areas competing theories may be cast as mathematical models. An advantage of this formal approach is that sometimes (e.g., Townsend, 1971; Estes, 1986) one learns that seemingly different models or theories are actually mathematically equivalent to each other! More often the formal analysis points researchers toward situations in which the models in question make different predictions.

At their best, mathematical models can be extremely useful. Even when they fail, the reasons for their failure are often informative and point the way to better models. Mathematical models are not, however, beyond criticism. To keep the models from getting too complex, one may have to simplify the experimental situation so severely that models describe the constraints of the situation rather than the constraints of the human mind. Like any theory, a mathematical model focuses on some phenomena and ignores others. For example, Bower's one-element theory said nothing about what would make the learning probability big or small—it just described and predicted (very successfully) the consequences of assuming that learning was all-or-none and that the learning probability did not change across trials. Recent mathematical models have placed a premium on breadth and applicability to a variety of situations (e.g., Hintzman, 1988).

Probably the safest generalization is that degree of formalism should vary with stage of development. Initial observations should make clear what the phenomena are; mathematical models might narrow attention prematurely to a subset of these phenomena. Frameworks serve to organize phenomena but their lack of testability means that they may drift into circularity unless they inspire more specific theories. It is a testimony to the vitality of cognitive psychology that there seems to be plenty of room for varying degrees of formality.

Simplicity versus Sufficiency—AI and Computer Simulation Models.

Testability is a fundamental principle associated with developing mathematical models, even if this requires simplifying experimental situations in some ways. A different perspective on cognitive modeling grows out of the AI tradition. This alternative view is that a researcher's primary goal should be to have a model that is sufficient to do something interesting, even if the model becomes so complex that it is not clear how to test it. Very often models that stress sufficiency take the form of computer simulations.

Computer simulation models are quite straightforward. Investigators attempt to describe some cognitive task in terms of a series of processes and then write a computer program in which the steps in the program correspond to the process. Then the outputs of the program can be compared with the actual data. A classic example of this approach is the

General Problem Solver (GPS) developed by Newell, Shaw, and Simon (1959).

True to its name, GPS was designed to have a core set of processes that could be applied across a variety of different problem-solving domains. The basic idea was that problem solving can be analyzed in terms of a starting point, a goal, and a series of operators or procedures that might reduce the difference between the starting point and the goal.

How does GPS know the starting point, the goal, things or objects to be operated on, and possible operations? The programmer has to provide them. GPS then transforms the starting point into the goal using a variety of strategies. Table 2.1 summarizes the major methods used by GPS. Because pursuing various goals leads to the generation of subgoals, GPS also has an executive routine that monitors the generation of new subgoals and sets up priorities for working on them.

GPS produces interesting behaviors and can solve problems and prove theorems. More significant for our purposes is that the subgoaling and other steps that GPS goes through seem to correspond to descriptions that humans provide when they are asked to "think aloud" as they try to solve the same problems (Newell & Simon, 1972). In other words, GPS can be thought of as a psychological theory of human problem solving.

Computer simulation models are falsifiable as psychological models. For example, the think-aloud protocols might not have matched the steps that GPS goes through. On the other hand, simulation models often involve what Smith (1978) refers to as the sufficiency/transparency trade-off. It is common to say in AI that the theory "is the program." But some aspects of a program are necessary just to make the program run. The general principles of the theory may be buried in the mass of detail needed to make the theory sufficient. Consequently, it may be difficult to isolate individual assumptions or components of a simulation-based theory and evaluate them separately. The trade-off between having theories that can handle complex problems and being able to understand and evaluate the theories is difficult in both cognitive psychology and AI.

Despite the sufficiency/transparency trade-off, models in the form of computer simulations, notably AI models, have made a number of contributions at both specific and general levels. Contributions at the specific level will be detailed in later chapters of this book. At a general level, we list here three major strong points of simulation models.

1. *The value of explicitness.* Computer simulations have a built-in safeguard against vagueness. Unless assumptions can be translated into steps in a program, the program will not run. Writing a program forces one

Table 2.1   A summary of the major goals of GPS and the associated methods used to achieve them. The goals of transforming object *A* into *B* leads to the subgoal of reducing one or more differences between them. To reduce a given difference, a relevant operator is found. The next subgoal is to apply the operator to *A*. If that cannot be done, then the next subgoal is to see how *A* differs from something to which the operator can be applied. At this point the sequence will repeat at this lower level.

Goal I: Transform object *A* into object *B*

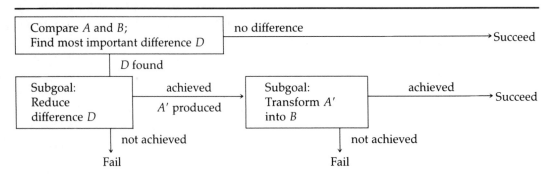

Goal II: Reduce difference *D* between object *A* and *B*

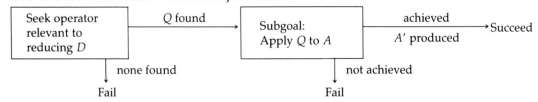

Goal III: Apply operator *Q* to object *A*

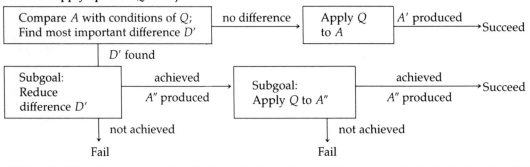

Source: Green, B. F. Jr., 1963.

to face issues and assumptions that otherwise might be hidden in less formal, verbal descriptions.

     2. *Appreciation of computational complexity.* A program might run but take forever to come up with an answer because there are too many possibilities to be considered. A standard question in AI programming is whether a program will "scale up," that is, continue to perform efficiently when given a larger problem or more knowledge. Many very plausible routines for accomplishing some goal run into complexity problems. It is a standard practice in AI journals to include computational efficiency as part of the description of the program.

     3. *Appreciation of the need to control relevance.* This point is directly related to the preceding one. A system cannot search and reason through its entire knowledge base to answer simple questions. It is important to organize knowledge so the *relevant* information can be brought to bear without getting bogged down in details.

Explicit versus Implicit Structure—Connectionist Models. A common practice, if not goal, of many computer simulation programs is to make structure as explicit as possible. Information resides in discrete locations and to understand how the program works, it is important to make transparent which structures are doing what. The representational system or language used to perform information processing operations is jointly specified by the programming language and the structures that programmers build into the simulation.

     Certainly explicitness has its virtues, but it comes at certain costs. Building structures directly into a program does not address the question of how structures are acquired by organisms. Standard computer simulation programs also may not represent plausible models of how the brain works, at least if one takes the analogy to be quite specific. For example, we know that information does not reside in single brain cells, but rather is distributed across thousands of neurons. If information were completely localized, we might wake up being unable to recognize our grandmother because the cell dedicated to recognizing her has "passed away."

     Recently there has been a renewed interest in developing computational models that are more directly inspired by knowledge concerning how the brain functions. These models are variously referred to as neural networks, parallel distributed processing (**PDP**), or simply **connectionist models**. The majority of these models have a more implicit structure in that what corresponds to a piece of information is a pattern of activation across many nodes or over a network of interconnected cells. Furthermore, in some models the various bits of information are all stored in the same network and it is far from obvious that the network can "keep the facts straight." As we shall see, however, it is precisely the distributed nature of these representations that gives them many of their interesting characteristics. Let's look at a specific example, a model for room schemas.

We have already alluded to **schemas** as devices for organizing knowledge. Schemas are used for representing concepts and act like models of the world. Furthermore, partial information leads to the activation of the relevant schema and it can be used to infer other information that is not directly specified. Thus, when we read "John went into the kitchen and got a soda" we can use our knowledge of kitchens and sodas to infer that there was a refrigerator in the room, that the soda was in the refrigerator, and that John opened the refrigerator to get the soda. We also assume other things that are "too obvious to mention" such as that the kitchen almost surely had a ceiling, floor, and walls.

Although it is clear that schemas are a good idea as a device for handling inferences, it is not always clear just how to implement them. Is there a single schema for kitchens that is retrieved whenever "kitchen" is mentioned? A problem with this approach is that the resulting schema might be too rigid. For example, one would expect that a *large kitchen* would be different from a *small kitchen* in more respects than simply size. A large kitchen might be more likely to have a television set or a fireplace in it than a small kitchen. A possible solution would be to have one schema for small kitchens and another one for large kitchens. The drawback to this approach is that it may lead one to postulate endless numbers of schemas. The connectionist approach to schemas is quite elegant and has a natural flexibility. As one example, we briefly outline Rumelhart et al.'s description of a PDP approach to room schemas (Rumelhart, Smolensky, McClelland, & Hinton, 1986).

From a connectionist perspective schemas are not explicitly stored entities that are retrieved from memory. Instead schemas are constructed or computed dynamically from a knowledge base, which takes the form of a pattern of interconnections in the network. These interconnections summarize the experience of the learning system with its environment. Retrieval begins when the initial input (maybe the word "kitchen" or fragments of information associated with kitchens) activates units and activation spreads through the network. Features that are unspecified in the input may nonetheless be activated or *filled in*. These features can be thought of as inferences or guesses about the environment.

Rumelhart et al. constructed a model for room schemas by asking people to indicate which of the 40 room descriptors shown in Table 2.2 applied for different rooms. For example, people said that all rooms have

Table 2.2   **The Forty Room Descriptors.**

ceiling	walls	door	windows	very-large
large	medium	small	very-small	desk
telephone	bed	typewriter	bookshelf	carpet
books	desk-chair	clock	picture	floor-lamp
sofa	easy-chair	coffee-cup	ashtray	fireplace
drapes	stove	coffeepot	refrigerator	toaster
cupboard	sink	dresser	television	bathtub
toilet	scale	oven	computer	clothes-hanger

Source: Rumelhart, Smolensky, McClelland and Hinton, 1986.

ceilings, that fireplaces were likely to be in living rooms and not in bathrooms, that sinks and refrigerators were almost always in kitchens, and so on. This information was used to construct a network summarizing the information. Items that tended to appear together had positive or excitatory connections to each other and the more often items appeared together, the greater the strength or weight of the connection between them. For example, refrigerators and sinks would have a strong positive connection whereas refrigerators and bathtubs would have a strong negative association. In short, the network consisted of the 40 descriptors or nodes connected by positive or negative links. That is, the room schema was just a jumble of positive and negative connections.

The resulting network is summarized in Figure 2.1. The figure looks a little forbidding but is actually fairly easy to understand. The white and dark squares inside the units indicate positive and negative connection strengths, respectively. The squares are spatially organized. The large white square in the top row and second column of the ceiling unit means, for example, that there is an excitatory connection between ceilings and walls (since the wall unit is in the top row and second column). Similarly there is an excitatory link between the refrigerator unit (fifth row, third column) and the sink unit (fifth row, second column) and an inhibitory link between the refrigerator unit and the bathtub unit (last row, second column), in the latter case because refrigerators and bathtubs are rarely in the same room.

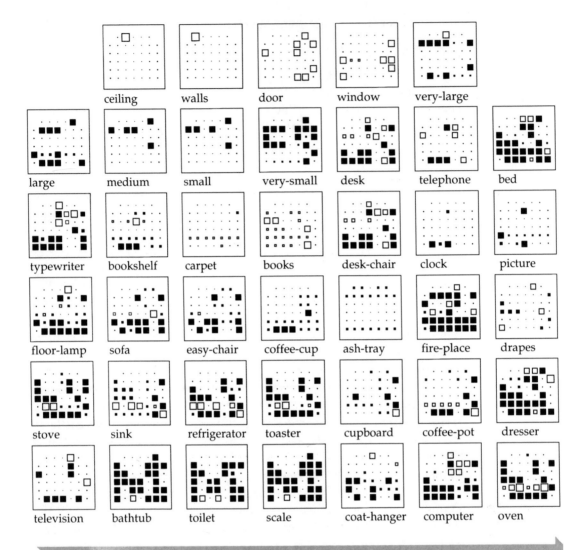

Figure 2.1   In the figure each unit is represented by a square. The name below the square names the descriptor represented by each square. Within each unit, the small black and white squares represent the weights from that unit to each of the other units in the system. The relative position of the small squares within each unit indicates the unit with which that unit is connected. *Source*: Rumelhart et al., 1986.

What do all these interconnections mean? Although nothing in Figure 2.1 is readily labeled as a schema, the network functions naturally as a schema. That is, when one activates some of the units this partial information leads to the activation of other schema-related information. For example, if one activates the ceiling unit and the oven unit, the patterns of activation soon begin to stabilize to that seen in Figure 2.2. One can see that (in addition to the oven), coffeepot, coffee cup, cupboard, toaster, refrigerator, sink, and walls are strongly activated (stove is less strongly activated, perhaps because people tended to mention either stove or oven but not both), whereas telephone, small clock, drapes, and window are moderately activated and units like sofa, desk, and bed are not activated at all. Thus the kitchen schema has been activated with the amount of activation corresponding to the certainty of inference about other properties. In general, if a typical property for a type of room is turned on or activated, then the entire room schema tends to be activated. In other words, the schema is not organized under a single heading (e.g., kitchen) but can be accessed by whatever properties tend to be associated with the schema. This is a very desirable property.

In addition, the network can potentially encode subtle interactions of properties within a given schema. For example, books and bookshelves are linked more closely than books and a telephone. If there are subtypes for a schema the appropriate subtype will tend to be activated. Looking again at Figure 2.1, we see that the *small* unit has an inhibitory connection to the *fireplace* unit (fourth row, sixth column) so that *sofa* might activate *fireplace* but *sofa* plus *small* would not. In our opinion, a major strength of connectionist models is their ability to integrate multiple sources of information naturally and to generate inferences in a flexible manner.

You will have noticed that the room schema example included abstract conceptual units (e.g., the oven unit) that were directly built into the network. As we shall see later on, however, in principle networks can construct or learn these units from experience (Anderson, Silverstein, Ritz, & Jones, 1977; Rumelhart & Zipser, 1985; Rumelhart, Hinton, & Williams, 1986).

As with AI models, we will not provide a separate chapter on connectionist models but we will incorporate their description into relevant content-oriented chapters. The two-volume work by Rumelhart and McClelland (1986) provides an extensive discussion and illustration of the virtues and strengths of connectionist models. The recent renewed interest in PDP models means that there are many developments to be explored and problems to be solved. Although PDP models have been criticized on a variety of grounds, it nonetheless seems like a safe bet that parallel distrib-

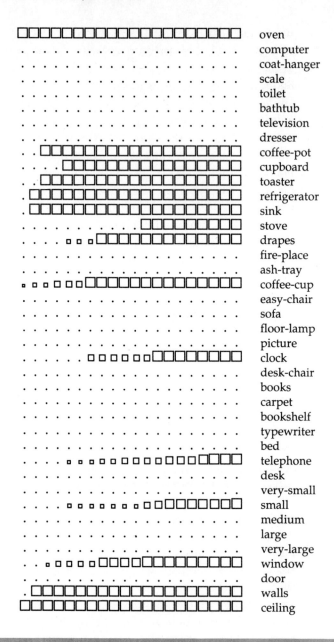

☐☐☐☐☐☐☐☐☐☐☐☐☐☐☐☐☐☐☐	oven
· · · · · · · · · · · · · · · · · · · ·	computer
· · · · · · · · · · · · · · · · · · · ·	coat-hanger
· · · · · · · · · · · · · · · · · · · ·	scale
· · · · · · · · · · · · · · · · · · · ·	toilet
· · · · · · · · · · · · · · · · · · · ·	bathtub
· · · · · · · · · · · · · · · · · · · ·	television
· · · · · · · · · · · · · · · · · · · ·	dresser
· · ☐☐☐☐☐☐☐☐☐☐☐☐☐☐☐☐☐	coffee-pot
· · · · ☐☐☐☐☐☐☐☐☐☐☐☐☐☐☐☐	cupboard
· · ☐☐☐☐☐☐☐☐☐☐☐☐☐☐☐☐☐	toaster
· ☐☐☐☐☐☐☐☐☐☐☐☐☐☐☐☐☐☐	refrigerator
· ☐☐☐☐☐☐☐☐☐☐☐☐☐☐☐☐☐☐	sink
· · · · · · · · · · ☐☐☐☐☐☐☐☐	stove
· · · · □ □ □ ☐☐☐☐☐☐☐☐☐☐☐	drapes
· · · · · · · · · · · · · · · · · · · ·	fire-place
· · · · · · · · · · · · · · · · · · · ·	ash-tray
▪ □ □ □ □□□☐☐☐☐☐☐☐☐☐☐☐☐	coffee-cup
· · · · · · · · · · · · · · · · · · · ·	easy-chair
· · · · · · · · · · · · · · · · · · · ·	sofa
· · · · · · · · · · · · · · · · · · · ·	floor-lamp
· · · · · · · · · · · · · · · · · · · ·	picture
· · · · · · · □ □ □ □ □ □□☐☐☐☐☐☐	clock
· · · · · · · · · · · · · · · · · · · ·	desk-chair
· · · · · · · · · · · · · · · · · · · ·	books
· · · · · · · · · · · · · · · · · · · ·	carpet
· · · · · · · · · · · · · · · · · · · ·	bookshelf
· · · · · · · · · · · · · · · · · · · ·	typewriter
· · · · · · · · · · · · · · · · · · · ·	bed
· · · · · ▪ □ □ □ □ □ □ □□□☐☐☐☐	telephone
· · · · · · · · · · · · · · · · · · · ·	desk
· · · · · · · · · · · · · · · · · · · ·	very-small
· · · · · ▪ □ □ □ □ □ □ ▪ □ □☐☐☐☐☐	small
· · · · · · · · · · · · · · · · · · · ·	medium
· · · · · · · · · · · · · · · · · · · ·	large
· · · · · · · · · · · · · · · · · · · ·	very-large
· · ▪ □ □ □ □ □☐☐☐☐☐☐☐☐☐☐☐	window
· · · · · · · · · · · · · · · · · · · ·	door
· ☐☐☐☐☐☐☐☐☐☐☐☐☐☐☐☐☐☐	walls
☐☐☐☐☐☐☐☐☐☐☐☐☐☐☐☐☐☐☐	ceiling

Figure 2.2 Runs of the network where the unit *ceiling* and the unit *oven* are clamped on. The clamping of *ceiling* represents information indicating that *room* is the domain of discussion. The system settles on properties that one would associate with a kitchen. *Source*: Rumelhart et al., 1986.

uted models focusing on implicit rather than explicit structures will continue to be an active medium for constructing models of cognition.

Summary.   As we have just seen, there are strikingly different ways to study cognition within a general information processing framework. Examples of these distinct styles of theorizing will be scattered throughout the remainder of this book. We conclude this chapter with two other fundamental issues with respect to the study of cognition: (1) levels and units of analysis; (2) relations between (artificial) laboratory experiments and the natural world. The issue of levels of analysis is important because it can help to organize findings and theories. For example, a network might function as a realization of a mathematical model (more on this later). Finally, the relation between artificial laboratory tasks and the world is important both for evaluating research and for linking our central themes to experimental research.

Levels and Units of Analysis

Units of Analysis.   A fundamental issue in the study of cognition is what the proper units of analysis should be. Some behaviorists thought that the proper units were the movement of individual muscles and tried to analyze thought as subvocal speech. From an abstract perspective we want the units we use to give us useful generalizations about whatever we are studying.

A common research strategy is to attempt to explain phenomena at one level by breaking down the units at that level into subunits or features. For example, suppose we are trying to explain why people are more likely to confuse the letter E with F than they are to confuse E with T. We might argue that the letters are made up of components or features and that E differs from F only in one feature (the bottom horizontal line), but E differs from T in multiple features. Of course, this particular featural analysis will not be helpful when we try to explain why the concept *dog* is more similar to the concept *wolf* than to the concept *dot*. That is to say, the relevant units or features are relative to the level of analysis that is of interest.

The issue of units is especially salient in analyzing computer simulation models. Presumably, the theory embodied in the program should not be taken seriously at the level of individual lines or statements because the same theory could be programmed in a variety of ways and what constitutes a line or statement may depend on the programming language chosen or even the machine. At the other extreme, one would not want to define a program strictly by its outputs because the same output could be achieved by fundamentally different underlying processes. So it seems that the proper units must be found at some intermediate level of abstraction.

Implicit in our discussion of units is the idea that we are interested in models that illuminate cognitive *processes*. This assumption may be too broad for some purposes and too narrow for others. It may be too broad in that it may be a mistake to ignore how processes actually are implemented in living organisms. Cognitive neuroscientists argue that cognitive psychologists generally have not taken the nervous system seriously enough. We may also be too narrow in not paying sufficient attention to what cognitive processes are for—that is, what problems they are designed to address. So let's take a closer look at levels.

Levels of Analysis.   The human brain is obviously very different from a digital computer, yet the two may be similar in certain respects, depending on the level of analysis. One interesting and influential way of thinking about complex information systems grows out of the work of David Marr.

Marr's Three Levels.   Although Marr's research was on vision, his analysis of levels of description is quite general. To illustrate a complex system Marr (1982) uses the example of a cash register at a checkout counter and we shall borrow heavily from his description.

The broadest level of analysis asks what the system or device does and why. What a cash register does is addition, so this level involves the theory of addition. This theory will tell us what is being computed in a way that is independent of both how numbers are written (e.g., Roman versus Arabic) and how the addition process will actually be executed. The why part of the question can be answered by noting that the constraints associated with our theory about making purchases corresponds to the operation of addition. For example, if you buy nothing you should pay nothing; there is a natural zero point; the total cost should depend neither on the order in which you purchase things nor on how things are grouped (the mathematical principles of commutativity and associativity); and if the purchaser returns an item, the net expenditure should be zero (i.e., there is a natural inverse). Questions about what is being computed and why characterize what Marr calls the **computational level** and what it yields, in this example, is a computational theory of cash registers.

To actually perform the operation of addition, a system needs to have some form of *representation* (a formal system for being explicit about the information operated on) and an algorithm or procedure to accomplish the operation. This second level, the **algorithmic level**, specifies how the computations are done. For addition, a system might use Arabic numerals for the representation and the algorithm might follow the rules about starting with the least significant digits and "carrying" if the sum is greater than nine. Just which algorithm is appropriate depends on the representation selected. In general, a variety of different representation algorithm pairs could accomplish the same computations (e.g., one could use either a decimal or binary system to do addition).

The third level of analysis is the **implementation level**. This is the level at which the algorithm is physically realized. A child who adds Arabic numerals in the manner we have described is using the same algorithm that is implemented by the wires and transistors in a cash register. Even different computers may realize the same algorithm in different ways—Marr points out that a computer programmed to play tic-tac-toe was implemented by W. K. Hissis and B. Silverman in a computer made from Tinkertoys!

These three levels are summarized in Table 2.3. Marr argues that to understand a complex system, scientists need to operate on all three levels. Knowing *what* is being computed often places important constraints on the algorithmic level (it must compute the right thing). Similarly, obser-

Table 2.3   The three levels at which any intelligent system carrying out an information-processing task must be understood.

Computational Theory	Representation and Algorithm	Hardware Implementation
What is the goal of the computation and why is it appropriate?	How can this computational theory be realized? In particular, what is the representation for the input and output, and what is the algorithm that does the computation?	How can the representation and algorithm be physically implemented?

* *Source*: Marr, 1982.

vations at the implementation level determine which algorithms can be realized.

Marr's three levels will come up again in later chapters. His framework allows us to see relationships among different research perspectives. For example, Chomsky's theories of grammar can be seen as applying at the computational level, research on language comprehension may correspond to the algorithmic level, and a neurolinguist focusing on the neural substrate of expressive aphasia (inability to speak associated with damage to Broca's area of the brain) can be seen as operating at the implementation level.

Recursive Decomposition.   For many purposes Marr's three-level distinction works fairly well. But a closer analysis suggests that there are actually many possible levels of description. Studies of text comprehension and studies of expressive aphasia are quite a few levels higher than microbiology or physics. Palmer and Kimchi (1986) suggest that information processing theories rely (among other things) on the principle of **recursive decomposition**. According to recursive decomposition, any complex (informational) event at one level of description can be specified more fully at a lower level of description by decomposing it into (1) a number of components and (2) processes that specify the relations among these components. An example of recursive decomposition is shown in Figure 2.3.

Neither the Marr nor the Palmer and Kimchi descriptions of levels should be equated with the notion of **reductionism**, which assumes that the best or correct level of description is the most specific one (e.g., at the level of physics). Different levels of description are not just quantitatively simpler but may also be qualitatively different. This is most evident in Marr's analysis. In general, however, higher level descriptions may manifest emergent properties that derive from how the system is organized. To borrow an example from Palmer and Kimchi, the states of matter corresponding to liquids, solids, and gases are properties of aggregates of molecules, not of individual molecules. No single molecule, by itself, has the property of being gaseous, liquid, or solid.

In cognitive psychology the ideal is to pick the level or levels that best illuminate the questions being asked. We say levels because there are likely to be limitations if only a single level of analysis is considered. Cognitive psychologists have been criticized (perhaps quite properly) for not giving sufficient consideration to Marr's most general level, the what and why question. Often this criticism has taken the form of pointing to the need to consider our human environment or ecology in conducting and evaluating experiments.

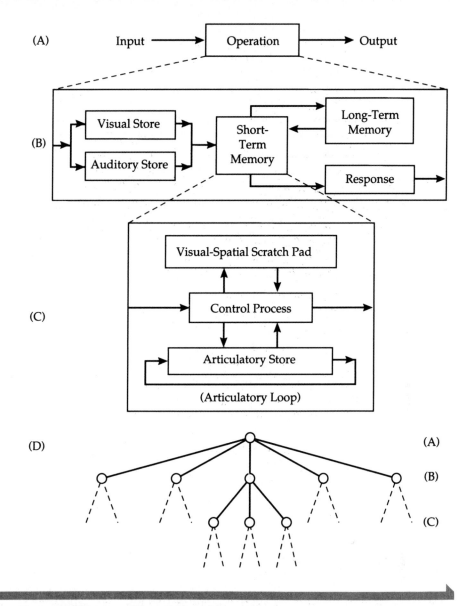

Figure 2.3 **Recursive Decomposition of Mental Processes.**
The mind can be described as a single, complex informational operation that maps input stimulation to output behavior (A). This operation can be decomposed into an information flow diagram of several simpler component operations (B), each of which can be further decomposed into still simpler operations (C). The resulting recursive structure of theoretical decomposition can be represented by a hierarchical graph (D) in which the nodes at a given level correspond to the component operations of the flow diagram at that level and the links (arcs) connecting them represent the decomposition relations between different levels of description.
Source: Palmer and Kimchi, 1986.

Ecological Validity

A common criticism of laboratory studies is that they are too artificial and lack **ecological validity**. We take ecological validity to refer to the idea of developing theories that describe cognitive processes operating in realistic, everyday situations. It is hard to fault this ideal.

Ecological validity, however, has also been used as a rallying point for a variety of related arguments, which, at best, we only partially agree with. One position is that any laboratory experiment that fails to capture the full complexity of natural situations will necessarily produce invalid results. It certainly is possible to be so concerned with controlling variables that one creates a very artificial, even impoverished situation. Any important variable left out of an experimental situation may limit the generality of any result obtained. But to argue that results are necessarily invalid is to ignore much of the history of science. One often has to resort to highly artificial situations (such as forcing people to say whether a sentence is old or new after 400 milliseconds) to contrast the predictions of alternative theories. The other side of the issue is that ecologically valid situations are very likely (or even necessarily) experimentally invalid because one cannot tease apart the contributions of different correlated factors to performance.

Another position correlated with ecological validity is that the research agenda of cognitive psychologists ought to involve "real" processes in "humanly understandable situations." One index of whether or not cognitive psychologists are meeting this goal is whether or not psychological research addresses questions that lay people would ask about the mind. Ulric Neisser (1982) chastised psychologists on precisely this point: "If X is an interesting or socially significant aspect of memory, then psychologists have hardly ever studied X" (p. 4).

Although we agree with some of Neisser's general arguments about considering the social context of memory, we do not agree with his specific suggestion that research should necessarily focus on the sort of practical questions that a lay person might pose about learning, memory, or thinking. We disagree because we believe that the most challenging questions about the mind typically involve processes that are so natural we tend to take them for granted. Perception does not seem to be a problem because it does not occur to us to ask how an ambiguous two-dimensional retinal projection is converted into the experience of a three-dimensional world. Nor does it occur to us to ask just how we bring our knowledge to bear in order to comprehend a sentence. Indeed, one index of whether some cognitive function is fundamental might be whether or not it operates so naturally and effortlessly that it does not occur to us to ask how it works. Of course, we have no strong prejudice against practical problems; it is often in analyzing such applied situations that one becomes aware of or is forced to deal with basic questions about the mind.

A third position on ecological validity can be seen in Gibson's ecological approach to perception. James J. Gibson (1979) argued that the view that we construct our percepts by combining sensory cues was a misguided consequence of elementaristic, ecologically invalid (impoverished) psychological experiments. Gibson's research program focused on an analysis of the information available in the environment, which he suggested provided enough valid information that the world could be perceived directly. That is, speculations about internal processes and inference were not needed because higher level invariants (or information) were directly available.

Gibson's devotion to analyzing the information available in the environment represents an important contribution to the study of perception. No analysis of perceptual processes can get very far without taking the environment and the information it affords seriously. David Marr was influenced by Gibson's work precisely because it addressed broad, computational-level questions. However, this focus comes at the cost of neglecting internal processes or mechanisms that enable organisms to extract invariants. In our view, an effective integration of concern about information in the environment and the organisms that interact in it is provided by Shepard's (1984) evolutionary perspective on ecological constraints.

Shepard agrees with Gibson that higher organisms are active explorers and manipulators of their environment. Shepard argues that this exploration is not just random but is guided by internal schemas that allow one to anticipate as well as notice events. The ability to develop appropriate expectations may be vitally important when there is little information or little time available before an organism must act.

Shepard draws an analogy between the perceptual system and biological or circadian rhythms. The activity pattern of many animals is guided by day–night cycles and it seems natural to assume that these rhythms are directly under the control of the sun. Researchers found, however, that when animals such as hamsters are placed under conditions of constant illumination (in an artificial laboratory situation) they continue to show cycles of 24 hours, plus or minus only a few minutes. In short, the periodicity has become internalized so that it continues in the absence of the external stimulus, freeing an animal from directly depending on it. This would be advantageous for animals on cloudy days or in environments (e.g., in the safety of a burrow) where the cues from the sun are not directly available.

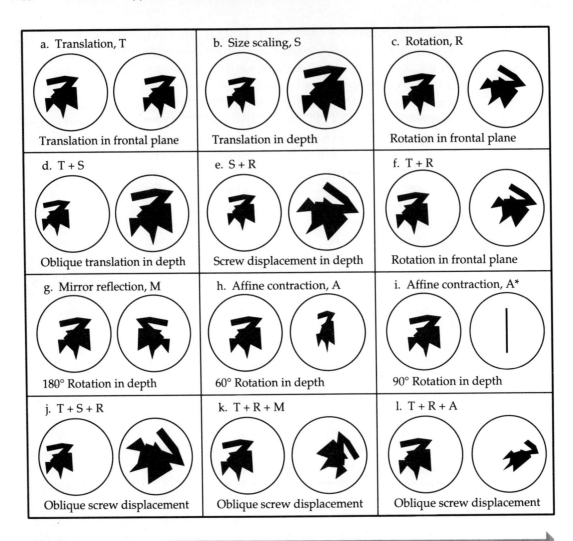

Figure 2.4 Pairs of two-dimensional shapes that when alternately presented in the indicated positions within the same (circular) field give rise to rigid apparent motion in space. (For each pair, the transformation that maps one shape into the other has the form indicated above the pair if the transformation is confined to the picture plane and the form indicated below if it is the simplest rigid transformation in space.) *Source*: Shepard, 1984.

Shepard suggests that the same situation holds for the perceptual system. The idea is that certain constraints associated with the environment (more properly the interaction of organisms with their environment) may become internalized or embodied in the perceptual system. To see what these constraints are and to evaluate their significance, researchers need to put organisms into artificial situations where the information is underdetermined. In these ambiguous situations natural constraints may be observed, just as circadian rhythms are observed under the noninformative situation of constant illumination.

Shepard illustrates this framework by his research on apparent motion. In apparent motion, the rapid alternating presentation of different views of an object gives rise to the experience of one object smoothly transforming back and forth. In the case of a dot appearing in two locations, the experience is of a single dot moving back and forth. In many situations there are a number of possible paths of motion (transformations) and the question is which ones are natural. For example, in Figure 2.4, panel b, one could perceive the figure as expanding and contracting in two dimensions, but (in experimental conditions) people perceive the figure as approaching and receding. Similarly, for panel h one could perceive horizontal compression and expansion but instead people perceive rotation in depth. The point is that this ambiguous situation, which takes people out of their normally rich environment, allows natural biases or constraints to emerge and provides important clues to how the perceptual system functions.

We suggest that Shepard's framework may hold, not just for the perceptual system but for the cognitive system in general. Note that this is support for a procedure for understanding the relation of cognitive systems to their environment by using artificial situations, not a blanket endorsement of artificial situations as ends in themselves.

In short, we believe that a concern with ecological validity is important not so much to ensure that experiments generalize to real-world situations but rather because ecological considerations are crucial to understanding cognition. We have been arguing that cognition must be heavily constrained if it is to function effectively and an analysis of natural situations provides a source of candidate constraints. Cognitive psychologists may profitably and explicitly violate ecological validity for certain purposes, but they cannot ignore ecological considerations.

Summary

We are a little uncomfortable with covering methods and approaches in such detail without talking very much about basic processes like learning, perception, memory, or problem solving. At the same time, however, we believe that you need a road map for the territory that we will be covering. In reading the later chapters it is important to bear in mind questions about levels of description and relationships of experimental situations to real-world contexts. Our brief review of the history of cognitive psychology and the different approaches to studying cognition should make it clear that cognitive psychology is a dynamic, exciting field and not a lumbering, monolithic enterprise. We hope our road map will not only help you avoid getting lost but also provide a perspective for evaluating the material to follow.

Key Terms

algorithmic level
behaviorism
chunks
cognitive psychology
cognitive science
computational level
computer simulation
  models

connectionist models
ecological validity
General Problem
  Solver
implementation level
information
  processing
introspectionism

mathematical models
PDP models
recursive
  decomposition
reductionism
schemas
Turing machine
Turing test

Recommended Readings

David Marr's book *Vision* (1982) provides a good overview of computational vision from an artificial intelligence perspective. He writes from a personal point of view that gives insight into how researchers think about problems. John Anderson's (1990) recent book illustrates the strategy of using computational level considerations to constrain cognitive models. Students with cognitive science interests will find Turing's (1936, 1958) articles to be fascinating reading. Shepard's (1984) paper is a very thoughtful analysis of an evolutionary approach to cognition. Finally, Chomsky's (1959) review of Skinner should be on the must-read list of any student of language.

II

ACQUIRING INFORMATION

3

LEARNING

Chapter Outline

"Why do you walk in such a crooked way, my child?" said an old crab to her son. "You must learn to walk straight."

"Show me the way, mother," replied the young crab, "and when I see you taking a straight course I will try to follow."

Aesop's Fables

Introduction

Among the several points in the above story about walking is the suggestion that crabs may have difficulty learning to walk straight. In this example, the problem is one of biophysical limitations. Even if a crab did somehow walk straight on one occasion, it would not necessarily know why. One of the various things it had been eating, thinking about, or looking at would all be possible causes, in addition to different component movements and combinations of movements. In general, organisms that are trying to learn "what goes with what" are faced with thousands and thousands of possibilities. Under these circumstances it is surprising that learning ever takes place. Organisms cannot, and therefore do not, consider all logical possibilities; instead they are born with certain biases so that learning some things is very easy. The cost of this bias is that learning other things is difficult if not impossible. As we shall see, these constraints generally work in a way that is adaptive for the organism.

Typically, when we think about learning our natural focus is on formal education. And it certainly is the case that the learning that takes place in school is vitally important and a central aspect of cognitive psychology. Material relevant to complex learning will be covered in chapters on memory, comprehension and inference, concepts and categories, expertise and creativity, and problem solving. In this chapter we shall concentrate on basic learning processes, drawing on examples from both human and animal learning.

Although the types of learning we shall be considering are indeed simple, the associated conceptual issues extend directly to complex learning. For example, in the branch of artificial intelligence concerned with machine learning (i.e., developing programs that can learn from examples rather than having knowledge directly programmed), one of the most important problems is **credit assignment**. When a program meets with success or failure it has to figure out why it succeeded or why it failed in order to make adaptive modifications. Again there are often many possibilities to be evaluated. AI researchers try to build into their programs biases that will lead their programs to pursue the most promising possibilities first. In the case of human and animal learning, nature has prepared us with certain heuristics (strategies) or biases that favor learning some things over others. The first section of this chapter reviews a range of learning strategies that nature has adopted.

Two Faces of Learning

The word **learning** is familiar to everyone, yet means different things to different people. Asked what is meant by learning, a person might offer as a first definition "profiting by experience." Learning in this sense refers to improvement in performance with respect to some standard, or, more broadly, an increase in the organism's adaptation to its environment.

This rough definition fits some cases well: a child learning to avoid a hot object, a puppy learning to find its water dish, a student acquiring facts and principles needed to pass an examination or the skills needed to compete in games. But in other cases the definition seems to miss the mark badly. Consider a person who has come to be mortally afraid of elevators. Presumably this fear developed through some learning process but it has no obvious element of adaptiveness or improvement with respect to a criterion of skill.

The crux of the matter is that learning in the sense of adaptation is learning to do something. But often we have reason to believe that a person or animal has learned something even though no specific change in performance can be identified. In this view, learning is conceived in terms of the storage of information in memory as a consequence of any experience the individual might have had. A separate body of theory is needed to explain how information is retrieved from memory and translated into performance in new situations.

Within this broadened framework, learning and memory are as two sides of a coin. We can never detect learning except by evidence that the organism remembers something. Conversely, there is no way to produce memory without learning. We separate these two aspects of a common basic process only for convenience. One of the main functions of living creatures—indeed, almost a defining property—is to process information continually from the environment and adjust behavior to take account of its significant aspects.

This chapter will focus on fundamental learning phenomena. In doing so, we will not hesitate to describe research with animals. Although this represents a departure from typical cognitive textbooks, it is very much in keeping with our central themes. Information processing approaches to cognition often rely on analogies between humans and computers but human beings are biological organisms with an evolutionary history. A major aspect of this history can be seen as responding to the need for constraints on learning in order to respond to complex problems in an adaptive manner. Nature helps with the problem of learning every step of the way.

The Biological Backdrop of Learning

One can learn to drive an automobile without having the slightest idea as to what goes on under the hood. Nonetheless, some understanding of how the machine is built and how its components operate may help us appreciate its limitations and deal with malfunctions. Similarly, we can study learning purely by observing how the actions of animals or people change with experience, but there are advantages in taking into account other information about the nature of the "machine" we are observing. In particular, it is often useful to know what kinds of adaptive behaviors appear without specific learning in an individual of a given species and age, what kinds are easy and what kinds are difficult or impossible to acquire through learning. Learning can provide flexible adaptation to environmental circumstances, but it can also be risky. The danger is that learning will take too long—even one-trial learning can be too slow for a prey avoiding a predator. We should not be surprised, therefore, that many behavioral adjustments to the environment reflect a "learning by the species" in which preprogrammed action sequences become incorporated into genetic equipment and do not require new learning in each new generation. In some cases these behaviors are quite complex. For example, the long-tailed tailorbird sews two large leaves together and builds its nest inside. It is able to perform this complex task correctly on the first attempt. The ability is considered to be inborn because it appears suddenly (does not require practice) and with adaptive results. Older birds with more practice, however, may build better nests than those nesting for the first time (Wallace, 1973).

Fixed Action Patterns and Releasers

Innate skills or behavior sequences that do not have to be learned by the animal are known as **fixed action patterns**. Newborn humans are equipped with a number of these functional behavior patterns. One example is the grasping reflex of the hand. If you touch the palm of an infant's hand, its fingers close tightly around yours in an ordered sequence of movements. This grasping is strong when an infant is nursing and is especially reactive to the mother's hair. The reflex is later lost as the nervous system develops.

Most of these fixed action reflexes are adaptive. Head-turning and sucking reflexes make it easy for newborn babies to be fed. Babies also have a respiratory occlusion reflex that is stimulated by a reduction of airflow. The first response is to pull back the head and if this is not effective the baby will move its hands in a face-wiping motion. If this does not work the baby will start to cry, and the resulting expulsion of air is often sufficient to remove whatever is obstructing the air passages. This exquisite pattern of reflexes is important for survival but it may complicate breast feeding. If the mother presses the baby too close during feeding so that the baby's nostrils are covered by the breast, the respiratory occlusion reflex may be triggered. Therefore, successful nursing may require a bit of experience on the part of both baby and mother.

Fixed action patterns are not limited to infants. For example, yawning may be triggered by the sight of another person yawning (Provine, 1986). Two characteristic features of fixed action patterns are that they are initiated by quite specific stimuli or **releasers** and then, once initiated, the behavior patterns often run their course almost automatically. If an egg is removed from the nest of the greylag goose, she will retrieve the egg by rolling it back under her bill. If the egg is removed by a human observer during this retrieval process, the goose will continue the egg-rolling motions until the egg would have been retrieved if it hadn't been removed.

When slight alterations are made in environmental settings, the resulting behaviors often seem bizarre and inappropriate. For example, in many cases exaggerated or "supernormal" stimuli are preferred to normal stimuli. Oystercatcher birds prefer eggs that are larger than normal and if presented with artificial eggs they will try to sit on ones that are much too large to incubate. "Learning by species" is based on the promise of stability in the environment and in nature. Where new circumstances do not intervene, these adjustments are quite effective. In some cases, members of one species exploit fixed action patterns in other species. The female cowbird locates the nest of some other bird (typically a smaller one) and then quickly lays an egg when the other bird leaves its nest. When the owner returns it often accepts the egg, incubates, and hatches it. Furthermore, the baby cowbird is generally larger than its nest mates and its size acts as a supernormal stimulus for (foster) parent feeding (Hamilton & Orians, 1965).

Critical Periods and Imprinting

Attachment.   A compromise between built-in behavior patterns and totally flexible individual learning is the occurrence of especially rapid learning during certain favorable periods (usually early periods) in an organism's life. **Imprinting** refers to a type of early learning that forms the basis of the young animal's attachment to its parents, and in many cases later on controls its selection of a mate. A newly hatched duckling reared without its mother will follow a human being, a wooden decoy, or almost any moving object it sees shortly after its birth. Even brief periods of following may result in relatively permanent attachment to the "imprinting object" and the duckling will prefer the object even to a live mother duck. Imprinting has been found in a number of species including dogs, sheep, and horses. Imprinting takes place only during certain sensitive or **critical periods**. According to recent theorists (e.g., Hoffman & Ratner, 1983), the end of the critical period for imprinting coincides with the development of fear reactions to novel stimuli.

It appears that critical periods occur in human as well as animal learning. There is also evidence that attachment or bonding between parents and their infants may have a critical period in that early separation (such as might occur during extended hospitalization) may impair the development of emotional attachment (see, e.g., Bowlby, 1969). It has been argued that the first minutes and hours after birth are crucial for bonding between mother and infant (Klaus & Kennell, 1976). More recent reviews, however, undermine this claim. The latest evidence does not suggest that the immediate postbirth period is in any way critical for human mother–infant emotional bonding (Myers, 1987).

Bird Song.   Although mynah birds and parrots are well known for their ability to mimic human speech, song learning in birds such as the white-crowned sparrow may actually show closer parallels to human language acquisition. The white-crowned sparrow will not develop a normal song if it does not hear the songs of other white-crowned sparrows as it matures. The sparrow must hear these songs between 10 and 50 days of age, even though it does not develop its own song until 150–200 days of age (Marler, 1970). If a white-crowned sparrow is isolated from members of its species and exposed to tape recordings of normal white-crowned sparrow song, the song will be acquired. Playing tape recordings of the song of the closely related song sparrow, however, has no effect; the isolated bird neither imitates the song sparrow nor develops the song of its own species. If sparrows are given a choice of two recorded songs, one from their own species and the other from a bird species living in the same habitat, they learn their own song and ignore the other one (Marler & Peters, 1977).

Can the study of song learning in birds tell us anything about human language learning? There are several intriguing possibilities. First, hearing particular songs at particular time periods is critical for the acquisition of bird song. Marler (1970) has suggested that birds have a "template" that acts as a crude guide for their species-specific song, much as other sign stimuli (chick distress calls) act as releasers for other behaviors (rescuing). The auditory input must be in roughly the right form to influence the template, although there appear to be differences across species and perhaps even across individual birds (Marler & Sherman, 1983; Marler & Peters, 1988). Human infants select human speech sounds from the vast array of sounds to which they are exposed, and they may also have an auditory "template" that constrains their speech development. The fact that birds may learn their song from tape recordings in the absence of any other social stimuli or external sources of reinforcement suggests the possibility that song learning depends on an intrinsic feedback or reinforcement system (i.e., the template). In a similar way many aspects of human speech acquisition may not depend on external reward. Thus parents may teach their children language not by rewarding them with smiles and attention for speechlike behaviors but rather by providing the appropriate auditory environment in which the infant's own language acquisition system can operate (see Miller & Jusczyk, 1989 for a recent review). As we shall see in the chapter on language acquisition, there is strong evidence that a critical period is associated with language learning.

Constraints on Learning

Early work suggested that learning did not depend very much on the particular stimuli, responses, and rewards used. If a reinforcer worked for some particular stimulus or response, it apparently would work for virtually all stimuli and virtually all responses.

This generalization proved to be overdrawn. Rats can readily be trained to press a bar for food and to run away from a signal to avoid shock, but it is difficult to teach a rat to press a bar to avoid shock or to run away from a signal for food in order to receive food (Bolles, 1970). The animal's response system seems to be organized to approach desirable outcomes and avoid undesirable outcomes, and these tendencies greatly constrain learning.

A related experimental result is shown in Figure 3.1. The rat is electronically wired to a circuit that produces an audible click when the rat licks from the bottle containing sweetened water. The rat can be punished either by experimentally inducing nausea or by electric shock administered to the paws. Thus there are two stimuli (the sweet taste and the click) and two outcomes (nausea and pain) that may be associated. The rat, however, readily learns only two of these associations: the click controls whether or not the rat drinks if the rat is punished by shock, while the sweet taste controls the rat's avoidance of drinking when illness-induction is the punishment (Garcia, Hawkins, & Rusiniak, 1974). That is, just what the rat learns is highly constrained by the particular cues and consequences. Sweetness can be associated with nausea but not pain, and the click can be associated with pain but not nausea.

There is clear experimental evidence that chemotherapy treatments become selectively associated with tastes and orders. In one study children were allowed to eat a novel flavor of ice cream (a mixture of maple and black walnut) in a clinic setting that was followed by a chemotherapy treat-

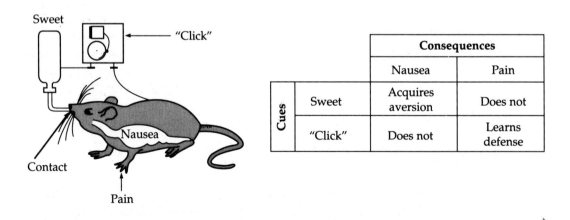

		Consequences	
		Nausea	Pain
Cues	Sweet	Acquires aversion	Does not
	"Click"	Does not	Learns defense

Figure 3.1   The effects of pairing a gustatory cue or an auditory cue with external pain or internal illness. *Source*: Garcia, Hawkins, & Rusiniak, 1974.

ment. One control group did not receive the ice cream prior to treatment and another control group received the ice cream but not the drug treatment. The children returned to the clinic a few weeks later and were given the choice of having the ice cream or playing a game. Both control groups were more than three times as likely to choose the ice cream as the group that had the ice cream followed by the drug treatment (Bernstein, 1978).

Learned taste aversions can create serious practical problems because nutritious hospital foods may become targets for aversions and result in loss of appetite. Viewing taste aversion from a learning perspective has the virtue of suggesting remedies. In a follow-up study Bernstein and her associates showed that a distinctive taste could serve as a "scapegoat." Children were given two different hospital meals each of which was followed by a chemotherapy treatment. Along with one of the two meals children were given a package of an unusual flavor of Lifesavers to eat (rootbeer or coconut). The idea was that the reaction to the chemotherapy might be associated with the distinctive flavor rather than the meal. In fact, children were twice as likely to eat foods later from the meal that was followed by the candy than foods from the meal that was not (Bernstein, Webster, & Bernstein, 1982). As Bernstein puts it, one could say that the Lifesavers were prophetically named! For a recent review of relations between learned taste aversion and appetite loss see Bernstein and Borson (1986).

Summary

These various observations suggest that we should conceive of learning as involving a continuum of flexibility. Where the environment is stable and where there is no time for learning (one-trial learning for avoiding some predators is one trial too many!), behaviors may be innate or preprogrammed. Where the environment is less predictable and organisms need to be able to adjust to changing circumstances, learning involving various degrees of flexibility may be observed.

Basic Learning

We continue our review of human beings as biological organisms by taking a brief look at basic learning. Certain forms of learning are so fundamental that we would expect them to be observed throughout the animal kingdom. Indeed, simple forms of learning occur even in single-celled organisms. Of course, one would not expect the mechanisms of learning to be the same in vertebrates as they are in single-celled organisms. Scientists interested in the physiological basis of learning typically focus on simple organisms and simple learning, based on the assumption that simple systems should be easier to understand than complex systems.

Some forms of learning appear to have extremely similar properties throughout the animal kingdom even when drastic differences in neurological organization make it unlikely that the neurophysiological basis could be the same. Presumably these instances result from evolutionary pressure, shaping the processes of adjustment of the organism to its environment in much the same way for very different organisms when the requirements of adaptation are similar. Among the best examples of these are the relatively simple forms of learning termed habituation and conditioning.

Habituation

Habituation refers to the ability of an organism to discontinue its response to highly repetitive stimuli. Consider the predicament of an organism that does not have a process of habituation. Suppose a deer is feeding near a farm where the silence is frequently broken by the bleating sound of the farmer's sheep. Initially, one would expect the sounds to interrupt the deer's feeding and put it on the alert. If the sounds were very frequent, little feeding would take place if the deer responded each time. What would be an adaptive reaction on the part of the animal? Ideally, the deer would respond less and less strongly to successive occurrences of the *same* sound until it finally ignored the noises entirely and continued eating. (Of course, the deer would need to remain alert to other sources of sound.) You are familiar with similar examples from your own experience. The ticking of an unusually loud clock can be very conspicuous when we first come into its vicinity, but we quickly "become used to the sound" and cease to hear it unless our attention is recalled to it for some reason.

One of the "lowest," that is, simplest organisms on which real behavioral experiments have been conducted is the *Stentor*, a single-celled organism that lives out its life attached to the bottom of a pond. This tiny animal has a single observable response, a contraction of its body that occurs either upon ingestion of a particle of food or upon contact with a possibly injurious object. Herbert Jennings, a nineteenth-century American biologist, studied habituation in a *Stentor* by touching it repeatedly with a fine hair. He noted that on the first touch the contraction occurred but that the magnitude of the contraction became progressively smaller with successive stimulations. Was this simply fatigue? Evidently not, for similarly repeated stimulation with food particles did not lead to similar habituation. Even more to the point, habituation progressed more rapidly after a weak than a strong stimulus, even though the response was not as intense in the former case and thus should have led to less fatigue.

The neurophysiological mechanisms responsible for habituation certainly cannot be the same in all species, for the process occurs in animals with and without nervous systems. It seems likely that in the very lowest organisms habituation is an independent, and in fact almost the sole, learning process available (see Kandel, 1976; Kandel & Schwartz, 1982, for work on the biological basis of habituation) but that in higher organisms it is simply a component of a more elaborate stock of related learning processes.

Elaborating this view, the Russian psychologist Sokolov (1963) has developed a theory of habituation in higher animals in terms of a "neuronal model." His idea is that upon repeated occurrence of any situation there forms in the brain a representation or model of the pattern of stimulation that is repeatedly encountered by the animal, and if the stimulation is repeated regularly, this neuronal representation similarly is aroused from internal sources at regular intervals. One manifestation of this formation of a neuronal model, or state of expectancy of a repeated situation, is that the animal's complex of alerting, attentional, and arousal reactions decreases progressively in magnitude. But if the situation changes so that on some occasions the animal's expectation as to what will occur is not confirmed, those reactions are immediately reinstated (that is, dishabituation occurs). You may be familiar with situations such as the following: A train always passes through a small town at 3:13 A.M. The residents, however, are not bothered by the sounds of the train and always sleep through the train's passing. One night the train is delayed by a snowstorm and promptly at 3:14 A.M. the residents wake up and wonder what has happened. According to Sokolov's theory this violation of expectancy (i.e., the absence of the train) has alerted the residents.

Although habituation is adaptive in its own right, it also may provide a useful bias for further learning. Suppose that some important event occurs and the organism is trying to determine what might have predicted or caused it. For a moment let's go back to the example of a rat that becomes ill. We know that rats are biased to associate illness with tastes. But a rat may have tasted many things in the hours before it became ill. If rats habituate to familiar tastes, then they should tend to associate their illness with those tastes that are more novel or unusual. Indeed, they do (see, e.g., Rozin & Kalat, 1971). Given that tainted foods typically have a distinct taste, this bias for associating a novel event with a novel taste serves rats very well. Holland, Holyoak, Thagard, and Nisbett (1986) argue that people generally follow an **unusualness heuristic** of linking surprising outcomes with unusual antecedent events.

Classical Conditioning

The aspect of expectancy or predictiveness emphasized by Sokolov in relation to habituation proves to be characteristic of a great part of the learning of all organisms, becoming progressively more conspicuous as we go up the phylogenetic scale. The basic properties of this pervasive process of developing anticipations of events are seen most clearly in experiments on conditioning. **Classical conditioning** is associated for both laypeople and scientists with the Russian physiologist Pavlov. Pavlov observed that a dog salivates when it sees or hears some cue that means food is imminent. The learning procedure was quite simple, as shown in Figure 3.2. It starts with a stimulus, such as food, that produces a response prior to any learning. The stimulus is referred to as the **US or unconditioned stimulus**, and the response (salivation, in this case) is known as the **UR or unconditioned response**. This is shown in the top part of Figure 3.2.

Next, a second stimulus is selected that is originally neutral in that

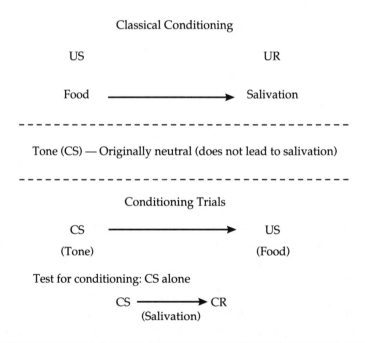

Figure 3.2 describes: Classical Conditioning — US (Food) → UR (Salivation); Tone (CS) — Originally neutral (does not lead to salivation); Conditioning Trials: CS (Tone) → US (Food); Test for conditioning: CS alone: CS → CR (Salivation)

Figure 3.2   **Procedures Used in Classical Conditioning.**

it does not lead to the unconditioned response. For example, dogs do not normally salivate when they hear a tone. Then the learning trials begin. On each of a series of conditioning trials the **CS or conditioned stimulus** (a tone) is presented and followed by the US (food). We know that conditioning has occurred in one of two ways. The dog may start to salivate after the CS comes on and before the US is presented. Of course, there will be no time for this to happen if the US follows the CS too closely. In that event we may check for learning by presenting the CS without the US, and any salivation to the CS alone is considered to be a learned or **conditioned response (CR)**.

Pavlov and others were able to use the classical conditioning procedure to learn a considerable amount about this form of learning. Is conditioning permanent? By no means. It is subject to forgetting just like any other learned association. But if following a series of tone–food presentations the administration of food (US) is discontinued and the tone (CS) is repeatedly presented alone, then the tendency to respond to the tone declines much more precipitously. In this case, we speak of **extinction** of the conditioned response (CR).

What Controls Conditioning? Is conditioning automatic and unselective? Following the early work of Pavlov and the popularization in this country of research on conditioning, the view became prevalent that conditioning does indeed occur automatically whenever some signal stimulus precedes a biologically significant event such as food, water, or painful stimulation. However, recent studies have shown that the relationships between signals and signaled events must be such that the occurrence of the latter has some *information value* for the organism.

Consider an experiment reported by Leon Kamin (1969). In a baseline experiment he used the well-established method for producing a "conditioned emotional response" by presenting rats with a certain stimulus A followed by shock. After only a few trials, he observed that presenting stimulus A when the animal was pressing a bar to obtain food produced a severe depression in responding, signifying that the stimulus aroused fear of the impending shock. In a second condition, Kamin presented two stimuli A and B (for example, a tone and a light) together followed by shock, then tested the two stimuli separately and found that each gave evidence of eliciting fear. In a third and critical experimental condition he first presented A followed by shock, then A and B together followed by shock, and finally tested A and B separately. The rather surprising observation was that in this last case, stimulus B, when tested alone, showed no evidence of evoking fear. His interpretation was that the inclusion of stimulus B on the A + B trials added no information as to when shock should be expected, and consequently conditioning to stimulus B was "blocked." **Blocking** is a robust phenomenon.

The idea that the information value of a CS regulates learning has had a major influence on our thinking about classical conditioning. Conditioning does not occur automatically whenever CS and US are paired— the CS must predict the onset of the US. A dramatic illustration of this principle comes from an experiment by Rescorla (1967), which is outlined in Table 3.1. Four groups of rats were tested under different contingencies. For two groups the probability that the US would follow the CS was high (80%) and for two it was low (40%). Also varied was the likelihood that the US would appear by itself in the absence of the CS. The results showed that whether or not learning occurred depended not simply on the probability that the US would follow the CS but on this probability *relative* to the probability that the US would appear alone. Thus the group for which the probability of the US was 80% in the presence of the CS and 80% in the absence of the CS showed no learning, whereas the group for which the US followed the CS only 40% of the time *but* did not appear in the absence of the CS did show conditioning.

Research on conditioning continues to be a very active area (see, e.g., Rescorla, 1988). Although Rescorla's study shows that contingency is more important to conditioning than cooccurrence, others have argued

Table 3.1   **Outline of One of the Rescorla (1967) Conditioning Experiments.**

Group	Probability that US follows CS	Probability that US occurs by itself
1	.80	.80
2	.80	.40
3	.40	.40
4	.40	.00

Results: Groups 2 and 4 show conditioning.
　　　　　　 Groups 1 and 3 do not show conditioning.
Conclusion: The CS must predict something.

that a different form of contingency plays a major role in conditioning. Specifically, the key factor may be the average temporal interval between CS and US relative to, for example, the average temporal interval between one US presentation and the next. If the former is shorter than the latter, then the CS helps to predict the occurrence of the US and conditioning should occur (e.g., Gibbon & Balsam, 1981; Wasserman & Neunaber, 1986). The key idea in all of these formulations is that the CS must have predictive value for conditioning to occur.

Conditioning as Adaptation.   In general, classical conditioning seems to be a form of adaptation. For example, salivation may serve to aid the digestion of food. Other digestive processes also show conditioning. Insulin is released by the pancreas as an unconditioned response to the presence of sugar in the digestive tract. The taste of sugar can become conditioned to the release of insulin as an anticipatory conditioned response. Interestingly, after such conditioning insulin may be released as an anticipatory response when subjects taste artificial sweeteners such as saccharin. This conditioned release of insulin causes a drop in blood sugar level and may account for the slight dizziness people may experience after drinking a diet soda on an empty stomach.

There is even evidence that the immune system is subject to principles of conditioning. That is, the presentation of a CS can influence the immune system, suggesting that the immune system is subject to neural control. One drug used to study conditioned taste aversions, cyclophosphamide, also tends to suppress the immune system by interfering with the production of antibodies. Robert Ader and his colleagues have been able to demonstrate that this suppression of the immune system can also be produced as a CR to a taste stimulus (e.g., saccharin previously conditioned to cyclophosphamide as the US; Ader, 1982; Ader & Cohen, 1985 and commentary; see also MacQueen & Siegel, 1989). Even more recently Siegel and his associates established conditioned enhancement of the immune system (MacQueen, Siegel, & Landry, 1990). This work is leading to the emergence of a new interdisciplinary field known as psychoneuroimmunology. If the immune system can be conditioned, we may be able to use principles of classical conditioning to fight disease.

Conditioning as Stimulus Substitution.   An early view of conditioning was that the CS comes to act as a "substitute" for the US and that the conditioned response (CR) takes exactly the same form as the unconditioned response (UR). For example, in Pavlov's experiments described earlier, both the UR and the CR were salivation. Today, we realize that this view is oversimplified. An alternative view is that the CR will take whatever form is most adaptive and may even be the opposite of the UR. There is some support for this **compensatory response model**. Consider the drug Dinitrophenol. The UR to this drug is increased oxygen consumption and increased temperature. Since this drug would tend to disturb the body's homeostatic balance, the body might try to compensate for this disruption by attempting to restore oxygen consumption and body temperature to normal levels. Indeed, when Dinitrophenol is used as a US in conditioning studies, the CR is *decreased* oxygen and *decreased* body temperature (Obal, 1966). In short, the CR takes the opposite form of the UR in the direction of what should be adaptive.

The compensatory response model has attracted a lot of attention because it may provide an explanation for the phenomenon of drug tolerance (Siegel, 1977a,b; Solomon & Corbit, 1974; Solomon, 1977). Development of drug tolerance is often a serious problem because progressively higher dosages are required to produce a given effect. The key idea in the compensatory response model is that the CR to the cues associated with the administration of a drug (e.g., the needle, smells present in the context, and other CSs) tends to counteract the effect of the drug. Therefore, the response to the drug becomes attenuated.

If this model is correct, then one ought to be able to alter the response to the drug if the CSs that elicit compensatory responses are absent. Siegel and his associates have found a considerable amount of support for this view. If an addict takes the same drug but in a different form so that the conditioned stimuli associated with drug tolerance are missing, then the same dosage that would have a very mild effect might produce an overdose (see Crowell, Hinson, & Siegel, 1981, for research based on this compensatory model and Siegel, 1989 for a general review).

Attractive as the compensatory response model is, it does not provide a full account of the form that CRs will take in a conditioning situation (see, e.g., Flaherty & Becker, 1984). If one measures several response systems one finds that some CRs are similar to the UR and some are opposite to it. It appears that the exact form of a CR depends not only on adaptive value but also on the particular CS employed and innate behavior patterns in organisms (see Holland, 1984; Domjan & Burkhard, 1986, for thoughtful discussions of this issue). What does seem clear is that classical conditioning is not an isolated phenomenon associated with primitive organisms but rather that it represents a form of adaptation relevant to human beings as well.

Research on conditioning is also important in that it may provide common ground for different approaches to learning and induction. For example, Sutton and Barto (1981) have pointed to close links between the contingency learning model of Rescorla and Wagner (1972) and the learning mechanisms of adaptive neural network models. Contemporary approaches to conditioning span the range between biological models that directly incorporate constraints associated with the nervous system to connectionist models, which are more loosely based on properties of neural networks (see Hawkins & Bower, 1989 for examples of these two approaches), up to theories of inductive learning in a rule-based system implemented in a traditional computer program (Holyoak, Koh, & Nisbett, 1989). Classical conditioning continues to be fundamentally important to our understanding of learning.

Trial and Error Learning or Instrumental Learning

We saw that in classical conditioning the unconditioned stimulus, or reinforcer, follows the presentation of the conditioned stimulus. In trial and error or **instrumental learning** the experimenter arranges things so that the reinforcer follows some required action of the organism. For example, one may reward a dog for "shaking hands" by patting it on the head.

Most psychologists think that much of everyday behavior is the result of instrumental learning and is under the control of **reinforcement**. Consider the following situation: A mother complains that her three-year-old boy is too demanding of attention and that she never gets a minute's rest. When she tries to ignore these demands the boy's behavior worsens until she finally loses her temper, screams at him, and ultimately complies with his request (perhaps feeling guilty about yelling).

How would you analyze the situation? The well-known psychologist B. F. Skinner would view these episodes as comprising **operant behaviors** regulated by rewards. Operant behaviors are actions that "operate" on the environment to produce some effect. Skinner distinguishes these acts from **respondent behaviors**, such as the knee-jerk reflex, which are under the control of specific stimuli and tend to occur regardless of their consequences. In the example, a distinct possibility is that the mother's attention, whether accompanied by positive or negative feelings, was rewarding to this little boy. If so, the mother should be able to change the boy's behavior by changing the payoffs. For example, she might pay special attention to her child when he engages in desired behaviors such as independent play, and withhold rewards when her boy becomes overdemanding, either by ignoring demands or by removing the child from the situation (sending him to his room for five minutes). In psychological jargon she would be reinforcing desired behaviors and extinguishing undesired behaviors. As Krasner and Ullman (1965) have documented, these techniques are often effective and quite likely would work for the mother in our example.

Studying Operant Behavior.   The mother-child interactions in the above example are doubtless too complex to serve as a beginning point for deriving principles of learning and behavior. A typical laboratory setup for studying operant behavior employs a *Skinner box*, an apparatus in which a rat may be taught to press a bar for food or a pigeon may be taught to peck a key for food. The apparatus can be programmed to record automatically some operant behavior (e.g., bar presses or key pecks). Note that selecting a measure always involves ignoring lots of behavior—the recorder does not care whether the pigeon was standing on one foot or two when the key peck was made—it's just a key peck. On the other hand, if we tried to record all of the pigeon's behavior, we would probably conclude that behavior is infinitely variable and too complex to be studied in the laboratory. In practice, we try to strike a balance and observe classes of behavior that are both meaningful and open to practical analysis.

Superstitious Behavior.   Operant behaviors need not always be causally related to reinforcement. Consider, for example, the prevalence of superstitions—baseball managers avoid stepping on the chalk line when coming out to talk with their pitchers, brides are expected to wear "something old, something new, something borrowed, something blue," hospitals have floor 12A but no floor 13, and so on. B. F. Skinner also found **superstitious behavior** in pigeons! He provided them with rewards at regular intervals *regardless* of their behavior. Nonetheless, the pigeons learned a variety of behaviors such as wing flapping and hopping. Of course, these behaviors are superstitious only from the experimenter's view. The pigeon is faced with the complex task of figuring out whether and when rewards depend on its behavior and which of its possible behaviors might be relevant.

Partial Reinforcement.   The alert reader may already have wondered why superstitious behavior does not quickly undergo experimental extinction since any particular superstitiously learned response often will not receive accidental reinforcements. Indeed, the same question might be raised about much behavior that occurs outside of the laboratory, for nature certainly does not always provide rewards for "correct" choices with 100%

assurance. A bird cannot afford to avoid visiting a tree that sometimes provides edible caterpillars merely because on some visits none are to be found. Nor do most people stop watching television shows because some samples turn out to be unrewarding.

Even during the period when the first major experimental studies of trial and error learning were being conducted, a number of investigators made the same observations and initiated a laboratory analog that has been termed intermittent or partial reinforcement (Brunswik, 1939; Humphreys, 1939; Skinner, 1938). If, for example, a laboratory rat is being rewarded with food pellets for pressing a lever, one can introduce partial reinforcement by setting the electrical control mechanism so that only a portion of lever presses actually yield reward. As might be expected, learning is typically slower under partial reinforcement, as a consequence of the fact that some responses go unrewarded, and thus some extinction occurs even during learning. However, the most interesting effects of partial reinforcement are observed when, following a period of partially reinforced responding, reinforcement is entirely discontinued and the investigator determines how long the animal will continue responding under conditions of experimental extinction. The result, termed the *partial reinforcement effect*, is that typically an animal that has received partial reinforcement will continue to respond much longer under conditions of extinction than an animal that has had consistent (100%) reinforcement. Thus the animal that acquires a superstitious response as a consequence of a few accidental reinforcements is actually learning under conditions that would be expected to lead to great persistence during extinction.

How can one explain the curious result that omitting a certain proportion of reinforcement during learning actually yields a stronger habit, in the sense of more resistance to extinction? The best supported explanation is one that calls on concepts of memory and patterning (Capaldi, 1967; Shimp, 1975). It must be assumed that even nonhuman animals do not respond solely to the stimulus and reward events that occur on a particular trial, but rather hold in memory the outcomes of one or more preceding trials of a sequence and learn to base their expectations on the way these are patterned. Thus, under a pure 100% reinforcement regimen, an animal would have the opportunity to learn only that a sequence of reward trials is followed by additional rewards; thus if reward is discontinued, it would be expected to shift quickly to an expectation of nonreward—that is, to extinguish its tendency to make the previously rewarded response. But if, say, rewards occur on only a random 50% of trials, then the animal would have opportunity to learn that a nonrewarded trial is sometimes followed by a rewarded one, and thus when reward was discontinued during extinction the animal would not shift quickly to an expectation of consistent nonreward.

Mixtures of Classical and Instrumental Conditioning.   Although experimental psychologists often act as if classical and instrumental conditioning can be easily separated, in almost all situations both forms of learning ought to operate.

Earlier we described operant behavior in the Skinner box as though it involved only trial and error selection of responses. However, this analysis may not be complete. Not only is reward contingent on some prior response, but also it is necessarily associated with the presence of certain stimuli, especially those occurring near where the response is made. These stimulus-reinforcer relations are just those conditions one uses in the study of classical conditioning.

This factor of stimulus-reward contingency can have a powerful influence on behavior. Brown and Jenkins (1968) studied a remarkably simple way of teaching a pigeon to peck a key, which has come to be referred to as **autoshaping**. The key was normally dark. At regular intervals the key was illuminated and free food was available in the food hopper. The light signaled when food was available, but the pigeon was not required to make any response to the key to get food. Yet the birds quickly came to peck the key when it was illuminated, even though that meant there was less time to eat the food. If the procedure is modified so that the illumination signals food only if the pigeon does *not* peck the key, pecking nonetheless develops and is maintained for hundreds of trials despite the fact that pecks cost the pigeons rewards. As soon as the light starts to predict food, the pigeons begin pecking; when as a result of pecking the light predicts food less well, pecking decreases. But as pecking decreases the light again becomes a better predictor of food and the cycle repeats as the pigeons begin to peck once more (Williams & Williams, 1969).

The phenomenon of autoshaping illustrates the fact that *stimulus-reinforcer relations are inevitably present whenever response-reinforcer relations are studied*. Much as one might like to study classical conditioning and instrumental learning separately, almost inevitably they are closely interwoven. Observed performance may reflect the organism's knowledge of stimulus-reinforcer relations and not the simple, automatic running off of a stimulus-response association.

Recognizing that situations may contain elements of both classical and instrumental conditioning may help us understand learning in some important applied settings. For example, millions of people undergo chemotherapy as a treatment for cancer. Chemotherapy is an aversive and often dreaded experience, in part because of the anticipatory nausea and vomiting associated with it. V. M. Whitehead, in an article in the *New England Journal of Medicine* entitled "Cancer Treatment Needs Better Antiemetics," describes the situation as follows: "After one or more courses [of chemotherapy], patients may begin to vomit on the morning of their treatment, or upon arrival at the physician's office, in anticipation of the injection, attesting to the abhorrence with which they regard the treatment. They confess to feeling ill for three weeks or more out of every four and may become deeply depressed and even suicidal" (1975, p. 199).

There is evidence that the chemotherapy situation contains important elements of classical conditioning. The odors and other cues (associated with the injection) may act as CSs with the illness produced by the drugs acting as the US. Nausea and anticipatory vomiting would be the UR. But the chemotherapy situation is quite different from the situation used by Pavlov in his studies. He arranged things so that the dogs would automatically be exposed to the tone CS. People in the same situation with cotton in their ears might show no conditioning because they did not hear the CS. In the chemotherapy situation people have at least some control over their exposure to potential CSs and, therefore, at least part of this (learning) situation is under instrumental control. The theoretical implication of this fact is that classical and instrumental learning are not readily isolated, and the practical implication is that this observation can be used to suggest possible treatments for conditioned vomiting.

If anticipatory vomiting is a classically conditioned response, then if the CS is not perceived, the CR (vomiting) ought not to occur. This idea is the basis for some work by William Redd and his associates on patients undergoing chemotherapy. He employed a combination of relaxation and guided imagery techniques (e.g., imagine that you are on a beach on a nice, sunny day, etc.) that, on the present interpretation, distracted patients from attending to the cues associated with the administration of the toxic chemicals. These techniques proved to be remarkably successful (see Redd, Jacobson, Die-Trill, & Dermatis, 1987, for a more detailed report). Related techniques might also be tried. For example, presenting the CS many times prior to conditioning greatly slows down the rate of learning, a phenomenon known as *latent inhibition*. If the cues associated with drug administration are repeatedly presented without the drug, then when the drug is given later, the association between the drug cues and the drug ought to develop more slowly (see Dafters, Hetherington, & McCartney, 1983, for some evidence related to this point). Of course, it may occur to you that all that might happen is that conditioning will occur to other cues. For example, might not the beach scene become associated with the drug? The principle of selective learning mentioned earlier seems to make it somewhat unlikely that this would happen. Tastes and odors are easily associated with illness but images are not.

Paired-Associate Learning

Paired-associate learning is a simple procedure for studying how people form associations. The experimental technique involves the pairing of previously unrelated words in much the same way as in the traditional method of learning a vocabulary of foreign words. A student of a foreign language pairs English and foreign words, typically on the fronts and backs of "flash cards," and practices anticipating the second member of each pair until eventually when the foreign word is presented, its English meaning comes to mind.

A question of theoretical importance in the study of paired associates is exactly what is learned in the experimental situation. It is obvious that some sort of mental link between the stimulus and response terms is formed. Experiments have shown that this link can be bidirectional; that is, the presentation of the response word alone can evoke memory for the stimulus word (the opposite of the usual order of presentation).

Techniques that make this mental link more obvious can remarkably facilitate learning. Atkinson (1975) has developed a *keyword method* to aid foreign language vocabulary learning. Starting with a foreign word one finds an English word that sounds like some part of the foreign word. Using this English word as the keyword, the learner then forms a visual image associating the keyword with the English counterpart of the foreign word. For example, the Spanish word for duck is *pato* (pronounced something like "pot-o"). Using the English *pot* as the keyword, one could imagine a duck walking around with a cooking pot over its head. Although the method seems somewhat elaborate, people using the keyword method acquire a foreign vocabulary twice as fast as control subjects not using the technique.

An important question about the nature of associative learning that has arisen within the framework of paired-associate procedures concerns the effect of repetition on the learning process. In the paired-associate paradigm, the list of stimulus-response pairs is presented many times until all the pairs are learned. A common view is that each time a pair is repeated, the connection between the items is strengthened. However, the situation turns out not to be quite that simple. The graphs in Figure 3.3 will help illustrate the problem.

Paired-associate learning curves (for that matter, almost all learning curves) are an average of the results for a number of subjects. These aver-

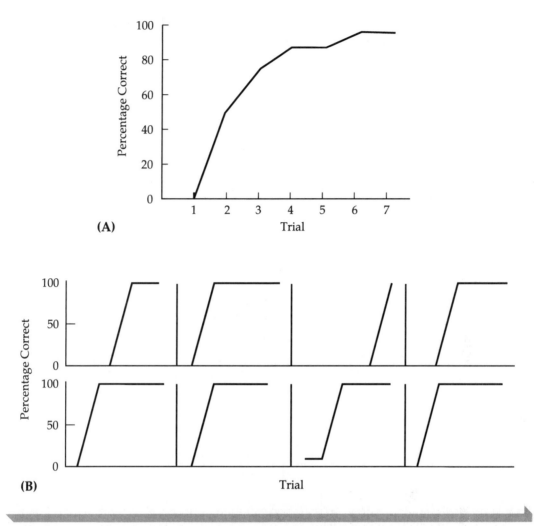

Figure 3.3   The curves below are data from a single subject learning eight different symbol-adjective pairs. The curve above is the average for that subject over all items. One can readily see that a gradual-appearing average curve does not imply that each item is learned gradually. *Source*: Unpublished study by W. K. Estes.

age curves show a smooth and regular improvement. However, smooth curves may arise from individual curves being gradual and smooth *or* they could as well arise from individual curves that exhibit an all-or-none transition from guessing to perfect learning. Indeed, paired-associate learning data collected by Bower (1961) conformed almost exactly to predictions arising from an all-or-none learning model. A possible interpretation of this finding is that, even without special training in the keyword method, a relatively sophisticated learner usually acquires a paired-associate item by searching his or her memory for a preexisting association linking the two members. For example, if an item were the word pair CAR-ICE, one might recall a recent experience of skidding on an icy pavement. On this interpretation, an error merely signifies that the learner has not yet found a suitable mediating association. On the average, performance improves over trials in Bower's experiment, but the reason is apparently that additional trials provide additional opportunities for all-or-none learning. This all-or-none learning depends on selecting an appropriate unit of analysis. Obviously we would not expect to learn the contents of a book on an all-or-none basis! One might, however, acquire isolated facts in an all-or-none manner. Although not everyone agrees on the relative importance of all-or-none versus gradual learning, looking at individual subject curves and even individual item curves can often yield important clues about the underlying learning process.

Simple associative processes have turned out to be not so simple. Clearly there is no process that automatically supplies a linkage between two words. Early work on paired-associate learning attempted to study learning in a pure form by using nonsense syllables as stimuli; instead of CAR-ICE, one might use pairs like BIV-GOH. The idea of using meaningless materials did not work, mainly because people are quite good at bringing their knowledge to bear to make nonsense materials meaningful. For example, one might note that BIV provides the first letters of blue, indigo, and violet and that GOH could be short for Van Gogh and link BIV and GOH by the theme of painting. Learning depends on the strategies employed and some words are much easier to associate than others. In short, there does not appear to be any learning process that forms associations independent of what is being associated. Selective associations are the rule, not the exception. Psychologists no longer think of paired-associate learning as a procedure for studying "elementary learning processes" because the performance observed depends on the knowledge brought to bear on the situation, as we have just indicated.

Probability Learning

Just as the simple conditioning paradigm was generalized to be more representative of situations outside the laboratory by the introduction of partial reinforcement, the same can be done with verbal association learning by allowing a stimulus to be associated with more than one response term, each response being correct on any trial with some probability. This generalization of the simpler paired-associate task has been studied under the label **probability learning**. The results are especially relevant to human behavior in situations where the outcome of a response is uncertain and fluctuates from instance to instance (e.g., gambling, weather forecasting, medical diagnosis).

In a typical probability learning experiment the task for the subject is to predict which of two events is going to occur (e.g., which of two "outcome" lights will turn on following a signal). After the subject has made a response, one of the possible events occurs. The events occur in a random sequence and there is no information available that would make perfect prediction possible. However, the overall probabilities with which the two events occur have been predetermined by the experimenter. Thus the situation is analogous to attempting to predict whether red or black will come up on successive spins of a roulette wheel.

Figure 3.4 reports data from a classic experiment by Grant, Hake and Hornseth (1951). In this experiment one of two outcome lights turned on with probability 1.00, .75, .50, .25, or 0 for different groups of subjects.

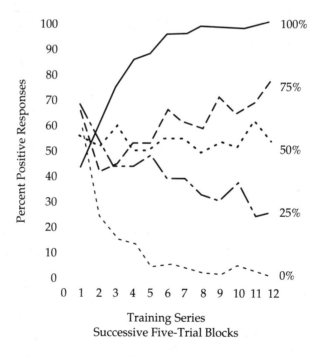

Figure 3.4   Percent frequency of predictions that a second light would follow a first as a function of the percent frequency that the second light actually did follow the first. At the end of training there is a close correspondence between frequency of occurrence and frequency of prediction. *Source*: Grant, Hake, & Hornseth, 1951.

(The other light turned on with the complementary probability.) All subjects started out predicting at chance level, guessing that each light would turn on about half the time. But as the experiment continued, their scores diverged until each group of subjects eventually came to predict the occurrence of each light with about the same probability as it actually occurred. Because the subjects' responding tends to match the probability of the event being predicted, this phenomenon has become known as **probability matching**.

Probability matching indicates that the subject has learned quite a lot about the experimental situation. However, if the subjects' aim is to be correct in their predictions as often as possible, they can make the best use of what they have learned about the event probabilities by always predicting the more frequent event. It has been observed that if subjects are rewarded for correct guesses or punished for incorrect ones they tend to move toward this optimal strategy (Estes, 1964).

Contingency Learning and Illusory Correlation

Earlier we described Rescorla's studies showing that rats were sensitive to whether or not a CS predicted something (contingency) rather than the sheer number of times that a CS and US were paired (cooccurrence). Experiments have also been done on people's judgments concerning correlation and contingency and some surprising results have been observed. Smedslund (1963) asked nurses to look through 100 cards that provided information about whether or not a particular symptom was present, then whether or not a particular disease was present. The various possibilities and the different combinations are shown in Table 3.2. The disease was

Table 3.2   Frequency (out of 100) of different patterns of presence or absence of symptom and disease in Smedslund's (1963) study.

		Disease		
		Present	*Absent*	Total
Symptom	*Present*	37	33	70
	Absent	17	13	30
	Total	54	46	100

Table 3.3   Abstract description of information relevant to judging correlation or contingency. The letters a, b, c, and d refer to frequencies.

		Property (e.g., disease)	
		Present	*Absent*
	Present	a	b
Property (e.g., symptom)			
	Absent	c	d

indicated as being present on a little more than half (54) of the cards and the symptom was present on 70 of the 100 cards. The nurses were asked to judge whether there was a relationship between the presence of the symptom and the disease.

From Table 3.2, one can see that there was essentially no relationship between the presence of the symptom and the disease. When the symptom was present the disease was present a little more than half the time (37/70 or 53%). When the symptom was absent the disease was also present a little more than half the time (17/30 or 57%). Even though there was no correlation between the symptom and disease 85% of the nurses judged that there was.

This difficulty in judging correlation is quite general (see, e.g., Ward & Jenkins, 1965; Shaklee & Mims, 1982; Arkes & Harkness, 1983; Shanks, 1986, 1989). A more abstract description of the correlation task is given in Table 3.3. One explanation of Smedslund's results is that the nurses may have based their judgments simply on the number of times that the symptom and disease were both present. This has come to be known as the "cell-a strategy" (again, refer to Table 3.3). By varying the values for a, b, c, and d investigators have been able to shed light on which particular strategies people employ. In addition to the cell-a strategy, people often make use of both the frequency with which the predictor is present and the outcome occurs and the frequency with which the predictor is present and the outcome does not occur (see, e.g., Shaklee & Tucker, 1980; Arkes & Harkness, 1983). If the property on the left side of Table 3.3 is taken to be the predictor, this strategy involves using both cell a and cell b. Note, however, that all four cells are relevant. The fact that the outcome might occur 80% of the time when the predictor is present is not in itself informative, because the outcome might occur 80% of the time when the predictor is not present (or even 100%, which would produce a negative correlation!).

What is responsible for people's poor performance on contingency or correlation tasks? One possibility is that the cell-a (and cell-a plus cell-b) strategy works most of the time and that keeping track of four frequencies is much more difficult than keeping track of one or two. A related possibility is that the covariation task does not reflect the full complexity of most learning tasks. In general, there is an unlimited set of potential antecedents in more realistic contingency judgment tasks. We have already seen that organisms have strong biases to select some antecedents over others (e.g., to associate illness with taste) in conditioning tasks. In more conceptually oriented domains we might expect that people's theories or expectations would tend to narrow down the set of potential antecedents. If the theory also included expectations concerning the strength of relationships between the predictor and outcome it might make sense to focus on cell a and cell b.

Actually, there is evidence that people's theories or expectations may dominate observations, leading observers to see correlations that are not objectively present. Consider a psychiatrist or clinical psychologist who gives a draw-a-person test (the patient is simply asked to draw a person) and is interested in whether characteristics of the drawing can be used to predict whether or not the patient is later diagnosed as paranoid or suspicious of others. That is, the basic question is whether or not there is a correlation between different properties of drawings and the diagnostic category. Tables 3.2 and 3.3 apply again. If some property, such as having significant body parts missing, is more likely to appear for patients later determined to be paranoid than for patients not found to be paranoid, then the property can be used to predict the presence of paranoia. In practice, however, as documented by Chapman and Chapman (1969), clinicians frequently fail to perceive correlations that are present and see correlations that are not objectively present. This latter phenomenon is known as **illusory correlation**. For example, in the case of the draw-a-person test people "see" associations between how the eyes are drawn and paranoia that are not true correlations. Illusory correlation is very much like a perceptual illusion in that different clinicians tend to see the same illusory correlations as do undergraduate students presented with drawings and diagnoses.

Illusory correlations may represent an instance of how properties of the memory system affect memory for associated events. Words that are highly associated (e.g., table and chair) tend to cue each other. Similarly, the concept of suspiciousness tends to be associated in our culture with things like "shifty eyes." Consequently, it may be far easier to recall cases in which the eyes were drawn in an unusual way and the diagnosis of paranoia was given (cell-a) than to recall cases in which paranoia was not the diagnosis (cell-b). Contingency learning continues to be an active area of research, in part because it is directly relevant to how people combine their prior expectations with new information (see Shanks & Dickinson, 1988 for a recent review of contingency learning).

Summary

Even within the narrow range of situations we have examined there is reason to believe that a diversity of underlying mechanisms may be determining performance. We seriously doubt, for example, that classical conditioning of salivation involves more or less identical processes as paired-associate learning. Nonetheless certain generalizations emerge from this body of work that seem to extend across diverse tasks. For our purposes the most obvious generalization is that "equipotentiality" never holds. That is, organisms seem to come prepared or biased to form certain kinds of associations and not others. Given the complexity of figuring out which of a large set of potential factors should be linked to some event, commitments favoring some possibilities over others are necessary if we are going to be able to learn the "right" things (where "right" is defined in terms of the adaptation of organisms to their environment).

Implications and Overview

Much of the progress in understanding learning has taken the form of overcoming limitations associated with behaviorism. In particular, the ideas that learning consists of forming stimulus-response associations, that these associations are formed more or less automatically, and that any two things are equally easy to associate are incorrect. They are wrong because they ignore both the active role that organisms play in organizing their experience and bringing their knowledge to bear on it and the evolutionary adaptations that favor learning some things over others. Let's take one last look at these issues before moving on.

The Learning-Performance Distinction

Early learning theorists such as Thorndike assumed that rewards tend to strengthen stimulus-response associations directly and automatically. In other words, reinforcement is the glue that connects stimuli with respon-ses. According to this viewpoint, any learning that takes place should be directly evident in changes in behavior—i.e., performance directly reflects learning. But common experience tells us that *not everything learned is im-mediately manifest in performance.* When a dog refuses to perform tricks that his trainer has taught him by using dog biscuits as rewards, it may reflect the fact that the dog isn't hungry, not that the dog has forgotten how to do the tricks. *Although learning is often inferred from performance, the absence of learning may not be inferred from the absence of performance.*

Once we draw the **learning-performance distinction** a natural question is whether reinforcement affects both learning and performance, mainly learning, or mainly performance. A variety of evidence suggests that reinforcement has its primary influence on performance rather than learning.

Observational Learning.   Much learning seems to require neither rein-forcement nor practice on the behavior in question. For example, Darby and Riopelle (1959) investigated the possibility that monkeys can learn purely by observation. Prior to the first trial on each of a series of different discrimination problems, monkeys witnessed another monkey execute a "demonstration" trial. Half of these demonstration trials were correct and rewarded and half were incorrect and not rewarded. The observer monkey was never rewarded on a demonstration trial. Over the series of problems, the observer's performance on the first trial following the demonstration rose from chance to above 75% correct. It appears that monkeys can learn simply from the opportunity of watching other monkeys.

Observational learning is an important phenomenon and is a mat-ter of much current debate, as for example in the question of whether the violence that children watch on television makes them more likely to be violent. The best evidence to date is that the answer may depend on the consequences of the behavior portrayed. Aggression that is rewarded is more likely to be imitated than aggression that is not rewarded (see Ban-dura, 1982).

Expectancy.   Our current view of reinforcement is that rather than en-slaving behavior with its irresistible power, reinforcement seems to act as a source of information about relations between actions and consequences. One implication of this view is that the tendency for behavior to occur in a given situation is a function of the individual's expectation of reinforce-ment in that situation. In other words, anticipation of reward, or *expec-tancy*, influences which responses will be selected by the organism rather than which ones will be learned. An experiment reported by Estes (1969) illustrates this point. College students were given repeated opportunities to choose between pairs of cards that differed in their reward value. However, the subjects' task was complicated; in order to receive the reward a subject had to choose the correct card and also correctly guess the precise reward value associated with that card. After several runs through the cards, new pairings of the cards were given for transfer tests. Certain of the transfer tests pitted a card of high value for which the reward had never been received (because the precise value had never been guessed) against a card of lower value for which reward had been received. The results clearly indicated that choices were determined by the magnitude of the reward anticipated and not by the amount of reward previously received. This experiment is another source of evidence that reinforcement does not operate in a direct and automatic manner to strengthen response tendencies (see also Levine, 1971).

Meaningful Learning

Although learning simple associations is a fundamental form of adaptation, one can still ask about the learning of more meaningful things. People master complex sets of material when they learn calculus, computer programming, or literary criticism. Children must acquire language and must learn how the words of the language map onto actions, objects, and events in their world. Clearly there is more to becoming an art expert than is captured by paired-associate learning. Cognitive psychologists should be able to say something useful about complex learning.

We looked at the indexes of three recent cognitive psychology textbooks and noted that "learning" did not have an entry in two of them and was only represented by "learning strategies" in the third. What's going on? The answer, we believe, is that meaningful learning is embedded in a variety of content areas. In the three textbooks we alluded to, complex learning is integrated into chapters on concept formation, comprehension and inference, language, and problem solving. We have also found it natural to discuss complex learning in particular content areas. So our discussion of complex learning will be scattered through many of the remaining chapters of this book.

The question about meaningful learning, however, also raises the issue of what appears to be a huge discontinuity between simple associative learning and complex meaningful learning. Do they have anything to do with each other? Our impression is that the answer lies, in part, on the level of description we adopt. We doubt that discovering the neural basis of habituation will take us very far toward understanding how children learn to read. And obviously classical conditioning is very different from language learning. At the same time, there are theoretical issues and challenges that apply directly to both types of learning. The learnability problem in classical conditioning (figuring out what goes with what) is paralleled by learnability problems in language acquisition and in both cases if learning is to succeed it must be guided or constrained. We believe that there are levels of description that will allow researchers to discover useful learning principles across a range of types of learning. One of the salient developments in formal theories of cognition is that they are increasingly broad in scope. To give but one example, the Holland et al. (1986) general theory of induction aims to account not only for human concept formation and induction but also for conditioning in rats and pigeons (see Holyoak, Koh, & Nisbett, 1989).

A final reason to expect meaningful learning to have something to do with simple learning is that simple learning is not simple. The most extreme efforts to get rid of meaning by using nonsense syllables only succeeded in showing how ingenious people can be in organizing highly impoverished situations. Learning is not an isolated process but rather consists of relating what is new to what is already known.

Summary

One can view learning as a gamble on Nature's part, a gamble that organisms will be able to learn quickly enough to profit from learning and that the right things will be learned. When environments are highly stable Nature may not gamble at all (as we see for innate behaviors) and when she does, Nature hedges her bets by providing various forms of guidance or constraints. Although "constraints" has the connotation of taking away opportunities, the other side of the coin is that constraints enable learning. The same biophysical constraints that prevent a crab from flying or even walking straight allow it to move about effectively in its environment.

Although individual species have diverse adaptations to their environments there is enough in common to foster hope for making broad generalizations concerning learning. These general principles, especially in the area of conditioning, are leading to increased interaction between cognitive psychologists and neuroscientists as part of the interdisciplinary field of cognitive neuroscience. These developments have led to a renewed interest in fundamental principles of learning and memory.

We are now ready to consider the information processing associated with complex cognition in greater detail. The next chapters, on attention and perception, describe work on how organisms take in information and make sense of it.

Key Terms

autoshaping
blocking
classical conditioning
compensatory
   response model
conditioned response
conditioned stimulus
credit assignment
critical period
extinction

fixed action patterns
habituation
illusory correlation
imprinting
instrumental learning
learning
learning-performance
   distinction
operant behaviors
probability learning

probability matching
reinforcement
releasers
respondent behaviors
superstitious behavior
unconditioned
   response
unconditioned
   stimulus
unusualness heuristic

Recommended Readings

The field of ethology provides an important perspective on both human and animal behavior. An excellent recent overview of this work is provided by Alcock (1989). Ilene Bernstein's (1978) work on chemotherapy and learned food aversions in children is both interesting and of great practical significance. Similarly, Shepard Siegel's research on conditioning and drug tolerance underlines the importance of basic learning processes to contemporary behavior. The Ader and Cohen (1985) article and the associated commentaries discuss the intriguing possibilities associated with the idea that the immune system may be conditioned. Finally, Rescorla's (1988) paper is a very accessible summary of modern developments in Pavlovian conditioning.

The review papers by Estes (1969) and Bandura (1982) raise a number of important issues about the control of human behavior by reinforcement. Holland et al. (1986) discuss the problem of learning what goes with what from the point of view of building computational models of learning and reasoning.

4

ATTENTION

Chapter Outline

Introduction

Some Initial Observations
Sensory Stores
Divided Attention

Capacity and Attention
Bottleneck Theories
Late Selection
Capacity Theories
Capacity and Automaticity

Attention and Action
Spatial Selection
What versus Where
Summary

Integration of Information: Feature Integration Theory

Summary

What holds attention determines action.

William James

Introduction

During every waking minute an individual is bombarded by an almost indescribable variety of stimuli. Complex as the human brain is, it is still far short of the capacity that would be needed to handle all of this enormous input in any effective way. In addition, much of the information is incomplete. People typically notice only a portion of the stimuli that impinge on them, and of those that they notice only a few affect their actions or have to do with events that they remember. The ways in which the total input of information is sifted, organized, and used are of fundamental interest to psychologists.

Of course, we do not only perceive the world, we also act upon it in the service of our plans and goals. There is a vast amount of potentially relevant information and a host of questions concerning how we deal with it. To decrease the chance that necessary information will become unavailable as the world rapidly changes, a person needs a way of keeping information available for a short time. In addition, to avoid becoming overloaded with all the stimulation, a way is needed to filter out what is irrelevant. An additional complication is that our world is inherently unpredictable so we must be able to balance the need to focus on goal-relevant information with the need to be sensitive to important changes in our environment. Much of the work addressed to these issues falls under the heading of attention.

This chapter provides a sampling of ongoing research on attention. Initially, work on attention was organized around the notion of capacity limitations but more recently investigators have stressed the role of attention in the coordination and control of action. One might even reverse the quote from William James at the beginning of this chapter and say that action determines attention. As we shall see in both this chapter and in the chapter on perception that follows, attention is also involved in integrating multiple sources and levels of information associated with perception.

The perspectives associated with thinking about attention in terms of capacity, control of action, and integration of information do not constitute mutually exclusive theories; instead they provide distinct views of the functions of attention. We begin with some observations and theories associated with attention as a limited capacity process.

Some Initial Observations

Sensory Stores

To process information, we need to ensure that it is available. Because the world is not under our control (there is no "instant replay") information may be changed before we are able to process it fully. To help overcome this problem, it is necessary to keep some internal record of the information. Our sensory stores accomplish this need by storing large quantities of information automatically for short periods of time in relatively "unprocessed" form.

Everyone is familiar with the rich but transient memory that persists for a second or so after a glimpse of a scene (as from the window of a vehicle) or following the end of interrupted conversation. In each case, an individual typically can provide a good deal of information about the scene or the conversation if interrogated immediately, but after even a few seconds filled with new inputs, the individual has almost entirely lost this ability.

Some of the earliest psychological experiments (e.g., Cattell, 1886) showed that when subjects are given a single brief look at an array of letters they typically can report no more than four or five of them. Whether this limited **span of apprehension** results from an inability to see more than a few letters at a time or from limited memory capacity remained a puzzle until 1960 when a doctoral student at Harvard University, George Sperling, devised an ingenious **partial report technique**. As illustrated in Table 4.1, subjects were shown a display of letters for a fraction of a second, then heard a tone indicating which row they were to report. To estimate how many letters the subject must have seen and had available in memory at the end of the display, Sperling reasoned as follows. Suppose that on the average a subject proves able to report three letters from any row of the display in Table 4.1. Since the row to be reported was not signaled until after the display went off, we can infer that the subject must have perceived three-fourths of the 12 letters presented. The results, shown in Figure 4.1, indicate that when more than four or five letters are presented, subjects actually perceive more letters than they can give in a whole report. Evi-

Table 4.1   **Sperling's Partial Report Technique.**

Present variable-size letter arrays for 50 milliseconds	Immediately following offset of array, present signaling tone telling subject which row to report	Subjects tries to report letters from the appropriate (signaled) row

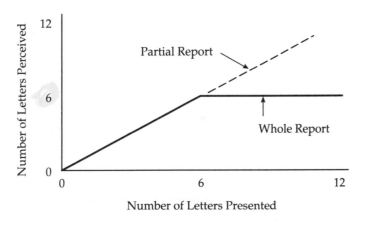

A D J E	—— High tone (top row)	**?**
X P S B	—— Medium tone (middle row)	
M L B H	—— Low tone (bottom row)	
(1)	(2)	(3)

* Source: Sperling, 1960.

Figure 4.1   **Results from Sperling's Partial Report Technique.**
Source: Sperling, 1960.

dently, much of the information in a brief visual experience never enters memory storage in a form that can survive even the short time needed to give a full report.

These results and a large body of subsequent research provide strong evidence for the idea of a sensory store. This store is assumed to record sensory experiences automatically, to persist beyond their duration, and to have a very large information capacity. Although we have concentrated on the visual sensory store (often called **iconic memory**), much research (e.g., Crowder and Morton, 1969; Crowder, 1982) has also examined the auditory sensory store (referred to as **echoic memory**). These sensory stores provide the information that can be used by later processes.

Divided Attention

How do we go from this large amount of information in the sensory store to an amount that can be reasonably processed? To illustrate some of the specific problems that call for investigation, consider a person at a party who is momentarily engaged in a conversation with a few friends concerning, say, a tennis match. Typically, the person would be oblivious to other conversations going on in the same room. Still, if someone in one of the other conversations remarked that one of the individual's friends had become sick, we might note a sudden shift of attention.

Many questions immediately arise concerning the processes and principles at work in this commonplace situation. Does the fact that the individual took cognizance of the mention of his friend's illness mean that he actually was following several conversations at once? Or did he begin to process information from the other conversation only at the point when the friend's name occurred? More generally, what are the limits on a person's ability on the one hand to select the most relevant input to attend to in such a situation and on the other hand to be aware of a significant event occurring outside his or her momentary focus of attention? This last question makes clear the fundamental problem: We need to focus attention to process relevant information adequately, but we also need to ensure that no crucial information is excluded.

One procedure that has been developed to obtain answers to some of these questions is the **dichotic listening experiment**. In this type of experiment, the individual who is being studied listens to tape-recorded messages with earphones. The connections of earphones to recorders are arranged so that different messages can be sent to the two ears. To start an analysis of one of the questions raised above, two messages can be sent simultaneously to the individual's two ears after instructing her that she is to follow only one of the inputs. Then by testing the person afterward one can determine whether she actually heard both messages or whether she ignored the irrelevant messages and heard only the relevant ones. For the experiment to be informative, the subject must be attending to the relevant input. Typically attention is ensured by having the subject *shadow* (that is, repeat aloud) the messages coming in over one of the earphones. Some pioneering experiments by Cherry (1953) showed that an individual is typically able to tell whether or not a voice was present on the unattended channel, and if a voice was present, something about the physical attributes of the nonattended message, but not much about its meaningful content. For example, the subject generally cannot even tell the language in which the nonattended message was spoken. Even in the absence of special instructions, it appears that an individual typically attends only to one channel at a time. Suppose that digits were presented simultaneously over both earphones, say the sequence 6, 2, 9 to the left ear and the sequence 4, 7, 5 to the right. If asked immediately afterward to repeat the digits, the listener would group together those heard over each channel, but even if asked to do so would find it very hard to alternate channels and report "6, 4, 2, 7, 9, 5." These and other observations have motivated a number of theories of attention.

Capacity and Attention

Bottleneck Theories

British psychologist Donald Broadbent (1958) used findings from dichotic listening experiments to formulate a "filter" or **bottleneck model** of attention as schematized in Figure 4.2. According to this theory, an individual's mental apparatus includes a central processing system that receives in-

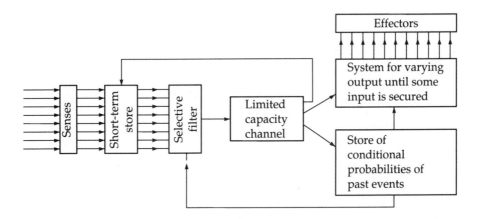

Figure 4.2   **Broadbent's Bottleneck Model of Attention.**
Source: Broadbent, 1958.

puts from sensory channels and compares them with items stored in the memory system to determine their meaning. Overload of the central processor is prevented by means of a selective filter interposed between the central processor and the outside world that sifts incoming stimuli, letting through those that have certain properties and excluding others. In the example of a person listening to a conversation at a party, the filter mechanism would be set to screen out all incoming auditory stimuli that did not have the properties of speech sounds. Of the sounds that pass this first filter, those having certain properties (say those characterizing the voice of the person with whom the individual is conversing) are admitted to the input channel to which the central processor is attending, thus enabling the individual to follow the conversation. An important characteristic of this filter is that it is flexible—one can readily shift attention to another conversation. The bottleneck is produced by the fact that the filter cannot shift back and forth across sensory channels fast enough to follow two conversations at once, for example.

The original conception of a filter proved oversimplified, as indicated by such findings as that the subject shadowing one channel in a dichotic listening experiment will nonetheless notice his or her name if it occurs in the nonattended channel (Moray, 1959). This observation is consistent with having a system be sensitive to high priority events that are not currently the subject of attention; one's name is a pretty good clue that the associated information will prove relevant. It has been necessary to amplify the model to incorporate several stages, as illustrated in Figure 4.3. At the first stage, the incoming sensory information is analyzed for its physical characteristics (pitch, speech versus nonspeech properties, origin in space, etc.). If required by demands of the task, a decision or response can be made on the basis of this analysis—for example, determining who is speaking. At the next stage, stimuli are checked against a list of high priority messages maintained in the permanent memory system, such as danger signals or the vocal pattern of an individual's name. If the stimulus proves to be high priority, attention is switched to the channel carrying the message. If the stimulus is not "flagged" at the permanent priority check, it is then matched against a list of current priorities. In the case of the conversation, a high current priority would be set for auditory inputs of the voice of the other person in the conversation, low priority for voices of other people or for nonspeech sounds. Stimuli passing this stage of the filter system receive futher processing, leading to comprehension of the meaning of the message, whereas those of low priority are ignored and typically receive no further processing.

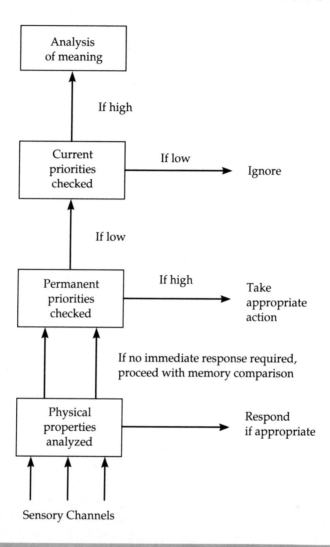

Figure 4.3   **Filtering Model Sensitive to Priorities.**

This attention theory (Treisman, 1960, 1964) allows for the possibility that the analysis of a message's semantic content occurs fairly early in processing. Also, it should be emphasized that the system is not conceived to operate in a passive, mechanical fashion. The early stage of analysis of physical properties may operate almost automatically, but the priorities at the higher levels are continually shifted in accord with the individual's purposes and expectations.

The role of expectations can be seen in an experiment of the following kind. Suppose that in a dichotic listening situation the subject is asked to shadow a message coming into his left ear:

"Give me liberty and shut the door."

while into the right ear comes a second simultaneous message:

"Please leave quietly or give me death."

If the subject had been actively attending to the words of a speech by Patrick Henry and had been generating expectations about its content, then following the passage "Give me liberty," current priorities would be high for words constituting the appropriate continuation and low for words that would not. Consequently, the subject would very likely report "Give me liberty or give me death" even though the task was to report only what was heard over the left earphone. Individuals' well-established habit of adjusting priorities so as to make sense out of what they hear leads them to extract the meaningful and in this case familiar message from the garbled input in spite of instructions to pay attention only to words coming over a particular channel.

Late Selection

An alternative view of attentional limitations is that they occur later in processing. Deutsch and Deutsch (1963) and Norman (1968) proposed models in which information is processed in parallel nonselectively until the results are placed in short-term memory. In brief, the bottlenecks of attention are the limitations of short-term memory. Not all the information sent to short-term memory can be stored and what is not rehearsed or elaborated is likely to be forgotten.

It has not proven easy to contrast **early selection** theories with **late selection** models. Tasks that prevent attention switching, such as shadowing, may impose an additional load on short-term memory. Therefore both types of theories seem consistent with poor memory for nonshadowed information, even at short retention intervals (see Kahneman & Treisman, 1984 for a review). We postpone further discussion of these competing theories until some additional relevant distinctions and observations are introduced.

Capacity Theories

Another approach to attention allows bottlenecks to vary with both the task and the strategy used to allocate attention. This perspective assumes that there is a general limit on people's capacity to perform mental work or expend cognitive effort but also proposes that people have a fair amount of control over how this capacity can be distributed across different tasks or task components (see Figure 4.4).

The model in Figure 4.4, proposed by Daniel Kahneman (1973), makes several straightforward predictions. One is that our inability to perform two tasks at once may not derive from a bottleneck at any particular stage of processing but rather from a nonspecific depletion of a limited pool of resources. Two tasks that do not demand much cognitive effort should

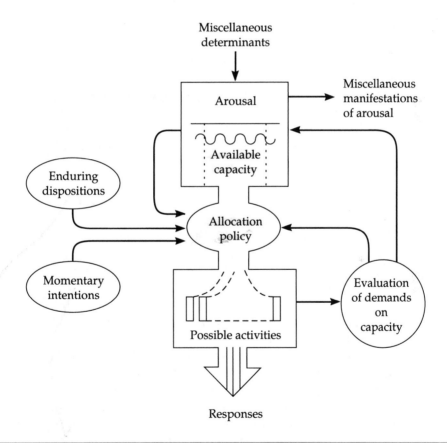

Figure 4.4　**Capacity Model of Attention.**
Source: Kahneman, 1973.

not interfere with each other. Since resources can be allocated, if one emphasizes the importance of one task versus another, there should be corresponding differences in performance.

The distinction between bottleneck and capacity theories is somewhat blurred by multiple resource theories (e.g., Navon, 1984; Wickens, 1984). The idea is that there are multiple pools each of which has limited resources that can be allocated. Whether or not two tasks interfere with each other, on this view, depends on how much they draw on the same resource pools. Just what constitutes a resource pool? One idea is that pools are different for different modalities. There is some evidence that auditory and visual tasks can be performed together more readily than two auditory tasks or two visual tasks (Wickens, 1980). Another idea is that the two hemispheres of the brain provide at least partially separate pools (Wickens, 1984). We will return to this multiple pools idea shortly.

Capacity and Automaticity

A person who is first learning to drive finds it very difficult to do anything else at the same time. With practice, however, people can drink a can of soda, carry on a conversation, and drive in traffic without any sense of stress. It seems that the more a process such as driving has been practiced, the less attention it requires. Informally, we say that the skill has become automatic.

There is strong experimental evidence that practice does produce **automaticity** and a reduction in resource demands. However, whether or not practice yields automaticity seems to depend on the structure of the task. The results from a memory search paradigm illustrate this point.

In the memory search task of present interest, participants are given a series of items (typically letters or digits) to memorize and then asked whether a particular item was in the set. For example, one trial might consist of the letters BKQR followed by the probe T. In this case the correct answer is "no" because T did not appear in the set. The contents and size of the memory set can be varied across trials. In early work on this task Sternberg (1966) noted that search times increased linearly with the size of the memory set with each item adding about 35–40 milliseconds to response times.

For present purposes we are interested in two major variants of the memory search task: **consistent mapping** and **varied mapping**. Under consistent mapping, targets from one trial are never distractors on another trial and vice versa. In the above example, since T appeared as a distractor on one trial it would never be in the memory set and probed on the same trial. That is, the target set and the distractor set do not overlap. Under varied mapping the target set and the distractor set overlap and a given letter may appear on some trials as a target and on other trials as a distractor.

Consistent mapping and varied mapping yield different results. Consider a study by Kristofferson (1972) in which participants were trained either on consistent mapping or varied mapping. Like Sternberg, Kristofferson found that reaction time increased linearly with memory set size. Reaction time did decrease across the 30 days of practice but the lines relating reaction times to memory set size were parallel. This means that the search time per item did not decrease. The reaction time increased about 36 milliseconds for each item in the memory set.

A different pattern of improvement was noted under the consistent mapping condition. In addition to an overall speedup, practice produced an interaction with memory set size. The difference in reaction time to a memory set of size 4 versus a set of size 1 early in training was more than twice the difference observed late in training. That is, the search time per item decreased substantially with practice. It appears that practice speeds up memory search in the consistent mapping case but not in the varied mapping case.

The difference between consistent and varied mapping is even more striking in a visual search task in which participants search through a series of rapidly presented slides or frames for particular targets (see Figure 4.5). As Figure 4.6 indicates, under consistent mapping conditions the reaction time functions become nearly flat across the range of memory set sizes and frame sizes. Participants in the consistent mapping condition report that after practice the targets seem to "pop out" and the search becomes effortless.

Walter Schneider and Richard Shiffrin (Schneider & Shiffrin, 1977; Shiffrin & Schneider, 1977) systematically explored the effects of varied and consistent mapping in developing their theory of automaticity. The empirical generalization is that search tends to become increasingly automatized in procedures involving consistent mapping. Furthermore, it appears that automaticity is not confined to low level visual features. Schneider and Fisk (1984) report automaticity effects when the memory set items are names of examples of categories, such as robin and canary. They even found evidence of transfer at the category level—that is, after training using items like robin and canary as targets, search was rapid for a new target (e.g., bluebird) belonging to an old category.

The Shiffrin and Schneider (1977) model for automatic and controlled processing is shown in Figure 4.7. Controlled processing has limited

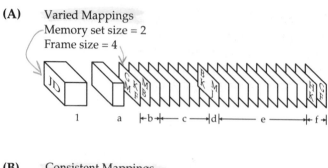

(A)   Varied Mappings
Memory set size = 2
Frame size = 4

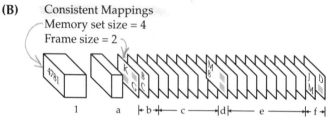

(B)   Consistent Mappings
Memory set size = 4
Frame size = 2

Figure 4.5   Two examples of a positive trial in the multiple-frame search paradigm of Experiment 1 from Schneider and Shiffrin (1977): (A) varied mapping with memory set = (JD); (B) consistent mapping with memory set = (4, 7, 8, 1). (1: presentation of memory set; a fixation dot goes on for .5 sec when subject starts trial; b: three dummy frames that never contain target; c: distractor frames; d: target frame; e: distractor frames; f: dummy frames that never contain target. Frame time is varied across conditions.) *Source*: Schneider & Shiffrin, 1977.

capacity and at least some comparisons and decisions must be serial in nature. As a function of consistent mapping, certain items may be automatically encoded and linked to automatic responses. Automatic encoding can take place in parallel and is not of limited capacity. The Shiffrin and Schneider model does not imply that automaticity comes without any costs. If consistently mapped stimuli automatically attract attention, they may interfere with processing when the task is changed. To test this idea, Shiffrin and Schneider (1977) introduced stimuli that previously had been consistently mapped into a varied mapping procedure. Subjects searched through rapidly presented four-item frames for memory set items. Only the items on one diagonal were relevant for the task but distractor items appeared on the irrelevant diagonal. Usually the distractor items on the irrelevant diagonal were items for the variably mapped set but sometimes an item that previously had been consistently mapped appeared on the irrelevant diagonal. This irrelevant, consistently mapped distractor could appear either on a frame that included the correct target or on some other frame. The results showed a 22% drop in the probability of the correct target being detected when a consistently mapped (automatic) item appeared in an irrelevant location on the same frame. As predicted, the consistently mapped item drew attention away from the target.

The Schneider and Shiffrin theory of automaticity has not gone unchallenged. For example, Hirst, Spelke, Reaves, Caharack, and Neisser (1980) argued that people could learn to perform two complex comprehension tasks simultaneously without either task being automatized. They trained people to read while taking dictation in the form of short sentences. After considerable practice, participants could write short sentences while reading aloud as well as answer complex comprehension questions about what they had read. Hirst et al. argued that their subjects were not alternating between tasks but had restructured it so that both tasks could be

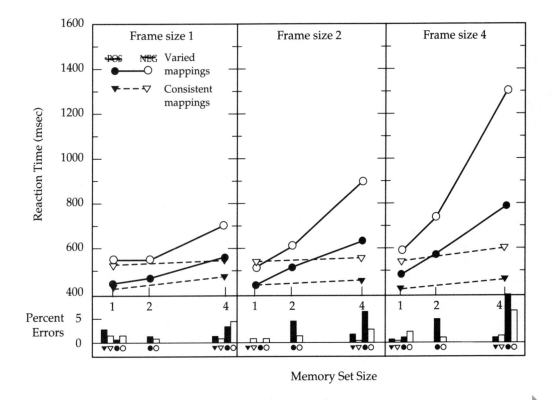

Figure 4.6   Mean reaction times for correct responses and percentages of error as a function of memory-set size for both varied and consistent search conditions from Experiment 2 of Schneider and Shiffrin (1977). *Source*: Schneider & Shiffrin, 1977.

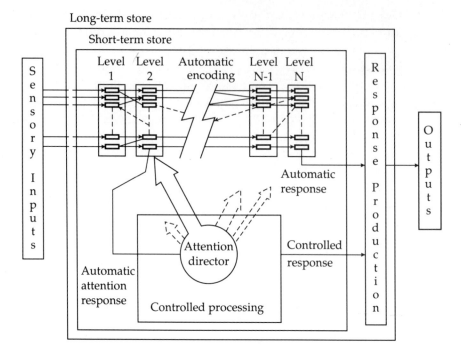

Figure 4.7   A model for automatic and controlled processing during tasks requiring detection of certain stimuli. The dashed arrows going from higher to lower levels indicate the possibility that higher level features can sometimes influence the automatic processing of lower level features. The small solid arrow from a node in Level 2 to the attention system indicates that this node has produced an automatic-attention response, and the large arrow from the attention system to Level 2 indicates that the attention system has responded. The arrow from level N to the Response Production indicates that this node has called for an automatic overt response, which will shortly be executed. The small arrow from Controlled Processing to Response Production indicates the normal mode of responding in which the response is based on controlled comparisons and decisions. Were it not for the automatic response indicated, detection would have proceeded in a serial, controlled search of nodes and levels in an order chosen by the subject. *Source*: Shiffrin & Schneider, 1977.

performed simultaneously. It is not entirely clear what "restructuring" means in this case, but Gordon Logan has developed a specific model based on the idea that what changes with practice is not the speed of operation but rather the type of operation that determines performance.

We will take a moment to describe Logan's (1988) instance theory of automaticity. His idea is that automaticity develops when performance associated with a task comes to rely increasingly on memory. Normally, a task will have some algorithm or procedure that can produce correct performance but this algorithm may take considerable time. For example, you can multiply 39 times 39 to arrive at the answer 1521. Having done so, if you are immediately asked what 39 times 39 is, you do not have to perform the computation again if you remember the result of the earlier computation. Logan views task performance as a race between the algorithm or procedure and memory for stored instances of the appropriate answer or response. Consistent mapping ensures that the retrieved instances will be useful (39 times 39 is always 1521) and performance improves with practice as one accumulates more stored instances. Logan developed a quantitative model for this presumed race process and demonstrated that it accounted for reaction time speedups with practice as well as the decreased variability of reaction times (see Cheng, 1985 for further arguments concerning changes in operations versus changes in their speed).

According to the instance theory, automatic processes can be controlled; one may not be able to control responding on the basis of automatic processes perfectly, however, because they tend to be fast and allow less time for the act of control to take place. Automatic processes may also be controlled by manipulating retrieval cues to make access to stored examples easier or more difficult. One challenge for the instance theory of automaticity is to specify just what an instance is and to describe how generalization from prior experiences occurs. Driving a car typically involves episodes (e.g., approaching a stop sign) that are in many respects similar to previous episodes but in other respects are unique. Some respects may matter and others surely do not. If you have been asked what 39 times 39 is in a written format, you could presumably retrieve the answer when the same question is asked orally. In brief, determining what an instance consists of is both a theoretical problem and an empirical question.

Whether or not automaticity effects reflect processes that are truly automatic (just what one means by automatic is itself a matter of debate; see Schneider & Detweiler, 1987; Shiffrin, Dumais, & Schneider, 1981; Shiffrin, 1988), they are important for understanding performance in attention tasks. In general, whether some irrelevant information interferes with or has no effect on processing of task-relevant information may depend on whether or not the relevant information, the irrelevant information, or both have become automatized.

Attention and Action

What is attention for? Alan Allport (1989) has argued for the value of addressing Marr's computational level question of what function attention serves. Allport suggests that attention is critically involved in selection-for-action. Consider what is involved in reaching for either a stationary or a moving object in a scene where many objects may be present. For the grasp to be successful one must determine the spatiotemporal coordinates of the goal object. Information about the position and size of other objects in the scene must not be allowed to interfere (that is, produce "**crosstalk**") with the relevant information. In short, selective processing is needed to map just those aspects of the scene to the goal object onto appropriate control parameters for action (or potential action).

As Allport notes, selection cannot consist simply of a split into two pools, relevant and irrelevant. Action may be complex and rely on multiple sources of information; frequently two or more categories of action must be coordinated. When conditions for two actions conflict, one or both must be modified to allow their continued execution or one action may take priority over the other.

Again the sets of information associated with concurrent, partially independent actions must be segregated so as to avoid unwanted crosstalk between them (information from one set intruding on the other). The interference associated with performing concurrent tasks may represent not so much capacity limitations per se as it does crosstalk where streams of relevant information are only partially segregated (Pashler, 1989).

Spatial Selection

One generalization concerning selection and interference is that interference varies inversely with the spatial separation of targets and distractors in the visual array (see, e.g., Johnson & Dark, 1986). This spatially based selectivity has led to the metaphor of a spatial "spotlight" notion of visual attention. The **spotlight metaphor** implies that attention cannot be simultaneously directed at two spatially distinct areas without also being directed at an area between the two points. Although there is evidence supporting spatial selection (see, e.g., Eriksen & St. James, 1986), other studies suggest that selection may be based on nonspatial perceptual grouping factors (see, e.g., Duncan, 1984; Driver & Baylis, 1989; see also Tipper, Brehaut, & Driver, 1990). Therefore, the spotlight metaphor is incomplete as a theory of selection for action.

What versus Where

There is good neuropsychological evidence that the "**what**" and "**where**" **systems** are functionally and neuroanatomically separable, parallel systems (see, e.g., Ungerleider & Mishkin, 1982; Ellis & Young, 1988), and even spatial attention may have functionally distinct subsystems (Posner, 1988). Note that these observations raise problems about the idea that there is an early selection based on location followed by later processing of the contents of information at that location. "What" and "where" appear to operate in parallel rather than sequentially and these sources of information may be coordinated only at a later stage of processing. In a moment we'll consider a specific theory of the role of spatial information in the integration of nonspatial information. For now, we simply note that there is increasing evidence for a variety of subsystems of attention (again, see Allport, 1989 for a general review).

Summary

Attention is needed for the coordination and control of action. A system must also be able to assign priorities in the case of conflicts and, as we argued at the beginning of this chapter, to be interruptible when unanticipated events of importance arise. The response to these various demands appears to involve functionally separable but partially overlapping attention subsystems.

For our purposes, this analysis casts a very different light on attention. From capacity framework we are led to focus on the limitations of information processing and we might wonder how much more effective we might be if we did not have these limitations. From the perspective of multiple goals and the need to coordinate and control action, attention becomes a positive enabler of intelligent action. If we were unable to select information or only able to select information in an all-or-none manner without further segregation, we would be unable either to think or to act. Potential crosstalk and the need to prioritize and coordinate tasks means that one can't always do two things at once as well as one could do either in isolation, but we believe that attention should be thought of as enabling organisms to properly organize relevant information and not solely as a limitation.

Integration of Information:
Feature Integration Theory

The work on automaticity considered earlier describes changes in the demands on capacity but it does not speak directly to the idea of multiple resource pools. Recently investigators have begun to identify specific resource limitations with functionally separable subsystems of attention. For example, the **feature integration theory** of Treisman and Gelade (1980) describes limitations associated with perceptual encoding processes. Specifically, the theory proposes that although individual features are encoded in parallel, *conjunctions* of features can only be encoded in a serial manner that demands attention. For example, people find it easy to search for green things (triangles or circles) against a background of red things or to search for circles (red or green) against a background of triangles (red or green). But it is difficult to search for *green circles* against a background of green triangles and red circles. Under consistent mapping, search time is fairly independent of display size for individual feature targets (as Schneider and Shiffrin found). For conjunctive targets, however, search time increases linearly with display size even though the mapping is consistent.

One might wonder what is so special about conjunctions of features. Part of the answer may lie in the distinction between what and where. One might be able to identify that some feature was present even if one were uncertain exactly where it appeared. But now consider a conjunction. There could be green present and circles present without necessarily a green circle being present, because the conjunction of features must appear in the same location. In fact, feature integration theory attaches special significance to spatial position information. The basic idea is that color information is indexed by location information and that shape information is also tagged with location information. Color information is not directly linked to shape information; rather, color and shape are indirectly linked through common spatial information. For example, when a blue triangle is presented at location X, blue and triangle are directly linked with X and their common location is used to integrate blue and triangle into blue triangle. In support of this proposal, Treisman and Gelade (1980) found that performance on detecting conjunctively defined targets was completely at chance on trials where subjects had poor information about where the target appeared (in some conditions people were asked to say both whether a target was present and, if so, where). In contrast, for simple feature detection people perform considerably above chance even when they do not know where the target appeared. Mary Jo Nissen (1985) has provided more direct evidence that spatial position is an obligatory intermediate link between color and shape information.

As usual, as research progresses things tend to get more complicated. It might have occurred to you that a person should be able to ignore all red things in looking for a green circle. As it turns out, the speed with which one can conduct a search for a conjunctive target depends on how distinctive each single feature is from possible distractors (Duncan & Humphreys, 1989). Consequently, modifications and alternatives to the feature integration theory have recently been advanced (see, e.g., Treisman, 1988; Treisman & Sato, 1990; Cave & Wolfe, 1990).

Summary

The study of attention underlines the joint problem of handling massive amounts of potentially relevant information and bringing knowledge to bear on it in the service of intelligent action. The coordination and control of action associated with different goals, motivational states, tasks, and sources of information require an attention system that simultaneously is able to select information in a coherent manner and to be sensitive to novel, potentially significant information. Human attention appears to be accomplished through overlapping but partially independent subsystems that operate on different types and levels of information. As we have seen in this chapter and will see in the next one, just how these sources of information are integrated to provide a unitary perceptual experience is a matter of great current research interest. Attention and perception are exquisitely adapted to allow us to move about in, act in, and make sense of our environment.

Key Terms

automaticity
bottleneck model
consistent mapping
crosstalk
dichotic listening
   experiment
early selection
echoic memory
feature integration
   theory

iconic memory
late selection
partial report
   technique
span of apprehension
"spotlight" metaphor
varied mapping
what system
where system

Recommended Readings

It is sometimes surprising to see just how modern certain "older" contributions to psychology can sound. A case in point is William James's (1890) book, which continues to inspire and influence attention researchers. Research on attention got a large boost from the human factors research associated with the Second World War. One practical problem was that of radar experts who had to maintain attention in order to detect infrequent (but important) targets. Broadbent's (1958) comprehensive and interesting book had its roots in that tradition.

There is a great current interest in the neuropsychology of attention. Ellis and Young (1988) and Posner (1988) offer detailed reviews of this literature. Recent surveys on the general topic of attention from two distinctive points of view are provided by Shiffrin (1988) and Allport (1989). Finally, interest in feature integration theory and its alternatives is sufficiently great that it's a good bet that if you pick up an issue of *Cognitive Psychology, Perception and Psychophysics,* or *Journal of Experimental Psychology: Human Perception and Performance,* you will find an article on feature integration.

5

VISUAL PERCEPTION

Chapter Outline

You can see a lot just by looking.

—Yogi Berra

The Problem of Perception

How do we perceive the structure of the world that surrounds us? As we have been emphasizing, at an intuitive level there is no problem—the world is there and we see it. It is only on closer examination that the true mysteries of perception become apparent. The challenge is to describe just how the two-dimensional projection of light onto the retina of the eye gives rise to the phenomenal experience of a three-dimensional world. An immediate problem is that any given input will be inherently ambiguous. Figure 5.1 shows just three out of an unlimited set of bars, each of which produces the same image on the retina. How is it that our perceptual system is able to resolve these ambiguities? Clearly this is one area where intuition is of little help, because our awareness is only of the *outcomes* of perceptual processes.

Given that the input underdetermines possible states of affairs in the world, additional assumptions (built-in constraints or biases) about the world are needed to arrive at a single, unambiguous perceptual experience. Jointly analyzing the nature of available information and the character of these additional assumptions is the primary agenda for much of the current work in vision.

On a more specific level, what problems does the perceptual system solve? Inferences from the structure of the retinal image to the structure of the outside world involve three natural subcomponents. We need to know *what* is out there, *where* it is, and *how* it is acting, both with respect to us and with respect to other things. In the last chapter we reviewed evidence suggesting that the subsystem for determining *what* is distinct from the subsystem determining *where*. In this chapter we add the further complication associated with perceiving relative motion. Obviously, it is vitally important to know whether some object is rushing toward us or away from us.

The perceptual system must also deliver information in such a way

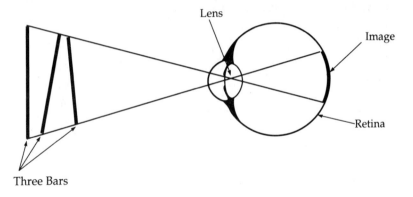

Figure 5.1   Three different bars that project the same image on the retina.

that relevant knowledge from memory can make contact with it. As we shall see, there is no one-way flow of information into a passive receiver. Rather, perception is an active process in which different levels of analysis interact to determine what we perceive and understand. Our focus will be on visual perception; auditory (speech) perception will receive a great deal of attention in the chapters on language.

It is virtually impossible to give a comprehensive description of perception in a single chapter. We talk of perception as a unitary thing because our phenomenal experience is coherent. But there is every reason to believe that perception is based on a multitude of parallel and hierarchically organized processes that at present are poorly understood. Industrial robots, for example, can only operate in highly constrained predictable environments and efforts to develop machines to read have met with limited success to date. Therefore, our goal will be to provide an overview of the problems of perception and some of the methods for addressing them. The amazing thing is that our perceptual system does what it does so automatically that we take it for granted.

The Constraints Perspective

As we stressed earlier, one of the central problems in perception is that two-dimensional image arrays on the retina underdetermine possible percepts. That is to say, retinal information is consistent with an infinite number of interpretations. Yet our experience of the world reveals nothing of this ambiguity. It appears that the perceptual system makes assumptions about the nature of the world and these assumptions, coupled with the input, allow for an unambiguous output or interpretation. Borrowing an example from Johnson-Laird (1988, p. 60), vision is like the problem of finding the value of X in the equation $5 = X + Y$.

One can see that X could take on any value, depending on the value of Y. If Y is -100, then X is 105; if Y is -95, then X is 100, and so on. It is as if the visual system makes certain assumptions about Y; for example, if Y is between 0 and 5, then X must be between 0 and 5, or if Y is 2, then X must be 3. Given that people seem to perceive the world fairly accurately (perceptual illusions are an exception), these assumptions typically must be approximately correct.

The framework motivating a large share of current research in the area of vision involves a search for what Brown (1984) refers to as natural constraints. In the case of computer vision the goal is to find constraints that will work; identifying the constraints adopted by living systems is a good place to start. For cognitive psychologists the goal is to see if plausible constraints (perhaps those identified by some theory) are, in fact, constraints guiding the human vision system. This latter goal often requires experimenters to construct highly artificial situations in which these constraints or assumptions are violated. If violating constraints alters perception, then the human perceptual system must embody the constraint in some way. An example of a constraint is that the perceptual system might assume that motion of objects is rigid (that is, that objects do not change shape as they move), which would allow one to determine shape from motion (for a proof, see Ullman, 1979). Rigid motion is a correct assumption for the movement of things like pencils but not for the movement of animals or artifacts like rubber bands, pieces of paper, or clothing. Perceiving animate motion accurately seems important, and we should perhaps not be surprised that several recent studies have questioned the generality of the **rigidity constraint** for human perception (see, e.g., Schwartz & Sperling, 1983; Todd, 1985; Braunstein & Andersen, 1986).

Now let's consider a positive example. The perceptual system clearly does use information from cast shadows to determine the apparent position of an object and its shape (see Figure 5.2). At the same time, however, colors, textures, and shapes of shadows are physically constrained in natural situations in ways that the human perceptual system seems to ignore. Cavanagh and Leclerc (1989) report that the only requirements for perceiving depth through shadow are that shadow regions be darker than surrounding nonshadow regions and that there be consistent contrast differences along shadow borders. It did not seem to matter much at all whether or not the shape of the shadow corresponded with the shape of its source object.

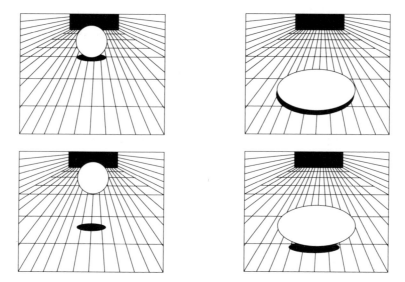

Figure 5.2   Cast shadows can influence the apparent position of an object and its shape. *Source*: Cavanagh & Leclerc, 1989.

The search for and evaluation of natural constraints continues to be a central theme in computational approaches to vision (see, e.g., Dannemiller, 1989; Todd & Reichel, 1989). Later in this chapter we will describe an example of how constraints may operate in computational models of perception so that you can understand this type of approach. We begin with the problem of localizing entities and then shift to the problem of how things are recognized.

Localization

To locate objects in our environment, we first have to segregate objects from one another and from the background. Associated with this task is the further problem of determining the position and movement of objects in the world. That segregation, fixing distance, and determining movement are closely related is supported by physiological evidence that these three functions are handled by the same part of the nervous system (Livingstone & Hubel, 1988).

Segregation

Much of the early work on object segregation was done by Gestalt psychologists who were opposed to the behaviorist tradition of focusing on the microstructure of behavior. Gestalt psychologists focused on the perception of whole objects and proposed a number of principles for how the perceptual system organizes objects. For example, they were very interested in **figure-ground relations**. *Figure* is determined by regions of contrast that are connected and cohesive. That *figure-ground* is not completely determined by the stimulus can be seen by reversible figures that allow more than one organization. Figure 5.3 can be seen either as a vase or as two profile faces.

The Gestalt psychologists also identified principles of grouping for organizing figures. For example, the closer two figures are to each other the more likely it is that they will be grouped perceptually (Figure 5.4a). This **proximity principle** also trades off with *similarity*. We tend to group things that are similar (Figure 5.4b).

The perceptual system also seems to prefer contours that continue smoothly along their course (see Figure 5.5a–c). Organization by **good continuation** does not even require that contours be continuous. Figure 5.5d is seen as a single rod and a rectangle rather than two rods and a rectangle or as a single, irregular object.

These assumptions made by the perceptual system tend to serve us well. In situations like those shown in Figure 5.5d there is an excellent chance that a single rod and a rectangular shape are really present. That is, these organization preferences reflect a certain "wisdom" of the nervous system. A natural question to ask is whether this wisdom is based on experience or whether it is present at birth. The answer is "a bit of both." As

Figure 5.3   **Reversible Figure-Ground Pattern.**
Reversible figure-ground pattern can be seen as either a pair of silhouetted faces or a white vase.

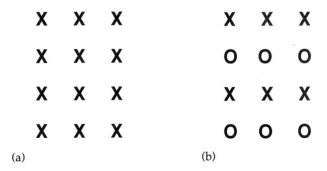

(a)   (b)

Figure 5.4   **Grouping by Proximity and Similarity.**
In (a) the pattern will tend to be organized as three columns whereas in (b) it will tend to be seen as four rows.

we shall see, however, it is remarkable how sophisticated perception is even in human infants.

An early view of infant perception was that it is piecemeal and disorganized. In a statement that is almost infamous William James (1890, p. 488) said, "The baby, assailed by eyes, ears, nose, skin and entrails at once, feels it all as one great blooming buzzing confusion." In contrast to this, we now know that infant perception is active, highly organized, intermodally coordinated, and coherent. (See Gibson, 1987 and subsequent articles in that special issue.)

How do researchers ask questions about infant perception, given that infants are relatively helpless and completely inarticulate? One ingenious technique relies on the phenomenon of habituation (discussed in Chapter 3). Infants direct their attention at informative or surprising events

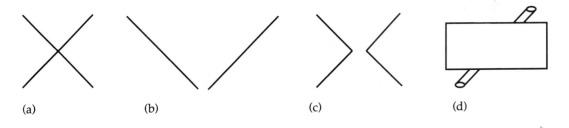

(a)   (b)   (c)   (d)

Figure 5.5   **Good Continuation.**
The line segments in (a) tend to be decomposed into the two lines in (b) rather than into the two lines shown in (c). The lines do not even have to be literally continuous. The figure in (d) is seen as a single rod and rectangle.

but with repeated exposure to the same event show less and less attention. One can evaluate infants' interpretation of an ambiguous event by first giving habituation trials and then showing the infants the event in various unambiguous ways. Infants should be surprised when the unambiguous event is contrary to their interpretation of the ambiguous event.

An example will serve to make this general idea clear. Consider the rod that is partially blocked by a white rectangle in Figure 5.6, panel A. If one repeatedly exposes infants to this pattern, the average amount of time they spend looking at it will rapidly decline, as the graph indicates. After habituation the white rectangle is taken away and infants either see a completely connected rod or a rod in two separate fragments. Adult observers expect the rod to be connected (based on "good continuation") and are surprised when shown the fragmented rod. Three-month-olds, however, look at the connected rod as much as they do the fragmented one (panel A test) suggesting that they had not interpreted the rod as connected (Kellman & Spelke, 1983).

Of course, negative results are not especially informative. Kellman and Spelke (1983) showed infants the same stimuli but moved the rod back and forth (in a coordinated manner) while the white rectangle remained

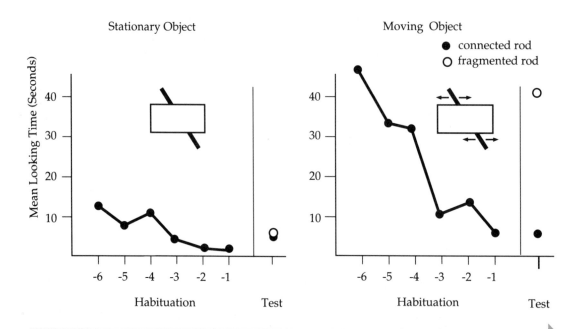

Figure 5.6   Looking time to complete and fragmented test displays, after habituation to stationary or moving center-occluded objects. *Source*: Spelke, 1990.

stationary. Again habituation occurred (albeit more slowly) as panel B of Figure 5.6 indicates and infants were again tested with either a connected or fragmented rod. The infants showed surprise at seeing the fragmented rod and spent a great deal of time looking at it. They spent little time looking at the connected rod. This suggests that infants perceive an object as unitary if its parts undergo common motion.

In an even more ingenious experiment Kellman, Gleitman, and Spelke (1987) demonstrated that the results just described do not depend on motion across the retina. They placed infants in moveable seats and when an object moved, they moved the infants' position to cancel motion across the retina. They also included a condition in which the infant moved while the object remained stationary. The results were that the object was perceived as coherent if and only if the object moved. Motion across the retina had no effect. Other studies using patterns of reaching in five- and six-month-old infants point to the same conclusion (e.g., Spelke, von Hofsten, & Kestenbaum, 1989).

These and related observations have led Elizabeth Spelke and her associates (see, e.g., Spelke, 1990) to the view that infants are born with an initial theory about the world that defines a concept of object. The infants' concept of object appears to be defined by four properties or constraints: (1) that surfaces of cohesive bodies must be connected; (2–3) that surfaces of cohesive bodies must move independently of their environment and on connected paths (the experiments we have just discussed support this claim); and (4) that surfaces must move through unoccupied space. These four assumptions appear to be central aspects of adults' intuitive conception of the physical world. Through learning, these assumptions become supplemented by further observations about objects that support principles like good continuation or the idea that objects tend to be homogeneous in color. The four assumptions cited by Spelke represent strong constraints on perception but they are also assumptions that are basically correct. In brief, instead of buzzing, blooming confusion, infants' perception is that of a world with bounded, unitary objects.

Distance

By now it should not surprise you to read that the visual system uses a variety of types of information to determine where objects are located. We will describe a number of these cues to distance and then analyze one particular cue, binocular disparity, in considerable detail. Although perceiving an object's depth seems effortless, it is a remarkable achievement given that the retinal image is flat and has no depth at all.

Monocular Cues.   A number of cues to depth require only a single eye. Three straightforward examples are interposition, linear perspective, and relative size. Interposition refers to the observation that when one object interrupts the contour of a second object, the first object is perceived to be in front of the second one. Linear perspective is often exploited by artists to create the impression of depth. When straight lines gradually converge (e.g., as in railroad tracks) they are perceived as parallel with the converging points seen as more distant. Relative size refers to the observation that people tend to perceive the smaller of two identical (or similar) objects as being farther away than the larger object.

We should note in passing that another remarkable property of the perceptual system is **size constancy**. That is, we tend to perceive an object as being the same size, even though its size on our retina varies with its distance from us. At extremes of distance size constancy may break down—from an airplane, cars on the ground may appear to be the size of ants. There is evidence that size constancy is present even in six-month-old infants (McKenzie, Tootell, & Day, 1980).

Texture Gradients.   So far we have described cues to depth that might allow the perceptual system to infer depth. The fact that we are not aware of these inferences has led to the idea, which can be traced back at least as far as Helmholtz around the turn of the century, that these inferences are unconscious. James J. Gibson (e.g., 1950, 1966) claims that people do not *infer* depth, but rather perceive it directly. His idea is that the perceptual system does not combine information from multiple cues; instead perception involves a direct sensitivity to higher order **invariants**. Invariants refer to properties of the proximal (retinal) stimulus pattern that remain unchanged despite various transformations of the distal stimulus or object. That is, there is information directly in the stimulus.

In the case of depth, Gibson demonstrated that **texture gradients** are a powerful source of information. A texture gradient arises when we view a surface in perspective. The elements that make up the textured surface appear to be packed closer and closer together as the surface recedes (see Figure 5.7). Gibson argued that size constancy is directly perceived as a higher order invariant. There is a constant ratio between the retinal size of an object and the retinal size of its adjacent textural elements.

Gibson's ideas about direct perception are controversial, especially his argument that invariants negate the need for any sort of internal, mental representations (for criticisms, see, e.g., Fodor & Pylyshyn, 1981). Nonetheless, Gibson's work has been very influential by focusing attention on the information that is available to the perceptual system. Gibson's criti-

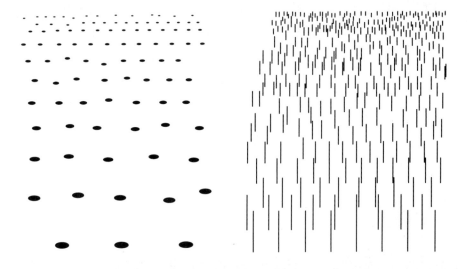

Figure 5.7   **Two Examples of Texture Gradients.**
Source: Gibson, 1950.

cisms of research restricted to two-dimensional stable stimuli have served to reinforce the study of the perception of objects and events in the world.

Motion Parallax.   So far in discussing distance perception we have only considered situations in which both the observer and the scene observed remain stable or stationary. Of course, in real life we are often moving about and motion provides an important source of information about the spatial arrangement of objects around us. As we move our heads from left to right, for example, the images projected by objects in our environment move across the retina from right to left. Relative motion or **motion parallax** provides a very effective depth cue. Nearby objects appear to move more quickly than objects further away.

Stereopsis.   **Stereopsis** arises from the fact that our two eyes view the visual world from slightly different angles. As Figure 5.8 illustrates, when we fixate on an object our eyes converge slightly so that the axes of vision meet at a point in the visual world. Any neighboring point in the visual field will then project to a point on each retina some distance from the center of vision. The distance generally will not be the same for both eyes but will vary with the depth of the fixated point. This means that information about **retinal disparity** can potentially be used to determine how far

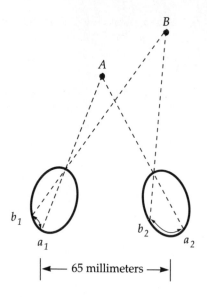

Figure 5.8   **Retinal Disparity.**
Two points, *A* and *B*, at different distances from the observer, present somewhat
different retinal images. The distance between the images on one eye, a_1b_1 is different (disparate) from the distance between them on the other a_2b_2. This disparity
is a powerful cue for depth. *Source*: Hochberg, 1978.

away the fixated point or object is. (You may recall from geometry or trigonometry that information about the length of one side of a triangle and its
two adjacent angles can be used to determine the lengths of the two other
sides. In short, depth or distance can be determined by triangulation.) We
will describe a procedure for computing stereopsis in some detail, because
it illustrates some important points concerning ways in which constraints
or assumptions about the world are embodied by the visual system.

To recover depth from retinal disparity, four steps are involved: (1)
a location in space must be selected from one retinal image; (2) the same
location must be identified in the other retinal image; (3) their positions
must be measured; and (4) the distance must be calculated from the disparity information (by triangulation). Although this procedure is straightforward to describe, under realistic viewing conditions the first two steps
are enormously complex, as Poggio (1984) points out. The retinal array
consists of patterns of raw light intensity and a given patch of surface
will not necessarily reflect the same intensity to both eyes. Furthermore,
patches of surface that do not correspond may happen to have the same
intensity. To begin to appreciate the full extent of the problem, consider

the random dot stereograms devised by Bela Julesz as shown in Figure 5.9. To create these **stereograms**, Julesz generated a random texture of black and white dots and made two copies of it. In one of the copies, he shifted a smaller square to the left and for the other he shifted the square to the right. When the pattern in Figure 5.9 is viewed through a stereoscope so that the left eye sees the left pattern of dots and the right eye sees the right pattern of dots, the brain fuses the two percepts into one and the phenomenal experience is of the smaller square being nearer and "floating"

Figure 5.9   Random-dot stereograms devised by Bela Julesz of AT&T laboratories are visual textures containing no clues for stereo vision except binocular disparities. The stereograms themselves are the same random texture of black and white dots (*top*). In one of them, however, a square of the texture is shifted toward the left; in the other it is shifted toward the right (*bottom*). The resulting hole in each image is filled with more random dots (*dark gray area*). *Source*: Poggio, 1984.

above the larger pattern (as in Figure 5.10). Demonstrations such as this indicate that stereopsis does not require the prior recognition of shapes or objects. The problem remains—how is the correspondence made between the dots seen by one eye to the dots seen by the other to create the impression of depth?

Clearly in Figure 5.9 any dot in the left pattern could be matched with any of a large number of dots in the other image. But somehow the brain consistently chooses the correct set of matches. Marr and Poggio (1976) proposed two constraints that would allow stereopsis to be computed. The first is that a given point has only one three-dimensional location at any given time, which means that each point can be matched with no more than one other point in the other image. The second key assumption is that variation in depth over a surface is generally smooth, with discontinuous changes occurring only at boundary lines. In short, changes vary smoothly except at object boundaries. An additional assumption employed by Marr and Poggio is that raw intensities are not matched but rather patterns of variation in intensity are (see Poggio, 1984 for details).

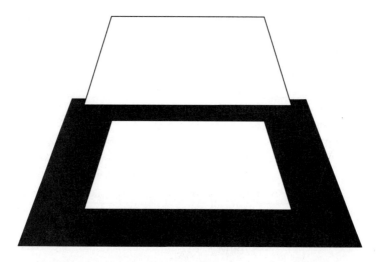

Figure 5.10   Vivid perception of depth results when the random-dot stereograms shown at the top of Figure 5.9 are viewed through a stereoscope, so that each eye sees one of the pair and the brain can fuse the two. The sight part of the image "floating" establishes that stereopsis does not require the recognition of objects in the visual world. *Source*: Poggio, 1984.

To test their proposal, Marr and Poggio embodied these constraints in a connectionist network that implemented a stereopsis algorithm. They set up a three-dimensional network of nodes that represented possible lines of sight from the eyes in the three-dimensional world. The uniqueness constraint was implemented by requiring that the nodes along a line of sight inhibit one another (that is, there is inhibition between competing interpretations). The continuity constraint was embodied by requiring that each node excite its neighbors (this produces reinforcement of consistent information).

The actual algorithm performs parallel constraint satisfaction to settle on an interpretation. It begins by setting up all possible matches between the information to one eye and information to the other eye. Candidate matches receive an initial activation, and excitation and inhibition are then passed on to other nodes in the network according to the rules described earlier. Next the algorithm sums the activation to each node by adding activation from neighboring nodes and subtracting activation from competing line of sight nodes. If the activation to a node exceeds a threshold that node responds again by sending out activation. After only a few such cycles the network settles on a stable pattern of activation. This stable pattern represents the interpretation of the pattern that is the candidate solution to the stereopsis problem. Marr and Poggio showed that this connectionist algorithm could solve random dot stereograms like those shown in Figure 5.9 and at least some natural images.

In terms of Marr's three stages we have described the problem of stereopsis at both the computational level and the algorithmic level. Although the Marr and Poggio algorithm was implemented as a computer program, they also provided some evidence and ideas about how these computations might be performed by the nervous system (again see Poggio, 1984). It is also important to note that the constraints embodied in the algorithm work to limit the search for solutions to the stereopsis problem, which otherwise would be intractable (because there would be too many possibilities to be considered and no way to decide among them).

Summary.   The visual system uses a variety of sources of information to determine depth. Normally only specialists such as vision scientists and artists are aware of these cues; our phenomenal experience is just of seeing things in depth. We have just seen, however, that even a single source of information about depth, stereopsis, involves complex computations. These are computations that the nervous system could plausibly perform, but they take place outside of our awareness.

Motion

A challenge to the problem of localizing things is that some of them may move. In addition, we care about whether things are moving toward us or away from us (for obvious reasons). So how do we perceive motion?

Illusory Motion.   The answer to the question of how we perceive motion is quite complex. First, the perception of motion cannot be equated with movement of an image across the retina. Recall, for example, Roger Shepard's work on apparent motion (discussed in Chapter 2). The rapid alternation of two isolated stimulus events is often not perceived as two isolated stimulus events but rather as continuous motion and transformation between the two images. The simplest case of apparent motion involves flashing a light in darkness and shortly thereafter flashing another light near the location of the first. When there is a short time interval between flashes, the perception is of a single light in motion. Only for long interflash intervals will the lights appear as isolated flashes. Apparent motion (also referred to as stroboscopic motion) is responsible for our seeing movies as involving action and motion rather than as a series of still photographs.

A second example of illusory motion occurs when a large object surrounding a smaller one moves. In this circumstance, the smaller object is often perceived to move even though it is static.

Real Motion.   Even when an image does move across the retina, the problem of motion perception remains complex. Movement across the retina could arise because the eyes rather than the object are moving. The visual system must integrate information from the motor system in order to "correct" for eye movements in determining real motion. These difficulties notwithstanding, the visual system is quite sensitive to real motion (Nakayama, 1985).

Just how the nervous system computes visual motion is a complex and difficult issue. Without going into details, one problem is that information provided by local changes in intensity values on the retina only weakly constrains possible speeds and directions of motion. One way to address this underdetermination is to posit that the visual system makes further assumptions about the world in order to further constrain things. Hildreth (1984a, b), for example, has explored a **smoothness constraint**; that is, the idea that the perception system assumes that the surfaces of objects are smooth relative to their distance from the viewer. Hildreth has constructed a technical proof that this assumption (along with the idea that the visual system assumes the minimum variation consistent with the input) can yield the direction and velocity of motion.

Actually, the problem is even more difficult because there is no guarantee that these constraints will yield the correct perception of motion. Of course, we have already noted that people are susceptible to certain visual illusions. Hildreth observed that if the human visual system follows the smoothness constraint, people should also misperceive motion under certain conditions. One such condition is the barber pole illusion. When a barber pole rotates, the winding stripe on the pole appears to move upward (or downward, depending on the direction of rotation), even though each point on the image of the stripe is moving horizontally. Hildreth's computational analysis indicated that following the smoothness constraint should lead people to misperceive this horizontal movement as vertical movement. Note also that the barber pole illusion does not disappear when we know what is objectively true. The computation of motion is apparently isolated from higher level knowledge that might inform it.

Use of Motion Information.   As complex as motion is, it does provide a rich source of information. When the perceiver is moving forward (as when a pilot is landing an airplane) the rate of expansion in the image specifies the perceiver's velocity, and the direction of motion of a point on the images specifies the trajectories of points relative to the perceiver.

Visual motion also may provide information about the shapes and boundaries of objects, as we saw in Elizabeth Spelke's studies of infant object perception. Ullman (1979) has shown mathematically that under certain conditions motion can specify the shape of an object.

Finally, patterns of relative motion may give rise to the perception that the motion of one object *caused* the motion of another. For example, when a square moves immediately next to another square and that second square begins to move, the first square is seen as having caused the second to move. This perception of causality depends on factors such as the speed of the first square, the speed of the second, whether the objects touch, and how soon after touching the second object begins to move (Michotte, 1963).

This ends our survey of the multifaceted problem of localization. Equally if not more challenging is the problem of identifying *what* something is. We turn now to some proposals concerning how object recognition is accomplished.

From Features to Structure

Much of the work in computational vision is directed at early vision processes such as edge detection, determining shape from information about shading and structure from information about motion, figuring out surface colors, and so on. So far, we have only touched on a small part of the early vision problem and said next to nothing about higher level processes that give rise to object and scene perception. Both Marr (1982) and Johnson-Laird (1988) provide very readable discussions and descriptions linking lower level and higher level vision (see Hildreth & Ullman, 1989 for a general review of computational vision).

In this section our attention will focus on one of the most central and difficult problems in perception: how shapes are recognized. The light entering the human eye is focused by the lens into a two-dimensional image on the rear of the eyeball or retina. A fundamental question is how information about the three-dimensional world is extracted from this (constantly changing) two-dimensional image. We will consider a number of ideas concerning how recognition is accomplished, beginning with some general ideas about pattern recognition and how it might be accomplished.

Feature Detection Theories

Feature-based models have enjoyed long-standing popularity. First, it seems intuitively natural to explain similarity between objects in terms of properties that they share. A pencil is similar to a pen because both are about the same size and shape and both can be used for writing. Furthermore, features provide a vocabulary for constructing objects. Just as the 26 letters of the English alphabet can be used to compose over 100,000 words, a small set of visual features may be sufficient to describe a large number of objects. The key idea of featural models is that all objects are composed of separable, distinct parts referred to as **features**.

There is even physiological evidence for features. In a now classic study Lettvin, Maturana, McCulloch, and Pitts (1959) used microelectronic recording techniques and determined that frog visual systems have four distinct kinds of feature detectors: edge detectors, which respond strongly to the border between light and dark regions; feature movement contrast detectors, which respond when an edge moves; convex edge or "bug detectors," which respond when a small circular dark spot moves across a frog's field of vision; and dimming detectors, which react when overall illumination is reduced.

Are all feature detectors innate? This is a difficult question. Recent work with neural network models raises the possibility that feature detectors may be acquired through experience.

Feature construction is possible for networks that have at least three levels of units, two of which correspond to an input layer and an output layer (see Figure 5.11). The intermediate layer contains what are known as "hidden units" which in effect compete with each other to pre-

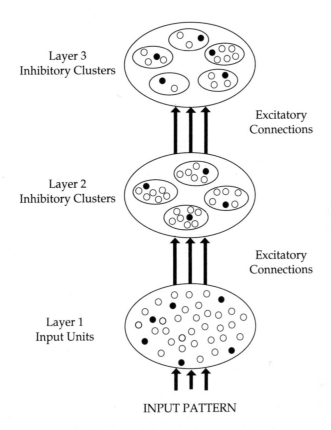

Figure 5.11   The architecture of the competitive learning mechanism. Competitive learning takes place in a context of sets of hierarchically layered units. Units may be active or inactive. Active units are represented by filled dots, inactive ones by open dots. In general, a unit in a given layer can receive inputs from all the units in the next lower layer and can project outputs to all the units in the next higher layer. Connections between layers are excitatory and connections within layers are inhibitory. Each layer consists of a set of clusters of mutually inhibitory units. The units within a cluster inhibit one another in such a way that only one unit per cluster may be active. A given cluster contains a fixed number of units, but different clusters can have different numbers of units. *Source*: Rumelhart & Zipser, 1985.

dict or interpret the inputs. As a consequence of the competition, these hidden units may become specialized so that a given unit tends to be activated only for certain types of input. That is, the hidden units begin to act as feature detectors. As an example, Rumelhart and Zipser (1985) trained a network model to discriminate horizontal from vertical lines. That is, one output was appropriate for patterns like A and B in Figure 5.12 and a different response or output was appropriate for patterns like C and D. Under these circumstances, the hidden units tended to become specialized for detecting either horizontal or vertical lines. In short, competitive learning can, in principle, lead to a set of feature detectors; features need not necessarily be built in (see also Anderson, Silverstein, Ritz, & Jones, 1977; Rumelhart, Hinton, & Williams, 1986).

Attractive as featural models are, they are incomplete as theories of object recognition. Feature models typically ignore spatial relationships among features. Featural descriptions may include spatial components, but they ignore spatial relations. Describing T as a letter with a horizontal line segment and a vertical line segment does not distinguish between a T and a +. In short, featural models face what could be termed an anagram problem. That is, if letters are features of words, then what distinguishes *atom* from *moat* from *otma* from *mtao*?

Featural models also seem to presuppose that objects have already been identified and isolated in complex scenes, otherwise the perceptual

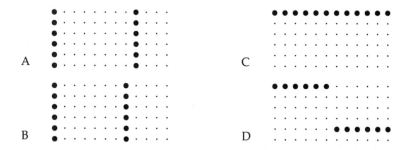

Figure 5.12   Stimulus patterns for the vertical/horizontal discrimination experiments with a correlated "teaching" input on the left-hand side. Without the teaching unit, the activation of a particular input node would give no information about whether a pattern is horizontal or vertical. With the teaching unit, some of the individual nodes do indicate the status of a pattern, for example, each of the five nodes under the upper left corner (see A) are only activated for vertical patterns. After learning, the teaching unit is taken away and the network still responds correctly. *Source:* Rumelhart & Zipser, 1985.

system would get lost trying to compose features from different objects into a single, coherent object. Even spatial segregation would not help very much—a cup of coffee with a spoon in it is not a single object. But if objects are already isolated and identified before a featural analysis is applied, how is this isolation accomplished? Also, one wonders if there is much work left for features to do. So it seems that, at best, featural models can only address part of the problem of object recognition or that feature detectors are only one aspect of an object recognition system.

Spatial Frequency Analysis

Another class of models proposes that object recognition is based on analyzing patterns of changes in intensity or contrast associated with an object. The idea is that the visual system performs a **spatial frequency analysis**. This approach is not as intuitive as the featural approach, and the details can get quite technical. Nonetheless, we will try to convey the general flavor. In spatial frequency analysis, the two-dimensional intensity array is analyzed into a set of components, each of which is specific to changes in intensity along a single orientation at a particular grid size or spatial frequency. Each spatial frequency can be thought of as a grid of parallel black and white stripes of a particular width oriented in a particular direction (see Figure 5.13), with the black and white stripes fading gradually into one another (in mathematical terms spatial frequency corresponds to performing a Fourier analysis). How well the array matches the grid yields an indication of the degree of contrast in the image corresponding to each step size and each orientation. The entire set of these numbers is the *amplitude spectrum* and the amplitude spectrum is roughly the same regardless of where in the visual field an object is located. Furthermore, this analysis segregates information about gross overall shape from small detail. In particular, gross shape is specified by low spatial frequency components. If the object recognition system selectively weighted low spatial frequencies, then a lot of minor variations and differences in patterns would not get in the way of successful recognition.

One reason why spatial frequency analysis is attractive is that it appears that the visual system computes something close to spatial frequency (Blakemore & Campbell, 1969). Pinker (1984a) notes that many researchers in psychophysics and visual physiology assume that spatial frequency analysis is the most promising theory of shape recognition.

But spatial frequency analysis also has its limitations. Most salient among them is that the amplitude spectrum of an object is (approximately) independent of its position only for isolated objects. When an object is in a

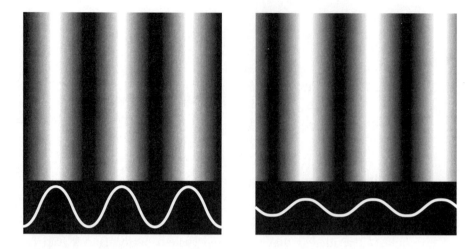

Figure 5.13   Sinusoidal gratings. (a) A high-contrast grating produced on a computer graphics system. A plot of the intensity variation is shown below the grating. (b) A lower-contrast grating with the same spatial frequency as (a). The intensity plot shows that intensity is varying at the same rate but within a smaller range.

scene, the spatial frequency components will be highly variable with position and there is no isolable component of the amplitude spectrum that corresponds to a single object. Furthermore, even for single objects there is nothing in the amplitude spectrum that corresponds to natural parts of objects. Finally, changes in orientation or rotation in three-dimensional space change the spatial frequency analysis in complex ways that make it difficult to match stored amplitude spectra to the presented object. Again, the visual system may use spatial frequency information but more must be involved.

Structural Theories

The third class of theory we shall consider assumes that shapes are represented as **structural descriptions**. The descriptions capture parts and their spatial relationships to each other (Sutherland, 1968; Palmer, 1975). Structural theories build upon and have many advantages associated with feature detection theories, but they imply that an object is more than a list of its parts.

Experiments by Steve Reed (1974) provide a nice demonstration of the need for structural analysis. Participants were shown patterns and then had to decide whether or not a second pattern was a part (subset) of the first one. Figure 5.14 shows some of the patterns used along with pos-

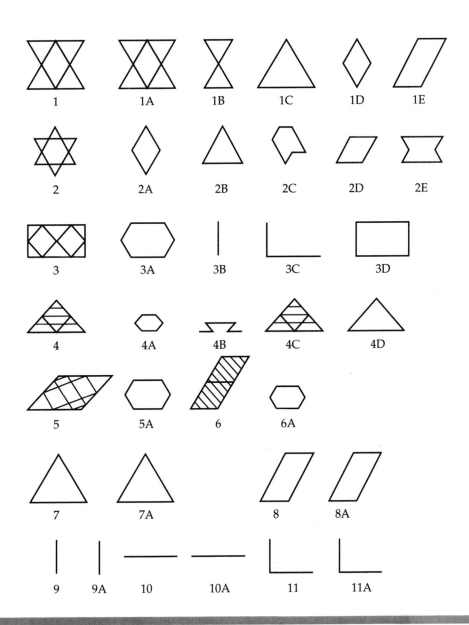

Figure 5.14   **Positive Pairs of Patterns Used by Reed (1974).**
A pattern is positive if it is a part or a subset of the pattern it is paired with. For
example, 1A, 1B, 1C, 1D, and 1E are each subsets of pattern 1.

sible parts. Note that some of the subsets involve natural parts (e.g., 3D) whereas others do not (3A). Reed (1974) found that people were much faster at identifying subsets that would correspond with a structural description than subsets that would not. For example, it took an average of 1.47 seconds to verify that 3D was a subset of 3 compared with 2.08 seconds for 3A. In addition, people made more than twice as many errors on 3A as on 3D.

As Pinker (1984a) notes, one of the major advantages of structural descriptions is that they can factor apart the information in a scene without necessarily losing information about the scene. Spatial information is not only a source of data for allowing inferences based on incomplete information but it also is important for interacting with objects. By representing the different parts of objects as separable elements in the description, structural models break up the recognition process into simpler subprocesses which may allow us to identify objects in a scene based on partial information.

An example of an approach that combines features with structure is Biederman's (1987) recognition by components theory. Biederman suggests that objects can be described in terms of a small set of parts called **geons**. Geons consist of simple three-dimensional shapes such as cylinders, cones, blocks, and wedges (see Figure 5.15 for examples). Complex objects are described in terms of constituent geons along with a description of the spatial relations between them.

If geons are to be the building blocks of objects, there must be a reliable procedure for identifying part boundaries. Biederman uses certain

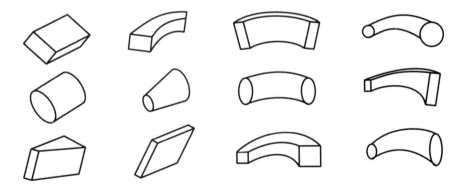

Figure 5.15   **Possible Set of Geons for Natural Objects.**
Cylinders, cones, blocks, and wedges may all be features of complex objects.
Source: Biederman, 1987.

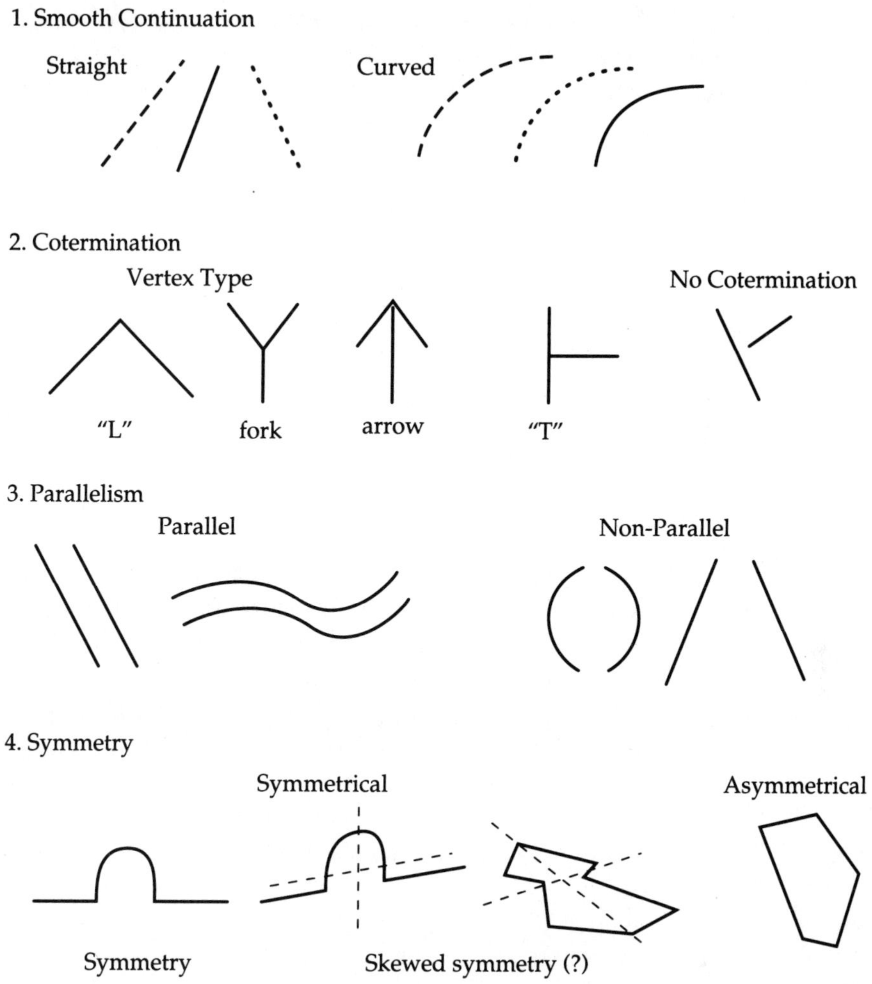

1. Smooth Continuation

Straight   Curved

2. Cotermination

Vertex Type   No Cotermination

"L"   fork   arrow   "T"

3. Parallelism

Parallel   Non-Parallel

4. Symmetry

Symmetrical   Asymmetrical

Symmetry   Skewed symmetry (?)

Figure 5.16   **Contrasts in Four Viewpoint-Invariant Relations.**
In the case of parallelism and symmetry, biases toward parallel and symmetrical
percepts when images are not exactly parallel or symmetrical are evidenced.
Source: Biederman, 1990.

"nonaccidental" relationships between contours in the image to determine
part decomposition. Smooth continuation, cotermination, parallelism, and
types of symmetry are examples of nonaccidental (informative) properties
(see Figure 5.16).

It is too early to provide a critical evaluation of Biederman's recognition by components theory or structural theories in general. Ullman

(1989) notes three potential limitations with structural approaches. One is that a decomposition of an object into geons may not be refined enough to distinguish between objects that have more or less the same parts (e.g., dog vs. wolf or cat). A second potential problem is that many objects (e.g., a loaf of bread) may be difficult to decompose into parts that will both characterize the object and be applicable to a variety of other objects. One could, of course, use more numerous, smaller units (Biederman suggests that there are about 36 geons) but the cost of adding more units is that the structural descriptions will become much more complex (there will be more geons in objects and more relations between geons to be coded). The final problem involves matching structural descriptions in the recognition stage. Remember, we not only have to represent objects but also to match these descriptions with previously stored memory representations. Matching structural descriptions leads to computational complexity problems; figuring out just which parts in the presented object should be compared with which parts in the stored representation involves a very large number of possibilities (Grimson & Lozano-Perez, 1984).

It is difficult to evaluate the above concerns. One obvious test is to see whether artificial intelligence systems for vision using structural descriptions prove to be successful. Because we are interested in human perception, a second basis for evaluation is how well a given theory accounts for results from experiments on perception. Here we face a different problem. As models become more complex it is harder to see just why they succeed or fail. For example, the recognition by components theory could be roughly correct but may fail to account for some observations because the objects have not been described in terms of the right set of geons. In this case, we need a different analysis of geons, not a new theory.

We turn now to a fourth approach to object recognition, template matching. Template matching has been a frequent target for criticism but it may prove more promising than is commonly assumed.

Template Matching and Alignment

The notion of **template matching** takes the two-dimensional image array quite seriously. That is, images or templates of patterns are stored in memory and shapes are classified by finding the best matching template. Optical scanners that banks use to read account numbers from checks employ template matching. Figure 5.17 gives a simple example of matching a test instance against either the J template or the T template. The instance matches the J template in 11 cells and mismatches in 2 cells; it also matches the T template in 8 cells and mismatches in 10 cells. Therefore, the instance more closely matches the J template and would be classified as a J.

Test Instance

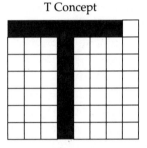
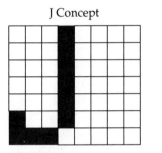

J Concept   T Concept

Figure 5.17   **Template Matching.**
If decisions are based on number of matching cells, then the test instance would be classified as a J. *Source*: Smith & Medin, 1981.

Of course the template matching procedure is too simple to be useful outside very special circumstances. An image may fall on different parts of the retina. If the test instance fell two columns to the right in the grid, it would match only 2 cells of the J template. Or the test instance might be slightly rotated or be a different size (larger or smaller) from the stored templates. To remain viable, a template theory might assume that some preprocessing "cleans up" the image and adjusts for differences in size and orientation. An alternative possibility is that the system does not have a single template for each concept but rather stores multiple templates (of different sizes and orientations) for each concept.

Even this liberalized view of templates faces serious difficulties. Consider what happens when we move from the two-dimensional world of letters and numbers to the three-dimensional perception of objects. In a three-dimensional world, changes in orientation or rotation have a major effect on apparent shape. An elongated pencil may turn into a tiny circle when it is turned on end and viewed from the top. Furthermore, objects appear in scenes with other objects, objects that can cast shadows or interfere with a viewer's line of sight to some object of interest.

Recently Ullman (1989) has tried to address many of these criticisms. Object recognition is assumed to consist of two stages, using a set of transformations to align the object presented with object templates or models stored in memory and then searching through these models to find the "best match" (most similar model) to the object. (See Ullman, 1989 for a detailed description of this approach.) Ullman has proved formally that one needs only partial information about an object (specifically, the location of three independent points) to determine whether or not two views (e.g., one presented and one stored in memory) belong to the same object. Therefore, one does not necessarily need to have a full, unrestricted view of an object for alignment to be successful.

One virtue of template models is that they implicitly include information about part relations and structure. This implicit information does not, however, lead to computational complexity problems as alignment need only involve three independent points.

Again, it's difficult to evaluate template models. There is some evidence that object recognition involves aligning viewed objects with stored models. For example, recognition latencies depend on the angle separating the orientation of the viewed object and the orientation of a previously viewed standard (see, e.g., Jolicoeur, 1985). So far these studies have looked at alignment in the two-dimensional image plane; stronger tests of the alignment idea might be provided by using three-dimensional stimuli.

Summary

Currently researchers are looking for models of object recognition that will be able to perform accurately across some nontrivial range of conditions. It is obviously not the case that we have a number of successful models and that we are trying to decide which model gives the best account of human object perception. Finally, bear in mind that these approaches are not mutually exclusive. Biederman's recognition by components theory employs features to construct geons and geons can be viewed as higher level features. Similarly, Ullman's alignment approach relies on features in segmenting objects and picking points to align. In brief, object recognition is an exceedingly difficult problem and it is nothing short of amazing that we do it effortlessly.

All of the proposed systems for object recognition are explicitly hierarchical in character. So far, however, we have paid little attention to the question of how different sources and levels of information are combined. We turn now to a couple of specific computational models that are concerned with integrating different levels of information in recognition. As we shall see, these two models are quite different in character.

Levels and the Integration of Information in Perception

Context Effects

So far we have described perception as if it proceeded in a single direction from the retinal array to complex percepts. We shall see, however, that the perception of some unit of information depends not only on lower level input but also on the surrounding context. In addition to so-called "bottom-up" processes there are "top-down" influences on perception. The perceptual system integrates a variety of sources of information in developing an interpretation.

Interactive Activation

In Chapter 2 we mentioned that one of the strengths of connectionist models is that they readily integrate multiple sources of information (by parallel constraint satisfaction). We will describe one such model proposed by Jay McClelland and David Rumelhart (McClelland & Rumelhart, 1981; Rumelhart & McClelland, 1982) in some detail.

The McClelland and Rumelhart **interactive activation** model operates at three levels, as indicated in Figure 5.18. The visual input is analyzed by feature detectors, which pass on information to the letter level, which in turn is linked to the word level. There are connections both within and across levels. For example, a horizontal line segment feature is consistent with the letter T but inconsistent with the letter N; therefore, there is an excitatory connection between the horizontal segment and the letter T and an inhibitory link between the horizontal segment and the letter N. Figure 5.19 shows a more detailed view of possible connections. Lines ending in arrows are excitatory or positive and lines ending in circles are inhibitory. Within the letter and word level connections are inhibitory, because the various letters or words represent alternative (mutually exclusive) interpretations. Across levels, connections can be both excitatory and inhibitory.

The general idea is that a unit at one level excites those units at another level with which it is consistent and inhibits those units with which it is inconsistent. For example, the word TIME inhibits all other words, excites T in the initial position, and inhibits letters other than T in the first position. The patterns of excitation and inhibition represent a set of constraints to be satisfied or sources of information to be integrated. This seems fairly chaotic but the patterns of activation stabilize to create a steady state in a fairly short time. This steady state corresponds to the interpretation made of the input.

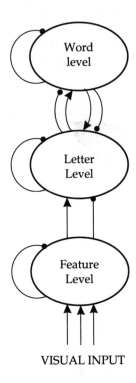

VISUAL INPUT

Figure 5.18   **The Simplified Processing System.**
Three hierarchically organized levels associated with letter and word perception.
The lines with arrows indicate excitatory connections and lines ending in a circle
indicate inhibitory connections. *Source*: McClelland & Rumelhart, 1981.

To illustrate how the interactive activation model works, consider
the stimulus of the printed group of four letters, WOR(?). Suppose that
some of the featural information is occluded and that the fourth letter is
consistent with both the letter R and the letter K. By providing specific
quantitative values (parameters) for the strengths of excitation and inhibition one can generate specific activation values, as shown in Figure 5.20.
At the word level, consider what happens to the activation of the candidates WORK, WORD, WEAK, and WEAR. Note that WORK is the only
word consistent with all the available information. The interpretation
WORD is consistent with most of the information and its activation initially
rises because of the excitatory input from the W, O, and R letter units.
Eventually, however, the activation of WORD falls below its resting level
mainly as a result of its competition with WORK. The activation of WORK
steadily increases. WEAR and WEAK are never very strongly activated be-

cause they receive little activation from the letter level. Note that WEAK eventually is slightly more active than WEAR. This is because WORK becomes highly activated and feeds back to the letter level to reinforce K rather than R in the final position.

At the letter level the inhibition from the featural level prevents the letter D from being activated. Note that although both K and R are consistent with the features available in the fourth position K quickly becomes more activated. This is because of positive feedback from WORK at the word level. Since WORR is not a word, it does not receive positive feedback from the word level. Although we have oversimplified the model, you nonetheless can get a fair idea of how interactive activation works to integrate information.

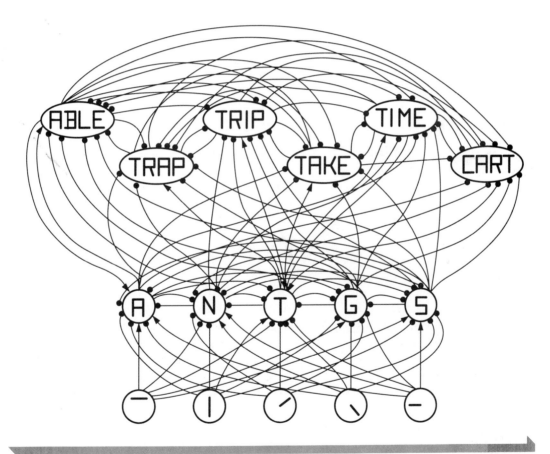

Figure 5.19   A few of the neighbors of the node for the letter *T* in the first position in a word and their interconnections. *Source*: McClelland & Rumelhart, 1981.

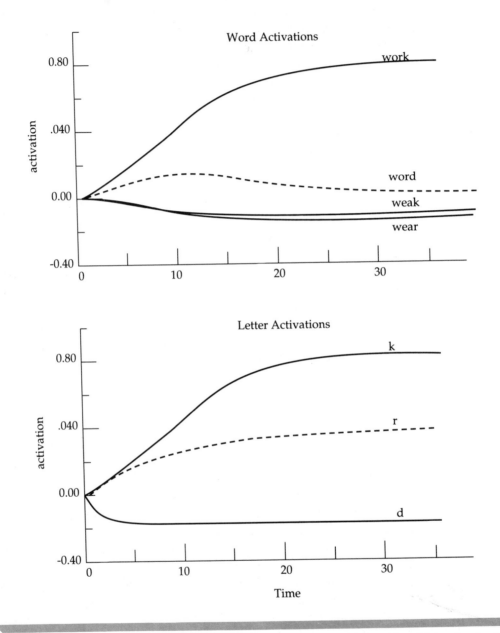

Figure 5.20   The time course of activations of selected nodes at the word and letter levels after extraction of the features. Time is based on number of cycles of activation. See text discussion. *Source*: McClelland & Rumelhart, 1981.

The interactive activation model successfully predicts a variety of phenomena concerning context effects on letter and word perception. One such observation is known as the word superiority effect (Reicher, 1969). A sample procedure involves brief exposure to a string of letters followed by a probe of one position. A participant must say which of two letters appeared in that position. For example, the stimulus might be ZORK and the probe in the fourth position might ask whether D or K was presented. Or the stimulus might be WORK with exactly the same probe. Reicher found that letter identification was more accurate in the context of letters comprising a word than for nonword sequences, even though each of the two choices (in this example, D and K) would produce a word. The interactive activation model is consistent with this result because without the word-level feedback processing might converge on some letter outside the choice set (e.g., R). In that event the participant would have to guess (between D and K). These and other observations provide good support for the ideas embodied in the interactive activation.

Connectionist models employing interactive activation have been extended to speech perception (McClelland & Elman's 1986 TRACE model) as well as naming and word recognition (Seidenberg & McClelland, 1989). The original interactive activation model directly built letters and words into the network, but by using hidden units it is possible for higher level features or units to be learned from experience (see, e.g., Seidenberg & McClelland, 1989).

Fuzzy Logical Model of Perception

Although connectionist models are a natural way of integrating information, they are not the only way. Greg Oden and Dominic Massaro have developed and tested a fuzzy logical model of perception (FLMP) (Oden & Massaro, 1978), which assumes that processing within a level is *not* directly influenced by processing at other levels. Integration of information across levels occurs at a later stage of processing.

FLMP assumes that there are three distinct phases to perception: feature evaluation, feature integration, and decision. In the case of speech perception, input provides (continuous) feature values that are matched against stored standards or prototypes for speech units (e.g., the syllable / ba/). For each feature and each prototype, the featural evaluation provides information about the degree to which the feature in the speech signal matches the featural value of the prototype. In FLMP, degree of match is represented as a "fuzzy truth value" that lies between zero and one. The fuzzy truth value roughly corresponds to the probability that one is certain that some feature was present.

Featural integration combines fuzzy truth values to determine the overall goodness of match to the target of interest. If the goal is to perceive a syllable, the fuzzy truth values of the constituent features of the syllable are combined. The combination rule involves multiplying fuzzy truth values together, which has the effect that the least ambiguous features have the greatest impact on the overall goodness of match.

During the decision stage the correct interpretation is likely to be selected to the extent that the goodness of match to it is high relative to alternative interpretations or prototypes. An important property of FLMP is that the effect of one cue is greatest when other cues are most ambiguous. In short, the more informative cues have greater impact on judgment. It is as if each piece of information gets to vote but the most confident sources of information have the most votes.

Like the interactive model for speech perception, TRACE (McClelland & Elman, 1986), FLMP is consistent with a large variety of observations concerning the integration of speech cues (see Massaro, 1987 for a review). The two models do, however, treat context effects or top-down effects in distinctively different ways. For FLMP the integration stage is independent of the evaluation stage. Therefore, FLMP predicts no systematic effects of top-down context on sensitivity at the lower level. Instead, top-down influences are completely captured at the integration stage where they are an independent source of information. The TRACE model, by contrast, involves interactive activation and top-down feedback affects the activation of lower level information. That is, the evaluation and integration processes occur simultaneously such that top-down influences do affect lower level sensitivity. Massaro (1989) systematically tested this difference between the two models and found evidence that favored FLMP over the TRACE model. Although Massaro's data are suggestive, the case can hardly be considered closed. More definitive conclusions await further experimental tests and further explorations of interactive activation models.

Although TRACE and FLMP are distinctly different models, they agree on several key issues. For example, both models view pattern recognition as involving the integration of multiple sources of information with top-down context exerting an important influence on perception. Both models also agree that perception is an active, dynamic process that uses whatever information it can get its processors on and uses it effectively (Massaro & Friedman, 1990).

Summary

The perceptual system must be able to provide a description of the relevant structure of information in the world. To do so is a daunting challenge because any perceptual input is consistent with an unlimited number of alternative interpretations. It should not be surprising, then, that the perceptual system is likely to be comprised of a variety of parallel as well as hierarchically organized subsystems for figuring out what is out there, where it is, and what it is doing. The constraints framework emphasizes the role of prior assumptions or expectations about the world in providing structure to the perceptual input. These assumptions give rise to certain illusions and misperceptions, but they also allow us to move about in and respond to our environment in a singularly impressive manner. Yogi Berra was right in saying we can see a lot by looking—just how we do so remains a challenging puzzle.

Key Terms

features

figure-ground relations

geons

good continuation

interactive activation

invariants

motion parallax

proximity principle

retinal disparity

rigidity constraint

size constancy

smoothness constraint

spatial frequency analysis

stereogram

stereopsis

structural descriptions

template matching

texture gradients

Recommended Readings

The area of perception has not been uncontroversial. Gibson's (1979) ecological approach to perception includes an attack on the idea of computations and internal representations in favor of "direct perception." Fodor and Pylyshyn (1981) offer a thoughtful critique of direct perception. Although the current consensus is that perception requires internal representations and processing mechanisms, the Gibsonian approach remains distinctive.

A good general introduction to computational vision and its goals is provided by Poggio (1984); Hildreth and Ullman (1990) offer a comprehensive overview. Two excellent reviews of theories of object recognition are those of Pinker (1984) and Ullman (1989).

Many of the most intriguing questions about perception concern its development. Gibson's (1987) article and the papers in the same journal issue that follow her introduction convey the flavor of excitement in this area. Elizabeth Spelke (1990) has also recently summarized her work on object perception.

The debate continues on the processes underlying context effects in perception. Massaro's (1989) critique of the McClelland and Elman (1986) TRACE model has not gone unanswered (McClelland, 1991) and McClelland's reply has led to a further response (Massaro & Cohen, in press). The communiques are instructive and offer distinct points of view.

Finally, Michotte's (1963) book on the perception of causality makes for wonderful reading. The experiments are ingenious and one can only marvel at Michotte's ability to carry out this program of research without the services of a computer (the bulk of the work was carried out in the early 1940s and Michotte's book was translated into English much later).

MEMORY

SPATIAL KNOWLEDGE, IMAGERY, AND VISUAL MEMORY

Chapter Outline

The general rule determining the ideas of vision that are formed whenever an impression is made on the eye, with or without the aid of optical instruments, is that such objects are always imagined as being present in the field of vision as would have to be there in order to produce the same impression on the nervous mechanism, the eyes being used under ordinary normal conditions.

Herman von Helmholtz, *Treatise on Physiological Objects*

Introduction

If we awaken in the middle of the night in our darkened bedroom, we can usually navigate around furniture or other obstacles that are in their usual places. Presumably, this ability is possible because we have knowledge about the spatial layout of the room that has been learned through much experience. If we were in a hotel room, such navigation would be more fraught with danger, or at least the possibility of stubbed toes. Knowledge of space is crucial not only for getting around dark bedrooms, but for any sort of navigation in the world.

In the case of darkened bedrooms, clearly we are relying on previously stored knowledge to get around. But what is the form of this stored knowledge about space and how did we come by it? In our discussion of perception, we noted that organisms must develop representations of the three-dimensional world from information in the form of two-dimensional projections on the retina. That is, organisms do not perceive the world directly but rather must figure out the connection between events associated with their perceptual system and events in the world. Informally, we could say that the perceptual system delivers a "mental model" of the world.

Our mental representations of our environment are typically so good that we are not even aware that they are representations. As the quote from von Helmholtz suggests, under "normal" conditions our representations mirror the world quite closely. But try a simple experiment (that you very likely performed in childhood) that creates "abnormal" conditions. Press on the corner of your eyeball with your eyes open. The scene in front of you seems to move (this is easiest to do with one eye closed) even though you "know" that it did not. But if you just move your eyes back and forth normally, the scene does not shift. The brain is able to take active movement into account in developing a representation but has no mechanism for dealing with the passive movement associated with pressure on the eyeball.

The point of the above example is that we *represent* our environment, and when we successfully make our way around the bedroom at night we are relying on previously stored representations of the layout of the room. A fundamental question concerns the form of mental representations of the environment and objects in it. A good deal of the research associated with this question has focused on imagery or mental images. Are images "pictures in the head" and, if so, what properties do they have? What is the relation between imagery and perception? Finally, are images fundamentally different from the mental representations of abstract propositions expressed through language?

In this chapter we describe work on imagery, visual memory, and spatial knowledge from the perspective of asking questions about mental representations. We first take a closer look at the notion of a mental representation and then provide a sampling of ongoing research on spatial knowledge, imagery, and visual memory.

Our evolutionary history suggests that we had to learn how to successfully move about in the world long before we developed any language skills. Therefore, it seems likely that understanding how we develop and use knowledge about our environment provides basic clues into the nature of human intelligence. Although the information processing tradition has found computers to be a useful metaphor for understanding intelligence, that metaphor may pay insufficient attention to the close link between organisms and their environment. Computers don't have to worry about the environment—the programmer puts information directly into the machine. Researchers in artificial intelligence are only beginning to worry about interfacing with an environment as they attempt to build robots capable of moving about in the world. As we shall see, useful representations are a crucial prerequisite for intelligent action.

Representations

Relations between Representations and Referents

We have already suggested that a stable internal model of the three-dimensional environment provides more effective support for movement and action than a two-dimensional retinal pattern. But there still is the question of what form this internal model must take. Some films on the nervous system, for example, seem to suggest that the internal representation is essentially a likeness of the external referent. In many cases the films also include a tiny person whose function is to perceive the internal representation! Of course, the films do not indicate how the perceptual system of the tiny person works.

Roger Shepard (1981, p. 290) has argued that a **representation** need not be literally similar to its referent any more than a lock must resemble a key. In his words,

> Just as the essential thing about a lock and its key is the unique functional relation between them whereby the lock is normally (i.e., from the outside) operated only by its corresponding key, the essential thing about a perceptual representation and its object is the unique functional relation between them whereby the percept is normally (except while dreaming or hallucinating) elicited only by its corresponding object.

To use another example, we often use a map to navigate between one part of the country and another. The fact that major highways are colored red while minor roads are black or gray tells us nothing about the color of the actual roads. Major highways with many lanes are drawn thicker on maps than two-lane highways. Representing more lanes with thicker lines is a natural convention, but we recognize that it is simply a convention. One could use the opposite coding scheme and people could adjust accordingly. Whatever the coding scheme, certain crucial information such as spatial relationships and type of roads must be preserved. But the map is not literally a likeness of the country. The key is that the functionally relevant information is preserved.

Analog Representations

To say that representations of referents must preserve relevant information does little to restrict the form that representations must take. Researchers such as Roger Shepard, Stephen Kosslyn, and Ronald Finke have argued that mental representations of objects and spatial relationships are *analog* in character. It is difficult to give a precise definition of an **analog representation**. Roughly speaking, a representation is an analog of a referent when it mimics or simulates the structure of the referent in a more or less direct manner. Immediately this definition runs into difficulty because we have not said what we mean by structure or a direct manner. In the case of space one can propose that two relevant structural properties are that space is continuous and that spatial relationships or configural properties are salient (e.g., that the nose is above the mouth on a face).

But what do we mean by "more or less direct manner"? Consider the simple map shown in Figure 6.1 which we will treat as the representation of a set of cities, A, B, C, D, E, and F. In this case true distance between cities is represented by distance on the map with some appropriate scale (e.g., 1 inch on the map may correspond to 10 miles). Similarly, spatial relationship between the cities is represented by spatial relationships on the map. City F is directly north of city E and on the map F is directly above E, and so on.

This same information could be represented as a series of languagelike propositions. **Propositional representation** approaches assume that representations are abstract and not tied to any particular sensory modality. Table 6.1 shows two different ways of using propositions to represent the information in Figure 6.1. The representation form on the left encodes city locations relative to some reference point, in this case city F (any reference point would do). This representation makes some information easy to determine. For example, one can directly look up (retrieve) the fact that A is 30 miles south and 10 miles west of F. Other information is less easy to come by. For example, what are the relative positions of C and D? To answer this question one would need to retrieve the facts that D is 10 miles south and 10 miles west of F and that C is 30 miles south and 10 miles

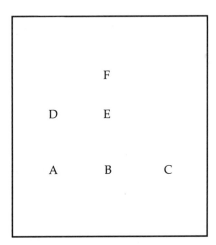

Figure 6.1   A Simple Map (Analog Representation) of the Relative Location of Six Cities.

Table 6.1   A set of propositions representing some of the same information represented in Figure 3.1.

F as a Reference Point	Route Information
E is 10 miles south of F	(A, B) 10 miles east
B is 30 miles south of F	(B, A) 10 miles west
	(A, C) 20 miles east
D is 10 miles south and 10 miles west of F	(C, A) 20 miles west
	(A, D) 20 miles north
A is 30 miles south and 10 miles west of F	(D, A) 20 miles south
	(A, E) 10 miles east, 20 miles north
	(E, A) 10 miles west, 20 miles south
C is 30 miles south and 10 miles east of F	(A, F) 10 miles east, 30 miles north
	(F, A) 10 miles west, 30 miles south
	(B, C) 10 miles east
	(C, B) 10 miles west
	(B, D) 10 miles west, 30 miles north
	(D, B) 10 miles east, 30 miles south
	(B, E) 20 miles north
	(E, B) 20 miles south
	(B, F) 30 miles north
	(F, B) 30 miles south
	(C, D) 20 miles west, 20 miles north
	(D, C) 20 miles east, 20 miles south
	(C, E) 10 miles west, 20 miles north
	(E, C) 10 miles east, 20 miles south
	(C, F) 10 miles east, 30 miles north
	(F, C) 10 miles west, 30 miles south
	(D, E) 10 miles west
	(E, D) 10 miles east
	(D, F) 10 miles north, 10 miles east
	(F, D) 10 miles south, 10 miles west
	(E, F) 10 miles north
	(F, E) 10 miles south

east of F and then combine these facts with some rules (e.g., if D is X miles south of F and C is Y miles south of F, then C is X minus Y miles south of D) to come up with the answer.

The propositional representation on the right side of Table 6.1 allows one to directly retrieve information about how to get from C to D (or from D to C). The cost is that many propositions have to be encoded. For 6 cities, we require 30 propositions; for 7 cities, 42 propositions; and for only 40 cities, 1,560 propositions. And even with all these propositions we have not exhausted all the information about spatial relationships. For example, the route information does not tell us that the most direct route from A to C requires that we pass through B. Again, we could develop a procedure for deriving this information.

The general point is that particular types of representations allow us to access some types of information easily and other types of information with greater difficulty. Analog representations are good for configural (spatial relationship) information and they allow for easy integration of new information. Adding a new city to the representation is simple and does not require that a large set of new propositions be encoded (as does a route representation).

Our story about analog representations is incomplete because we have not specified processes that operate on these representations to derive information. A representation does not tell us anything until it is interpreted by a processing system. As we shall see shortly, other researchers (e.g., Kosslyn & Shwartz, 1977) have developed computational models using analog representations and have shown that they are viable theories of visuo-spatial cognition.

The idea that there may be both analog and propositional representations has been controversial (Anderson, 1978; Minsky, 1975; Palmer, 1978; Pylyshyn, 1973, 1978, 1979, 1981; Finke, 1985; Kosslyn & Pomerantz, 1977; Shepard, 1981; Shepard & Podgorny, 1978) with scientists such as Zenon Pylyshyn arguing that the mind employs only propositional representations. We will not presume to resolve this debate but to be honest we must admit to a bias favoring both types of representation. The motivation for our view is perhaps best summarized by a quote from Shepard (1981, p. 288):

> So when Pylyshyn (1978) and Minsky (1975) ask why we should suppose that a human or other higher organism uses an analog system when a propositional system is so much less constraining—is, in fact, capable of any specifiable sort of computation whatever—I answer, "that's why!" By definition, a completely unconstrained system cannot be more competent at any one kind of thing than any other. As a result, it cannot excel at any one. Being a "jack of all trades" it necessarily is a master of none. In particular, such a general purpose system will not be suited to the rapid prediction of and preparation for external developments in a three-dimensional, Euclidean world than a Turing machine will provide for the safe and efficient control of air traffic. The more nearly the constraints prevailing in the world have been "hard-wired" into the system, the greater will be the effectiveness of the system in that particular world.

The above quote is not so much an argument for analog representations as it is for constraints. That is, there may be a constrained form of propositional representation that allows for easy and natural access to computation of visuo-spatial information. Although such a representation system would not be an image or even visual in character, it would satisfy our broad (perhaps too broad) definition of an analog representation.

We have belabored the subject of representation because it is crucial to understanding the basis of much of the ongoing research on imagery and spatial knowledge. The issue of representation sounds a bit esoteric but it is central to the problem of how organisms interface with or relate to their environment. We turn now to related empirical work, beginning with spatial knowledge.

Spatial Knowledge

Maps and Navigation

Our mental representations include information about spatial relationships and about how to navigate in our environment. Let us begin with two simple examples from Thorndyke and Hayes-Roth (1982): "Point to the Statue of Liberty from where you are sitting. Now point to the local airport from where you are sitting." These two cases are accomplished by most people in very different ways. For the first case, we remember that the Statue of Liberty is in New York, where New York is relative to our town, and what direction we are facing. For the local airport case, we may simply remember how we get there and point in that direction. These examples illustrate two of the main types of knowledge we have about space: **survey knowledge**, a bird's-eye view often learned from maps, and **route knowledge**, gained from navigating through the environment. Researchers are interested in characterizing these types of knowledge and in understanding when and how they might be learned. What sorts of experiences lead to survey as opposed to route knowledge? We can begin by noting that the different types of knowledge are useful for different spatial tasks.

Survey knowledge is very useful for making judgments involving global spatial relations, such as distance judgments between two points. Survey knowledge allows fast scanning and measuring. It can often be acquired quite easily. However, if knowledge is acquired from maps, some judgments, such as those involving orientation, may be difficult. For example, Thorndyke and Hayes-Roth (1982) tested people on their spatial knowledge of the floor of a large, irregularly shaped office building. Some subjects had been working in the building for up to two years, while others had never been in the building and were just shown a floor plan. Simplifying the results, subjects just shown the floor plan were able to perform many tasks quite well, such as estimating distances, but had great difficulty with orientation tasks, such as pointing to one location when standing in another.

Route knowledge may require more time to learn, but does allow people to perform well on tasks that are difficult if the knowledge is learned only from maps. Direct experience with the routes appears to lead to a more orientation-free representation, so that people can use their knowledge of the route very flexibly (see, e.g., Presson, DeLange, & Hazelrigg, 1989). If the environment is irregular (e.g., the streets are winding and cross at unusual angles) the knowledge acquired through navigation may distort the overall view (Tversky, 1981; Byrne, 1982). However, if the environment is regular (i.e., a city with a grid of streets, a building with a simple layout) experience in navigation is often sufficient for learning survey knowledge as well. An interesting proposal is that this greater navigational experience may lead to a different type of survey knowledge than that acquired from maps in which the full layout may be seen from a navigational perspective (Thorndyke & Hayes-Roth, 1982) or in a more integrated model-like way (Presson, DeLange, & Hazelrigg, 1989). For both theoretical and practical reasons, the way in which navigational experience affects the representation of space is of great interest and is under much current investigation.

Hierarchical Representations of Space

It is tempting to view our representations of spatial layouts being like a map. However, there is evidence that our representations of space are influenced by nonspatial knowledge. Answer the following question: Is Seattle north or south of Montreal? Most people believe Seattle is south of Montreal, although in fact it is more north. In this case, most of us do not know the latitudes of both cities or their relative latitudes, but we do know that Canada is generally north of the United States, that Seattle is in the United States, and that Montreal is in Canada. We then make the reasonable inference that Montreal is north of Seattle. This type of plausible reasoning will usually lead to the right answer, but not always, especially given irregular boundary lines. (Try your friends on "Which is more east: Reno or Los Angeles?" Again, Nevada is east of California, but L.A. is east of Reno.) These errors suggest that people use hierarchically organized information (Reno is in Nevada, Nevada is east of California) to answer questions about spatial relationships.

Stevens and Coupe (1978) provide further experimental evidence

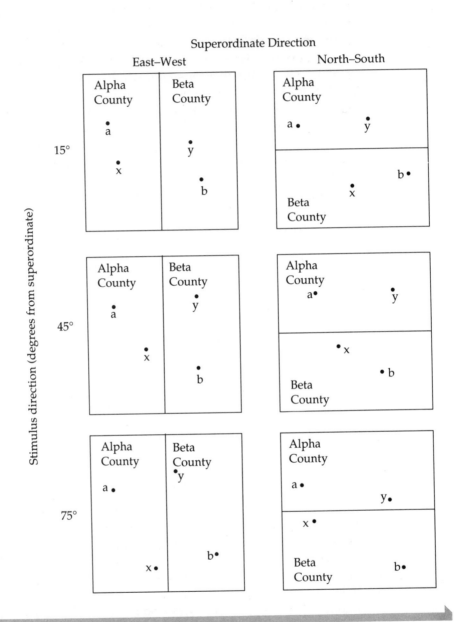

Figure 6.2   **Prototypical Stimuli from Experiment by Stevens and Coupe (1978).**
After a short study period, the map was taken away and participants were asked
to indicate the relative direction between pairs of cities, including the x-y pair.
Source: Stevens, A., & Coupe, P., 1978.

of the use of superordinates (Nevada is superordinate to Reno) in making spatial judgments by showing systematic distortions with this type of material. In addition they found that even after learning from simple new maps such distortions occur. For example, in one study subjects learned one of the maps shown in Figure 6.2, then had to judge, from memory, the relative positions of x and y. Performance was much better when superordinate information was congruent with the question. For example, subjects were more accurate at saying that x was west of y when the superordinate was east-west (left side of Figure 6.2) and more accurate at saying that x was south of y when the superordinate was north-south (right side of Figure 6.2). Thus, it appears that the superordinate units are being used to make spatial judgments.

A number of other studies show that such nonspatial influences do not depend on having some unambiguous hierarchical structure. For example, Hirtle and Jonides (1985) conducted some studies on residents of Ann Arbor, Michigan involving various locations in Ann Arbor. They found that each of the residents had a hierarchical representation that was used for making spatial judgments, though the particular hierarchy differed from person to person. McNamara (1986), using a layout of objects in a simple rectangular space, found that people tend to organize such a layout and that the organization is evidenced in spatial judgments about the layout. (For further reading, a very interesting paper by Tversky, 1981, provides some demonstrations of heuristics that people employ in remembering maps that lead to other types of systematic distortions.)

Thus, evidence suggests that a simple spatial map view of spatial knowledge is not correct. Rather, learners organize the spatial information to include nonspatial knowledge as well.

The Brain and Spatial Cognition

Stephen Kosslyn (1987) has suggested that the human brain has at least two distinct kinds of representations for spatial relations. One type is categorical in nature and determines relations such as "inside of" or "above." The second form of representation specifies distances in a continuous or analog form. In support of Kosslyn's theory, Hellige and Michimata (1989) report evidence that the left hemisphere of the brain is specialized for categorical information and the right for metric information concerning space (see Kosslyn, 1987, for other arguments and evidence on this point).

The importance of spatial cognition to our normal lives is underlined by studies of people who have suffered brain injury and have impaired spatial cognition. A particularly striking phenomenon is **spatial ne-**

glect. Patients appear behaviorally unaware of objects or events on the neglected side—as if part of their world effectively ceased to exist (see, e.g., Chedru, 1976). In some patients unilateral neglect includes or may be confined to their own limbs and body surface (Bisiach, Perani, Vallar, & Berti, 1986). For example, when such patients put on a shirt they may not put their arm through the shirt sleeve on the neglected side. Even more striking, when their attention is called to a neglected limb, such patients may deny that it is theirs and express puzzlement concerning how it got there.

Given the importance of spatial cognition to our getting along in the world, it is surprising that we know so little about it. It is encouraging that there is increasing interaction among neuroscientists and cognitive psychologists in efforts to understand the neural basis of spatial cognition (see, e.g., Kosslyn, 1987; O'Keefe & Nadel, 1978). Researchers are using findings from neuroscience to construct computational models of spatial information processing.

Imagery

In modern society, it is clear that much of our knowledge is learned through reading books and listening to verbal presentations of one type or another. But it is also true that much of what we learn comes from visual information other than words on a page. Our memory for this type of information often seems qualitatively different from verbal information. Let us take some examples. First, imagine a capital letter F and then imagine it rotated clockwise 90° (1/4 turn). Second, picture what your high school looked like, or picture the face of a good friend or the Statue of Liberty. Third, imagine yourself walking from one friend's house to another's or that you have to give someone directions for getting from the grocery store to your school. Almost all people experience visual images in performing these tasks. In this section we examine various results and ideas about how such images occur and are used.

Our knowledge about space is used in accomplishing many goals. Imagine you are in a room with objects. Shut your eyes and take two steps forward. You are able to easily compute where you now are in relation to many of the objects. As in all memory tasks, you are augmenting the incomplete information available by bringing relevant knowledge to bear. Furthermore, what knowledge you bring to bear and how it is represented will have a large impact on the complexity of processing and your ability to accomplish your goals. Images are one form of representation that appears to preserve much about the spatial relations among objects, making it easy to know the relative positions of the objects even as we move.

At the most general level we would like to know what the relation is between imagery and perception. Furthermore, research on imagery is of central importance to the debate concerning whether the human mind employs both propositional and analog representations. For this reason, research on imagery has received unusually close scrutiny as researchers have worried about potential confounding factors that might undermine parallels between imagery and perception.

By its nature, imagery is a totally internal event. As discussed in Chapter 2, psychology went through a long period in which internal events were not studied. No one doubted that people could have mental images, but there was much doubt about whether these images were psychologically relevant. That is, although the phenomenology of imagery was not in doubt, its effects were. For example, imagine a robin. Do robins have beaks? Do robins lay eggs? It may seem that you answer the first question by inspecting your image and that you answer the second by the use of some other knowledge in your memory. Nonetheless, it is possible that even the first question was answered by your use of other knowledge. You presumably know either that robins have beaks or that robins are birds and birds have beaks. If you are able to answer the question without the image, what is the evidence that you in fact used the image to answer it? Let's take a closer look at this question.

Evidence for Use of Visual Imagery

A great deal of evidence exists for the importance of images in performing various tasks. A full discussion of such evidence and its implications would be a book in itself (see, e.g., Kosslyn, 1983; Richardson, 1980). A brief discussion of several different types of evidence may provide you with an appreciation of the case for visual imagery.

Selective Interference.   The earliest pieces of evidence in the modern work on imagery relied on the idea of *selective interference*. In these studies (see, e.g., Brooks, 1968) subjects would be asked to perform some task while imaging or not. If imaging led to a decrease in task performance, the argument goes, there is evidence that imagery is using related processes. Most important, however, is the idea that the influences would be selective. That is, interference should be greater between tasks using the hypothesized same processes than on tasks thought to use different processes. The work by Segal and Fusella (1970) provides a clear example.

Before each trial, the subject was asked to either form a visual image of a common object (e.g., a tree), form an auditory image of a common sound (e.g., a typewriter sound), or form no image. Then the subject was presented with a very weak visual signal (a small blue arrow), a very weak auditory signal (a chord from a harmonica), or no signal. The subject's task was to say whether there had been a visual signal, an auditory signal, or no signal. The results were quite clear. First, imaging led to worse detection performance than not imaging. Second, and most important, the two types of imagery selectively interfered with detection of their corresponding signals. That is, visual imaging led to worse performance on detecting visual signals and auditory imaging led to worse performance on detecting auditory signals. Not only were subjects less likely to detect a signal in these cases, but when no signal was presented they were also more likely to report a signal of the type they had been imaging (i.e., a false alarm). Thus, these results show that imagery can selectively interfere with the detection of signals.

Manipulation of Mental Images.   Some striking regularities are observed from studies of **mental rotation** conducted by Shepard and his associates (see, e.g., Cooper & Shepard, 1973, 1978; Shepard & Metzler, 1971; Shepard & Cooper, 1982). In these studies, subjects are presented with an object and asked whether another object is merely a rotation of the first. Figure 6.3 provides an example of the objects used. The forms in A and B can be rotated into correspondence but the forms in C cannot be aligned through rotation. Therefore, the correct answer would be "yes" for A and B and "no" for C. Data from a typical experiment are also shown in the figure. The larger the required rotation, the longer it took to answer the question. The time needed to decide whether the second object was a rotation of the first was a linear function of the extent of the required rotation. This suggests that mental rotation takes place at a fixed rate. These results are consistent with the idea that the internal representation is not a structure corresponding to the object independent of its position but rather that structure as seen from a particular direction. Otherwise the reaction times would not be such a systematic function of the extent of rotation.

Marcel Just and Pat Carpenter (1976) have raised the possibility that the linear reaction time effects are artifacts of eye movements. Just and Carpenter found that when patterns in a mental rotation task are presented simultaneously, participants move their eyes back and forth between the patterns and do so more with increasing angular disparity. This interpretation would not, however, explain results from studies in which the probe stimulus is delayed and the patterns do not appear at the same time. Even

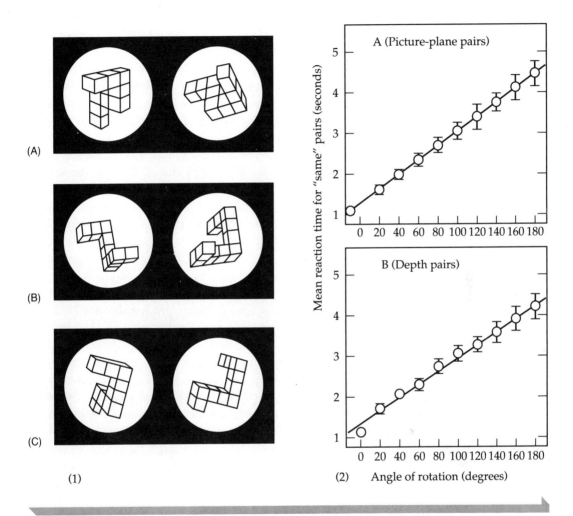

Figure 6.3   (1) Examples of pairs of perspective line drawings presented to the subjects: (A) a "same" pair, which differs by an 80 degree rotation in the picture plane; (B) a "same" pair, which differs by an 80 degree rotation in depth; and (C) a "different" pair, which cannot be brought into congruence by *any* rotation.

(2) Mean reaction times to two perspective line drawings portraying objects of the same three-dimensional shape. Times are plotted as a function of angular difference in portrayed orientation: (A) for pairs differing by a rotation in picture plane only, and (B) for pairs differing by a rotation in depth. The vertical bars around each circle indicate a conservative estimate of the standard error of that mean.

Source: Shepard, R. N., & Metzler, J., 1971.

when the probe appears by itself, reaction time continues to be a linear function of degree of rotation (e.g., Cooper & Shepard, 1973; Cooper, 1975, 1976).

Pictorial Properties of Mental Images.   Stephen Kosslyn has demonstrated that people's scanning of mental images shows effects similar to scanning physical scenes or maps (Kosslyn, 1973; Kosslyn, Ball, & Reiser, 1978). For example, in one study (Kosslyn, Ball, & Reiser, 1978) subjects learned a simple map in which seven locations were marked by objects. The test trials began with the naming of one of the objects. Subjects were asked to image the entire map and focus on the location of the named object. Another object was then named. If the object was not on the map, subjects pressed one button. If the object was one of the ones marking a location on the map, subjects scanned to it and pressed another button when they reached it. (The instructions were to image a black speck moving in the shortest straight line from the first object to the second.) The results showed that longer distances took longer to scan just as it might be if one moved one's eyes across a scene or map from one location to the next.

Further parallels between images and the manipulation of physical objects come from another clever set of studies by Kosslyn (1975, 1976) examining the effect of image size. This research begins with the observation that the smaller an object, the harder it is to see any attribute of it. Is the same true of images? In these studies, subjects were told to image objects at different sizes. After they had an image, subjects were asked whether the object had some physical attribute (e.g., ears, a beak). Kosslyn found that the smaller the image, the longer it took to verify that this attribute was present (when it was) and to decide that it was not present (when it was not). Although these and other studies have received some sound methodological criticisms (Intons-Peterson, 1983; Intons-Peterson & White, 1981; Mitchell & Richman, 1980), on the whole, the main findings appear to survive (see Finke, 1985 for a balanced review).

Perceptual-like Effects of Images.   Some results from imagery experiments suggest that images behave very much like visual perception. For example, Wallace (1984) found that the Ponzo illusion, in which two identical horizontal lines appear different in length when two converging diagonal lines are placed on either side of them, could be produced when the diagonal lines were merely imagined. Finke and Schmidt (1977) reported that the McCollough effect (an orientation-specific color aftereffect; if one stares at green horizontal bars and red vertical bars, then later looks at black and white bars, one sees a red afterimage when looking at horizontal bars and a green afterimage when looking at vertical bars) could occur after participants imagined bar gratings superimposed on a field of color. Although these findings seem immune to criticism in terms of the sort of demand characteristics we discussed in Chapter 1 (because participants could hardly know what effects they should produce), we cannot be fully confident of them because they have not been easy to replicate (see, e.g., Broerse & Crassini, 1984).

Representation of Images

How Equivalent Are Imagery and Perception?

The findings just reviewed make a good case that images are analog representations but it is far from clear just how closely imagery mirrors perception. Chambers and Reisberg (1985) argued that perceptual stimuli must be interpreted but images are already interpretations. In support of their position they produced strong evidence that visual stimuli and images behave differently. In one experiment they presented participants with ambiguous stimuli such as the one shown in Figure 6.4. Take a quick look at the figure and see what it depicts. If you look at the figure for a while you will be able to interpret it differently. Chambers and Reisberg showed this figure for 5 seconds, asked people to form a clear mental image of it, and then removed it. This brief presentation did not give people time to reinterpret the figure. None of the 15 participants was able to come up with a second interpretation using just their mental image of the figure. When, however, the participants were asked to draw the figure (from memory) and then reinterpret it, all 15 were able to see the second interpretation! (If you have not yet

Figure 6.4   **Ambiguous Figure from Chambers and Reisberg's Experiment (1985).**
Source: Chambers, D., & Reisberg, D., 1985.

seen both possibilities, it may help to know that one interpretation is a rabbit—the left side is its ears—and the other a duck—the left side is its bill.)

Finke, Pinker, and Farah (1989), however, were able to demonstrate some ability of people to reinterpret visual images. For example, participants asked to imagine the letter D on its side and placed on top of the letter J spontaneously report "seeing" an umbrella. Therefore, mental images can under some circumstances be given new construals or interpretations; therefore reinterpretation does not constitute a qualitative difference between imagery and perception. It may, however, be a quantitative difference. The critical factors determining when and how mental images may be reinterpreted remain unknown.

Are Visual Images Visual?   It seems clear from the studies we have reviewed that images encode analog spatial information. The results are consistent with either of two very different ideas about the nature of this representation. One possibility is that these visual images are really *spatial* representations. By this view, the knowledge we use to generate and use images is abstract and not tied to any specific modality. It is more like knowledge about the general layout of an object or scene, rather than just the type of information we could get by looking at the scene. The contrasting idea is that these visual images are truly *visual* representations. That is, the visual images are tied to the visual modality and we have encoded knowledge about the literal appearance of the objects or scenes. By this view, a visual image requires some of the same representations usually engaged when that same object is seen.

This distinction addresses the question of whether or not visual imaging involves the visual system. In addition to its centrality in research on visual imagery, the question has important implications for a number of theories of cognition (see Farah, 1988 for some examples). The results from research on this issue have been somewhat mixed. In favor of spatial representation, a number of arguments have been advanced. One impressive argument is that congenitally blind subjects show a number of imagery effects. For example, Kerr (1983) conducted research patterned after Kosslyn's scanning and size experiments just discussed. In one study, similar to the Kosslyn, Ball, and Reiser (1978) scanning study, she had blind and sighted subjects learn a simple layout of seven different geometric figures on a board. Following learning (the figures were raised so that blind subjects could learn by feeling them), subjects were read the name of an object and asked to imagine the board and "focus" on the name object. They were then given the name of another object and asked to imagine a raised dot going from the first to the second object. When the dot reached the second object, they were to push a button. The results revealed that both blind and sighted subjects showed the usual increase in response time with distance. Because the blind subjects have been blind from birth, it is assumed that they do not have visually based representations (though they can encode spatial information). Thus, finding that the scanning effects are similar for blind and sighted subjects suggests that there is no reason to believe a visual representation is necessary for imagery.

Although these findings seem problematic for the idea of visual representations, other results provide strong support for such an idea. Martha Farah has marshalled several strong arguments in favor of visual representations (see also Finke, 1985). First, relying on neuropsychological studies of brain-damaged patients, she notes that when cortical lesions from brain damage lead to selective visual deficits, there are often parallel imagery deficits (Farah, 1988). For example, if cortical damage leads to central color blindness, the patients lose their ability to image in color. Second, she provides some interesting data combining reaction times and brain potential recordings which are consistent with visual representations (Farah, Peronnet, Gonon, & Giard, 1988). This study used a procedure similar to the selective interference paradigm, but looked for facilitation of imaging and detecting the same content. In particular, subjects were asked to image a capital H, a capital T, or not to image. They were then given a very brief (20 milliseconds) presentation of one of these letters or nothing, followed by a masking stimulus. The subjects' task was to report whether they had seen a letter or not. These researchers found that people were better at detecting a letter if they had been imaging the same letter. That is, if they were imaging H, they were more likely to detect H than T. Thus the facilitation was specific to the content of the image, suggesting that at some point the visual and imaginal representations joined (or fed into the same process). In addition, event-related potentials were recorded by putting electrodes to various scalp areas of the subjects. These recordings from the visual cortex showed systematic effects of this match between the image and the stimulus (i.e., whether they were the same, H-H or T-T, or were different) less than 200 milliseconds after the stimulus was presented. This finding provides strong support for the idea that the representation of the image involves the visual cortex and is truly visual.

Thus, we have evidence for both spatial and visual representation of images. Farah, Hammond, Levine, and Calvanio (1988) suggest that the evidence is mixed because the representation is neither entirely visual nor entirely spatial. Rather, *both* spatial and visual representations of images exist, but which is used depends on the task. In addition to accounting for the number of mixed findings and some other general arguments, they describe two further pieces of relevant evidence. First, they note that there may well be two anatomically distinct cortical systems for dealing with visual representations. One system is involved in representing the appearance of objects and the other with the location of the objects in space (the what and where systems discussed in Chapter 4).

A second piece of evidence in favor of this compromise solution comes from neuropsychology. Of most relevance, Farah, Hammond, Levine, and Calvanio (1988) present results from a patient who suffered brain damage from an automobile accident. Although the patient does well in intelligence and simple visual acuity tests, he suffers from severe deficits in visual recognition. Not only is he unable to recognize a number of common objects and animals, he often has trouble recognizing his wife and children. In various imagery tasks, he sometimes performed at normal levels and sometimes at far below normal levels. Most interesting, normal performance was found on all seven of the spatial imagery tasks for which he was tested. These tasks, such as the scanning and mental rotation tasks, clearly require spatial information but have sometimes been shown not to require visual representations (such as from the work with congenitally blind subjects). In contrast, on the four visual imagery tasks that require specifically visual representations (that is, asking about a visual property such as the color of objects), the patient performed much below normal.

In summary, the evidence appears to favor the compromise view in which both spatial and visual representations exist. This is not, however, an uninteresting compromise and it may serve as inspiration for integrative computational models of visuo-spatial representation (see, e.g., Kosslyn, 1987).

Visual Memory

Many people feel that their memory for visually perceived objects, scenes, and faces is quite good. We can remember what our car looks like, the inside of a restaurant, and the faces of friends and acquaintances. If we have been only briefly acquainted with someone, we may not be able to remember his or her name, but we are confident that we would at least know we had seen the person somewhere before. In this section we examine some research on memory for visual stimuli.

Remembering Details

Our confidence in our visual memory abilities is generally not misplaced. Before examining the impressive memory we have, however, let us consider a potential problem illustrated by the following two examples. First, picture the front of a public building that you are very familiar with. How many windows does it have on the front? Many people are able to picture the building but when trying to answer this question find that their image of the building does not include any definite number of windows.

For the second example, draw the front of a penny. Most people find this hard to do, but still might feel that they know what it looks like. Nickerson and Adams (1979) asked subjects (all American citizens) to perform this task. When asked to draw a penny, they omitted far more than half the features or located them in the wrong place. When asked to choose the real penny from 15 possibilities, less than half the subjects picked the correct one. Jones (1990) performed some related experiments with British coins (and British subjects) and found similar results. In fact, slightly less than half the subjects even knew the number of sides on a 50 pence coin (seven).

These results are quite surprising. As Nickerson and Adams note, however, the details that are not remembered are almost always irrelevant to one's use of a penny. People don't mistake a penny for a quarter or a button because they cannot remember where the date is on the penny. Memory is being used to accomplish goals; details that are without function with respect to these goals often may not be remembered as well as goal-relevant details.

Memory for Pictures

Suppose that you are allowed to look through 612 color pictures of common settings. When you finish, after about an hour (averaging about 6 seconds per picture), you are then shown two pictures at a time and asked to pick out which of the two were in the 612 pictures you had already seen. One picture is one of the 612 and the other picture is selected from the same general pool (i.e., it is of the same type). How well do you think you would be able to do this?

Shepard (1967) ran this experiment and found that people were correct about 97% of the time. If they were not tested for three days, they were still 92% correct. In fact, 120 days later, they were still 58% correct.

It is important to realize that we are not claiming that subjects are remembering all the details of these pictures. As we just saw from the study on pennies, memory for details is not always good. Many different types of knowledge could allow subjects to perform well in this picture memory experiment. For instance, they might remember one unusual detail from a picture. However, to do this well on recognition, they clearly are making use of *some* memory for the pictures seen. When we remember that they saw over 600 one after the other and for a very brief time each, such memory seems quite impressive.

The results of Standing (1973) show even more impressive memory for pictures. He presented up to 10,000 pictures for 5 seconds each over several days. Two days later, he tested for memory by presenting two pictures and asking subjects to pick the old one. The correct picture was chosen 83% of the time. Clearly, much can be remembered from very short exposures to visual stimuli.

The Picture-Superiority Effect

A common intuition is that pictures are better remembered than words. This is generally correct. As one example, in the Shepard (1967) study just mentioned, another group of subjects looked at words rather than pictures. Even though there were fewer words than pictures (540 vs. 612), words were not recognized as well (88% vs. 97%). Many studies in the last 25 years have carefully controlled various factors and still found better memory for pictures, using a variety of picture types and testing conditions. This advantage for pictures over words is called the **picture-superiority effect**. This difference is found even if the memory test involves simply the names of the pictures rather than the pictures themselves.

Much of the research has been connected to the ideas of Allan Paivio, which are reviewed in Paivio (1971). He proposes a **dual coding** hypothesis in which pictures are more likely to be stored in two independent codes (verbal and imaginal) than are words. As a further indication of distinct codes, Schooler and Engstler-Schooler (1990) found that verbal rehearsal of pictures can *interfere* with memory for them. Although other hypotheses have been suggested for this effect as well, a common assumption is that picture superiority is caused by a richer coding in the case of pictures than in the case of words. (Though Weldon & Roediger, 1987 present some evidence that the effect can be reversed with tests that tap less conceptual aspects of the materials.)

Face Recognition

Despite the fact that most faces have the same set of features (nose, eyes, etc.), our memory for faces is excellent. In one fascinating study, Bahrick, Bahrick, and Wittlinger (1975) tested the memory of people for their high school classmates. For all 392 subjects, the experimenters obtained their high school yearbooks. These subjects ranged in age from 17 (newly graduated) to 74 (not so newly graduated). Of interest here is the face recognition test. Ten pictures were randomly chosen from each yearbook and photocopied. Each picture was put on a card with four other pictures taken from other yearbooks (but chosen so that fashion changes over the years and differences in picture type could not be used as a clue). Subjects were then asked to pick the face of their classmate from the set of five. The correct choice was made 90% of the time and this accuracy persisted even in groups that had graduated about 35 years earlier. The group that had graduated nearly 48 years earlier still chose the correct face 71% of the time. Our memory for faces is quite incredible.

Given this impressive memory, it is tempting to speculate that our memory for faces may be special, perhaps based on a memory system specialized for faces. As one example of the type of finding that seems consistent with such a speculation, Yin (1969) tested recognition of faces and other complex visual stimuli when they were presented upright or inverted. He found that the decrement caused by inversion was 30% for faces, but only 10% for the other types of stimuli. Although this result is suggestive both it and other evidence used to support the idea of a specialized capacity for face recognition have been criticized on a number of grounds (see Cohen-Levine, Banich, & Koch-Weser, 1988, for a brief review of these arguments).

Diamond and Carey (1986) argued that the greater effect of inversion for faces may not be due to any inherent differences in our processing of faces, but rather to our considerable expertise with processing faces as opposed to other types of stimuli considered. To test this hypothesis, they found a stimulus type for which people had considerable differences in expertise, recognition of dogs. In their study, they found that people who were "dog experts" showed an inversion effect as large for dogs as for people faces, while nonexperts showed much less of an inversion effect for dogs.

Even if faces are processed similarly to other complex visuo-spatial stimuli, the evolutionary specialization argument may still be partially correct. It is possible that the capacity for such processing came about because of the need to individuate other members of our species, but that the capacity was flexible enough to be used for processing other patterns as well (see Cohen-Levine et al.). Nonetheless the evidence suggests that at least part of the usual advantage for face recognition is due to our great deal of experience in processing and remembering faces.

Mnemonics

The last topic in this section on visual memory is the use of visual images for remembering other information. Many strategies for remembering (**mnemonic devices**) make use of visual or spatial images for remembering, though the reasons why such strategies work are still under investigation (see, e.g., McDaniel & Pressley, 1987). Numerous popular books provide detailed descriptions of mnemonic strategies and how to use them (e.g., Bellezza, 1982; Lorayne & Lucas, 1974).

As many people know, to remember something it is sometimes useful to imagine some strange or bizarre image that includes whatever you want to remember. For example, to remember to call the vet to make an appointment for your dog, you might imagine your dog dialing the telephone (although in this case a note in some often used location might be even more helpful). Einstein and McDaniel (1987) review a great deal of the large literature on such effects. Although such bizarre images do not always improve memory, they do under a wide variety of conditions.

A mnemonic technique for remembering a set of items in order, known as the **method of loci**, also relies on visual imagery. With this technique you imagine moving along a familiar path (e.g., from your dormitory room or apartment to the chemistry building) and "depositing" to-be-remembered items at each of the landmarks you cross. Then you recall the items later by mentally traversing the path again. As you will see if you try it, the method of loci is quite effective.

Summary

We have argued that spatial knowledge and mental representations of visual information are fundamental to cognition. We have further suggested that, despite the controversy between analog and propositional theories of representation, the evidence favors the idea that human cognition uses both analog and propositional representations. Our definition of an analog representation was that it mimics or parallels the structure of what is being represented in a more or less direct manner. Both the notion of structure and "more or less direct manner" allow for considerable leeway in how literally imagery mirrors perception. Any particular representation scheme allows a system to access some forms of knowledge easily and other forms of knowledge only with difficulty. Studies of visuo-spatial cognition suggest that what the human conceptual system accomplishes easily is consistent with representations having many analoglike properties.

On a broader level the study of visuo-spatial cognition is important because other cognitive mechanisms may have evolved by modifying existing systems. Given that the spatial representation system is probably one of the oldest, one might expect that other cognitive systems show a "spatial bias." The representation of spatial relations does appear to be fairly ubiquitous in human thought. Many of the metaphors that we use to describe how we think and feel rely on spatial relations (feeling up, feeling down, feeling close to another person, "higher" level thinking, placing a plan on the back burner, and so on; see Lakoff & Johnson, 1980). We also find it natural to discuss the similarity of entities such as color in terms of being "close to" or "far from" each other.

Finally, in our discussions of comprehension and reasoning we will make frequent reference to "mental models," which centrally employ spatial representations. To close our argument that spatial cognition may bias other forms of cognition we offer another spatial metaphor: The apple may not fall far from the tree.

Key Terms

analog representations
dual-coding hypothesis
mental rotation
method of loci
mnemonic devices
picture-superiority effect

propositional representations
representations
route knowledge
spatial neglect
survey knowledge

Recommended Readings

We have not done justice to the debate concerning image versus propositional representations. For further discussion see articles by Kosslyn and Shwartz (1977), Pylyshyn (1979, 1981), Anderson (1978), and Shepard (1981). Steve Kosslyn's (1983) book offers an extensive overview of the structure and function of images.

Spatial cognition is a topic that is receiving increasing attention. Tversky (1981) and Byrne (1982) report interesting limitations in memory for spatial information. The phenomenon of spatial neglect is as intriguing as it is disturbing. Descriptions of neglect can be found in Chedru (1976) and Bisiach et al. (1986).

There continue to be careful analyses of parallels between imagery and perception. Chambers and Reisberg (1985) and Finke et al. (1989) have written an interesting pair of papers. Ronald Finke (1985) provides a thoughtful, balanced review and Martha Farah (1988) analyzes this issue from a neuroscience perspective.

If your goal is to improve your memory, there are very good popular books by Bellezza (1982) and Lorayne and Lucas (1974). Finally, skeptics may wish to consult the Einstein and McDaniel (1987) review of mnemonic strategies.

7

MEMORY: REMEMBERING NEW INFORMATION

Chapter Outline

I distinctly remember forgetting that.

Clara Barton

Introduction

Centrality of Memory

The importance of memory frequently goes unnoticed. Often we think of memory as a repository in which names, dates, and the like can be kept until they are needed. Close analysis, however, shows memory to be a far more pervasive aspect of mental activity.

To appreciate the centrality of memory to mental life, we need only imagine what it would be like to be deprived of our memory for a time—or even more effectively, to observe someone who has had this unhappy experience. Consider the following dramatic case of a brain-injured man whose ability to store new information was virtually lost following surgery (Milner, 1966, pp. 112–115):

> This young man (H. M.) . . . had had no obvious memory disturbance before his operations, having, for example, passed his high school examinations without difficulty. . . . The patient was drowsy for the first few post-operative days but then, as he became more alert, a severe memory impairment was apparent. He could no longer recognize the hospital staff . . . , he did not remember and could not relearn the way to the bathroom, and he seemed to retain nothing of the day-to-day happenings in the hospital.

> . . . ten months after the operation the family moved to a new house which was situated only a few blocks away from their old one, on the same street. When examined . . . nearly a year later, H. M. had not yet learned the new address, nor could he be trusted to find his way home alone, because he would go to the old house. Six years ago the family moved again, and H. M. is still unsure of his present address, although he seems to know that he has moved. . . .

> One gets some idea of what such an amnesic state must be like from H. M.'s own comments. Between tests he would suddenly look up and say, rather anxiously,

"Right now, I'm wondering. Have I done or said anything amiss? You see, at this moment everything looks clear to me, but what happened just before? That's what worries me. It's like waking from a dream; I just don't remember."

Not surprisingly, psychology gives memory a critically important status. Memory is conceived as an extremely complex set of processes and mechanisms for accessing old knowledge and encoding new information. It is inextricably involved in every cognitive task from the simplest to the most difficult—from the memorization of a person's name to understanding speech to formulating and following personal goals. In fact, memory influences will be discussed in almost all later chapters of this book. Before discussing memory in detail it is useful to consider some of the different functions that memory may serve.

Uses of Memory

It is common to view memory as something that allows one to store and to retrieve facts: What is the capital of Oregon? What did you have for dinner last night? Furthermore, we tend to equate having a "good memory" with the ability to retrieve obscure or detailed facts.

Clearly, we do store and remember facts, but our memory is not used simply for the recollection of facts we have learned. Even in situations in which some fact is being queried, we often do not (or cannot) retrieve the exact fact, but rather retrieve relevant information that may allow us to answer the question. For example, what about questions like:

1. What is George Bush's telephone number?

We do not have to search through all our knowledge concerning George Bush to realize that we do not know his phone number.

To further complicate the picture, consider the following question:

2. How many windows are there in your current residence?

Most people can answer this question correctly but they do not do so by directly retrieving this information (unless they have recently washed or painted their windows). Instead, people typically employ mental imagery and may imagine themselves walking through their house or apartment and counting the windows. In brief, our old knowledge is often used to derive some new knowledge.

Finally, consider questions like the following:

3. Did Julius Caesar have toes?

4. Do elephants eat more in a day than lions?

Both questions could be readily answered, but again not on the basis of fact retrieval only. In the case of Caesar our answer is based on a plausible inference from our knowledge that most people have toes. Similarly, the answer that elephants eat more than lions may derive from the general rule that there is a positive correlation (though not a perfect one) between size and how much an organism eats.

These examples suggest that there is a lot more to memory than retrieving facts. In fact, our memory is needed in all acts of interpreting objects and events. Even to understand the questions we have just been considering requires access to (stored) knowledge about English grammar and the meanings of the associated words.

These observations provide clues to some of the central functions that memory serves. First, we cannot store every fact or conclusion that follows from the facts we already know—there are just too many of them. Our memory system is organized as a natural inference system that allows us to store a few facts and derive others as needed. We will take a closer look at such inferences in Chapters 8 and 11. A second major function of memory is to relate new events to prior knowledge in order to understand them. Just how this is done is addressed in Chapters 11 and 12. A third general function of memory is to deliver relevant knowledge when it is needed. Even with our heavy reliance on inference, we have stored a tremendous number of facts and other bits of knowledge in memory. Just how we access that knowledge is a fundamental question. If we see a black widow spider, we need to access the knowledge that it is possibly poisonous. It will not help us to retrieve the fact that Thanksgiving is on a Thursday or that spiders spin complex webs. Furthermore, we need to access this knowledge quickly—and for this to happen, memory must be organized. The amazing thing is that memory is used so automatically that much of the time we are scarcely aware of it. Our understanding of memory needs to include not only the cases where it fails (where did I park my car *today*?), but also the countless times when it succeeds.

Although our knowledge is used in many ways, it is also true that one of the ways is the usual sense of remembering or recollection— to store and retrieve new information. In this chapter we examine this memory for new information. Even here we will see that the use of prior knowledge has a major influence on the acquisition of new knowledge. We begin by investigating how information may be retained over very short periods, the study of short-term memory. We then examine a variety of findings on how information is retained (and forgotten) over longer periods, the study of long-term memory. With this background we can discuss some explanations or models for the remembering of new information. Finally, we end the chapter with an investigation of individual differences in memory.

Short-Term Memory

Introduction

Suppose that someone tells you the combination to a bicycle lock or how to operate a burglar alarm, and you cannot write it down. How would you try to keep from forgetting it? A common (and useful) strategy is to keep repeating the numbers over and over to yourself. The idea is that by repeating the numbers you are keeping them active and available. This active, available information is what psychologists call **short-term memory** (also often called *primary memory* or *working memory*). It is helpful to think of two ways in which this type of short-term memory may be useful. First, if you attend carefully to some information, such as the lock combination, it is registered in this short-term memory, making the information available for further processing and/or more permanent storage. Second, if you recall some information from permanent memory into short-term memory (e.g., the birthdate of a sibling), it is available for further processing (e.g., figuring out the age of your sibling). As we have repeatedly mentioned, much of the information in the world is incomplete and requires augmentation by memory. Short-term memory is a crucial link in this augmentation, keeping available the information from the world to be augmented by memory. Short-term memory allows different information to be compared and integrated. In addition, it helps deal with the complexity problem (i.e., of knowing what information may be relevant) by keeping available recent information. Although any information is potentially relevant to a task (e.g., solving a problem, understanding a story), it is more likely that recent information will be relevant.

Short-term memory is biased toward keeping recent information available. However, if information in short-term memory is to be available immediately, short-term memory needs to be limited. These limitations surface in the forgetting that occurs, the errors people make, and the way in which much more information can be stored.

Characteristics of Short-Term Memory

Short-Term Forgetting and Rehearsal.   Events occurring both during and immediately following an experience are critically important determiners of short-term forgetting. Consider the following classic experiment by Peterson and Peterson (1959). The experimenter would say a three-letter consonant group (e.g., BKF) and then immediately say a three-digit number (e.g., 397). The subject then counted backward by threes (or fours) from this digit (i.e., 397, 394, 391 . . .). At the end of a preset interval (3, 6, 9, 12, 15, or 18 seconds) the subject was asked to recall the consonant group. The proportion of correct recalls for each interval is presented in Figure 7.1. As can be seen, the proportion of items recalled decreased sharply over the interval. If subjects cannot rehearse the items, they do not remember them for more than a matter of seconds.

In or out of the laboratory, it is universally observed that one can

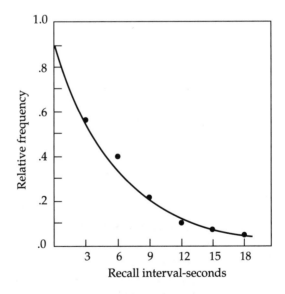

Figure 7.1   Proportion recalled in short-term memory task as a function of delay during which subjects are counting backward by three. *Source*: Peterson, L. R., & Peterson, M. J., 1959.

maintain memory for a few letters, numbers, or words just seen or heard almost indefinitely if one rehearses them repeatedly. By simply repeating the items to oneself over and over (termed *maintenance rehearsal* or **primary rehearsal**), one in effect imprints the items anew in short-term memory on each repetition, much as one can prevent a watch from running down by winding it at intervals.

It cannot be assumed, however, that experiences with interfering tasks produce forgetting solely as a consequence of preventing rehearsal. In many memory theories (e.g., Atkinson & Shiffrin, 1968) it is assumed that short-term memory has an extremely small capacity, limited to a few items at a time. Consequently, if immediately after seeing or hearing some to-be-remembered items a person is presented with additional items, these new items may enter short-term memory and, in effect, crowd out some of those earlier items he or she is trying to retain. Rehearsal may take place, but only of the items still in short-term memory.

Coding in Short-Term Memory.   How is information in short-term memory coded? Some of the processes involved are brought out nicely in a simple experimental situation developed by the British psychologist Conrad (1964). On any one trial, the subject views a series of items, typically a string of 4–6 consonant letters that appear one after another on a display screen at a relatively rapid rate. Following a retention interval during which the subject reads aloud a series of rapidly presented random digits, a recall signal tells the subject to report as many of the letters as possible.

To find out how information about the visually displayed letters is recorded and stored in short-term memory, we may examine the nature of the errors made in recall. When a subject makes errors in recalling a string of letters, he or she is most likely to replace a letter that was shown on a particular trial with another letter that *sounds like* the one presented (for example, T with V). If the subject is prevented from pronouncing the letters as they appear (for example, by being required to say something else), these auditory confusion errors do not appear at the time of recall. A striking consequence of preventing the formation of auditory memory codes in this way is that short-term memory for the letters is greatly reduced.

Conrad's experiment shows that information may be coded (or recoded) into acoustic codes in short-term memory. For some time such coding was thought to be a necessary characteristic of short-term memory. However, other research has now shown that other codings of information are also prevalent in short-term memory (for example, the visual codes discussed in Chapter 6 on spatial knowledge, imagery, and visual memory).

In addition to acoustic and visual codes, the semantic aspects of items affect short-term memory. A clear demonstration of semantic effects may be seen in a clever paradigm used by Delos Wickens and his colleagues (Wickens, 1972) called **release from PI** (proactive interference). The procedure is as follows. Subjects are given a triad of category members (e.g., flowers such as rose, tulip, daisy) to remember, but a distractor task is given so that subjects cannot rehearse the items. Recall is then requested. This test is followed by another triad from the same category (e.g., three new types of flowers) with the same procedure. A third triad is then presented with the same procedure. The recall of the second triad is lower than the recall of the first and the recall of the third triad is lower than the recall of the second, a phenomenon known as proactive interference. The interest, however, is in the recall of a fourth triad, which is either from the same category or from a new category. As shown in Figure 7.2, when the triad is from a new category, recall increases back to the level achieved for the first triad. When the triad is from the same category as the first three triads, its recall is even lower than the third triad recall. Clearly, knowledge about the category is affecting the short-term memory recall, evidence for some type of semantic coding.

Limitations and Chunking.   Consider again the example involving a lock combination. If it was a long combination and the numbers were 10, 20, 30, 40, 50, 60, 70, and 80, would it be easier to remember than if they were 50, 30, 60, 20, 80, 10, 40, and 70? Almost everyone would agree that the first

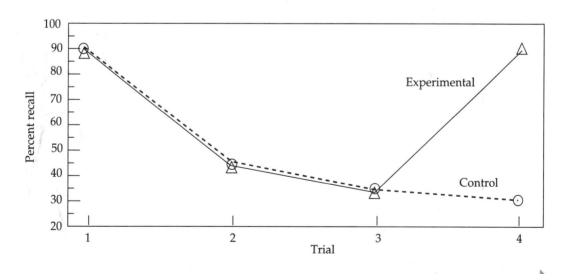

Figure 7.2   **Illustration of Typical Results Obtained in Release from PI Studies.**

combination would be easier to remember. To give another example, compare your ability to remember the following:

A string of 10 letters: R, P, L, B, V, Q, M, S, D, G
A set of 52 letters: I pledge allegiance to the flag of the United States of America.

Although the words include 52 letters, most people find them much easier to remember than the string of 10 letters. Why?

The answer for both of these examples is fairly obvious. In the first case, you can simply remember (i.e., keep in short-term memory) the idea that the numbers went from 10 to 80 in increments of 10 rather than remember the exact order in which the numbers occurred. In the second case, you need remember only that the sequence is the opening to the Pledge of Allegiance, rather than remembering the exact letters and their order. The coding you use to store these easy-to-remember groups of information is called **chunking**. A chunk refers to any meaningful group of information. Rather than storing each piece of information in the chunk in short-term memory, you can store the idea that the pieces of the chunk occurred. When you need to retrieve the information, you can remember that the pieces of the chunk occurred (because this idea is in short-term memory) and then you can bring the constituents of the chunk from more permanent memory. For example, if you were asked to recall the set of words in the second example, you would use the chunk "first sentence of Pledge of Allegiance" to retrieve the sentence from memory. If you were asked to recall the letters in that set of words, you would first retrieve the words and then, for each word, spell out the letters (again using information from more permanent memory).

The idea of chunking was outlined by George Miller (1956) in a famous paper ("The magical number seven plus or minus two . . .") in which he pointed out that a large number of seemingly disparate findings could be reconciled if we computed memory limitations not in terms of some physical entity, such as letters, but rather in terms of a psychological entity, chunks. Counting this way, he identified the short-term memory span to be about seven (or five to nine) chunks. Although the exact limits are controversial, the idea that people chunk information is widely accepted. This chunking allows us to keep track of much more information and have it available for processing. This ability becomes even more important as we deal with complex situations for which a great deal of information may be relevant.

In addition, it is important to realize that chunking is a function of our prior knowledge. What is meaningful depends on what we know, as well as what we are currently experiencing. For example, consider these two sequences of letters and try to remember them (adapted from Bower and Springston, 1970):

F BIV IPG NPC BS   versus   FBI VIP GNP CBS

Our knowledge does not provide chunks to be readily used for most of the first letter sets, but does for the four later letter sets.

Working Memory

We have been concentrating on short-term memory effects as if short-term memory was simply a "storage device." That is, we have been concerned with how information is coded, retained, and accessed, but not with the actual *use* of this information in any complex task. Baddeley and Hitch (1974) began a series of experiments addressing the question "what is short-term memory for?" In some clever studies, they showed that short-term memory should not be thought of as a unitary storage area, but rather as a set of interactive temporary storage systems that are coordinated by a single central "executive."

The evidence for such a **working memory** view comes from a variety of sources, but can be illustrated by the following study (Logie, Zucco, & Baddeley, cited in Baddeley, 1988), which shows that the verbal memory and visual memory for items are not part of a single storage system. A dual-task paradigm was used in which subjects' ability to do two tasks at the same time is used as an indication of the extent to which the two tasks call on some similar limited capacity (such as a short-term store). Of greatest interest in this study was performance on a simple recognition memory span test, presented either as a verbal span of letters or a visual span of a simple 2 × 2 array. In each case, one letter or cell was changed between the two presentations (2 seconds apart) and subjects had to say which had changed. These tasks are quite easy and subjects could perform without error, except that they were also asked to do a secondary task at the same time, either involving a visual array of letters or a simple arithmetic task in which they kept a running sum of a set of single digits. The logic was that if the visual span task involved a different store than the verbal letter span task (i.e., if it involved a visual store of some type), it would be more interfered with by a visual secondary task. The opposite would be true for the verbal span task—it would be more interfered with by a secondary task that involved verbal material (such as maintaining a running sum of numbers). This prediction was supported.

Baddeley has continued in this line, investigating these different types of subsystems to understand their function. For example, he has argued (Baddeley, 1983, 1988) that the auditory codes are part of what he calls the *articulatory loop* system, which holds speech-based material as a necessary part of speech comprehension. In addition, he describes a *visuo-spatial sketch pad* that can be used to maintain and manipulate visuo-spatial images. Such a system would be used, for example, to mentally rotate items or to answer the question of how many windows there are in your house or apartment. Much still remains to be learned about this working memory view, especially about the critical central executive component. Nonetheless, it seems that a simple view of short-term memory as a single unitary store is unable to account for many of these findings.

Long-Term Memory

Introduction

Items that enter a person's memory system and survive the critical first few seconds may be retained for very long periods. In fact, there is a real question whether memories, once established, are ever completely lost. But if **long-term memory** is permanent, why does it sometimes fail or even mislead us, as when different eyewitnesses remember conflicting accounts of the same event? Why do nearly all of us often have difficulty in recalling names and dates or the details of lectures or textbook chapters?

Even a partial answer to the central question of the fallibility of memory has many aspects. We need to keep in mind two general themes. First, people are faced with great complexities in figuring out what of their huge store of knowledge might be relevant to any situation. Second, the information they are given is often incomplete and must be augmented. Together, these ideas lead to a conception of the human as an active as opposed to passive processor of information. The ability to remember will be affected by the processes that occur at the time the information is learned (i.e., how it is encoded and organized) as well as the processes that occur at the time the information is retrieved. Let's start with a simple example of remembering, which will also illustrate active processing of the material.

One technique that has proven useful in analyzing memory is known as **free recall**. In the simplest form of a free recall experiment, the subject is presented with a list of words and asked to reproduce from memory as many of the words as possible. Though the task sounds simple, even extremely intelligent and literate adults can typically remember only

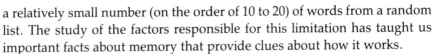

a relatively small number (on the order of 10 to 20) of words from a random list. The study of the factors responsible for this limitation has taught us important facts about memory that provide clues about how it works.

For example, the probability of recalling an item depends on where it appeared in the list, a phenomenon referred to as the **serial position effect** (see Figure 7.3). Items at the beginning and at the end of the list are more likely to be recalled than items in the middle of the list. The increased recall for items at the beginning of the list is referred to as the **primacy effect**, while the increased recall for the last items is the **recency effect**. If we delay recall for half a minute or so while distracting the subjects by, for example, asking them to solve an arithmetic problem or to count out loud, recall of items at the end of the list suffers but performance on the items in the beginning and middle positions remains unaffected (see Figure 7.3). One interpretation of this finding is that the recency effect occurs because items at the end of a list are being recalled from short-term memory and the arithmetic task presumably eliminates this advantage. Since recall of items in other positions is not similarly affected, they presumably are being recalled from long-term memory. (An interesting recent complication of this picture is that one sometimes gets recency effects even after long delays [see, e.g., Glenberg, Bradley, Kraus, & Renzaglia, 1983]. Although the exact cause of these long-term recency effects is still under investigation, they appear to be due to the retrieval of context, a topic we will discuss in detail later in this chapter.)

What causes the primacy effect? One explanation relies on the idea

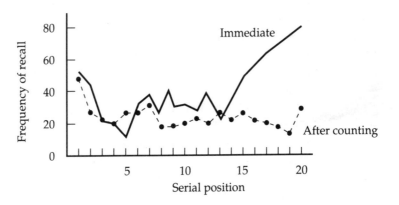

Figure 7.3   Serial position functions for free recall tests given immediately after the presentation of a 20-word list as compared to a test given after a 30-second delay during which subjects were counting backward. *Source*: Postman, L., & Phillips, L. W., 1965.

discussed earlier that short-term memory is influential in determining what information is transferred into long-term memory, but is limited in the number of items it can hold. By this account, subjects may actively rehearse items to try to remember them, but can only rehearse a few items at a time. When the early part of the list is being encoded, items may be added without bumping out other items, because the short-term memory limit has not been exceeded. Thus, items very early in the list generally will be retained longer in short-term memory, leading to more rehearsal and better long-term memory for these items. This robust finding is one illustration of how people may actively process material and how it may affect their memory for the material. We now consider more complex cases of how information is encoded and retrieved, as well as the important relationship between the two processes.

Encoding

Everyone understands that what activities we engage in when an event occurs affect the probability that the event will be remembered. For example, quickly reading a section of text (such as this one) while thinking about some personal problem will lead to far worse memory for the text than if you had concentrated and written a summary of the text after reading it. In this section we consider four of these **encoding** effects: levels of processing, memory for meaning, organization, and elaboration.

Levels of Processing.   Craik and Lockhart (1972) proposed that an item could be processed in a number of different ways and the resulting memory depended on how the item was processed. This approach, referred to as **levels of processing** or sometimes *depth of processing*, argued that we should be focusing not only on the material being learned, but on the way in which the person is encoding such information. They further argued that these different processings could be viewed as a continuum that ranges from the shallow analysis of physical characteristics of the item to the deeper level of meaning. These differences in encoding processes are crucial because they can have large effects on what is remembered.

As one example, Craik and Tulving (1975) presented subjects with a list of 60 concrete nouns about which the subjects had to answer one of three questions (see Table 7.1 for examples). The questions required subjects to examine the *case* (capital vs. lowercase) in which the word was typed, the sound of the word for a *rhyme*, or the meaning of the word to see if it fit in a *sentence*. These questions were chosen to induce increasingly deeper levels of processing by the Craik and Lockhart account. The

Table 7.1   **Study Conditions for a Levels-of-Processing Experiment***

Condition	Question	Response Yes	No
Case	Is the word in capital letters?	TABLE	table
Rhyme	Does the word rhyme with weight?	crate	market
Sentence	Would the word fit the sentence: "He met a ———— in the street"?	friend	cloud

*Typical questions and words presented. Subjects would see one of the two possible words (e.g., crate or market) and then be tested on their memory for the words that had been presented. Adapted from Craik and Tulving, 1975.

questions were presented auditorily and were followed two seconds later by a brief (200 msec) presentation of the word. Following this question-answering procedure, subjects were given 180 words and asked to check off the words they had been asked questions about. The results are quite straightforward. The probability of recognizing a word increased substantially from the case condition (17%), to the rhyme condition (37%), to the sentence condition (65%). Thus, even though the word was presented for only a short time and the encoding manipulation was simple, there was a large difference in recognition.

The Craik and Tulving study used an **incidental learning** procedure in that the subjects were not aware that they would be required to remember the words for a later test. Does this levels analysis make the correct predictions even when subjects know about the later test? The answer is yes. As one example, Hyde and Jenkins (1969) presented words to subjects and asked them either to indicate the number of letters in the word (a low level of processing) or to rate the pleasantness of the items (requiring a deeper analysis of meaning). The subjects were then given a surprise free recall test. As in the Craik and Tulving study, the deeper analysis group (pleasantness) remembered substantially more, 68% vs. 39%. In addition, two other groups were tested with the same tasks, but were told there would be a final recall test. These groups showed almost exactly the same difference as the groups not told about the final recall test (69% vs. 43%).

Knowledge about a final test appears to have little effect on memory, whereas the level to which the material is processed has a large effect.

Although many studies showed effects of processing on memory, the levels of processing approach was criticized by a number of researchers (e.g., Baddeley, 1978). One criticism is that the idea of different levels of processing was based on intuition and no independent measure of depth was provided. Thus, the interpretations of experiments had a circularity—those types of processing that led to better memory were deeper and deeper processing led to better memory. A second criticism, which we will discuss in detail shortly, is that what is better remembered often depends on how the memory is tested. Despite these criticisms, however, we believe that the levels of processing framework helped to focus researchers on the important question of how the processing of material affects memory for it.

Memory for Meaning.   We have been considering how people may remember an unrelated set of words, but such remembering is rarely the case in our real-world uses of memory. We often do not need to remember a precise set of words, but rather their meaning.

The extent to which the goal of understanding affects what is remembered can be understood by the errors people make when tested for their memory of meaningful material. One type of error occurs because the act of comprehending sentences often includes plausible inferences and the results of these inferences may be indistinguishable in memory from information actually given. For example, if a few minutes after you read the sentence "Three turtles rested on a floating log and a fish swam beneath it" you are asked whether you had read that the fish swam under the turtles, you are very likely to say yes. In fact, Bransford, Barclay, and Franks (1972) showed that when people were tested for exactly what they had read they were generally unable to distinguish between the literal information and natural inferences based on the information. On the other hand, the subjects detected even small changes in sentences when these altered the meaning. For example, if subjects saw the sentence above substituting "beside" for "on," they would not have difficulty saying that they had not seen a sentence about a fish swimming under the turtles.

Organization.   So far we have focused on memory for single items or events. Often, however, our encoding of and memory for an item depends critically on other items that are present. In particular, if the items can be *organized* in some way, performance often increases.

An experiment by Bower, Clark, Lesgold, and Winzenz (1969) shows that organization improves memory. They presented groups of about 28 items either organized by their category (e.g., rare metals such as silver and gold; common metals such as lead and iron, etc.) or in a random order (the presentation was in terms of a hierarchy, but this is not of importance here). They found that the grouped presentation led to much better performance. On the first trial, the average proportions recalled for the grouped and random conditions were .65 and .18, respectively. The grouped condition recalled .95 of the words on the second trial and all the words on the third and fourth trials. The performance of the random condition also improved with trials, but by the fourth trial recall was .63, less than the grouped condition's performance on the *first* trial. Clearly, organization of the information at encoding can greatly improve memory performance. (Halpern, 1986 presents an interesting similar experiment involving memory for song titles with the organization by genre, such as Christmas songs.)

Elaborations.   Often when we are presented with some information we not only encode its meaning, but we elaborate or explain it. For example, on seeing someone at a door opening an umbrella, we may make a simple elaboration that the person is doing so because they are about to go out, it is raining, and they do not want to get wet. These elaborations provide a means of integrating and retaining information to the extent that they help relate the current information to our knowledge.

The effect of such relevant elaborations is nicely illustrated in a study by Stein and Bransford (1979). Ten sentences were presented that had a simple idea (e.g., "The fat man read the sign"), an irrelevant elaboration (e.g., "The fat man read the sign that was two feet high"), or a relevant elaboration (e.g., "The fat man read the sign warning about thin ice"). After a short delay, subjects were given the simple idea sentences with the adjective (e.g., "fat") blanked out and asked to fill in the appropriate adjective. The adjective was recalled 42% of the time by subjects who had read the simple sentences, but 74% of the time by subjects who had read the sentences with relevant elaborations. Therefore, elaborations that help to integrate the materials with prior knowledge facilitate memory for the materials. (Also of interest, the subjects who read the irrelevant elaborations recalled the adjective only 22% of the time, a reliable decrease from the simple sentence condition.)

These elaborations can be viewed as helping to interpret the information. That is, we take the incomplete information presented and interpret it by adding further information from our memory. Thus, prior knowledge may greatly influence what we remember (also see Reder, 1979 for the role of elaborations in memory for prose).

Retrieval

Let us now assume that you have encoded information and want to re-member it. Suppose you had just taken a vacation and someone asked you what you had done. How would you retrieve the various memories for the vacation? One possibility would be to start thinking about the vacation and tell the person about whatever events "pop" into your head. The problem with this approach is that less accessible events may not come to mind. Depending on what events are remembered, it is possible that an entire part of your vacation will not be recalled. A very different means of describ-ing the vacation events would be to think about your vacation in chrono-logical order and recall events in the order that they occurred. Although such an approach does not guarantee that all events will be remembered, it will often increase the number of events recalled.

As an experiment, time someone to see how many animals he or she can name in one minute. Then give them a minute to name states as fast as they can think of them. Although there are many more animals than there are states, chances are very good that the person will name more states than animals in the minute. It is easy to generate states rapidly be-cause one can use a natural retrieval plan based on geographic location (e.g., Washington, Oregon, California, etc.). Of course, there are many ways of organizing the generation of animal names (e.g., farm animals, zoo animals), but they do not provide for a systematic order of recall and one often finds that names already recalled come to mind again. One person who was able to generate a large number of animal names in a minute imagined himself walking through a particular zoo and recalled the ani-mals in each area as he (mentally) passed by.

In both of these examples, recall is much higher if the person has a **retrieval plan**—an organized set of cues to use in helping to retrieve the information. One of the main difficulties in recalling information concerns developing an organized plan for retrieval. The plan needs to have two main characteristics. First, the various cues in the plan should be organized so that no cue is likely to be forgotten. In the states example, if you remem-bered the states by regions, you would be better off using adjacent regions such as Northeast, then Middle Atlantic, rather than jumping from Pacific Northwest to Southeast. Second, each cue in the plan should be able to lead to the recall of a number of items not recallable from other cues and also do so in as systematic a way as possible (so items are not recalled more than once or missed altogether). With an appropriate retrieval plan, the organized cues will guide retrieval and lead to more items being recalled.

Encoding-Retrieval Interactions

We have been considering how encoding and retrieval may affect memory for events. However, the picture is more complicated than that. It is useful to consider an analogy between human memory and a library. The remarkable fact about a large library is that one is normally able to obtain quickly almost any one of the millions of volumes stored in the stacks. The secret of this capability lies in the organization and retrieval systems. Books can usually be found regardless of the number of books stored because they are coded; books having the same codes are shelved together; and the codes are related to "pointers" filed in the card catalog. It is crucial that the same cues used for encoding information also be used for retrieving that information. One cannot get rapid access to a book if all one knows is that it has a green cover and was written by a person whose middle initial is E. Memory works in a similar way.

A major principle of memory is that recall or recognition of an event usually increases with the amount of the original context that is supplied at the time when retention is tested. If one thinks of a primary use of memory as retrieving relevant information, then the retrieval of information in a similar context to the current situation (as opposed to a different context) is a good guess as to its relevance.

This importance of context is nicely illustrated in the difference between recognition and recall. Recognition is generally believed to be easier and more accurate than recall. One reason is that the individual being tested is presented with more of the context of the original experience than would be the case on a recall test. Thus, if a student has read in a text assignment that John B. Watson was the founder of behaviorism and we wanted to test the student's knowledge of this fact, we might present the statement "The founder of behaviorism was John B. Watson" and ask the student to respond "true" or "false." Because nearly all of the elements that the individual was attending to at the time of the original learning are supplied as part of the test, conditions are optimal for retrieving the relevant long-term memory. We might, on the other hand, ask "Who founded behaviorism?" In that case part of the original context is missing and conditions are less favorable for reactivating the relevant memory.

Encoding Specificity.   How can we be sure that this difference between recognition and recall reflects encoding-retrieval matching of context rather than simply the fact that recognition is easier than recall? The answer is quite simple: because it is possible to find situations in which recognition is worse than recall and these situations occur when the match between encoding and retrieval contexts is greater for recall than for recognition.

Much of the work in this area is due to the efforts of Endel Tulving and his colleagues. The methodology and ideas are quite complicated, so we start here with a simpler situation (based on a study by Light & Carter-Sobell, 1970). Suppose you were given a list of word pairs (e.g., river bank) and asked to remember the second word of each pair. Later you might be given one of two tests. In the recognition test, you would be given a word pair (e.g., piggy bank) and asked if you remember having seen the second word on the original list. In the cued recall test, you would be given a cue (e.g., river) and asked to recall a word from the original list that it had been paired with. On which test do you think you would do better? In fact, performance is usually higher on the cued recall test.

Clearly, the difficulty in the recognition test is that the word "bank" has two very different meanings. Even though you are being asked to recognize the word you saw before, if you encode it very differently (i.e., with a different meaning) you may be unable to remember having seen it earlier. The cued recall task, on the other hand, asks you to recall a word consistent with the meaning you encoded earlier. Thus, recognition may be harder than recall, because the encoding is not consistent with recognition, but it is consistent with recall.

Tulving and his associates have conducted a large number of studies that show the same **encoding specificity effect** (i.e., that retrieval depends on matching the specific encoding), where the differences between the encodings are much more subtle. For example, the word "light" can be thought of as having a number of related meanings such as "a bulb" and "not dark." Tulving showed that a biasing of the sense used in encoding and retrieval would allow recognition to be worse than recall, analogous to the finding with different meanings of "bank."

Consider the example illustrated in Table 7.2 (in fact, the experiment [Tulving & Thomson, 1973, ex. 2] was quite a bit more complex than illustrated). For the 24 critical items, subjects were shown the target word (e.g., "LIGHT") in capital letters and a weakly associated word (e.g., "head") in lowercase letters. Subjects were instructed that their task was to learn the words in capital letters but they might find it useful to use the words in lowercase letters. Following this study task, subjects participated in a free association task that included generating six words to a strong

Table 7.2   **Phases of an Encoding Specificity Experiment***

1. Study list: Learn target words in capital letters.

Cue	Target
head	LIGHT
grasp	BABY

.
.
.

2. Free association: Generate 6 words to each word presented.

Word	Possible generated responses
dark	light, black, room, . . .

.
.
.

| infant | sleeping, bottle, baby, . . . |

.
.
.

3. Recognition: Mark any generated words that were on the study list in capital letters.

4. Recall: Recall the words from the study list in capital letters, using these cues that they were studied with.

grasp _____

.
.
.

head _____

.
.
.

*Based on information from Tulving and Thomson, 1973.

associate of each target word. For example, the word "dark" may have been given for which a large proportion of subjects generated the word "light" (the target) as one of the six words. Subsequently, subjects were asked to look over the words that they had generated and mark any that had been target words in the first part of the experiment (i.e., a recognition test). Finally, they were given a cued recall test in which the word studied with the target word was provided (e.g., head) and were asked to generate the target word studied with this word. Therefore, when checking off the free associates that had been target words, the exact target word was provided and subjects needed only to decide if it had been in the first part of the experiment (a recognition test). In the final cued recall task, the subjects needed to generate the target word given the word with which it had been studied. If recognition is easier than recall, one would expect higher performance in marking words which were old than in generating old words from the cues. However, contrary to this expectation, only 22% of the generated targets were recognized, while 59% of the targets were recalled when cued by the word with which they had been studied (e.g., recall of "LIGHT" when cued by "head"). Thus, the context in the cued recall test matched the study encoding better than did the context of the recognition test and performance was higher in the cued recall test. The match between encoding and retrieval context is crucial for understanding how well items are remembered—the encoding specificity effect.

Encoding-retrieval interactions are powerful enough to override some other types of memory effects. Remember that in our discussion of encoding effects we described a study by Craik and Tulving that showed semantic processing of words led to better memory than did processing for a rhyme (Table 7.1). Fisher and Craik (1977) argue that the better memory for semantic processing may be because when no retrieval cue is specified, people are likely to use semantic cues. They conducted a study in which some of the cues were rhymes. In this case, memory for words learned under the rhyming condition were recalled better than words learned with the sentence encoding condition (40% to 29%). This result does not negate the importance of encoding condition. In fact, even in the Fisher and Craik study the sentence condition led to substantially higher overall recall than did the rhyming condition. Nonetheless, it does show that the encoding-retrieval interactions can be quite strong and are important to an understanding of memory.

Context Change.   The work just discussed shows that memory for an item is affected by the match of encodings at learning and retrieval. Other research has examined how less integrated aspects of the learning and retrieval context may affect memory. This work has distinguished between two types of **context** cues, external cues such as the physical environment and internal cues such as body states. Each research area has yielded some evidence for the importance of context in remembering.

The research on environmental context shows that being in the same physical setting for the learning and testing of new material benefits recall. The most dramatic example of this idea is the research of Godden and Baddeley (1975). They had scuba divers learn lists of words either on land or about 20 feet underwater and then tested them in one or the other setting. The recall was almost 50% better if the test occurred at the same setting as the learning. Less dramatically, Steven Smith (Smith, 1979, 1986; Smith, Glenberg, & Bjork, 1978) has shown that recall is facilitated if the test occurs in the same room as the learning.

How might internal cues affect memory? At one extreme one may observe **state-dependent recall**. For example, a person who has too much to drink one night may have little memory for the evening's events the next day. Nonetheless, this memory failure is not permanent and the individual may well recover this memory the next time he or she drinks too much.

Besides anecdotal reports, much research has examined the effects of internal cues such as drugs or mood. Gordon Bower (described in Bower, 1981) conducted a number of studies (see Eich, 1980 for a review) on the effects of mood on memory, showing that people sometimes recalled more if they were in the same mood as when they learned the lists. (These moods were induced in the subjects either through hypnosis or some other induction procedure.)

Thus, a number of experimental results show the effects of external and internal context on memory. Unfortunately, these results do not replicate consistently (Eich & Metcalfe, 1989; Fernandez & Glenberg, 1985), suggesting that our understanding of context is incomplete. This difficulty should not obscure the fact that context can have large influences on memory nor the consensus that an understanding of context is necessary for understanding memory. Memory is very sensitive to the subtle changes of how an item is encoded and retrieved.

Spacing Effect.   Although the encoding specificity and context change experiments may appear to be contrived situations, the importance of matching conditions between study and test is evident in many situations. We present one illustration here that also allows us to discuss an interesting empirical finding, the **spacing effect**.

The spacing effect refers to the common observation that memory is better for repeated information if the repetitions occur spaced over time than if they occur massed, one after the other. This effect is remarkably robust, being found with a variety of materials, study conditions, types of tests, and in many situations outside the laboratory (see, e.g., Glenberg, 1976; Hintzman, 1976; Smith & Rothkopf, 1984). As one example, an early study by Melton and Shulman (cited in Melton, 1970) involved presenting subjects with lists of 48 words, 24 of which appeared twice in the list. The twice-presented items were repeated after either 0, 2, 4, 8, 20, or 40 intervening items. Different groups of subjects were shown the items at different rates of presentation before a free recall test. The data are presented in Figure 7.4. As the number of events between repetitions increased, the probability of recall increased.

What causes this spacing effect? Recent evidence suggests that it may depend on several different factors (see, e.g., Glenberg, 1979; Greene, 1989). One cause particularly relevant here is the effect of varying encodings and context. Suppose you are presented with a list of words to remember. When repetitions occur, the further apart they are the more likely you will encode the word differently (you can imagine what would happen with multiple meaning words such as bank, but as we saw with encoding specificity, even single meaning word encodings change). A number of studies have shown that experimentally manipulating the encoding of items changes the spacing effect. For example, Madigan (1969) manipulated encodings by a technique similar to that used in encoding specificity

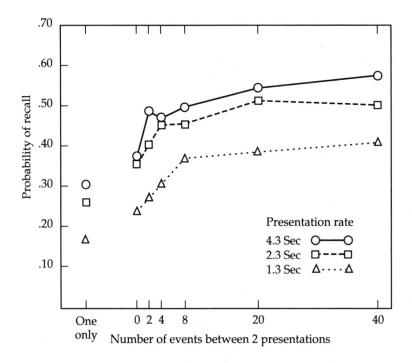

Figure 7.4   **Illustration of the Spacing Effect.**
The figure shows the probability of recalling words occurring once or twice with varying number of other words between the two presentations. The three curves each represent data for different rates of visual presentation of the words. From data of Melton and Shulman. *Source*: Melton, A. W., 1970.

(i.e., presenting the critical word with another word next to it to influence its encoding). He found that (a) different encodings led to better recall and (b) that the effect of the different encodings was larger on the massed items, which would usually be encoded in the same way otherwise.

Some recent work suggests that the spacing effect may depend importantly on the repetition reminding the learner of the earlier presentation (see, e.g., Bellezza & Young, 1989). By this account, the learner then stores some information about the changes in the encoding and context from the prior presentation. At some later test, this reminding may provide additional information that might be retrieved and used in remembering that the particular word was presented. A finding consistent with this interpretation is that spacing effects only occur for items recognized on the second presentation (Bellezza, Winkler, & Andrasik, 1975). Whatever the future evidence about this particular explanation, the variations in the spaced presentations appear to be an important component of the spacing effect. Because the changes in encoding and context will be greater with greater spacing, spaced presentations will tend to be better remembered than massed presentations (Greene, 1989).

The spacing effect is not due simply to the encodings, however; it also depends critically on the retrieval conditions. As one simple example, Glenberg (1976) finds that long spacings lead to worse memory than shorter spacings at short retention intervals. At short retention intervals the test context is more similar to the learning context than at long intervals. Thus, the spacing effect depends on the change in encoding and context between presentations, as well as their relationship to the retrieval context.

Forgetting

Every student has had the experience of studying a lesson but being unable to remember some of the material at the time of a later test. We all have had experiences in which we know the answer to a question but the answer seems to have temporarily "slipped our minds."

Two main theoretical questions come to mind concerning these common incidents. First, what has happened to the missing items—that is, have they been erased from memory or are they still there? Second, what caused the forgetting?

Is Memory Erased?   Current thinking concerning the nature of forgetting is that once entered in long-term memory, items are not lost but under some circumstances become temporarily or perhaps permanently irretrievable. Although a controversy exists about whether information may be lost or overwritten by later experiences, in many cases information that appeared to be lost can be shown to be retrievable. (See Loftus & Loftus, 1980 and Zaragoza & McCloskey, 1989 for part of this controversy.)

One of the observations suggesting that "forgotten" information may not be lost is fascinating, although not very convincing. In the course of some neurosurgery, various parts of the brain are stimulated, in part to ensure that areas serving vital functions will not be destroyed. Brain surgery often requires only local anesthetics, so patients are conscious during these surgeries. A number of reports are available in which these patients offer a "long forgotten" memory in response to a particular stimulation. For instance, in response to an electrode in the temporal lobe, one patient mentioned, "There was a piano over there and someone playing. I could hear the song you know" (Penfield, 1959, p. 172). These reports suggest that forgotten memories may not be lost, but it is important to note that these reports are rare and the memories cannot be verified.

The difficulty with assessing whether real-life events that cannot be remembered are truly lost has led to studies of forgetting in laboratory experiments. These studies ask whether information that seems to be forgotten might be retrievable using other cues or under other circumstances. Although the question of whether memory is permanent probably cannot be given a definite answer, research does show that retrieval failure cannot be equated with loss from memory.

One of the many kinds of experiments leading to the idea that memory is permanent has to do with the possibility of intentional forgetting. When we are dealing with a mechanical or electromagnetic memory, as in the case of a tape recorder, we know that we can erase items from the memory of the device just as easily as we can enter them, but we don't seem similarly able to erase material from our own memories at will. Some researchers have investigated the problem of **intentional forgetting** with special experiments (see, e.g., Bjork, 1972). For instance, subjects were shown a number of lists of items to remember, but on some trials, partway through the list a signal would appear informing the subjects that they should try to forget everything preceding this signal. The results showed that whether the items to be forgotten were forgotten or remembered depended on the measure. The items preceding the "forget" signal proved not to take up short-term memory capacity—the items following the signal were remembered as well as if they had been presented alone. Also, if the subjects were later given an unexpected recall test for the full list, they proved unlikely to remember any of the items preceding a "forget" signal. If, however, the subjects were given a recognition test they were perfectly able to recognize the "forget" items as belonging to the list. From the capacity and recall results, we would have believed that the items preceding the "forget" signal were lost from memory storage. However, from the recognition test it is clear that these items were not lost.

Sometimes when it appears that forgetting is complete, other more indirect and more sensitive measures may reveal a residual memory influence. For example, even unrecognized information from an earlier learning session will sometimes show a **savings in relearning**. Nelson, Fehling, and Moore-Glascock (1979) presented subjects with a series of digit-word pairs such as 27-hates. A month later subjects were tested on their memory for these pairs. For pairs that were not remembered, the digits and words were presented again, either with the original pairing or switched (i.e., the digits were paired with different words). Despite the fact that the subjects had been unable to recognize the original pairing, pairs that were presented again were learned better, with performance of 57% correct as opposed to 22% for the switched pairs. If the earlier memory was truly lost, such savings would not occur.

Burtt (1941) provides another example of this savings. In this study, conducted during the 1920s and 1930s, Greek passages were read to a toddler aged 15 months. Three short passages were read once a day for three months, then another three passages were read once a day for three months, and so on, until the child was three years old. He was then tested at ages 8½, 14, and 18 years. For these tests, Burtt measured the time it took the child to learn new passages versus these old passages (one-third of the old passages were tested at each test age). The old passages were learned considerably faster than were the new ones for the first test at 8½, somewhat faster at 14, and only a little bit faster at 18. The details of the materials and statistics are not provided (a not uncommon occurrence in some older articles), so we should perhaps be a little skeptical of this particular finding. However, savings in relearning is a very sensitive measure that often supports the idea that some observed forgetting may not be due to the memory being lost permanently. Overall, the evidence favors the idea that memories are not lost, but that forgetting is instead due to retrieval difficulty.

Causes of Forgetting. One of the earliest hypotheses about the causes of forgetting was the "law of disuse," according to which items that are not recalled or studied for a period of time tend to lose strength in memory as a result of an automatic process of decay. Anecdotally, if you have not thought of an event for awhile, it often seems that the longer this period has been the less likely you are to be able to remember the event. In the laboratory, the evidence for this forgetting with time is very easy to demonstrate and quite robust, going back to the earliest systematic study of memory (Ebbinghaus, 1885). No one argues that memory does not get worse with delay; the question is whether this decrement in performance reflects the effect of decay or some other cause.

It has been very difficult to find support for the **memory decay hypothesis** because in real life any period of time during which decay for memory might be occurring is filled with activities that might in themselves influence the course of forgetting. A famous experiment by Jenkins and Dallenbach (1924) pointed up the possible importance of other activities. These researchers had two intensively studied subjects learn lists of items and then measured retention after varying numbers of hours of sleep and compared their results with retention after similar periods of ordinary waking activity. The rate of forgetting was much greater when the subjects were awake than when they were asleep.

The slower forgetting during sleep is not a very encouraging result from the standpoint of the theory that disuse leads to decay. However, this experiment by itself cannot lead to a decision about the hypothesis one way or another. Conceivably, differences in an individual's rate of metabolism in the sleeping and waking states might have something to do with the rate of decay from memory. An alternative to decay is that an individual who is awake is likely to encounter new material similar in some respects to the items being retained, thus generating some kind of interference with memory retrieval. This latter possibility seemed more likely to earlier experimental psychologists and led to the development of an experimental scheme termed the **retroactive interference** paradigm that was designed to check more decisively on the role of interference.

As this type of experiment is typically conducted, one group of subjects learns certain material such as a list of vocabulary words—call it List A—and then after an interval is tested for recall. A second group of subjects learns List A, then learns a different List B, and then after the same interval is tested for recall of List A. The experimental design, then, takes the form:

Group	Original Learning	Interpolated Learning	Test
Experimental	List A	List B	List A
Control	List A	Rest	List A

The typical finding is that recall of List A is poorer for the experimental than for the control group.

Somewhat surprisingly, however, it also proves to be the case that earlier learning may interfere with memory for related material learned later. The process is termed **proactive interference**, as was used in the release from PI studies discussed earlier. It is easy to see how to design the experiment to bring out the effect.

Group	Prior Learning	Learning	Test
Experimental	List B	List A	List A
Control	None	List A	List A

Again it is characteristically found that recall of List A is poorer for the experimental than for the control group.

At first thought it may seem strange that forgetting of material can be influenced by learning that went on earlier. At least a partial explanation of these interference effects is that the more items a cue is stored with, the less effective it is in retrieving any *particular* item (see, e.g., Watkins, 1975). For example, suppose that you are trying to remember what you ate for dinner two months ago when you had dinner with a friend. If this was your only dinner with this friend, the friend is a useful part of the retrieval cue. But if you have dinner with this friend a couple of times a week, then all the dinners the friend has had with you make it much harder to retrieve the particular dinner being queried. The experimental group has more items learned with the context "cue" so performance is lower.

Separate Short- and Long-Term Memories?

Now that we have discussed long-term memory, how is it related to short-term memory? Early conceptions of short-term memory assumed that it was a separate buffer from the long-term memory. At the time such a division seemed quite reasonable: short-term memory involved acoustic codes and forgetting by decay, while long-term memory involved semantic codes and forgetting by interference. However, it is now clear that short-term memory can use semantic codes and that much (all?) of the forgetting is by interference.

If there is no strong evidence for two separate memories, what is the difference between short-term and long-term memory? A number of contemporary theories (see, e.g., Anderson, 1983) view short-term memory as the temporarily activated (i.e., more readily available) portion of long-term memory. That is, under these views, short-term memory is not a separate buffer but is a transient portion of long-term memory, which changes as we think of new concepts. Although these two views are quite different, it is difficult to distinguish them with empirical tests. First, many of the characteristics of short-term memory can be handled by either view. Second, even when one considers predictions on which these views should differ, any particular empirical test may involve additional processes as well, making the predictions less clear-cut. For example, the separate buffer alternative would predict that short-term memory would not reflect the various ways these items are related to other items in more permanent memory (i.e., because the short-term memory items are in a separate buffer). In designing an experiment, however, one must keep in mind that the separate buffer view would allow short-term memory contents to be transferred to long-term memory (and vice versa), so effects of other items may occur during these transfers. Although it is an important issue, there is no consensus about whether to view these short-term memory effects as arising from a separate buffer or the activated portion of long-term memory.

Models of Memory for New Information

General Approach

In this section we examine some models of memory aimed at explaining the basic memory effects just reviewed. Memory models consist of hypotheses about the structure of memory and the processes that operate on this structure. Presumably it will ultimately be discovered that information that enters memory is encoded somehow in entities within the brain. But for the present we know little about bases of particular memories in the brain. When we speak of *structure* we mean that we are trying to form a picture of the way in which the contents of memory are organized. The memory structure is the person's internal representation. The memory *processes* specify how the structure is used to store and retrieve information. The development of models can help us to understand the ways in which information is stored, organized, and retrieved in the normal and impaired functioning of memory. In this section we begin with some simple models and progress to a more complex model.

Simple Association Models

Consider the sketch of three successive types of association models of memory structure illustrated in Figure 7.5. All three models represent attempts to understand what happens when an individual is presented with a list of words such as the input list at the left (hat, star, dog, . . .) and is expected to recall the words after an interval of time. In the earliest form of association theory, the *chain association* model, it was conceived that the successive items of the list are linked together by single associations or connections, hat with star, star with dog, and so on. In this scheme the first word is associated with a symbol for the list and at the time of recall that symbol is brought to mind by the instruction to try to remember the words, leading to recall of hat, which in turn leads to recall of star, and so on. However, the model predicts that if in the course of recalling the list people failed to remember some item, say the word dog, then they would be unable to remember any of the items that followed. This implication has been shown to be false by many experiments.

The next level of complexity is the *multiple association* model illustrated in the middle of Figure 7.5. Here it is assumed that each of the words of the list is associated with a common list symbol. This model does not

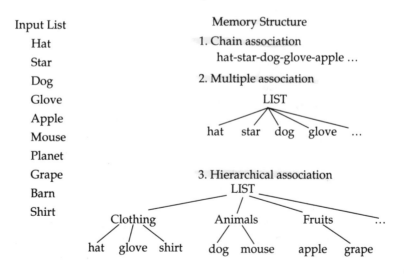

Input List	Memory Structure
Hat	1. Chain association
Star	hat-star-dog-glove-apple …
Dog	2. Multiple association
Glove	
Apple	
Mouse	
Planet	
Grape	3. Hierarchical association
Barn	
Shirt	

Figure 7.5   Three alternative association models for the memory structure underlying free recall of the list of words shown at the left. *Source:* Estes, W. K. (1976). Structural aspects of associative models for memory.

run into the same problem as the first one if the individual omits a word during recall. Still, there is no way to predict from this model that words with similar meanings would tend to be grouped together during recall, which is an important property of performance in this task. This last fact, however, can be accommodated by the third try, the *hierarchical association* model illustrated at the bottom. Here the individual words of the list are associated with category names (clothing, animals, fruit) and these in turn are associated with the list symbol. Now when the individual thinks of the list symbol at the time of recall he or she is likely to remember one of the category labels, which in turn leads to recall of the members of the category that appeared on the list, then another category label and so on. This hierarchical association is one means of limiting complexity and will lead to the clustering by semantic categories that often occurs in these situations. It is also consistent with many of the results on organization discussed earlier.

The above associative models assume that the connection between items, the association, is simple with no real meaning attached to it. These associations capture the powerful intuition that when we are thinking of one idea we may be very likely to think of a particular other idea (e.g., black may lead to white). Although these simple associative models have difficulty in accounting for some of the complexities of human memory, such as people's ability to deal with embedded sentences (e.g., see Anderson & Bower, 1973, Chapter 2), they have led to the development of more sophisticated models, such as the SAM model to be described next.

The SAM Model

Introduction.   The Search of Associative Memory (**SAM**) Model has been developed by Richard Shiffrin and his colleagues (Raaijmakers & Shiffrin, 1981; Gillund & Shiffrin, 1984) to account for a large number of different memory effects. The model begins with some basic assumptions that build on the results we have been discussing. First, short-term memory is viewed as a limited buffer that (a) is used to access knowledge from long-term memory and (b) affects what information is stored in long-term memory. Second, long-term memory is assumed to consist of a large set of interconnected concepts. Third, memory retrieval is assumed to be cue-dependent, meaning that what is retrieved depends on the cue used to probe the memory. Fourth, memory is assumed to be nonerasable, with forgetting due to retrieval failure. Fifth, context is considered to be a crucial determinant of memory retrieval. These general assumptions are not a model, but rather provide some guiding principles for construction of a model. Although the SAM model is far more complicated than the simple associative models, it is able to account for a much greater number of memory effects.

Description of the Model.   Memory is assumed to consist of a large number of interconnected feature sets called *images*. These images contain information about (a) the context in which the learning occurred, (b) the item, such as its meaning, name, etc., and (c) the relation to other images. To remember something, a person is assumed to gather a set of cues or probes in short-term memory and use them to activate associated images in long-term memory. This probe results in various images being activated to varying degrees as a function of their connections to the probe.

With this overview, we now go into a little more detail. The images are assumed, as in many explanations, to be encoded from short-term memory. In particular, short-term memory is assumed to be a limited buffer (e.g., four items). Suppose a person is given a list of words to learn, such as the list given in Figure 7.5 (hat, star, dog, glove, apple, . . .). The first few words are retained in short-term memory until its capacity is reached. After this, new items put into short-term memory bump one of the old items out. For example, with a buffer of four items capacity will not be reached until the word apple is read, meaning that hat will have been retained for three additional items, star for two, and so on. When apple enters the buffer one of the items, say dog, will be bumped out. After reading the list, the person will have a set of interconnected images in long-term memory. Those items that were retained for a long time in short-term memory (e.g., hat) will be strongly connected to the study context. In addition, any pairs of items that were retained together in short-term memory will have strong interimage strengths (e.g., hat star). Thus, the longer an item is retained in short-term memory, the greater its association to the study context (and some images) and the more images to which it is associated.

The probes will activate these images as a function of (1) these context-image and interimage strengths and (2) the match between the probe and image (i.e., how similar they are). Thus, activation will be a function of how strongly associated the image is to the study context and other learned images, as well as how similar it is to the probe. Finishing our example, if star is the probe item it will lead to much activation for its image and also for the image of hat (as well as for other items it co-resided with in the buffer).

To understand how the activated image is used it is necessary to consider the task. In recognition, the implied question is "Did you see this word in this list?" so the probe consists of the context and the item being asked about (e.g., star). This probe activates all the images that are strongly connected to *both* the context and the item. In recognizing whether you saw the word star in the list, you want to know whether an image of the concept star is strongly associated to the context, not just whether there is a strong image of star. In addition, other images may be activated if they were learned in this list (so had strong context connections) and have strong interimage connections because of being in short-term memory with the probed item. Although the details are complex, the main point is that recognition is assumed to be based on the overall activation, which the researchers call *familiarity*. The more a probe activates all the images, the more likely it is for the person to say he or she recognizes the probe item was on the study list.

A depiction of the necessary processes for recall is given in Figure 7.6. It is assumed that the recall uses the context or context plus some previously recalled item as the probe to "search" the long-term memory for relevant images (i.e., items studied on the list). The search includes two stages, *sampling* and *recovery*. There are many possible relevant images. Sampling is the selection of an image. Once an image is chosen for retrieval, it does not mean that the relevant information can be figured out or retrieved. Recovery is the process of getting the information. As an analogy, we return to the library example. Suppose you want some information but you are not sure where it is likely to be. You might come up with a set of keywords or indexes and then use the card catalog. If each keyword led to a large number of choices, a reasonable strategy would be to choose those books that were found with many of the different keywords. Once you choose a book, however, it does not mean that you have the information you want. Rather, it means that you have some probability of being able to find the desired information. Presumably, by choosing a book related to many keywords, your chances are much better than if you had randomly chosen a book. Sampling is analogous to finding the book and recovery is analogous to finding the desired information in that book.

SAM Model Account of Effects. The reason for providing this description of the SAM model is to show how it is able to accommodate a large number of memory effects. In this section we illustrate how it accounts for a few important findings presented in this chapter.

First, primacy effects are accounted for by the short-term memory assumptions. As a reminder, primacy effects refer to the finding that the early words in a list are better remembered than the middle items in the list. By the SAM account (and similar to some other explanations that have been offered) the probability of recall is a function of context-to-image

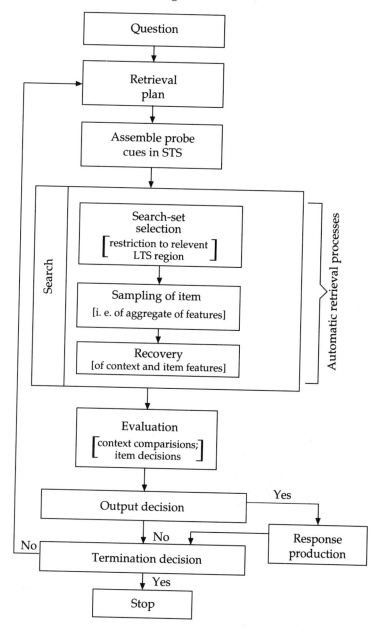

Retrieval From Long-Term Store

Figure 7.6   A sketch of the retrieval processes used in the SAM model for recall. STS = short-term store; LTS = long-term store. *Source*: Raaijmakers, J. G., & Shiffrin, R. M., 1981.

strength and interimage strength. The first few items on a list have an advantage in that they are retained in the buffer until its capacity is reached. Thus, if we assume a four-item buffer, the first item will be retained at least until the fifth item is read. It then has a 3/4 chance of being retained until the sixth item, a 9/16 (i.e., 3/4 × 3/4) chance of being retained until the seventh item, and so on. However, an item from the middle of the list immediately has the chance of being bumped by a new item (because the buffer is already full). Therefore, on the average the early items have more time in short-term memory, leading to greater context-to-image strengths and interimage strengths. Although the SAM account is similar to other accounts of the primacy effect, it is important to note that the short-term memory assumptions are also being used in other ways to help account for a number of other effects.

Second, encoding specificity effects are accounted for because the remembering requires the image to be associated to all the probe cues. Encoding specificity effects refer to the finding that the retrieval depends on a match between the encoding and retrieval cues. As mentioned earlier, recognition can be worse than recall if the cues in recall match the study cues better than the ones in recognition do. Such a finding is predicted by SAM because the activation of images requires a strong connection to *all* the probes (see the earlier discussion). In recognition, the probe includes contextual cues and the item. Thus, recognition could be hurt by changes in the context from study to test or by changes in the encoding of the item (so the match of the item to its image is hurt).

Third, context effects are accounted for because context is included in all the probes. Again, the retrieval depends on the association of the image to *all* the cues, so a change in context will decrease the activation of the image.

Fourth, interference effects are accounted for because the sampling of images is proportional to total activation. Thus, if an additional image is strongly associated to the probes it will decrease the probability of other images being sampled. Suppose you are interested in the probability of recalling a particular item, given the context as a cue. The more items associated with the context, the less likely the particular item of interest is to be sampled (see, e.g., Watkins, 1975). This interference occurs both for items studied before the item of interest (i.e., proactive interference) and for items studied after (i.e., retroactive interference).

Final Comments.   The SAM model is far more complicated than the simple models with which we began this section, but it accounts for far more results. We believe that the SAM model has two important strengths.

First, it demonstrates that these simple assumptions, when elaborated in clever (but reasonable) ways, can provide detailed quantitative accounts of a variety of memory data. It is difficult to know how best to convey the impressiveness of the model's success, but Figure 7.7 shows an example of how well SAM can fit the data from a memory experiment (Roberts, 1972)

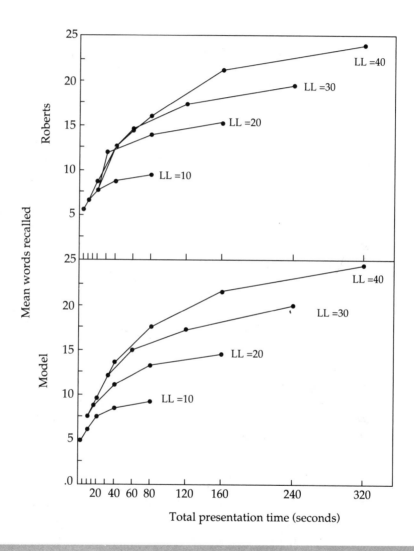

Figure 7.7   Example of a fit of the SAM model to some memory data. The top panel shows data from Roberts (1972) in which the recall was measured as a function of presentation time and list length (LL). The bottom panel shows the fit of the SAM model. *Source*: Raaijmakers, J. G., & Shiffrin, R. M., 1981.

that varied the length of the list and presentation time. As you can see, the fit is quite good.

A second important strength of SAM is that it provides a unified account of a wide variety of memory phenomena. We have only mentioned a few effects that it deals with, but research papers provide a large number of additional results that SAM can model using the same set of assumptions. The use of a single model to account for a wide range of findings has two important consequences. First, because the model needs to account for different results simultaneously, it cannot be tailored for a particular task. That is, if researchers argue that a particular process is used in free recall of word lists, they must also use this process in predicting the results of word lists of different lengths or different relatedness.

Second, the constraints imposed by accounting for various effects with the same general assumptions may lead to surprising explanations. Consider a counter-intuitive finding called the part-list cuing effect. Suppose two people each learned a list of words and were later tested on their recall of those words. One person was given some of the words from the list as cues and the other person was not. Who do you think would recall more uncued words? Contrary to expectations of many people (and researchers), the person given some of the words does not recall more words and sometimes recalls fewer of them. Why? This finding was taken to mean that the associations between items on the list are not being used to great advantage (or else the word cues, by allowing greater use of these associations, would have led to greater recall). However, Raaijmakers and Shiffrin (1981) show that this seemingly reasonable interpretation may well be incorrect. They demonstrate that SAM can account for the part-list cuing effect, but does so by making use of interword associations as well. (The details are complex, but the general idea is that list items are organized into clusters, and if there is no word cue provided for a given cluster, none of its items may be recalled.) The general point is that although it may be easier to construct separate models for each task, a unified model not only forces one to have a framework in which all the models are compatible, but also may lead to unexpected (and testable) explanations of empirical results.

Individual Differences

Introduction

For the most part, research on memory is concerned with processes that are believed to be common to all normal individuals, at least beyond the very earliest stages of development. Given the complexity of the brain and the relatively small range of differences in human memory ability (relative to what one might imagine could be the case), this approach seems a reasonable one. It is also true that we all know people who are particularly good (or bad) at remembering. Perhaps you have had the experience of going with someone to a movie, lecture, or athletic event and find later in discussing this event that the other person's memory for exactly what happened is more (or less) accurate than your own. The question then arises, if we all have essentially the same basic machinery, why do people differ in their abilities to remember? Three common answers might be that (1) some people are more motivated to learn, (2) some people are just better at remembering things, and (3) some people are just more interested in that sort of thing. As in many commonsense answers, there may be some truth to these assertions, but they do not really serve to explain the differences. Although we believe that the commonalities of human memory are much more striking than the differences, an examination of these differences helps to point out some important issues that might not be noticed when thinking about the common aspects.

The growing weight of evidence favors the idea that a great part of the individual differences we see in memory performance is a consequence of the strategies used and differences in prior knowledge. We examine these differences and then discuss some cases of extraordinary memory.

Strategies and Knowledge

Earlier we examined the influences of encoding and retrieval plans on memory. Although many books explain various techniques for improving your memory (e.g., Bellezza, 1982; Lorayne & Lucas, 1974), much can be done with the ideas we have already discussed. The first step toward effective remembering is always carefully attending to the material at the time of original presentation. Then most newly presented items fade quickly into inaccessibility unless one takes the trouble to bring them back into short-term memory for rehearsal so that they can be related to other aspects of the situation in which recall may be needed.

Further, we have noted that effective rehearsal is not simply a matter of rote repetition but rather of noticing potential retrieval cues and integrating these with the items to be remembered. Still more effective is the procedure of forming a retrieval plan—that is, thinking in advance of the situation in which recall may be needed. A talk that is to be given in class or at a dinner meeting would be remembered best if practiced in the classroom or at the table with audiences actually present. That is not ordinarily feasible, but one may provide a substitute by imagining the classroom situation or the dinner meeting and the cues that are likely to be present in that situation while rehearsing the material of the talk. Finally, one should organize the material into higher order units or chunks.

Individual differences in memory are often due to differences in the use of strategies. Why doesn't everyone use the best strategies all the time? Part of the answer is that considerable effort is required to learn and use many of these methods. In addition, in order to learn these strategies, one must be able to monitor how well one is able to remember. Indeed, over the last decade there has been a great deal of attention paid to **metamemory**, that is, people's ability to know how likely they are to be able to remember something or how effective some strategy may be (see Brown, Bransford, Ferrara, & Campione, 1983 for an extensive review and discussion of research on metamemory). Consider a student who studies for an exam by poring over notes and acquiring a good feeling of familiarity for the material. If this feeling of familiarity is used as a measure of preparedness, there is danger that the student will not do well on the test because of failing to take into account the difference between the study conditions (being able to look at notes and readings) and the test conditions. A more effective study technique might be to make up sample test questions (or better yet, to trade sample test questions with another student) and then try to answer them.

Perhaps the largest source of individual differences in memory performance is differences in knowledge in a particular domain. It is much easier to remember something if we have a framework in which to embed that new knowledge. For example, when we (the authors) read a technical journal article in our research areas, we often remember the authors, the year of publication, the journal in which the article was published, and the gist of the findings for a long time. Yet when we read novels, we seldom remember the main characters long enough to finish the book.

There is clear evidence that the ability to acquire new facts about some domain depends a great deal on what one already knows. For example, Spilich, Vesonder, Chiesi, and Voss (1979) found that people who knew more about baseball were much better able to remember descriptions of baseball games. They read a description of a half-inning of baseball to people and later examined their memory. For the 98 game-relevant facts, the people with more baseball knowledge recalled twice as many (24 vs. 12). For the facts that were not relevant to the game, the groups showed no difference in recall. Thus, having prior knowledge allows one to understand (and remember) the relevant information better. Such an effect may not be surprising if you have ever sat through a game of a sport you did not understand well. As discussed in more detail in Chapter 11 on inference, this previous knowledge allows one to interpret new information more easily to make it meaningful, to incorporate it into what one already knows, and to retrieve it easily using prior retrieval schemes.

Extraordinary Memories

There may be upper limits on the amount of information that can be stored in the human memory system, but there is no reason to believe that the limits are ever approached. Rather, we see case after case in which new efforts to improve encoding and retrieval lead to increases in what have seemed to be upper limits for particular situations.

Short-Term Memory Span.   Consider the simple **memory span** test that appears in nearly all intelligence scales and is commonly used by neurologists to check on memory functioning. The examiner simply reads a list of random digits aloud at a rate of about one per second, and at the end of a sequence the person being studied is asked to recall them in order. For normal adults, the average memory span is about seven digits. Thus, if presented with the sequence 3, 2, 9, 4, 6, 7, 1, most students would be able to recall the sequence correctly, but if one additional digit, say 5, were added, many would fail. But if the same individuals thought to group the digits into subgroups of chunks of two or three adjacent elements, say 329 467 15, most would be able to remember eight digits without difficulty. More dramatically, mentally retarded children who ordinarily score very low on the test have been brought up to nearly normal levels when they were encouraged to use this technique of chunking.

An extreme example of the role of strategies comes from a study showing that an individual was able to achieve a memory span of more than 80 digits (Chase & Ericsson, 1981)! The person, a runner, organized the digits into chunks that would correspond to running times for different distances. For example, the sequence 2141034084750 might be broken into chunks corresponding to running a marathon (2 hours, 14 minutes), a hundred-yard dash (10.3 seconds), a mile (4 minutes, 8 seconds), and 10 miles (47 minutes, 50 seconds). Although it might be tempting to believe that this person has some unique ability, Chase and Ericsson showed that another person taught this same strategy was able to get up to a span of 40 (before the study was stopped) and improved at about the same rate as the original subject. How were they able to do this? In fact, this ability made use of a number of principles we have discussed in this chapter. The subjects were able to quickly chunk the numbers to access long-term memory (for running times) and could provide a hierarchical structure for organizing these chunks.

Mnemonists.   **Mnemonists**, people who are able to remember great amounts of information, have long provided entertainment with their extraordinary feats of memory. Most of these mnemonists use well-known methods to perform their feats. Lorayne and Lucas (1974) provide some wonderful examples. For example, Lucas (the ex-New York Knickerbocker forward, for basketball fans) memorized the first column of names and phone numbers on a few hundred pages of the Manhattan telephone book! These mnemonists spend a great deal of time and mental effort to learn to use these mnemonic techniques so well.

Although they play an important role in individual differences, strategies may not be the whole story. Even if people are taught the same strategy and appear to learn it equally well, most of us would not be surprised if some people performed consistently better than other people. (In addition, we all are aware of some changes in memory performance with age.) Luria (1968) describes an unusual mnemonist whom he refers to as S, whose remarkable ability was not simply due to strategies. S was a journalist who annoyed his editor by never taking notes of the lengthy assignments he was given. In response to the editor's command to repeat the assignment, S did so flawlessly, apparently unaware that his memory was anything out of the ordinary. Once he had been examined in the laboratory, the remarkableness of his memory was quite apparent. S could repeat back lists of 70 words in a memory span test (longer lists were not tried). In addition, he could produce these lists in reverse order as easily as in the order given and could rapidly produce the successor or predecessor of any word in the list. Finally, and amazingly, he could recall lists that had been presented 16 years earlier (he was studied periodically over a very long time), even though by then he had become a professional mnemonist and had memorized many thousands of lists.

How did he do it? S converted every item to a visual image. (In fact, he appeared to have to a fantastic extent an ability we all have, called *synesthesia*, to experience stimuli in one sense using a different sense. For example, certain colors look hot and certain sounds feel smooth.) Every word, number, or sound would lead to a rich image. Thus, his ability to encode new information was quite unusual, but he was faced with the difficulty of organizing his images in some reasonable way to encode the order in which items appeared. Even in his case, strategies were important and he used the method of loci (see Chapter 6) to organize these images. When he became a professional mnemonist, the strategies became even more important because people would give him extremely difficult lists to memorize. He developed his own method, a combination of several mnemonic techniques, for taking advantage of his imagery ability.

In fact, his memory was so image-oriented that he was often unable to use simple logical organization. For example, when given the following table of numbers to remember:

```
1 2 3 4
2 3 4 5
3 4 5 6
4 5 6 7   and so on
```

he did not notice that each line's first number was the next whole number and that the rest of the numbers in the line were immediate successors. Rather, he just remembered the table in the same way he would have if the numbers had been in a totally random order.

Amnesia

After considering the processes and structure of memory as well as the feats of mnemonists, we end this chapter by returning to the problem of amnesia mentioned in the beginning of the chapter. We have been examining the role of memory in allowing us to deal with incomplete information and to reduce the great complexity of information. Amnesias provide cases in which this role is greatly reduced.

A number of texts describe the many types of amnesia in great anatomical, neurological, and neuropsychological detail, but here we will be interested only in characterizing the symptoms of a general type of permanent amnesia. Butters (1979) lists four symptoms of most cases of permanent amnesia. First, there is severe **anterograde amnesia**, meaning that new information cannot be learned. Second, there is some **retrograde amnesia**, the loss of memory for events before the trauma (e.g., operation, injury), though this is often patchy and variable. (It is interesting to note that television shows usually portray amnesic people with profound retrograde but with little if any anterograde deficits.) Third, some amnesic patients, especially near the time of trauma, show considerable confabulation (mentioning "facts" that are not true) when faced with questions they are unable to answer. Finally, despite these severe memory deficits, other intellectual functions are often relatively intact.

Although we have presented this single characterization of amnesia, amnesias vary in many ways. It is clear that the memory deficits differ greatly and depend on the nature of the problem and the anatomical loci (see, e.g., Squire, 1982). For present purposes we will have to be satisfied with a brief look into anterograde and retrograde amnesia.

Anterograde Amnesia.   The beginning of this chapter included a long quote from one of the many papers that documented the memory deficits of H. M. His amnesia is among the most severe of any documented case, with great anterograde and retrograde deficits as well as some short-term memory impairment. H. M. is unable to remember people he has met many times since his operation. His performance on new tasks that require him to consciously remember something is always awful. For example, although he can perform well on perceptual tasks, if they require him to find some figure in a complex picture his performance deteriorates greatly because he is unable to remember the figure he is searching for. In addition, although he is able to learn short tactile mazes, his performance on longer mazes is abysmal. He showed no improvement at all over 215 learning trials of a maze and made over 2800 errors, whereas normals learn this maze with an average of 17 trials and 92 errors (Milner, 1965).

Although he has been studied for over 25 years, H. M. shows little change. He has been able to learn a few significant facts after great amounts of repetition, such as the floor plan of the house he now lives in and the fact that his father has died (Corkin, Sullivan, Twitchell, & Grove, 1981). However, he is unable to keep track of most of what is going on in his world.

Retrograde Amnesia.   Retrograde amnesia refers to the inability to remember information from before the trauma. In general, retrograde amnesia occurs less frequently than anterograde and in most amnesic cases is completely limited to the few years before the trauma. One group of amnesic patients, those with Korsakoff syndrome, show large retrograde deficits. These patients have usually developed this syndrome after severe and prolonged alcoholism (the cause appears to be a thiamine deficiency resulting from their poor diet). At the onset of the syndrome these people change dramatically. Although many have a history of violence, they become passive, apathetic, and uninterested in alcohol (Butters, 1984). In addition, they have little ability to learn any new material (i.e., severe anterograde deficits) and experience difficulty recalling events from the past (i.e., retrograde deficit).

Cohen and Squire (1981) examined the retrograde deficits of several types of amnesic patients, including Korsakoff patients. The study of retrograde amnesia can be quite tricky, because the experimenter has no control over what was learned by the patients and has no knowledge of the extent or conditions of learning. Nonetheless, a number of tests have been devised that appear to be good indicators of past memory. Cohen and Squire had seven different tests, including (1) television programs that had aired for only one year between 1963 and 1977, (2) photographs of people who had become famous between 1930 and 1979, and (3) famous public events from the 1930s to the 1970s. The Korsakoff patients averaged about 54 years of age in 1980, meaning they were born around the mid–1920s. Although the other amnesic patients showed mild retrograde deficits limited to the few years before the trauma, the Korsakoff patients' retrograde amnesia was severe and extended back several decades to when the patients were quite young. In addition, the forgetting was slightly graded, with Korsakoff patients having more difficulty remembering recent events and faces than with remembering ones in the distant past. This result has many possible explanations. For example, prior to the onset of Korsakoff syndrome many of these patients had been drinking heavily, which is known to lead to some anterograde deficits. If new information was learned increasingly less well as drinking progressed, the graded effect may simply be due to less information being learned during the latter premorbid stages.

Butters and Cermak (1986; see also Butters, 1984) present some very interesting data to show that this possibility will not explain all the graded effect. In particular, they describe some research on a patient, P. Z., who had been an eminent scientist at a university before he developed Korsakoff syndrome when he was 65. In addition to having written many research articles, chapters, and books on his specialty, he had also written an autobiography that had been finished a couple of years before the onset of Korsakoff syndrome. Butters and Cermak conducted tests on his knowledge of various types of information contained in his autobiography. For example, P. Z. had discussed a number of scientists in his book and these names were given to him for identification. These scientists were categorized by whether they had achieved prominence before 1965 (17 years before the onset of P. Z.'s amnesia) or after 1965. Compared to another scientist of his age in his specialty, P. Z. showed forgetting of all the scientists, but this difference was greater for scientists who had become famous after 1965. Even more dramatically, he was tested about more personal information in his autobiography, such as about relatives, colleagues, or research assistants. As can be seen in Figure 7.8, those events from the distant past were remembered quite well, but recent events were not remembered at all. Because these test items were taken from his autobiogra-

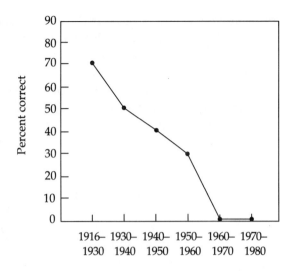

Figure 7.8 **Retrograde Amnesia for Recall of Information from P. Z.'s Autobiography.**
Source: Butters, N., & Cermak, L. S. (1986). A case study of the forgetting of auto-
biographical knowledge: Implications for the study of retrograde amnesia. In
D. C. Rubin (Ed.), *Autobiographical memory* (pp. 253–272). Cambridge: Cambridge
University Press.

phy, we can be confident that they had been learned originally. The exact
explanation for this temporal gradient is still uncertain.

Summary

Memory has many functions. In this chapter we addressed the remembering of new information. We began by considering short-term and long-term
memory with a focus on how each helps us to deal with the problems of
complexity and relevance. Short-term memory allows the augmentation of
incomplete information, the integration of information, and the transfer
of information to long-term memory. Long-term memory depends critically
on the encoding and retrieval processes used as well as how the encoding
and context at learning match the encoding and context at the time of retrieval. In addition, forgetting appears to be largely due to retrieval failure
rather than the permanent loss of information.

How can such effects be explained in a unified way? We examined
one important current model of memory, SAM. SAM incorporates many of
the ideas about short-term and long-term memory to account for a variety

of memory effects such as primacy, encoding specificity, and interference.

The final section of this chapter examined individual differences in memory. Many differences in memory are due to effects of knowledge and strategy. People who know more about a topic can better remember new information about that topic. People who use more effective memory strategies can better remember new information, in some cases leading to incredible feats of memory. We ended by considering amnesic patients and the difficulties they have in remembering new information as well as retrieving some old information.

We hope that you now have a better appreciation of how complex (and marvelous) your memory really is. Rather than being a storehouse of passively received information, memory involves the active interpretation of events, its augmentation with knowledge, and often its reorganization or elaboration. In addition, memory retrieval often provides relevant information and is sensitive to a variety of factors to increase the likelihood that retrieved information will be relevant.

Key Terms

anterograde amnesia
chunking
context
encoding
encoding specificity effect
free recall
incidental learning
intentional forgetting
levels of processing
long-term memory
memory decay hypothesis
memory span
metamemory
mnemonists

primacy effect
primary rehearsal
proactive interference
recency effect
release from PI
retrieval plan
retroactive interference
retrograde amnesia
SAM
savings in relearning
serial position effect
short-term memory
spacing effect
state-dependent recall
working memory

Recommended Readings

Miller (1956) has written the classic (and charming) paper on chunking. Baddeley (1990) provides a thorough and interesting review of short-term memory and working memory research and theory.

Readers interested in levels of processing should look at Craik and Lockhart (1972) and Craik and Tulving (1975), and also at the criticisms such as Baddeley (1978). The research and ideas on encoding specificity are reviewed in Tulving (1983). Bower (1981) provides a general discussion of his work on mood and memory and Eich (1980) reviews the work on drug effects on memory.

Whether memory is unerasable or not has long been a topic of debate. Loftus and Loftus (1980) argue that memories can be erased or overwritten. Many psychologists have argued the other side, with Zaragoza and McCloskey (1989) being a useful recent reference.

Readers who want to improve their memory (and are willing to work at it) should read the brief books by Lorayne and Lucas (1974) or Bellezza (1982). Luria (1968) provides a fascinating and readable description of the mnemonist S, examining not only his remarkable memory feats, but also how this ability affected his life and personality.

8

REPRESENTATION OF KNOWLEDGE AND ITS USE

Chapter Outline

Knowledge is of two kinds. We know a subject ourselves or we know where we can find information upon it.

Samuel Johnson

Introduction

How can people know so much and use this knowledge so easily? One of the authors was recently treated to a monologue by his preschool daughter. She talked about recent and distant past events and gave considered opinions about these events. Included in this monologue were the rules of her preschool, the injustice done to her that morning by her sister, and the fact that the Statue of Liberty had been a real person. (When queried whether she meant that the model for it had been real, she emphatically insisted that the statue itself had been real.) Examples like this raise issues about the many different things people know (or think they know). In this chapter we begin an examination of knowledge people have, how it is represented, and how it is used.

Much of this book can be viewed as examining our use of knowledge in perception, language, reasoning, and so on. Here we investigate knowledge representation and use for a particular task—answering questions about well-known objects in the world. First, we address how people can answer simple questions about objects and their superordinates. We then ask how different types of memories may be distinguished and what it means to have different memory systems. Following this, we discuss some recent memory models that attempt to integrate the results of the last chapter on remembering new information with the findings of this chapter on the representation of knowledge and its use. Finally, we reconsider the issue of memory distinctions in these recent models.

Models of Semantic Knowledge

Introduction

How is our knowledge about the many things in our world stored? One possibility is that the knowledge is not organized. Each fact is stored separately. A more plausible possibility is that the knowledge is organized. If so, we must deal with the nature of this organization and its consequences for memory.

Let us examine this issue by considering some questions:

1. Is a robin a bird?
2. Is a robin a living thing?

To answer the first question, most of us have the intuition that we know this fact. That is, we already have stored the information that a robin is a bird. The second question, however, seems to require us to make an inference. That is, while we certainly "know" that a robin is a living thing, we may never have stored that fact. To say yes to this question, we infer the answer from knowledge we do have stored. For example, you may have learned that robins are birds and birds are living things. Because these categories are nested (i.e., all robins are birds and all birds are living things), you can make the inference that a robin is a living thing. Clearly, memory allows us to retrieve information that we have stored. But much of the power of memory comes not from the retrieval of this stored information but from the fact that we can use this information to compute or infer new information that we may never have learned. *That is, a crucial function of memory is not only to retrieve previously learned knowledge, but to retrieve relevant knowledge from which the desired information may be computed.* This section addresses how such uses of memory can occur. We will discuss two different accounts of knowledge representation and use and then a third account that attempts to provide a compromise solution.

The Hierarchical Model

One of the most influential early views of long-term memory, the **hierarchical model** of Collins and Quillian (1969; 1972), assumes that a person's relatively permanent accumulation of knowledge about the meaning of the words is organized in a hierarchical network of associations. Network models are successors to simple associationist models (such as the ones discussed in the previous chapter). Before elaborating on the Collins and Quillian model, a brief discussion of network models is necessary.

Networks consist of nodes and links. The **nodes** correspond to concepts or ideas. Although these nodes are often represented by a word, it is important to realize that the node does not represent the word but rather the concept. The **links**, or pointers, designate the relation between any two nodes. This network provides a metaphor, much as the associationist models did, for capturing the intuition that some thoughts often lead to other thoughts and that concepts are related in various ways.

Description of the Model.   A key assumption is that the meaning of words is hierarchically organized in a network. For example, as illustrated in Figure 8.1, a concept such as *living thing* is represented by a high-level element in the network. This concept is associated with subordinate categories *animal* and *plant*, the concept *animal* is associated with *mammal*, *bird*, etc., the concept *mammal* with *dog*, *cat*, *lion*, and so on. However, the links between the subordinates and their superordinates indicate the nature of the relationship, not just that they are associated. Although the artificial intelligence work of Quillian (1968) and its subsequent application to human memory are considerably more complicated than this simple sketch, the basic idea is that the meaning of a concept is determined by its relationship to the other concepts in the network. Clearly, if all one knew were the relationships among concepts, there would be no way to relate one's knowledge to the world, so properties must make some contact with sensory experience. Still, the important claim is that in usual understanding and memory use one thinks about concepts in terms of their relations to other concepts.

Predictions.   How would one proceed to determine whether the hierarchical model has some actual correspondence to the inner workings of memory? One of the most important methods that has been developed uses as a measure an individual's *reaction time* when asked to answer a question or verify a sentence.

Suppose, for example, that you're asked on one occasion to say yes or no to indicate whether the sentence "A robin is a bird" is true and on another occasion to say yes or no to indicate whether the sentence "A robin is an animal" is true. According to the theory, one must predict that the first of these sentences will be verified more quickly than the second because the pathway through the memory network from the word *robin* to the category label *bird* is shorter than the pathway from *robin* to the category label *animal*. Experiments confirming this hierarchical effect prediction gave a major boost to the idea of a hierarchical network model (Collins & Quillian, 1969; Landauer & Freedman, 1968).

The reason why the length of the pathways between the points in the network corresponding to the subject and predicate of a sentence is so critical can be seen by reference to Figure 8.1. It is assumed that when you encounter the lower level word, say robin, in a sentence of the form "A robin is an X," you recognize from the grammatical form that X must be a

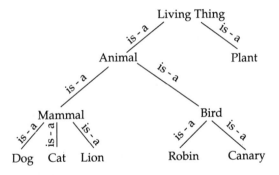

Figure 8.1   Hierarchical memory structure for meanings of familiar words belonging to the familiar categories. If an individual is presented with an example of a particular word such as "robin," it is assumed that a message travels upward along the associated paths, activating first the memory representation of the category label "bird," then the representation of "animal," and so on.

category label and start a search of your memory to see whether there is an "is-a" association leading from robin to X. In terms of the network model, a message is transmitted upward through the network. If there is an intact pathway from robin to X, then when the message arrives at the node in the network representing X, this means that robin and X are associated in the queried way and the response will be that the sentence is true. In the illustration, the message would arrive at the label *bird* in the sentence "A robin is a bird" before it would arrive at the label *animal* in "A robin is an animal." Consequently, reaction time would be shorter for the first sentence than for the second. If the first sentence had been "A robin is a plant," the message traveling upward through the network from robin would never arrive at the category element *plant* and you would judge the sentence to be false.

Evaluation.   When models fail to make the correct predictions it is often possible to understand the reason for their failure and to try to improve subsequent models. The Collins and Quillian work generated much further research, and a number of mispredictions were found (though see Collins & Quillian, 1972, for some counterarguments). One problem may be illustrated quite easily. People are faster to verify that a robin is a bird than they are to verify that a penguin is a bird. This difference is an example of the **typicality effect**: Instances that are more typical of a category are verified more quickly than atypical instances of that category. This result suggests that it is incorrect to assume each concept has stored with it equally accessible knowledge about its superordinate and subordinates, as the Collins and Quillian model assumes.

A second problem for the Collins and Quillian model is that the basic hierarchical effect (i.e., that robin-bird is verified more quickly than robin-animal) sometimes reverses. For example, "A chicken is a bird" takes longer to verify than "A chicken is an animal." This violates the presumed hierarchy and one would need to explain why the hierarchy works for robin but not for chicken. The only solution to this problem in this type of network is to allow another path between chicken and animal that can be traversed more quickly than the chicken-bird path, but such a change would violate the hierarchical nature of the model.

A third problem for this model concerns the description of how false responses are made. Although Collins and Quillian noted that there were a few possible ways in which subjects might decide a sentence was false, their model did not allow easy descriptions of these possibilities. Because the simple view is that one would respond false if the category label was not found in the upward search (e.g., the robin-plant example), the only variable that should make a difference is how far down in the hierarchy the first term is. The problem is that there are systematic differences among false sentences that this model cannot account for. For example, "A bat is a bird" takes longer to respond false to than does "A bat is a plant." In general, false responses in which the subject and category are related or have similarities (such as wings and flies for bat and bird) often lead to longer reaction times. This difference is called the relatedness effect.

All three of these failures can be viewed as stemming from the same assumptions: Superordinate information is equally available for all concepts and is the only information used to make category judgments. Later theories have revised both assumptions.

Feature Comparison Model

To understand the differences between the hierarchical model and our next model, the feature comparison model, it is useful to think about the meaning of "meaning." This idea will be elaborated a little later in this chapter and in the chapters on language and concepts, but basically we may distinguish two general views. In one view, the meaning of a concept is defined by its relation to other concepts, as used in the network analyses. In the other view, the meaning of a concept is defined by its values on a set of primitive attributes. That is, the meaning is viewed as a *decomposition* into some set of values on these more primitive attributes (e.g., animate-inanimate, color, etc.). In this section we will consider one implementation of a decomposition view that accounts for the results, the feature comparison model of Smith, Shoben, and Rips (1974).

Description of the Model.   The **feature comparison model** assumes that each word is represented by a set of semantic features that vary in their importance to the meaning of the concept. That is, some features are essential to the concept and are called **defining features**, while others are less defining but generally true and are called **characteristic features**. Smith, Shoben, and Rips suggest that this distinction is more of a continuum, but for ease of exposition we will treat it as a binary distinction. (We will consider this issue in detail in Chapter 12; also see McNamara & Miller, 1989.) As an example of each type for the concept *bird*, defining features might be animate and feathered because a nonliving or unfeathered object is not a bird. Characteristic features for bird might be flies or sings. Clearly, not all birds fly and not all birds sing, but these are features that for us are generally true of birds. For a specific type of bird, such as *robin*, the mental representation would always include the defining features of bird (animate, feathered) and would have some defining features of its own, such as red breast, flies, and sings. Note that some of the characteristic features of bird are defining features of robin. Now consider the features of a bird such as *penguin*. While its defining features would include those of bird (animate, feathered), its other defining features would be unlike the characteristic features of bird and might include black and white, does not fly, lives in cold climate, etc.

To make predictions from the feature comparison model we also need to examine its processing assumptions. The model assumes that people may make decisions by including information that is not technically relevant, perhaps because such use is fast and usually accurate. The processing assumptions for the feature comparison model are presented schematically in Figure 8.2.

The model assumes that two stages may occur. The first stage is a fast, holistic comparison of all the features of both the subject (robin) and the predicate (bird), without taking into account how defining any of the features are. If the feature overlap is very high, the person can respond "true." If the feature overlap is very low, the person can respond "false." The underlying idea is that if the features of one concept (the predicate) are largely included in the features of the other concept (the subject), the subject is likely to be a member of the predicate category. In addition, if they have almost no features in common, the subject is very unlikely to be a member of the predicate category. If the overlap is intermediate, the deci-

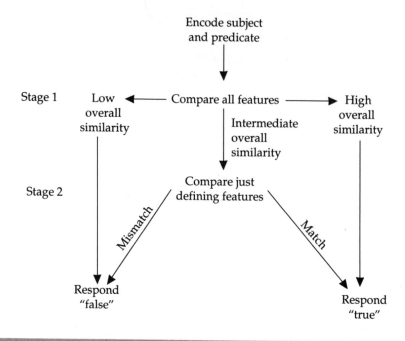

Figure 8.2   **The Two Stages of Decision Processes for the Feature Comparison Model.** If the overall similarity is very high (or low), then immediately respond true (or false, if similarity is low). For intermediate similarity, a second stage examining defining features is executed.

sion proceeds to a second, more analytic stage in which the defining features are isolated. In this stage, if the defining features of the predicate are matched in the subject, a "true" response is given (e.g., if the defining features of bird are included in the defining features of robin). If the predicate has defining features that are not included in the subject's defining features, a "false" response is made. It is assumed that this last stage is error-free and that differences in response time are due to differences in the probability of having to go to the second stage.

Predictions.   Before examining the predictions of this model, it is important to realize that there is one basic problem with it—no one knows exactly what features are represented for each concept and how defining each of the features is. Without this information, how can we generate the predictions? This problem is serious, but Rips, Shoben, and Smith (1973) argue that rated typicality is a reasonable index of the extent to which two items share characteristic features. That is, robin will be rated as a more typical bird than will penguin, because although both include the defining features of bird, robin shares far more characteristic features. In the same vein, the more similar two items in a category are (e.g., robin-sparrow are more similar than robin-penguin), the more characteristic features they are assumed to share. The ratings can be transformed into a more pictorial representation by a procedure known as *multidimensional scaling*, an example of which is presented in Figure 8.3. The full scaling procedure is too complicated to explain here, but it represents similarity in terms of distance. More similar instances are closer in space than less similar instances. For example, robin and sparrow are close to each other and far away from goose and duck. The scaling solutions depict a category (and two superordinates) with the idea that the closer two items are on the figure, the more features they share.

With this scaling solution, the feature comparison model can now make predictions of the basic results. It can predict the basic hierarchical effect of Collins and Quillian (i.e., that robin-bird is faster than robin-animal) because robin and bird are more similar (closer in Figure 8.3), than are robin and animal. Processing can often stop after the first stage for the robin-bird questions, but will need to include a second stage for robin-animal. Thus, the model explains the hierarchical effect not in terms of searching up the hierarchy, but in terms of feature similarity. Far superor-

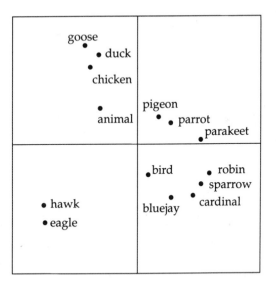

Figure 8.3   **Multidimensional Scaling of Birds from Rips, Shoben, and Smith (1973).**
The more similar two concepts are, the closer they are in the space. *Source:* Rips, L. J., Shoben, E. J., & Smith, E. E., 1973.

dinates will generally have less feature similarity to an item than will near superordinates.

In addition, the feature comparison model handles typicality effects, reversals of the hierarchical effect, and the relatedness effect in false responses (all of which were problems for the Collins and Quillian model). First, consider typicality effects (i.e., typical instances are verified more quickly than atypical instances). As can be seen in Figure 8.3, robin is much closer to bird (i.e., has more features in common) than chicken is to bird, so a second stage will be needed less often for the robin-bird decision, leading to faster responses. That is, typical instances (robin) have high overall similarity to their superordinate (bird) and will tend to be responded to on the basis of the first stage comparison, while atypical instances will usually require a second-stage comparison of defining features.

Second, the model can account for reversals of the hierarchical effect by arguing that this will happen when the feature similarity is reversed. Put another way, some instances will be more similar to far superordinates than to near superordinates. In these cases, the far superordinates should be responded to more quickly than the near superordinates. For example, as can be seen from Figure 8.3, chicken is closer to animal than it is to bird, thus one would predict that chicken-animal should be faster than chicken-bird, and it is.

Third, this model can account for the relatedness effect of false responses. Many false responses (e.g., bear-bird) have few similar features and a fast "false" response may be made on the basis of the very low first-stage similarity. However, false responses in which the instance has some moderate similarity to the superordinate may require a second stage. For example, bat-bird takes much longer to say "false" to than does bear-bird. By the feature comparison account, this difference is because the many features that bat and bird share (wings, flies, etc.) are sufficient to force the decision to a second stage, while the few features in common between bear and bird often allow first-stage decisions to be made.

Evaluation. The idea of feature similarity can be used to explain many results that seem to require more hierarchical explanations. As we will see in Chapter 12 on concepts, the idea that similar features organize concepts is a popular one. The reason is that superordinates and subordinates share many features. Despite these successes, the feature comparison model has also been criticized on a number of grounds. First, it is unclear whether the ratings used are a truly independent measurement of feature similarity. It may be that the process used for verifying statements is similar to that used for determining similarity ratings. Similarity judgments may reflect direct comparison of the features of examples, but we do not know exactly how people make similarity judgments. If they use other information, for example about the relations of the instances to the category (e.g., robin and sparrow are typical birds), then the findings are not evidence for the importance of feature similarity. Rather, they simply show that if you have two related measures, one can be used to predict performance on the other.

Second, the claim of this model is that all decisions are made by comparing feature sets, never by retrieving a learned fact. However, later findings (e.g., Holyoak and Glass, 1975) showed that there were multiple ways that subjects used for responding "false," such as thinking of counterexamples (e.g., "All birds are canaries" could be rejected if the subject found information that a robin is a bird and that a robin is not a canary), which could not be accounted for by the feature comparison view.

Third, most of the effects are attributed to different probabilities of first-stage responses, but some of the effects can be obtained even when the situation makes it unlikely that subjects could respond on the basis of the overall similarity of the first stage. McCloskey and Glucksberg (1979) included questions in which some of the instance and category terms were switched (i.e., "All birds are robins"), so that high overall similarity could not be used as an indication of a "true" response. They still found typicality effects on true responses and relatedness effects on false responses.

Although the feature comparison model has been criticized on a number of grounds, it has advanced our understanding of knowledge representation and use in at least three important ways. First, it showed that hierarchical effects do not require one to posit a hierarchy. Second, it focused attention on the importance of feature similarity in knowledge representation. Third, it illustrated that even in what seem to be simple decisions, people may make use of knowledge that is not strictly relevant to the decision.

Comparison of Models.   We have been focusing on the particulars of the models, but it is often useful to take a step back and ask what is being accomplished by each model. Smith (1978) distinguishes between *prestored* and *computed* knowledge. Using this distinction, it appears that each of these models is emphasizing part of the picture at the expense of the other part. That is, as the hierarchical model emphasizes, some of our knowledge is prestored and we may use that knowledge to answer some questions or to make simple inferences to answer other questions. In contrast, the feature comparison model suggests that quick computations can be done to determine category membership if overall similarity is used as a guide or heuristic. The first stage of the model bases decisions on similarity rather than on direct knowledge of category membership. The research to support or falsify each model led to a much better understanding of the phenomena in the area (of which we have just given a few) and the important points about each model. Some later models (e.g., McCloskey & Glucksberg, 1979) have attempted to elaborate on the featural view. In the next section we consider a model that extends the network approach but also incorporates many of the ideas we have just examined from the feature comparison model.

Spreading Activation Model

Description of the Model.   Collins and Loftus (1975) present a more powerful network model than the hierarchical model by making different assumptions about the representation and the retrieval process. First, the representation is not strictly hierarchical, but allows various other types of relations between concepts. These additional relations include verb relations and even negative superordinate relations (e.g., information that a bat is not a bird). Second, the links differ not only in type but also in how crucial they are, with more crucial links traversed more quickly. Because of these two changes, the notion of organization changes dramatically. Rather than by hierarchy, memory is organized by the total interconnectedness between concepts (i.e., how many links and how quickly traversed), which Collins and Loftus call **semantic relatedness**. Figure 8.4 provides a sample portion of this network representation.

This change in representation forces a change in our understanding of the retrieval process. Because the hierarchical information is only a part of the knowledge, the retrieval process is not limited to using just this hierarchical information. Collins and Loftus want to allow for the cases in which nonhierarchical information may be accessed as well. For example, if one had stored the information that "A bat is not a bird" it would seem that responding false to "A bat is a bird" should be accomplished quickly, but it is not. The claim, along lines related to the feature comparison model, is that the semantic relatedness of bat and bird is high because many important (accessible) links from each are connected, such as having wings and flying. Because we cannot know beforehand what information may play a role in the decision, all information linked to the concepts must be searched. Collins and Loftus conceptualize this as a **spreading activation** search, in which the activation at each initial concept (from reading the sentence) spreads through the links to the closely related concepts and then the concepts related to those concepts, and so on. (An analogy may help make this idea clearer. Activation spread can be viewed as information

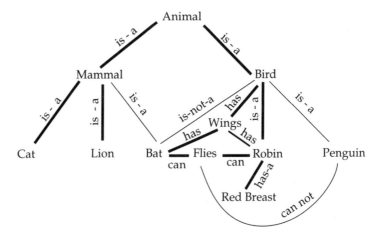

Figure 8.4   **Sample of a Network Using Spreading Activation.**
Activation spreads from mentioned concepts to their neighbors, with intersections of activation providing evidence for a positive or negative response. Thicker lines represent links that would be more accessible (i.e., more quickly activated).

being broadcast (e.g., yelled) to all close neighbors, who in turn broadcast it to their neighbors, and so on.) The process is complicated because a node can be activated from multiple paths, but the basic idea is that if a path is found that connects the two initial concepts (bat-bird), this **intersection** is evaluated. The evidence from this evaluation is then added to any other evidence until a threshold is reached indicating that enough evidence of one type has been found to give an answer.

Lexical decision studies (e.g., Meyer & Schvaneveldt, 1971) also suggest that related information may be activated by a probe. In the Meyer and Schvaneveldt study, subjects were asked to classify letter strings as words or nonwords (a decision about whether the letter string is in the lexicon, or mental dictionary). The time to classify a letter string as a word (e.g., doctor) was faster if the previous trial had just been a semantically related word (e.g., nurse) than if it had been a semantically unrelated word (e.g., butter). Their interpretation was that the semantically similar previous trial had *primed* the target word (doctor) because accessing it had led to activation spreading to its related words.

Predictions.   Three examples may make the workings of this model clearer. Suppose "A robin is a bird" is given in the experiment and the subject must respond "true" or "false." The concepts for robin and bird would be activated. Because birdiness is an important property of being a robin, activation would traverse quickly in this direction. Also, because robin is a typical bird, activation would traverse quickly in the opposite direction too, often leading to a quick intersection. This intersection provides diagnostic information (i.e., that a robin is a bird) so that a "true" decision can be made quickly. (Note that at the same time much other information would be activated that would also lead to positive evidence, such as flies, has wings, lays eggs, etc.)

Now suppose "A penguin is a bird" is to be verified. Activation would go quickly from penguin toward bird, but because penguin is a very atypical bird, it would not go quickly from bird toward penguin, increasing the time before an intersection. In addition, other possible paths would not be activated as quickly either and some may provide negative evidence (e.g., penguins cannot fly). All of these differences from the robin-bird case would lead to slower "true" responses.

Finally, suppose "A bat is a bird" was given as the sentence to be responded to. As outlined before, activating bat may lead to the activation of the information that a bat is not a bird. In addition, Collins and Loftus postulate several strategies (such as the use of counterexamples) that might provide additional negative evidence. At the same time, however, other intersections giving positive evidence would also be evaluated, such as has wings and flies. These positive intersections would often slow a response.

Evaluation.   Spreading activation can be viewed as a mechanism for heuristically determining relevance. That is, often when one uses a concept the most relevant knowledge will be knowledge closely related to the concept. Spreading activation makes this knowledge more accessible. As with any heuristic, it may sometimes lead one astray (as in the bat-bird case), but it often helps.

The model allows both the use of prestored knowledge and the computation of information that was not stored, but this combination of mechanisms comes at a price. As some researchers have noted, the model is quite complex and unconstrained in its accounts of the data (see, e.g., Smith, 1978). The model has so many possible ways of responding to any query that its predictions in many cases are not clear.

This spreading activation model has nonetheless been quite influential in conceptions of our organization of knowledge. Although the model has not been followed up directly, many later models have been influenced by its combination of different mechanisms and its use of spreading activation.

You may have noted that the models just discussed were primarily investigated during the 1970s. Research on the representation of knowledge and its use has not ended. Rather, such research has become applied to many areas other than what is usually referred to as memory research. As will be shown in later chapters, investigators in language, decision making, reasoning, and problem solving have also examined how memory is used in their domains of interest.

The work on knowledge representation seems quite distinct from memory for new information discussed in the last chapter. In the next section we take up the relationship between knowledge and memory for new information.

Are There Distinct Memory Systems?

We remember lots of different things. We remember phone numbers, items to shop for at the grocery store, whether we did an errand, the street names and street locations of our hometown, multiplication tables, whether robins lay eggs, how to ride a bicycle, and much, much more. A natural question to ask is whether our memory for all these different things is one system or whether we may have different memory systems corresponding to at least some of these differences. If the latter, the question then becomes which distinction(s) correspond to distinct memory systems. (See Brewer & Pani, 1983 for a further discussion and proposal of distinctions.)

Although most psychologists accept a number of classifications of memory, it is not clear whether these classifications correspond to distinct systems. For example, many psychologists would consider short-term memory to be the currently activated aspect of long-term memory. In the last several years the focus has been on two general distinctions that seem to separate important classes of memories: episodic vs. semantic memory and declarative vs. procedural memory. In this section we consider the first distinction in some detail. Later in the chapter we return to the second distinction.

The most controversial issue in this area has been whether or not episodic and semantic memory are separate systems. (See Tulving, 1972 for an introduction to this distinction and Tulving, 1983 for a review of more recent evidence.) **Episodic memory** refers to memory for autobiographical events, including the context (time, place, setting) in which they occurred. Examples include remembering whether you took your suit to the cleaners yesterday or remembering watching the last Rose Bowl game. In contrast, if you should be asked such questions as "Are penguins birds?" or "Is the term of a United States senator six years?" you would answer on the basis of what is termed **semantic memory**. Here the relevant information stored in memory has to do not with any particular incidents in your past history, but rather with your knowledge concerning relationships between objects and their properties or words and their meanings.

These types of memory seem rather different, and this distinction has led to a great deal of research examining episodic and semantic memory. Much of the research discussed in the previous chapter concerned how people learn about new events (e.g., word lists), which would be part of the study of episodic memory. In contrast, work concerning the representation of knowledge about concepts, as discussed so far in this chapter, would be part of the study of semantic memory.

There is suggestive evidence that the amnesic syndrome produces a functional dissociation between systems (see Tulving, 1983, 1985, for reviews). One idea is that amnesia leaves semantic memory more or less intact while grossly impairing episodic memory. This idea is consistent with the description of H. M. given in the previous chapter. H. M. remembers episodes prior to his operation but basically has no episodic memory for postoperative events. However, this distinction does not seem to capture a number of findings in the amnesia literature. First, the retrograde amnesia of Korsakoff syndrome patients includes both past autobiographical memories (episodic) as well as world knowledge (semantic). Second, the research on anterograde amnesias suggests that both new episodic and semantic memories are hard to acquire. Under near optimal learning conditions, Glisky, Schacter, and Tulving (1986) were able to get amnesic patients to learn some computer-related vocabulary words. But many of the words were not new ones and had technical definitions related to their usual meaning (e.g., SAVE). Even so, learning was very slow compared to controls. Gabrieli, Cohen, and Corkin (1988) performed a number of sensitive experiments trying to detect semantic knowledge that might have been learned by H. M. since his amnesia, but found little learning.

Others have argued that the boundaries between episodic and semantic memory are not clear-cut (e.g., Anderson & Ross, 1980; Hintzman, 1984; McKoon, Ratcliff, & Dell, 1986). Our view, similar to the view outlined in Anderson and Ross (1980), is that by definition there is a clear *content* distinction between the two types of memories. That is, we can discuss the two different types of information as semantic and episodic with general agreement about each. But we do not believe that there is any convincing evidence of a *functional* distinction, with each type of information requiring different structures and processes to be involved in encoding and retrieving.

Why should a decision about this distinction be important? The semantic–episodic distinction has been an influential one and one, we think, that has helped to further our understanding of memory. But, to the extent that similar principles underlie memory for the two types of information, treating them as distinct may delay our understanding of these principles. In addition, one of the main reasons for wanting distinctions is to allow the principles to be as detailed as possible. It appears from some comprehensive theories, however, such as the ones to be discussed in the next section, that similar principles may apply to both episodic and semantic memories.

Two Models of Memory Including Episodic and Semantic Information

Introduction

The models in the last section focused on how questions about our world knowledge (semantic information) could be answered. In this section we present two different types of models that encompass memory for both semantic and episodic information. The first one, a network model called ACT, extends the network metaphor discussed in the spreading activation model and provides an account of various types of memory phenomena. The second, a PDP or connectionist model, also provides an account of many memory phenomena, but does so in a very different way. (Also see Hintzman, 1988 for another approach to modeling.)

The ACT Theory

The final network model we will consider combines the storage and retrieval of episodic and semantic knowledge. The **ACT** (adaptive control of thought) theory of John Anderson (1976; revised as ACT* in 1983) is an attempt to account for a wide variety of phenomena and data in memory, learning, language, problem solving, and reasoning within the same framework. Although this ambitious project can be dealt with only briefly here, Anderson's view of memory has been very influential and has helped in understanding the interrelations among a number of memory topics. Here we examine his view of memory structure and retrieval.

Description of the Model.   Anderson conceptualizes memory as a network of nodes and links, but the nodes (concepts) and links (relations) are organized into propositions. **Propositions** can be thought of as the smallest unit of meaning about which one can reasonably assert truth or falsity. For example, if one sees the word "pretty" one cannot find it either true or false without knowing what "pretty" is being asserted about. In contrast, "The flower is pretty" is a proposition, because it makes sense to say that it is either true or false. Thus, propositions can be viewed as encoding a fact. Note that a sentence can have multiple propositions. For instance, "The flower is pretty and red" contains two propositions, one claiming the flower is pretty and one claiming the flower is red. Each proposition can be said to be true or false. In addition, propositions can be embedded to express complex ideas, such as "Bill thinks that the flower is pretty." Figure 8.5 gives samples of different simple propositional networks. The propositions have labels that identify semantic relationships among the elements (e.g., agent, object).

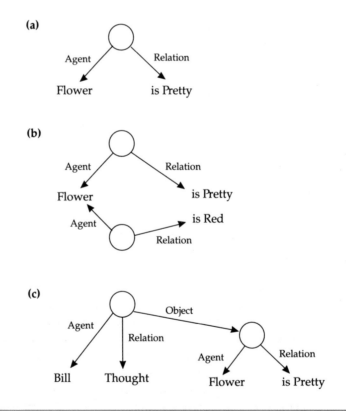

Figure 8.5   ACT propositional encoding for three propositions: (a) The flower is pretty. (b) The flower is pretty and red. (c) Bill thinks that the flower is pretty.

The idea that memory consists of propositions is important when one realizes that Anderson is trying to account not only for semantic knowledge, but new episodic knowledge as well. The claim is that people encode the meaning of new information, not the exact wording; thus it is important to have a memory organized around the meanings. As we have seen, people often do forget the exact wording and remember the meaning or gist of new information (Bransford, Barclay, & Franks, 1972).

Two more points about representation are needed for us to consider memory retrieval in this model. The first point about the representations is that links differ in their strength, with more frequently encountered information being more strongly linked. Second, the concepts are really general concepts (e.g., the idea of a chair), whereas the information learned is often about specific instances of the concept (e.g., a particular chair you are looking at). Network models that incorporate all types of information need to keep track of what each fact means. For example, if you said "The chair is blue" you would not want to attach this assertion to the concept of chairs in general. So far our simplified representations have not made this distinction (see Figure 8.6a). To handle this difference, network models make a **type-token** distinction. A *type* refers to the general concept while the *token* refers to the particular use of the concept. One way to accomplish this distinction is to view the type as a category (e.g., chairs in general) and each token as a member of the category (e.g., a chair). In Figure 8.6b, X marks the place of some specific token, which is represented as a member of the category of chairs. This representation encodes that there is an entity that is a particular chair and that it is blue. Because this token is linked to the type node, knowledge about chairs in general is often available when considering your favorite chair. Now, if you learn any additional information about the blue chair, you store it linked to the token node referring to that chair (i.e., the X). Figure 8.6c shows a representation that includes the additional fact that the chair is small.

Retrieval of information from this network works by spreading activation, similar to the Collins and Loftus model. The activation varies in amount, with the activation level at any concept a sum of the activation it receives from the other concepts. It is simplest to consider how this retrieval works for a recognition question (i.e., "Have you seen this sentence: . . ."). When a sentence is given for recognition, the concepts contained in the sentence are activated and activation spreads from these concepts to the neighboring concepts (i.e., concepts that are linked to them). Recognition occurs when the activation from the concepts has intersected

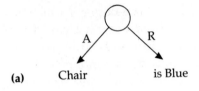

(a)

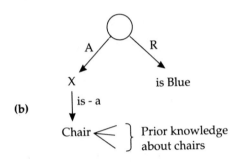

(b)

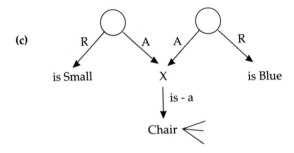

(c)

Figure 8.6 **The Type-Token Distinction.**
Panel (a) shows the simplified representation with no distinction made between types and tokens. X is a token, a specific chair that is blue. The "chair" node is the type node, encoding knowledge about chairs in general. Panel (b) shows how the distinction is represented. Panel (c) shows how new information about the token, X, is represented off the token node.

(i.e., the appropriate proposition or propositions are activated) and the level of activation is above some threshold. The final point is that the activation that spreads from any concept is divided among the links from the concept, with the strongest links (i.e., those encoding more frequently occurring relations to that concept) receiving more activation. Thus, the activation that arrives at any concept is a function not only of how many activated concepts it is linked to, but also how strongly linked it is to these concepts. (Though see Ratcliff & McKoon, 1981, 1988 for arguments against spreading activation and in favor of an alternative.)

It is worth noting that this activation takes the place of any separate short-term memory buffer. That is, Anderson views short-term memory as being simply the activated portion of long-term memory.

This discussion of activation and its spread is rather abstract but an example should help to make the ideas clearer. Suppose you had learned a number of sentences about a doctor and a number of sentences about a lawyer, and you were queried about whether you had learned the sentence "The lawyer fought the doctor." Figure 8.7 provides a schematic of this portion of the assumed propositional network. The concepts "lawyer," "fought," and "doctor" would be activated. The activation would spread from these concepts and, given their connectedness, it is likely that an intersection would occur in which the proposition that includes all three of them would be activated. The time to the intersection would depend on how long it took for the activation from these three concepts to intersect at a level above some threshold, which in turn would depend on how much activation spread from each concept down the relevant links. The amount of activation that spreads down a link (1) increases, the stronger (more frequent) the link, and (2) decreases, the more links from the concept with which the activation needs to be shared.

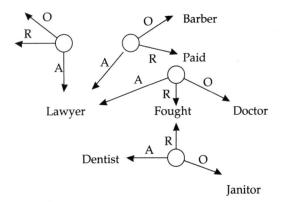

Figure 8.7   ACT propositional encoding for the sentence "The lawyer fought the doctor," as well as for a number of other sentences that include the concepts lawyer, fought, and doctor. The fan off each concept is the number of other propositions in which it occurs, so the fans of lawyer, fought, and doctor are 3, 2, and 1, respectively.

Explanation of Predictions.   Because ACT assumes that frequency affects the strength of the links, which in turn affects the speed with which knowledge is accessible, it predicts the well-researched finding that more frequently occurring information is accessed more quickly (e.g., see Anderson, 1976, pp. 283–290). ACT also provides one explanation for how memories interfere with one another, called the **fan effect**. Connected to any concept are a number of links, which Anderson calls the *fan* of the concept (because in a network picture the lines for links resemble the structure of a fan). The claim is that the more links emanating from a concept the more divided the activation, and thus the longer for an intersection to occur. Interference is assumed to be due to this fanning of information from a concept. (Although we discuss this interference in terms of time to retrieve information, interference also includes cases in which the asked-for information is not found within a reasonable time and the person decides he or she cannot remember.) Anderson and his colleagues have provided a great deal of empirical support for the fan effect (see Anderson, 1976, 1983 for reviews). A typical experiment would vary the fan from the different concepts in each sentence. Using Figure 8.7 as an example, concepts might be included in one, two, or three other learned sentences, such as doctor, fought, and lawyer, respectively. The results show that the time to recognize a sentence increases with the number of other sentences learned about the different concepts.

We have considered the ACT model as applied to learning episodic information, but the importance of the model is that the same representation and retrieval principles are used for explaining memory for semantic information, such as historical knowledge (Lewis & Anderson, 1976) or knowledge about concepts (Anderson & Ross, 1980). A brief discussion of the Lewis and Anderson study may illustrate the power of the ACT theory in incorporating both semantic and episodic information. In this study subjects learned fantasy facts about well-known historical figures, such as "George Washington wrote *Tom Sawyer*." The fan, or number of these facts, learned about each historical figure varied from zero to four, as shown in Table 8.1. At a later test, the time to verify well-known historical facts (e.g., "George Washington crossed the Delaware") increased with the more fantasy facts learned about the individual. Thus, the more episodic facts one learned about the individual, the more interference in retrieving well-learned semantic knowledge.

This last result has an interesting implication. Everything else equal, the more you learn about a concept the longer it should take you to retrieve any particular fact about that concept, because the fan has increased. Yet often it seems that when we know much about a topic we have

Table 8.1   **Examples of Material Used in the Experiment.**
The numbers before the test facts indicate the number of study sentences which included this famous person.

Examples of artificial facts studied
    George Washington wrote *Tom Sawyer*.
    Napoleon Bonaparte was from India.
    Napoleon Bonaparte was a singer.
    Napoleon Bonaparte is a liberal senator.
    Napoleon Bonaparte had a ranch.

Examples of test probes
  Actual facts
    0 Fidel Castro is Cuban.
    1 George Washington crossed the Delaware.
    4 Napoleon Bonaparte was an emperor.
  Fantasy facts
    1 George Washington wrote *Tom Sawyer*.
    4 Napoleon Bonaparte was from India.
  False
    0 Fidel Castro was a Texan politician.
    1 George Washington is a swimmer.
    4 Napoleon Bonaparte was a humorist.

Source: From Lewis, C. H., & Anderson, J. R., 1976.

quick access to a large number of facts. Although there are a number of reasons for this increased availability (some of which will be discussed in Chapter 11 on inference), one reason may have to do with how we use our memory in real-world situations. Often we are not concerned with whether we recognize having learned a particular fact, but rather whether a particular fact is true or not (or if we believe it is true). If you learn that "A dax is a bird" and "A dax flies," and you were asked if a dax has wings, you would respond yes. You would not care whether you had learned that a dax has wings as long as it is a strong inference from what you do know.

    Reder (1982) has proposed that memory judgments are often made along the lines of these plausible inferences rather than by retrieving the exact information queried. Reder and Ross (1983) provide evidence that if people respond on the basis of plausibility, as opposed to the strict recognition of the sentence, then the more facts one knows about a concept the faster the response. In their study, subjects learned a number of sentences about some person and some activity (e.g., Steven, moving):

Steven called to have a phone installed.

Steven read and signed the lease.

Steven unpacked all of his boxes.

Subjects were then queried about a sentence that was related to these activities, such as "Steven mailed out change of address cards" or new sentences about Steven that were unrelated to moving. (During the experiment, the subjects had learned about two other people who had mailed change of address cards.) In one condition, subjects were required to make strict recognition judgments about whether they had studied the exact sentence. As in the previous fan effect research, the more facts they learned about the queried concepts, the longer the time to respond that they had seen that exact sentence (e.g., Steven read and signed the lease). In another condition, subjects were presented with these same test sentences, but now had to respond whether this test sentence was plausible given the other facts they knew about this person. In this condition, the more facts they had learned about the queried concepts the *faster* the response. This result is important in showing that people can often base their judgments on plausible inferences. In real-world use, one is rarely concerned with whether a literal fact has been learned at a particular time but rather whether the information is likely to be true. Under these circumstances, the number of relevant facts may aid rather than hinder the judgment.

The ACT theory has focused researchers on a variety of questions, such as the use of strict recognition versus plausibility judgments. According to this theory, the same representation used to make one type of judgment has to be suitable for predicting effects in the other type of judgment. Using a single representation for both judgments greatly constrains possible explanations (see Reder and Ross, 1983, for one way to account for these results within the ACT framework).

General Points.   Part of the reason for providing such detail on ACT is that this theory provides possible answers to two important questions about the flexibility of memory related to our themes of relevance and complexity: (1) How do we determine what knowledge is relevant? (2) Once we have determined relevance, how do we find the exact information we are looking for?

First, given all that one knows, how is the relevant knowledge retrieved? As discussed for the spreading activation model, the use of spreading activation is a type of relevancy heuristic. In ACT, knowledge that is closely related to the activated information (i.e., frequent and/or low fan) is available more quickly. Thus, this model claims that the relevant knowledge can often be determined as a function of the knowledge that has been related to it in the past.

Second, this model gives an interesting partial answer to the question "How is it, given all the knowledge that we possess, that we are often able to retrieve quickly the knowledge asked for in a question?" The answer is that we may not. Rather than viewing the use of memory as retrieving exactly the information queried, this model takes the view that other information may be relevant as well and that sometimes one may respond without having the exact information queried. For example, a person may answer that a bat is not a bird, not because they know that it is not a bird but because they retrieve various information suggesting that it may not be and/or that it may be more similar to some mammals. Similarly with episodic materials, they may answer a query about a particular event by retrieving other knowledge about that event or related events. In short, remembering is not simply retrieving stored facts, but rather memory may be used in a variety of ways in the service of accessing relevant knowledge quickly.

A Parallel Distributed Processing Model of Memory

A very different approach to modeling memory with combined episodic and semantic information is a *parallel distributed processing* (**PDP**) model. McClelland and Rumelhart (1986a) argue that we should conceive of memory in terms of each new event changing the knowledge that can be used to respond to a situation. As a very loose analogy, each experience when we are driving a car affects our knowledge of driving, which in turn affects how we may respond to new driving situations. Applied to memory retrieval, prior experiences affect our remembering not simply by being retrieved and inspected, but by changing our whole knowledge base that is used to answer all queries. Although this may sound like doublespeak when described at such an abstract level, the McClelland and Rumelhart proposal is quite specific in how prior experiences can affect memory and the results of memory retrievals.

General Description of the Model.   Similar to the PDP models discussed in Chapters 2 and 5 (for examples that examined room schemas and an interactive activation model of word recognition), the model involves many processing units whose combined activation determines the output. As in the network models, memory is assumed to consist of a large set of interconnected units, each of which can take on some activation value. Unlike the network models we have considered in this chapter, each unit does not represent a concept (such as "bird"). Instead, concepts are represented as a *pattern of activation* over the network. The connections between units are weighted. These **connection weights** determine how much influence the activation of one unit has on the activation of another unit. The weights between two units, A and B, may be (1) positive, in which case the activation of A leads to the activation of B, (2) negative, in which case the activation of A leads to the inhibition of B, or (3) zero, in which case the activation of A has no effect on the activation of B. The weights vary in absolute value as well, with greater weights providing more excitation or inhibition. These weights are set so that units that tend to occur together in many patterns will activate each other and units that tend rarely to occur together will inhibit each other. McClelland and Rumelhart assume that there are many simple sets of units like these, called *modules*, which combine to make up the memory system.

Because of the complicated interactions that arise from many units working together, it is often hard to intuit or to simply describe the detailed workings of this model. We shall first provide a general description of the process, then examine a very simple example in detail. Finally, we will address some general issues of this approach.

We can present a general description of the model by discussing (1) how new information is represented, (2) the short-term effect it has on the pattern of activation, and (3) the long-term effect it has on the network. First, as is common in a number of memory models, each input is represented as a vector (i.e., an ordered set of values). To be able to encode rich information, the vectors need to be quite large, but a simple illustrative four-element vector might be $(1 \; -1 \; -1 \; \; 1)$. The positive and negative 1's simply indicate two distinct values. The general idea is that this vector stands for, or represents, some new information to be encoded by the network. Items that are similar will tend to share more values in the vector than items that are not similar. For example, for the vector $(1 \; -1 \; -1 \; \; 1)$, $(1 \; -1 \; -1 \; -1)$ is similar (three of four elements overlap) and $(-1 \; \; 1 \; \; 1 \; -1)$ is very dissimilar (zero of four).

Second, this input vector is "given" to the system and changes the pattern of activation. It is convenient to think of this process as similar to a short-term memory. The pattern of activation before the input vector is presented can be viewed as a representation of what is being thought about. Clearly, we want the input to affect what the system is thinking about, but how? For present purposes it is important only to realize that the input vector and weights are multiplied together in some way and the old activation values are also taken into account to get new activation values. These new activation values represent the new short-term memory information. Thus, the new activation is a function of the old activation, the knowledge (weights), and the input. We can think of this as the input leading to some new thought.

Third, the long-term effects of any input occur only through its change of the connection weights between units. Thus, the set of weights can be thought of as the long-term memory. After affecting the activation, each new input can cause a small change in the connection weights, which can be thought of as the encoding of that item in memory. (See the appendix to this chapter for a specific example of how this works.)

An important idea in PDP models is that rather than each memory being some new, separate trace or some new nodes in a network, the memories are all stored in the same set of weights (as will be illustrated shortly). This idea may seem strange and fraught with difficulties in that one expects there to be lots of confusion about what was stored. The contribution of this work, however, has been to show how well information can be retained in such a scheme. Further, the researchers argue that even the types of confusions that do occur are important and also occur when people are remembering.

We will first explain how a very simplified model of this type works and then examine some general issues that are illustrated. Although these finer points are a bit complicated, they are important to show how the model works.

A Simple Example.   In this example, borrowed from McClelland, Rumelhart, and Hinton (1986), we will make some simplifying assumptions. First, we will assume that the stimuli can be represented as vectors with only four values. Second, we will assume that the network is quite simple with the four-value input leading to a four-value output vector. The input vector will represent the stimulus and the output vector will represent the system's response to the input (i.e., we will not include cycles of activation or add these changes to the old activation). Each of the four elements of the input vector is connected to each of the four elements of the output vector, as shown in Figure 8.8a. Figure 8.8b shows the weights of the simple network in matrix form. (The chapter appendix explains how these weights were computed.) This network was trained to learn two different arbitrary associations with the following input-output pairings:

	Input Vector	Output Vector
PAIR1	(1 -1 -1 1)	(-1 -1 1 1)
PAIR2	(-1 1 -1 1)	(-1 1 1 -1)

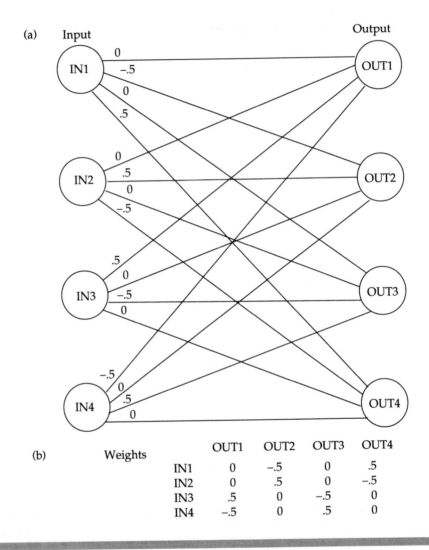

(b)   Weights

	OUT1	OUT2	OUT3	OUT4
IN1	0	−.5	0	.5
IN2	0	.5	0	−.5
IN3	.5	0	−.5	0
IN4	−.5	0	.5	0

Figure 8.8   **A simple example of a PDP network with four input elements and four output elements.**
(a) This network perfectly responds to the PAIR1 and PAIR2 associations given in the text. The input-output weight is indicated by the number on the line connecting them. (b) The matrix provides another way of showing the weights on the input-output connections of the network. For example, the weight of the connection between IN1 and OUT2 is − .5.

Assuming we have this network, how is it used? To determine the value of the output vector, we multiply the value of the input element by its weight and add all the values for a given output element. (It may be helpful for you to refer to the figure.) For example, using PAIR1, the first output element (OUT1) gets an activation of 1 from the first input element (IN1) times the weight between IN1 and OUT1 of 0, so it is 0. OUT1 also gets -1 times 0 from IN2, -1 times .5 from IN3, and 1 times $-.5$ from IN4. Thus, the value at OUT1 is:

$$0 + 0 + (-.5) + (-.5) = -1$$

The second element, OUT2, gets an activation of 1 from IN1 times the IN1 to OUT2 weight of $-.5$, plus -1 from IN2 times the IN2 to OUT2 weight of .5, plus -1 from IN3 times 0, and 1 from IN4 times 0, with the sum being $-.5 + (-.5) = -1$. Using this same method, the output for the remaining two elements of the output vector are as desired, 1 and 1. Thus, this set of weights does encode the PAIR1 association. That is, given the input $(1\ -1\ -1\ \ 1)$, the network responds with $(-1\ -1\ \ 1\ \ 1)$.

This example shows that these weights will transform the input vector of PAIR1 to the appropriate output vector. However, memory systems usually encode more than one stimulus. The power of the PDP approach is that the same weights can be used to encode multiple associations. For example, the simple network we have presented was constructed by also having it learn the association PAIR2 given above. Referring again to Figure 8.8, the input $(-1\ \ 1\ -1\ \ 1)$ leads to the desired output $(-1\ \ 1\ \ 1\ -1)$. To do one calculation here:

$$OUT1 = (-1 \times 0) + (1 \times 0) + (-1 \times .5) + (1 \times -.5) = -1$$

This example can be used to illustrate four points about the PDP approach: (1) its distributed nature, (2) the encoding of specific and general information, (3) the use of partial information, and (4) the effects of learning.

Distributed Representation.   First, this example shows the knowledge is distributed (hence the D in PDP) in two ways. One, the knowledge does not reside in any single location but is encoded throughout the network in the weights. Two, the same sets of weights can be used to encode multiple pieces of knowledge. As we shall see, distributed representations facilitate generalization and the use of partial information.

General and Specific Information.   A basic problem in memory is how one deals with both remembering specific information and learning abstractions. For instance, as we meet new people, we may want to remember each person, but at the same time use these people to learn more about people in general and also about specific categories of people. Many theories would assume that specific and abstract learning would require separate connections. In the PDP approach, however, the same set of weights can lead to remembering specific information and learning abstractions.

If we look at the two input and output vectors in PAIR1 and PAIR2, we see that certain values are the same. In particular, IN3 (-1) and IN4 (1) occur in both pairs, as do OUT1 (-1) and OUT3 (1). Although this example is a simple setup, we may imagine far larger vectors in which subsets of common elements could encode, for instance, those features in common between many members of a category. We wish to point out two aspects of the encoding.

First, if this network is given the input (0   0 -1 1) (the 0 input is the same as saying there is no known value), the output responds (-1 0   1   0). That is, given the two input elements in common, the two common output elements are generated. Thus, although this general pattern was never before presented, the network has captured the regularities of the two patterns.

Second, if the network is given a new full input that includes these two "general" input elements, the output will include the two general output elements. For example, the input (.75   .25 -1 1) leads to the output (-1 $-.25$ 1   .25).

Partial Information.   An important feature of our memory is that we may use partial information about an event or association to retrieve further information. You may have learned to associate the appearance of a dog with its name, but if you see just the face of the dog, you can often recall its name. As we noted in the last chapter, the more of the encoding context one has at retrieval the better, but an exact match is not usually needed to retrieve some information. PDP models allow the use of partial inputs to retrieve partial outputs.

For example, again using Figure 8.8, suppose one just had the first three elements of the input for PAIR1, (1 -1 -1 0). The output would not be the exact association learned, (-1 -1 1   1), but a similar output ($-.5$ -1 .5   1). Thus, partial input allows one to retrieve some relevant information, but often not exactly the encoded information. How close to the original output one gets depends on how much of the input is missing and how much that missing input could be made up for by the regularities already encoded into the network.

Learning More in the Same Network.   How do these systems learn additional information? The learning details are described in the chapter appendix, but we provide a characterization of one general learning procedure here. The output activation values, corresponding to short-term memory, are a function of the input values times the weights (what the system knew before the input). These output values are then compared to some target values. (Learning requires some feedback. This feedback about performance may come from an outside source, such as a teacher or parent, or from the system itself noticing discrepancies between the input and output.) The error, the difference between the output and target values, is used to change the weights, with more change being made to weights that led to greater error or that were from high input values. These weight changes *are* the long-term memory encoding of that presentation.

We chose the particular network in Figure 8.8 to illustrate how two different associations could be perfectly stored together in the same network. Perfect remembering is not usually the case in PDP models. Rather, as more information is stored it begins to affect the retrieval of earlier information. For instance, suppose we had the network in Figure 8.8 also learn another pattern pair:

PAIR3:   input (1   1   1 $-$1) and output (1   1   1   1)

The new weights (again, see the chapter appendix for learning details), in matrix form, are given in Figure 8.9. Given the input (1   1   1 $-$1), this network would give the output (1   1   1   1). However, the earlier pair outputs would suffer. PAIR1 output would be ($-$1 $-$1.5   .66   .5) instead of the earlier ($-$1 $-$1   1   1) and PAIR2 would be ($-$1   .5   .66 $-$1.5) instead of ($-$1   1   1 $-$1). The reason is that the changes to the weights made to accommodate the new pair were inconsistent with some of the

After learning

(1 1 1 –1) → (1 1 1 1)

	OUT1	OUT2	OUT3	OUT4
IN1	0	−.25	.83	.75
IN2	0	.75	.83	−.25
IN3	.5	.25	.33	.25
IN4	−.5	−.25	.99	−.25

Figure 8.9   **New Matrix Values for Input-Output Connections after Learning PAIR3.**

weights needed to generate the earlier pairs. This large interference problem (this is a case of retroactive interference) can be quite severe in some cases (McCloskey & Cohen, 1989).

General Properties.   The PDP model views retrieval as the bringing to bear of relevant knowledge, which can come from multiple sources. Because all the memories are encoded together in the same set of weights, every memory influences the "remembering" of every other memory. The advantages of interactive memory structures come from the need for flexibility and multiple purpose. In the future, we may see only partial inputs and need to "remember" the rest. Or we may see new items and have to "remember" similar old items and respond in similar ways. The PDP approach argues that these needs are met by storing new experiences in the same set of weights.

Remembering is often thought of as a retrieval of a memory trace, but such a view is inappropriate when there is no separate memory trace to retrieve. Rather, PDP models take the view that one should think about the circumstances of remembering—one is given some cue or partial information about the memory and must reproduce the rest of it. For example, you may be asked, "Do you remember what John said about Mary's bike?" You use the cue to probe memory for some episode in which this cue is incorporated. Similarly, PDP models would claim that all remembering is a matter of taking some partial information and reproducing the information that was stored with it. Remembering, then, is a type of pattern completion in which the original pattern must be reproduced from some subset of it. PDP models can be quite good at such pattern completions. In fact, weight adjustments could be made to perfectly reproduce a pattern, except that the same weights also have to reproduce all the other patterns experienced before. The "memory trace" is an adjustment in these weights, with the extent of the change depending on how well the old weights did in reproducing the pattern. If the new pattern was "consistent" with much of your previous knowledge, it could be well reproduced with little adjustment of the weights, whereas if it was very different, greater adjustments might be required. Thus, memory can be viewed as incorporating weights that provide a compromise between recalling old information and adjusting for recall of new information.

McClelland and Rumelhart argue that such a model allows the learning of generalizations and the remembering of specific instances. The generalizations occur naturally. Because the same set of weights are used to encode all the different instances, those units that tend to participate in multiple instances of a given type will mutually activate each other, forming a generalization of those instances. This same explanation works in considering the related distinction of semantic and episodic memories. This model incorporates both in the same way. The model encodes each episodic memory as an adjustment to the weights. The semantic memory is claimed to arise from the fact that many of the episodic memories will have similar subpatterns of activation that will be repeated. For example, experiencing different dogs in different contexts would lead to some units being activated in all of these cases (which together would represent the pattern for "dog") as well as some specific subpatterns that would be activated as a function of some specific properties of the dog (e.g., color brown) or context (e.g., met in park).

Evaluation.   The development of PDP models has increased greatly in recent years and many of their properties are not yet fully understood. The presentation here is far simpler than most current models in terms of the representation, the interconnectedness of units, the activation and learning functions, and a number of other important features.

On the positive side, PDP models of memory incorporate rather simple processing assumptions to perform complex tasks. Each unit is quite simple, but when configured appropriately, the models can be very powerful. In addition, they provide an alternative view to the idea that cognition is a type of symbolic computation.

On the negative side, it is still unclear whether these models are consistent with certain memory phenomena. For instance, McCloskey and Cohen (1989) argue that interference effects are problematic for PDP models in that when the models adjust the weights to try to reproduce the new pattern, they may lead to very poor memory of the earlier patterns. Using the same weights to capture multiple memories has the advantage of leading to generalizations, but the flip side is that it leads to interference. McCloskey and Cohen argue that such interference can be catastrophic in that the earlier memories are essentially lost. (Also see Ratcliff, 1990 for some related criticisms of the learning algorithms). Not surprisingly, there have been attempts to address these problems (see Hetherington & Seidenberg, 1989 and Kruschke, 1990 for some possible solutions). This area of research has attracted many investigators and the next few years should see substantial development and clarification of advantages and criticisms.

Summary

We have examined two models that encode episodic and semantic information together. Models that argue for a single scheme for these memories highlight some issues that are problematic for models positing separate memory systems. In particular, if one posits separate systems, then what is the interaction between the systems that allows us to use our semantic knowledge in understanding new events and our episodic knowledge in answering queries about semantic information?

Models proposing separate systems also do not seem to address the question of how semantic memories are acquired. Models proposing a single system generally have semantic information resulting from the accumulation of similar episodic events. The PDP model argues that they arise naturally from the episodes through an interferencelike property of the systems, as the generalizations arise from the specific experiences. (The ACT theory is less clear about this, but an interference explanation is one possibility here as well.) The point is not that these theories incorporating both types of knowledge are correct, but rather that by their nature they have been forced to deal with a number of issues that have not been dealt with by investigators arguing for multiple systems.

Implicit and Explicit Memory

Even if an experience is not recollected, it may be "remembered" in the sense that it exerts an influence. A clear example of such nonrecollected influence occurs all the time in sports. You may practice your tennis swing, guided by some instruction. However, you are not practicing this swing so that you can recollect this particular episode at some later time, but rather so that, with sufficient good practice, you will be able to swing in the appropriate way when a ball is hit to you.

This general distinction has been discussed in terms of implicit versus explicit memory (Graf & Schacter, 1985). **Implicit memory** refers to cases in which some previous experience affects performance without necessarily being associated with any conscious recollection of the experience. **Explicit memory** refers to cases that require the conscious recollection of the experience. Most memory research since the early work of Ebbinghaus in the late 1800s has used explicit memory tasks such as recall or recognition (although Ebbinghaus also used savings in relearning, a type of implicit memory task). But memory has a number of functions, only one of which is the conscious recollection of an experience.

Dissociations Between Implicit and Explicit Measures

After years of emphasizing recollection, many memory researchers have begun to investigate implicit tasks and how the memory in such tasks might be related to memory on more explicit tasks. Many of the analyses of implicit memory can be considered together as types of **repetition priming**—a recent exposure to a stimulus affects its subsequent processing. For example, suppose you were asked to name the first three fruits that come to mind. Now, further suppose that before that task you were shown a list of words, one of which was "banana." It might not surprise most people that the probability of generating banana when asked for three fruits would be much higher than if you had not seen banana in the previous list. Less obvious is the fact that this increased probability can occur even if a person no longer remembers seeing banana on the list. One reason for the interest in the distinction between implicit and explicit memory is the possibility that they may be separate memory systems.

In one of the first studies in this area, Jacoby and Dallas (1981) examined the effect of a presentation of the word on its subsequent recognition (an explicit task because it requires remembering the word) and perceptual identification, the ability to identify a word presented for a very short time (an implicit task because it does not require recollecting any specific experience). They presented a list of 60 words, asking questions that forced subjects to consider the meaning, rhyming, or particular letters in the word (as in the Craik and Tulving, 1975 study discussed in the previous chapter). Following this study list, subjects were presented with 80 words at test, 60 that had been presented on the study list and 20 that had not. Half the subjects were given a perceptual identification test for each word, in which the word was presented for 35 milliseconds (about 1/30th of a second). The other half of the subjects received the 80 words one at a time and had to respond whether they had seen the word on the study list.

Jacoby and Dallas found a repetition priming effect on perceptual identification. Words presented on the list were identified correctly 80% of the time, while words that were not presented on the list were identified correctly 65% of the time.

By itself that result may not seem surprising. Perhaps subjects simply were more likely to guess a word from the list if they were unsure of what they had seen in the brief perceptual identification trial. That is, perhaps this implicit measure is also being influenced by recollection. A problem for this explanation is that Jacoby and Dallas found that manipulating the question asked at study (meaning, rhyme, or letter) affected recognition but had *no* effect on perceptual identification. Questions about meaning led to much better later recognition than did questions about rhyme, which in turn led to better recognition than did questions about whether a particular letter was present (95%, 72%, and 51%, respectively, for yes responses). But this manipulation had no effect at all on the perceptual identification task, with the probability of reporting the correct word being 80%, 82%, and 78% for these same three study conditions. Thus, the repetition priming effect on perceptual identification was not due to subjects' explicit guesses of words on the list, because they would have guessed much better in the meaning condition than the rhyme condition and better in the rhyme condition than the letter condition. Somehow, the prior experience had an effect on perceptual identification that did not depend on the variables that influenced its effect on an explicit memory task.

Some researchers have argued that implicit tasks may simply reflect sensitivity to a temporary activation of the concept. So, if you see a word on a list, it may simply activate its corresponding concept for a short time, leading to a facilitation in implicit tasks. Such a view would argue that levels of processing manipulations have no effect, because implicit tasks are simply sensitive to activation of the concept, not the details of the activation or later memory trace. This activation view cannot be all there is to the implicit memory tasks. First, effects on implicit tasks can be quite long-lived, in many cases surviving for a week or more (see, e.g., Tulving, Schacter, & Stark, 1982). Second, other experimental variables affect implicit measures but not explicit measures. For example, the physical similarity between the study and test presentations (e.g., whether the word is presented in the same font or modality) affects implicit memory measures (see, e.g., Roediger & Blaxton, 1987) but has little or no effect on explicit measures. If the presentation of an item activated the concept, it is difficult to see why such physical manipulations would affect implicit memory measures.

In the last decade a large number of experiments have been conducted using many different implicit and explicit memory tasks (see Richardson-Klavehn & Bjork, 1988 and Schacter, 1987 for reviews). The pattern is often that some variables affect performance on one type of task but not the other. It is also true that these tasks sometimes show similar effects of some variables. Still, the pattern of differential effects is striking.

Despite general agreement about the effects, there is a great deal of disagreement over how to interpret them. Some researchers believe that the large number of differences suggest different memory systems, with conscious recollection relying on different representations than that used by implicit tasks. Other researchers argue that these tasks are better seen as falling on a continuum, with the effects due to some encoding-retrieval interaction. That is, implicit and explicit tasks may rely on different kinds of encoding information or processes. These investigators argue that such interactions are quite common within the literature examining explicit memory (see the previous chapter for some examples), so should not lead us to believe that separate systems are involved.

For example, Roediger, Srinivas, and Weldon (1989) proposed that explicit memory tasks tap the encoded meaning of the concepts, whereas implicit memory tasks often rely heavily on more perceptual matches between study and test. Thus, recall or recognition may emphasize meaning, which is why a levels of processing effect is found. Perceptual identification is not affected by that variable but is affected by the physical similarity of items at study and test because of its perceptual emphasis. Although their suggestion may also have problems (see, e.g., Tenpenny & Shoben, 1992), Roediger and colleagues do point out that the logic of experimental manipulation effects is not wholly consistent for the implicit/explicit distinction: sometimes different implicit tasks are differentially affected by the same experimental manipulations and sometimes different explicit tasks are. These inconsistencies make it more difficult to argue that the findings are strong support for distinct memory systems. (See Roediger, 1990 for a very readable presentation of these arguments.)

Spared Learning in Amnesia

Patients with amnesia have great difficulty learning new information, but their learning on some tasks is largely spared from amnesia. Specifically, learning tends to be spared on tasks that do not require conscious recollection. Such effects clearly are crucial to our understanding of amnesia, as well as our conceptions of memory.

For example, Milner (1966) found that the amnesic patient H. M. showed steady improvement in both errors and time in a mirror-tracing task across three days, although he was unable to explicitly remember having learned the task. Such sparing of memory has also been shown with problem-solving tasks and perceptual tasks (see Cohen, 1984; Schacter, 1987 for reviews).

To illustrate this spared learning in perceptual tasks, Cohen and Squire (1980) had amnesic patients and normal controls learn to read mirror-reversed words. This task is difficult at first, but people improve with practice and become quite proficient (see, e.g., Kolers, 1975). Each person was shown triads of words and had to read 50 of these triads on each of three days and then once more about three months later. Korsakoff patients, despite being unable to recognize having seen many of the words (far fewer than normals were able to recognize), showed improvement in this skill at about the same rate as the normals. Other studies with different perceptual and cognitive tasks have found similar sparing of learning, although the amnesic patients often learn at a slightly slower rate than normals.

In addition to the findings with learning of new skills, amnesic people often show repetition priming effects even though they may be unable to explicitly remember the earlier experience. For example, Graf, Squire, and Mandler (1984) presented amnesic patients and control subjects with a list of words two times and then tested the subjects in a variety of memory tasks. The words were chosen so that the first three letters of each word (e.g., mar____ for the word market) occurred in a number of words (e.g., marry, marble, marsh). Although their experiments involved several different tests, we consider here the cued recall and word completion tests. In the cued recall test subjects were given the first three letters and asked to recall a word from the earlier list that began with the same three letters. In the word completion task they were given the first three letters and told to make these into words by writing the first English word "that comes to mind." Thus, the subjects received exactly the same cues and the only difference was in the instructions. In both tasks, the dependent measure was how often the words from the list were given as responses.

As expected, amnesic subjects were worse on the cued recall test. But on the word completion test, the amnesic subjects performed at least as well as control subjects. Thus, these repetition-priming effects also show preserved learning in amnesia. Notably, the amnesic performance on word completion was almost exactly the same as in cued recall (57.2% vs. 57.6%). Control subjects were much more likely to give the study word to the cue when asked to do so. Although it is an open question as to whether these repetition priming and skill learning effects are due to the same processes, both suggest that some learning may be spared in amnesia.

We have discussed differences between implicit and explicit tasks, as well as spared learning in amnesic patients. These findings clearly are central ones for memory theories to account for. What is the correct explanation for these results? The true answer is easy—we do not know. Various possibilities have been offered, including the encoding-test interaction explanation discussed earlier. In the next section we focus on one influential possibility in more detail, in which it is argued that many of these differences are due to distinct *procedural versus declarative* memory systems.

The Procedural-Declarative Distinction

Numerous investigators have argued that we need to have distinct memory systems to account both for what learning is spared in amnesia and for the implicit-explicit differences. Although the ideas differ greatly in their details, a common theme is that different functions of memory may be served by these different systems. Here we focus on the proposal by Neal Cohen and his colleagues (e.g., Cohen, 1984; Cohen & Eichenbaum, in press).

Cohen and his colleagues argue that the division of implicit and explicit memory is not quite the right way of dividing memory functions. The implicit-explicit distinction is a poor one in two ways. First, the distinction is used with respect to tasks, but tasks are almost never a pure measure of what the investigators would refer to as explicit and implicit memory. For example, perceptual identification, an implicit task, can be influenced by subjects' explicit memory of the previous word list. Therefore, using results from these tasks as if they tap distinct memory systems will be misleading. Second, even if this purity of tasks was not an issue, the implicit-explicit distinction is really a description of the phenomena, not an analysis of the underlying mechanisms. What is it that leads to explicit measures being sensitive to some variables and implicit measures being sensitive to other variables? Cohen proposes, as have some other researchers, that the extant distinction between declarative and procedural memory can be used to understand many of these differences.

Declarative memory refers to memory for facts, such as *knowing that* Des Moines is the capital of Iowa or that you ate spaghetti for dinner last night (i.e., it includes both semantic and episodic memories). These memories can be thought of as the outcomes of processes, the things that we think about. They can often be verbalized or imaged and may be used in multiple activities. **Procedural memory** refers to *knowing how* or the memory that subserves activities such as getting dressed, reading a word, driving a car, performing a surgery, and so on. Such memories are not verbalizable, but rather involve knowledge about the actual doing. For example, in tying your shoelaces you do not think about the sequence, you just do it. To see this distinction, ask yourself whether you begin by putting the left part of the lace under the right or the right under the left. To answer this question, most people need to imagine themselves tying the shoelaces. Even though at one time you were taught explicitly how to start and continue the tying, the procedure has become so well learned that it no longer requires accessing this earlier declarative knowledge.

Cohen and his colleagues argue that the procedural-declarative distinction is supported by both behavioral and neuroscience data (e.g., Cohen & Eichenbaum, in press). Our reading of the literature is that although a great deal of support is provided for these ideas, the strong claims of this view are yet to be fully tested. It does provide one way of trying to incorporate both the findings from the burgeoning research on implicit-explicit memory and the findings of spared learning in amnesic patients.

Implications for ACT and PDP models

Now that we have briefly examined the procedural-declarative distinction, what implications does it have for the models discussed in the last section? The ACT model makes a fundamental distinction between procedural and declarative representations (see Anderson, 1976, for an early discussion and 1983 for a later exposition). The theory represents the two types of memories differently and independently, although any particular task may make use of both. The network representation is the declarative representation. Anderson views this representation, along with the spreading activation, as a heuristic for activating relevant information. The procedural part of memory, however, is the part that takes this possibly relevant information and makes use of it. The details of the procedural memory in ACT, a representation called *productions*, are discussed in more detail in the chapter on expertise and creativity.

The PDP model of McClelland and Rumelhart (1986a, 1986b) is not committed to such a procedural-declarative distinction. They argue that this distinction is plausible, but the data do not rule out other possible interpretations. For example, they suggest that perhaps differences in the amount of weight change could account for a procedural-declarative distinction. By this account, procedural tasks would be sensitive to small weight changes because they are modifications of previously existing memories. Declarative memories, on the other hand, would involve large weight changes because they require the learning of a new pattern of activation. McClelland and Rumelhart (1986b) further speculate that the spared learning in amnesic patients could reflect an ability to still make small weight changes, whereas the loss of conscious recollection could reflect a loss of the ability to make large weight changes. These ideas have yet to be fully evaluated. An alternative possibility is to consider the PDP model to be a model of something like procedural memory, in which small changes are made to previously learned interconnections (also see Schacter, 1989). Because of the recent advances in both PDP models and the exact nature of the memory distinctions, it is not yet clear how (or whether) the model might accommodate these results.

Evaluation

What have we learned from this work on memory distinctions? The research on implicit-explicit measures and their relations has provided new findings that are challenging current theories. Although new findings will eventually lead to better theories, in the course of doing so they also lead to disagreements. These disagreements reflect differences of opinion about the importance of different types of evidence and what it means to argue that memory systems are distinct.

Important memory distinctions are not going to be decided on the basis of a single study. Rather, what has developed over the last decade is an appreciation of how different sources of evidence may all be used together to help understand and refine the important distinctions. Thus, memory researchers incorporate results from neuropsychological studies of amnesia (some of which have been discussed), from studies using psychophysiological measures (such as brain blood flow), from other neurosciences involving models of animal memory (in which the hippocampus has been suggested as important for declarative memories), and from evolutionary arguments (see, e.g., Sherry & Schacter, 1987).

Summary

We began this chapter with some models of how knowledge about objects and their superordinates might be represented and used. We then examined two models incorporating both semantic and episodic information: ACT and a PDP model. An important idea in many of these models is that our knowledge allows us to make inferences beyond the specific information we have encoded. By organizing our knowledge, we greatly increase our ability to apply this knowledge to new situations.

Intuitively, we might think that it would be best if we could use all the knowledge that is relevant. However, it should be noted that the use of relevant knowledge might have a cost as well. To the extent that our memory works to have all relevant knowledge available to be used, it may be difficult to recollect a single experience without being influenced by other knowledge. In many models there is a trade-off between retrieval of specific information and the use of more general knowledge.

In addition to the general knowledge issues that arise from this chapter, we have also investigated a number of disparate models. An examination of models can sometimes be frustrating to the beginner. We think it important to answer directly two common complaints. First, if the goal of models is to simplify, doesn't it seem as if the models are getting very complex? Second, if people cannot agree on the correct model, where is the progress?

It is true that models are becoming more complex and they are likely to continue to be even more so. On the other hand, memory is quite complex and it may take a complex model to give a reasonable account. Despite their increasing complexity, our understanding of the important characteristics of models has increased as well. Although many current models require the use of computers for figuring out their predictions, extensive analyses of these models provide a clear idea of which characteristics are affecting which aspects of the predictions.

It is important not to confuse disagreement with lack of progress. Throughout this chapter, we have described very different models that attempt to account for roughly the same set of results. This competition among models leads to new tests, which may lead to new findings, which may lead to an even better understanding of memory. Disagreements about the types of memory distinctions are part of the fuel of progress.

Key Terms

ACT
characteristic features
connection weights
declarative memory
defining features
episodic memory
explicit memory
fan effect
feature comparison model
hiearchical model
implicit memory
intersection

links
nodes
PDP
procedural memory
propositions
repetition priming
semantic memory
semantic relatedness
spreading activation
type-token distinction
typicality effect

Recommended Readings

The early work on semantic memory models is well presented in the articles discussed here, but Smith (1978) presents a very clear and integrative review. Smith and Medin (1981) also review much of this work in the context of research on concepts and categories.

The ACT theory is presented in great detail in the original monographs (Anderson, 1976, 1983), which also contain references to the many experimental studies examining this theory. The research and theory on plausibility judgments is provided in Reder (1982), and further extensions in Reder and Ross (1983).

The PDP work is gaining great influence in a number of fields and has led to the development of some new journals. Some of the most influential papers so far are contained in a two-volume set called *Parallel Distributed Processing* (McClelland & Rumelhart, 1986c; Rumelhart & McClelland, 1986).

Memory distinctions are presented in many readings. Tulving (1983) presents evidence of the semantic/episodic distinction, though a number of criticisms have been presented (e.g., Ratcliff, McKoon, & Dell, 1986). Schacter (1989) reviews evidence for the implicit/explicit distinction. A very different perspective on this research is given by Larry Jacoby (e.g., Jacoby, Kelley, & Dywan, 1989; Jacoby, Woloshyn, & Kelley, 1989). The procedural/declarative distinction is discussed in Anderson (1976, 1983) and Cohen (1984). Cohen and Eichenbaum (in press) provide an extensive up-to-date treatment.

Appendix: Learning in a Parallel Distributed Processing Model

In this appendix we present an example of the learning processes in a PDP model by showing how it can learn the weights used in the example given in the chapter. As in the chapter, we assume that each of the four input values (IN1, IN2, IN3, IN4) is connected to each of the four output values (OUT1, OUT2, OUT3, OUT4). The weight on each connection (e.g., IN1–OUT2 as the weight between IN1 and OUT2) is what changes with learning. To simplify the illustration we will assume a very simple weight-change method.

To begin, let us assume all weights are zero. We want to teach the pattern association PAIR1, that when $(1 \; -1 \; -1 \; 1)$ is given as input, $(-1 \; -1 \; 1 \; 1)$ should be the output. To determine the value of each output we multiply the value of the input element by the weight between the input and output and add all the values for a given output element. In this case, because all the weights are zero, the output from this input (or in fact any input) is $(0 \; 0 \; 0 \; 0)$.

For any single input it is easy to change the weights to get a particular output. However, we want the knowledge about each output value to come from multiple sources, so that if any one source cannot contribute (e.g., because of missing input), the others can at least partially make up for it. That is the reason for a more complicated weighting scheme—to *distribute* the knowledge.

Let us go back to our example now. If we were to present the same

Want association   Input   (1 –1 –1 1)
                                     Output   (–1 –1 1 1)

Start with 0 weights

IN1 (1) ══════ (0) OUT1

IN2 (–1) ══════ (0) OUT2

IN3 (–1) ══════ (0) OUT3

IN4 (1) ══════ (0) OUT4

Target (T)	–1	–1	1	1
Output (O)	0	0	0	0
Error (T-O)	–1	–1	1	1
(×Learning parameter .33)	–.33	–.33	.33	.33

Weight changes	OUT1	OUT2	OUT3	OUT4
IN1	–.33	–.33	.33	.33
IN2	.33	.33	–.33	–.33
IN3	.33	.33	–.33	–.33
IN4	–.33	–.33	.33	.33

Figure 8.A1   The first pass at learning the PAIR1 association presented in the chapter. The network starts with all 0 weights and gets the output (0 0 0 0). The middle part of the figure shows the determination of error and the bottom part shows the weight changes made.

input again, we would want the system to respond with something closer to the desired pattern. The learning of the system is in terms of the weight changes. The idea behind the weight change is simple, although the details can get complex. The basic idea is that we compare the output value with the expected value or *target* [in this case, $(-1 \ -1 \ \ 1 \ \ 1)$] and the difference is the "error." Learning then consists of changing weights to reduce this error. The method used is to assume that each weight between an input and output element contributed to that error. However, knowing each weight contributed does not tell you how to change them. A common method for determining weight changes is to assume that weights from large input values contributed more to the error than weights from lower input values. Thus the change made to each weight is determined by the size of the error and the input activation.

For instance, OUT1 was expected to be −1 but was 0, so the error was target (−1) minus output (0), or −1. The rule used (referred to as the *delta rule*) is to multiply the error (−1) by the activation value of the input element and then multiply it by some learning parameter, which for purposes of illustration we will set to .33. (The learning parameter is important in the mathematics for keeping the change from being too great, but we will not explain it further here.) Thus, by this scheme, the weight on IN1-OUT1 would be changed by the error (−1) multiplied by the input value (1) multiplied by the learning parameter (.33),

$$-1 \times 1 \times .33 = -.33$$

In Figure 8.A1 we have calculated the weight changes for each input-output connection. The errors were all equal except for sign and the inputs were all equal except for sign, so the weight changes in this example are all

Using weights in bottom of Figure 8A.1 for Pair 1

Input   (1 −1 −1 1)

Output   (−1.32 −1.32 1.32 1.32)

Target (T)	−1	−1	1	1
Output (O)	−1.32	−1.32	1.32	1.32
Error (T-O)	.32	.32	−.32	−.32
(×.33)	.10	.10	−.10	−.10
Weight changes	.10	.10	−.10	−.10
	−.10	−.10	.10	.10
	−.10	−.10	.10	.10
	.10	.10	−.10	−.10
New Weights	−.23	−.23	.23	.23
	.23	.23	−.23	−.23
	.23	.23	−.23	−.23
	−.23	−.23	.23	.23

Figure 8.A2   Continuation of the example from Figure 8.A1 showing the error, the matrix of weight changes, and the new weights after the weight changes are added to the old weights (which are presented in Figure 8.A1).

Using weights in bottom of Figure 8A.2

Input   (1 −1 −1   1)

Output   (−.92 −.92 .92 .92)

Target (T)	−1	−1	1	1
Outout (O)	−.92	−.92	.92	.92
Error (T-O)	−.08	−.08	.08	.08
(× .33)	−.02	−.02	.02	.02
Weight changes	−.02	−.02	.02	.02
	.02	.02	−.02	−.02
	.02	.02	−.02	−.02
	−.02	−.02	.02	.02
New Weights	−.25	−.25	.25	.25
	.25	.25	−.25	−.25
	.25	.25	−.25	−.25
	−.25	−.25	.25	.25

Figure 8.A3   Continuation of the example from Figure 8.A2 showing the error, the matrix of weight changes, and the new weights after the weight changes are added to the old weights (which are presented in Figure 8.A2).

equal except for sign. Since the original matrix of connections was all zero, this weight change matrix added to the original matrix leads to a new matrix that is equal to the weight changes. In general, the new weight is equal to the old weight plus the product of the error and input activation values (and the learning rate). The smaller the error (or input activation), the smaller the change to the weight.

Figure 8.A1 shows the set of weights after the first presentation. If the same stimulus (1 −1 −1   1) is presented again, the activation for the output vector is (−1.32 −1.32   1.32   1.32), a much closer fit to the desired pattern of (−1 −1   1   1) (see Figure 8.A2). The error is (.32   .32 −.32 −.32) and the weight changes are made again (input × error × learning parameter), with the resulting weight changes given in Figure 8.A2. In the bottom of the figure we show the result of adding these weight changes to the weights given in Figure 8.A1.

If the input were presented a third time, the output vector would be quite close, (−.92 −.92   .92   .92). As shown in Figure 8.A3, the weight changes made are getting smaller (.02 or −.02). The matrix given at the bottom of Figure 8.A3 will take the input of (1 −1 −1   1) and give the desired output (1 −1 −1   1). Thus, the weights have "learned" the association of these two patterns.

This example shows that this simplified scheme will work in converging on the correct output with practice. One might wonder how the same system would learn the other pattern association given in the chapter, PAIR2, that (−1   1 −1   1) leads to an output of (−1   1   1 −1). We use exactly the same procedure as when learning the first association. If (−1   1 −1   1) is given as input to the matrix, the output is (0   0   0   0). (The weight changes encoding PAIR1 have no effect on the output of PAIR2 because the two input vectors are uncorrelated or, more technically, *orthogonal*. As was shown earlier in the chapter with two examples involving PAIR3, if the input vectors are correlated, weight changes to encode one input-output pair do affect the output when the other input vector is presented.) Thus the error from the target of (−1   1   1 −1) is (−1   1   1 −1) and we determine weight changes for each input-output

Learning a new association pair   (–1 1 –1 1) → (–1 1 1 –1)

Input   (–1 1 –1 1)

Output   (0 0 0 0)

Target (T)	−1	1	1	−1
Output (O)	0	0	0	0
Error (T–O)	−1	1	1	−1
(×.33)	−.33	.33	.33	−.33

Weight changes				
	.33	−.33	−.33	.33
	−.33	.33	.33	−.33
	.33	−.33	−.33	.33
	−.33	.33	.33	−.33

New Weights				
	.08	−.58	−.08	.58
	−.08	.58	.08	−.58
	.58	−.08	−.58	.08
	−.58	.08	.58	−.08

Figure 8.A4   The effect of learning PAIR2 on the matrix from Figure 8.A3, showing the error from using the weights from PAIR1 for responding to PAIR2. The matrices encode the weight changes and the new weights. (Compare to Figure 8.8 to see how the learning is converging on the matrix of weights presented there.)

connection. These weight changes are given in the middle of Figure 8.A4. When they are added to the matrix learned from the first pattern, the resulting matrix has changed dramatically. In fact, the matrix is quite close to the one given in Figure 8.8, which perfectly associates both pairs of patterns. It would take a couple more weight changes to get to the exact matrix, but we will leave that to the interested reader.

IV
LANGUAGE AND UNDERSTANDING

9
LANGUAGE

Chapter Outline

Every language is a temple in which the soul of those who speak it is enshrined.

—Oliver Wendell Holmes

Introduction

To the best of our current knowledge, language is uniquely human and perhaps our most impressive accomplishment. Analyses of the structure of language reveal enormous complexities and subtle regularities that people, even infants, nonetheless seem to master effortlessly. Many cognitive scientists believe that language is an important window to the mind. Relative to the visual system, the language system seems less constrained by how the world is than by distinctly human characteristics.

Levels and Structure

Levels.   One of the more striking aspects of language is the different levels that are involved in both production and comprehension. In speaking, we start with some thought or idea, put it into the form of a sentence, and then transform it into sounds that express the sentence. In listening, we hear speech sounds, understand them in terms of words, combine the words into sentences, and then go from sentences to the underlying thoughts or ideas. To a considerable extent, the link between sounds and underlying ideas is arbitrary because different languages use different individual speech sounds, combinations of speech sounds, and different rules for word order. In the case of sign languages the visual modality replaces the auditory modality as the medium for communication. This chapter is organized around the different levels associated with language production and comprehension.

Structure.   Language is organized into a hierarchy of levels. At the lowest level are **phonemes**, which are the smallest significant sound units in language. English has about 40 phonemes (see Table 9.1). Languages differ from one another to some extent in the particular phonemes they employ.

Table 9.1 **Phonetic Symbols.**
The major consonants, vowels, and diphthongs of English and their phonetic symbols.

Consonants				Vowels		Diphthongs	
p	pill	θ	thigh	i	beet	ay	bite
b	bill	ð	thy	ɪ	bit	æw	about
m	mill	š	shallow	e	bait	ɔy	boy
t	till	ž	measure	ɛ	bet		
ḍ	dill	č	chip	æ	bat		
n	nil	ǰ	gyp	u	boot		
k	kill	l	lip	ʊ	put		
g	gill	r	rip	ʌ	but		
ŋ	sing	y	yet	o	boat		
f	fill	w	wet	ɔ	bought		
v	vat	ʌ	whet	a	pot		
s	sip	h	hat	ə	sofa		
z	zip			ɨ	marry		

Source: Clark, H. H., & Clark, E. V. (1977).

For example, Japanese does not distinguish between *r* and *l* (that is, the two phonemes in English become a single phoneme in Japanese), which explains why *r* often becomes *l* and vice versa when Japanese people speak English words. By the same token English does not distinguish between aspirated and unaspirated *p*, although other languages such as Hindi do. An aspirated *p* is accompanied by a slight puff of air, as when you say "puff." (You can verify this by placing your hand in front of your mouth to feel the puff or by holding up a match or candle to see the puff.) An unaspirated *p* as in the word "spill" does not produce a puff. The French language does not aspirate *p* at all. One of the tasks of acquiring a language is to learn which sound units make a difference and which don't.

Morphemes are the smallest units of language that carry meaning. A morpheme can constitute an entire word, but need not. Morphemes correspond to units that we often refer to as prefixes, suffixes, roots, or stems. For example, the suffix *s* typically indicates more than one and the prefix *pre* means before. The position of a morpheme determines its meaning. *Steam* does not mean more than one team and *gamepre* does not mean anything. The typical English speaker knows about 50,000 morphemes.

Words, phrases, and sentences are higher levels of organization. Words are the building blocks of phrases and phrases are organized building blocks of sentences. By combining words into sentences we express thoughts. We learn labels for different types of words (*the* is an "article," *strangers* is a "noun," *talked* is a "verb," etc.) and phrases (the noun phrase versus the verb phrase).

It is important to distinguish between the **surface structure** of a sentence and its *underlying representation,* sometimes called its **deep structure**. The surface structure refers to natural groupings of words based on the literal order of words in the sentences. The underlying representation refers to a grouping of words that represents the basic meaning of the sentence. Two sentences may have different surface orders but (essentially) the same meaning as in "John hit Bill" versus "Bill was hit by John."

At a general level the study of language can be broken down into four major branches: phonology, syntax, semantics, and pragmatics. **Phonology** is concerned with the structure and processing of the sounds of language, **syntax** with the way that words combine to form sentences, and **semantics** with meaning. Finally, language includes **pragmatics**, which refers to the sort of (practical) knowledge that a language user needs to know to communicate effectively. For example, "Can you close the door?" is a request, not a question about ability. This observation leads naturally to a consideration of what language is for and how it is used. In this chapter we will focus on phonology and syntax. Chapter 10 is on various aspects of language acquisition. Pragmatics forms an important part of Chapter 11 and semantics receives considerable attention in Chapter 12.

Functions of Language

Everyone would agree that languge is for communication but it is worth saying a bit more. Language does serve to convey meanings, but it is also used to teach and to issue requests and commands.

An important feature of the functions of language is referred to by Hockett (1963) as *displacement.* Language enables us to talk about ideas and events that are taking place in other contexts, have taken place in the past, or may take place in the future. Among other things the property of displacement opens up new avenues for social interchange.

Language supports goals that are facilitated by communication. Language is used to persuade, to coerce, and to bargain as well as to solve problems and to make decisions. Most of the time communication is a cooperative effort in which the parties involved establish a ground of common knowledge before moving on to new information.

And language also has an aesthetic function. We appreciate the beauty of a Shakespearean sonnet and are charmed by the turn of phrase. Language entertains us when we read a mystery and it allows us to "escape" into an endless variety of alternative possible worlds. Language is a marvelous thing. And just how is all of this accomplished? Before turning to a detailed analysis of comprehension and production, we consider some other respects in which language is distinctive.

Important Properties of Language

In addition to levels and structure, language has a number of other properties that strongly constrain theories of language use. These properties provide a useful background to our survey of language comparison and production.

Productivity and Novelty.   Language is productive in that units at one level of analysis allow the generation of many more units at the next level of analysis. For example, English has about 40 speech sounds that can be combined (according to certain rules) to generate thousands of words. Rules for combining words make it possible to generate an unlimited number of sentences. Obviously language is capable of novelty. When you hear or read the sentence, "The little green man had eaten too many four-leaf clovers," you understand the ideas being expressed, even though you doubtless have never seen this particular combination of words before. Of course language does not permit all possible combinations of words—the sequence "four-leaf the too eat green many man little clovers had" is not a possible sentence.

Ambiguity.   Language is full of ambiguities that scarcely attract our attention. Although normal conversational speech seems perfectly intelligible most of the time, typical speech is actually not at all clear when presented word by word. For example, Pollack and Pickett (1964) surreptitiously recorded people in spontaneous conversation and then played single words cut out from these tape recordings to other people for identification. Single words were correctly identified less than half the time! This is ambiguity at the *phonetic* (speech sound) level.

Segmenting the stream of speech into individual words is very difficult. Speech does not provide natural breaks between words and is essentially continuous. Anyone who listens to a conversation carried out in a foreign tongue can appreciate some of the difficulty. And anyone spending much time around children will be able to come up with examples of incorrect segmentation. One well-known example is the hymn "Gladly the Cross I Bear," which was understood by a child as "Gladly, the cross-eyed bear!"

Individual lexical items or words are also semantically ambiguous. For example, *saw* and *files* have very different meanings in the following two sentences:

1. Bill saw the files.
2. Bill files the saw.

Phrases can also be ambiguous. Consider the following sentence:

3. They are visiting relatives.

This sentence could refer to a type of relative, namely those who are visiting, or to a situation in which some unidentified "they" are paying a visit to relatives.

Yet another type of ambiguity is illustrated by the sentence:

4. Visiting relatives can be a nuisance.

This sentence says either that the relatives who are visiting can be a nuisance or that a visit to relatives can be a nuisance.

In normal conversation the context usually specifies the intended meaning and almost always the ambiguities we have been describing go unnoticed. These ambiguities are, however, quite important when attention shifts to the question of how languages are learned and how language is understood.

Integration of Information.   The language system must have resources for coping with limited information and resolving ambiguity. People must be sensitive to contextual information and must employ knowledge about the world, word meanings, and syntax in the service of understanding. Just how this integration is accomplished is a challenging puzzle. Jerry Fodor (1983) has argued that language is one of several cognitive "modules" that operates in isolation from other aspects of cognition. The idea of **modularity** is that only the products or outputs of the language module are accessible to the rest of the mind. Therefore, any influence of world knowledge on comprehension must occur only after the language module has done its work. In contrast, other researchers have argued that world knowledge is immediately and closely integrated with syntax and semantics (see Winograd, 1972). Integration clearly does take place; the question is when. We will take up this problem in detail later in this chapter.

These observations reveal some of the complexities of language and language use (there are also clear implications for language learning, which we discuss in the next chapter). They constitute the entry points to a number of issues for researchers who wish to describe the organization and structure of language. Here we provide an overview of language production and comprehension, beginning with phonology.

Phonology

Normally, we pay little attention to either how we produce or how we understand speech. The details are complex and fascinating. Our analysis begins with a description of the structure of speech sounds.

Structure

Phoneme Production. When people speak, air from the lungs is expelled through the larynx and vocal tract, including the pharynx (throat), mouth, teeth, lips, and sometimes the nose (see Figure 9.1). Sound is primarily produced in the larynx where the vocal cords vibrate and release a rapid series of puffs of air into the vocal tract. (Not all speech sounds involve this process, only so-called *voiced* sounds; we consider voiceless sounds shortly.) We talk by moving the various parts of the vocal apparatus while expelling a column of air up from the lungs and out of the mouth. Each of these movements shapes the column of air differently and this produces a distinctive speech sound. The vocal tract acts as a filter or resonator that reinforces some frequencies of vibration and inhibits others. People can produce and understand speech at a rate of upwards of 250 words per minute, which corresponds to a very rapid 16–20 phonemes per second.

The facts of speech production and perception are somewhat technical but nonetheless straightforward. Studies of speech perception have demonstrated that the general shape of the sound spectrum (see Figure 9.2C) is what listeners use to identify which vowel has been spoken. The resonant frequencies of the vocal tract (those multiples of the fundamental frequency that are enhanced by the shape of the vocal tract) are called **formants**. The first formant of the vowel [ə] or "schwa" (as the a in the word *about*; see Table 9.1) is at 500 hertz (cycles per second), the second is at 1500 hertz, and the third is at 2500 hertz. Formant frequencies are important for intelligible speech. Men and women have different fundamen-

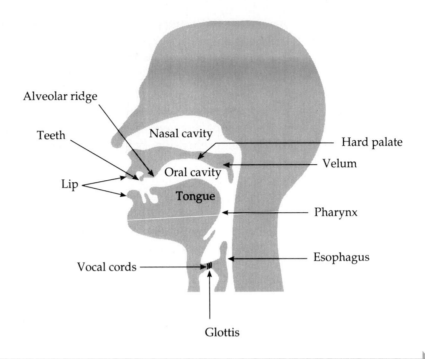

Figure 9.1 **Positions of Articulation in the Mouth.**
Source: Clark, H. H., & Clark, E. V. (1977).

tal frequencies in their voices but the formants will not vary much at all. For example, the fundamental frequency of 100, shown in Figure 9.2A, is in the range of a man's speech. Suppose that a woman rather than a man had spoken the word *about*. Because a woman's vocal tract is likely to be shorter than a man's the fundamental frequency would probably be higher, say 200 hertz. However, the general pattern or envelope of the sound spectrum would be similar (compare Figure 9.3 with Figure 9.2C).

Figure 9.2 (At right on facing page) In speech production the lungs function as a power supply, the vibrating vocal folds (cords) as an oscillator, and the vocal tract as a resonator. The acoustic spectrum for a source with a fundamental frequency of 100 hertz (A) shows the amplitude decreasing uniformly with frequency. The filter is the vocal tract, which modifies the source in a predictable way. For the vowel [ə] the filter function (B) has resonant peaks at 500, 1,500, and 2,500 hertz. When the source is filtered, the resonant peaks are imposed on the output spectrum (C) of the vowel. *Source*: Miller, G. A., 1981.

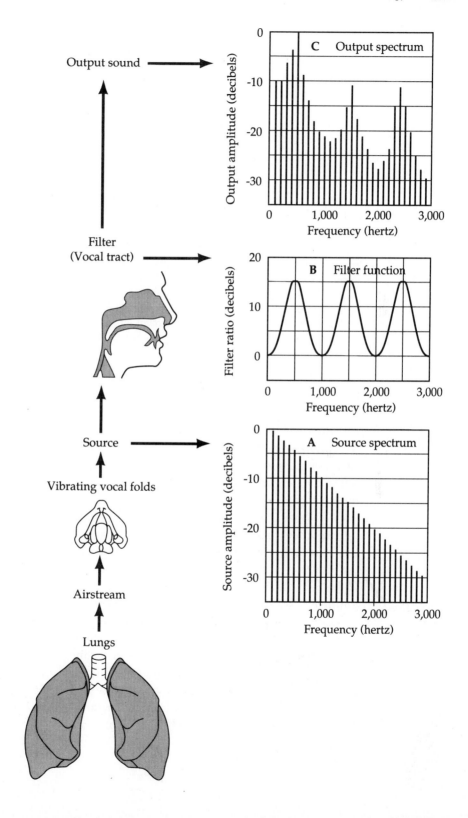

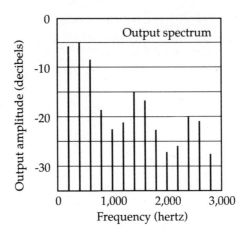

Figure 9.3   When someone with a high voice says "about" and produces the vowel [ə] at a fundamental frequency of 200 hertz, the output spectrum has no overtones at the resonant frequencies 500, 1,500, and 2,500 hertz. Yet it has the same general shape as the output spectrum for the same vowel when it is produced with a fundamental frequency of 100 hertz (see Figure 9.2C), and the vowel has the same phonetic quality. *Source*: Miller, G. A., 1981.

Other vowels are produced by changing the shape of the vocal tract to make it vibrate at different frequencies. For example, [i] (as in beet; refer back to Table 9.1) is produced by moving the tongue forward and up, [a] (as in pot) by moving the tongue back and down, and [u] (as in boot) by a high tongue position with the tongue drawn back and the lips slightly constricted. These alterations in the vocal tract produce distinct first and second formants.

Vowel sounds tend to be static in that little movement is involved during vowel production. Consonants are more dynamic. Consonants differ from each other in three ways: (1) the *place of articulation*, which concerns which part of the mouth is constricted to produce the consonant (Table 9.2 lists the possibilities for English); (2) the *manner of articulation*, or the means by which the sound is produced (see Table 9.3); (3) **voicing**, whether or not consonants are accompanied by vibration of the vocal cords. For example, [s] and [z] differ from each other in that [s] is voiceless while [z] is voiced. (Place a finger on your Adam's apple and say out loud "sip" and "zip.") As Table 9.4 indicates, many pairs of English consonants are identical in place and manner of articulation and differ only in voicing.

So far we have seen that phonemes are not the ultimate constituents of speech but rather are themselves comprised of combinations of features having a particular structure. Chomsky and Halle (1968) formalized this analysis of speech sounds into a set of 13 distinctive features. Each phoneme can be characterized by the particular combination of constituent features it manifests. The features developed by Chomsky and Halle correspond to or are refinements of the features we have been discussing (see Table 9.5). For example, *anterior* determines whether a segment is made at the front or the back of the mouth; *coronal* whether it is made in the top center ("crown" or "corona") or periphery of the mouth; *strident* indicates whether or not a buzzing quality is involved; and the features *voice* and *nasal* correspond exactly to our earlier discussion.

With two possible values for 13 distinctive features, one could, in principle, have 2^{13} or 8,192 distinct phonemes. In English there are only about 40 phonemes, which means that the values on some distinctive features are predictable from others. For example, from Table 9.5 one may note that if a phoneme is + anterior it is also + consonantal (i.e., look at the value for anterior for p, b, t, f, v, and so on and then check their value for consonantal). The fact that some features provide some information

---

Table 9.2 **The Place of Articulation.**

1. the two lips together (*bilabial*)
2. the bottom lip against the upper front teeth (*labiodental*)
3. the tongue against the teeth (*dental*)
4. the tongue against the alveolar ridge of the gums just behind the upper front teeth (*alveolar*)
5. the tongue against the hard palate in the roof of the mouth just behind the alveolar ridge (*palatal*)
6. the tongue against the soft palate, or velum, in the rear roof of the mouth (*velar*)
7. the glottis in the throat (*glottal*)

This division breaks up the consonants into seven major groups:
1. *bilabial:* p, b, m, w
2. *labiodental:* f, v
3. *dental:* θ, ð
4. *alveolar:* t, d, s, z, n, l, r
5. *palatal:* š, ž, č, ǰ, y
6. *velar:* k, g
7. *glottal:* h

Source: Clark, H. H., & Clark, E. V. (1977). *Psychology and language.* New York: Harcourt Brace Jovanovich.

Table 9.3 **Manner of Articulation.**

1. *stops:* p, b, t, d, k, g
2. *fricatives:* f, v, θ, ð, s, z, š, ž, h
3. *affricates:* č, ǰ
4. *nasals:* m, n, ŋ
5. *laterals:* l
6. *semivowels:* w, r, y

1. *stops:* complete closure at a point of articulation
2. *fricatives:* construction at a point of articulation which can produce sustained turbulence or vibration
3. *affricates:* sequence of complete closure followed by a fricativelike rush of air through a constriction
4. *nasals:* complete closure of the mouth at some point of articulation along with an opening of the nasal cavity to let air rush through the nose
5. *laterals:* shaping the tongue so that the main opening is at the sides of the tongue
6. *semivowels:* shaping the tongue so that the main opening is at the middle of the tongue

Table 9.4 **The English Consonants.**
Symbols on the left side of each column are voiceless;
those on the right side are voiced.

	Bilabial	Labio-dental	Dental	Alveolar	Palatal	Velar	Glottal
Stops	p b			t d		k g	
Fricatives		f v	θ ð	s z	š ž		h
Affricates					č ǰ		
Nasals	m			n		ŋ	
Lateral				l			
Semivowels	w			r	y		

Source: Clark, H. H., & Clark, E. V. (1977).

Table 9.5 Distinctive Features for English Consonants and Vowels.

Consonants and Liquids

Distinctive Feature	p	b	t	d	č	ǰ	k	g	f	v	θ	ð	s	z	š	ž	r	l	m	n	ŋ
Consonantal	+	+	+	+	+	+	+	+	+	+	+	+	+	+	+	+	+	+	+	+	+
Vocalic	−	−	−	−	−	−	−	−	−	−	−	−	−	−	−	−	+	+	−	−	−
Anterior	+	+	+	+	−	−	−	−	+	+	+	+	+	+	−	−	−	+	+	+	−
Coronal	−	−	+	+	+	+	−	−	−	−	+	+	+	+	+	+	+	+	−	+	−
Voice	−	+	−	+	−	+	−	+	−	+	−	+	−	+	−	+	+	+	+	+	+
Nasal	−	−	−	−	−	−	−	−	−	−	−	−	−	−	−	−	−	−	+	+	+
Strident	−	−	−	−	+	+	−	−	+	+	−	−	+	+	+	+	−	−	−	−	−
Continuant	−	−	−	−	−	−	−	−	+	+	+	+	+	+	+	+	+	+	−	−	−

Vowels and Glides

Distinctive Feature	i	ɪ	e	ɛ	æ	ɨ	ə	ʌ	a	ʊ	u	o	ɔ	y	w	h
Vocalic	+	+	+	+	+	+	+	+	+	+	+	+	+	−	−	−
Consonantal	−	−	−	−	−	−	−	−	−	−	−	−	−	−	−	−
High	+	+	−	−	−	+	−	−	−	+	+	−	−	+	+	−
Back	−	−	−	−	−	+	+	+	+	+	+	+	+	−	+	−
Low	−	−	−	−	+	−	−	−	+	−	−	−	+	−	−	−
Round	−	−	−	−	−	−	−	−	−	+	+	+	+	−	+	−
Tense	+	−	+	−	−	−	−	−	+	−	+	+	+	−	−	−

Source: Clark, H. H., & Clark, E. V. (1977).

about others suggests that perception and production processes may take advantage of this redundancy or predictability.

Additional support for the idea of distinctive features comes from studies in which isolated sounds are presented to listeners. Just which sounds are confused with which forms a systematic pattern that makes sense in terms of features. For example, consonants are most likely to be confused when they have similar articulatory features (Miller & Nicely, 1955; Shepard, 1972).

The general support for distinctive features does not necessarily mean that speech perception is accomplished by means of feature detectors in the nervous system (Remez, 1987). As we shall see, the properties associated with a particular phoneme feature may vary widely with the speaker and the phonetic context; therefore, it is unlikely that there are discrete feature detectors responding to invariant properties of the speech signal.

We admit to finding the preceding observations concerning phonemes to be pretty amazing. Normally one does not think about speech production—one just talks. On closer examination, however, we see that there are a limited number of possibilities for sound production which languages exploit. There is a distinct code (or pattern of articulation) that determines what sounds are produced and certain properties of these sounds (e.g., the first and second formants) are similar enough across speakers that distinct phonemes can be identified. The information needed for speech production and perception is not in the form of explicit knowledge. Researchers have been able to identify and make explicit this knowledge, but for most of us, the critical information for speech is largely implicit. The picture become much more complex and fascinating when we consider speech in context.

Speech in Context.   We are all well aware of the fact that speech does not consist of single phonemes punctuated by temporal gaps. People readily speak at a rate of 16 phonemes per second and speech is essentially continuous. An important tool for analyzing speech structure is the sound spectrograph, which provides a visual representation of sound energy for different frequencies as a function of time. The left side of Figure 9.4 shows a spectrograph for the consonant vowel combination [su] produced by a male speaker of English. Although it looks as if there are two distinct segments corresponding to the consonant and to the vowel, more detailed analyses reveal a more complex picture. One can use computer-editing techniques to separate the two segments and play them individually to a listener. Upon hearing segment A, the listener will be able to identify the

[su]   [šu]

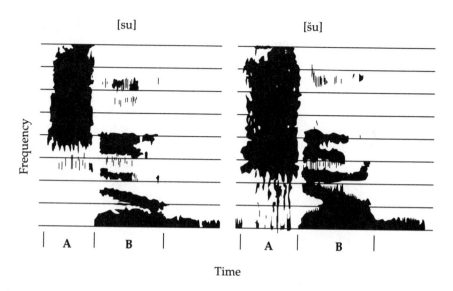

Frequency

| A | B | | A | B |

Time

Figure 9.4   Spectrogram of [su] and [šu], produced by a male speaker of English. *Source*: Miller, J. L. (1990). Speech perception. In D. N. Osherson & H. Lasnik (Eds.), *Language: An invitation to cognitive science*, Vol. 1, p. 72. Cambridge, MA: MIT Press.

consonant [s]. However, the listener is also able to identify the vowel on the basis of segment A. That is, segment A contains information about both the consonant and the vowel that was spoken (Yeni-Komshian & Soli, 1981). This parallel transmission of information results from **coarticulation**; when the consonant is being pronounced the articulators are already being shaped in preparation for the vowel sound. That is, the articulatory movements for the different sounds within a word overlap one another in time. Because of the coarticulation, individual phonetic segments do not correspond in a simple way to distinct acoustic segments in the speech signal.

It is worth underlining a principal implication of coarticulation: *There is no single invariant property in the acoustic signal that corresponds uniquely to a given phonetic segment of the language.* Instead, the acoustic signal associated with a phoneme changes with the context in which it is uttered. Consider the spectrogram of consonant vowel pair [šu] on the right side of Figure 9.4. Note first that the frication noise for [š] has its concentration of energy at relatively lower frequencies than does the frication noise for [s]. (Compare the two A segments of the sounds.) But the precise frequency composition of the frication noise of [š] and [s] changes depending on which vowel follows the fricative during production. For example, for both [š] and [s] the energy of the frication noise is concentrated at a relatively higher frequency region before [a] than before [u]. This means that the frequency region for [ša] will be very similar to the frequency region associated with frication for [su]. In short, in order to identify whether a speaker produced [š] or [s], the listener must take into account the identity of the following vowel. Hence the perception of phonemes is context-dependent (Diehl & Kluender, 1987; Miller, 1990). *This means that speech perception entails the integration of multiple sources of information rather than the discrete identification of isolated segments of the acoustic signal.*

There is even a further complication—there is more than one speaker in the world. The mapping of acoustic cues is highly variable from one speaker to the next. People's speech differs in pitch, quality of articulation, and more broadly, in style. In addition, people sound different depending on whether they are excited or calm, shouting or whispering, talking to adults or children, and so on. Apparently listeners are able to adjust and adjust quickly for these differences.

A nice illustration of the above point comes from work by Ladefoged and Broadbent (1957). They presented listeners with one of six artificially generated versions of "Please say what this word is," followed by one of four artificially synthesized words, *bit, bet, but,* or *bat.* The short introductory sentence had a remarkable influence on the identification of the test words. When the introductory sentence was spoken in a relatively high-pitched voice the test word *bit* was correctly identified 87% of the time. But when the introductory sentence was spoken in a low-pitched voice, that same word was (incorrectly) identified as *bet* 90% of the time! Ladefoged and Broadbent demonstrated that listeners use the introductory sentence to determine the characteristics of the speaker and adjust their perception of the test word to fit these characteristics. A theory that claims that words are identified by means of presorted templates or patterns would be completely unable to account for these results. Speech perception involves a dynamic adjustment that takes into account differences among speakers.

With these observations on context and structure in hand, we turn to an analysis of operating principles. The rules and regularities associated with phonology are also quite impressive.

Rules or Operating Principles of Phonology

Phonology is centrally concerned with the rules that determine how linguistic representations are pronounced. This statement contains the implication that rules are, in fact, determining pronunciations. An alternative possibility is that one simply memorizes the pronunciation of each of the 50,000 or so morphemes of English. Actually, this will not work because how a morpheme is pronounced depends on what it is paired with. For example, the plural of dog is pronounced with a final [z] whereas the plural of cat has a final [s]. So if one wants to maintain that pronunciations are simply memorized, one must assume that each combination of morphemes is memorized, which would involve many hundreds of thousands if not millions of distinct items.

Even if we grant that people could memorize the pronunciation of all combinations of morphemes, the strict memorization position fails to account for other regularities or generalizations. Consider how you would pronounce plurals of the following nonwords: *loap, fambish,* and *plur.* Almost everyone would apply the suffix [s] to *loap,* [iz] to *fambish,* and [z] to *plur.* The strict memorization position cannot predict this consistency. It appears that our pronunciation of words is principled and the search for rules has the goal of describing these principles.

One could concede that there are phonological regularities without necessarily agreeing that pronunciation is determined by directly represented rules. For example, one might suggest that nonwords remind people of known words and that people pronounce the nonword by analogy with the known word (see, e.g., Glushko, 1979). *Loap* might remind one of *soap* and *plur* of *blur.* We confess that nothing comes immediately to mind for *fambish* (perhaps *faddish?*). This analogical process would have to have a fortuitous similarity structure that would prevent *loap* from reminding one of *loaf* (with its plural of loaves) or *loan,* leading one to add [z] as the suffix. We could restrict remindings to favor similar word *endings,* but that reinforces the point that unconstrained remindings will not work. Although the analogical mechanism is, in principle, a possibility, we suspect that the necessary guidance to ensure appropriate remindings would, in effect, build rules into the mechanism. Technically, such a sophisticated analogical mechanism would not have rules directly represented. Nonetheless the rule structure would be embodied in the system. (We'll say more about this point in the next chapter.)

There is a way in which pronunciation could follow rules without rules being represented at all. It could be that there are constraints associated with producing morpheme combinations that may favor some realizations over others. It is difficult to add [s] or [z] to *fambish.* On the other hand, children often pluralize incorrectly. For example, a child may say *sock*[ziz] or *sock*(z) rather than *sock*[s]. Therefore, production or articulatory constraints are, at best, part of the story (and likely only a small part at that).

Still other observations simultaneously undermine the idea that constraints are solely articulatory and demonstrate the role of rules of syntax in phonology. Consider these sentences:

5. I am going to leave.
6. I am going to New York.
7. I'm gonna leave.

This is perfectly acceptable speech but note that one cannot say:

*8. I'm gonna New York.

(The asterisk is a convention used in linguistics to indicate an unacceptable or nongrammatical sentence.)

In terms of articulatory requirements sentences (5) and (6) are essentially the same. In sentence (5), however, the *to* is part of an infinitive verb whereas in (6) *to* is a preposition. It is the syntactic role of *to* that determines whether or not *going to* can be contracted into *gonna*.

The distribution of English plural morphemes is, in fact, quite regular. For example, [iz] is used for words like *places, porches, cabbages, horses,* and *ambushes;* [s] for words like *soaps, lists, books,* and *graphs;* and [z] for words like *pies, plums, turns, holes,* and *lions.* The choice of suffix is governed by the last sound in the word. One can describe the regularity as follows:

[iz] if the noun ends with [s, z, č, ǰ, š, or ž]

[s] if the noun ends with [p, t, k, f, or θ]

otherwise [z]

One can also state the regularity in terms of properties shared by features of the words within a category (Halle, 1990):

[iz] if the ending is strident and coronal, otherwise

[s] if the ending is voiceless, otherwise

[z] if the ending is voiced (and nonstrident)

Note that these rules apply in order. You may recall that [s] and [š] are voiceless and that the second rule should apply to them. Note, however, that they are also strident and coronal (refer to Table 9.5) and meet the conditions for the first rule. In short, to operate successfully, rules need to be organized to apply in the proper order. For present purposes, the significant observation is that there are regularities of pluralization that are captured in terms of phonological features present in the stem noun. The general characterization of phonology in terms of systematic rules holds fairly uniformly across languages.

Speech Perception

The fact that we can carry on a conversation is proof enough that speech perception is possible. But how, in general, is it done? Over the past few decades two principal theories have been presented, referred to as the **motor theory** of speech perception and the **auditory theory** of speech perception. The motor theory is associated with Liberman and his colleagues at Haskins Laboratories (Liberman & Mattingly, 1985). It makes two claims: (1) that there is a close link between the system responsible for perceiving speech and the system responsible for producing speech (this is why it is called a motor theory). The key idea is that we perceive speech by virtue of our tacit knowledge of how speech is produced, so that we naturally adjust for the lack of invariants in the speech signal associated with context and coarticulation effects. In other words, in perception, we determine which articulatory gesture the speaker has made and, by virtue of this, we are able to determine which phonetic segments have been produced. (2) Perception is innate. Our speech perception is inborn and species-specific. Given that humans are the only known organisms who produce speech and who would have knowledge about articulation, only humans should perceive speech as a structured sequence of phonemes. A shorthand description of the motor theory is that it claims that "speech is special."

The auditory theory is the logical antithesis of the motor theory. Its claims are: (1) that speech perception derives from general properties of the auditory system and (2) that speech perception is not species-specific. This claim follows from the observations that the human auditory system is similar to that of many other animals. The auditory theory is neutral with respect to which perceptual distinctions are innate or learned.

It is not clear how to provide critical tests that would distinguish between these two theories. Nonetheless, the contrast between these two orientations has provided a framework for an intriguing series of observations on speech perception. A sampling of research follows.

Recall that one consequence of coarticulation effects is that energy concentration at the higher frequencies of phonemes like [s] and [š] varies with the associated vowel context. Despite this, listeners have no difficulty recognizing which fricative, [s] or [š], has been produced. Mann and Repp (1980) showed that when context is carefully varied by employing synthesized speech sounds, the identification of [s] versus [š] varies systematically with the vowel context. This observation is compatible with the motor theory of speech perception because knowledge of articulatory constraints is assumed to guide perception of speech. These same findings pose a challenge to the auditory theory to specify properties of the auditory system that could give rise to context effects.

Another observation that was initially taken as favoring the motor theory is **categorical perception**. In the pronunciation of consonants such as [b] and [p] the closed lips are opened, releasing air, and the vocal chords begin vibrating. The time between release and vibration is known as **voice onset time**. In the case of the voiced consonant [b], the release and vibration are nearly simultaneous. For [p] the voicing is delayed. Lisker and Abramson (1970) performed experiments with computer-generated variations of voice onset time. They asked participants to identify whether a [b] or a [p] had been presented. Over most of the range of voice onset time, identification was unambiguous. That is, two categories could readily be distinguished, one corresponding to [b] and one corresponding to [p]. The main changes in identification were at a narrow category boundary in the neighborhood of a voice onset time of about +.02 sec to +.04 sec. The most striking data concern the ability of listeners to discriminate between two sounds varying in onset time. Unless the two sounds fell on opposite sides of the category boundary, discrimination was very poor. That is, a small difference across categories was readily perceived but listeners had great difficulty distinguishing larger differences that were *within* a category. It appears that a continuous variation in voice onset time is perceived in a largely all-or-none or categorical manner (Studdert-Kennedy, 1976). Again the challenge to auditory theory is to explain why perception should be categorical.

Recent evidence on categorical perception is more favorable to auditory theory. First, it is now clear that categorical perception is not unique to humans. Chinchillas have an auditory system similar to ours and Kuhl and Miller (1978) found that identification functions for chinchillas showed the same sharp category boundaries that were noted for humans. In addition, there is both theory and data that suggest that categorical perception arises from rapid decay of auditory memory, not something special about speech (see, e.g., Fujisaki & Kawashima, 1970; Pisoni, 1973). Later evidence also suggests some ability to discriminate speech sounds within a category and that sharp boundaries may derive not from perception per se but rather from the decision rule mapping perception onto judgments (see Massaro, 1987). Overall, then, the observations on categorical perception seem consistent with the auditory theory.

Still other findings, however, are clearly inconsistent with any theory of speech perception that relies solely on auditory information. A particularly fascinating observation comes from a study by McGurk and MacDonald (1976). They developed a videotape showing a speaker mouthing /pa-pa/ paired with the speech sound /na-na/. Observers report hearing neither of these, but rather an integration of the two, /ma-ma/. (Say each of these out loud and try to identify the sense in which /ma-ma/ is a compromise between /pa-pa/ and /na-na/.) This has come to be known as the **McGurk effect**. Somehow the perceptual system integrates the information from the auditory and visual modalities to yield the unitary experience of a single speech sound. There is even evidence that infants have knowledge of the correspondences between articulatory movements on a speaker's face and the acoustic speech signal (Kuhl & Meltzoff, 1982). Obviously the pure auditory theory cannot account for this observation. The auditory theory must be supplemented with some visual information and some means of integrating vision and audition (see, e.g., Massaro & Cohen, 1983).

We will mention just one other phenomenon, the **phonemic restoration effect**. Warren (1970) presented people with the following recording: "The state of governors met with their respective legi*latures convening in the capital city." The asterisk indicates a .12 second interval that was cut out of the tape and replaced with an ordinary cough. When asked if there were any missing sounds from the recording, 19 out of 20 listeners said no and the remaining listener guessed incorrectly where the break was. When the cough was replaced by silence, people had no difficulty locating the silence. People seemed to automatically fill in the missing phoneme over the cough. It appears that people rely on syntactic and semantic constraints to replace the missing phoneme. Even more surprising are the findings of Warren and Warren (1970). They presented the following sentences:

It was found that the *eel was on the *axle*.

It was found that the *eel was on the *shoe*.

It was found that the *eel was on the *orange*.

It was found that the *eel was on the *table*.

The only difference across the sentences was the last word. And what people heard over the cough depended on the last word; they heard *wheel*,

heel, *peel*, and *meal*, respectively, for the four sentences. In other words the phonemic restoration effect exploits information that appears *after* the missing information. This observation underlines the interactive, constructive nature of speech perception.

The debate between the motor theory and the auditory theory has not been resolved but many advances have been made in our understanding of speech perception. There are important observations that any theory must be able to address. The most salient is that speech perception involves the integration of a variety of sources of information, including information from both the auditory and visual modality (as in the McGurk effect). It should be said that it is not entirely clear at what stage of processing these integration effects occur. One could argue for an early stage involving separate modules (visual vs. auditory; syntactic vs. phonological) followed by a later integration stage. Questions about early versus late integration require more fine-tuned experiments, some examples of which will be seen later in this chapter. The remarkable thing is that integration takes place so smoothly that we are scarcely aware of it.

Speech Production

We have already seen some of the complexities associated with the fact that speech is not uttered one phoneme at a time. Not surprisingly, people sometimes make speech errors such as intending to say "barn door" but instead saying "darn bore." Both psychologists and linguists have used error data as a source of evidence concerning the structure of language (see, e.g., Fromkin, 1971) and the nature of language generation (see, e.g., Garrett, 1975; MacKay, 1970, 1972, 1982). The motivating idea is that speech errors result from the mistiming or misapplication of linguistic rules. (Here and elsewhere in this chapter we sidestep the question of whether language use involves directly following *rules* or whether language use is best described "as if" people were following rules. This question will be a central issue in the next chapter.)

One reason for thinking that speech errors may provide insights into language processing is that errors are associated with distinct linguistic levels. The "darn bore" error, for example, is a phonological error. The exchanged phonemes are phonologically similar and they occupy phonologically similar positions (i.e., initial position of a stressed syllable). Errors also occur at the morpheme level (e.g., "self-destruct instruction" leading to "self-instruct destruction") and at the word level (e.g., "Writing a letter to my mother" going to "Writing a mother to my letter"). Within each level a variety of types of errors have been noted (see Table 9.6).

Another generalization about speech errors is that the major "rule systems" associated with a linguistic level usually are not violated by an error occurring at that level. For example, at the phonological level errors may create nonwords (e.g., "spill beer" to "speer bill") but the errors almost always are consistent with the phonological rules of language (Fromkin, 1971). Notice also that errors at the word level preserve the syntactic structure of the sentence (Garrett, 1975). In short, the pattern of errors and preservations seems to reflect the regularities of language.

Garrett (1975, 1976) has taken error data as reflecting two distinct processing levels. As we prepare to speak, words are assembled into an underlying syntactic or thematic structure at what Garrett calls the *functional level*. Later, at the *positional level*, phonological forms of words are inserted into slots in a surface syntactic and phonological frame. Distinct and independent error types are assumed to be associated with each level. For example, word errors, which occur at the functional level, should be sensitive to the thematic and syntactic properties of words. Word errors should not be sensitive to positional-level information such as the phonological form of words. The data on speech errors are generally consistent with Garrett's theory (see Bock, 1986).

Although the idea of distinct functional and positional levels has received a fair amount of support, there is some evidence that errors at one level of processing can be affected by factors outside that level. Phonological errors often create nonwords, but there may be a bias favoring words over nonwords (Baars, Motley, & MacKay, 1975; Dell & Reich, 1981) and meaningful phrases over nonmeaningful phrases (Motley, Baars, & Camden, 1982). Similarly, although word level errors may preserve the appropriate syntactic category, they may also show influences of sound similarity and associative similarity (Harley, 1984).

Recently Gary Dell (1986, 1988) has proposed a model for speech production that aims to reflect both linguistic structure and rules as well as the interactive influence of multiple levels of structure. Interactive influences are handled by a connectionist network. The network consists of both a lexical component and a "wordshape" component, reflecting a distinction associated with linguistic theory (see Figure 9.5, which provides a simplified view of Dell's theory). Wordshape involves a decomposition of a word into an ordered set of phoneme categories, as in the two lower levels of Figure 9.5. The lexical connections between words and phonemes are excitatory and bidirectional (refer to the upper two levels of the figure), which allows positive feedback between levels, as in the Rumelhart and McClelland (1982) interactive activation model described in Chapter 5.

Following Dell (1988), we will describe how the model might en-

Table 9.6   Types of Speech Error.

Type	Examples	Unit involved[a]
Sound errors		
Misordering		
Substitution		
Exchange	*York library—lork yibrary*	Phoneme
	Spill beer—speer bill	Rime constituent
	Snow flurries—flow snurries	Consonant cluster
	Clear blue—glear plue	Feature
Anticipation	*Reading list—leading list*	Phoneme
	Couch is comfortable— comf is . . .	Syllable or rime
Perseveration	*Beef noodle—beef needle*	Phoneme
Addition		
Anticipatory addition	*Eerie stamp—steerie stamp*	Consonant cluster
Perseveratory addition	*Blue bug—blue blug*	Phoneme
Shift	*Black boxes—back bloxes*	Phoneme
Deletion[b]	*Same state—same sate*	Phoneme
Noncontextual errors	*Department—jepartment*	Phoneme
(substitution,	*Winning—winnding*	Phoneme
addition,	*Tremendously— tremenly*	Syllable
deletion)		
Morpheme errors		
Misordering		
Substitution		
Exchange	*Self-destruct instruction—self-instruct de . . .*	Prefix
	Thinly sliced—slicely thinned	Stem
Anticipation	*My car towed—my tow towed*	Stem
Perseveration	*Explain . . . rule insertion— . . . rule exsertion*	Prefix
Shift	*Gets it—get its*	Inflectional suffix
Addition	*Dollars deductible— dedollars deductible*	Prefix
	Some weeks—somes weeks	Inflectional suffix

Table 9.6   Continued

Type	Examples	Unit involved[a]
Noncontextual errors (substitution, addition, deletion)	*Conclusion— concludement*	Derivational suffix
	To strain it—to strained it	Inflectional suffix
	He relaxes—he relax	Inflectional suffix
Word errors		
Misorderings		
Substitution		
Exchange	*Writing a letter to my mother—writing a mother to my letter*	Noun
Anticipation	*Sun is in the sky—sky is in the sky*	Noun
Perseveration	*Class will be about discussing the test— . . . discussing the class*	Noun
Addition	*These flowers are purple—these purple flowers are purple*	Adjective
Shift	*Something to tell you all—something all to tell you*	Quantifier
Noncontextual errors		
Substitution	*Pass the pepper—pass the salt*	Noun
	Liszt's second Hungarian rhapsody—second Hungarian restaurant	Noun
Blend	*Athlete/player—athler*	Noun
	Taxi/cab—tab	Noun
Addition	*The only thing I can do—the only one thing*	Quantifier
Deletion	*I just wanted to ask that—I just wanted to that*	Verb

Note: These errors are taken from Stemberger (1982), Fromkin (1971), Garrett (1975), Shattuck-Hufnagel (1979), and Dell and Reich (1981). In the examples, the text to the left of the error is the intended utterance and the text to the right is the actual utterance.
[a] The units involved in the examples for a given type do not exhaust the set of possible units for that type. In general, a given type can occur with many different units.
[b] The deletion category appears both under the heading of sound misorderings and sound noncontextual errors. This is because some deletions, such as the *same state* example, seem to involve a contextual influence, whereas other deletions do not.
Source: Dell, G. S., 1986.

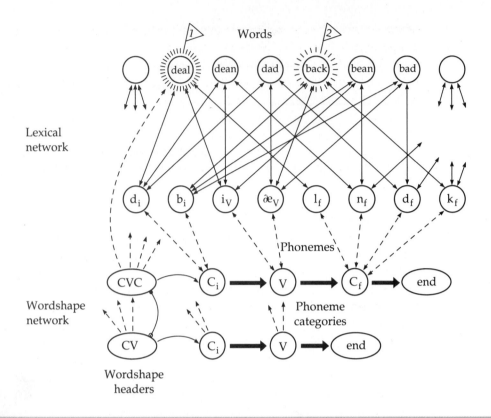

Figure 9.5   The lexical and wordshape networks in Dell's model. The intended phrase is *deal back* indicated by numbered flags on the word nodes. The word *deal* is the current word. All connections between nodes in the lexical network are excitatory and two-way. The dotted lines indicate connections between the lexical and word-shape networks. The arrows between phoneme category nodes in the wordshape network indicate their sequence of activation. *Source*: Dell, G. S., 1988.

code the phrase "deal back." The first word, *deal*, becomes activated and upcoming words in the same phrase that are already flagged (refer again to Figure 9.5) are primed by a lesser amount of activation. Activation spreads through the network and every node sends some fraction of its activation to nodes with which it is directly connected. The spread of activation allows activated words to retrieve their associated phonemes in the lexical network. Note, however, that since activation spreads in both a top-down and bottom-up manner, many words and phonemes other than the correct ones become activated to some extent and this influences the retrieval process.

   After activation has spread, the most highly activated phonemes are selected, subject to constraints associated with the wordshape network. Activated word nodes also send activation to their associated word-shape nodes (e.g., *deal* sends activation to the CVC wordshape header) and the most highly activated header selects the phoneme for each of its category nodes. If *deal* controls most of the activation, the selected sounds would be [d], [i], and [l]. After selection has taken place, the activation of selected phoneme nodes is set to zero. This inhibition keeps the network from reselecting the same phonemes. (Without inhibition the network would stutter.) Then activation shifts from the initial word to the new current word, in our example *back*, and the activation and selection process repeats.

Phonological errors occur when the wrong phoneme is more active than the correct one of the same phoneme category and is selected. If [b] is more activated than [d] when the network is encoding *deal*, the resulting response may be *beal back*. This is known as an anticipation error. The exchange error, *beal dack*, might occur because when [b] is selected for the first word, the [d] that was not selected remains active. Incorrect sounds might become more activated when upcoming words are primed and contribute to patterns of activation. In addition, spreading activation may activate words and phonemes that are not part of the intended phrase.

Investigators have developed a number of techniques for producing speech errors in the laboratory (see, e.g., Baars & Motley, 1974). In one procedure, participants see word-pairs at a fairly rapid rate and are asked to *be prepared to say* each pair as it is shown. At some unexpected time they receive a signal to actually pronounce the current word pair as quickly as they can. Early pairs in the list are a source of priming and interference and that, combined with a deadline, leads to speech errors. Participants are also asked to repeat slowly what they intended to say after the trial so that speech errors can be separated from reading errors.

Dell has used the above technique to evaluate the network model. He draws a useful distinction between predictions that are more or less built into the model and predictions that are generated by the dynamics of activation. The latter are of greater interest and provide a good test of the model. And the model has fared very well in this regard. For example, the model correctly predicts that different patterns of errors will be associated with different deadlines or speech rates. The model also predicts that more slips will be made on words that do not appear often in the language than on words that appear frequently. Although this prediction is built into the model (frequent words are assumed to have a higher resting level activation than infrequent words), the model does make an interesting prediction concerning homophones, two words pronounced in the same manner (e.g., him, hymn). Because both words have the same sounds, they connect to the same lower level nodes. This means that *hymn* activates the

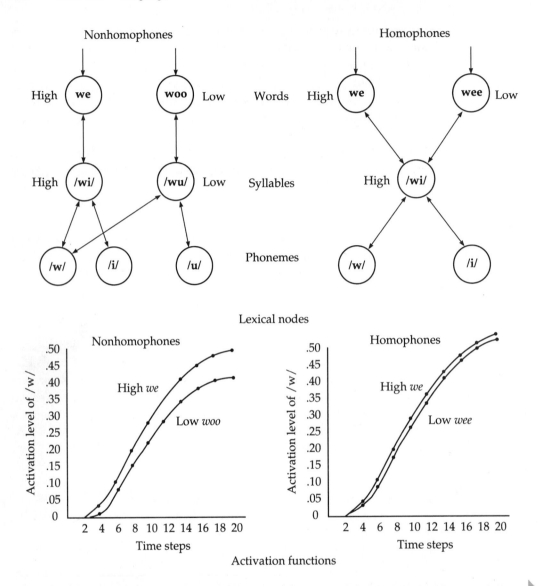

Figure 9.6 Word, syllable, and phoneme nodes for the homophones *we* and *wee*, contrasted with the nonhomophones *we* and *woo*. The resting level of activation for the low-frequency word nodes *wee* and *woo* is assumed to be − .1. A resting level of 0 is assumed for all other nodes. Below are the activation levels of the node for /w/ as a function of time and intended word for each network. *Source*: Dell, G. S., 1988.

same network structures as *him*. The consequence of this may be seen in Figure 9.6, which shows the activation of *we* versus *wee* and *we* versus a nonhomophone, *woo*. The model predicts that low-frequency homophones will have the same lower rate of slips manifested by their higher frequency counterparts. Data on speech errors agree with this prediction. Overall, Dell's model has been fairly successful.

We have only presented a tiny sample of ongoing work on speech errors and language production. The pattern and nature of errors observed provide strong support for certain linguistic distinctions, such as Garrett's separation of the functional and positional levels. Dell's combination of linguistic structure with connectionist ideas concerning interactive activation promises new insights into the processing side of language production.

This ends our survey of phonology, speech perception, and speech production. So far syntactic structure has made an occasional appearance but it has been mainly in the background. It is time to take a closer look at syntax.

Syntax

The Need for Structure

We have already said that sentences involve more than a string of words. In English, the order in which words appear strongly affects meaning. "John hit Bill" means something different from "Bill hit John." It is easy to see that these regularities cannot be correctly described by surface rules of the form "the actor always comes first and the acted upon comes second" because this rule would provide the wrong interpretation of the sentence "Bill was hit by John." Clearly a deeper analysis of sentence structure that goes beyond word order is needed.

The need for structure is also revealed in the use of pronouns or pronomalization. Consider the following two sentences:

   9. John thinks he passed the exam.
   10. He thinks John passed the exam.

The standard reading of the first sentence is that *he* refers to John; that is, John thinks that John passed the exam. (Other readings are possible if, for example, the preceding sentence were, "How did Bill do on the exam?"). In the second sentence, however, *He* and *John* do not refer to the same individual. Speakers of English clearly know this but it is not obvious how to describe the rule or principle that is involved. A surface order analysis will not work. One could offer the generalization that when a pronoun appears first in the sentence it is not co-referential (does not refer to the same individual) with the proper noun that follows it. But this generalization is violated by sentences like:

11. After he studied very hard, John was able to pass the exam.

Yet another problem for surface level analyses concerns the principles associated with converting a declarative sentence into a question. Consider sentences 12 and 13:

12. John is going to sleep.
13. Is John going to sleep?

It looks as if all one needs to do is to move the helping verb *is* to the front of the sentence to create a question. Again, however, this simple rule will not work. Consider the next pair of sentences:

14. John who is very tired is going to sleep.
*15. Is John who very tired is going to sleep?

Sentence 15 does not work. Although the second "is" can be moved, the first cannot; this indicates that the principles involved in question construction require a deeper analysis of sentence structure.

Structure

We will begin this section by reviewing some of the critical properties of syntactic structure. First, sentences are *hierarchically organized*. That is, sentences can be divided into their main parts and then further subdivided. Consider the following sentence:

16. The woman won the marathon.

It is natural to break this sentence into two parts, (the woman) and (won the marathon). The first chunk is known as a *noun phrase* and the second chunk as a *verb phrase*. The noun phrase can be broken down into an article, *the*, and a noun, *woman*. The verb phrase *won the marathon* can be subdivided into (won) (the marathon), where *won* is a verb and *the marathon* is another noun phrase which can be subdivided into an article and a

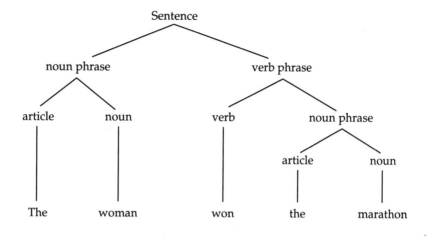

Figure 9.7   Tree structure of the sentence, "The woman won the marathon."

noun. An easy way to represent this hierarchical structure is in terms of a tree diagram as in Figure 9.7.

Not only is a hierarchical structure intuitively natural but also we can show that the meaning of a sentence depends on the chunks or clusters that are constructed. Consider the sentence:

17. Susan saw a man eating shark.

The meaning of this sentence hinges crucially on whether one takes the chunks as (man) and (eating shark) versus (man eating) and (shark). The former chunk supposes a restaurant scene; the latter, an ocean scene or an aquarium. In short, there is more to meaning than a string of words because how the string is chunked is important. Understanding a sentence involves figuring out the intended structure. The subtlety of our intuitions about grammar is quite remarkable, especially in light of the observation that people have great difficulty describing the "rules" of their language. Consider the following pair of sentences, both of which involve the word *that*:

18. The marathon that she won was exciting.
19. The marathon that allowed her to qualify for the Olympics was exciting.

The two sentences are similar in that they both link *that* with a relative clause. Note however, that the word *that* may be deleted from the first sentence without producing loss of meaning but *that* is critically important to the second sentence and may not be omitted. The crucial difference seems to be that marathon is the object of the verb *won* in the first sentence but the subject of the verb *allowed* in the second sentence. The intuitions are obvious to any fluent speaker of English but the underlying rules certainly are not.

Phrase Structure.   The tree structure shown in Figure 9.7 illustrates what is referred to as **phrase structure**. One major aspect of acquiring a language is learning its phrase structure rules. For example, English can be described in terms of rules. (The arrows below mean "can be written as or consisting of" and parentheses indicate a form which is optional):

>   **1.** Sentence → noun phrase + verb phrase
>   **2.** Noun phrase → (article) + (adjective) + noun
>   **3.** Noun phrase → pronoun
>   **4.** Verb phrase → verb + noun phrase
>   **5.** Verb phrase → verb + preposition
>   **6.** Verb → auxiliary + verb
>   **7.** Prepositional phrase → preposition + noun phrase

If we add a list of words categorized as verbs, nouns, articles, adjectives, pronouns, prepositions, and auxiliaries, we have a procedure for generating sentences. The general goal of grammar is to be able, in principle, to generate all the acceptable sentences of a language and not generate any unacceptable sentences. The rules we have just sketched are clearly inadequate. For example, they would not distinguish between

>   **20.** The man thought.

which is perfectly acceptable and

>   **21.** The man solved.

which is not. The point is that some verbs (so-called transitive verbs) require explicitly stated objects whereas others (intransitive verbs) do not.

Phrase structures are a considerable advance over viewing sentences solely in terms of a linear sequence of words (surface structure). Chomsky (1957) has argued that phrase structure grammars are nonetheless inadequate as complete descriptions of natural language. One source of evidence for this claim is again the problem of ambiguity. Recall sentence 4 from the beginning of this chapter,

    4. Visiting relatives can be a nuisance.

This sentence could refer either to the act of visiting relatives or it could be relatives who are doing the visiting. But our chunking strategy will not solve the ambiguity in this case because in either event *visiting* modifies *relatives* (see Figure 9.8). That is, the ambiguity is at the level of underlying structure. Observations such as this suggest the need for further analysis and motivated Chomsky's description of transformational grammars.

Transformations.   How can one disambiguate or show the difference in meaning for the two readings of sentence 4? Figure 9.9 gives us a rough representation of the two readings. Both representations suggest that sentence 4 contains an unstated *someone* whose role is crucial to determining the intended meaning. One could think of an underlying word string like that shown in Figure 9.9 as providing the meaning. This underlying structure was referred to by Chomsky as the deep structure. His idea was that different transformations are applied to deep structures to convert them into surface phrase structures. These transformations will differ as a function of whether the speaker wishes to make an assertion, ask a question, and so on.

    An example of a transformation is the wh-question formation. A

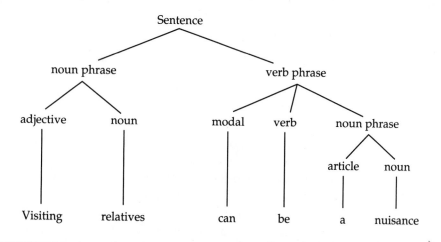

Figure 9.8   Tree structure for the sentence, "Visiting relatives can be a nuisance."

(1)

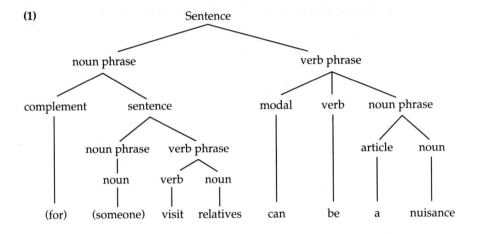

(2)

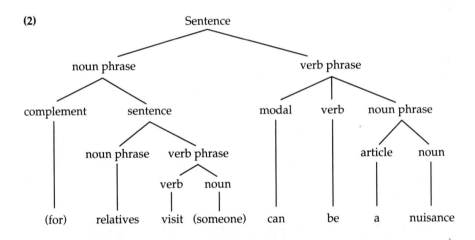

Figure 9.9   Two readings of the sentence "Visiting relatives can be a nuisance."

wh-question is one that asks who, where, which, why, what, or how (how is included even though it does not start with *wh*). According to a transformational analysis, one formulates a question by moving a constituent from its normal "deep structure" syntactic position to the sentence-initial position; this movement is the transformation. In this analysis, when a question word appears at the beginning of a sentence there is a *gap* or missing constituent within the sentence. Thus if one converts sentence 16 to the question "What did the woman win?" there is a gap corresponding to the object of the verb after the word *win*. You might wonder what evidence would support such a claim. The answer is that this analysis predicts that certain word strings should be judged to be ungrammatical. Specifically, filling the gap while retaining the question form should yield an ungrammatical sentence. It does, as the following example shows:

22. What did the woman win the marathon?

Our description of syntax in general and transformations in particular is vastly oversimplified. As in the case of phonological rules, some of the strongest evidence for rules comes from intuitions and evidence concerning the order in which rules apply, as in the joint application of case (e.g., he versus him) and questions or so-called wh-movement. Overall, there is excellent psychological evidence for the distinction between surface and deep structure (Fodor, Bever, & Garrett, 1974).

More recently **transformational grammar** theory has been substantially altered. One major trend has been to assign more structure or information about roles to individual lexical items. For instance, it is assumed that part of the semantic function of verbs is to include information about whether they take a direct or indirect object (e.g., *solved* requires an object). The net effect of assigning more structure or information to the lexicon is that the syntactic rules can involve less structure and consequently can be simplified. In Chomsky's (1981) most recent **government and binding theory** there is only one transformation, which is abstractly described as "move x." One of the goals of Chomsky's theory is to reduce differences between languages to differences in a small number of parameters, each of which can take only a few values. In this conceptualization the problem of language acquisition (more properly, acquiring syntax) reduces to discovering the parameter settings that distinguish one language from another.

We are unable to go into the complexities of government and binding theory or any of its main alternatives (Gadzar, Klein, Pullum, & Sag, 1985; Bresnan, 1978; see Wasow, 1989 for a review). As we shall see in the next section of this chapter, there is good psychological support for the idea of movement or transformation. There are several ways besides wh-movement for "gaps" to be created and there is strong empirical evidence that "gap-filling" links antecedents with these so-called empty categories (Bever & McElree, 1988). We'll take up this topic again later on.

It is important to bear in mind that Chomsky's analysis aims at describing a model of language *competence* without making strong claims about actual human *performance*. That is, his goal is to account for the structure of language, represented by rule systems. How people actually use language is a separate issue, one of performance. In this sense, his analysis corresponds to Marr's computational level, with the goal of describing what and why without necessarily worrying about how. Nonetheless, Chomsky's ideas have been extremely influential and there has been a fair amount of psychological research on syntactic processes, to which we now turn.

The Psychological Reality of Syntax

A variety of evidence supports the psychological reality of syntax. For example, one can show that memory is linked to syntactic processing. Sachs (1967) demonstrated that memory for sentences is very different from memory for strings of words. Sachs presented participants with recorded passages and later tested for verbatim memory of particular sentences. The new sentences or lures consisted of various transformations of original sentences. For example, a sentence might be altered from active to passive voice. New-old recognition performance was strongly affected by the types of changes made. The participants were quite good at detecting changes that altered the meaning of sentences at all retention intervals. In contrast, the ability to distinguish active from passive sentences dropped rapidly with the delay interval. Overall, recognition errors could be predicted much better on the basis of whether a transformation preserved meaning than on the basis of how much of the original word order was preserved.

Jarvella (1971) read subjects passages that were interrupted at different points for a recall test. Participants were instructed to write down as much of the passages as they could remember. Jarvella reasoned that recall would not simply depend on the ordinal position of a word but also on whether or not it was a constituent in the phrase currently being processed. For example, one passage read, "The confidence of Kofach was not unfounded. To stack the meeting for McDonald, the union had even brought in outsiders." Jarvella observed two discontinuities or jumps in the pattern of recall as a function of word position. One was between the seventh and eighth word, the former being recalled less than 40 percent of the time and the latter being recalled more than 80 percent of the time. This inflection point corresponded to the end of the preceding sentence and the beginning of the current one. A second jump in recall corresponded to the end of the first phrase of the second sentence and the beginning of the second phrase (between the thirteenth and fourteenth words). This pattern of recall is consistent with the idea that when processing of a phrase is complete, attention shifts to the next phrase and verbatim memory for preceding material drops off rapidly.

Operating Principles

The structural principles of language ought to have quite a bit to do with how we generate and understand sentences. In producing sentences people presumably map from their intended underlying meaning onto some surface structure that is uttered or written as a string of words. In understanding sentences the process is reversed. That is, listeners or readers must be able to break a string of words into appropriate chunks and apply rules and strategies to try to derive the appropriate meaning. The fact that we normally have little difficulty in understanding sentences conceals the considerable underlying complexity of sentence comprehension. Let's take a closer look.

First of all, it seems clear that we try to understand sentences online as we hear or read them. That is, we do not wait until the end of a sentence, encode that sentence as a single chunk, and then send the sentence off to some pattern recognition device or sentence analyzer. Rather, comprehension processes start with the first word and (for English sentences) move from left to right. Presumably our language comprehension device (we'll abbreviate it as LCD) looks up the meaning of the first word of the sentence in the mental dictionary or lexicon and attempts to determine the role it plays in the sentence. For example, the word *the* is an article or determiner that suggests the presence of a noun phrase and makes it unlikely that the next word will be a verb. One might say something like:

23. The ruined John's public speaking career because he could never pronounce it.

This sentence in which *the* is followed by a verb may be borderline acceptable. Adding quotation marks to *the* or placing stress on it in speech would move it into the clearly acceptable range but note that the quotation marks or stress provide a strong clue that the word *the* is being used as a noun.

Suppose that *the* is followed by *bank*. The LCD would identify *bank* as a noun but would face difficulty determining whether the correct meaning involved a financial institution, a piggybank, or the border of a river. Presumably the ambiguity will be resolved later in the sentence but the LCD must either select a meaning and backtrack if it is wrong or keep each of the candidate meanings active as possibilities. If the next word is an auxiliary such as *is* or *was*, the LCD should determine that the first two words, *the bank*, represent a noun phrase and that a verb phrase is beginning. If the fourth word is *overflowing* the LCD is justified in believing that *bank* refers to river bank but the LCD must also be able to deal with sentences like:

24. The bank is overflowing with customers.

In certain respects sentence comprehension is like the game, Charades, in which one person acts out an intended meaning and the others try to determine it from nonverbal clues. Since meaning can only be indirectly conveyed through signs or symbols, the LCD must make its guesses from the clues left by the speaker or writer in generating strings of words from an underlying intended meaning. Clark and Clark (1977) provide an extensive list of a variety of syntactic clues that might be exploited by the LCD.

The LCD presumably uses both syntactic and semantic information. For example, we can understand a sentence like "watered girl flowers" even though the word order is ungrammatical. Or consider the following sentence:

25. John wrote letters to the customers on his list.

Presumably the LCD does not understand this sentence as meaning that there are a group of customers who are literally standing on a (necessarily) large list owned by John. Instead, it ought to assume that the list contains names of customers. The correct interpretation depends on world knowledge about customers and lists. If we substitute the word *island* for *list* a different reading is appropriate.

Heuristics and Strategies.   As we have been emphasizing throughout this book, one way to understand how a system works is to try to identify constraints or strategies that make some tasks easy and natural and other difficult and unnatural. Language researchers have followed this approach in their efforts to understand how the LCD works.

There is evidence, for example, that the LCD is biased to expect active rather than passive sentences. For example, Slobin (1966) gave children and adults active sentences like "The dog is chasing the cat" or passive sentences like "The cat is chased by the dog" and then immediately showed one of two pictures—for this instance a dog chasing a cat or a cat chasing a dog. The task was to decide whether or not the sentence described the action. Both adults and children were faster for active sentences than for passive sentences. This suggests that the LCD assumes that the first noun refers to the actor and that it needs to revise this hypothesis when it meets a passive sentence.

Sentences that lack the clues that help the LCD should be harder to understand than normal, and sentences that remove ambiguous cues should be easier to understand. Consider the following two sentences:

26. John went to school and he played tennis.
27. The princess kissed the frog whom the king knighted.

Sentence 26 would be easier to understand if *he* were omitted because the LCD must consider the possibility that *he* refers to someone other than John. Sentence 27 becomes more difficult when *whom*, which is a clue to a second proposition, is removed:

28. The princess kissed the frog the king knighted.

These conjectures have been confirmed in comprehension tests with adult subjects (see, e.g., Bever, 1970; Wanner & Maratsos, 1978).

Minimal attachment.   One idea of how parsing proceeds is that the LCD follows a strategy of taking the first available structural option for attaching new input to old. The **minimal attachment** strategy represents a bias toward attaching a new phrase to an old node rather than building a new phrasal node (see Frazier, 1979). Figure 9.10 illustrates two sentences, only one of which allows for minimal attachment. In the first sentence the phrase *with binoculars* is directly attached to the verb phrase whereas in the second a new noun phrase is constructed and the prepositional phrase is attached to it. According to minimal attachment, the second sentence should be more difficult to parse in the binocular/revolver area than the first because of the initial bias simply to attach the propositional phrase to the verb phrase. Rayner, Carlson, and Frazier (1983) recorded eye movements of people while they read sentences like these. Reading times proved to be longer in the revolver/binoculars area for the sentence in which the correct interpretation violated minimal attachment (as the second sentence does). The Rayner et al. results are therefore consistent with the idea that the LCD follows the minimal attachment strategy (but see also Osterhout & Swinney, in press, for data which fail to support minimal attachment).

Garden path sentences.   Consider a sentence like the following well-known example:

29. The horse raced past the barn fell.

(a)

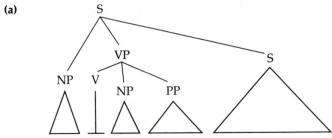

The spy saw the cop with binoculars but the cop didn't see him.

(b)

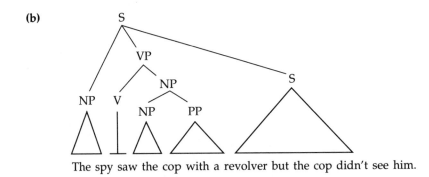

The spy saw the cop with a revolver but the cop didn't see him.

Figure 9.10 Minimal (a) and nonminimal (b) attachments for prepositional phrases. *Source:* K. Rayner, M. Carlson, and L. Frazier, 1983.

This **garden path sentence** seems to totally throw off the LCD when it arrives at the word "fell." The sentence seems ungrammatical because the LCD has taken *raced* to be the main verb. The observation that the LCD is fooled by garden path sentences reinforces the idea that sentence processing is incremental and that the LCD makes certain commitments that it sometimes has to retract later. Keep in mind, however, that garden path sentences are fairly rare and that the LCD makes the right guesses most of the time.

A Second Look at Modularity

The various interactions between syntax, semantics, and pragmatic knowledge in the service of comprehension do not seem to be the sort of stuff out of which modularity would be constructed. Recall that Fodor (1983) proposed that syntactic processing is performed by a language-specific (encapsulated) module. The notion of an encapsulated module is that processing is automatic, mandatory, rapid, and not influenced by other sources of information (in the case of language, not influenced by world knowledge). Somewhat surprisingly, there is actually some fairly good evidence that information is encapsulated early in processing.

First, consider the role of pragmatic knowledge in comprehending active and passive sentences. Slobin's (1966) study, described earlier, included subjects and objects that were either reversible or nonreversible. A reversible sentence is one in which pragmatic knowledge would not constrain the interpretation. For example, dogs can chase cats or cats can chase dogs. A nonreversible sentence would be one like, "The ice cream was eaten by the policeman," where pragmatic knowledge rules out the ice cream consuming the policeman. Slobin found that passive sentences were harder to comprehend than active sentences only for reversible sentences. Apparently pragmatic knowledge facilitated comprehension in the case of the passive, nonreversible sentences. So far this does not sound like modularity. However, Forster and Olbrei (1973) used a rapid serial visual presentation (RSVP) procedure and obtained a different result. In RSVP the words of a sentence are presented one at a time at a fast rate (e.g., 10 words per second) on a screen. Under this procedure passive sentences were more difficult to comprehend than active sentences and reversibility had no effect at all. Apparently the effect of pragmatic knowledge enters at a later (slower) stage of sentence processing.

Dave Swinney and his associates have also found evidence of information encapsulation early in processing. Swinney uses a technique in which people hear sentences as they are watching a screen where strings of letters may be presented. Participants have to say as rapidly as possible whether the string is a word (a lexical-decision task). Processing the sentence can serve to make some words more accessible and produce priming effects on the lexical decision task. Subjects might hear a sentence such as: "Everyone watched the enormous heavyweight boxer that the small 12-year-old boy had$_1$ beaten$_2$ (t) so badly." Footnotes 1 and 2 indicate possible points at which a lexical decision probe might be presented. Possible probes might include *boxer* or *boy*. In this particular example, syntactic theory suggests that the verb *beaten* leaves a trace (t) or gap that should trigger a search for its antecedent. Pragmatic knowledge would suggest that an enormous heavyweight boxer would defeat rather than be beaten by a small boy and one might on these grounds expect some priming or facilitation for lexical decisions for *boy* at point 2. On syntactic grounds one would only expect priming for *boxer*, the correct antecedent. Swinney and his associates observed priming for *boxer* but not *boy* at point 2 (see Swinney & Osterhout, in press for a general description of this line of re-

search). Again it seems that pragmatic knowledge fails to affect performance early in processing.

Another example of encapsulation concerns how the LCD fixes the
meaning of words. Although context ultimately allows the LCD to determine correct meanings, it appears that access to representations of words
operates as a module that initially delivers an unconstrained set of possible
meanings. For example, when the crossmodal (auditory plus visual) priming technique is used to present probes immediately after the word *port* in
the sentence, "The waiter poured the port into the glasses," both *wine* and
ship show significant priming effects (Swinney, 1979). Initial processing appears to be highly modular and only in a later stage of processing are the
various sources of constraint integrated to establish meaning.

We have only scratched the surface of ongoing research on syntactic processing. There is still considerable debate concerning the relative
roles of syntax, semantics, and world knowledge in sentence comprehension. Chapter 11 will provide another look at inference generation as we
take a broader view of comprehension. So far we have also had relatively
little to say about semantics or word meanings. The structure of lexical
concepts is the central topic of Chapter 12. Before moving on to these chapters, however, in Chapter 10 we turn to the question of how all of this
structure we have been discussing applies to the question of language
acquisition.

Summary

This has been a long chapter yet we feel that, if anything, we have given
language less coverage than it deserves. The next three chapters also
deal with language but a proper treatment would seem to require a complete book.

A spirit of excitement pervades the study of language. The more
we look at phonology or syntax, the greater is our appreciation of their
subtle complexities. Our experience is somewhat akin to that of a biology
student taking a first look at a drop of water under a microscope. In both
cases the closer view reveals teeming life and structures that otherwise
would be outside our awareness.

A central aspect of language is that we use it. The "teeming life"
includes a variety of strategies and heuristics for a language processing that
can get thrown off by garden path sentences but that nonetheless serve us
so well that communication appears to be effortless. Beneath our conscious
awareness are intricate mechanisms and modules that work together to

conceal the enormity of the task they accomplish. Language is both a remarkably complex creation and an accomplishment that all cultures share. It may truly prove to be a window on the human mind.

Key Terms

auditory theory	phonemes
categorical perception	phonemic restoration effect
coarticulation	phonology
deep structure	phrase structure
formants	pragmatics
garden path sentences	semantics
government and binding theory	surface structure
McGurk effect	syntax
minimal attachment	transformational grammar
modularity	voice onset time
morphemes	voicing
motor theory	

Recommended Readings

For a general introduction to language the Clark and Clark (1977) textbook is still very helpful. George Miller's (1981) *Language and Speech* is both fairly brief and very readable. Fodor, Bever, and Garrett (1974) is also an excellent source, especially with respect to syntactic processing. The collection of chapters on language in the book edited by Osherson and Lasnik (1990) provide a more recent review.

A key issue in language is the question of modularity. Fodor's (1983) book lays out the modularity issue while Massaro's (1987) book focuses on the integration side of things. These two perspectives need not be incompatible because modularity is not opposed to integration—the issue is *when* integration takes place. Swinney and Osterhout (1990) provide a methodological overview and a sampling of results on modularity and integration.

The striking phenomenon of categorical perception is analyzed from a variety of perspectives in a book edited by Steven Harnad (1987). To get a better idea of how speech errors are used to make inferences about language structure see articles by Garrett (1975), Dell (1986, 1988), and MacKay (1972, 1982). Finally, those interested in plunging into the complexity of grammatical theory will find Wasow's (1989) review article to be a good guide.

10
LANGUAGE ACQUISITION

Chapter Outline

Language learning is doubtless the greatest intellectual feat anyone of us is ever required to perform.

—L. Bloomfield (1933)

Introduction

To call language learning a great intellectual achievement may strike readers as odd because we know that learning a language is "so easy that a child can do it." One of our primary goals in this chapter is to convey an understanding of just why Bloomfield was so impressed with such a common accomplishment.

Two important facts about language acquisition are that more or less everyone learns at least one language and that just how this acquisition takes place is a deep mystery. It is a mystery because the closer we look into the conditions under which language learning occurs, the more evident it becomes that the information needed for correct language learning just is not there. Another striking observation is that children are better than adults at acquiring a language. Given that adults seem more likely and more able to employ sophisticated learning strategies than children, it is a further mystery that children excel over adults in language learning. In this chapter, we will take a look at the learning problem, discuss its implications, and then describe some ideas about factors or biases that may facilitate language learning.

The Learning Problem

Units and Segmentation.   An initial question is how language learners segment continuous speech into appropriate chunks or units. As we noted in Chapter 9, anyone who has listened to a foreign tongue can appreciate the difficulty of isolating individual words in continuous speech. Furthermore, the goal of isolating individual words presupposes a concept of a word and a bias to assume that words are, in part, carriers of meaning. A learner hears a series of sounds in some context and must decide that those sounds, as opposed to various forms of movement such as gestures (except in the case of sign language), are what is relevant to the scene.

In short, the child must solve the **segmentation** problem (hit upon the right units of analysis for sounds and meanings) and reflect the appropriate sensitivity to syntactic principles. And when we take a closer look, things get even more complicated. For example, we noted in the last chapter that the constraints associated with generating speech prevent any invariant mapping between acoustic segments and phonetic segments. Recall that how a consonant is pronounced depends in part on the particular vowel that follows it. Somehow the listener must take this into account.

Of course, language involves more than individual words. The learner must be able to create chunks corresponding to phrases, clauses, and sentences. The significance of two words appearing in succession will depend on factors such as whether they are part of the same clause or phrase.

Reference.   Even if the learner can isolate individual words, the task has just begun. Consider a benevolent teacher who points to an object and utters a single word. The situation is still ambiguous. Suppose the teacher is pointing to a coffee cup. The single word could be referring to the handle or some other part of the cup, to the material out of which the cup is constructed, to its color, to some defect in the cup, or to any set of superordinates that might be applied (e.g., drinking vessel, container, piece of artwork, human artifact). Usually situations do not even involve a benevolent teacher and, therefore, are still more ambiguous.

Generalizations.   It is important to remember that generalizations about grammar operate at the level of phrases and clauses and not in terms of the specific order of words in a sentence. There are no useful generalizations concerning the relationship between the first and fourth words of sentences. The idea is that there is an unlimited set of hypotheses about the structure of language that are very wrong and we need to account for how learners always seem to be in the right ballpark. The strategy of looking for relations between first and fourth words in sentences may seem silly but that is precisely the point. Our natural biases direct us toward more promising hypotheses. In general, there are so many possible syntactic and semantic rules that could be considered that it is possible to *prove* that an unbiased hypothesis testing system will not be able to acquire a language in a finite time period. See Gold (1967), Wexler & Culicover (1980), Pinker

(1984), and Osherson, Stob, and Weinstein (1986) for formal treatments of learnability theory, which address conditions under which learning is or is not possible.

Input Conditions

It seems obvious that language is *learned* because whether a child comes to speak English or French (or both) depends on the language to which he or she is exposed. But exactly what feedback does a child receive to shape his or her language learning? The evidence suggests that the feedback is quite limited. For example, parents rarely correct the grammatical mistakes of their children (Baker, 1979). Brown and Hanlon (1970) looked at parents' tendencies to correct children's utterances and found that the crucial variable was whether or not it was correct in terms of meaning rather than whether or not the child's statement was grammatical. This observation further complicates the language learnability problem because **negative evidence** (i.e., that a string of words is *not* grammatical) is needed to converge on the correct language.

The importance of negative evidence is illustrated in Figure 10.1, which shows various possible relationships between a child's hypothesis about language and the correct language. In diagram a of the figure the child's guess is completely wrong, as any sample of the correct language

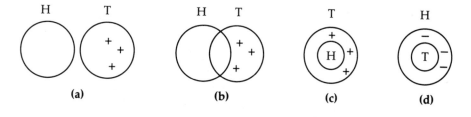

Figure 10.1   Four ways that a child's hypothesis about language could be incorrect. (a) The child's hypothesis language (H) is disjoint from the language to be acquired (the "target language" T). (b) The child's hypothesis and the target language intersect. (c) The child's hypothesis language is a subset of the target language. (d) The child's hypothesis language is a superset of the target language. In cases a through c the child can realize that his or her hypothesis is incorrect by hearing sentences ("positive evidence," indicated by +) that are in the target language but not the hypothesized one. This is impossible in case d; negative evidence would be needed. *Source*: Pinker, S. (1990).

will reveal. In diagram b the child's guess is partly right and the child may hear sentences that he or she thought did not belong to the language. The same situation holds in diagram c, where the child's guess is correct as far as it goes but is only a subset of the true language. But in diagram d the child's guess is too broad. In this case, any sentence the child hears will be consistent with the hypothesis. It is not clear how the child could narrow down the hypothesis without receiving negative evidence. Learning would be straightforward if the child uttered an ungrammatical sentence (one that fit the too broad hypothesis) and was told that it was not grammatical, but we have noted that children rarely receive this type of feedback. In short, if the child's conjecture about the correct grammar is more general than it should be, the child will not receive the feedback needed to narrow down the hypothesis appropriately (see Pinker, 1990). Some researchers have suggested that learners have a bias to avoid hypothesizing overly general grammars, the **subset principle** (Berwick, 1986), but as we shall see, there are clear cases where children seem to overgeneralize (that is, produce forms that are not part of the language). Just how children recover from these overgeneralizations is a question of great interest and importance (see Pinker, 1989, 1990 for review and discussion).

In exceptional circumstances the linguistic input may be limited in an even more dramatic sense. Deaf children whose parents do not know a sign language or only have limited signing abilities receive inadequate input for both a spoken language (because they are deaf) and a sign language. When there is no sign input, deaf children invent a rudimentary gesture system that shares many formal properties with that of language (Feldman, Goldin-Meadow, & Gleitman, 1978). When the input consists of a noisy and impoverished version of American Sign Language (ASL), the learners are capable of *surpassing* their models. That is, a child whose parents are poor signers and provide the child's only linguistic input may nonetheless outperform his or her parents in ASL (Singleton & Newport, unpublished manuscript).

Innateness

The learnability analyses alluded to earlier underline the fact that language learners cannot test all the possible grammars that are consistent with linguistic input (there are too many of them). Therefore, language researchers see no alternative to the view that language learning is innately constrained so that children only hypothesize a very restricted set of grammars. This restricted set presumably includes all human languages but excludes a vast number of potential linguistic systems that humans do not (presumably because they cannot) employ. The dramatic cases in which deaf children improve upon their input may reflect the influence of innate constraints.

One view of innate constraints is that they are specific to language learning. Chomsky (1965, 1980) argues for the view that there is an innately given "language organ" which consists of a universal grammar that specifies the grammatical properties that hold across all human languages, referred to as **linguistic universals**. This universal grammar acts as a constraint on the hypotheses a learner considers. The idea is that the learner is born knowing the set of properties that are true across languages and simply has to learn the parameters that distinguish his or her language from others. In short, it is as if the child innately knows about languages in general and just needs to figure out the particular details of the language of his or her environment.

An alternative idea is that language learning is constrained by general processing principles that are not unique to language (see, e.g., Anderson, 1983). Later we will describe the intriguing idea that the limited processing capacities of children are what actually allow them to acquire a language (Newport, 1990).

It is too early to draw any firm conclusions with respect to whether the constraints associated with language acquisition are or are not language-specific. The combination of learnability problems and children's accomplishments in the face of them puts the burden of proof on those who only posit general constraints. There are some subtle regularities in morphology and syntax to which human learners are sensitive that might prove difficult to capture in a system without some language-specific biases (see Pinker, 1989, 1990). By now the reader should appreciate the fact that language acquisition is vastly more complicated than the common intuition that all there is to language learning is children imitating their parents.

Productivity and the Status of Rules

We have repeatedly noted the productive character of language; from a small number of basic units and rules an infinite number of sentences can be constructed. A classic example of **productivity** comes from some early studies of language development by Berko (1958). Young children were given novel words and asked about appropriate plural and past tense forms. For example, they might be shown a picture of a cartoon bird and be told that it was a "wug." Then they would be shown a second picture with two cartoon birds and told, "Now there are two of them, there are two ___." Most of the time four- to seven-year-old children completed the sentence with the word *wugs*. This performance suggests that the children had learned the regularities associated with pluralization and could apply them productively to completely new examples (other tests showed that they had also learned past tense regularities).

What knowledge did the children in Berko's study have? The most straightforward and natural answer is that they had learned *rules*. For example, a child might initially encode *dog, dogs, pig,* and *pigs* as complete forms and later note that *dog* and *dogs* differ only in the final consonant sound and that *pig* and *pigs* differ in the same way. At this point the child could form a generalization or rule covering plural forms. (Recall in the last chapter that we described three forms of plural suffixes depending on whether the ending is strident and coronal [e.g., porches], voiceless [e.g., books], or voiced [e.g., plums]). It is not assumed that these rules are consciously and explicitly formulated—the claim is that the language system has induced the appropriate rule from experience with examples. Until a few years ago examples of productivity (like Berko's) had been taken as evidence for internalized rules.

Recently, Rumelhart and McClelland (1986) have proposed a parallel distributed processing (connectionist) model for past tense learning where no words are stored and no rules are induced. In their model the network encodes mappings between phonological patterns in the stem and corresponding patterns for past tense. The response to new stems is based on the similarity of the stem to previously encoded stem patterns. In short, the network may produce rulelike behavior without directly representing rules. This description is somewhat terse but we take up the Rumelhart and McClelland model in detail later in this chapter.

The contrasts between these two differing conceptions of productive behavior have given rise to considerable controversy. The question "what is learned?" is a central one for language acquisition and the interest attached to the rule-based versus connectionist models is hardly surprising.

Overview

Figuring out how languages are learned is clearly a challenge. In the remainder of this chapter we first provide a general description of language development and then review some ideas and clues concerning how different aspects of language (phonology, syntax, semantics) might be acquired. Our review will only be able to supply bits and pieces of the puzzle, each of which is flavored with the constraints perspective. In the final section of the chapter we focus on past tense learning as a case study of some of the complexities of language acquisition.

Course of Language Acquisition

Early Development

Infant language shows a fairly consistent pattern of development. We are all familiar with the cooing and babbling of young infants. Babbling does not seem to depend on auditory feedback as even congenitally deaf babies babble. At about eight months (everything we say about timing shows considerable individual variability) the babbling begins to show intonational patterns that depend on an infant's language environment and show sound patterns consistent with the parents' language (Weir, 1966).

At about one year (again the normal range of variability is quite large) the infant begins to produce single words. These initial words tend to be simple nouns like *duck* and *doggy*, names such as *mama* and *dada*, or references to interactions with adults such as *bye-bye*, *peekaboo*, *more*, and, of course, *no*. Early vocabulary is biased toward actions and active things rather than large, stable objects such as *sofa* (Nelson, 1973).

The one-word stage is often referred to as the **holophrastic speech** stage because the child seems to use a single word to stand for an entire sentence. Thus given an appropriate context, "more" is to be understood as "I want more juice." Context is crucial in understanding the infant's intentions.

The one-word stage provides a direct opportunity to see how the infant's concepts map onto adult concepts. Logically, infant concepts can differ from adult concepts in two ways. The infant may *overgeneralize*, as when every adult male is called *daddy*, or *undergeneralize*, as when only some dogs are called *doggy*. Some cases of overgeneralization may arise because the beginner does not know the correct label and says the closest word from his or her working vocabulary. These generalization errors are fairly common in initial stages of vocabulary development but rapidly become rare (Rescorla, 1980). Just how beginners are so successful is a puzzle to be explained.

Very young children show some sensitivity to syntactic cues. Hirsh-Pasek, Golinkoff, Fletcher, DeGaspe-Beaubien, and Cauley (1985) showed 17-month-old children two simultaneous videos of familiar cartoon characters (Big Bird and Cookie Monster) interacting. Some children were given the sentence "Big Bird is tickling Cookie Monster" whereas others were given the sentence "Cookie Monster is tickling Big Bird." The children spent more time looking at the video where the action matched the sentence than at the scene in which the acting roles did not match the sentence. This preferential looking shows that 17-month-olds were able to use syntactic order to construct the appropriate meaning. What is especially striking is that these children were still at the stage of only speaking single words.

Somewhere around the age of 18 months the young child begins to combine words into two-item strings. In this two-word stage the young child is better able to express intentions and we see the beginnings of syntax. Inessential words (articles, pronouns, auxiliary verbs) are omitted and for this reason the two-word stage is referred to as **telegraphic speech**. Bloom (1970) argued that two-word utterances show syntax; for example, sequences are almost always in an order that would be correct in the adult language (Brown, 1973).

There is evidence that children in the two-word stage know more about linguistic structures than they can say. Consider the following observation by Shipley, Smith, and Gleitman (1969). They found that children at the two-word stage followed their mother's instructions better when she said "Throw me the ball!" than when she said "Throw ball." That is, using normal adult speech was more effective than mimicking the child's own normal speech. It appears that children appreciate propositional structures that they are unable to produce. One speculation is that problems of memory limitation, planning, and producing complex sentences are simply too demanding at this stage.

At approximately the age of two the child's vocabulary undergoes explosive growth. It has been estimated that an average child's vocabulary goes from about 25 words at 18 months to more than 15,000 by the age of 6. This works out to about 10 new words a day! Bear in mind that each word corresponds to a concept, so children are simultaneously forming concepts and learning labels for them at the rate of 10 a day.

Later Development

By two and a half years of age (more or less) children progress beyond the two-word stage. The average length of their utterances increases systematically and their speech undergoes a dramatic increase in complexity. Closed class words (e.g., *a, the, of, that*) become part of their vocabulary.

The most striking aspect of toddlers' speech is that they begin to make errors on word formations and syntactic patterns that they previously produced correctly. They may say *feets* instead of *feet* and *goed* instead of *went*. That is, many of their errors consist of applying a general rule ("add *s* to form a plural") to lexical items that are exceptions. At this stage the child's performance may be inconsistent, as if the child has learned the exception but sometimes misapplies the rule. Eventually these **overgeneralization errors** drop out. By the time a child is five, his or her speech corresponds closely to that of adults (though more subtle forms of syntax may not be learned until years later; see Chomsky, 1969).

Summary

In this section we have given a descriptive account of the course of language learning. Although we referred to stages of development, it is not clear that there are stages in a deep psychological sense. That is, just because we can describe development in terms of stages does not mean that a theory of language acquisition necessarily needs to include stages. To better appreciate both what children accomplish and how constraints guide language acquisition, we need to examine how children learn the sounds, grammar, and word meanings of their native language.

Constraints and Interactions

Phonology

Human infants have a head start on the problem of phonological analysis. There is good evidence that even very young infants perceive acoustic signals in terms of phonetic segments. Consider the striking observations of Peter Eimas and his associates (Eimas, Siqueland, Jusczyk, and Vigorito, 1971) on the perception of stop consonants by one- and four-month-old infants. They varied voice onset time over the range of −.20 sec to +.80 sec. To assess perception, they used a habituation paradigm. Infants appear to seek novel stimulation and to habituate or show less interest in repeated stimulation of the same type. The researchers used a procedure in which infants could suck on a pacifier to produce speech sounds. Whenever the infant sucked, the speech sound was presented. When the same sound was repeatedly presented, infants sucked less to produce it (they habituated). When a new sound was presented, the infant dishabituated and sucking increased once again. Therefore, one measure of an infant's ability to discriminate between two speech sounds is whether or not dishabituation occurs when repeated presentation of the first sound is followed by presentation of the alternative speech sound. For both age groups, Eimas et al. found that a difference in voice onset time of 20 msec. led to dishabituation only if the two sounds were from opposite sides of (what for adults is) the category boundary. This result suggests that infants perceive stop consonants and perceive them categorically.

If children already are sensitive to phonetic segments, they need only learn which phonetic distinctions matter in their language environment. Japanese babies will habituate to [ra] and then dishabituate to [la] despite the fact that Japanese adults do not distinguish between the two (Eimas, 1975). Similarly, English-speaking adults disregard the pitch of a sound that would have been relevant if the language in question were Zulu rather than English. That is, adults lose distinctions that are not important for their native language. In short, young children are "biologically prepared" to pick out pieces of their acoustic environment that will be important in language learning (see Kuhl, 1987, 1990 for recent reviews on the development of speech perception).

Syntax

Segmentation. Are there constraints or biases that help the language learner to isolate chunks larger than phonemes? Gleitman and Wanner (1982) proposed that stressed syllables represent the learner's initial word-like conceptual unit. Newport, Gleitman, and Gleitman (1977) provided correlational evidence from their study of "motherese" (parents' speech to children) that the rate of learning auxiliary verbs was increased when they appeared in stressed positions in utterances. There is also evidence that prosodic cues (e.g., speech timing, rising and falling of fundamental frequency) are correlated with phrase boundaries and that both adults (Streeter, 1978) and infants (Fernald, 1984) are sensitive to prosody. An infant with a bias for treating intonationally circumscribed segments of speech as chunks (phrasal constituents) would have an enormous advantage over an unbiased learner in figuring out appropriate phrase boundaries and learning the regularities associated with them. Finally, there are reliable acoustic cues to clause boundaries in speech, such as lowered tones, longer pauses, and stress (Klatt, 1976; Cooper & Paccia-Cooper, 1980). In brief, there do appear to be acoustic cues that could be used to identify words, phrases, and clauses as units—cues that could be exploited by a learner with a bias to attend to them (see Morgan, 1986 for an extensive review and analysis).

Sequence and Distributional Information. Fairly early in development children show sensitivity to word order. For example, Bloom (1970) observed that children who can say "Mommy throw" and "throw ball" do not say "ball throw" to describe the situation. Michael Maratsos (1982; Maratsos & Chalkley, 1981) has argued that children learn concepts of noun and verb by their patterns of occurrence or **distributional information** in speech. For example, nouns tend to appear after *the* and verbs tend to appear after *can* and *have* and before *-ed*. There are two complications with this view, one minor and one major. The minor concern is that the correlations are not perfect (-ed can follow words that are not verbs; e.g., the *melted* crayon ruined the table). The major problem, however, is the question of how the child comes to evaluate these informative correlations rather than the enormous number of alternative possible correlations. The number of possible correlations is far smaller if the child considers only correlations within a phrase (a refinement suggested by Gleitman & Wanner, 1982).

Bootstrapping.   So far we have considered phonology, segmentation, syntax, and semantics one at a time. The learner does not have this luxury and must face the additional complexity of acquiring these mutually interdependent aspects of language simultaneously. How is this possible? It may be that Nature turns necessity into a virtue; learners may use syntax to learn semantics and vice versa.

One view has emphasized what may be called **semantic bootstrapping**. The key idea is that this semantic information gets the syntactic learning process going (see, e.g., Pinker, 1984; Grimshaw, 1981; Bowerman, 1982). Though not all nouns are physical objects, all physical objects are described as nouns. Similarly, a word describing an action is probably a verb. If children assume that semantic and syntactic categories are correlated in restricted ways in their input, they could use semantic properties of words and phrases to infer corresponding syntactic categories. With these categories in hand, they would be in a position to learn, for example, that in English the subject usually comes before the verb and the object usually comes after the verb. Pinker (1990) suggests that semantic, correlational, and prosodic cues may combine to facilitate syntactic learning.

Landau and Gleitman (1985) have argued for **syntactic bootstrapping**. The general idea is that if meaning can be used to make conjectures about form, then, because form and meaning are correlated, form can be used to infer meaning. One strong motivation for syntactic bootstrapping is that real-world contexts do not provide sufficient constraints to fix meaning. The same action can be described with many alternative verbs (e.g., *perceive, look, see, eye, face, orient, attend, notice*). Landau and Gleitman

(1985) studied language acquisition in both sighted and blind children and one of their surprising results is how sophisticated and appropriate the language of blind children is, even when the seemingly necessary visual input is not available. For example, blind children know that orange is intermediate between red and yellow and that purple lies between red and blue. They also understand the difference between *look* and *see* and distinguish between both of these verbs and the verb *touch*.

How is it that blind children come to know that *look* describes the dominant means of discovering objects in the world and that *see* describes the state that results from this observation? Not from looking and seeing. This problem extends to sighted children as well as blind children. There does not appear to be anything like adequate information that would serve to allow a child to learn and distinguish verbs like *know*, *guess*, and *think*.

Landau and Gleitman (1985) suggested that many verbs may be learned from their privileges of occurrence in syntactic structures. For example, the verb *see* requires two noun phrases (John sees the ball) whereas *give* requires three (John gave the ball to Mary). Similarly, a parent may say "I will *look* for it" but not "I will *see* for it." Landau and Gleitman presented evidence that syntactic and observational information available to a blind child together were sufficient to distinguish the interpretation of the common verbs. Neither source of information by itself would have been adequate, they argue. Overall it appears that both semantic and syntactic bootstrapping serve to facilitate language learning (see also Gleitman, Landau, & Wanner, 1988).

Critical Period Effects.   As we mentioned in Chapter 3, there is strong evidence that language learning has a critical period associated with it. Elissa Newport and Ted Suppalla have studied the signing abilities of deaf adults who acquired American Sign Language (as their first full language; at best they had only limited skills in English) at different ages. Although all groups were successful on basic word order tests, performance on tests for correct use of syntax decreased as the age at which language learning started increased (Newport, 1984, 1988, 1990). These differences in performance were very pronounced despite the fact that the adults had been using ASL for at least 10 years (see Figure 10.2). Similar results are observed for ability to learn a second language as a function of when second language learning begins (Johnson & Newport, 1989). If one does not learn a language very early (during the critical period), one's language abilities may never be as good as those of someone who did.

Why should there be a critical period for learning a language? The most straightforward idea amounts to a redescription of the results—

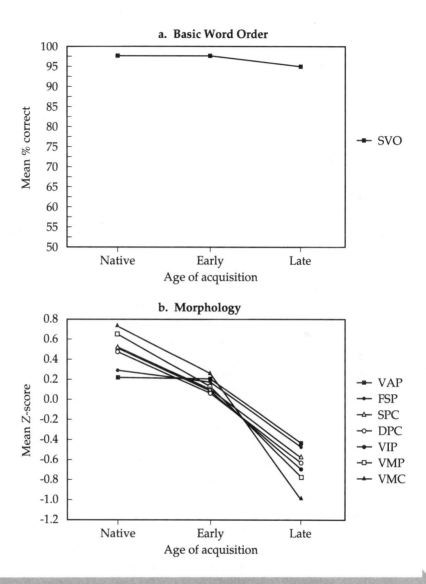

Figure 10.2 (a) Score on ASL basic word order for native, early, and late learners of ASL. Native signers were exposed to ASL from birth on. Early learners were first exposed to sign at ages 4–6, and late learners encountered sign after the age of 12. (b) Z-scores on seven tests of ASL morphology for native, early, and late learners of ASL. The Z-scores provide a measure of relative performance. *Source*: Newport, E., 1990.

namely, that there is some language learning capacity that is present only early in development. It is conceivable that neural development closes off some possibilities even as it opens up others.

Elissa Newport (1990) has offered an intriguing conjecture concerning language learning that is known as the **less-is-more hypothesis**. The key idea is that the limited processing capacity of children may be precisely what allows them to learn a language. This possibility takes a little explaining. Following Newport (1990), consider a simple situation in which there are three sign components (call them a, b, and c) and three meaning components (call them m, n, and o). The learner has to figure out how sign components map into meaning components and even in this very simple example there are 49 possibilities (the relevant sign components could be a, b, c, $a+b$, $a+c$, $b+c$, or $a+b+c$ and there are also seven ways to combine the meaning components to produce a total of 7×7 or 49 possibilities). For example, the sign components a and c together might correspond to meaning component m. For a slightly more complex sign with five components there are nearly a thousand possible mappings.

So far we have only made things sound more challenging. The less-is-more hypothesis entails the idea that children will pick up fewer sign and meaning components than adults and examine many fewer possibilities. A child who only encoded sign component b and meaning components m and n could only consider a few possibilities (that b corresponds to m, that it corresponds to n, or to $m+n$). A child would be unlikely to encode enough sign and meaning components to consider the idea that abc as a whole corresponds to mno as a whole. In short, the child is only able to search in a tiny part of the space of possibilities. That's the "less" part.

The "is more" part is that the tiny part of the space of possibilities that a child can examine is more or less the right part. In the case of ASL the correct correspondences involve a one-to-one mapping of sign components to meaning components rather than any of the more complex combinations and possibilities that the child is unable to consider because of limited processing capabilities. Given that the more complicated possibilities are wrong, the child actually benefits from being unable to consider them.

At this point the reader may wonder how children could know the right units or sign components. One answer is that ASL (and other languages) has developed linguistic components (in this case, morphemes in ASL) that correspond to natural perceptual segments. See Newport, 1990, for a detailed discussion of this point and some evidence bearing on it.

The less-is-more hypothesis suggests that maturational or critical period effects are attributable to nonlinguistic factors. As we hinted earlier, the general issue of whether language learning is driven by a special language facility or by nonlinguistic constraints is far from settled. What is clear is that constraints are needed to explain why children (and not adults) uniformly achieve full competence in learning a language.

Word Meanings

We will say a little bit about how children learn word meanings but again the constraints theme is prominent. Recall that even a benevolent teacher nonetheless would leave the learner in a quandary with respect to figuring out what meaning is intended when the teacher points to some entity and utters a word. Ellen Markman (1989, 1990) has suggested three constraints that children place on the meaning of words and provided empirical support for each of them.

The first bias is that children tend to assume that a novel term applies to the entire object rather than to its parts or properties, the **whole object assumption**. That is, if a parent points to a red ball and says "ball," the child tends to assume that "ball" refers to the object, not its color. This assumption requires that even young infants have a well-defined notion of object and there is good evidence that they do (Spelke, 1990).

The second bias is that children consider labels as referring to objects of like kind rather than to objects that are contextually or thematically related. This **taxonomic constraint** is important because generalizing on the basis of thematic relations will not work. For example, a dog and a bone are thematically related. If a child learns that a particular animal is a *dog*, to generalize correctly he or she must apply the label *dog* to other dogs and not to bones. What complicates matters is that children are sensitive to thematic relations. For example, when they are asked to categorize objects they often do so on the basis of thematic relatedness rather than taxonomic relations. Markman proposes that a linguistic context shifts biases away from thematic relations and toward taxonomic relations.

Markman and her associates have demonstrated that young children do show a taxonomic bias in word learning. In one study (Markman & Hutchinson, 1984), four- and five-year-olds were shown objects of the type listed in Table 10.1. In the no word condition children were asked to find a picture that was the same as the target. The novel word condition used the same instructions except that a nonsense syllable was used to label the target picture. One choice was always thematically related (e.g., a cow and milk) and one taxonomically related (e.g., a cow and a pig).

The linguistic context provided by the novel word (nonsense syl-

Table 10.1 Triads Used in Markman & Hutchinson's Study.

Standard Object	Taxonomic Choice	Thematic Choice
Cow	Pig	Milk
Ring	Necklace	Hand
Door	Window	Key
Crib	Adult bed	Baby
Bee	Ant	Flower
Hanger	Hook	Dress
Cup	Glass	Kettle
Car	Bicycle	Car Tire
Sprinkler	Watering Can	Grass
Paintbrush	Crayons	Easel
Train	Bus	Tracks
Dog	Cat	Bone

lable) had a very large influence on the children's choices. In the no word condition the taxonomic choice was made only 25% of the time, a testimony to the salience of thematic relations. In the novel word condition the taxonomic choice was made 65% of the time. Other studies by Markman and Hutchinson (1984) demonstrated that this taxonomic bias holds even for completely unfamiliar objects.

The third assumption or bias is that children expect objects to have only one label. Children might, for example, assume that a second novel label for an object refers not to the object but rather to a part or property of it (for evidence on this point, see Markman & Wachtel, 1988). Note that this **mutual exclusivity assumption** is not objectively correct—objects can be labeled at varying levels of abstraction (e.g., dog, animal, living thing). Still, this bias may be useful to a language learned in some contexts. For example, suppose a child sees two objects and hears a novel label whose referent is ambiguous. If the child knows a label for one of the objects, he or she might (according to the mutual exclusivity hypothesis) assume that the novel label applies to the other object (again see Markman & Wachtel, 1988 for evidence). Of course, eventually children must learn that objects can have more than one label.

These three constraints or biases may work to guide children's hypotheses or assumptions about word meanings. Although there is fairly good evidence for these three constraints the general point is that biases or guiding principles are needed if the child is to successfully figure out what words mean.

Summary

We hope we have conveyed the flavor and excitement of the ongoing work on constraints and interaction associated with language acquisition. Investigators are beginning to piece together various constraints and to address the question of how these guiding principles work together to allow children to master the complexities of language. Before ending this chapter we take a detailed look at children's learning of the past tense. Our specific focus will be on a connectionist model of past tense learning that embodies the claim that rulelike regularities do not require one to assume that the linguistic system uses rules.

A Connectionist Model of Past Tense Learning

The catalyst for much of the recent discussion of rules and regularities is a model for the learning of past tense developed by David Rumelhart and Jay McClelland (1986). They suggested that linguistic rules are not directly represented but rather that the interaction of multiple sources of information gives rise to behavior that can be described as rulelike. That is, the mechanism that produces certain regularities that conform to the past tense rule does not contain any like a statement of this rule. In short, it is very different from a computer program that would look up a rule in order to generate a past tense.

To support this general claim Rumelhart and McClelland offered a connectionist model of past tense learning. As we suggested earlier, children's learning past tense appears to go through distinct stages. In the first stage children use the past tense for only a small number of verbs and these verbs tend both to have high frequency in our language and to be irregular. By irregular we mean verbs that do not follow the typical rule of adding *ed* to form the past tense. For example, common verbs like *is, go, have,* and *come* have irregular past tenses (*was, went, had, came*). Generally children form the past tense correctly for the limited number of verbs that they use.

The second stage is striking. Children use many more verbs, most of which are regular. The children not only perform correctly on these regular verbs but also can generate the correct past tense for a newly invented word. Berko's (1958) study showed that if children were taught to use the word *rick* to describe an action, they would spontaneously say *ricked* when describing the action in the past tense. This was true even though the children had never heard the word *rick* before. Even more striking is the observation that children in the second stage will now often give the incorrect past tense for the same irregular verbs that were produced correctly in the first stage. For example, they will say *goed, wented, comed,* or *camed*, rather than *went* or *came*. These observations have been taken as evidence that children have acquired and are using the past tense rule.

In the third stage children produce both correct regular forms and correct irregular forms. That is, they now produce the past tense correctly. One should also note that certain irregular verbs themselves form subclusters that have regularities. For example, verbs ending in *eep* may use *ept* as the past form (*keep, sleep, sweep, weep*).

Can a model without rules account for these stages of past tense learning? Let's see. The basic structure of the Rumelhart and McClelland model is shown in Figure 10.3. The figure and model are complex but we can at least convey the general ideas. After learning is complete the network is supposed to take any word stem as its input and produce the correct past tense form as its output. This model is analogous to the connectionist model of memory we discussed in Chapter 8, which also learned the correct output for a given input. The first layer encodes the phonological representation of the root or stem and converts it to a featural representation and the final layer converts the featural representation of the past tense form into a phonological representation. The learning component or pattern associator is a network with two layers of nodes (the two inner layers in Figure 10.3), one representing the input and the other the output. Each node represents a different property that an input item may have. Nodes may be "on" or "off" to mark the presence or absence of particular properties.

On a very general level, the model operates as follows. It first encodes a stem as a pattern of activation over the input units. The input units then pass on activation to the output units. The net input activation to an output unit is simply the (weighted) sum over all input units linked to it. The greater the weight an output unit receives, the more likely it is to be turned on. This is just the sort of interactive activation model we considered earlier in the chapter on perception. Learning involves adjusting the weights on connections so that the correct output units are turned on for each different root form.

We need to say a bit more about encoding. Words are comprised

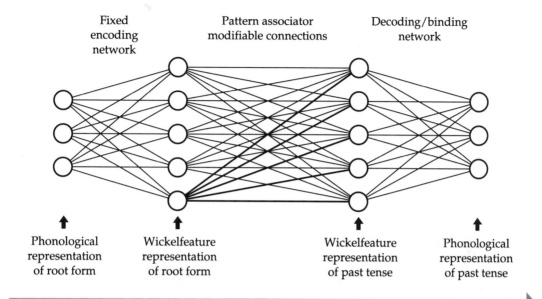

Fixed encoding network

Pattern associator modifiable connections

Decoding/binding network

Phonological representation of root form

Wickelfeature representation of root form

Wickelfeature representation of past tense

Phonological representation of past tense

Figure 10.3   **The Rumelhart-McClelland Model of Past Tense Acquisition.**
The network converts the phonological input into a distributed coding of Wickel-phones, referred to as Wickelfeatures. The Wickelfeature layer then passes on activation to the output layer in accordance with the learned connection strengths. Finally, the representation of past tense in terms of Wickelfeatures is converted or decoded into the phonological representation of past tense. *Source*: Rumelhart, D. E., & McClelland, J. L. (1986).

of a series of letters presented in a particular order. Given that a network consists of units that are turned on or off simultaneously, one might wonder how order could be encoded. Rumelhart and McClelland adopted a scheme proposed by Wickelgren (1969) whereby a string is represented by the set of trigrams it contains. Thus *depart* would consist of (dep), (epa), (par), and (art) trigrams, where the order of trigrams does not matter. To locate word edges, it is assumed that word boundaries are also encoded (represented by #) so that *depart* would have the two additional trigrams (#de) and (rt#). The system then knows that #de has to be the start of a word and that rt# has to be the end and with either point fixed it can integrate the other trigrams to form #depart#. Rumelhart and McClelland refer to these trigrams as **Wickelphones**. Figure 10.3 refers to Wickelfea-tures rather than Wickelphones. Recall that network models often encode an item as a pattern of activation over a number of nodes rather than assigning them to a single node. That is, the representation is distributed.

Wickelfeatures represent a distributed coding of Wickelphones so there is no unit that corresponds exactly to a given Wickelphone. Wickelphones have the property of capturing enough of the context in which a phoneme occurs to provide a basis for differentiating between the different cases of the past tense rule and for determining subregularities of irregular past tense verbs.

The past tense model was trained on 420 different root–past tense pairs. After these teaching inputs were given, Rumelhart and McClelland tested the network by presenting both old and new roots and observing what output was generated. To someone unacquainted with connectionist models, the first surprise is that the network produced correct responses for the roots on which it was trained. Thus, it gave *melted* from *melt*, *looked* from *look*, but also *lived* from *live*, *hit* from *hit*, and *sang* from *sing*. This performance derives from the connection weights but there is nothing at all in the system that one can point to and call a rule. Furthermore, the network operates the same way on regulars and irregulars—they do not have separate networks. The next surprise is that the network responded correctly to many stems on which it was not trained. This was true for both new regular verbs and to a fair extent for new irregular verbs.

Rumelhart and McClelland (1986) were also able to mirror stages in past tense acquisition by presenting the network initially with frequent, irregular verbs and then giving the network a large set of (mostly) regular verbs. When the regular verbs were added, the network overgeneralized the regularities and began to make errors on the frequent irregular verbs that it had earlier produced correctly. In short the network, though it had no explicit rules, produced the pattern of performance that previously had been taken as unequivocal evidence for rule use.

Our description does not do justice to the detailed evaluations of the network model performed by Rumelhart and McClelland. They concluded their paper by writing,

> We have shown that a reasonable account of the acquisition of past tense can be provided without recourse to the notion of a "rule" as anything more than a *description* of the language. We have shown that, for this case, there is no *induction problem*. The child need not figure out what the rules are, nor even that there are rules. (1986, p. 267)

These are very strong conclusions and they have not gone unchallenged. The Rumelhart and McClelland past tense model was criticized in papers by Pinker and Prince (1988) and by Lachter and Bever (1988). The criticisms are extensive, thorough, and detailed. We will provide a sampling of these concerns and then focus on the issue that is central to the themes of this book.

One set of problems derives from the use of Wickelphones. The fact that pairs of words like *silt* and *slit* have no Wickelphones (three-letter sequence) in common has the implied consequence that they have no phonological properties in common. In short, the Wickelphone representation may be an unsatisfactory measure of psychological similarity. The Wickel-system also has difficulty representing generalizations like "add [d] to the end of a word when it ends in a voiced consonant." The reason is that Wickelphones involve triplets, whereas this generalization involves only a pair of adjacent elements (see Lachter & Bever, 1988 for a pointed discussion of how the network model attempts to get around this and related problems). A major problem is to represent enough of the context to make the system work but not so much that it will be unable to generalize. Finally, it is probably a mistake not to distinguish between words and their featural decomposition because the correct past tense form may depend on whether a verb has been derived from a noun or verb. Consider the word *brake*, which can be either a noun or a verb. One can say "He broke the bottle" but not "He broke the car to avoid the crash." That is, the correct past tense form depends on more than phonological information alone.

Pinker and Prince (1988) also criticize the Rumelhart and McClelland model on empirical grounds. They note that the network often gives incorrect answers at a high rate (by their count, 28%), including errors that children do not make. For example, *membled* was derived from *mail*, *brawned* from *brown*, *slept* from *slip*, *mappeded* from *map*, and *maded* from *mate*.

Pinker and Prince further note that the stages in children's learning of past tense are not associated with changes in the proportion of irregular verbs in linguistic input or in a child's vocabulary (Brown, 1973; Kuczaj, 1977). Recall that the network simulation assumed that the input changed dramatically; it is changes in the input that were responsible for the emergence of overregulations.

We believe that these (as well as other) criticisms of the past tense model are well taken (see also Massaro, 1988), especially if normal standards of evaluation are applied. On the other hand, it is impressive that the model does as well as it does, given the various simplifying assumptions embodied in it. As an illustration of what a relatively crude system can accomplish, the model must be considered a success that will no doubt stimulate the development of more refined connectionist models.

Our principle reservation lies not with the network model per se but rather with one of the claims that Rumelhart and McClelland made about induction. They stated that "there is no *induction problem.*" Rumelhart and McClelland did make a valuable contribution in demonstrating that induction need not involve explicit rule search or evaluation of hypothesis. But there still is a very serious induction problem. Many models, connectionist models included, have assumptions about similarity built into them and it is assumed that generalizations are formed in terms of this similarity. Suppose that instead of using phonemes and phonetic features we constructed a network that encoded the semantic features of words and that we attempted to learn past tense rules in terms of semantic similarity. Such a system would, for example, be biased to expect that *run* and *trot* would have the same past tense form because of their semantic similarity. And such a system would fail. Phonemes and phonetic features work better than semantic features for learning past tense, but that kind of knowledge is what the problem of induction is all about!

The crucial question is how a system can learn from limited experience when that limited experience is consistent with so many distinct possibilities. The reason the network system "knows" that past tense does not depend on whether or not it's raining outside or whether the speaker blinks is because that possibility has not been built in or allowed by the simulation. In the case of children learning how to form past tense, there must be innate or acquired biases that keep them from even considering these unprofitable possibilities. (Note, incidentally, that rain and blinking may be relevant to some other learning task—they just aren't relevant to learning past tense.) The upshot is that all learning systems, whether connectionist or symbolic, need strong constraints, constraints that work to guide the learner in addressing the problem of induction—a problem that will not go away.

Summary

Language acquisition represents a paradigmatic case of the themes that serve to organize this book. Language learning in its general form is impossible because there are too many possibilities or hypotheses to be considered. Despite these computational complexity problems, children do acquire language and acquire it even more readily than adults. The search for constraints and figuring out how various constraints may be coordinated with one another have been the central organizing themes for research on language acquisition. What is clear is that there are sufficient constraints or guiding principles to turn an impossible task into one that any kid can do.

Key Terms

distributional information
holophrastic speech
learnability theory
less-is-more hypothesis
linguistic universals
mutual exclusivity assumption
negative evidence
overgeneralization errors
productivity

segmentation
semantic bootstrapping
subset principle
syntactic bootstrapping
taxonomic constraint
telegraphic speech
Wickelphones
whole object assumption

Recommended Readings

Pinker (1990) offers a good general introduction to the language learnability problem and readers who want to probe further should look at his (1989) book. The edited volume by Wanner and Gleitman (1982) represents a thoughtful survey of issues in language acquisition. Readers with a particular interest in phonological learning are referred to review papers by Miller (1990) and by Kuhl (1987, 1990).

In a couple of recent papers Elissa Newport (1988, 1990) reviews evidence that language acquisition has a critical period associated with it and discusses alternative mechanisms that might mediate such efforts. The Johnson and Newport (1989) paper on critical periods in second language learning has a very thorough and instructive discussion of methodological issues in interpreting critical period effects.

The controversy continues over whether rulelike behavior is necessarily governed by a rule mechanism, prompted by the Rumelhart and McClelland (1986) connectionist model of past tense. The special issue of *Cognition* containing articles by Fodor and Pylyshyn (1988), Lachter and Bever (1988), and Pinker and Prince (1988) provides criticisms of connectionist approaches to language and one may anticipate that the debate will continue.

11

COMPREHENSION AND INFERENCE

Chapter Outline

I took a speed reading course and read *War and Peace*. It involves Russia.

—Woody Allen

Introduction

In the chapters on memory, we claimed that people often remember the meaning of some information rather than the exact information that was presented. In this chapter we address the question of how this meaning is figured out. What is understanding and how does it depend on background knowledge? As we shall see, prior knowledge has a major influence on the inferences brought to bear in the service of understanding. For example, suppose we hear someone mention a kickoff. To someone who knows American football this term would refer unambiguously to the initiation or beginning of an event. To the listener more acquainted with soccer, however, the term would conjure up visions of overtime and a dramatic conclusion to a long contest. These are two very distinct understandings, only one of which is correct in a particular context. In this chapter we focus on what it means to understand and comprehend information.

Why is understanding a problem at all? Reading involves far more than understanding the information that is explicitly conveyed. Read the following few sentences (adapted from Charniak, 1973):

> Jane heard the jingling of the ice cream truck.
> She ran to get her piggy bank and started to shake it.
> Finally some money came out.

This passage appears to be quite straightforward, but it is easy to show that readers generate a number of inferences in understanding this passage that might be wrong at least some of the time. How old is Jane? Why did she get the money? Did she turn her piggy bank upside down?

Was the money that came out in the form of coins or bills? How big was the piggy bank? None of this information is explicitly stated, but we would be quite surprised to find that Jane was 87, owned a piggy bank the size of a car, and shook out a handful of thousand dollar bills in order to make an offer to purchase the truck.

This passage illustrates a number of important points about comprehension. First, the meaning of these sentences is not simply the words in the sentences, but also includes the knowledge that you bring to bear to understand these sentences. In this case, you used your knowledge about ice cream trucks and selling to understand the sentences. Put more generally, *meaning is a function of both the input and activated knowledge*. Second, meaning does not come through some passive assimilation of the meaning of the sentences, because the meaning of the sentences is partly in the reader. Thus, *comprehension is an active, not passive process*, with the reader constructing the meaning from the input and his or her activated knowledge. Third, and perhaps less obvious, *understanding consists of constructing an integrated representation*. That is, we understand this passage when we are able to figure out how all this information fits together to make sense.

Imagine that the preceding passage included, after the first sentence, the additional sentence "She had thrown away yesterday's paper." Even though the rest of the sentences fit together nicely as before, most readers would feel that they did not fully understand the story, not because they could not understand this additional sentence by itself but rather because they do not know how this sentence fits with the others. Suppose, however, the readers knew that the preceding day's paper included a coupon entitling the person to a free ice cream cone. This additional knowledge would allow the readers to integrate the new sentence with their understanding of the other sentences. Thus, understanding consists of integrating presented information with previously acquired knowledge to construct a unified representation. The meaning consists not just of the presented information but also of the activated knowledge, including any inferences needed to connect this structure.

This chapter will further illustrate the themes that (1) information in the world is incomplete and ambiguous, and (2) completing this information by using our knowledge to generate inferences introduces the problem of computational complexity yet again. Given that so much knowledge is potentially relevant, how do we come to use the appropriate information? After outlining the problem we discuss some partial solutions, ranging from social rules for communication, known as conversational maxims or pragmatics, to cognitive processes such as schema formation and the construction of "mental models."

The Active Nature of Understanding

Let us begin with a simple case. What do people understand when they read a sentence? What is the meaning of a sentence? Or, to make the issue more concrete, suppose you wanted to build a computer program that would translate a sentence in Russian into English. What would you do? In fact, this was the question addressed by a number of research projects in the early 1960s, when the government hoped that computers would help us better understand what the Soviets were thinking. One answer, which seemed promising, was to access the definition of every Russian word in a sentence and then translate the words into their best English match. This system, though it may sound simple, requires a great deal of work to try to get the right meanings of words and the right grammatical constraints. To test this idea and evaluate the output, the researchers had English sentences translated into Russian and then translated back into English. An often quoted illustration of the inherent problems in such a task is the following: "The spirit is willing but the flesh is weak" was translated into Russian and then translated back into English as "The vodka is good but the meat is rotten." Although this sentence does provide a meaningful (if not particularly useful) message, most readers would agree that it does not capture the meaning of the original sentence. What *is* the meaning?

The meaning of a sentence is not simply a combination of the definitions of the words. To begin with, many words have multiple meanings, so at the very least the meaning of sentences includes some decisions about the appropriate meaning of the words. For example, "Mary went to the ball" could mean that Mary walked over to retrieve some playing ball, but when read in isolation it is usually interpreted to mean that Mary attended a formal dance.

However, the active nature of understanding even a simple sentence involves much more than resolving the ambiguity of words with multiple meanings. Our understanding includes many inferences that go beyond the information given. For example, suppose you were asked the meaning of the sentence, "Mary kicked the ball." Here there is little doubt that the intended meaning of ball is the spherical object, and certainly most readers would understand this sentence to mean that some female had used a fast movement of her foot to propel a spherical object. But understanding goes beyond these observations. Readers would be quite surprised to learn that the ball was twice the size of Mary. That is, understanding the sentence included an inference about the ball size. Why might this be so?

It is always possible to suggest an alternative explanation of a single example. Perhaps the meaning of ball includes information about its usual size. However, consider the following sentences, focusing on the word "caught."

    1. The python caught the mouse.
    2. John caught the mouse.

Note that the sense of caught and the inferences about how the catching was done change in these two sentences. Although it is natural to assume that the python caught the mouse in its mouth, the same inference is very unlikely for John! We might also assume that the python intends to eat the mouse but John does not (Brewer, 1977 shows that people often misremember the python sentence as having included eating). Thus, the inferences made about the word "caught" do not depend simply on its meaning (as the alternative explanation for the earlier example proposed) but upon what it is that is doing the catching. In addition the meaning of *caught* changes again when sentence 2 is changed to:

    3. John caught the ball.

Now, the physical actions involved in catching are quite different (although most readers would still not make the inference that catching led to eating). What does all this show? The basic point is that one cannot view understanding as some passive process in which the presented information is taken in and understood. Rather, understanding consists of actively making inferences to represent the presented information. The reason that understanding involves going beyond the information given is that one rarely is trying to understand words or sentences in isolation. Rather, we are trying to understand complex events, texts, arguments, and so on that consist of many simple events, sentences, and utterances. Thus, appropriate inferences made in understanding one part may help greatly in fully understanding the next part. If you look back at the Jane–ice cream sentences, the true meaning of the last sentence depends crucially on inferences made in understanding the earlier sentences, such as that the piggy bank had money and the money was to be used to buy ice cream. If the meanings of the first two sentences were taken simply to be indications of Jane's hearing abilities and interest in shaking objects, the last sentence would not be understood in the way it is.

So far we have considered only one half of the inference and prediction problem. A simple sentence like "John caught the mouse" is consistent with any number of inferences. Without some control over the inferencing process, a single sentence could leave us lost in thought for days (some early AI systems that generated inferences were susceptible to this problem). Just which kinds of inferences are drawn during reasoning is a topic that has been studied systematically. For example, people appear to make inferences involving causal relations, where one event mentioned in the story is connected by a causal inference to another explicitly mentioned event (Keenan, Baillet, & Brown, 1984). On the other hand, Singer and Ferreira (1983) found that causal inferences are not made unless the consequence of the to-be-inferred event is explicitly stated (see Trabasso, Van den Broek, & Suh, 1989 for a detailed analysis of comprehending causal structure in text).

How can one tell when an inference is drawn? Gail McKoon and Roger Ratcliff have employed a variety of techniques (or converging operations) that generally agree with each other with respect to conclusions about inferencing. One technique is to present a paragraph for comprehension and then give a speeded word recognition test in which the task is to indicate as quickly as possible whether a word appeared in the paragraph. If a word has been inferred, people should be slower to indicate that it did not appear in the paragraph. For example, participants might be given the sentence, "The director and the cameraman were ready to shoot closeups when suddenly the actress fell from the fourteenth story" and then probed with the word "dead." A control sentence might use many of the same words but not include death as a predictable inference. For the preceding sentence a control sentence might be, "Suddenly the director fell upon the cameraman, demanding closeups of the actress on the fourteenth floor." Using these materials and others like them, McKoon and Ratcliff (1986) found evidence that these predictable but not explicitly described events are encoded into memory only minimally. Responses to probes like "dead" were slow only on an immediate test as if the inference had been only partially activated or considered only briefly. McKoon and Ratcliff suggest that the sort of minimal coding that took place would be roughly that "something bad" happened. (We know from other experiments by McKoon and Ratcliff that their procedures are sensitive enough to detect the influence of inferences when they are drawn.) As we shall see, it makes sense for an inference system to be somewhat conservative about its guesses because otherwise we might often be forced to retract inferences. For example, the next sentence in the story involving the actress might have been, "Miraculously, an awning broke her fall and she survived." We say *somewhat* conservative because the inference system clearly is making plausible guesses most of the time (think back to Jane and the ice cream truck or John catching the mouse).

Although most situations are underdetermined and ambiguous, a striking observation is that we are normally unaware of any ambiguity. Consider the following phonetic ambiguity (borrowed from Garrett, 1990); the phonetic information is consistent with the main text but is also consistent with the string of words within the brackets.

> Remember, a spoken sentence often contains many words
> [ream ember us poke can cent tense off in   men knee
>
> not intended to be heard.
> knot in ten did tube bee herd]

The comprehension process must be able to use background knowledge and partial information to resolve these ambiguities and it does so most of the time without our being aware of any problem. We have seen that understanding is an active process that constantly must cope with ambiguity and draw needed relevant inferences.

As we move from single sentences to the level of paragraphs and organized passages of text, the comprehension process involves further complexities. For example, that van Dijk and Kintsch (1983) characterize text understanding as involving the construction of four distinct types of representation:

1. the *microstructure,* which is a set of propositions representing what the text says more or less literally
2. the *macrostructure,* which is derived from the microstructure and represents the "gist" of the text
3. the *superstructure,* which represents the rhetorical form or style of the text (this is needed because the form or style may influence how the reader should interpret the text)
4. the *situation model,* which is a set of knowledge structures representing what the text is about

The van Dijk and Kintsch model has been tested in a variety of ways. The model makes predictions about how long it will take to read different passages (as a function of their microstructure and macrostructure), what information from a text will tend to be recalled and what forgotten, and what propositions will be included when people are asked to write a brief summary of a text (Kintsch & van Dijk, 1978; Keenan, 1986; see also Kintsch, 1988). These predictions have generally been supported. Developmental research has demonstrated the value of distinguishing between microstructure, macrostructure, and the situation model (see, e.g., Brown & Day, 1983; Keenan, 1986; Weaver & Dickinson, 1982).

In brief, one can see that text comprehension involves vastly more than looking up word meanings in some mental dictionary.

Pragmatics and Comprehension

Pragmatics refers to the practical matter of making sure that people understand each other. There are numerous rules and guidelines that people seem to follow to facilitate communication.

The Given-New Strategy

Haviland and Clark (1974) proposed that the organization of sentences supports a **given-new strategy**. Speakers or writers normally are trying to relay new information and do so by relating it to what is already known or given. The listener (or reader) assumes that the speaker (or writer) knows and is able to gauge what the listener (or reader) does not know. Consider the following sentence: "The jokes that Horace tells are awful." The given information is that Horace tells jokes and the new information is that the jokes are awful. The sentence presupposes that the reader knows who Horace is and without that shared knowledge the sentence may seem strange.

Haviland and Clark (1974) found that the time it took people to comprehend sentences varied as a function of whether or not the given-new principle was violated. For example, people were faster at comprehending the second sentence in the first of the following sentence pairs:

1. Last Christmas Eugene became absolutely smashed. This Christmas he got very drunk again.
2. Last Christmas Eugene went to a lot of parties. This Christmas he got very drunk again.

The word *again* presupposes that Eugene had gotten drunk before, an assumption that is directly stated only in the first pair of sentences. This example and others like it reveal that there are numerous strategies that can be used to promote (see, e.g., Clark & Schaefer, 1987a) or inhibit (Clark & Schaefer, 1987b; Schober & Clark, 1989) effective communication.

Presupposition and Assertion

The given-new strategy works well when a sentence includes a shared presupposition or background followed by an assertion of new information. Because greatest attention is directed at the new or asserted information it may be possible to slip misleading information into the presupposition part of a sentence. Elizabeth Loftus has shown that presuppositions can be manipulated in such a way as to affect eyewitness testimony. For example, Loftus and Palmer (1974) showed undergraduate students films depicting a traffic accident and then asked a variety of questions about them. In different films two cars collided and these collisions took place at speeds of 20, 30, or 40 miles per hour. The specific verb used to ask the question about speed was also varied. For example, some students might be asked "About how fast were the cars going when they hit each other?" whereas others might be asked "About how fast were the cars going when they smashed into each other?" The verb *smashed* seems to presuppose more speed than the verb *hit*. Loftus and Palmer found that the verbs used had a clear effect on estimated speeds. For the verb *hit* the mean estimated speed was 34.0 miles per hour and for *smashed* the mean estimated speed was 40.8 miles per hour. Differences in actual speed had little effect. The mean estimates for the speeds of 20, 30, and 40 miles per hour were 37.7, 36.2, and 38.3 miles per hour respectively.

Conversational Maxims

Making the right inferences may also depend on common conventions or rules. Grice (1975) proposed that cooperative communication requires adherence to a set of **conversational maxims**. He refers to these maxims as *quantity, quality, relation,* and *manner*, which can be approximately translated into *be informative, tell the truth, be relevant,* and *be clear*. An important aspect or consequence of these **Gricean maxims** is that they often require that we do not take statements literally. For example, if John says to Bill, "Can you close the door?" and Bill responds by saying "yes," then Bill has violated the principle of relevance. Both John and Bill know that Bill is capable of closing the door and therefore Bill should understand John's question as an *indirect speech act* or request to close the door. Consider the following interchange:

> Parent: Where did you go?
> Teenager: Out.
> Parent: What did you do?
> Teenager: Nothing.

This may violate the principle of informativeness but so obviously that it might be best read as an indirect speech act intending to convey "none of your business."

Sometimes we use a literal mode of response to violate the maxim of quality or truthfulness. For example, a parent might say to a child, "Did you walk into the kitchen and take some cookies?" The child might say "no," because the truth is that he *ran* into the kitchen and took some cookies.

One of the interesting aspects of conversational maxims is that people seem to know them even though they are not explicitly taught. As we have just seen, people use conversational principles in subtle ways in the service of communication (or sometimes miscommunication).

Interpreting and Integrating Information

In the earlier chapters on memory we discussed how the organization of information may affect memory for that information. When this occurs at encoding, one may think of the earlier items as setting up some framework in which the latter items are interpreted and remembered. For example, the word "orange" is interpreted differently depending on whether the context consists of "apple, banana, pear" or "yellow, green, red." Such effects are not limited to these words with multiple meanings but can occur at all levels of understanding. The framework we are using or the knowledge that has been activated affects our understanding of new information. What we learn depends on what we already know. Recall the research mentioned in our discussion of memory showing that what is learned from a baseball game depends on how much a person knows about baseball.

However, it is not only the knowledge a person has that is important. As we have often seen, we possess so much knowledge that a crucial consideration is how the relevance of information is determined. That is, how do we get to the right information without getting lost in a sea of irrelevant possibilities? It is not total knowledge that is crucial but rather the knowledge that the reader *brings to bear* in understanding. Read over and think about the following paragraph from Bransford and Johnson (1972):

> The procedure is actually quite simple. First you arrange things into different groups. Of course one pile may be sufficient depending on how much there is to do. If you have to go somewhere else, due to lack of facilities, that is the next step; otherwise you are pretty well set. It is important not to overdo things. That is, it is better to do too few things at once than too many. In the short run this may not seem important but complications can easily arise. It is difficult to foresee any end to the necessity for this task in the immediate future, but then one never can tell. After the procedure is completed one arranges the materials into different groups again. They can be put into their appropriate places. Eventually they will be used once more and the whole cycle will then have to be repeated.

Do you understand this passage? As one indication of your understanding, how well do you think you would be able to remember this passage an hour from now? Probably not very well. But suppose that in addition to the paragraph you were given a title for it. This seems like a pretty minor change that ought not to affect things very much, but in fact it does. The title of the above passage is "Washing Clothes." Now go back and reread the paragraph. It seems obvious that you would now remember it much better. Although you knew about laundry the first time you read the passage, this knowledge was not activated and did not influence your understanding of the passage. The title serves to activate such knowledge and makes the passage sensible and easier to remember.

The idea that activated knowledge affects understanding is not limited to contrasts between cases in which we have relevant activated knowledge and cases in which we do not. Rather, the *particular* knowledge that is activated can influence our understanding. Consider the story in Table 11.1 (from Anderson, Reynolds, Schallert, & Goetz, 1977). Most people would interpret this story as one in which Rocky is a prisoner. If, however, people read this story with knowledge activated about wrestling (e.g., just having watched a wrestling match), then they might be likely to read this as a passage about wrestling. In one experiment, physical education majors were much more likely to interpret this passage as about wrestling and remember those facts consistent with that interpretation.

The activated knowledge we bring to bear in understanding has a large effect on our understanding. What is this activated knowledge? The next two sections deal with two broad types of activated knowledge. First, we examine how general knowledge about situations may be used in un-

Table 11.1   **Wrestling/Prisoner Story.**

> Rocky slowly got up from the mat, planning his escape. He hesitated a moment and thought. Things were not going well. What bothered him most was being held, especially since the charge against him had been weak. He considered his present situation. The lock that held him was strong but he thought he could break it. He knew, however, that his timing would have to be perfect. Rocky was aware that it was because of his early roughness that he had been penalized so severely—much too severely from his point of view. The situation was becoming frustrating; the pressure had been grinding on him for too long. He was being ridden unmercifully. Rocky was getting angry now. He felt he was ready to make his move. He knew that his success or failure would depend on what he did in the next few seconds.

Source: From Anderson, Reynolds, Schallert, and Goetz, 1977.

derstanding a particular instance of that type. Second, we investigate how knowledge concerning a particular situation may be used in reasoning about that situation.

Schemas

Motivation

How are we to understand understanding? First, as we hope is clear by now, understanding is not simply a matter of decoding some input, but rather requires an active supplementing of the input with knowledge. For example, if the input is some linguistic material such as a written sentence or an utterance, it is not understood simply by linguistic analyses (though as we have seen, these too are far from simple). Often a true understanding of what is meant will require a substantial amount of nonlinguistic knowledge as well. The sentences about Jane and the ice cream truck illustrate the extent to which world knowledge may be used in understanding.

Second, the knowledge that is often brought to bear in understanding is not just a relevant fact or two, but more of a body of knowledge. For example, in understanding the earlier passage about ice cream it was not enough to have one or two facts about ice cream, but rather a whole set of facts about ice cream trucks, money, and children. To understand something requires fitting it into some integrated representation. Furthermore the information in the world is often incomplete and other knowledge must be accessed and integrated to form some unified representation. In many cases, such as the ice cream passage, the amount of knowledge needed to make sense of the input is great. The need for large amounts of relevant knowledge greatly complicates the computational complexity problem. By this we mean that if knowledge is a set of separate small units (e.g., propositions) and richly interconnected, then determining which units are relevant and which connected ones are not is going to be impossibly difficult.

We have seen that understanding requires the careful integration of new input with a potentially vast amount of prior knowledge. The amazing thing is, however, that we don't find ourselves sitting around mulling over thousands of interpretations and inferences every time someone says something to us. Quite the opposite. In fact, the realization that little effort is involved in complex situations is an important clue to the nature of comprehension processes. That is, certain units of knowledge and inferences are often used together. It appears our comprehension system has learned to access and use them as a whole. These large units of knowledge are called schemata (plural of *schema*; we'll also refer to them as *schemas*).

What Is a Schema?

The term **schema** is used to refer to a wide variety of different constructs, but almost all of them have several points in common (also see Rumelhart & Ortony, 1977). Simply put, *a schema is a general knowledge structure used for understanding*. Let us look at these ideas in some greater detail.

First, a schema is knowledge. It does not refer to information in the world but rather to one's knowledge about the world. Second, a schema is general. It does not encode information about one particular situation but rather about a particular *type* of situation. Third, a schema is structured. That is, a schema does not just consist of some set of facts but also includes how these facts are related. This structure is part of what allows a schema to be used for inferencing. Fourth, a schema is used in comprehension. The structure of the schema is such that it includes how the knowledge is related in this type of situation, but it does not include information about any exact situation. Therefore, some knowledge is incomplete. For example, if you had a schema for buying ice cream, your understanding of a particular event would require you to know who bought the ice cream and probably which flavor was chosen. Although your schema would include knowledge that someone buys some type of ice cream, it is general and would not contain the particular person or the particular ice cream. That is, the schema would include the general expectation that purchasing ice cream involves an exchange in which one person pays money to another person to receive some quantity and type of ice cream.

A schema is often viewed as consisting of a **frame** that includes **slots** for particular information. An ice cream purchase frame would have slots for the buyer, the seller, amount paid, and type of ice cream. Understanding consists of filling in these slots or incomplete knowledge. A frame also contains **default assumptions** concerning slot values. If a text fails to mention some piece of information, the default value may be assumed. For example, if we read "John went to the ice cream store and left with a vanilla cone," we assume that John paid for it (a default value) rather than stole it and that vanilla was the flavor of ice cream he selected (instantiating or filling in the slot for type) and not the color of some cone-shaped object. Finally, slots contain restrictions about what information can fill them. For example, in the ice cream buying schema it is not permissible to have the buyer slot filled in by "chocolate-vanilla swirl" or the ice cream type to be "Jane."

The idea of a schema is complex and puts a very different perspective on understanding. Previously in our discussion it seemed that the difficulty in understanding was figuring out what relevant knowledge to bring to bear and how to have some control over the inferences. Now the difficulty is knowing what schema to use. As we saw in the washing clothes passage, the determination of the appropriate schema is not always simple. We will discuss this issue shortly. First, however, we will take a more detailed look at schemas.

Schemas can occur at various levels of abstraction and can be embedded. For instance, if you have a schema for ice cream buying, this schema may include much knowledge that comes from your schema about buying in general (e.g., what money is) and some that is applicable only to ice cream buying (e.g., what the truck bells signal and the menu, often with pictures, of the different ice creams available).

What are the advantages of schemas? They help us to understand. Rather than having to figure out what knowledge is relevant, how it all fits together, what inferences to make, and how likely each piece of knowledge is alone and in all possible combinations, we can rely on schemas. Once selected, a schema contains all this knowledge and the task is now to simply figure out what information relates to what slots in order to understand. In addition, schemas *generate expectations* about what is likely to happen. These expectations are invaluable to us in helping us to understand later events and also to notice if something unusual is happening. The power of these schemas arises because they include information about how all the different aspects of the situation are related. Thus, they can be used for predicting what will occur. These ideas can best be understood by examining a particular type of schema for stereotyped events, a script.

Scripts

Consider the following passage, adapted from the work on scripts by Schank and Abelson (1977):

> John was hungry.
> He went into a restaurant and ordered a sandwich.
> He paid his bill and left.

Almost all readers find these sentences easy to understand. Although these sentences contain only 18 words, they allow you to make a large number of inferences with varying degrees of certainty. Did John eat his sandwich? From whom did he order a sandwich? What was the bill for? Many of these questions seem silly because the answer is so obvious, but in fact none of these answers is stated in the sentences.

A **script** is a knowledge structure containing the sequence of events that usually occurs in a particular stereotyped situation. Thus, scripts are a type of schema for mundane or routine events. They have slots and requirements as to what can fill these slots. In addition, the scripts are structured, with the events causally linked to one another. This causal linking allows us to make inferences to understand events and to make predictions about future events.

To make this idea concrete, Table 11.2 gives an outline of the script for restaurants (adapted from Schank & Abelson, 1977). The actions can be broken down into what are referred to as *scenes*, such as entering, ordering, eating, and exiting. Although Table 11.2 looks much like a simple sequence, it is important to remember that the events are causally linked so that changes in one may lead to changes in another. For example,

> John was hungry and ordered a hamburger.
> It was burned.
> He would not pay.

In addition to all the usual inferencing (e.g., pay what?), this passage introduces a deviation in the usual script routine: The food was badly prepared. Because we understand that the payment at the end of the meal is directly linked to the food, it is easy for us to understand that the food preparation can affect the payment.

Table 11.2   **Restaurant Script.**
This script version is a particular version of the Coffee Shop track.

Script: Restaurant
Track: Coffee Shop
Props: Tables, menus, food, check, money
Roles: Customer, cook, owner, waiter, cashier

Entry Conditions: Customer is hungry.
Customer has money.

Results: Customer has less money.
Customer is not hungry.
Owner has more money.

Scenes:
1. Entering
Customer goes into restaurant.
Customer looks around.
Customer decides where to sit.
Customer goes to the table and sits down.
2. Ordering
Customer picks up menu.
Customer decides on food.
Customer orders food from waiter.
Waiter tells cook the order.
Cook prepares food.
3. Eating
Cook gives food to waiter.
Waiter gives food to customer.
Customer eats food.
4. Exiting
Waiter writes out check.
Waiter brings check to customer.
Customer gives tip to waiter.
Customer goes to cash register.
Customer gives money to cashier.
Customer leaves restaurant.

Source: Adapted from Schank and Abelson, 1977.

Although it may seem that this knowledge and its use are straightforward, the process is actually quite complicated. The causal connections between all the parts of the script have to be present to allow us to understand not only the normal script actions but any of a large number of possible problems or unusual events that can occur. For each of these events, we can often quickly understand its implications for other script actions (such as how the burning of the hamburger affects the payment). Programming computers to make such inferences, even for a relatively small number of possibilities, is difficult and painstaking.

Because of the highly structured nature of the knowledge, scripts allow us to generate predictions about what is going to happen (see Charniak & McDermott, 1985 for a discussion of this issue). The slot values are highly correlated, such that knowing the value in one slot allows you to predict the values of other slots. If you went to a restaurant with red and white checkered tablecloths, you would be more likely to expect a candle on the table in a Chianti wine bottle. If the tablecloth and candle were present, would you expect Chinese or Italian food? In fact, the number of inferences one can make from just a small sample of what the restaurant is like is quite large. We use this information to help fill in gaps in what we read or observe, as well as to predict what is likely to occur.

People presumably have scripts of a large number of stereotyped events, though some appear to be more stereotyped than others. For example, consider the script for a doctor's appointment. The scenes might include arriving, waiting in a waiting room, entering an examination room, being examined, paying, and leaving. Note, however, that the exact events that occur within each scene and the order of the events seem far less stereotyped than in the restaurant script. For example, one does not necessarily receive or pay the bill before leaving a doctor's office. This observation, as well as others, have led to further investigation of the exact nature of the knowledge used in understanding stereotyped events (e.g., Schank, 1982). Despite controversies concerning the details of how schemas are organized, most researchers would agree that people's understanding and memory for these events are influenced by some type of general knowledge structures (see, e.g., Bower, Black, & Turner, 1979).

Schema Learning and Use

Although schemata may be very helpful in comprehension and prediction, a number of issues are not yet resolved. Schemas may exist but they have little effect unless they are used. In addition, assuming our knowledge about restaurants is not innate, how do we learn it? In this section we consider how schemata are acquired and then how they are used.

Schema Acquisition. If schemata are used for understanding and predicting in a wide variety of situations, how are they learned? A common view is that these schemata are learned in two ways. First, as we experience events, we remember them. If later events are very similar to these earlier events, we may be reminded of the earlier events and use them to help understand the current event. For example, suppose you experienced some new event that does not seem to fit into any of your schemata. The next time you experience a similar event, you are likely to think back to the earlier time. If you want to understand the current event or, in particular, if you want to make predictions about what will happen next, this past event seems the most relevant knowledge. Assuming that this is an appropriate earlier event and helps you to understand and predict the current event, you may store some knowledge about events of this type that captures the commonalities of these two events (Schank, 1982). Later instances of this event type may be understood using this common part. Thus, schemas may develop from noticing commonalities among particular events.

Second, schemas may be learned from modifying other schemas (see Rumelhart & Norman, 1978 for a detailed example). As has been stated often, we learn in relation to what we know. If a new event is not an instance of any schema, it may still be related to a known schema. The person could then use this existing schema as a basis for constructing some new schema. The advantage of such learning is that we can make use of a great deal of previous knowledge. The disadvantage is that some of this imported knowledge may lead one to make inappropriate inferences for the new situation. For example, suppose you had many experiences with restaurants and had developed a reliable script, but had never been in a fast food restaurant. The first time you did, you would presumably follow your restaurant script and sit at a table waiting for a menu and someone to take your order. You could get quite hungry before a waiter or waitress came by.

Schema Activation.   Although we have focused on the effects of activated schemata, a crucial first step is to activate the appropriate schema. If one uses a restaurant schema to understand a home-cooked meal, many of the inferences and predictions will be inappropriate. This problem is the usual complexity problem, with a focus on schemata: Given all the knowledge one possesses, how is the relevant schema determined?

Although this issue is far from resolved, several possible ways in which schemas are activated have been proposed. First, certain key words (or objects if one is not reading or listening) may help to *trigger* the appropriate schema. In the case of the restaurant script, these key words may include restaurant, out to dinner, waiter, chef, and so on. Second, in addition to the words that are distinctively associated to restaurants, other words may provide at least some support for this schema being appropriate (e.g., hungry). Third, events often occur in a context that can also provide support for the relevance of particular schemata. If you knew John was in town for a convention and was hungry, restaurant would become more activated than if he were sitting home and was hungry. As in the memory retrieval work discussed previously, it may be reasonable to conceive of this activation as coming from multiple sources, with some sources more strongly associated and thus contributing more activation and more support.

Schemas and Action

Although we will be unable to say much about action in this book, action is a fundamental issue because intelligent organisms act and behave in relation to their environment. There is good evidence that the organization of action involves coordinated schemas that are triggered by events. Recently action schemas have been studied by analyzing "slips" or mistakes in planned actions such as pouring orange juice rather than milk on top of one's cereal (e.g., Reason, 1979; Reason & Mycielska, 1982; Norman, 1981; Heckhausen & Beckmann, 1990). Slips may involve fairly elaborate patterns of action. Heckhausen and Beckmann (1990) cite an anecdote involving the mathematician David Hilbert:

> Shortly before the arrival of their dinner guests, Mrs. Hilbert noticed that her husband was not wearing a suitable tie. She sent him to the bedroom to change it. When she checked on him because he failed to return, she found him in bed, undressed and fast asleep. (p. 41)

Apparently removing his tie triggered undressing and going to bed because this sequence of behaviors often had been linked in Hilbert's earlier experience. Action schemata offer the advantage that one need not pay close attention to every detail of one's actions but, as the above example illustrates, sometimes a triggered action schema can lead us astray.

Problems with Schemas

You will have noticed that our discussion of schemas has been full of examples and general description but short on details that would necessarily be part of a computational model. The reason for our vagueness is that it is not entirely clear just how to implement the desired properties of schemata. For example, it is straightforward to have slots with default values but exceedingly difficult to implement the idea that the values in some slots constrain the acceptable values in other slots. One needs to be able to do this to capture correlated slot values, as in the example of Chinese versus Italian restaurants discussed earlier.

This kind of observation is what motivated David Rumelhart and his associates to implement schemas within a neural network model (recall the room schema example in Chapter 2—in fact, you may wish to go back and review it now). Network or connectionist models for schemas do have the advantage that they readily handle correlated values and offer more flexibility than more traditional approaches. To our knowledge connectionist systems have not successfully embedded schemas within other schemas. Nonetheless, the flexibility of connectionist models for schemas gives them considerable promise.

A variety of perplexing puzzles associated with the use of schemas still remains. Sometimes, for example, situations may involve a mixture of schemas. One wouldn't want to disrobe when one meets one's physician in a restaurant nor would one want to stand in front of the cash register waiting to pay for one's meal in the event of fire. Although the notion of schemas represents a powerful approach to constraining relevant knowledge, there still are some subtle mysteries to be solved. As of this writing there still is no implemented system that handles the relevance problem with anything like people's gracefulness and flexibility. We shift now to another tool for generating expectations, mental models.

Mental Models

Introduction

We have been considering cases in which people use very general knowledge schemata to understand a situation and make predictions. However, sometimes people have much more specific knowledge about a particular situation or object that they use to understand, predict, and explain. As we shall see, these systems of relevant knowledge, or **mental models**, greatly influence our understanding and behavior. Mental models can be distinguished from schemata in the following ways:

1. Mental models are not simply a filling in of expected values on the basis of prior experience but rather are actively constructed in the service of understanding and explaining of experience.

2. Mental models are often constructed spontaneously to under-

stand situations and to make predictions (via mental simulation of these models) about the future.

✓3. Mental models are often constrained by theories about the world rather than empirically derived through experience (see also Gentner & Stevens, 1983; Johnson-Laird, 1983).

Mental models often are used to describe the knowledge one has of how some object, such as a thermostat, works or how some situation is a function of a set of interacting processes and objects. For example, Nussbaum (1979) examined children's conception of the planet Earth. The children had various facts about the Earth (e.g., Columbus sailed around it, space photographs, perceived flatness, sky) that they put together into some mental model to capture as many of the facts as possible. Some of these mental models are illustrated in Figure 11.1. For some children, this mental model consisted of a flat disc in the middle of water, whereas for some older children the earth was viewed as a half-sphere, with the sky completing the sphere. These mental models would be used to understand observations and other information, as well as to reason about related phenomena. Thus, because of its focus on the workings of some particular object, system, or situation, a mental model can be a powerful reasoning tool (see also Vosniadou & Brewer, 1987).

Mental Models and Health Behavior

To give an idea of both the theoretical and practical importance of mental models, we describe a detailed example from the domain of health and medicine. Patients frequently develop models or beliefs about disease symptoms, causes, health threats, and treatments and these models greatly influence their behavior when they are ill. A major difficulty in combating certain diseases is the high rate of patients not following physician-prescribed treatments or regimens and, as we will see, a major reason for this nonadherence is the mental models that patients have of their diseases.

To illustrate this point, we describe a particular medical problem, hypertension. In 1988 the National Heart, Lung, and Blood Institute estimated that 58 million Americans had hypertension, with 30% of those having greater than mild severity. Hypertension is asymptomatic (there are no symptoms a person can use to tell if his or her blood pressure is or is not high) so compliance is particularly important and patient understanding is crucial.

We know quite a lot about the mental models associated with people's understanding of hypertension due to the important work by Meyer

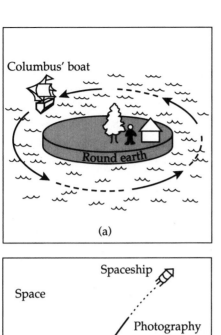

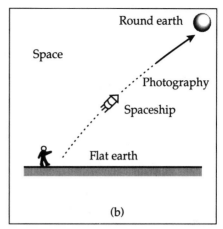

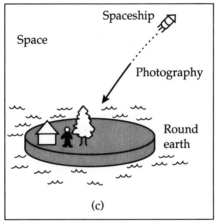

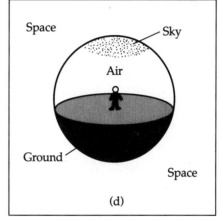

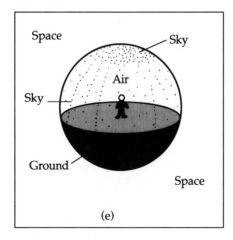

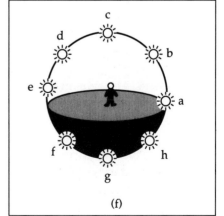

Figure 11.1   Children's Conceptions of Earth.
Source: Nussbaum, J., 1979.

and Leventhal (e.g., Leventhal, Meyer, & Gutmann, 1985). First of all, despite the fact that patients were told that hypertension is asymptomatic, about 80% of patients indicate that they can detect some symptoms. For these patients, three general types of models have emerged from the extensive interviews.

One model, which Leventhal et al. (1980) refer to as the *acute episodic model*, appears to be derived from the representations or mental models of many other illnesses. Patients with this model believe that treatment will be short and lead to a cure of the disease. More than half of these patients claim to be able to specify the time and place for the onset of their hypertension and feel that it is caused by specific stress at home or work. A common focus of this group is on the speed of the heartbeat as an indication of hypertension.

A second group of subjects, using a *cyclic model*, expects the symptoms to subside and then recur. They report random or repetitive symptoms and generally attribute the disease to their behavior in terms of their drinking and diet. These patients often explain the disease in terms of arterial problems caused by excess blood or clogging of the veins.

The final model that emerged from these interviews was referred to as the *chronic model*. These patients view the disease as being due to the body's running down, either from age or hereditary factors. Because of this "cause," they expect the symptoms will be long lasting, if not permanent.

The beliefs about the causes affect the perception of symptoms assumed to covary with the illness (Pennebaker & Epstein, 1983). If patients view hypertension as a disease of the heart, they monitor their heart rate. If they believe the cause is emotional stress, they monitor changes in emotion; if they attribute the hypertension to arterial disease, they are sensitive to any feelings of numbness or coldness in their extremities.

These representations of hypertension are important because they affect whether or not people stick to physician-prescribed medication. Meyer et al. (1985) examined how patients followed recommended treatments. The general finding was quite simple: If hypertensives believed that the treatment was affecting the symptoms they thought indicated hypertension (as described above), over half of them followed the treatment plan sufficiently to bring their blood pressure under control. If they did not believe that the treatment was affecting the "relevant" symptoms, only 24% followed the treatment and brought their blood pressure under control. For example, if a patient attends to heart rate as a symptom, when the heart rate is high the patient is likely to take the medication (Pennebaker & Epstein, 1983). Medications for controlling high blood pressure do not necessarily decrease heart rate and patients who focus on heart rate may discard their medication as ineffective. Similarly, patients who subscribe to the cyclic model may only take their medications in a cyclic manner rather than in the (continuous) manner prescribed. In short, people's mental models of hypertension have a large influence on their health-related behaviors.

Intuitive Theories

Where do mental models come from? We said earlier that mental models are not simply passive accumulations of expected events but rather are actively constructed theorylike structures. A dramatic demonstration of this phenomenon is provided by a recent study by Kaiser, McCloskey, and Proffitt (1986). They examined developmental changes in intuitive theories of motion using the so-called curved tube problem (see Figure 11.2). Grade school students and college students were shown a clear plastic tube in the shape of Figure 11.2A. The interior end of the tube was elevated such that a steel ball dropped into the elevated end would roll through at a moderate speed. Participants were asked to draw the path that the ball would take as it left the tube. The correct response is shown in Figure 11.2B but a very common error is to draw the path indicated in Figure 11.2C. Another version of the problem substituted a "C-curve" for the full spiral but again the correct answer remains the same. The most striking result concerns performance as a function of age, shown in Figure 11.3. Preschool and kindergarten children perform as well as college students but the performance of third through sixth grade children is substantially worse than that of either older or younger participants. Other controls ruled out the possibility that the youngest children performed well simply because they could not draw curved lines.

 Kaiser et al. suggest that grade school students are constructing theories of motion and that a precursor to the principle of inertia (that things in motion will stay in motion unless acted on by an outside force such as friction) is an idea about the persistence of motion. That is, the children act as if they have formed the generalization that an object tends to persist in moving the way in which it was moving. Empirically this is the case for the example of a bouncing ball (it continues to go both up and down for a while) and children may overgeneralize from situations like bouncing balls to the curved tube problem. Thus, the curvilinear motion error may arise as a by-product of the development of a general motion persistence principle that, although not completely correct, is very often useful in predicting and understanding motion.

 Yet to be explained is how incorrect theories of motion are replaced

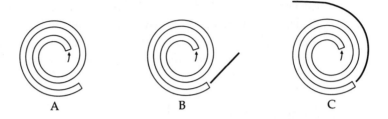

Figure 11.2 The curved tube problem (A), its correct solution (B), and the most common incorrect response (C). *Source*: Kaiser, M. K., McCloskey, M., & Proffitt, D. R., 1986.

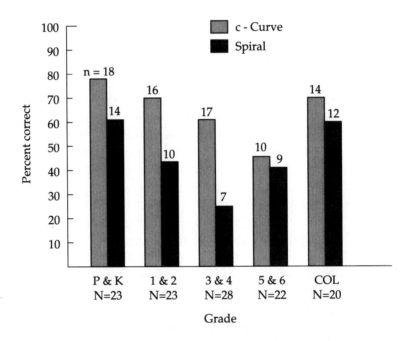

Figure 11.3 Proportion of correct predictions on the C-curve and spiral tube problems by age group. (P = preschool, K = kindergarten, COL = college.) *Source*: Kaiser, M. K., McCloskey, M., & Proffitt, D. R., 1986.

by correct expectations. Another look at Figure 11.3 will reveal that even college students are likely to make the error of expecting curvilinear motion, which suggests that the answer is that it is not easy to replace useful but incorrect theories. Incorrect **intuitive physics** theories often persist in adults even after they have taken college courses in physics (see, e.g., McCloskey, 1983; Gentner & Stevens, 1983; Di Sessa, 1982). The question of how naive mental models are acquired and changed remains a fascinating problem. It also has clear implications for education. The idea that learning involves a passive accumulation of information is clearly wrong and understanding of naive mental models is fundamental to the goal of replacing initial **naive theories** with more accurate explanations.

Just as theories in psychology can range from highly specific models to very broad conceptual frameworks, there is also some range in the scope of mental models. So far we have considered mental models having a theorylike character. More generally, mental models can be thought of as constructed working models of the world used in the service of understanding. This broader definition suggests that mental models may be used in comprehending fairly specific situations. For example, suppose one reads that Bill is taller than John and that John is taller than Larry. One could construct a mental model representing these facts together and, by inspection, note that Bill must also be taller than Larry. In short, mental models may also serve to support reasoning, in this case about the transitivity of the relation *taller than*. Phillip Johnson-Laird (1983) has argued that mental models are a fundamental tool in reasoning. We will take a much closer look at mental models in the chapter on reasoning.

Summary

The information in the world is incomplete. Understanding is not just an accretion of facts, but a much more active process that depends heavily on the (previously stored) knowledge brought to bear on the situation. The information in the world seems to trigger relevant knowledge and associated inferences in the service of comprehension. The interaction and integration of these factors leads to coherent interpretation. This integrated knowledge structure is then further used to explain and make predictions about later events in the world. It leads us to attend to some facts and not others, to give a particular interpretation to ambiguous information, and to understand the implications in a particular way. Schemas are a very important tool for accessing and organizing relevant knowledge. Finally, mental models reflect the fact that people actively construct theories about their world. Comprehension and inference are truly creative processes.

Key Terms

conversational maxims
default assumptions
frame
given-new strategy
Gricean maxims
intuitive physics

mental models
naive theories
schemata
script
slots

Recommended Readings

The Schank and Abelson (1977) book is a good introduction to the role of scripts and goals in everyday understanding. Implications of knowledge structures for theories of text comprehension are detailed and illustrated by van Dijk and Kintsch (1983) and Kintsch (1988). General conversational maxims are laid out by Grice (1975) and their subtle consequences traced in papers by Clark and Schaefer (1987a,b) and Schober and Clark (1989).

Mental models are of particular interest, in part because they are often incorrect. For clever but incorrect models of the earth and solar system see Nussbaum (1979) and Vosniadou and Brewer (1987). Meyer, Leventhal, and Gutmann (1985) describe alternative adult models of blood pressure. The edited book by Gentner and Stevens (1983) offers a general survey of work on mental models and Johnson-Laird's (1983) book develops the widespread implications of a mental models approach to cognition.

12

CONCEPTS AND CATEGORIES: REPRESENTATION AND USE

Chapter Outline

Mind and world in short have evolved together, and in consequence are something of a mutual fit.

William James

Introduction

Why Categorize?

Our world seems to be full of categories. We have names for groups of things such as dogs, cats, cars, computers, birds, birthdays, and balloons. Furthermore, we can combine single words to create an unlimited number of new categories like green-garbed grumpy golfers and camel-carted carpets. But why do we need categories?

 The answer is that without categories we would be unable to make any sense of our experience or to profit from it. If each thing we encountered was totally unique and unlike anything else we had ever known, we would not know how to react to it or make any useful predictions about its properties. We would be literally lost in a sea of new experiences, helpless to employ any of our prior knowledge to navigate.

Imagine a clinical psychologist unwilling to form or use any diagnostic categories who argues that every individual is unique and requires a totally individualized plan of treatment. Unique treatments for every individual seems reasonable, even commendable, but when implemented it is completely self-defeating. Following Kendall (1975), suppose we have available treatment A and treatment B (and presumably more). What is our rationale for selecting which treatment to give? We are trying to predict which treatment will be more effective but if each individual is completely unique, we have no basis for making predictions at all! If we knew only that a patient seemed to be more similar to people who had responded well to treatment A than to people who had responded to treatment B, we would have some rationale for thinking that treatment A would be more effective. Of course, to draw on our experience in this way is to categorize. Even before medicine had any sort of effective set of treatments, a major conceptual advance was made when people began to reject the idea that every instance of illness was unique. It seems inevitable, then, that to have any basis for providing (and even tailoring) a treatment we need to categorize, even if we do not necessarily use formal diagnostic categories.

The need to categorize is not specific to clinical diagnosis but rather applies wherever relevant knowledge might be brought to bear. When we recognize some entity as a dog, our knowledge about dogs (e.g., that they sometimes bark, usually like to be petted, and so on) allows us to make predictions about and understand their actions. Categorization is pervasive.

Computational Complexity

It is easy to show that categorization quickly runs into problems of computational complexity. Suppose we have a set of only n things. We can determine that the number of ways of assigning those things to categories increases very rapidly with n. With two objects a and b we can set up two categorization schemes: (a) (b) and (ab), where the parentheses define category boundaries. If we double the number of objects we can have 15 distinct category structures: (a)(b)(c)(d), (ab)(c)(d), (a)(bc)(d), (a)(b)(cd), (ac)(b)(d), (ad)(b)(c), (a)(bd)(c), (abc)(d), (a)(bcd), (acd)(b), (abd)(c), (ab)(cd), (ad)(bc), (ac)(bd), and (abcd). And by the time we get up to 10 objects, there are more than 100,000 possibilities!

The fact that there are so many possibilities makes it natural to ask why we have the categories we have rather than others. One answer is that our categories are produced because of the way the world is. The world comes organized into natural "chunks" and our concepts mirror those natural groupings or categories. An alternative possibility is that we have the categories we have because we are the sort of creatures we are. Another way of putting it is that the categories we have represent a solution for a set of problems (e.g., coping with ignorance) and that perhaps we can better understand human concepts by asking what problems they address and what functions they serve. We will review these functions, describe a body of research on category learning, and then return to the question of why we have the categories we have.

By this time you may wonder about the difference between a concept and a category. We use **concept** to refer to a mental representation and **category** to refer to the set of entities or examples "picked out" by the concept. Some researchers suggest that categories have independent existence in the world (independent of the organisms that conceive of them).

We do not endorse this view because we believe that in many cases (if not all) categories are constructed by the human mind. As we'll see, however, our categories have to be linked to the world if they are to prove useful.

Functions of Concepts

So far we have described concepts at a relatively informal level. When we try to be more precise we see that concepts serve a number of distinct roles.

Classification.   We can define a *concept* as a mental representation or idea that includes a description of important properties of a class (as we shall see, there is a lot of disagreement about what counts as an "important property"). This representation must include information that allows one to determine whether a particular example is an instance of a concept. That is, one function of a concept is to classify, a function that allows the mind to make contact with the world.

Understanding and Explanation.   Classification allows intelligent organisms to parse their experience into meaningful chunks and to construct an interpretation of it. A major facet of this understanding is bringing old knowledge to bear on the current situation. For example, a person on a hike in the mountains who recognizes an animal as a *rattlesnake* will interpret the situation as dangerous. Concepts also support explanations; understanding why a friend reacted to a stick with alarm is explained with the knowledge that he or she initially classified it as a rattlesnake.

Prediction.   A key aspect of classification is that it allows one to make predictions concerning the future, predictions that can be used to select plans and actions. For example, after we identify an animal as a *rattlesnake*, we can act so as to avoid it.

Reasoning.   Concepts support reasoning. One does not need to store every fact and possibility if inferences can be derived from information that is stored. From the knowledge that all animals breathe, that reptiles are animals, and rattlesnakes are reptiles, one may reason (deductively) that rattlesnakes must also breathe, even though one may never have directly stored that fact. Furthermore, people can combine concepts to describe novel situations and to envision future states of affairs. You probably have never thought about or seen a *paper bee*. We asked a few people about this novel concept and most of them came up with the idea that a paper bee is a bee made out of paper. Furthermore, everyone who arrives at this interpretation also envisions that such a bee would not be alive and could not breathe. To get an idea of how complex conceptual combination is, try to figure out the concept *paper committee*. Now it seems natural to interpret it as a committee *concerned* with paper (but presumably not made out of paper).

Communication.   To the extent that people share knowledge and index it in terms of the same categories, they will be able to communicate with each other. Communication allows learning on the basis of indirect experience. When an expert tells us to avoid sudden movements in the presence of *rattlesnakes* we can follow this advice the very first time we are confronted with a rattlesnake.

One can readily see that concepts function in multiple ways and are essential to mental life. Understanding, explanation, and prediction are at the core of intelligent behavior. Before turning to the question of how categories are structured, we focus on an important consequence of categorization.

Concepts and Misconceptions

Our use of categories is not without its problems. We may have the wrong categories or categories that are too broad for our purposes. Our conceptions of categories seem to be the sort of mental shorthand that inevitably leads to some oversimplification and misperception. In order to develop and use categories, it must be the case that each individual not be unique in every respect. On the other hand, the fact that examples share enough properties to make categorization useful does not mean that category examples are similar in every respect. Both pit bulls and poodles are dogs but one would not want to treat them in identical ways.

Concepts seem to do more than summarize—they also lead to systematic misperceptions. This phenomenon is observed even for the perception of lines. Tajfel and Wilkes (1963) showed people four short lines labeled "A" and four long lines labeled "B" and asked them to estimate the lengths of the lines. A control group was given the same task without the category labels (see Figure 12.1). Relative to the control group, people given labels rated the short lines as more similar in length to each other and more different from the long lines.

Consequences of categorization are also evident in the important domain of social categorization. When people are brought into laboratories

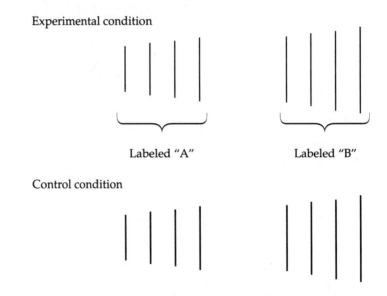

Figure 12.1   **Stimuli like those used in the Tajfel and Wilkes (1963) study.**

and divided into groups based on an arbitrary dimension (e.g., whether they over- or underestimated the number of dots in a picture), in-group favoritism results. For example, Howard and Rothbart (1980) used the dot estimation procedure to assign people to two groups and then gave them favorable and unfavorable information about their group (in-group) and the other group (out-group) members. On a later recognition test people showed significantly better memory for negative out-group than for negative in-group behaviors. In short, these more or less arbitrary categories affected people's perceptions in a way that favored the in-group.

The results just described are somewhat sobering and certainly do not leave the impression that categorization is necessarily a good thing. The process of categorization leads only too naturally to stereotypes and misperceptions of other groups (see Tajfel, 1981; Devine, 1989 for examples). Perhaps knowledge of the fact of human propensity for forming stereotypes can moderate or weaken our reliance on them. On a more optimistic note, there is evidence that stereotypes may yield to more concrete, specific information. Locksley, Borgida, Brekke, and Hepburn (1980) asked people to rate the assertiveness of target individuals who were described in one of three ways: (1) name only (conveying gender information); (2) name plus a descriptive paragraph irrelevant to assertiveness; or (3) name plus a descriptive paragraph relevant to assertiveness. In the first two conditions, male targets were rated as more assertive than female targets, but in the third females were rated as being as assertive as males. That is, when relevant information was provided it was used and gender information was not used. In some cases it seems stereotypes are treated as default values that are employed only when no other information is available.

As we have seen, categorization is far from being universally beneficial. Still, categorization is necessary for all the reasons listed at the beginning of this chapter. We turn now to work on the structural underpinnings of categories, beginning with natural object categories like bird, fish, and tree.

Structure of Natural Object Categories

Almost all theories about the structure of categories assume that, roughly speaking, similar things tend to belong to the same category and dissimilar things tend to be in different categories. For example, *robins* and *sparrows* both belong to the category *bird* and are more similar to each other than they are to *squirrels* or *pumpkins*. Similarity is a pretty vague term and most commonly it is defined in terms of shared properties or attributes. For example, *robins* and *sparrows* are similar in that they are *living, animate,* have *feathers, wings,* and *hollow bones,* and can *sing, fly, build nests,* and *lay eggs*. Squirrels have only some of these properties and pumpkins have fewer still. Although alternative theories assume concepts are structured in terms of shared properties, theories differ greatly in their organizational principles. Let's take a look at the main views concerning category structure.

The Classical View

The **classical view** assumes that concepts have defining features that act as criteria for determining category membership. For example, a *triangle* is a closed geometric form with three sides with the sum of the interior angles equalling 180 degrees. Each of these properties is necessary for an entity to be a triangle and together these properties are sufficient to define *triangle*. According to the classical view, concepts have rigid boundaries in that a given example either does or does not meet the definition. All members of a category are equally good examples of it, and learning involves discovering what these defining features are.

Most of us have the initial intuition that our concepts conform to the classical view and have defining features. But think a bit more about a concept like *chair* or *furniture*. What makes a chair a chair? We might start by saying that a chair is something an individual can sit on, but that definition does not exclude *sofas*, *benches*, or even *rocks*. Next one might add the proviso that chairs must have four legs, but that would exclude beanbag chairs. The more we think about it, the trickier it becomes. For example, we might start to worry about the difference between *stools* and *chairs* and ultimately decide either that we do not know exactly what a chair is or that we may be unable to describe it.

There has, in fact, been a fair amount of research done on people's knowledge about natural object categories like *bird*, *chair*, and *furniture*. Not only do people fail to come up with defining features but also they do not necessarily agree with each other (or even with themselves when asked at different times) on whether or not something is an example of a category (McCloskey & Glucksberg, 1978; Bellezza, 1984). For example, is a rug considered furniture? A parquet floor? A telephone?

Philosophers and scientists also have worried about whether naturally occurring things like plants and animals (so-called "natural kinds") have defining features. And the current consensus is that most natural concepts do not fit the classical view. Even the concept of *species* is not well defined (see Sokal, 1974). For example, a species might be defined as an interbreeding population. But in some species the males of one group are fertile with the females of the other but the females of the first group are not fertile with the males of the other. Although some concepts like *triangle* may be well defined, many concepts do not appear to be, and for this reason cognitive psychologists have pretty much abandoned the classical view.

The Probabilistic View

The major alternative to the classical view is the **probabilistic view**. It argues that concepts are organized around properties that may be only typical or characteristic of category members. For example, most people's concept of *bird* may include the properties of *building nests*, *flying*, and having *hollow bones*, even though not all birds have these properties (e.g., ostriches, penguins).

The probabilistic view has major implications for how we think about categories. First, if categories are organized around characteristic properties, some members may have more of these properties than other members. In this sense some members may be better examples or more typical of a concept than others. For example, people judge a robin to be a better example of a bird than an ostrich is and can answer category membership questions more rapidly for good examples than for poor examples (see, e.g., Smith, Shoben, & Rips, 1974; and see Medin & Smith, 1984,

Mervis & Rosch, 1981, and Oden, 1987 for reviews). You may recall that the feature comparison model of Smith, Shoben, and Rips (1974) discussed in Chapter 8 can account for these typicality effects. A second implication is that category boundaries may be fuzzy. Nonmembers of a category may have almost as many characteristic properties of a category as do certain members. For example, whales have a lot of the characteristic properties of *fish* and yet they are *mammals*. Third, learning about a category cannot be equated with determining what the defining features are, because there may not be any.

Features and Typicality. In some pioneering work aimed at clarifying the structural basis of fuzzy categories, Rosch and Mervis (1975) had subjects list properties of exemplars for a variety of concepts such as *bird, fruit,* and *tool*. They found that the listed properties for some exemplars occurred frequently in other category members, whereas other examples had properties that occurred less frequently. Most important, the more frequently an exemplar's properties appeared within a category, the higher was its rated **typicality** for that category. The correlation between number of characteristic properties possessed and typicality rating was very high and positive. For example, robins have characteristic bird properties of flying, singing, eating worms, and building nests in trees, and they are rated to be very typical birds. Penguins have none of these properties, and they are rated as very atypical birds. In short, the Rosch and Mervis work relating typicality to number of characteristic properties put the probabilistic view on fairly firm footing.

Mental Representations of Fuzzy Categories. If categories are not represented in terms of definitions, what form do our mental representations take? The term probabilistic view seems to imply that people organize categories via statistical reasoning. Actually, there is a more natural interpretation of fuzzy categories that has been referred to as a **family resemblance** principle. Many people in an extended family might share features such as a distinctive chin, certain expressions, a high forehead, and so on. Of course, not everyone in the family would have all of these characteristics and some members might have more than others. The general idea is that category members resemble each other in the way that family members do. Category members tend to share characteristic properties with each other but there is no set of properties that each and every example has to have. That is, different examples would tend to share different properties.

A simple form of summary representation for such a family resemblance structure would be an example or ideal that possessed all the characteristic features of a category. The best example or ideal is referred to as the **prototype** which can be used to decide category membership. If some candidate example is similar enough to the prototype for a category it will be classified as a member of that category. The general notion is that, based on experience with examples of a category, people abstract out the central tendency or prototype that becomes the summary mental representation for the category. Note that no individual need have all the properties that are represented in the prototype. In that sense a prototype is like a stereotype which also may be true of no individual.

Actually, prototype models are probably too rigid to account for how people use concepts. People may use any information available to improve their understanding and predictions about the future. Prototype theories assume that categories are organized around what is, on the average, true. But an average may not be enough. For example, people seem to know that small birds are more likely to sing than large birds—a prototype does not capture this awareness of correlational information (Malt & Smith, 1983). In addition, how well an item belongs to a concept depends on the context in which it is presented (Roth & Shoben, 1983). For example, a harmonica is a typical *musical instrument* in the context of a campfire, but is atypical in the context of a concert hall. People seem to adjust their expectations in a very sensitive manner to different settings.

Laboratory studies of categorization using artificially constructed categories also raise problems for prototypes. Normally many variables relevant to human category learning tend to be correlated with each other and it is hard to determine which variables really are important. For instance, typical examples tend to be more frequent and people's ability to classify typical examples quickly may be related to typicality, frequency, or both factors. The general rationale for laboratory studies with artificially created categories is that one can isolate some variable or set of variables of interest by breaking these natural correlations. Experiments with artificial categories reveal a number of salient phenomena associated with fuzzy categories, and several of these are consistent with prototype theories. For example, one observes typicality effects in learning and on transfer tests using both correctness and reaction time as the dependent measure (see, e.g., Rosch & Mervis, 1975). A striking result, readily obtained, is that the prototype for a category may be classified more accurately during transfer tests than are the previously seen examples that were used during original category learning (see, e.g., Homa & Vosburgh, 1976; Medin & Schaffer, 1978; Peterson, Meagher, Chait, & Gillie, 1973).

Typicality effects and excellent classification of prototypes are consistent with the idea that people are learning these ill-defined categories by forming prototypes. More detailed analyses, however, show that there are problems with prototypes as mental representations. As we noted earlier, prototype theory implies that the only information abstracted from categories is the central tendency. A prototype representation discards information concerning category size, the variability of the examples, and information concerning correlations of attributes. The evidence suggests that people can use all three of these types of information (Estes, 1986; Flannagan, Fried, & Holyoak, 1986; Fried & Holyoak, 1984; Medin, Altom, Edelson, & Freko, 1982; Medin & Schaffer, 1978). In short, prototype representations seem to discard too much information that can be shown to be relevant to human categorizations.

Exemplar Theories.   Exemplar theories provide an alternative way of representing probabilistic or fuzzy categories. **Exemplar models** assume that people initially learn some examples of a concept and then classify a new instance on the basis of how similar it is to particular examples of a concept. The idea is that a new example reminds the person of similar old examples and that people assume that similar items will belong to the same category. For example, you might classify one animal as a rodent because it reminds you of a rat (which you know is a rodent) but classify some other animal as a rodent because it reminds you of a rabbit (which you also know is a rodent). Furthermore, the knowledge that large birds are less likely to sing than small birds may be derived from retrieving examples of small and large birds.

The exemplar models that have received the most attention (Hintzman, 1986; Medin & Schaffer, 1978) assume that examples that are most similar to the item to be classified have the greatest influence on categorization. This could arise either because highly similar examples are differentially weighted or because the likelihood of retrieving an example depends on its similarity to the item. The idea that retrieval is similarity-based and context-sensitive is in accord with much of the memory literature (see, e.g., Tulving, 1983 and Chapter 7). Surprisingly, exemplar models can even account for the observation that the prototype may be more accurately classified on a transfer test than examples seen during original learning. The reason is as follows: the prototype will tend to be similar to a number of examples from its own category and not very similar to examples from alternative categories. Therefore, the prototype should reliably remind the learner of examples from the correct category. In contrast, a training example may not be highly similar to other examples from its own category and may be similar to examples from other categories. In this case the example may remind the learner of examples from alternative categories. It is important to bear in mind that exemplar models do not assume that people are necessarily able to retrieve individual examples one at a time without confusing them. Instead, the idea is that a test example will tend to activate a number of similar stored representations.

Quite a few experiments have contrasted the predictions of exemplar and prototype models. In head-to-head competition, exemplar models have been substantially more successful than prototype models (Barsalou & Medin, 1986; Estes, 1986; Nosofsky, 1988a, 1988b, 1991; but see Homa, 1984 for a dissenting opinion).

Why should exemplar models fare better than prototype models? One of the main functions of classification is that it allows one to make inferences and predictions on the basis of partial information (see Anderson, 1990). Here we are using classification loosely to refer to any means by which prior (relevant) knowledge is brought to bear, ranging from a formal classification rule to an idiosyncratic reminding of a previous case (which, of course, is in the spirit of exemplar models; see also Kolodner, 1984). Relative to prototype models, exemplar models tend to be conservative about discarding information that facilitates predictions. For instance, sensitivity to correlations of properties within a category enables finer predictions: From noting that a bird is large, one can predict that it cannot sing. It may seem that exemplar models do not discard any information at all, but recall that they do not assume that people necessarily can access a specific stored example without activating other examples. In fact, examples may be so similar that new-old recognition is very poor even while performance is based on stored examples. But, generally speaking, exemplar models preserve more information than prototype models, information that people seem to be able to use. This does not prove that exemplar models are correct but it suggests that learning depends more on examples than prototype models have assumed (Medin & Ross, 1989). Instance-based ideas have also been incorporated into AI categorization models (see, e.g., Kibler & Aha, 1987; Stanfill & Waltz, 1986). Finally, we note that there have been formal proofs that classifying on the basis of the single most similar example (a "nearest neighbor" principle) is not far from the optimal classification (Cover & Hart, 1967).

Although exemplar models have the virtue of being conservative with respect to discarding potentially relevant information, the exemplar notion is incomplete as a theory of categories. Items are assumed to be placed in the category with the exemplars they are most similar to, but exemplar theories do not explain how concepts are created in the first place. There are no constraints on what can be a concept. Furthermore, the only explanation for why a new example should be placed into a category is "because it is similar to an old example"—a very limited form of explanation. As we shall see, these two problems are true for probabilistic view theories in general. The concern about whether and when people use prototypes or examples should not mask the strong consensus that many concepts are fuzzy rather than well defined (see Smith & Medin, 1981).

So far we have focused exclusively on within-category structure. We turn now to some ideas concerning between-category structure before worrying again about why we have the categories we have and not others.

Between-Category Structure

Most things have membership in numerous categories. In this section we consider two types of between-category structure. Many categories (e.g., taxonomic categories) have a hierarchical structure: higher level categories subsume lower level categories (e.g., *animal* includes all birds and *birds* includes all robins). A second type of categorization scheme yields multiple overlapping categories. For example, someone can be a female, chess-playing banker. The lack of membership in one category does not preclude membership in either of the other categories. There are some important properties of each type of between-category structure.

Basic Levels. Often categories are organized taxonomically at different levels of abstraction where at each level an example belongs to one of a set of mutually exclusive categories (as we saw in our discussion of models of semantic knowledge in Chapter 8). A poodle is also a canine, a mammal, an animal, a living thing, and an object. (See Figure 12.2.) A poodle is a mammal and not a reptile, an animal and not a plant, and so on. One of these levels, known as the **basic level**, appears to be psychologically privileged. For example, basic level concepts are the first to be learned, the natural level at which objects are named, show cross-cultural consistency, and are the highest level in which the instances all share the same parts and overall shape (Rosch, Mervis, Gray, Johnson, & Bayes Braem, 1976). Interestingly, the basic level is neither the most specific nor the most abstract level, but rather is intermediate. For example, *rocking chair* is a subordinate category, *chair* would be the basic level, and *furniture* would be at the superordinate level. There is some evidence that as one becomes more expert in an area, what was previously the subordinate level becomes the basic level. For example, *dog* might be a basic level category for most people, but *poodle* might be at the basic level for dog trainers (Tanaka & Taylor, 1991).

If we could understand just why the basic level is basic, we might

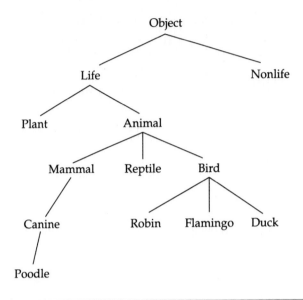

Figure 12.2   Part of a simple taxonomic structure.

gain further insight into what types of categories are natural or cohesive. One possibility is that the basic level is the highest level at which entities tend to share parts (Tversky & Hemenway, 1984). Another idea is that levels higher than the basic level have different purposes. For example, superordinate categories may serve to organize scenes (Murphy & Wisniewski, 1989) and superordinate category members may tend to share common functions more than perceptual similarities (see, e.g., Rosch et al., 1976; Murphy & Smith, 1982). Probably the most honest answer is that we do not know exactly what makes the basic level basic.

Nonhierarchical Categories.   Many of the categories that we use do not fit into a taxonomic hierarchy. This is particularly true in the domain of socially relevant concepts. One can be a mother, a psychologist, a Democrat, a golf player, and a Mexican-American all at the same time, and no one category is either superordinate or subordinate with respect to the others.

    If there is no clear hierarchy, then by definition there is no basic level. Given that people tend to use categories to understand their experience, one can think of the various categorization schemes as competing for attention. We already know from the memory literature that it is implausible to think that to understand some behavior, people access all the potentially relevant categories they have and reason with them. So what does determine which categories people access and use? Two factors that determine category access are the frequency and recency with which a category has been used. For example, in one study (Srull & Wyer, 1979, experiment 1) people first performed a sentence construction task that was designed to activate concepts associated with hostility. Then in an ostensibly separate experiment the participants were asked to form impressions of people based on reading a description of behaviors. The behaviors were ambiguous with respect to hostility. Ratings of the descriptions with respect to hostility increased directly with the number of times hostility-related concepts had been activated on the presumably unrelated sentence construction task. The Srull and Wyer study illustrates the point that category accessibility has an important influence on how social information is encoded and interpreted.

Does Similarity Explain Categorization?

Similarity is a very intuitive notion but it is very difficult to pin down. One problem with using similarity to define categories is that similarity is too variable. An example of the context-dependent nature of similarity is shown in Figure 12.3 (taken from Tversky, 1977). People are asked to judge which of three alternative faces is the most similar to a standard face. What varies between Set 1 and Set 2 is the middle face. Although the middle face is rarely picked, its status strongly influences which of the two outside faces is judged to be most similar. Observations such as this suggest that similarity is quite flexible.

Formal models of similarity allow similarity to be quite flexible. For example, Tversky's (1977) influential contrast model defines similarity as depending on common and distinctive features weighted for salience or importance. According to this model, similarity relationships will depend heavily on the particular weights given to individual properties or features. For example, a zebra and a barber pole would be more similar than a zebra and a horse if the feature "striped" had sufficient weight. This would not necessarily be a problem if the weights were stable. However, Tversky and others have convincingly shown that the relative weighting of a feature (as well as the relative importance of matching and mismatching features) varies with the stimulus context, experimental task (Gati & Tversky, 1984; Tversky, 1977), and probably even the concept under consideration (Ortony, Vondruska, Foss, & Jones, 1985). For example, a person from Maine and a person from Florida will seem less similar when they meet in Washington, D.C. than when they meet in Tokyo.

Once we recognize that similarity is dynamic and depends on

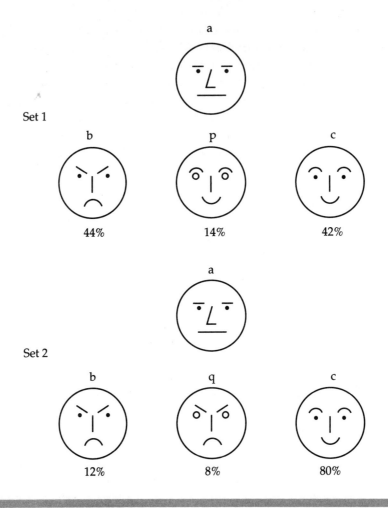

Figure 12.3   **Two sets of schematic faces used to test the diagnosticity hypothesis.**
The percentage of subjects who selected each face (as most similar to the target) is
presented below the face. *Source*: Tversky, A., 1977.

some (not well-understood) processing principles, earlier work on the
structural underpinnings of fuzzy categories can be seen in a somewhat
different light. Recall that the Rosch and Mervis (1975) studies asked subjects to list attributes or properties of examples and categories. It would be
a mistake to assume that people had the ability to read and report their
mental representations of concepts in a perfectly accurate manner. Indeed
Keil (1979, 1981) pointed out that examples like robin and squirrel share
many important properties that almost never show up in attribute listings
(e.g., has a heart, breathes, sleeps, is an organism, is an object with

boundaries, is a physical object, is a thing, can be thought about, and so on). In fact, Keil argued that knowledge about just these sorts of predicates serves to organize children's conceptual and semantic development. For present purposes, the point is that attribute listings provide a biased sample of people's conceptual knowledge.

To take things a step further, one could argue that without constraints on what is to count as a feature, any two things may be arbitrarily similar or dissimilar. Thus, as Murphy and Medin (1985) suggested, the number of properties that plums and lawn mowers have in common could be infinite: both weigh less than 1000 Kg, both are found on the earth, both are found in our solar system, both cannot hear well, both have parts, both are not worn by elephants, both are used by people, both can be dropped, and so on (see also Goodman, 1972; Watanabe, 1969). Now consider again the status of attribute listings. They represent a biased subset of stored or readily inferred knowledge. The correlation of attribute listings with typicality judgments is a product of such knowledge and a variety of processes that operate on it. Without a theory of that knowledge and those processes that use it, it simply is not clear what these correlations indicate about mental representations.

If similarity is so flexible, how can it provide the basis for determining categories? One possibility is that children are not as flexible about similarity as adults. Linda Smith (1989) has proposed that there is a developmental increase in the tendency of children to weight dimensions differentially with the youngest children biased toward responding in terms of overall similarity. If flexibility arises only after most perceptual categories are learned, then similarity might be stable enough to support the initial development of many categories.

Even if similarity can be constrained, it still may not explain categorization. We believe that similarity is properly viewed as a general guideline or heuristic for categorization but that it does not provide the backbone of conceptual structure. Things that look alike do tend to belong to the same category. Furthermore, things that look alike superficially also tend to be alike in other, deeper ways (e.g., structure and function tend to be correlated). Overall similarity is a good but fallible guideline to category membership. When additional information (or a closer look) suggests that overall similarity is misleading, it is readily abandoned.

A nice illustration of the fact that even young children are not strongly constrained by overall similarity comes from a set of experiments by Gelman and Markman (1986). They pitted category membership against perceptual similarity in an inductive reasoning task. Young children were first shown pictures of two animals and taught that different novel properties were true of them. Then they were asked which property was also true of a new (pictured) example that was perceptually similar to one alternative but belonged to the category of the other alternative, from which it differed perceptually. For example, children might be taught that a flamingo feeds its baby mashed-up food, and that a bat feeds its baby milk, and then asked what a blackbird feeds its baby. The blackbird was perceptually more similar to the bat than to the flamingo, but even four-year-olds made inferences on the basis of category membership rather than similarity. That is, they thought that the blackbird would feed its baby mashed-up food. Therefore, even for young children, similarity acts as a general guideline that can be overridden by other forms of knowledge.

It does not seem that similarity, at least in the form that it takes in current theories, is going to be at all adequate to explain categorization. Similarity may be a by-product rather than a cause of categorization. To use a rough analogy, winning basketball teams have in common scoring more points than their opponents, but one must turn to more basic principles to explain why they score more points. One candidate for a set of deeper principles is the idea that concepts are organized around theories. In the next section, we will briefly summarize some of the current work on the role of knowledge structures and theories in categorization and then turn to a way of relating similarity and knowledge-based categorization principles.

Concepts as Organized by Theories

Recently, a number of researchers have argued that the organization of concepts is knowledge-based (rather than similarity-based) and driven by intuitive theories about the world (see, e.g., Carey, 1985; Keil, 1986, 1987; Murphy & Medin, 1985; Rips, 1989; Schank, Collins, & Hunter, 1986). Murphy and Medin suggested that the relation between a concept and an example is analogous to the relation between theory and data. That is, classification is not simply based on a direct matching of properties of the concept with those in the example, but rather requires that the example have the right "explanatory relationship" to the theory organizing the concept. Classification may be more like an inference process than a similarity judgment. We may induce that a man is drunk because we see him jump into a pool fully clothed. If so, it is probably not because the property "jumps into pools while clothed" is directly listed with the concept *drunk*. Rather it is because part of our concept of *drunk* involves a theory of impaired judgment that serves to explain the man's behavior.

One of the more promising aspects of the theory-based approach is that it begins to address the question of why we have the categories we have or why categories are sensible. In fact, coherence may be achieved in the absence of any obvious source of similarity among examples. Consider the category comprised of children, money, photo albums, and pets. Out of context the category seems odd. But if we are told that the category represents "things to take out of one's house in case of a fire," the category becomes sensible (Barsalou, 1983). In addition, one could readily make judgments about whether new examples (e.g., personal papers, magazines) belonged to the category, judgments that would not be based on overall similarity to category members.

Susan Carey (1982, 1985) has shown that children's biological theories guide their conceptual development. In one study, six-year-old children rated a toy monkey to be more similar to people than is a worm. But they also judged that the worm was more likely to have a spleen than was the toy monkey (a spleen was described as "a green thing inside people"). Although worms may be less similar to people than are toy monkeys, they are more similar *in some respects*, namely common biological functions. And Carey's work shows that children's biological theories help them determine which respects are relevant. Thus, the four-year-old children's rudimentary biological knowledge influences the structure of their concept of *animal*.

The idea that concepts might be knowledge-based (or theory-driven) rather than similarity-based suggests a natural way in which concepts may change—namely, through the addition of new knowledge and theoretical principles. We have a different set of psychodiagnostic categories now than we had one hundred years ago, in part because our knowledge base has become more refined. Often knowledge of diseases develops from information about patterns of symptoms to a specification of underlying causes. For example, the advanced stages of syphilis were treated as a mental disorder until the causes and consequences of this venereal disease were better understood.

Putting Similarity in Its Place

Although we have severely criticized the notion of similarity we believe that it has a very important role to play. Our idea is that similarity does not provide structure but that a constrained form of similarity may guide learners toward structure.

The impact of more direct perceptual similarity on the development of causal explanations is evident in the structure of people's everyday theories. Frazer's (1959) cross-cultural analysis of belief systems pointed to the widespread character of two principles, homeopathy and contagion. The principle of **homeopathy** is that causes and effects tend to be similar. ✗

One manifestation of this principle is homeopathic medicine, in which the cure (and the cause) are seen to resemble the symptoms. In the Azande culture, for example, the cure for ringworm is to apply fowl's excrement because the excrement looks like the ringworm. Shweder (1977) has provided strong support for the claim that resemblance is a fundamental conceptual tool of everyday thinking in all cultures, not just so-called primitive cultures. In our culture people reject acceptable foods shaped into a form that represents a disgusting object (Rozin, Millman, & Nemeroff, 1986). We will spare you a concrete example.

Contagion is the principle that a cause must have some form of contact to transmit its effect. In general, the more contiguous (temporally and spatially similar) events are in time and space, the more likely they are to be perceived as causally related (see, e.g., Dickinson, Shanks, & Evenden, 1984; Michotte, 1963). People also tend to assume that causes and effects should be of similar magnitude. Einhorn and Hogarth (1986) pointed out that the germ theory of disease initially met with great resistance because people could not imagine how such tiny organisms could have such devastating effects.

It is important to recognize that homeopathy and contagion often point us in the right direction. Immunization can be seen as a form of homeopathic medicine that has an underlying theoretical principle supporting it. Our reading of these observations, however, is not that specific theoretical (causal) principles are constraining similarity but rather that similarity (homeopathy and contagion) acts as a constraint on the search for causal explanations. Even in classical conditioning studies, the similarity of the conditioned stimulus and the unconditioned stimulus can have a major influence on the rate of conditioning (Testa, 1974).

One way of integrating similarity and explanation is in terms of a notion of **psychological essentialism** (Medin & Ortony, 1989; Wattenmaker, Nakamura, & Medin, 1988). The main ideas are as follows: People act as if things (e.g., objects) have essences or underlying natures that make them the thing that they are. Furthermore, the essence constrains or generates properties that may vary in their centrality. For example, people in our culture believe that the categories male and female are genetically determined, but to pick someone out as male or female we rely on characteristics such as hair length, height, facial hair, and clothing that represent a mixture of secondary sexual characteristics and cultural conventions. Although these characteristics are more unreliable than genetic evidence, they are far from arbitrary. Not only do they have some validity in a statistical sense, they are also tied to our biological and cultural conceptions of male and female.

It is important to note that psychological essentialism refers not to how the world is but rather to how people approach the world. Wastebaskets presumably have no true essence, although we may act as if they do. Both social and psychodiagnostic categories are at least partially culture-specific and, therefore, may represent constructions rather than discoveries about the world (see also Morey & McNamara, 1987).

Why should people act as if things had essences? The reason is that it may be a good strategy for learning about the world. One could say that people adopt an essentialist heuristic, namely, the hypothesis that things that look alike tend to share deeper properties (similarities). Our perceptual and conceptual systems appear to have evolved such that the essentialist heuristic is very often correct (Medin & Wattenmaker, 1987; Shepard, 1987). This is true even for human artifacts such as cars, computers, and camping stoves because structure and function tend to be correlated. Surface characteristics that are perceptually obvious or are readily produced on feature listing tasks may not so much constitute the core of a concept as point toward it. This observation suggests that classifying on the basis of similarity will be relatively effective much of the time, but that similarity will yield to knowledge of deeper principles. Thus, in the work of Gelman and Markman (1986) discussed earlier, category membership was more important than perceptual similarity in determining inductive inferences.

Summary

We have presented one way of relating similarity to knowledge structures and theories. It would be misleading to state that there is any form of consensus on this general issue. Indeed, in the area of machine learning a great deal of attention is being directed at the question of how to integrate similarity-based and explanation-based learning (see, e.g., Ellman, 1989; Rajamoney & DeJong, 1987; Flann & Dietterich, 1989). What does seem clear is that similarity has a role to play but that, by itself, it is inadequate to explain our categories and concepts.

Category Learning

So far we have focused on the question of how categories are organized. We turn now to a brief look at the learning side of things. Aside from the natural question of how learning takes place, data from category learning studies are useful for evaluating alternative theories of categorization.

Constraints and Category Learning

We have already described developmental research on concept learning which suggests that concepts are organized around theories. Furthermore, these theories undergo changes with development. Susan Carey, for example, has evidence that children initially organize their biological knowledge with human beings as the central focus and later shift to a less anthropocentric view. Young children are more likely to infer that a property true of humans is true of bees than that a property true of bugs is true of bees (Carey, 1985, 1988). Later the bug to bee inferences are stronger than human to bee inferences.

Analyzing concept learning in natural settings is quite difficult. Learning may be based on experience with examples, word meanings are often acquired from context (see, e.g., Klausmeier & Sipple, 1980), and in other cases learners may be directly taught or told category-relevant information. Laboratory studies of category learning do not approximate the complexity of learning in natural environments. Nonetheless, learning procedures can be isolated and controlled in a manner that allows tests of models or theories of category learning. We turn briefly to one example of this approach.

To our knowledge, every model for category learning has some constraints or biases associated with it in the sense of predicting that some kinds of classification problems should be easier to master than others. As mentioned earlier, one way to evaluate alternative learning models is to see if the problems they predict should be easy or difficult to acquire are in fact, easier or more difficult for people to learn.

One constraint of interest is known as **linear separability**. Prototype models imply that categories must be linearly separable to be learnable. One way to conceptualize the process of classifying examples on the basis of similarity to prototype is that it involves a summing of evidence against a criterion. For example, if an instance has enough features characteristic of birds it will be classified as a bird. More technically there must be some weighted, additive combination of properties (some similarity function) that will be higher for all category members than for any nonmembers. What this means is that a prototype process requires that all bird examples be more similar to the bird prototype than to alternative prototypes and that nonbirds must be more similar to their respec-

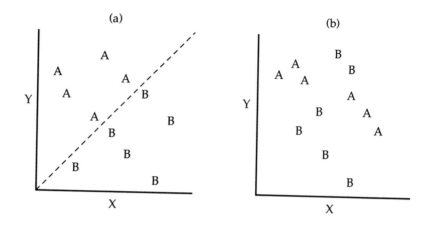

Figure 12.4   **Two-dimensional example of two categories that are linearly separable (panel a) and are not linearly separable (panel b).**

In each graph, category members in categories A and B are denoted by the letters A and B, respectively. The position of each letter corresponds to its value on the X and Y dimensions.

tive prototypes than to the bird prototype. If a bat were more similar to the bird prototype than to the mammal prototype, it would be incorrectly classified.

Figure 12.4 gives a more intuitive description of linear separability for examples that have values on two dimensions. The categories are linearly separable if there is a straight line that perfectly partitions the categories (Figure 12.4a). If no straight line will partition the categories (Figure 12.4b), there is no way to construct prototypes such that all examples are closer to their own category prototype than to the prototype for the contrasting category. A number of neural network models of learning favor categories that are linearly separable because, in effect, they add up the evidence favoring a classification decision (Minsky & Papert, 1988).

If linear separability acts as a constraint on human categorization, people should find it easier to learn categories that are linearly separable than categories that are not linearly separable. However, studies employing a variety of stimulus materials, categories, subject populations, and instructions have failed to find any evidence that whether or not categories are linearly separable influences the ease with which people learn categories (see, e.g., Kemler-Nelson, 1984; Medin & Schwanenflugel, 1981).

Artificial Grammars and Implicit Learning

So far we have focused on categories that have corresponding objects in the world. We can, however, view the learning of a grammar as a categorization task in which strings of words are classified as grammatical or ungrammatical. A number of studies have been done involving the learning of artificial grammars and they have produced some intriguing results. Specifically these studies have raised the possibility that there are unconscious or implicit learning mechanisms that may be quite powerful.

Grammars involve a complex set of rules for generating strings of words or sentences. Artificial grammars often involve strings of letters. They can produce an unlimited number of strings but certain (ungrammatical) patterns are not permitted. Let's look at a specific example. Figure 12.5 shows what is referred to as a finite-state grammar that can be used to generate strings of letters. S_1 is the initial state and, according to the figure, either P or T must begin the sequence. If the string begins with T then one is in State 2 (S_2) and either X or one or more S's followed by X will come next. This leads to State 4 where the sequence will terminate with S (going to State 6) or may follow with another X and go to State 3, and so on. By this grammar TSSXS is a possible string but TSXXP is not (because a string cannot end with P). There are an unlimited number of possible string

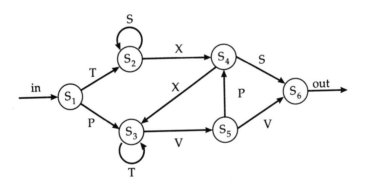

Figure 12.5   **Schematic diagram of a finite-state grammar.**
Stimuli are generated by following any path of arrows leading from the initial State 1 to the terminal State 6. The following are the five basic strings of the grammar with loops or recursion in brackets: (1) T[S]XS; (2) T[S]XX[[T]VPXVV; (3) T[S]XX[[T]VPX]VPS; (4) P[[T]VPX]VV; (5) P[[T[VPX]VPS. *Source*: Reber, A. S., 1989.

sequences (just as there are an unlimited number of possible sentences in English).

A typical training procedure involves exposing participants to grammatical strings and then presenting new strings for grammaticality judgments. One notable finding concerns the effect of different learning strategies, as studied by Art Reber and his associates. One group of participants, the Rule group, is told that the strings shown during learning were generated according to a grammar or complex rule system and that they should try to figure out the rules. A second group, the Memory group, is simply told to memorize strings of letters as part of a rote memory experiment. Later, the Memory group is told that the strings were generated by a grammar and both groups are asked to make grammaticality judgments on new strings. The surprising result is that the Memory group outperforms the Rule group (see Brooks, 1978; Reber, 1976; Reber, Kassin, Lewis, & Cantor, 1980)! A second result of interest is that participants in the memory group have difficulty describing how they are making their judgments, as if the knowledge supporting their judgment is implicit or unconscious rather than explicit.

Reber (1989) has argued that results such as those described above indicate that there are powerful implicit learning mechanisms that may be interfered with by explicit learning strategies. This unconscious abstraction mechanism may subserve complex tasks such as mastering the syntax of a language or acquiring an artificial grammar.

Reber's claims have not gone unchallenged. Dulany has argued that grammaticality judgments are driven by explicit, consciously available rules (Dulany, Carlson, & Dewey, 1984, 1985; but see also Reber, Allan, & Regan, 1985). Dulany correctly notes that people do not have to have determined the exact grammar in order to perform well on grammaticality judgments. Any limited set of sample strings will be consistent with a very large (actually unlimited) set of grammars or rule systems and if one allows grammars to be correct most rather than all the time, then the set of candidate grammars is still larger (this is the constraints issue once again). Therefore, it should not be surprising if the rules participants give do not seem to correspond to those of the grammar that generated the strings (as Reber, 1989b also concedes). Dulany et al. (1984, 1985) assess rules by asking participants to circle the part of the string that makes it ungrammatical or grammatical. Although one might argue that this measure of rule use implies a very broad concept of "rule," it is the case that one can predict performance extremely well on the basis of what participants circle.

Another controversial issue concerns the learning process itself. Lee

Brooks, who is well known for his work on exemplar models of categorization, has proposed that participants in artificial grammar experiments are basing grammaticality judgments on the similarity of new strings to stored examples of old strings (Brooks, 1978; Vokey & Brooks, in press). The memory group performs better than the rule group, on this account because it has more accurate memory for the old strings.

We will not presume to resolve the controversies concerning artificial grammar learning on these pages. The case for powerful, unconscious learning mechanisms activated by strings of letters constructed by an artificial grammar is yet to be made convincingly, but it seems premature to reject this possibility out of hand.

Use of Categories in Reasoning

So much attention has been paid to the structural nature of categories that only modest attention has been given to the question of how categories may be used in reasoning. The promising results from the few studies that have been done suggest that this question is worthy of much more attention.

Goals and Ad Hoc Categories

Larry Barsalou (see Barsalou, 1985, 1987, 1989) has studied the organization of **ad hoc categories** constructed in the service of goals. "Things to take on a camping trip" and "foods to eat while on a diet" are two such ad hoc categories. Barsalou has found that such goal-derived categories show the same typicality or goodness-of-example effects that are seen with more established categories. The basis for these effects, however, is not overall similarity of examples to each other or to a prototype, but rather similarity to an ideal. For example, typicality ratings for the category of things to eat on a diet is determined by how closely examples conform to the ideal of zero calories. As we have already seen, goals can serve to make categories comprised of very dissimilar examples psychologically coherent (e.g., "things to take out of your house in case of a fire").

Conceptual Combination

Concepts provide "mental tokens" that enable the construction of new concepts from old ones. For example, people use their knowledge of *chocolate* and *rash* to interpret chocolate rash as a rash caused by chocolate even though they may never have seen the term *chocolate rash* before. **Concep-**

tual combination allows us to produce a virtually unlimited set of new concepts. Given that we hear novel combinations of concepts all the time an important question is how people are able to understand them.

To our knowledge, there does not exist anything like a complete theory of how people combine concepts. Basically, we know that the most straightforward ideas are incomplete. One idea is that adjective-noun combinations are understood by constructing modified prototypes (Smith & Osherson, 1984). For example, according to their model, to understand the term *brown apple*, the apple prototype would be retrieved, the dimension of color would receive extra attention, and the prototypical value of red would be replaced with brown. In effect, one would be constructing a new prototype, *brown apple*, and the typicality of examples could be judged with respect to this constructed prototype. This modification model accounts for a number of phenomena associated with typicality judgments for combined adjective-noun concepts (Smith, Osherson, Rips, & Keane, 1988).

But conceptual combination is more complex than the modification model (or any other current model) implies. One problem is that the typicality of combined concepts cannot be predicted from the typicality of constituents. As an illustrative example, consider the concept of *spoon*. People rate small spoons as more typical spoons than large spoons, and metal spoons as more typical spoons than wooden spoons. If the concept *spoon* is represented by a prototypic spoon, then a small metal spoon should be the most typical spoon, followed by small wooden and large metal spoons, and large wooden spoons should be the least typical. Instead, people find large wooden spoons to be more typical spoons than either small wooden spoons or large metal spoons (Medin & Shoben, 1988). The only way for a prototype model to handle these results is to argue that people have separate prototypes for small spoons and large spoons. But this strategy creates new problems. Obviously one cannot have a separate prototype for every adjective-noun combination, because there are simply too many possible combinations. One might suggest that there are distinct subtypes for concepts like *spoon*, but one would need a theory describing how and when subtypes are created.

Another problem is that combined concepts may have properties that do not appear as properties of either constituent concept (Hampton, 1987; Murphy, 1988). For example, a salient property of the concept *pet bird* is that they live in cages, but this property is very atypical of either pets or birds by themselves.

A third problem is that people may use a variety of strategies for comprehending combined concepts, and this may complicate analyses. Even for a single strategy such as using analogies, interpretations may seem confusing unless one knows further details. *Bread money* may be understood as money used to purchase bread by analogy with milk money but also understood as profits gained from selling bread by analogy to oil money. So far it seems that conceptual combination is as difficult as it is important.

Induction

Finally, we note that categories play an important role in inductive reasoning. **Induction** will be an important part in our chapter on reasoning but we include a sample here to illustrate the combined influence of similarity to examples and category membership in reasoning. Recently, Osherson, Smith, Wilkie, Lopez, and Shafir (1990) developed a formal model of category-based induction. The main idea is that judgments are based on both similarity to examples and knowledge of category membership. The model is formulated in terms of "argument strength," going from a premise or premises to the conclusion (candidate inference). For example, a premise might be "Robins have property X" and the conclusion "Sparrows also have property X" or "All birds have property X." Osherson et al. used what they referred to as "blank properties" where "blank" means that participants in experiments would have no knowledge concerning whether or not these properties are true (e.g., "birds have sesamoid bones"). The task of the participants was to judge which argument form is stronger. For example, people judge the argument involving the conclusion that sparrows have the property to be stronger than the argument involving the conclusion that all birds have the property for the above mentioned case.

Argument strength is assumed to depend on two factors: the similarity of premise categories to the conclusion category and the similarity of the premise categories to examples of the lowest level category that the premise and conclusion categories share. For example, the strength of "robins have X" for the conclusion "all birds have X" is based on similarity of robin to bird (assumed to be perfect, since robins are birds) and the similarity of robin to other birds. It follows directly that "robins have X" should be stronger than "ostriches have X" for the conclusion that all birds have X, because ostriches are less similar to other birds. The model also correctly predicts that going from "robins have X" to "ostriches have X" should be stronger than going from "ostriches have X" to "robins have X" (Rips, 1975). Again the reason for this prediction is that robins are more similar to other birds than are ostriches.

Many of the predictions of the Osherson et al. model make intuitive sense but a few predictions are quite surprising. The model predicts that going from the premise "bears have X" to the conclusion that "all mammals have X" will be stronger than the same premise with the conclusion "rabbits have X," even though rabbits are mammals. Note that whatever is true of all mammals must also be true of rabbits. The reason for this prediction by the model is that going from bears to rabbits involves weighting separately the similarity of bears to rabbits whereas going from bears to mammals is based only on the overall similarity of bears to other mammals (which should be fairly high since bears are typical mammals). The results agree with this counterintuitive prediction.

Overall, the category-based induction model is quite successful. As we said at the beginning of this section, psychologists are just starting to explore the use of categories in reasoning.

Summary

Concepts serve to organize our mental life. Analyses of conceptual structure provide some important conclusions for our understanding of human cognition. Contrary to one's initial impression, many categories do not have defining properties but rather are fuzzy or probabilistic. In general, things that are superficially similar tend to be similar in deeper ways, but similarity does not provide the basis for conceptual coherence. Concepts are often organized around theories and are knowledge-based rather than similarity-based.

What about the questions and problems with which we began this chapter? Why do we have the particular categories we have out of the virtually unlimited number of possibilities? Are categories in the world to be discovered or are they imposed on the world by our minds? We have suggested that perceptual similarity may serve as an initial classification strategy that is refined and deepened by knowledge and developing theories about the world. If our perceptual and conceptual systems suggested to us categorization schemes that did not serve our goals and did not allow for predictions and explanations, we would be poorly adapted. Therefore, it is tempting to say that categories are organized around our goals and that different organisms with different goals would have very different categorization schemes. Although this may be true, it is equally important to recognize the importance of our environment. If we lived in a very different world, we would need a different perceptual and conceptual system to pick out categories that would be useful in that world. In our opinion, William James was correct when he suggested that mind and world "are something of a mutual fit."

Key Terms

ad hoc categories
basic level
category
classical view
concept
conceptual combination
exemplar models
family resemblance

homeopathy
induction
linear separability
probabilistic view
prototype
psychological essentialism
typicality

Recommended Readings

Since both authors do research on categorization we are tempted to say "read everything!" Fortunately a number of reviews of the literature exist. For basic background the edited volume by Rosch and Lloyd (1978) and the book by Smith and Medin (1981) is recommended. More recent analyses and overviews are provided by Homa (1984), Medin and Smith (1984), Oden (1987), Estes (1991), and the edited volumes by Neisser (1987) and Vosniadou and Ortony (1989). For analyses that focus on contrasts between particular models of categorization see Hintzman (1986), Anderson (1990), Estes (1991), Medin and Florian (in press), and Nosofsky (in press).

The theory-based approach to concepts is represented in developmental work by Carey (1985), Gelman and Markman (1986), and Keil (1987). Other papers on knowledge-driven learning include Murphy and Medin (1985), Schank, Collins, and Hunter (1986), Barsalou (1987), Medin (1989), and Rips (1989). For a review of AI systems for explanation-based learning see Ellman (1989).

The question of whether or not there are unconscious processes capable of complex learning is a fascinating one. The reader would do well to begin with Reber (1976) and Brooks (1978) followed by Dulaney et al. (1984, 1985), Brooks (1987), Reber (1989), and Vokey and Brooks (in press). This topic will be of continuing interest.

Finally, there is increasing interest in the use of categories in reasoning. A good place to start is Rips (1975) and Osherson et al. (1990), and for developmental work, Gelman and Markman (1986) and Gelman (1988).

V

THINKING

13

JUDGMENT AND DECISION MAKING

Chapter Outline

There is no more miserable human being than in whom nothing is habitual but indecision.

William James

Introduction

One of the hardest things about decision making is to define it, for it is so pervasive that we could equate it with virtually all voluntary human behavior. If a behavior is voluntary then it might have been different, and the processes that led to that behavior rather than another can be thought of as involving decision making. On the other hand, brushing one's teeth in the morning seems to be more a matter of habit than a conscious selection from a set of potential behaviors. And just what constitutes this set? Certainly the fact that a person did not pour oatmeal into his coffee, stir it with scissors, and then attempt to use the mixture as shaving cream does not mean that he explicitly decided not to do so. So it seems that we would want to restrict decision making to choosing among alternatives that are in some sense explicitly available.

But equating decision making with selecting among explicit choices may be too narrow. Part of good decision making may involve generating new options. A commuter faced with traffic jams or crowded public transportation may learn that there is another route or realize that she could work at home. Gettys, Manning, Mehle, and Fisher (1980) noted that even experts were not very good at generating a full set of hypotheses about the cause of a problem such as a car failing to start. Furthermore, field studies indicate that people in flood plain areas do not know much about the range of options for reducing the risk of flood damage or insuring against it (Kunreuther, Ginsberg, Miller, Sagi, Slovic, Borkan, & Katz, 1978).

A key aspect of decision making is that it involves risk in one form or another. A person offered a choice between buying a car for $15 versus $15,000 finds the task so obvious that the first reaction would surely be "What's the catch?" or "What else haven't you told me?" To make effective decisions, one must assess risks. We criticize the captain of the

Exxon Valdez for turning control of his oil tanker over to the third mate (resulting in a spill of over 200,000 barrels of oil) because we think that the captain did not weigh the risks properly. Overall, then, decision making can be roughly defined as generating, evaluating, and selecting among a set of relevant choices, where the choices involve some uncertainty or risk.

It will take only a moment's thought to realize that decision making is rife with issues of computational complexity. How do people select from a potentially infinite set of choices only those that are relevant in a particular situation? And for each alternative there may be a vast if not unlimited amount of information that one could collect and evaluate prior to reaching a decision. To make the objectively optimal choice in these circumstances, a person would need an infinite amount of time to decide. To cope with these complexity problems, people seem to adopt strategies or heuristics that are efficient (in that they reduce the complexity) and effective (in that many undesirable alternatives are eliminated and the alternative selected satisfies the goal even if it is not optimal).

If you find the above arguments to be plausible, then you might be surprised to find that much of the history of research on decision making has been organized around the question of whether human decision making is perfectly rational or optimal. The study of decision making owes much of its origins to philosophy and economics. Traditionally, theories of economic behavior have assumed that people's purchasing decisions follow a **rational model** leading to optimal rules. From the perspective of these theories the question was not *whether* people optimized but *what* they optimized. Therefore, studies were aimed at different ways of measuring what people value because, knowing that, one ought to be able to predict what choices people will make.

A major contribution of psychological research on decision making has been to undermine the view that computational complexity and the associated demands on resources in decision making can be ignored. Decision making has its costs and they must be given important consideration in theories of human choice behavior. Some people continue to have the bedrock faith that human decision making is always optimal or at least rational (in a bit we'll define what we mean by rational), and attribute any nonoptimality or irrationality to the researcher's failure to analyze the task properly (see Cohen, 1981 for a modest version of this view). The body of research on choice behavior, however, motivates the consensus view that human decision making often shows clear departures from optimality.

Just as researchers in the area of perception may study visual illusions to get an idea of how the visual system works, decision researchers often focus on situations in which strategies and heuristics may fail or be misleading. These failures are illuminating but they should not be read as indicating that, in general, human decision making is ineffective any more than visual illusions prove that our perceptual system is ineffective. On the other hand, human shortcomings in decision making can be quite serious. Furthermore, decision making can be improved, so it behooves us to understand it better. At the same time, however, we would argue that decision making must be understood in the context of computational complexity and that, for the most part, the procedures used in decision making serve people well. Herbert Simon has suggested that decision making might show **bounded rationality**; that is, rationality from the perspective of costs and computational limitations of decision makers.

This chapter first focuses on reasoning involving uncertainty and describes cases in which people's decisions depart from what is optimal or normative. Next we evaluate normative models of decision making as psychological models and show that even very weak assumptions do not fully describe human decision making. Then we shift to a consideration of some of the strategies people employ to address computational complexity in terms of both their shortcomings and their strengths. Finally, we describe research on probabilistic reasoning.

Normative or Rational Models

First, let's define what we mean by rational. Following the lead of Dawes (1988), we can define *irrational* by the **law of contradiction**: Reasoning processes based on the same evidence that reach contradictory conclusions are irrational. That is, a person who believes that overall choice A is better than B, and that overall choice B is better than A, is being irrational. This definition focuses on consistency. By this same criterion, if a person prefers A to B and B to C, he or she ought to prefer A to C. That is, choices should show **transitivity**. Rationality is not based on what most people value. If John would rather have a paper clip than a stereo set and would rather have a stereo set than a free trip around the world, then John meets the consistency criterion for rationality as long as he prefers a paper clip to a free trip around the world (regardless of how silly his choice may seem to us).

Models that provide an ideal standard or norm hold people to a stricter criterion. Given certain assumptions about a person's goals and values and a description of some task, normative models prescribe what choice should be made. That is, normative models are prescriptive and they set norms by which human decision making can be evaluated. Sometimes normative models are treated as candidates for psychological models, but people's performance departs sufficiently from optimality to undermine this practice.

Expected Value Theory

An example of a normative model is **expected value** theory. Expected value theory applies to choice situations in which different outcomes and probabilities are associated with alternative choices. For example, one might be offered a choice between

1. Winning $40 with probability .20, versus
2. Winning $30 with probability .25.

It is easy to determine the *expected values* of these two choices because it is simply the outcomes multiplied by their probabilities. The expected value for the first choice is $40 times .20 or $8 and for the second choice is $30 times .25 or $7.50. An expected value of $8 means that if the choice were selected numerous times one would expect an average gain of $8.

It is well known that people's behavior often violates expected value. People gamble in casinos and buy lottery tickets even though the expected value for playing is less than the expected value for not playing.

Expected Utility Theory

In their classic book, *Theory of Games and Economic Behavior*, von Neumann and Morgenstern (1944) offered a theory of decision making based on the idea of expected utility. The notion of *utility* refers to personal value rather than objective monetary value. The theory is formulated in terms of a set of axioms and if people's choices satisfy these axioms then their decisions could be described as maximizing **expected utility**. Therefore, the von Neumann and Morgenstern theory can be seen as providing a normative theory for expected utility.

It is important to note that expected utility is not the same as expected value. Most people do prefer choice 1 to choice 2 in the above example and in this case one would say that expected utility and expected value lead to the same choices. But one could imagine situations in which expected utility and expected value disagree. Consider a college student who needs $25 for bus fare to return home. Both of the above choices provide at least that much money and the extra $10 associated with the first choice may have little additional utility. If that were the case, the extra probability associated with the second choice could make it the preferred decision. The college student in the above example would have violated expected value but the choice would be perfectly consistent with expected utility.

Unless we know what the utilities are for a particular person, we cannot say whether option 1 or option 2 should be chosen. In fact, one might think that expected utility theory would prove impossible to test or falsify. But the theory is quite testable, mainly because of the consistency it implies across choices. Consider the following two alternatives:

3. Winning $40 with probability .40 versus
4. Winning $30 with probability .50.

It is easy to see that choices 3 and 4 are just like choices 1 and 2 except that the probabilities have been doubled. Expected utility theory assumes that utilities and probabilities are independent so that the utility of $40 would be identical for the first and third choices as would the utility of $30 for the second and fourth choices. Therefore, expected utility theory imposes a consistency constraint: If you prefer choice 1 over choice 2 then you should also prefer choice 3 over choice 4; if you prefer choice 2 to choice 1 then you ought to prefer choice 4 to choice 3. In fact, for the four choices outlined here, people generally are consistent, as expected utility theory predicts.

But now consider two more choices:

5. Winning $40 with probability .80 versus
6. Winning $30 with probability 1.00.

Again we have left the amount unchanged but doubled the probabilities once more. In this circumstance many people who prefer choices 1 and 3 to choices 2 and 4 nonetheless prefer choice 6 to choice 5. This observation is inconsistent with expected utility theory, so the theory is not only testable, it is incorrect. As we shall see, people show a tendency to prefer certain sure gains (and to avoid certain losses) and a preference for choice 6 over choice 5 is consistent with this observation. This tendency is known as the **certainty effect**. Let's take a closer look at violations of expected utility.

Limitations of Expected Utility and Alternatives to It

A number of observations suggest limitations of expected utility and even of the weaker criterion of consistency. We begin with a more detailed discussion of the certainty effect.

Violations of Expected Utility

The Allais Paradox.   Allais (1953) proposed the following hypothetical pair of decision problems:

Pair 1:

    Choice 7 $1,000 with probability 1.00 versus
    Choice 8 $1,000 with probability .89,
            $5,000 with probability .10,
            and $0 with probability .01.

Pair 2:

    Choice 9 $1,000 with probability .11
            and $0 with probability .89 versus
    Choice 10 $5,000 with probability .10
             and $0 with probability .90.

Most people pick choice 7 over choice 8 but select choice 10 over choice 9. The second pair is related to the first by taking an equal amount ($1,000 with probability .89) away from both choices. In pair 1 people are not willing to give up the certainty of the $1,000 payoff to take a chance on winning $5,000. (If you would be inclined to pick choice 8, then reduce the $5,000 in choices 8 and 10 to $2,000 or $1,500 and you will likely find yourself preferring choices 7 and 10 to 8 and 9, respectively.) This example illustrates what is known as the **Allais paradox**.

Tversky and Kahneman (1981) found that in questions dealing with the effects of a hypothetical epidemic, most people preferred an 80% probability of losing 100 lives to a sure loss of 75 lives (that is, they preferred to avoid a certain loss). The subjects also preferred a 10% chance to lose 75 lives to an 8% chance of losing 100 lives. Note that the second situation is just the first one with each probability reduced by a factor of 10. The key difference (psychologically) is that the first situation involves certainty and the second does not. The certainty effect shows that outcomes perceived with certainty are overweighted relative to uncertain outcomes.

Preference Reversals.   Many theories of decision making view judgment and choice as equivalent measures of preference. Slovic and Lichtenstein (1968) reported, however, that ratings of a gamble's attractiveness and choices among pairs of gambles were influenced primarily by the probabilities of winning and losing, but the amount people would pay for a gamble or sell a gamble for was mainly a function of the amount to be won or lost. Expected utility theory requires that both measures be equivalent and agree with each other. Consider the following pair of gambles:

> Bet A: 11/12 chance to win 12 chips
> 1/12 chance to lose 24 chips

> Bet B: 2/12 chance to win 79 chips
> 10/12 chance to lose 5 chips

Lichtenstein and Slovic (1973) asked people which bet they would choose and to give a minimum price they would sell each bet for. Overall, bets A and B were selected equally often but bet B received a higher selling price 88% of the time. Even the people who selected bet A gave a higher selling price to bet B 87% of the time. (By the way, this study was conducted on the floor of a casino in Las Vegas!)

As an interesting sidelight, two economists were skeptical about these **preference reversals** and ran a series of studies (Grether & Plott, 1979) with the explicit goal "to discredit the psychologists' works as applied to economics" (p. 623). They developed a number of criticisms of earlier work and ran a number of "improved" studies. Despite their considerable efforts and much to their surprise, they also observed preference reversals. Preference reversals continue to be of theoretical and empirical interest (see, e.g., Tversky, Sattath, & Slovic, 1988).

Framing.   Perhaps the most direct way to demonstrate an irrational (that is, inconsistent) component to human decision making is to show that the same information presented in different forms can lead to different decisions. Changes in decision associated with different presentation forms are known as **framing effects.** Consider the following problem originated by Daniel Kahneman and Amos Tversky (see Tversky & Kahneman, 1974; Kahneman, Slovic, & Tversky, 1982).

> 1. Imagine that the U.S. is preparing for the outbreak of an unusual . . . disease which is expected to kill 600 people. Two alternative programs have been proposed. Assume that the exact scientific estimate of the consequences of the programs is as follows:

If Program A is adopted, 200 people will be saved.

If Program B is adopted, there is a 1/3 probability that 600 people will be saved and a 2/3 probability that no people will be saved.

Which of the two programs would you favor?

2. Imagine the identical situation with the following choices:

If Program C is adopted, 400 people will die.

If Program D is adopted, there is a 1/3 probability that nobody will die, and a 2/3 probability that 600 people will die.

Which of the two programs would you favor?

In reading over the problem you probably realized that program A and program C are identical, as are program B and program D. On logical grounds, then, and according to expected utility theory, people who prefer program A to program B ought to prefer program C to program D. Usually this problem is presented to one group of subjects which is shown the first phrasing and another group of subjects which is shown the second phrasing. The typical result is that people prefer program A over B, and program D over C. Deaths seem to loom larger in program C than in program A. We have presented this problem to different groups of medical school students and they show this same pattern of results, but they show a higher overall willingness to gamble (select programs B and D). It is not clear how to interpret this willingness to take a risk, but we prefer to think of it as a sign that idealism is not dead and that these students want to save everyone. On a more serious note, McNeil, Pauker, Cox, and Tversky (1982) found that both physicians and patients varied their ratings of how preferable different treatments were as a function of whether they were described in terms of probability of living versus probability of dying. Obviously, this is a problem if we want decisions to be based on objective properties of choices rather than how we talk about them. In facing situations in which framing effects are likely to be present, it may be a good strategy to try to develop multiple frames.

On the lighter side of framing effects, one of the authors (DLM) recently experienced buying a new car. It is easiest to tell the story in first person. I read various reports about the quality and performance of various candidate cars to narrow down the range of choices (e.g., cars that did not pass the crash test were eliminated). And obviously some features seemed a lot more important than others—for me, a front windshield affording a clear view (some are too slanted, in my opinion) is more important than the color of the car. After selecting the make and model of car I wanted, I discovered that the color I preferred was not available. Although color is not especially important I could not help thinking, "For this amount of money I should at least get the color I want!" Psychologically, I was assigning most of the price of the car to color, a very inappropriate framing effect indeed. (The story had a happy ending—I found the color I wanted.)

Another version of the framing effect is referred to by the name of **sunk costs**. Imagine that you are watching a play after having paid $10 or after having paid $50 for a ticket. Suppose the play is lousy. Does whether or not you walk out depend on whether you paid $10 or $50? Logically, it shouldn't—the money is paid and nonrefundable and the only issue is how you wish to spend your time. Nonetheless, if you paid $50 rather than $10 you are probably more likely to stay. (One weak rationale might be to argue that a play that people pay $50 to see is more likely to get better in the next act than a play that people pay $10 for.) Or imagine the following situation (taken from Thaler, 1980): "A man joins a tennis club and pays a $300 yearly membership fee. After two weeks of playing he develops a tennis elbow. He continues to play (in pain) saying 'I don't want to waste the $300.'" Note that the man probably would not have played if given a free membership! The point is that our ideas about sinking resources into choices seem to influence our future choices in ways that, objectively speaking, do not appear to be very logical. Sunk costs should not influence decisions about the future. If the man would rather not be playing tennis in pain, he should stop.

Although these framing effects meet our criterion for irrationality, they should not be used to decry human decision making in general. Although one can recognize sunk costs' effects as maladaptive in certain situations, such situations may be difficult to distinguish from those in which persistence is adaptive; for example, those that involve initial modest negatives followed by strongly positive outcomes (e.g., starting out completely incompetent at tennis and then developing skill). We believe that these various effects reflect strategies and policies that people develop to organize and cope with difficult choices. We turn now to a pair of theories that attempt to address some of these phenomena.

Prospect Theory

Kahneman and Tversky (1979) proposed a descriptive theory of human decision making. **Prospect theory** can be seen as a modification of expected utility theory but prospect theory aims to account for the nonnormative aspects of decision making. There are two key assumptions in the theory. One is that utilities are not evaluated in an absolute sense but rather with respect to a reference point. Framing effects can be interpreted as affecting the reference point. Consider again the example of the disease expected to kill 600 people. Programs A and B take the anticipated loss of 600 people as the reference point. Subjects are reluctant to give up saving 200 lives for sure to gamble for the chance to save 600 lives. For programs C and D the current situation is provided as the reference point. Subjects apparently see the loss of 400 lives as not too different from the loss of 600 lives and so appear willing to gamble on the chance that no one will die.

The second major assumption is that utilities are not multiplied by objective probabilities but rather by a distorted "psychological probability" that Kahneman and Tversky call the π function. Figure 13.1 illustrates this function (p refers to objective probability and π refers to the weight associated with a given probability). According to this function very low and very high probabilities are overweighted relative to intermediate probabilities. To see this, note that the middle part of the function is bowed so that the π value associated with a probability of 1.00 will be more than twice as large as the π value associated with a probability of .50. The π function can account for the Allais paradox discussed earlier, because objective probabilities cannot simply be broken down into additive constituents. That is, the π value associated with a probability of 1.0 is greater than the sum of the π value for probability .11 plus the π value for probability .89. In brief, prospect theory handles certainty effects and framing effects by assuming

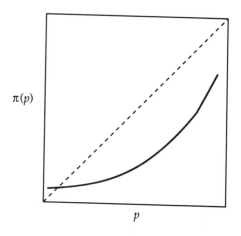

Figure 13.1 π, the weight applied to the utility of each outcome, as a function of p, the probability of the outcome, according to prospect theory.
Source: Kahneman, D., & Tversky, A., 1979.

a π function that departs from objective probabilities and by the idea that reference points can be altered by how a problem is described.

Regret Theory

Another way to address certainty effects is to describe decision situations in terms of anticipated reactions to various outcomes. For example, a reason for preferring choice 7 to choice 8 in the Allais paradox is that one may focus on the 1% chance of obtaining nothing for choice 8 and imagine how miserable one might feel about not getting $1,000 that one could have had for sure. **Regret theory** suggests that we overweight anticipated feelings of regret when the difference between outcomes is large (Bell, 1982; Loomes & Sugden, 1982).

A clever observation in support of regret theory comes from a recent experiment by Loomes (1987). Subjects were given choices like the ones given in Table 13.1. Participants were told that a ticket had been randomly selected from a set of tickets numbered from 1 to 24. They were given a choice between options A and B and between options C and D. The amount won would depend on the ticket selected. Options A and C are identical and options B and D both offer a 50% chance to win $16.

Table 13.1 Two sets of options with identical probabilities and outcomes but with different possibilities for regret. For simplicity we have changed the monetary units from pounds to dollars.

	Ticket Number		
Option	1–9	10–21	22–24
A	$24	$ 0	$0
B	$ 0	$16	$0

	Ticket Number		
Option	1–9	10–12	13–24
C	$24	$ 0	$0
D	$16	$16	$0

Source: Loomes, G., 1987.

Despite the parallels between the two sets of options people choose A slightly more often than B and D more often than C. According to regret theory, Option A might be preferred because the regret associated with drawing a ticket number between 1 and 9 approximately offsets the regret associated with a ticket number between 10 and 21. But for options C and D, the major regret factor involves the possible drawing of ticket numbers 10 through 12, which would favor option D (the difference between $24 and $16 for ticket numbers 1 through 9 would produce only modest regret). This observation is exactly as predicted by regret theory.

Prospect theory and regret theory represent two interesting attempts to capture the irrationality of human decision making. In fact, one might argue that anticipated feelings (e.g., regret) are an important ingredient in a decision-making situation and that these reactions must be included in the evaluation of utilities and probabilities. (For an interesting discussion of this issue see Chapters 16 and 17 of Baron, 1988.) Again we wish to emphasize that decision making in a single situation must always be viewed in the broader context of strategies that people develop to deal with the problem of having limited resources for processing a vast amount of potentially relevant information.

Dealing with Complexity

Imagine that Leigh has just received her Ph.D. in clinical psychology and must decide where to set up her practice. Obviously there are many, many choices available and for each choice there is a wealth of potentially important information she might gather (e.g., cost of living, quality of schools, number of other clinicians practicing, cultural events available, malpractice insurance costs, types of restaurants, access to recreation, and so on). It would take several lifetimes to completely evaluate all the choices, so obviously some shortcuts or strategies must be employed to make the decision manageable. There are two aspects to this problem. Leigh must decide how much information to gather and then how to combine this information to make a choice. Several strategies have been identified for dealing with this sort of informationally rich situation.

Strategies for Dealing with Complexity

Satisficing. Herbert Simon (1957) has argued that people and organizations often abandon the goal of making the optimal choice in favor of one that is satisfactory. The idea is to search through a set of alternatives until a satisfactory one is found. A related idea is to sample a set of n alternatives and pick the best one, provided that at least one is satisfactory. For example, a company hiring a secretary would not examine the complete pool of potential employees, but might set up interviews for eight candidates and pick the best of these. This **satisficing** strategy implies a very strong sensitivity to the exact sampling procedure. Getting into the pool of n alternatives is critically important and for satisficing, the exact order of considering choices is crucial.

Elimination by Aspects.   The **elimination by aspects** procedure focuses not on the overall desirability of choices but rather the individual aspects or components (Tversky, 1972). The idea is that some dimension or aspect is selected and all alternatives that fail to meet some criterion with respect to this dimension are eliminated. Then a new aspect is picked and further unsatisfactory alternatives are eliminated until one is left with a single choice. For example, Leigh might decide first to live in the Midwest and eliminate from consideration all alternatives that are not in the Midwest. Next she might choose to locate within 100 miles of a university, and then to require a city with a population of between 100,000 and 300,000, and so on until either just one alternative remains or until the choice set is small enough that it can be examined in detail. Elimination by aspects is also nonoptimal in that it depends on the order in which various aspects are considered. An optimal decision rule would pick the "best" choice regardless of order.

Clustering.   A closely related idea is that people reduce the set of choices by first clustering the choices and then picking indifferently within a cluster once the most desirable cluster has been identified. This procedure is very similar to elimination by aspects except that the decision procedure stops when a satisfactory cluster has been identified. Choice behavior will depend on the factors that determine which clusters are created.

Adaptive Decision Making

There may be situations in which the choice set is small and the amount of relevant information concerning each alternative is modest. In this case it would be sensible for people to examine each alternative fully and weight each aspect by its (psychological) importance, as expected utility theory would prescribe.

Is there evidence that people adjust their decision-making strategies in an adaptive manner? There is. Payne, Bettman, and Johnson (1988) combined computer simulation with experimental investigations to demonstrate this point. They first ran simulations of different decision procedures under various time constraints. That is, they assumed that each step in a decision procedure would take one unit of time and then cut off the decision-making process after various time periods had passed. For example, when satisficing was simulated, if no satisfactory choice had been identified by the cutoff time, the program randomly selected from the remaining alternatives. In addition to heuristics such as elimination by aspects and satisficing, the Payne et al. simulations included normative decision procedures (e.g., examining all aspects of all alternatives and picking the one with the best overall weighted average). They found that under time pressure some of the non-normative heuristics such as elimination by aspects actually performed much better than the normative procedure. The reason is that the normative procedure may take too long and the simulation often had to pick at random when time ran out.

These simulations demonstrate that heuristics which technically are irrational procedures may be better than normative procedures when time limitations are significant. That is to say, normative models do not take into account the costs associated with gathering and evaluating information. Where time costs are critical, normative models may be inappropriate.

Payne et al. (1988) went on to conduct experiments with human subjects in which they varied the complexity of the choice task and time pressure. They found that people adjusted their decision procedures in an adaptive manner. When there was little time pressure and the decision task was not overly complex, strategies shifted in the direction of normative procedures. Under time pressure in complex environments, strategies shifted toward simplifying heuristics (see also Payne, 1976; 1982). These observations provide an appreciation of some of the positive aspects of heuristics.

In the next section we take a more extensive look at the use of heuristics in judgment and decision making. Although the examples reveal systematic biases and misperceptions, bear in mind that, for the most part, they represent adaptive responses to computational complexity.

Further Heuristics and Biases

Cognitive heuristics are easy or natural ways of thinking that are very often useful and powerful. Because they are shortcuts, however, they represent oversimplifications and, consequently, may lead to systematic biases or misperceptions. In the last section we considered strategies for dealing with complex information. In this section we describe strategies for generating and evaluating information used in judgments as well as heuristics for monitoring the decision-making process itself.

An important aspect of cognitive heuristics or biases is that they are very strong in two senses: (1) they are used by experts in technical areas such as medicine, as well as by novices, and (2) they are difficult to overcome. Cognitive heuristics are two-sided. They can be both very effective in some cases and very misleading in others. We shall focus on the biases associated with cognitive heuristics, as most heuristics do not come equipped with warning labels. Bear in mind, however, that in general these strategies are efficient and effective, especially in relation to the complexity of judgment and decision-making tasks. Still, the consequences in terms of systematic biases must be taken seriously.

Research over the last two decades has led to a major shift in our thinking about human bias. The earlier view was that human thought could be neatly partitioned into a logical, rational component and an irrational, blind, emotion-laden component, the latter giving rise to certain human shortcomings such as racial prejudice. Although we still do not understand the role of emotion in cognition, it has become increasingly clear that normal cognitive processes frequently give rise to nonrational by-products that are associated with systematic misperceptions of other individuals and groups. In some respects this newer view is more sobering than the earlier one because it suggests that human rationality is not segregated from processes that lead to cognitive biases.

Many of the examples that follow are based on the pioneering work of Kahneman and Tversky (e.g., Tversky & Kahneman, 1974; Kahneman, Slovic, & Tversky, 1982). As we noted earlier, initial work on decision making or judgment in uncertain situations was based on determining what the optimal decision-making procedure would be in a given situation, but it soon became clear that people typically do not perform optimally (Edwards, Lindman, & Savage, 1963; see Einhorn & Hogarth, 1981 and Fischhoff, 1988 for more recent reviews). Kahneman and Tversky demonstrated that many violations of what would be rationally or optimally correct can be traced to the use of cognitive heuristics.

Availability Heuristic

The **availability heuristic** refers to a tendency to form a judgment on the basis of what is readily brought to mind. For example, a person who is asked whether there are more English words that begin with the letter *t* or the letter *k* might try to think of words that begin with each of these letters. Since a person probably can think of more words beginning with *t*, he or she would (correctly) conclude that *t* is more frequent than *k* as the first letter of words. So far, so good.

As long as the retrieval process is unbiased, the availability heuristic works quite well. Of course, anything that biases the retrieval process may lead to incorrect judgments. Consider the following experiment. We ask different groups of subjects to judge how many English words fit either this pattern: _ _ _ _ n _ or this pattern: _ _ _ i n g. Objectively, the answer has to be greater in the first case because the first pattern includes the second pattern as a special case. On the other hand, the group shown the first pattern may not think of the *ing* ending, which the other group is given. In fact, groups of subjects give higher estimates for the second pattern than the first. One recent demonstration produced a median estimate of 125 words fitting the first pattern and a median estimate of 880 words for the second pattern.

The above finding might be mildly disturbing to a producer of Scrabble sets using subjective estimates to decide how many different letter tiles to make of a given type, but why should it bother anyone else? The reason is that this phenomenon is quite general. Many factors can influence the accessibility of information and consequently influence judgments.

"Solo" or Token Members.   One robust finding from memory research is that if one word in a list of words to be remembered is different from the others in some way (e.g., an animal name in a list of plant names), that word is much more likely to be remembered than any other word. This is known as the Von Restorff effect (after its original investigator).

Consider the situation of a black person in an otherwise all-white group, or a female in an otherwise all-male group. They will be distinctive in that group context. Taylor, Fiske, Etcoff, and Ruderman (1978) showed that the perception of a group member is strongly influenced by the member's status as a solo. The subjects in their experiments listened to a tape recording of a group discussion. As the tape was played, subjects were shown slides of the participant who presumably was speaking at the time. By using the same tape but varying the slides shown, Taylor et al. were able to change the assumed group composition while keeping the content of the discussion constant. For example, in one condition the slides indicated that the discussion involved five whites and one black, and in another that the discussion involved three whites and three blacks. The observers then rated the group members on a number of scales. These ratings showed that solo members were perceived as having been more active and influential during the discussion than the same stimulus person in the fully integrated group. Subjects also remembered more of what the solo person said. Ratings on evaluative dimensions were also more extreme for solo members. If the rating was slightly negative in the fully integrated group, it became far more negative for the same stimulus person in the solo context. These findings and others (see, e.g., Hamilton, 1976) suggest that people tend to systematically misperceive minorities, simply on the basis of the Von Restorff effect and the availability heuristic.

Representativeness Heuristic

The **representativeness heuristic** refers to a tendency to judge an event as likely if it "represents" the typical features of (or is similar in its essential properties to) its category. As a consequence, people may use similarity as a guideline in situations where, objectively, they should focus on probability. This can lead to errors in judgment.

Conjunction Fallacy.   Which of the following events is the most likely?

1. that a man is under 55 and has a heart attack
2. that a man has a heart attack
3. that a man smokes and has a heart attack
4. that a man is over 55 and has a heart attack

Many people might select the third or fourth choice as most likely because these alternatives seem to conform most closely to their ideas about typical heart attack victims. The correct answer is the second choice, as a moment's reflection will reveal. The reason is that the second alternative encompasses all the others, or more formally, the *conjunction* of probabilistic events (such as smoking, being over 55, or having a heart attack) cannot be more probable than any individual events. In short, people seem to use similarity to some prototypical example rather than probability as the basis for judgment (see Tversky & Kahneman, 1983). This tendency is known as the **conjunction fallacy**.

Misconceptions of Chance.   A key problem with the use of the representativeness heuristic is that random patterns will appear nonrandom and people may inappropriately attribute the apparent pattern to a cause. For example, people tend to think extremes are less likely to occur than they actually are. If a baseball player fails to get a hit 12 times in a row, people assume that he is in a "batting slump" even though it might be that he continues to have the same probability of getting a hit in each turn at bat.

The other extreme is the notion that a batter who has not had a hit in several at bats is somehow "due to get a hit" such that the probability of his getting a hit is much greater than normal. This idea that prior outcomes can influence the outcome of an independent probabilistic event is known as the **gambler's fallacy**. Because of this belief, a person who believes that the airline with the best safety record is "due for a crash" might make an unwise choice in picking an airline for a trip.

Anchoring and Adjustment

A common strategy in making estimates is to start with some initial estimate or anchor and then adjust it in light of new information to come up with an answer or final estimate. Again this is a useful strategy, but frequently people fail to make sufficiently large adjustments to appropriately overcome the influence of the initial anchoring. For example, in one study of **anchoring and adjustment** by Tversky and Kahneman (1974), two groups of high school students were asked to estimate within a few seconds the value of a numerical expression written on the board. One group estimated the product

$$1 \times 2 \times 3 \times 4 \times 5 \times 6 \times 7 \times 8$$

whereas the other group estimated the product

$$8 \times 7 \times 6 \times 5 \times 4 \times 3 \times 2 \times 1$$

The initial numbers ought to act as an anchor and, therefore, Tversky and Kahneman predicted, the second group would come up with higher estimates. The median estimate for the first sequence was 512 whereas the corresponding estimate for the second group was 2,250. (The correct answer is 40,320.)

An important aspect of anchoring is that we may be influenced by initial anchors even when these anchors are generated by an arbitrary or biased source. This tendency is exploited by salespeople and auctioneers to influence people's willingness to pay higher prices for goods. An auctioneer who starts the bidding for a lamp by saying "Who will give me $300?" may have no expectation of selling the lamp for $300, but he or she may have succeeded in inserting a high anchor that will not be adjusted downward appropriately as the bidding proceeds.

Causal Schemas

Causal schemas is a term used to refer to a tendency to expect predictions to be more accurate when they are presented in a way that is consistent with one's expectations about causes or notions about underlying stability. Consider the following two questions. Which would be more accurate:

1. Predicting a daughter's eye color from her mother's eye color or predicting a mother's eye color from her daughter's eye color?
2. Predicting scores on a short quiz from performance on a 10-hour exam or predicting scores on a 10-hour exam from scores on a short quiz?

People are very likely to indicate that the first prediction would be more accurate on each of the two questions. In fact, since both directions of prediction involve just a correlation, the predictions would be equally accurate in either direction. Apparently this bias arises because, based on our understanding of genetics, we think of a mother as causing or directly influencing her daughter's eye color and, based on notions of stability, we think that a 10-hour exam would better predict quiz performance than vice versa. This bias may lead people to interpret correlations in ways consistent with prior expectations and to fail to consider alternative possibilities (e.g., the idea that smoking does not cause cancer but rather that cancer causes the urge to smoke—of course, proper experiments can disentangle such correlations). A key aspect of the use of causal schemas is that it can lead people to ignore other potentially relevant information (as we shall see later in this chapter).

Hindsight Bias

Hindsight bias refers to the tendency for people to think *after the fact* that they would have known something *before the fact* when in actuality they would not have. This problem seems intuitively plausible but one might wonder how it could be established experimentally. Again we will take an example from medicine, but the phenomenon appears to be quite general (see Fischhoff, 1982). Arkes, Wortmann, Saville, and Harkness (1981) gave the same medical history to five different groups of clinicians. The *foresight group* was asked to assign a probability estimate to each of the four possible diagnoses. The four *hindsight* groups were asked to do the same thing but were told the correct diagnosis. Specifically, they were asked to disregard their knowledge of the correct diagnosis and give estimates only on the basis of other information presented. The hindsight groups that were told that the least likely diagnoses were correct (likelihood was determined by the judgments of the foresight group) assigned probability estimates for these "correct" diagnoses that were two or three times higher than the probabilities given by the foresight group. That is, the hindsight groups were unable to disregard information about the correct diagnosis. This hindsight bias may lead to an inadequate appreciation of the original difficulty of a diagnosis.

Overconfidence

For reasons that are not entirely clear, both novices and experts appear to be more confident in their judgments than is objectively justifiable (see Lichtenstein, Fischhoff, & Phillips, 1982 for a review). Part of the problem may be hindsight bias and part of the problem is that experts often do not receive feedback on their judgments (see, e.g., Einhorn & Hogarth, 1978) and therefore do not know when they are in error. Figure 13.2 is taken from a study by Christensen-Szalanski and Bushyhead (1981) that involved diagnosis of possible pneumonia at an outpatient clinic. In the study, physicians interviewed the patients and then estimated the probability that the patients had pneumonia. In all cases, regardless of the probability estimates, X-rays were given to determine radiographically whether or not a patient did have pneumonia.

As Figure 13.2 indicates, as the probability estimates increased so also did the objective likelihood that the patients had pneumonia, indicating that the physicians were sensitive to the predictive value of different

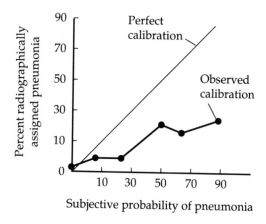

Figure 13.2   **Relationship between physicians' subjective probability of pneumonia and the actual probability of pneumonia.**
Source: Christensen-Szalanski, J. J. J., & Bushyhead, J. B., 1981.

symptoms. However, subjective probabilities were far higher than objective likelihoods. For example, when the physicians were 90% sure that pneumonia was present there was less than a 20% chance that the diagnosis would be confirmed by the X-rays. There has been, for obvious reasons, a fair amount of effort to figure out how to make expert judgments more accurate. Interestingly, among populations of experts, meteorologists' predictions of precipitation appear to be least susceptible to overconfidence effects (Murphy & Winkler, 1977). Meteorologists are directly trained to reason with probabilities and they receive accurate feedback about their judgments (they also have computer models to help them). As another way of adjusting for biased estimates, in the United Kingdom the Electricity Board has a policy of doubling engineers' chronic underestimates of the time needed for production (Kidd, 1970).

Relativity of Judgment and Use of Norms

Kahneman and Miller (1986) have argued that judgments are often based on norms or standards that are recruited or retrieved by the events themselves. Consider the following scenario:

> Two business people, John and Jill, are sharing a cab to the airport where they intend to take separate flights each of which is scheduled to leave at 11:00 A.M. Traffic proves to be very heavy and the cab arrives at 11:30 A.M. Both miss their flight, but Jill finds out that her flight left on time and John finds out that his flight left at 11:25 A.M. Which traveler will experience greater regret?

Most people judge that John, who missed his flight by five minutes, will be more upset. Given that the flights were scheduled to leave at the same time, that they shared the cab, and that they both missed their flight, it is clear that this judgment is based on more than outcomes alone. According to Kahneman and Miller, John is more upset because he can imagine similar possible worlds (e.g., less traffic) in which he would have made the flight than can Jill.

The general idea is that people form judgments based on comparisons of alternative possible worlds where the possible worlds are based on imagined changes from the present world. Certain changes are easier to imagine than others, and judgments should tend to reflect influences of changeability or what Kahneman and Miller (1986) refer to as *mutability*.

What determines mutability? One factor is that information that is part of the background of a scenario may be less mutable than the aspects that are the focus of attention. This can lead to systematic biases. As Kahneman and Miller note, the idea that the actions of an individual who is in focus are mutable may help explain the well-established tendency for victims of violence to be assigned an unreasonable degree of responsibility for their fate (Lerner & Miller, 1978). Imagine that a victim took an unusual rather than a typical route on just the evening that he was robbed on the way home. The ready availability of an alternative scenario can lead to the victim's receiving a disproportionate responsibility for being robbed.

In related work Pennington and Hastie (1988) have argued that often complex decision making involves the construction of explanations. The idea is that information is not weighed in some objective manner but rather that the information plays a role in determining the explanation that is constructed. In some of their research on juror decision making they found that participants spontaneously evaluate evidence in a legal judgments task by constructing an explanation in the form of a narrative story. To show that these stories play a direct role in decisions, Pennington and Hastie varied the order in which evidence was presented so as to favor the construction of one story over another. The order manipulation shifted choices in the direction of the more easily constructed story. The key idea is that the representation that enters into decisions is not an algebraic or probabilistic quantity but rather a rich representation of the situation comprising key relations among important events. Participants appear to be confident in their decisions to the extent that there are no coherent competing explanations that would lead to a different decision.

Summary

We have deliberately presented the strongest case for paying attention to cognitive heuristics and biases, because we believe they are very important. At the same time, however, we should add the caution that we really know far less about these phenomena than we would like. So far, work in this area has the character of being more like a list of ingredients than a recipe. That is, we do not have a procedure that is guaranteed to tell us when one heuristic rather than another will come into play, or precisely how a heuristic may influence judgments. This is not a satisfying state of affairs, particularly from the point of view of improving human judgment. Again, we emphasize that heuristics are often efficient and effective in many realistic decision-making circumstances. Hogarth (1981) points out that most judgment research has focused on discrete situations. He argues that many decision tasks are continuous and interactive, where one's initial decisions can be modified and refined on the basis of feedback. Therefore, it may often suffice to get the decision process headed roughly in the right direction rather than exactly on target. Although it is very important to keep in mind the limitations of various cognitive heuristics, there may be compensatory factors associated with the decision context that keep us from being led too far astray.

Probabilistic Reasoning

We shift attention now to the question of how people reason with probabilities about uncertain events. The short answer to this question is "not nearly so well as they might." Let's start with an example. Suppose we are trying to diagnose a fairly rare but serious disease. A treatment exists for the disease but it is both costly and risky. Therefore it is important to make sure that the disease is present before giving the treatment. A new diagnostic test is developed that has the following two properties:

> If the disease is present, 98% of the time the test will be positive.
>
> If the disease is absent, only 1% of the time the test will be positive.

Suppose that we perform this diagnostic test on a patient and it turns out positive. How likely is it that the patient has the disease?

In general, people have difficulty in reasoning about uncertain events like the one outlined here. When we give the above problem to first-year medical school students, the most common answer is that the odds are about 98 to 1 that the patient has the disease. As we shall see, the correct answer is that we cannot tell without knowing the prevalence of the disease in the population of people being tested. We said the disease was rare and under that circumstance, the actual probability could easily be less than 1%!

We are constantly faced with the need to do probabilistic reasoning and to revise prior beliefs in light of new information. Therefore, it is important to understand probabilistic reasoning.

Test Quality

Should a bus driver who shows a positive drug test be fired? Two important pieces of information for debates about such questions are the quality of the drug test and the prevalence of drug use among bus drivers. Let's see why. The quality of a test depends on two factors: the likelihood of a true positive test result and the likelihood of a false positive test result. In the earlier example the true positive rate was 98% and the false positive rate was 1%. An easy way to think about test quality is in terms of the following table:

| | | Disease | |
		Present	Absent
Test Result	Positive	a	b
	Negative	c	d

The table indicates the possible test results and the possible true state of affairs with respect to disease. Cell a corresponds to patients who show a positive test result and have the disease, whereas cell d corresponds to patients who show a negative test and do not have the disease. The bigger a and d are, the better the test. The proportion of positive tests among those with the disease is equal to $a/(a + c)$. The false positive rate among patients who do not have the disease is $b/(b + d)$. The quantity $(a + c)/(a + b + c + d)$ corresponds to the **base rate** of the disease among the population being tested. Note that the probability that a patient has the disease given that he or she shows a positive test corresponds to none of these quantities—it is equal to $a/(a + b)$. Similarly, the probability that a patient does not have the disease given a negative test is $d/(c + d)$.

It is easy to see how base rate influences the likelihood of having a disease given a positive test. If the disease appears in half the population being tested, our table might look like this:

| | | Disease | |
		Present	Absent
Test	Positive	98	1
	Negative	2	99
	Total	100	100

In this case the true positive rate is 98%, the false positive rate is 1%, the base rate 50%, and the probability of having the disease given a positive test is 98/99 or about 99%. This corresponds to most people's intuitions concerning the answer to our initial problem. But remember we started by stating that the disease is fairly rare. Suppose it has a base rate of 1 out of 100 patients (or, to stick with whole numbers in the table, a prevalence of 100 out of 10,000). Then our table would look like this:

		Disease	
		Present	**Absent**
	Positive	98	99
Test	Negative	2	9801
	Total	100	9900

Now for the same true and false positive test rates, the probability that the disease is present given a positive test is 98/(98 + 99) or a little less than 50%. If the disease were present in only 1 in 10,000 patients tested, this probability would further shrink to less than 1%.

There is a simple, intuitive way to understand the influence of base rates on the probability that a disease is present when a positive test appears. Even if false positive tests are rare, when one tests a large population of healthy people the false positive tests start to mount up. Since what matters is the relative number of true positive and false positive tests, when a disease is rare the number of false positive tests can overwhelm the number of true positive tests. Thus, many (or even most) of the people who test positively for *rare* diseases may not actually have the disease.

Many screening tests have lower true positive and higher false positive rates than in the present example. For diseases that are not very common among the population of people being tested, a positive test may raise the likelihood that a disease is present only from less than 1% to less than 10%. Therefore, it is absolutely essential to consider base rates in reasoning from diagnostic tests. When one reads about tests for drug use among athletes or in certain occupations (e.g., driving a bus) one needs to consider true positive rates, false positive rates, and base rates before jumping to any conclusions from a positive test. Unless the false positive rate is zero, decisions can be made that unfairly harm innocent people.

Bayes's Theorem

By making up tables, we have been able to combine test quality with base rate information to determine the likelihood that a disease is present given a positive test. Basically, we were considering the initial probability that the disease was present and then adjusting our estimate according to the results of the test. Mathematically speaking we were using **Bayes's theorem**, which is a general formula for revising beliefs or probabilities in light of new information. This theorem says that the new odds for some event happening are just the old odds multiplied by the odds associated with the new information. More formally for our examples:

$$P(\text{disease} \mid \text{positive test})$$
$$= P(\text{disease}) \times \frac{P(\text{positive test} \mid \text{disease})}{P(\text{positive test})}$$

P(disease | positive test) is a conditional probability and the "|" sign is read as "given." The left-hand term is the probability of the disease being present given that the test is positive. In more familiar terms the formula reads:

$$P(\text{disease} \mid \text{positive test})$$
$$= (\text{base rate}) \times \frac{\text{true positive probability}}{\text{overall probability of a positive test}}$$

In terms of our 2 × 2 matrix, this formula would read:

$$P(\text{disease} \mid \text{positive test})$$
$$= \frac{a + c}{a + b + c + d} \times \frac{a/(a + c)}{(a + b)/(a + b + c + d)}$$

which looks complicated, but we can cancel out some terms to reduce the formula to:

$$P(\text{disease} \mid \text{positive test}) = \frac{a}{a + b}$$

the formula we were using before. Another way to see the relationship is to directly substitute values into the Bayes equation. For example, using the same test quality as before and a base rate of 50%, we would have:

$$P(\text{disease} \mid \text{positive test}) = \frac{1}{2} \times \frac{98/100}{99/200} = 98/99$$

as we found before.

There are a number of decision aids or computerized expert systems that use Bayes's theorem as a basis for diagnosis. These procedures have the obvious advantage of combining the new diagnostic information with base rate information, which we have seen is crucial in evaluating the results of a test.

Perhaps the single most important contribution of Bayesian analysis is simply to underline the distinction between two conditional probabilities:

> The probability of A given B.
>
> The probability of B given A.

If A is a symptom and B a disease, only the second provides the information that is crucial to diagnosis. It is fundamentally important to distinguish these two conditional probabilities because the former may be high at the same time that the latter is very small. For example, the probability of being tall given that you are a professional basketball player is very much higher than the probability of your being a professional basketball player given that you are tall. Eddy (1982) documents the tendency of health professionals to confuse these two and to treat the first as if it were the second. His analysis of the use of mammography to decide whether or not to perform a breast biopsy to determine if a mass is malignant shows that these conditional probabilities are sometimes confused even in technical medical journals. These confusions can lead to a very inefficient decision strategy. For example, along with the usual recommended biopsy if the mammography is positive, some medical articles include the advice that biopsy should be used when the mammography is negative, "just to make sure." Of course if the biopsy is to be performed regardless of the outcome of the mammography, there is no point in doing the X-ray. In general, a person who bases the decision on the probability of a symptom given a disease is not only ignoring base rates but also neglecting the false positive tests.

Base Rate Neglect

So far our analysis of Bayes's theorem has been prescriptive. How well do people conform to Bayes's theorem? Not well. We began this section with an example in which base rate information was not presented. Tversky, Kahneman, and others have noted that even when base rate information is presented, it is frequently ignored. Consider the following problem taken from Tversky and Kahneman (1981):

> A cab was involved in a hit-and-run accident: Two cab companies, the green and blue, operated in the city. You are given the following data:
> 1. 85% of the cabs in the city are green and 15% are blue.
> 2. A witness identified the cab as a blue cab. The court tested his ability to identify cabs under the appropriate visibility conditions. When the witness was presented with a sample of cabs (half of which were blue and

half green) the witness made correct identification in 80% of the cases and errors in 20% of the cases.

Question: What is the probability that the cab involved in the accident was blue rather than green? (p. 63)

According to Bayes's theorem the correct answer should be 12/29 or .41. In contrast, the modal answer in a typical experiment is .80, which corresponds to the reliability of the witness. This suggests that the base rate information simply was ignored. Base rate neglect may derive from the use of the representativeness heuristic, discussed earlier in this chapter. Given that so many situations involve combining prior information with new information, it is not surprising that the use of base rate information has been extensively studied. In general, it appears that base rate information is more likely to be used when it is made salient (Fischhoff, Slovic, & Lichtenstein, 1979), when there is clear conceptual relationship or causal linkage between the base rate information and the problem outcome (see, e.g., Bar-Hillel & Fischhoff, 1981; Gigerenzer, Hell, & Blank, 1988), and when the base rate information is conveyed through experience with examples rather than being presented in summary form (Manis, Dovalina, Avis, & Cardoze, 1980; Medin & Edelson, 1988). To give but one example, Gigerenzer, Hell, and Blank (1988) found that base rate information was used effectively on the following problem:

> In the 1978/79 season of the West German soccer "Bundesliga," Team A won 10 out of 34 games. We have selected some of the games that season randomly and checked their final results as well as their half-time results. For instance, on the 7th day of the season the half-time result was 2:1 in favor of Team A. What is your probability (estimate) that this game belongs to those 10 games won out of 34?

The base rate of winning was varied from a low of 7 to a high of 19 out of 34 games. Gigerenzer et al. observed that estimates of winning increased systematically as base rate increased.

There are several important differences between the cab problem and the soccer problem. The most obvious one is that the two pieces of information in the soccer problem are conceptually related in that both the base rate and the new information are directly linked to winning and losing. Of course, base rate information is relevant to both the soccer problem and the cab problem.

Summary

People experience considerable difficulty when they are asked to reason explicitly with information that is probabilistic in character. Base rates are often ignored and the distinction between the probability that a disease is present given a positive test and the probability of a positive test given a disease is present is often confused. Probability is hard and conditional probability is even harder. One speculation is that there are some situations in which the use of appropriate probabilistic reasoning is naturally triggered but for others probabilistic reasoning is labored and becomes easy only after long, explicit training. This speculation is empty unless one can describe what "natural" means. For some ideas along these lines, see Nisbett, Krantz, Jepson, and Kunda (1983) and Gigerenzer et al. (1988).

Summary and Overview

Human judgment and decision making is fallible. In psychology this is not major news. As early as 1954 Paul Meehl published a book summarizing comparisons of the diagnostic skills of expert clinical psychologists with the predictions generated from a simple statistical formula (a linear regression model, to be specific). The ground rules were that both statistical formuli and the clinicians would have access to the same information (results of diagnostic tests). Meehl found that the statistical formula consistently outperformed the experts (Meehl, 1954).

Subsequent studies confirm that simple linear models perform better than experts in areas ranging from decisions concerning who to admit to graduate school to loan risk assessments by bank officers (see Dawes, 1988 for a review and discussion). In fact, Dawes and Corrigan (1974) found that (statistical) models of what expert judges said they were doing made better predictions than the judges themselves! The reason that this technique leads to improvements is that experts may not apply their rules consistently. Many factors could affect consistency such as information processing or working memory demands (we calculate better on calculators and computers than we do "in our head") or being distracted by irrelevant information. For example, judges might feel that some unique information turns a decision into a special case and consequently may depart from the decision policy (to their peril, if we use comparisons with the performance of the model of the expert as a guide).

As we suggested at the beginning of this chapter, the shortcomings of human decision making have come as big news and have had a major impact in economics and in a variety of applied areas ranging from stock market forecasting to medical decision making. Cognitive biases can produce serious errors. Normative models of decision making are not, in general, very accurate models of human choice behavior.

But optimality is a very tough standard given the complexities of decision making. Although we may be accused of taking too charitable a view, it is surprising to us how effective and efficient human decision-making strategies often prove to be. When one considers computational costs and time limitations, as we have seen, heuristics may outperform normative strategies because the "correct" or optimal strategies take too long to compute. In short, human decision processes can be seen as adaptive, even if they are not flawless.

Key Terms

Allais paradox
anchoring and adjustment
availability heuristic
base rate
Bayes's theorem
bounded rationality
certainty effect
cognitive heuristics
conjunction fallacy
elimination by aspects
expected utility
expected value

framing effects
gambler's fallacy
hindsight bias
law of contradiction
preference reversals
prospect theory
rational model
regret theory
representativeness heuristic
satisficing
sunk costs
transitivity

Recommended Readings

Decision making is an important and intriguing subject. Even though one may understand framing effects they may remain compelling. For a review and survey of work on judgment heuristics see the edited volume by Kahneman et al. (1982), Fischhoff's (1988) article, and the textbooks by Dawes (1988) and Baron (1988).

A more salient reason to be intrigued by decision making research is that it raises questions about human rationality. To get a flavor for the different perspectives on this issue, see Simon (1975), Hogarth (1981), and Cohen's (1981) article and the associated commentaries. Readers interested in clinical judgment should look at Meehl (1954), Dawes and Corrigan (1974), and Dawes (1988).

14

REASONING

Chapter Outline

If J. Edgar Hoover had been born in Russia, then he would have been a communist.

If J. Edgar Hoover had been a communist, then he would have been a traitor.

Therefore, if J. Edgar Hoover had been born in Russia, then he would have been a traitor.

> D. K. Lewis, *Counterfactuals*

Introduction

There is something wrong about the above line of argument concerning the former head of the FBI, J. Edgar Hoover, but it may not be easy to say exactly what it is. The first and second statements seem plausible in isolation but when they are put together the implied conclusion does not make sense.

Suppose we try to formalize things. Let A represent Hoover being born in Russia, B represent his being a communist, and C represent his being a traitor. The first two statements are known as *premises* and the third the *conclusion*. The term *therefore* is often represented by $\therefore$. Then we can represent the line of argument as:

(Premise 1) If A, then B.

(Premise 2) If B, then C.

(Conclusion) $\therefore$ If A, then C.

Alternatively, if-then or conditional statements are often represented by an implication symbol, $\rightarrow$. Then we can write:

$$A \rightarrow B$$
$$B \rightarrow C$$
$$\therefore A \rightarrow C$$

which again seems perfectly reasonable.

So what is the problem? The problem is that the two premises have different background conditions or assumptions that make it inappropriate for us to combine them. The second premise, fully specified, would need to be something like "If J. Edgar Hoover had been living in the United States, head of the FBI and a communist, then he would have been a traitor to the United States." Now the argument structure would look like this:

$$A \rightarrow B$$

$$B \text{ and } L \text{ and } H \rightarrow C$$

$$\therefore A \rightarrow C$$

which does not follow because A leads to B rather than B and L (living in the United States) and H (head of the FBI).

The laws of logic or deductive reasoning specify valid argument structures. That is, principles of deductive reasoning tell us whether or not some conclusion logically follows from some set of premises. The laws of logic are abstract and are not empirical—that is, they tell us which beliefs follow from other beliefs strictly on the basis of their form, not their content. They are not concerned with the state of affairs in the world. The argument from the premises $A \rightarrow B$, $B \rightarrow C$, and A to the conclusion C is valid in that it necessarily follows that if the premises are true, the conclusion must be true.

The example involving Hoover illustrates a central issue concerning reasoning in general and deductive reasoning in particular. Although the laws of logic are not empirical, human reasoning is typically embedded in the world. Part of the problem concerns mapping states of affairs in the world onto abstract symbols. Our initial pass at the Hoover example could be represented as $A \rightarrow B$ and $B \rightarrow C$, respectively. A closer look, however, reveals that the second premise should actually be represented as B and L and $H \rightarrow C$.

A second major aspect of the problem is that people often evaluate arguments not only in terms of whether they are valid but also on the basis of whether they are empirically true. Logical validity and empirical truth do not necessarily agree. Consider the following argument:

Premise 1: All doctors are professional people.

Premise 2: Some professional people are rich.

Conclusion: ∴Some doctors are rich.

A moment's reflection will reveal that this argument form is not valid because it may be the case that all of the professional people who are rich are nondoctors. The fact that the conclusion may be empirically true does not mean that the argument structure is a **valid argument**. A fair amount of the research on reasoning has been concerned with content effects on reasoning. The observation that people are less than perfect at separating structure from content may, in part, reflect the fact that reasoning is almost always embedded in a context in which both validity and truth are at issue. Note, however, that content effects do not necessarily imply a failure to distinguish truth from validity. It may be that some contents facilitate or interfere with people's ability to draw valid conclusions by, for example, facilitating or interfering with short-term memory.

A third significant aspect of reasoning is that people expect arguments to be not only logically correct and empirically true, but also *relevant*. Consider the following argument:

Premise 1: If it is raining, the picnic will not be held.

Premise 2: It is raining.

Conclusion: ∴The picnic will not be held or cats have six legs.

The conclusion is deductively valid because if X is true then X or Y must also be true, regardless of what Y is. The problem with the conclusion is that the number of legs cats have has nothing to do with the premises. Even if the conclusion were that "the picnic will not be held or cats have four legs" we still would have a relevance problem. Typically researchers supply the conclusions and ask participants to judge their validity; only rarely have psychologists studied which conclusions seem intuitively natural (and presumably relevant) to people (see Johnson-Laird, 1983 for a notable exception).

Deductive vs. Inductive Reasoning

Deductive reasoning can be contrasted with inductive reasoning in terms of necessity versus probability. **Deductive reasoning** is concerned with which beliefs are licensed or entailed by other beliefs by necessity. **Inductive reasoning** is concerned with certain beliefs *supporting* or being supported by (rather than being logically required by) other beliefs. Given that John has no alibi for where he was last night and that he possesses a crowbar and that 15 television sets are found in his apartment, it is more likely that he broke into a local appliance store last night than if he had an alibi and possessed neither a crowbar nor 15 television sets. But the conclusion that John robbed the appliance store is not deductively valid. The deductive argument might be something like:

> If John committed the robbery, then he has 15 television sets.
>
> John has 15 television sets.
>
> Therefore, John committed the robbery.

This argument form error is known as **affirming the consequent**. It is not valid to conclude from $P \rightarrow Q$ and Q that P must be true (P = John committed the robbery; Q = John has 15 television sets).

John's possession of the 15 television sets makes it more likely that he committed the robbery but there may be other explanations. For example, John may be the apartment manager and may have purchased the television sets to furnish other apartments, or John may have a larcenous roommate, or John may run a television repair business from his apartment. Inductive reasoning involves "going beyond the information given" to beliefs about what is likely to be true. The general point is that people employ both inductive and deductive reasoning to arrive at beliefs and the same argument that is inductively strong or powerful may be deductively invalid.

Deductive Reasoning

In this section we review evidence that human deductive reasoning departs from what is normatively correct by showing both content and structure effects. These shortcomings will be viewed from the perspective of integrating logical and empirical truth as well as processing limitations.

Conditional Reasoning

Conditional reasoning concerns what outcomes can be expected if certain conditions are met. The if-then examples we discussed earlier are instances of conditional reasoning.

Modus Ponens and *Modus Tollens*.   The most well-known conditional argument form is referred to as **modus ponens**. It has the structure:

1. $P \rightarrow Q$
2. P
3. $\therefore Q$

As an example, let P equal "John gets B or better on the final test" and Q equal "John passes the course." We can see that it follows from the first two premises that John passes the course.

A closely related form is **modus tollens**, which has the following structure:

  1. $P \rightarrow Q$
  2. not Q
  3. $\therefore$ not P

In the above example involving John the first premise, coupled with the observation that John did not pass the course, lets us conclude that he did not get a B or better on the final test.

Now consider the following argument:

  1. If it is sunny, the picnic will be held.
  2. It is not sunny.
  3. $\therefore$ The picnic will not be held.

Although this argument form seems plausible, whether or not it is logically valid depends crucially on the meaning of "if" and in our language "if" is ambiguous. It might mean "if and only if," an interpretation known as the *biconditional* (because both $P \rightarrow Q$ and $Q \rightarrow P$), in which case the argument form would be valid. Alternatively, *if* might be given a conditional reading ($P \rightarrow Q$ only), in which case the argument is not logically valid. Conditional implication is represented by a unidirectional arrow ($\rightarrow$) and the biconditional is represented by a bidirectional arrow ($\leftrightarrow$).

The convention in logic is to assume that *if* is conditional unless the biconditional is explicitly stated. By this standard the preceding argument form is invalid and constitutes an error known as "**denying the antecedent**." (The antecedent of $P \rightarrow Q$ is P.) What the argument commits us to is the belief that if the first premise is true and it is sunny that there will be a picnic. If it is not sunny then the first premise is not relevant and any state of affairs may hold. Only in the case where *if* means both $P \rightarrow Q$ and $Q \rightarrow P$ (if and only if) would this argument's form be valid.

Unfortunately, natural language does not necessarily conform to logic and just which sense of *if* is intended often can be understood only in context. For example, the parent who says "If you pick up your toys I will read you a story" intends *if* to mean *if-and-only-if*; whereas a sports fan who says "If our quarterback is injured, then our team will lose" very likely has in mind a unidirectional inference. Given this ambiguity of *if*, it is not surprising that a fair proportion (more than 20%) of college students in reasoning tasks make the error of denying the antecedent (Marcus & Rips, 1979).

Modus ponens appears to be an intuitively correct and natural rule. College students are nearly always correct regardless of the contents of P or Q and regardless even of whether they have meaningful contents (P and Q work just fine; see, e.g., Evans, 1977). *Modus tollens* is a different story— a third or more of the time college students fail to agree that the conclusion is logically (necessarily) correct. It is not clear why *modus tollens* is so difficult. One speculation is that people often treat logical implication as reasoning from causes to effects. *Modus tollens* requires backward rather than forward reasoning and it is probably easier to reason from causes to effects than from effects to causes. The fact that college students also have considerable difficulty with affirming the consequent (incorrectly concluding from P $\rightarrow$ Q and Q that P must be true) is consistent with this suggestion. Consider again the example involving a quarterback. It is easy to imagine that an injury to a quarterback could lead to the loss of a game. Consequently, one may be tempted to conclude from the observation that the team lost that the quarterback was injured. But this conclusion does not follow as a deductive consequence.

We might also expect that *modus tollens* might be very susceptible to content effects (see Rips, 1990, for a review). Although *modus tollens* is difficult when presented abstractly, the following example seems natural enough:

    1. If the horses had been to the waterhole, we would see their tracks.
    2. We see no tracks.
    3. Therefore, the horses have not been to the waterhole.

But wait, something is not right here! Our example heavily biases the reading of *if* as the biconditional *if-and-only-if* (see also Marcus & Rips, 1979 for examples of content influencing the interpretation of the conditional). To see this, change the argument form so that we affirm the consequent:

    1. If the horses had been to the waterhole, we would see their tracks.
    2. We see their tracks.
    3. Therefore, they have been to the waterhole.

This argument seems virtually ironclad empirically, but it is not logically valid. What makes this example tricky is that when the conditional reasoning is embedded in a causal framework, whether or not there are compelling alternative explanations of Q may determine how natural it is to interpret *if* as a biconditional. Let's try modifying the example a bit beginning with *modus tollens*:

1. If the horses had been to the waterhole, then the food we left out would be gone.
2. The food we left out is still here.
3. Therefore, the horses have not been to the waterhole.

This example seems reasonable and valid. Furthermore, we would not necessarily fall for affirming the antecedent when the argument form is changed to:

1. If the horses had been to the waterhole, then the food we left out would be gone.
2. The food we left is gone.
3. Therefore, the horses have been to the waterhole.

The reason we might not fall for this argument is that we could think of alternative reasons why the food might be gone. For example, other animals may have taken it.

Note that this discussion of content has nothing to do with the validity of the *modus tollens* argument form. These examples do serve to illustrate some of the difficulties associated with keeping argument contents distinct from argument form, especially when the conditional, *if*, is itself somewhat ambiguous. Although the if-then argument form is not to be equated with cause-effect relations, it appears that cause-effect relations influence whether or not *if* is interpreted as a biconditional and the difficulty of *modus tollens*.

Conditional Reasoning in Hypothesis Testing: The Selection Task.   Consider the following example from Wason (see Wason & Johnson-Laird, 1972):

You are given the four cards:

$$\boxed{E} \qquad \boxed{F} \qquad \boxed{4} \qquad \boxed{7}$$

each of which has a letter on one side and a number on the other side. The question is which cards you should select to test the hypothesis that "If a card has a vowel on one side, it has an even number on the other side."

Many people make the error of selecting E and 4 rather than E and 7. E is a reasonable choice because if there is an odd number on the other side, the hypothesis would be falsified. The 4 card combined with a vowel would be consistent with the hypothesis but combined with a consonant would be irrelevant to it. Note that a vowel on the other side of the 7 card would disprove the hypothesis. This error of choosing the 4 card and neglecting the 7 card cannot be explained as a bias for interpreting *if* as a biconditional because in that case all four cards would be relevant to the hypothesis. Selecting E is analogous to evaluating a *modus ponens* argument whereas selecting 7 (which people do not commonly do) is analogous to evaluating a *modus tollens* argument.

Why do people fail on the Wason selection task? One idea is that the most natural way to link the hypothesis with the cards (or data) is to match terms in the hypothesis with states of affairs in the data (Evans, 1982). The hypothesis mentions vowels and even numbers and the most common response is to select E and 4. If the matching hypothesis is correct, then if we change the wording of the hypothesis to "If a card has a vowel on one side then it will *not* have an even number on the other side," we might expect performance to improve. Now the correct response is E and 4 and both vowels and even numbers are mentioned in the conditional. In fact, performance is considerably better on problems having the "if P, then not Q" format (Evans & Lynch, 1973; Mankelow & Evans, 1979; Wason & Evans, 1975).

Why should matching be important? In a general review of the literature Evans (1982, 1983) suggests that two factors are involved. One is simply attention. The fact that terms are mentioned in the conditional statement draws attention to them. Why? Part of the answer may be that people are sensitive to Gricean principles or maxims for communication (as we discussed in the comprehension and inference chapter) and they expect information to be relevant. If this analysis is correct, it suggests that the bias to attend to terms that are mentioned derives from the fact that most of the time information that is mentioned is relevant. A second factor suggested by Evans is that people generally find it more difficult to reason with negative statements than positive statements. For example, people apparently do not spontaneously convert "not an even number" into "odd number" or else the matching hypothesis would not have been supported in the Evans (1982) study. In short, the matching hypothesis appears to be at least part of the story about why the four-card problem is so hard.

The Wason and Johnson-Laird task is also very susceptible to content effects, though their interpretation is not always clear. Johnson-Laird, Legrenzi, and Legrenzi (1972) showed English adults a drawing of sealed and opened envelopes stamped with either a 4d or a 5d postage stamp (the d stands for penny) in a format analogous to the E, F, 4, 7 problem. Participants were asked which of the envelopes should be examined to test the rule "If a letter is sealed, then it has a 5d stamp on it." Their subjects were quite successful in figuring out that the envelope with the 4d stamp (in which the sealing is not visible) and the sealed envelope (on which the stamp is not visible) were relevant. One might think that these results show that concrete forms of the problem are in general easier than abstract versions, but this is not the case (see Griggs, 1983). Griggs and Cox (1982) replicated the Johnson-Laird et al. experiment with college students in the United States and found no differences between the envelope condition and a control condition using abstract materials. One important difference between the Griggs and Cox and the Johnson-Laird et al. experiments is that the English subjects may have been familiar with an earlier postal regulation that associated different rates with sealed and unsealed envelopes. Indeed, Golding (1981) found that English subjects over the age of 45 (who presumably remember the postal regulation) performed well on the envelope task, whereas subjects under the age of 45 (who presumably do not remember the regulation) performed no better with the envelopes than with abstract materials.

Although relevant experience may improve performance on the selection task, other evidence suggests that what is essential is that people think about the problem in terms of *permission*, *obligation*, or *authorization*. For example, people perform well when the rule is "anyone consuming Coca-Cola on these premises must be at least 100 years old" or even a completely unfamiliar rule such as "Any lengths of red wool must be at least 6 meters long," as long as permission or authorization is involved (Wason & Green, 1984). Patricia Cheng and her associates (e.g., Cheng & Holyoak, 1985; Cheng, Holyoak, Nisbett, & Oliver, 1986) have argued that conditional reasoning is organized around these sorts of **pragmatic reasoning schemas** rather than "syntactic logical rules." That is, reasoning skills are not completely abstract forms independent of contents. Semantic contents, such as permission, are said to "trigger" particular reasoning schemas. Rips (1990) does not agree with the idea that pragmatic reasoning schemas are less abstract than formal rule systems; he notes that a particular form of logic, known as modal logic, involves terms like obligation and permission. Although it is clear that contents yield powerful effects, the underlying basis for these effects remains controversial (see, for example, Cosmides, 1989; Cheng & Holyoak, 1989; Klaczynski, Gelfund, & Reese, 1989 for further arguments and counterarguments).

One final factor influencing performance in the selection task is whether or not the hypothesis or rule encourages a unified representation rather than a disjoint representation. In the standard version of the task the relevant sources of information are on opposite sides of the cards, which Wason and Green (1984) argue should lead to disjoint representation. They offer the following rule as an example that encourages a unified representation: "If the figure on the card is a triangle then it has been colored red." In fact, the representation is so unified that it's not clear how one could present shapes without revealing their colors. Wason and Green (1984) got around this problem by describing possible colors and shapes and asking their subjects to imagine the stimuli. An example of a rule that should lead to a disjoint representation would be, "All the triangles have a red patch above them" or the alternative wording, "All of the cards which have a triangle on one half are red on the other half." They found that about 80% of their subjects solved the problem for the description that should lead to a unified representation compared with about 40% for problems that should lead to a disjoint representation.

Many of these phenomena may seem to you akin to Russian dolls; for each explanation it seems that there is a deeper explanation inside it. Does a unified representation have anything to do with the matching hypothesis described by Evans? Are pragmatic reasoning schemas special or are they just effective because they lead to unified representations? What is clear is that conditional reasoning tasks are underspecified in the sense that research participants bring a variety of types of knowledge to bear on them, ranging from conversational rules, to causal reasoning, to specific, relevant prior experiences.

Some researchers have taken these observations on content effects to mean that people have limited (or no) abstract reasoning abilities. Our reading of this literature is that content and logical form interact in terms of the way in which abstract forms are linked to or instantiated in particular contents. This observation does not, however, mean that people cannot reason abstractly. For example, people are perfectly capable of reasoning from A $\rightarrow$ B and B $\rightarrow$ C that A $\rightarrow$ C. But when this reasoning structure is embedded in content, there are challenging issues concerning how one decides that an A, B, C, or an implication has been instantiated and whether the B in the first term is really equivalent to the B in the second term (recall that in the example involving J. Edgar Hoover the terms were not equivalent when they were examined more closely). In short, a central question is not so much whether people use reasoning schemas but how people go from specific contents to instantiate conditions for abstract rules. That is, the terms in rules need to be linked with real world contents when we reason about events in our environment.

So far we have ignored any potential limitations on people's ability to draw out all the relevant implications or possibilities associated with a set of assertions. This becomes an important issue in the domain of reasoning with syllogisms, to which we now turn.

Categorical Syllogisms

The Greek philosopher Aristotle is credited with being the first to develop formal logic and a good part of his studies was directed at syllogistic reasoning. Perhaps the most famous and well-known **categorical syllogism** is:

Premise 1: All men are mortal.

Premise 2: Socrates is a man.

Conclusion: Therefore, Socrates is mortal.

The following syllogism also seems very straightforward:

Premise 1: All As are Bs.

Premise 2: All Bs are Cs.

Conclusion: All As are Cs.

Now consider the following syllogism:

Premise 1: Some As are Bs.

Premise 2: Some Bs are Cs.

Conclusion: Some As are Cs.

Many people find this syllogism compelling but it is easy to see that the conclusion does not logically follow: let A be men, B be psychologists, and C be women. In this section we first review evidence on human success and failure with categorical syllogisms and then try to integrate these perspectives and relate them to the overall themes of this book.

Some Errors.   Woodworth and Sells (1935) suggested that syllogistic reasoning is susceptible to an **atmosphere effect**. The idea is that people are prone to accept arguments as valid if the quantifiers (e.g., some, all, no) in the premises and in the conclusions agree with each other. In the case of all As are Bs, all Bs are Cs, therefore all As are Cs the conclusion is correct but, as we have seen, it is not correct for the quantifier *some*. Nor is the argument structure valid for the quantifier *no*, as in:

> No As are Bs.
>
> No Bs are Cs.
>
> ∴No As are Cs.

If it is not obvious why this argument is invalid, then let A be women, B be robots, and C be ballerinas.

Another suggestion is that people often "convert" or reinterpret one of the premises (Chapman & Chapman, 1959), the **conversion hypothesis**. For example, "all As are Bs" may be converted to include the assumption that all Bs are As (which is obviously not true—let A be airline pilots and B be people). Conversion would lead to errors on arguments like:

> All As are Bs.
>
> Some Cs are Bs.
>
> ∴Some Cs are As.

which is not valid because the Cs that are Bs might not be As (try letting A be ocean liners, B be vehicles, and C be toys).

A third type of error consists of content or *belief-bias* effects on judgments. Markovits and Nantel (1989), for example, found that people were more likely to agree that:

> All things that have motors need oil.
>
> Automobiles need oil.
>
> Therefore, automobiles have motors.

is a valid argument than that the following is a valid argument:

> All things that have a motor need oil.
>
> Opprobines need oil.
>
> Therefore, opprobines have motors.

Neither argument structure is valid, but in the former case the conclusion is empirically (but not logically) true.

The errors discussed so far can be described as attributable to superficial processing (the atmosphere effects), comprehension problems (the conversion hypothesis), or to the intrusion of prior beliefs. Other errors and biases may be more intrinsic to the process of reasoning.

For the three-term argument structures being discussed in this chapter there are a large set of conclusions that could be, but are not, drawn. For example, it follows from all As are Bs, and all Bs are Cs that some As are Bs, some Bs are As, some Bs are Cs, some Cs are Bs, some As are Cs and some Cs are As, but the only conclusion people typically give is that all As are Cs. A complete theory of human deductive reasoning ought to be able to account for which conclusions are drawn and which aren't.

One bias in formulating conclusions is referred to as the **figural effect** (Johnson-Laird, 1983). In illustration, consider the following premises and ask yourself what conclusion follows:

Some artists are beekeepers.

All of the beekeepers are chemists.

Two equally valid conclusions are "some of the artists are chemists" and "some of the chemists are artists" but it is very likely that you drew the first conclusion rather than the second. Furthermore, this bias does not seem to depend on the order in which the premises are given. Rather, it appears that it is more natural to go from the subject of a premise to the predicate of another premise in formulating a conclusion than vice versa.

Figural effects can also lead to errors. Consider the following, more difficult argument structure:

All of the beekeepers are artists.

None of the chemists are beekeepers.

What conclusion follows from these premises? Almost no one arrives at the valid conclusion "Some of the artists are not chemists." The artists that are not chemists are the artists who are beekeepers. It is not necessarily true that "some of the chemists are not artists." All of the chemists may be artists but consist exclusively of artists who are not beekeepers. Again it appears that the figural effect is operating. The premises have the form of

B - A

C - B

and the invalid conclusion takes the form C - A. The valid conclusion A - C runs in the opposite direction of the figural effect. In brief, figural effects are quite powerful.

Processing Limitations. Reasoning is highly subject to processing limitations. As we noted at the beginning of this book, checking the internal consistency of only a modest set of beliefs presents enormous computational problems simply because there are so many possibilities to be considered. Another form of processing limitation involves failure to consider all the possible ways in which a premise may be realized or instantiated (Johnson-Laird, 1983; Erickson, 1974; Harmon, 1986; Newell, 1981). One example of a theory that incorporates processing limitations is Phillip Johnson-Laird's mental models theory. The general idea is that people reason by constructing mental representations or *mental models* corresponding to the premises and then use these models to reason about possible conclusions. According to this view, reasoning relies on concrete instantiation of possibilities rather than the abstract application of rules.

Following Johnson-Laird's example, we begin with a simple argument structure:

All artists are beekeepers.

All beekeepers are chemists.

The first premise is represented by setting up some mental tokens of actors as:

artist = beekeeper

artist = beekeeper

artist = beekeeper

(beekeeper)

(beekeeper)

The equals sign indicates that there is an "actor" who is both an artist and a beekeeper. The parentheses around the fourth and fifth tokens are designed to indicate that there may be beekeepers who are not artists. Now we can add in the effect of the second premise as:

artist = beekeeper = chemist

artist = beekeeper = chemist

artist = beekeeper = chemist

(beekeeper) = (chemist)

(beekeeper) = (chemist)

(chemist)

The parentheses around the final three tokens of chemist indicate that if there are additional beekeepers they must be chemists and that there may be chemists who are neither beekeepers nor artists.

Now if one is asked whether the conclusion that all artists are chemists is valid, one could inspect the mental model and verify that it is true (because all tokens for artists have a corresponding token for chemists linked to them). One could also verify other conclusions such as that some of the chemists are artists. Next let's try a slightly more complicated example:

No authors are burglars.

Some chefs are burglars.

The first premise can be represented as

author

author

_____

burglar

burglar

where the line means that the set of authors and the set of burglars do not overlap (are disjoint). Now we add the second premise to get:

author

author

_____

burglar

burglar = chef

(burglar) (chef)

From this model one would judge the conclusion that none of the authors are chefs to be valid or that none of the chefs are authors (as did a fair proportion of subjects in the Johnson-Laird & Steedman, 1978 studies). But there is another way to represent the second premise:

author

author = (chef)

_____

burglar

burglar = chef

(burglar) (chef)

This alternative model is also consistent with the premises but it invalidates the previous conclusions that none of the authors are chefs and that none of the chefs are authors.

There is even a third possibility:

author = (chef)

author = (chef)

_____

burglar

burglar = chef

(burglar) (chef)

This third model shows that even the conclusion that some of the authors are not chefs is not valid! A conclusion that survives all three models is, "Some of the chefs are not authors." Johnson-Laird and his associates (e.g., Johnson-Laird, Bryne, & Tabossi, 1989) have found that the difficulty of reasoning tasks is highly correlated with the number of different models that must be constructed to establish a conclusion as valid.

The mental models approach to reasoning has been applied mainly to syllogisms. Recently, however, it has been extended to conditional reasoning (Johnson-Laird, Bryne, & Schaeken, 1990; Johnson-Laird & Bryne, in press). Content effects, for example, may arise either indirectly through memory limitations (meaningful materials are easier to remember) or directly in terms of influencing how the mental models are explicitly set up (see also Oakhill & Johnson-Laird, 1985). Overall, the mental models approach has proven fairly successful.

One advantage of the mental models framework is that individual differences in reasoning ability may be understood in terms of differences in the number of different models that are constructed on problems that require multiple models. Galotti, Baron, and Sabini (1986) found that good reasoners did construct more alternative models than less successful reasoners. They also report, however, that some participants, especially experts, reported applying abstract rules. One possibility is that after a certain amount of practice with a particular mental model, people may not go through all the steps but rather directly retrieve the conclusion. This might provide a transition from mental models to rules.

Do People Have Abstract Reasoning Structures or Rules?

One reason that there has been such a fuss about whether people can reason abstractly is that analyses of other aspects of higher cognition often require an underlying abstract system for deduction that includes rules such as *modus ponens* (Rips, 1988). Research conducted from this perspective focuses on correct reasoning and treats errors and limitations in reasoning as secondary (see, e.g., Henle, 1962).

Johnson-Laird has offered mental models as an alternative to abstract reasoning rules. Lance Rips has argued, however, that mental models presuppose deduction principles in order to set up models in accordance with the premises and to interpret and draw conclusions from them (Rips, 1986). This would seem to imply that mental models represent an instantiation of a deductive reasoning system rather than an alternative to it. The crucial issue, however, is the status of rules. Lance Rips has proposed a reasoning model in which formal rules of inference are directly represented. The mental models approach uses procedures for constructing models that evaluate the validity of arguments but do not explicitly represent rules.

Which view is correct? We know that under certain circumstances people can use rules directly—logicians may use abstract rules for complex problems, and the rest of us may use them for simple problems. But there is also considerable support for the idea that people may reason by trying to think of concrete examples or the sort of mental tokening suggested by the mental models approach. Just which strategy is used may vary across reasoning tasks. We can also repeat our earlier speculation: It may be most natural to reason using examples or mental tokens but with repeated experience with a particular argument form or with expertise, one may convert or "compile" these reasoning procedures into directly represented rules. We hasten to add that repeating a speculation should not enhance its credibility—prominent researchers in the area of reasoning might well argue that abstract rules are fundamental and mental models secondary.

Another perspective on errors in deductive reasoning grows out of the observation that we employ reasoning to think about events in our world. This basic fact provides a rationale for understanding observations pointing to the conclusion that people may be only partially successful in separating logical validity from empirical truth. As Rips (1990) notes, people may use empirical truth as a quick check on the accuracy of their reasoning. Normally, logical validity and empirical truth would tend to be highly correlated. For example, John may reason that Jill is either in the kitchen or in the dining room, note that she is not in the kitchen, and conclude that she is in the dining room. When he then walks into the dining room and sees her, his conclusion receives empirical support and reinforces his reasoning.

We will close this discussion with an analogy. Normally the weight of objects in our experience is highly correlated with their size. Furthermore, studies of weight judgment show that people are susceptible to a size-weight illusion such that our judgments of weight are influenced by size. (This illusion can be reduced or eliminated by giving people experience with objects where size and weight are not correlated; Anderson, 1970.) No one takes the size-weight illusion as proving that people cannot distinguish between size and weight. Rather, it is the case that the illusion normally serves people well, as it allows them to anticipate the weight of objects before (or without) lifting them. The same situation may hold for logical and empirical truth. Our experience may be such that it is advantageous to exploit the correlation between logical and empirical truth. But this need not mean that people are incapable of separating the way things are in the world from how we reason about them.

Inductive Reasoning

Abstractly speaking, inductive reasoning is concerned with how observations and beliefs support other beliefs. In certain respects inductive reasoning runs in the opposite direction of deductive reasoning. In illustration, the argument structure for inductive reasoning seems to be something like the following:

1. $P \rightarrow Q$
2. Q
3. $\therefore P$ is more likely

P can be a set of beliefs or a theory linked to certain expectations (Q) and if these expectations are satisfied (Q occurs), then we are more confident of P. For example, P may be the belief that all dogs bark and Q the observations of a particular dog barking. Or P may be Einstein's theory of relativity and Q may be the outcome of an experiment designed to test his theory. Inductive reasoning is inherently uncertain: One may always run into a variety of dog that does not bark and some other prediction of Einstein's theory might turn out to be incorrect. We have already discussed inductive reasoning associated with concepts and categories in Chapter 12. In what follows we focus more directly on some conceptual and computational problems associated with the use of inductive reasoning.

Argument Structure

Suppose that some thinker X has the belief that "Zebras are striped and the moon is made of cheese." Now suppose that X observes a zebra and notes that it is striped. By our definition of inductive reasoning, this observation should increase X's belief that zebras are striped and the moon is made of cheese. But this argument seems a bit strange in that zebras don't seem to have much to do with the composition of the moon.

Let's take another example, this time from Goodman (1955). Let grue be the color of an object at time t if and only if the object is green and t is before the beginning of the year 2000 or the object is blue and t is on or after the beginning of 2000. Now consider the following pair of arguments:

1. All emeralds so far observed have been green; therefore, the first emerald to be observed after the beginning of 2000 will be green.
2. All emeralds so far observed have been grue; therefore, the first emerald to be observed after the beginning of 2000 will be grue.

Argument 1 predicts that the first emerald observed after the year 2000 will be green whereas argument 2 predicts that it will be grue (that is, blue). People find the first argument more compelling than the second, yet the abstract structure of the arguments is the same (Sternberg, 1982; see also Osherson, Smith, & Shafir, 1986). It seems that inductive strength depends on more than the argument structure per se.

One could argue that one should favor the concept green over the concept grue because the concept green is more simple than the concept grue. But as Goodman (1955) notes, simplicity is relative to a descriptive system. Suppose we have as our basic concepts grue and the concept bleen, which applies if t is before the year 2000 and an object is blue or if t is after the year 2000 and the object is green. Relative to this system, the concept green will be defined as an object that is grue before the year 2000 and bleen after the year 2000, a fairly complex concept!

Again the point is that argument structure is an incomplete measure of inductive power. Whether or not a concept seems natural (green vs. grue) is tied to our theories about categories, objects and their properties. For example, there is nothing odd about the concept of *leaf* that specifies that they be green in the summer and brown (or yellow or red or purple for that matter) in the fall (see Tetewsky & Sternberg, 1986). Similarly, there is clear evidence that people's certainty about an inductive argument depends crucially on the properties and categories in question. For example, people are more confident that having a particular color will be true of all examples of a species than they are that having a particular weight will be true of all examples of that species (Nisbett, Krantz, Jepson, & Kunda, 1983). Perceived variability will presumably vary with specific contents; one-pound boxes of chocolate vary more in color than in weight whereas bags of oranges would vary more in weight than in color.

Inductive Strength, Similarity, and Analogy

Similarity is a rough and ready guide to inductive possibilities. The general argument form might be something like this:

> Object 1 has properties A and B.
>
> Object 2 has properties A, B, and also C.
>
> Therefore, it is likely that object 1 also has property C.

In general, the more properties that object 1 and object 2 share, the more likely it is that some new property (C in the above example) will be shared. Similarity-based induction is anything but ironclad. For example, suppose we have two cars that are alike in many ways (e.g., same style, same manufacturer, etc.). We still might not be confident that if one car is red, the other car is also red.

Recent research on analogy suggests that what is crucial in analogical reasoning is not overall similarity but rather relational or structural similarity (Gentner, 1983). Relational similarity is to be contrasted with attributional similarity. Roughly the distinction is as follows: Attributes are predicates or statements taking one argument (e.g., x is red, x is large) whereas relations are predicates taking two or more arguments (e.g., x collides with y, x is larger than y). Overall similarity is similarity in terms of both attributes and relations.

Early work on analogy assumed that the question of "what goes with what" in an analogy depends on overall similarity (see, e.g., Winston, 1980). Dedre Gentner has argued, however, that relational similarity has a special status in analogical reasoning. To illustrate her theory, consider the analogy "an atom is like the solar system" shown in Figure 14.1. The central question is what is analogous to what; that is, how are analogies interpreted? Does the fact that the sun is yellow lead us to assume that some part of an atom is yellow, and if so, which part?

According to Gentner's structure-mapping theory, interpreting an analogy involves the following steps:

1. Setting up correspondences between the two domains.
2. Discarding attributes (e.g., yellow, hot, and massive for sun).
3. Mapping relations (e.g., more massive than, revolves around) from the base domain (solar system) onto the target domain (atom).
4. Observing **systematicity** by discarding isolated relations such as *hotter than* and keeping systems of relations that are governed by higher order relations (relations on relations), which can themselves be mapped.

These steps lead to a mapping from the solar system onto the atom shown in the bottom of Figure 14.1. Neither the fact that the sun is hotter than planets or that it is yellow enters into the analogy. The structure-mapping principle operates to give special weight to systems of relations that often involve causal relations. To maximize the likelihood of an analogy picking out relevant structures, causal connections are favored over connectives like *and*. Gentner's structure-mapping theory has been implemented as a computer program and has received a fair amount of empirical support (Gentner, 1989; Falkenhainer, Forbus, & Gentner, 1990). For example, people's judgments about the soundness of analogies is well predicted by relational similarity (Gentner & Landers, 1985; Rattermann & Gentner, 1987; Gentner, 1989). Although there are differences between alternative theories of analogy, there appears to be a consensus that relational structure is at the core of interpreting analogies (see, e.g., Holyoak & Thagard, 1989). In short, work on reasoning by analogy suggests that inductions are guided by systems of relations rather than simply by number of similarities

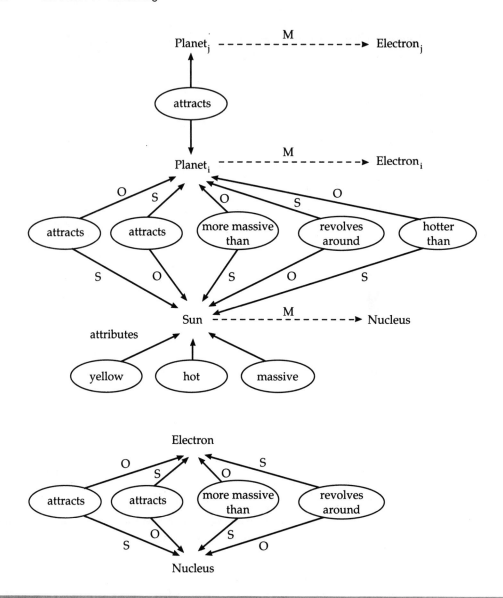

Figure 14.1 Partial depiction of the analogy between solar system and hydrogen atom, showing a person's presumed initial knowledge of the solar system and the mapping of that knowledge to the atom. *Source*: Gentner, D., 1983.

or overall similarity. This bias tends to serve people well in that it should direct people toward underlying causal relations.

Hypothesis Testing and Scientific Reasoning

An important aspect of reasoning is the evaluation of hypotheses. A number of procedures have been used to study how people construct and test hypotheses. In one very simple but intriguing procedure, Wason (1960) told subjects that the sequence of 2, 4, 6 followed a rule and that their task was to discover this rule. The participants were allowed to generate sequences of three numbers and for any sequence they would be told whether or not the example followed the rule. Very loosely, the situation is like a scientist trying to determine the "correct theory," where generating a sequence is like conducting an experiment.

A common result was that a participant would hypothesize that the rule was "number ascending by 2" and provide test sequences such as 1, 3, 5 or 101, 103, 105, or -80, -78, -76 or 6.5, 8.5, 10.5. For each such sequence the answer would be that it follows the rule and often a participant would state with high confidence that he or she had discovered the rule. Note, however, that these test sequences all match the hypothesized rule. This ignores the procedure of producing a sequence inconsistent with the rule. For example, if a participant generated the sequence 10, 11, 14 and was told that it also followed the experimenter's rule, the hypothesis "numbers ascending by 2" would have to be rejected. Actually the rule that Wason had in mind was "any ascending sequence," which many participants failed to discover. The tendency to construct tests that are consistent with our hypothesis has been referred to as **confirmation bias**.

Other studies have used more realistic simulated research environments. For example, Mynatt, Doherty, and Tweney (1977) asked subjects to try to account for the motion of a particle that was "fired" from a position on a computer screen. The displays could be quite complex and featured a variety of objects occupying a variety of positions. The rule was that the particle stopped moving when it was near any gray figure (until fired again). Subjects were given an initial display and thereafter allowed to choose one display out of two to test their hypotheses. Again a tendency was observed for subjects to select tests that were consistent with their hypotheses rather than those that might falsify it. This is further evidence of a confirmation bias.

An interesting perspective on confirmation bias is provided by Klayman and Ha (1987). They argue that confirmation bias should be thought of as a **positive test strategy** and that it can be a very good heuristic under many realistic conditions. Testing cases that are expected to show some properties of interest (the positive test strategy) is only clearly bad when the current hypothesis is a subset or special case of the correct hypothesis. In realistic circumstances one would expect that hypotheses would either partially overlap with the correct state of affairs or not overlap at all. In both of these cases the positive test strategy would provide useful information. The general point is that what looks like a poor strategy in a particular context may nonetheless be an effective strategy in broader contexts.

One should not be surprised that people do not consistently discover the "correct" rule. As Klayman (1988) notes, these simulated research environments are underconstrained in that any limited set of experiments will be consistent with an unlimited set of hypotheses. The fact that some people do succeed is probably testimony to the fact that what experimenters consider to be reasonable rules and what participants find natural overlap to some extent. These simulated research environments are very useful in bringing out the natural preferences or biases people have in formulating and testing hypotheses (see also Tweney, Doherty, & Mynatt, 1981; Klayman, 1984, 1988).

One might also wonder how and whether reasoning strategies are acquired. Given work by Susan Carey, Frank Keil, and others which suggests that children's conceptual knowledge is organized by theories (as discussed in Chapter 12) it makes sense to ask how good children are as intuitive scientists. It appears that young children may not be very good at testing hypotheses or at linking them to evidence (Kuhn, 1989). The sort of theory testing that we associate with scientific theories is slow to develop.

Summary

We have only been able to sample from the literature on reasoning. And the pool on which our sample is based is itself probably not very representative of the variety of situations in which human reasoning is employed. There is far more to deductive reasoning than *modus ponens* and categorical syllogisms. For example, a major subfield in artificial intelligence is concerned with proving theorems by means of deductive logic. Nonetheless, our review does bring out some of the central issues in reasoning.

Deductive reasoning is embedded in the sense that it is applied to objects and events in the world. It is one thing to know that if P implies Q and that P is true then Q must be true but quite another to know what statements (or events) constitute a P and a Q and that the P in the first premise is identical to P in the second premise.

Although researchers find it useful and important to distinguish between inductive and deductive reasoning, bear in mind that reasoning is embedded in contexts where it is in the service of goals. Appropriate reasoning is reasoning that provides accurate answers regardless of whether the road to these truths is logical necessity, procedures operating on models, or plausible conjecture. Therefore, we should not be surprised at many of the errors made in deductive reasoning tasks because the same argument (e.g., affirming the consequent) that is logically invalid can be a powerful inductive reasoning strategy.

Although philosophers and scientists have studied inductive reasoning for many centuries, it is only recently that cognitive psychologists have begun systematic research on the psychology of inductive reasoning. We mentioned earlier in this book that the hardest thing to get a computer to do is not to perform complex calculations but rather to exhibit common sense. Only very recently have researchers attempted to program plausible (inductive) reasoning into a computer program (see, e.g., Collins & Michalski, 1989) or to detail the variety of reasoning strategies that people employ. As just one example Gentner and Collins (1981) observed that people often use a lack-of-knowledge inference rule to answer questions like "Is rice a major crop in Florida?" That is, people often suggest that this answer is "no" because if rice were a major crop in Florida they probably would have heard about it. What is most impressive to us is the resourcefulness that people use in integrating logic and strategies to come up with plausible answers about their world.

Key Terms

affirming the consequent
atmosphere effect
categorical syllogism
confirmation bias
conversion hypothesis
deductive reasoning
denying the antecedent
figural effect

inductive reasoning
modus ponens
modus tollens
positive test strategy
pragmatic reasoning schemas
systematicity
valid argument

Recommended Readings

We admit to a modest prejudice. Prior to doing our review of this area we thought that work on reasoning was a bit dry, if not dull. But we were very wrong!

A central issue with respect to understanding the human mind concerns the extent to which logical truth and empirical truth can be separated. Do people have abstract rules which they use in reasoning? "Yes," according to Rips (1988, 1990) and "No," according to the mental models approach associated with Johnson-Laird (1983; see also Johnson-Laird and Bryne, in press). The pragmatic reasoning schemas view of Cheng and Holyoak (1985, 1989) is that rules may be tied to fairly abstract social schemas, whereas Cosmides (1989) argues strongly in favor of content-specific reasoning abilities. A firsthand reading of the above paper will serve to convey some of the controversy and excitement linked with these distinct points of view.

Less drama but equal interest attaches to studies of inductive reasoning. Goodman's (1955) paper is a classic and the psychological implications of Goodman's paper are examined by Sternberg (1982) and Tetewsky and Sternberg (1986). For contributions from analogy, see the recent papers by Gentner (1989) and Holyoak and Thagard (1989). Finally, psychologists are, by necessity, interested in scientific reasoning. The Tweney et al. (1981) book provides a good introduction to research on scientific reasoning and the Klayman (1988) and Klayman and Ha (1987) papers are important additions. Kuhn (1989) looks at scientific reasoning from a developmental point of view.

15

PROBLEM SOLVING

Chapter Outline

The biggest problem in the world

Could have been solved when it was small.

—*Witter Bynner,* "The Way of Life According to Laotzu"

Introduction

Problems, Problems, Problems

Problem solving occurs throughout life. A young child may be trying to figure out how to stack blocks to make a tower that does not topple over. An older child may be trying to solve a mathematical word problem. Someone may be attempting to decide on an anniversary gift. An architect may be designing a house or a mathematician attempting to prove a theorem. Despite the diversity of these problems, the ways people go about solving them show a number of common characteristics. This chapter examines these commonalities and what they tell us about human thought and intelligence.

What Is a Problem?

Before proceeding to a discussion of how people solve problems, it is important to first define what is meant by a problem. For our purposes, we can consider a person to have a problem when he or she wishes to attain some goal for which no simple, direct means is known. To elaborate, we consider a **problem** to have four aspects: goal, givens, means of transforming conditions, and obstacles. The *goal* is some state of knowledge toward which the problem solving is directed and for which at least some criterion can be applied to assess whether the problem has been solved. Using some of the examples above, the goal might be to have a stack of blocks that does not topple or to have a house properly designed. The *givens* include the objects, conditions, and constraints that are provided with the problem, either explicitly or implicitly. A mathematical word problem explicitly provides the objects and initial conditions, while the specifications for a house contain only some conditions to which the architect may add.

Problems need to have some *means of transforming conditions*, of changing the initial states. This requirement excludes those situations for which no problem solving may be attempted. In the examples above, we assume that the older child can understand the words in the word problem and has at least some relevant mathematical knowledge that might be applied, and that the mathematician and architect have some relevant knowledge for transforming the initial conditions. Finally, problems have some *obstacles*. A goal that can be attained simply in one single known step is not usually considered to be a problem. For example, if you were asked the name of your mother and could immediately retrieve her name, you have attained the goal, but we exclude such cases from our discussion of problem solving. Thus, if the math student is given exactly the same word problem two times in a row and gives the answer to the second by remembering the exact answer to the first, problem solving is not involved. We do not want to exclude any problems for which memory use is important, only those for which the exact solution may be retrieved in a single step.

In short, problem solving is said to be taking place if a person is (1) trying to attain a goal, (2) starting from some set of conditions, (3) with some means of transforming these conditions, but (4) no immediately available knowledge of a solution.

Types of Problems

Despite the idea that problems have common aspects, figuring out how to fix a flat bicycle tire seems very different from figuring out how to have an interesting career. Clearly, these two problems have many differences, such as their importance to the person, their time scale, and their difficulty. Just because two problems are different, however, does not mean that the problem solving is different in important ways. Rather, a crucial activity in understanding problem solving is to analyze which problem differences are important and which ones are not.

In this section we consider one distinction that has had considerable influence in the field, that drawn between well-defined problems and ill-defined problems (Reitman, 1965). **Well-defined problems** have completely specified initial conditions, goals, and means of transforming conditions. Many games and puzzles are well defined (though some tricky puzzles appear to be well defined, but are not). For example, a maze puzzle is usually well defined. The initial condition is the starting point. The goal is some well-specified ending point, such as the middle of the maze which has a bench to sit on. Thus, you will know when you have attained the goal. Finally, the means of transforming the conditions are by walking on any path in the maze. **Ill-defined problems** are ones in which some aspects are not completely specified. The problem of having an interesting career is clearly ill defined. Even if you knew how to tell whether you would have an interesting career, you wouldn't know how to transform the current situation to achieve this goal. Problems may differ on how well defined (or ill defined) they are, so it is best to consider this distinction as a continuum rather than a dichotomy.

Much of the early work on problem solving studied well-defined problems. However, this focus does not mean work on problem solving is irrelevant to how people solve ill-defined problems. For example, Voss and his colleagues (see Voss & Post, 1988 for an overview) have examined how people solve social science questions such as how to improve crop productivity in the Soviet Union (taking the role of the Russian Minister of Agriculture). Although this is a very ill-defined problem, the results show many of the same processes that were discovered and analyzed in the research on well-defined problems. Simon (1973) has argued that a crucial part of problem solving is the changing of ill-defined problems into well-defined problems.

Methods for Studying Problem Solving

Before proceeding to a discussion of problem-solving results, it is useful to consider the methods used in problem-solving research. Many of the studies use measures of accuracy and/or latency (time to complete the problem). Unlike other research areas, however, the latency can be on the order of many seconds or even many minutes. If our goal is to try to understand the cognitive processes associated with problem solving, obtaining a single measure for the whole problem-solving episode is problem. The number of possible explanations that could lead to the same accuracy level or latency is quite large. To reduce the number of possibilities, data are often obtained throughout the process of problem solving. Three methods that are often used in problem-solving research are (1) intermediate products, (2) verbal protocols, and (3) computer simulations.

Intermediate Products.   Intermediate products simply mean that instead of recording only the answer to the problem, we observe some of the work the subject does in getting the answer. If we are interested in how people solve puzzles, we would collect information about the various moves they make in getting to the goal. If we are interested in mathematical problem solving, we would collect and analyze the equations and other information the subject writes down in the course of problem solving. These intermediate products provide much finer constraints on possible explanations.

Verbal Protocols.   The second method often used in problem-solving research is a **verbal protocol**. Although there are a number of possible ways to collect such data, the most common is to ask the subjects to "think aloud" as they go about solving the problems. That is, they are asked to say whatever they are thinking about, but not to embellish or explain it for the experimenter's benefit. The idea behind this measure is straightforward: People's thoughts provide further information about the course of their problem solving.

As you might suspect, not all verbal protocols provide useful information. For example, one of the authors was watching "Sesame Street" with his preschool daughter when the addition problem of 5 + 3 was presented. She closed her eyes, paused, and finally said "Eight." He was quite impressed, given that she had never counted without her fingers before, and asked her if she knew how she had done that. She replied that she did—"I used the brain." True, but not very informative. It is common for subjects to be quiet in the crucial part of the problem solving. When these quiet subjects are then prompted as to what they were thinking, they sometimes reply, "I was thinking how to solve the problem."

Despite the difficulties with collecting useful protocols, they have proven a vital source of information. Simply put, they provide information that is near impossible to gain from other current methods. Because of their usefulness, some research has also examined how to collect protocols and the validity of these protocols (see Ericsson & Simon, 1980, 1984 for a good review and theoretical framework). Some means of soliciting protocols clearly lead to distortions. For example, asking subjects to think back to how they solved a problem (a mistake made by one of the authors in the example above) or why they used a particular method requires the subjects to go beyond articulating their current thoughts. Although thinking-aloud protocols may seem intrusive, the use of such protocols usually appears to have no effect on the solution of the problem other than slowing down the performance (though see Russo, Johnson, & Stephens, 1989 for some exceptions). Verbal protocols have provided a great deal of insight into the problem-solving processes and can often be followed up by more traditional dependent measures.

Computer Simulation.   Verbal protocols may be used as direct evidence for some hypotheses or to generate new ideas that are then tested by other methods. However, a common goal in problem-solving research is to build a computer simulation that is meant to mimic the problem-solving process as revealed by the protocols.

Verbal protocols allow us to see the products of thought, not the processes that led to that thought. That is, we can see that a person thought of moving a certain piece in a puzzle or about performing a certain calculation, but we cannot see the full details of what led to considering that move or calculation. With computer simulations, researchers make hypotheses about what processes led to these products and program them. This programming has three advantages. First, it forces the researcher to be *explicit* about the processes. One cannot program that the process "finds some relevant information" but must specify how this is done and what is found. Second, it allows a check of whether the posited processes will work together at all—that is, are they *internally consistent*? One process may end up undoing the work done by another or interfering in some unexpected way. Third, the simulation allows one to see whether the posited processes are *sufficient* to lead to the protocol behavior observed. That is, when the simulation runs, does it lead to behavior similar to the protocols?

What can one say if a simulation meets all these goals? There is no way to ensure that the simulation is leading to the results for the same reason that the person is. There may be many ways to get a certain behavior, so finding one way does not *prove* that people do it that particular way. At the very least, the simulation provides one strong hypothesis that can be tested by later work. In addition, often the act of designing and experimenting with the simulation helps the researcher to understand the ideas better and see other ways of testing them.

Now that we have an idea of what a problem is and the methods used for examining problem solving, it is time to consider current conceptions of how people solve problems.

Problem Solving as Representation and Search

Introduction

Consider the problem presented in Figure 15.1. This problem, which may be familiar to some of you, is called the Tower of Hanoi problem or the three-disk problem. As you can see, there are three disks of different sizes stacked one upon the other by size on the left peg. The problem is to get the disks stacked in the same arrangement on the right peg. To make this task a little more difficult than simply picking up the three disks and putting them down on the right peg, there are two rules. First, only one disk

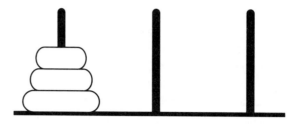

Figure 15.1   **Tower of Hanoi Problem.**
The goal is to move the tower from the left peg to the right peg, moving only one disk at a time and never putting a disk on a smaller disk.

may be moved at a time. The next disk may not be moved until the previous one has been put on a peg. Second, a disk may not be stacked on a smaller disk. Take a minute to try to solve this problem.

What do you need to do to solve this problem? First, you need to keep track of the current situation, that is, which disks are on which pegs. To start, all disks are on the left peg, but with each move, the new configuration needs to be known. Second, for the updated configuration, you need to consider what the possible moves are and how they may help you to reach the solution.

At a simplified level, these two aspects are what a theory of problem solving needs to explain. First, how are the problem and the various possible configurations represented? That is, how does a person take the (incomplete) information given in the problem, elaborate it, and represent it? Second, how is this representation operated on to allow the problem solver to consider the possible moves? Although the number of possible moves in the Tower of Hanoi problem is quite small, most problems have an exceedingly large number of possibilities. In this section, we first consider a particular view of problem solving by Newell and Simon (1972) that has been very influential in both psychology and artificial intelligence. Then, using the ideas from this view, we examine both of these questions in more detail.

The Problem Space Analysis

Starting in the late 1950s, Allen Newell, Herbert Simon, and their colleagues began a long series of investigations on problem solving in both humans and computers. Much of their theory and evidence is presented in their gigantic 1972 book, *Human Problem Solving* (for an overview, see

Simon, 1978). Newell and Simon were pioneers in the detailed use of verbal protocols and the use of computer simulations to model underlying cognitive processes. For the various tasks they described in their book they collected extensive protocols, programmed simulations, and analyzed the underlying commonalities of problem-solving behavior. They consider problem solving in terms of an information processing system (i.e., the problem solver) and the particular task environment (i.e., the problem). We briefly outline each of these influences and then describe how they interact.

Information Processing System.   Newell and Simon view problem solvers (whether people or machines) as systems that are processing information. In addition, they argue that a few main characteristics of the human information processing system influence how it may solve problems. Very briefly, these characteristics concern the processing and storage limitations of the problem solver. First, information is generally processed in a serial fashion. Second, we have a very limited-capacity short-term memory in which four to seven "chunks" (i.e., meaningful units) may be stored for immediate availability. Third, we have an essentially unlimited long-term memory in which other information may be stored, but it takes time to access and store information in long-term memory. For our present purposes, it is sufficient to realize that the problem solver is limited in how much can be kept track of and processed at any one time, so that any problem solving will be affected by these limitations.

Task Environment.   The task environment is the term Newell and Simon use for the problem. They use a different term to make it clear that they are talking about the objective entity presented, not how it is encoded by the problem solver. Any problem, before it can be solved, must be represented in memory in some way. The task environment influences problem solving by influencing this representation, which is called the problem space.

Problem Space.   The **problem space** is the problem solver's internal representation of the problem. It consists of states and operators. The **problem states** are states of knowledge, that is, what information is available to the problem solver about the current situation. A problem space has an initial state, which is the representation of the givens in the problem (as well as any additional knowledge used to elaborate the givens); a goal state, which is the representation of the desired outcome; and a number of intermediate states, which represent knowledge states that may be "passed through" in going from the initial to the goal state. The **problem operators** are the means of moving from one state to another. Because of the seriality of the information-processing system and the limitations of short-term memory, it is assumed that problem solvers focus much or all of their attention on the current state and on evaluating the possible operators that can be applied.

Before proceeding further, let us return to the Tower of Hanoi problem given in Figure 15.1 and examine its problem space, given in Figure 15.2. As we noted in discussing this problem, a problem solver needs to keep track of which disks are on which pegs. Thus, the states of knowledge in a problem space for this problem would include these facts. The initial state would include the information that all three disks are on the left peg. The goal state would include the information that all three disks are on the right peg. The intermediate states would be all possible configurations of disks on pegs that could be produced by legal moves. The operators would be these legal moves. The only permissible means of moving from one state to another would be a move in which a disk from the top of a stack is picked up and put on a peg that contains no smaller disk. Because of the small number of disks and pegs, the number of legal moves from any state is quite small. As may be seen in Figure 15.2, many states may be arrived at by multiple routes (i.e., through different sequences of moves) but there does exist a unique solution for solving this problem in the minimum number of moves (seven).

Although this is a simple problem space, it is important to keep in mind that for many problems the space can be very large. From the starting position in chess there are 20 possible first moves for the first player, then for each of these 20 possible moves for the second player. Thus the problem space would have an initial state plus 20 times 20 intermediate states (401 total states) just for the first move of each player.

Newell and Simon's framework transformed the idea of problem solving into one of representation and search. Although the representation of the problem precedes the search through this representation, until recently much of the research was concerned with how problem spaces are searched. In the next section we consider this search problem and in the succeeding section we examine how problems are represented.

Problem Solving as Search

How might people search a problem space? We first need to distinguish between an algorithm and a heuristic. An **algorithm** is a systematic procedure that is guaranteed to lead to a solution. For example, if you are trying to find your way through a maze, it is easy to get lost and find that you

Initial State

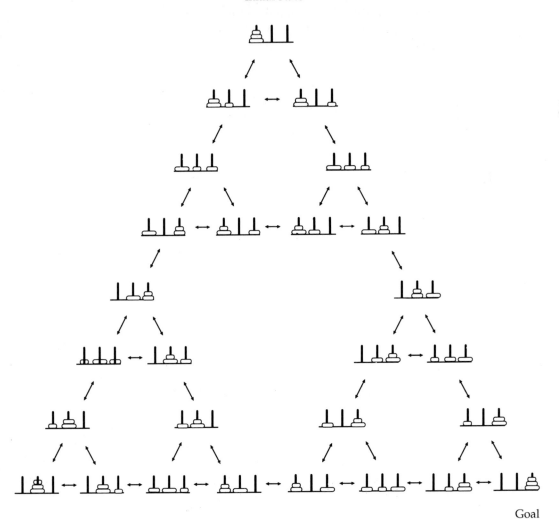

Figure 15.2   **Problem space for Tower of Hanoi. Each drawing represents a state of the problem.**
The arrows indicate that one can move from one state to the next by applying a legal operator. *Source*: Kotovsky, K., & Fallside, D. (1989).

have returned to a dead end that you have visited before. However, an algorithm exists for finding your way out of the middle of a maze (if there are no unconnected walls). Put your left hand on a wall of the maze. Then walk, making sure never to remove your hand from the wall. This method will allow you to find your way out, since in the worst case you would eventually touch all the surfaces of the maze, including the ones on the exit path. This method may also take you down many dead ends. For any problem space, assuming there is a solution, an algorithm would be to consider all the possible moves from all states until one gets to the goal state. Although algorithms guarantee solutions, they can be extremely time consuming, if not infinitely long. In the Tower of Hanoi problem space it may not be too cumbersome to examine every possible move because the number of possible operators is small. However, if one considers all the possible moves for a game of chess, the time involved is astronomical. For example, although white has only 20 opening moves, after white's third move the number of possible board positions is 7.5 million; after black's third move, 225 million (Holding, 1985).

It is not feasible to exhaustively search through very large problem spaces, so some means is needed to reduce this complexity and guide the search. In the field of problem solving, **heuristics** refer to those methods that can be used to guide the search so that a complete search is not needed. Heuristics do not guarantee a solution, but usually allow one to have a good chance at a solution with much less effort than when using an algorithm. To the extent that individual differences in problem-solving ability are due to differences in search, the claim would be that these differences are largely due to differences in the ability to select and apply heuristics. How we can overcome the complexities of search may be an important component of problem-solving skill. We first consider a simple heuristic and then examine some alternatives that overcome some of its limitations.

Simple Search.   Assume you are at some state in the problem space. How do you decide which of the possible states to proceed to next? One possibility would be to choose a state randomly. Although there are times when one has no alternative but to choose randomly, a better alternative is usually available. One reasonable heuristic might be to look at all the possible next states and choose to go on to the one that is "best," the one closest to the goal. Given that the goal of the problem is to reach the goal state, the determination of best should take this goal into account. The determination of what is best can vary, so there are a number of heuristics that could fit under this type.

One form of this heuristic is called **hill climbing**. The term refers to the following analogy. Suppose that you were blindfolded, put in some unfamiliar terrain, and told to find the highest point in the terrain without taking off your blindfold. How would you do it? A good method would be to move your foot around, feel the angle of the terrain in all directions, and then move in the direction with the steepest incline. When you get to a location in which you find that no direction leads to an incline, you stop. Using this method is reasonable given the situation. It is possible, however, that when you take off your blindfold you may see that you are on top of a hill, but there may be other higher hills elsewhere. That is, you may have ended up at a local maximum.

In a problem-solving setting, hill climbing would mean that you would examine all possible operators to see the possible next states. Each of these states would be compared to the goal state. For example, in the Tower of Hanoi problem you would make the move to the state that looks most like the goal state. The decision about how to evaluate which state is closest to the goal (called the *evaluation function*) can be quite complex in some settings because there may be multiple criteria. For instance, in chess one would need to include pieces and position strengths.

Hill climbing takes into account the goal and chooses the next state that is closest to the goal. This method requires the problem solver to consider all possible next moves, but may not lead to a solution (because of a local maximum). The main problem (but also the reason why it is a relatively easy heuristic to employ) is that one is selecting operators based only on the very local consideration of the next state.

Overcoming Problems with Simple Search.   The difficulty with simple search heuristics is that not all problems can be solved by constantly moving toward the goal. Some problems require the problem solver to move away from the goal for awhile. An example may help to illustrate this point. Imagine that you are in a restaurant in New York City and you find out that you need to go to San Francisco immediately. How would you solve this problem using the hill-climbing heuristic? At each step, you go in the direction that takes you closest to the goal. Thus, you would always move to the west. Even if we were to assume that you could get to your car (i.e., that it was parked directly west of your location in the restaurant and that no walls blocked your exit), you would end up driving all the way to San Francisco unless you happened to drive through an airport on your way. Clearly, this heuristic fails to capture the full power of human problem solving, even in this fairly simple situation. No heuristic that bases its decision on a single step would be able to solve such a problem reasonably.

The same difficulty occurs in a large number of other situations. As one further example, we may consider a case in which exploratory surgery is performed to help in diagnosis. Clearly such surgery in itself is a step away from the goal of curing the patient. Most patients feel worse, not better, immediately after such a procedure. Nonetheless, most people have no difficulty understanding that such a procedure can be crucial for attaining the goal. Sometimes we must move away from the goal in order to attain it.

To be able to solve problems of this sort, the problem solver needs to plan beyond a single move ahead. The determination of what state to go to is not based simply on how that state relates to the goal, but rather how that state fits in some plan to reach the goal state. These planning heuristics require the problem solver to break the problem down in some way and try to find solutions for these subproblems. We concentrate here on a particular heuristic called **means-ends analysis** because of its importance in current AI systems and its frequent occurrence in human problem solving (Newell & Simon, 1972).

Means-Ends Analysis.   The basic idea of means-ends analysis is quite simple. The first step is to compare the current state with the goal state and characterize this difference. Then use this difference to help decide what operator should be chosen, concentrating on removing the largest part of the difference first. This technique is then applied to the new difference (i.e., between the new state and the goal) and so on until all the differences are reduced and the goal state is reached. The elimination of some differences may produce additional differences, but these can be eliminated just as any other difference can be. The assumption is that if one eliminates the largest differences first, any differences that are produced will be relatively minor. This assumption will not always be true, but because it often will be, this heuristic has a reasonable chance of succeeding.

This presentation may be somewhat abstract, so let us return to the earlier example in which you are at a restaurant in New York City and you find out that you need to go to San Francisco immediately. How would means-ends analysis proceed? You compare your current state to your goal state and determine that the difference is over 3000 miles. You consider your operators for reducing mileage differences and determine that for such a large difference an airplane is the best operator. Given that airplanes usually leave from airports, not restaurants, you now produce the subgoal of reducing the difference between being at the restaurant and being at the airport. You might decide to reduce this difference by using a taxi, which produces a further difference to reduce between being inside the restaurant and having a taxi to get into outside. As you can see from this example, although the elimination of differences does produce other differences, by eliminating the largest difference first it will often be true that any further differences are relatively minor. Of course, it is possible that no taxi could be found or that some other difference could not be reduced. Means-ends analysis is a heuristic, so one has to realize that it may not always succeed.

Although this is a general technique, it does require that the problem solver know what operators can reduce what differences. The restaurant example was solvable only because we know what types of transportation can reduce what mileage differences. Even general techniques may not be able to help without some relevant domain knowledge. In summary, means-ends analysis is a useful planning heuristic. It is simple but quite powerful. In addition, it is a very general heuristic in that it can be applied at any level of abstraction or representation of the problem and it has been widely used in computer simulations.

Working Backward.   Another heuristic that can be helpful is **working backward** from the goal. In some situations the number of possible directions to go from the givens (i.e., operators to apply to the initial state) is quite large and it is difficult to know which to choose. Rather than approach the problem that way, it may be better to start at the goal and ask what would need to be true for the goal to be true. Then one may take each of these "prior-to-the-goal" statements and ask again what would need to be true for each of these statements to be true. The intention is to keep working backward in that way until you are able to satisfy a set of these statements by the givens. Once that set of statements is true, you know that it implies that the next set is true, which in turn implies that the next set is true, and so on up to the goal.

Consider this simple example: Prove that the product of any two consecutive whole numbers (i.e., 1, 2, 3, . . .) is even. Just for fun, try it. If you start working forward from the givens, you may represent the problem as one number, n, and the next number, $n + 1$. The product would be $n(n + 1)$. There are ways to solve this example by working forward from these givens, but they are not obvious. Let us see how one might work backward from the goal. The goal is to prove the product is even. For a number to be even, it must be represented as $2w$, where w is a whole number. Thus, w must equal the product of the two numbers divided by 2. For this to be true, one of the numbers must be divisible by 2, meaning it must be even. Now the proof will be complete if you can show that the givens imply that one of the numbers must be even. But odd and even numbers alternate, so for any two consecutive numbers, one of them must be even. The proof is complete.

The basic point is that if the number of directions from the goal is small and the number from the givens is large, you may want to consider working backward from the goal. (Wickelgren, 1974 provides a detailed elaboration of this method and advice about when it may be useful.)

Summary.   The difficulty with searching a problem space is that the number of possibilities is often far too large to try them all, so some shortcut or heuristic is needed. Although we have contrasted some different means of searching problem spaces, it is important to realize that problem solving may make use of more than one heuristic. For example, it is quite common to work both forward and backward on a given problem, setting up statements that imply the goal, then working from the givens to these statements. Even within means-ends analysis, some subgoals may be solved by using a working backward, forward, or hill-climbing heuristic. The switch between different heuristics serves to reduce the computational complexity of search.

Problem Solving as Representation

Some Examples.   Try to solve the following problem (which is taken from Wickelgren, 1974). You are given a five-by-five checkerboard, as shown in Figure 15.3. Starting with the square that has the dot, try to draw a line through all the squares of the checkerboard. You may only go horizontally

Figure 15.3   **The 5 × 5 Checkerboard Problem.**
The goal is to start at the dot and draw a line through all the squares without picking your pencil up, without passing through a square more than once, and without using diagonal lines. *Source*: Wickelgren, W. A. 1974.

or vertically, you may not lift the pencil off the paper or go outside the checkerboard, and you may pass through each square only once. Show how to do this or prove that it is impossible.

If you are like most people, and like the authors, you probably tried various solutions without success, but were not sure whether it could be solved or whether you had not yet found the solution. In fact, there is a simple means of determining that this problem cannot be solved. However, this determination requires that you concentrate not on the visible checkerboard, but rather on a more abstract representation of the board. First, note how many black and white squares there are (13 and 12, respectively). Second, note that any horizontal or vertical line passing through two squares will pass through one black square and one white square. Third, note that because you are starting on a white square, you will always have passed through at least as many white squares as black squares (i.e., the same or one more white). Fourth, note that if you are to pass through an odd number of squares (i.e., 25), you need to end on the same color that you started. Since you start on a white square, you need to end on a white square. But since there are more black squares than white squares, you cannot pass through all the black squares while only passing through each white square once. Therefore, it is not possible to accomplish this goal.

A second problem is to play a game called number scrabble (Newell & Simon, 1972). The rules are quite simple. The numbers 1 to 9 are written on separate pieces of paper and laid face up on a table. Two players alternate choosing numbers. A player wins when she has three numbers that total 15 (e.g., 9, 4, and 2). Try playing it against yourself or a friend for awhile.

This game is often difficult for people playing for the first time. There is a lot to keep track of and it is easy to fail to recognize that the opponent can win on the next draw. The game becomes much easier if a different problem representation is used. In particular, if you imagine the numbers laid out as in Figure 15.4, you will realize that this game is equivalent to tic-tac-toe. That is, while the other person plays number scrabble, you can play tic-tac-toe, for which you probably have many well-practiced strategies. You are trying to get any three numbers horizontally, vertically, or diagonally, such as 8, 3, 4, or 8, 5, 2. With this hint, the game is much easier and you should now be able to beat your friends often.

The Importance of Representation. Although much of the early work on problem solving examined how people search a problem space to find a solution to a problem, the likelihood that one solves a problem also de-

4	3	8
9	5	1
2	7	6

Figure 15.4   **Number Scrabble Square for Isomorph to Tic-tac-toe.**

pends on the way in which the problem is represented. As Simon (1978, p. 276) points out, "The relative ease of solving a problem will depend on how successful the solver has been in representing critical features of the task environment in his problem space."

The lesson we wish you to draw is that *the problem representation is crucial.* In the five-by-five checkerboard problem, the representation of the problem needs to have information about the alternating color of the board *and* information about the alternating color coverage of a horizontal or vertical line. If one represented the board as just a 25-square grid, it is unlikely that one would be able to solve the problem. (See Kaplan & Simon, 1990 for a detailed discussion as to how including these alternations in the representation can lead to insight in a different problem using a checkerboard.) In the number scrabble problem, the representation of the problem as tic-tac-toe makes the problem much, much easier.

In addition to the problems that we have presented, there are a number of other demonstrations in which a problem cannot be solved until it is thought about in the "right way." You almost surely have had the same type of experience in some course in which you have been trying to solve a problem to no avail, but found that once you looked at it in a different way (i.e., re-represented the problem), its solution was obvious. The new representation of the problem allowed you to access and apply operators that were not available from the earlier representation. Our demonstrations are rather extreme examples to make a point, but even subtler variations in representation may have a large effect on problem solving. Much current research is focused on how people generate problem spaces and how the problem space affects performance.

Why Does Representation Matter?   The representation of the problem is the problem space, which consists of states and operators. The particular representation used makes a difference because different problem spaces may contain different information. The key difficulties are incomplete information and computational complexity. First, if crucial information is missing from the states, the problem may be impossible to solve. The problem is often incomplete and information must be added from the problem solver's memory to arrive at an adequate representation. In the checkerboard problem, if information about the color of the squares is not included in your representation, you may be stuck with only being able to say that you have not come up with a solution.

Second, some representations may affect the operators by making it difficult to apply and evaluate possible moves. Keeping track of all the irrelevant information may make it too hard to process the relevant information well. The number scrabble problem is very complicated if all the numbers are represented. You constantly have to check whether you or your opponent have any triples that add to 15 or any doubles that add to a number that can be made to 15 by the addition of one available digit. These calculations and bookkeeping chores are very difficult to do accurately in your head and in a reasonable amount of time. Even if you can keep track of all the necessary information of possible operators, this bookkeeping means that less time and effort are spent on planning the search through the space or on the strategy. Again, in number scrabble, once the relation to tic-tac-toe is understood, the player may concentrate on planning ahead to get two numbers each from two triplets so that the opponent will not be able to block both. This planning is possible if you have the states and operators efficiently represented, but is much harder if you do not.

In short, some problem representations allow problem solvers to apply operators easily and traverse the problem space in an efficient way; other representations do not. Although we have stressed the importance of representation, note that a good representation is crucial but not sufficient to solve a problem. In most cases a good representation does not immediately lead to a solution, but rather allows the problem solver to proceed with an efficient search of the problem space.

Other Examples of Representation Effects.   The idea that the representation of the problem is crucial is easy to illustrate with simple puzzles; however, it is important to realize that these effects of representation extend to all of problem solving. We will see a number of examples in the section on expertise in the next chapter, but here we point out some effects of different types of representation on problem solving.

Functional fixedness.   Consider the following task, presented by Duncker (1945). Subjects were asked to attach a candle to a wall to provide light. They were given a box of tacks, candles, and matches. The tacks were too small to go through the candle. How could the subjects accomplish the goal? Try to solve this problem yourself.

The solution, illustrated in Figure 15.5, is to empty the box of tacks, tack it to the wall, melt the bottom of the candle a little and stick it to this box. The problem can be solved by using the box as a platform. Very few subjects solve this problem. It appears that most participants do not think of the box as a possible part of the solution but rather as a container for objects. **Functional fixedness** refers to this inability to use objects in ways other than they are typically used. (For later research see, for example,

(a)

(b)

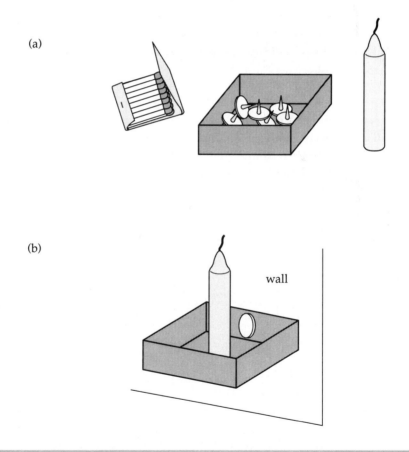

Figure 15.5   **Duncker's (1945) candle problem (panel a) and solution (panel b).**

Glucksberg & Danks, 1968; Weisberg & Sulls, 1973.) The basic argument is that if the representation of the problem does not include the box, then a solution that requires the box will never be attained.

Content Effects in Problem Solving.   The clearest examples of representation effects are cases in which two problems are formally equivalent but show large differences in difficulty. Such problems are called *problem isomorphs*. Thus, number scrabble and tic-tac-toe are problem isomorphs, though they are usually represented quite differently by most people. A large number of isomorphs have been constructed for the Tower of Hanoi problem (see Kotovsky, Hayes, & Simon, 1985 for detailed descriptions). For example, in some isomorphs three different-sized monsters have different-sized balls that they exchange according to certain rules. In fact, if one realizes that the monsters are like pegs and the balls like disks, one can see that the rules map exactly to the rules for the standard Tower of Hanoi problem. Formal equivalence is not psychological equivalence, however. The different isomorphs vary greatly in their ease of solution, with one taking 16 times as long to solve on the average as the peg-disk version. Kotovsky et al. (1985) provide evidence for a number of sources of difficulty. A primary source, as in the number scrabble problem, is the heavy processing load imposed by the operators in the more difficult problems. The point of this work is that the problem solving is very sensitive to many nonformal aspects, such as how the problem is stated, because these aspects affect how the problem is represented.

Reliance on Specific Relevant Knowledge

Introduction

Experience plays a central role in problem solving. Many of the cases we have looked at so far required the problem solver to use knowledge that was very general. That is, besides the information presented with the problem, the problem solutions mainly called on general problem-solving methods. Often we have more specific relevant knowledge that we can use to improve our problem solving. In this section we consider a very important and often used type of relevant knowledge, the solution of earlier problems.

Consider the following case that Kolodner and Kolodner (1987) adapted from the DSM-III Casebook (Case #125):

> Dr. X sees a patient who seems to show classic signs of Major Depression. She also reports that she has previously been diagnosed for Major Depres-

sion and was treated in a mental hospital with antidepressants. She was sickly as a child, has had a drinking problem, and has had a number of unexplainable physical illnesses. Dr. X concludes that she is suffering from Major Depression, Recurrent without Melancholia and treats her with antidepressants. They seem to work, but the woman comes back complaining of additional major physical disorders. Taking a further history, the doctor finds that her unexplained medical problems have been numerous. Realizing that this is important to consider, he makes a second diagnosis of Somatization Disorder.

Kolodner and Kolodner (1987) claim that if Dr. X were to see a second patient who had been diagnosed for major depression but who also had unexplained medical problems, he might first take a full history and consider somatization disorder.

This issue of how problem solving transfers to similar problems is a crucial one. Much of education is spent having students solve problems. The goal of this problem solving is not to have the student learn to solve the specific problems given but rather to have students learn to solve related problems. This section addresses the issue of how knowledge of the solution of one problem can affect the solution of a later related problem.

The Influence of Related Problems

To benefit from earlier experience with a related problem, the problem solver must first *access* some knowledge about the earlier problem and then *apply* that knowledge to the current problem. The application or analogical mapping between an earlier situation and current situation was discussed in the last chapter. Now we consider access: the process by which a problem solver may notice that the current problem is similar to one that had been solved earlier.

The Difficulty of Accessing Relevant Knowledge.   Consider the following problem, which was introduced by Duncker (1945) and used in an important set of studies by Gick and Holyoak (1980, 1983). Try to come up with solutions to the problem.

> Suppose you are a doctor faced with a patient who has a malignant tumor in his stomach. It is impossible to operate on the patient, but unless the tumor is destroyed the patient will die. There is a kind of ray that can be used to destroy the tumor. If the rays reach the tumor all at once at a sufficiently high intensity, the tumor will be destroyed. Unfortunately, at this intensity the healthy tissue that the rays pass through on the way to the tumor will also be destroyed. At lower intensities the rays are harmless

to healthy tissue, but they will not affect the tumor either. What type of procedure might be used to destroy the tumor with the rays, and at the same time avoid destroying the healthy tissue?

There are many possible solutions to this problem, but the one that we will be interested in is what Gick and Holyoak call the convergence solution. In this solution several machines use the low radiation, but they are placed around the patient and converge simultaneously at the tumor. Thus, the healthy tissue receives only low doses while the tumor receives the sum of several low doses (enough to destroy the tumor). If people are simply given the problem and asked to solve it, about 10% of them offer such a solution.

Gick and Holyoak were interested in how a similar solution in an earlier story might affect the proportion of convergence solutions. They had one group of subjects read the following story, which they called the General story.

> A small country was ruled from a strong fortress by a dictator. The fortress was situated in the middle of the country, surrounded by farms and villages. Many roads led to the fortress through the countryside. A rebel general vowed to capture the fortress. The general knew that an attack by his entire army would capture the fortress. He gathered his army at the head of one of the roads, ready to launch a full-scale direct attack. However, the general then learned that the dictator had planted mines on each of the roads. The mines were set so that small bodies of men could pass over them safely, since the dictator needed to move his troops and workers to and from the fortress. However, any large force would detonate the mines. Not only would this blow up the road, but it would also destroy many neighboring villages. It therefore seemed impossible to capture the fortress.
>
> However, the general devised a simple plan. He divided his army into small groups and dispatched each group to the head of a different road. When all was ready he gave the signal and each group marched down a different road. Each group continued down its road to the fortress so that the entire army arrived together at the fortress at the same time. In this way, the general captured the fortress and overthrew the dictator.

As you can see, this story uses a solution very much like the convergence solution for the tumor problem. After subjects read and summarized this story, they were asked to solve the tumor problem under the guise of a separate experiment. Given the clear analogy, you might think that performance would be near ceiling. Surprisingly, only 30% of the subjects offered a convergence solution. Moreover, when these same subjects were given the suggestion that they should use the General story, 80% provided a convergence solution. This finding demonstrates that subjects could apply the General story to the tumor problem when they were instructed to, but did not do so on their own. Many subjects do not spontaneously notice that the General story is similar to the tumor problem.

Why is this analogy so difficult for problem solvers to notice? Remember, the problem is solved very shortly after the story is read and the story and problem do seem rather closely analogous. Given the difficulty in spontaneously noticing the analogy, what do these results mean for more natural problem-solving situations?

These questions are currently the focus of much research, but we may offer some tentative answers. First consider the experiment from the subject's point of view. The subject reads a story about a general who overcomes a dictator through a tricky solution. Then the subject is asked to solve a problem in which a person has a tumor but the radiation machines are too strong or too weak. Given these characterizations of the story and problem, why would one think of the General story? In addition, most subjects have knowledge about medical procedures and X-rays that they might believe is more relevant to the solution of the tumor problem than is a story about a general.

More succinctly, a major part of the difficulty with noticing the analogy may be that the story and problem are stored in a content-dependent way. That is, the General story is not stored as a convergence solution that happened to have a military setting, but rather as a military story. The convergence solution is embedded within this story, not abstracted out in a way that might make it more available for later noticing. When the subject is trying to solve the tumor problem, which has a medical cover story, the underlying similarity to the General story is masked by the great amount of dissimilarity in the contents. In determining what knowledge might be relevant to the current problem, the memory processes will tend to suggest medical-related knowledge (e.g., see the discussion of spreading activation in memory in Chapter 8).

One might think that this content-dependence would not be a problem when people were solving problems within just a single domain, because the relevant knowledge is so circumscribed. But, even in the learning of new domains, people will often learn in a much more restricted way than intended. For example, consider a common textbook in a mathematical or scientific field. The chapter may start with some principles and formulas and then provide an illustration of each principle. Although these illustrative examples are intended to help learners understand the principle, it appears that the principle is often understood in terms of the example (see, e.g., Ross, 1987, 1989). In one study, Ross (1984) found that by simply varying the story line of word problems in elementary probability theory, performance would change dramatically. In particular, if a word problem had the same story line as a problem that illustrated a given principle (e.g., they were both about golfers in a tournament), subjects would solve 77% of the problems. However, if the problem had the same story line as a problem that illustrated a different principle, subjects would often try to apply the inappropriate principle, resulting in performance of just 23%. Clearly, these problem solvers were using the superficial story line content to think back to and make use of earlier problems.

It is important to mention that this content-dependence has certain advantages. If the current problem has similar contents to a relevant earlier problem, spontaneous noticing is much more likely (see, e.g., Holyoak & Koh, 1987; Novick, 1988; Ross, 1984). In this case, rather than acting to make the two problems seem dissimilar, the superficial similarity acts to make the two problems seem more similar. Thus, even if the deep underlying similarity between two problems is not sufficient to make a person notice the analogy, having similar contents may increase the similarity enough so that the earlier problem is accessed. So content-dependence can hurt the access of superficially dissimilar problems but help the access of superficially similar problems. The overall utility depends on how often one needs to apply problems with very different contents versus problems with similar contents. Although analogies to very different contents occur and seem creative when they do, most times when one has a relevant earlier problem it is likely that the content of that problem is not unrelated to the current problem contents. Earlier successful military strategies will usually be most relevant when one is trying to formulate a military strategy. Such use of earlier problems in problem solving persists far beyond early learning and may often be a common technique of experts.

Overcoming Access Difficulties.   There are at least two reasons why access is so difficult. First, as we have seen, much of the knowledge is stored in a content-dependent way, not abstracted away from many of the formally irrelevant details. Second, part of the difficulty may be that we have the knowledge, but we have not represented *when* such knowledge might be relevant. Simon (1980) observes that it is not enough just to know facts—one needs to access the facts *at the relevant point* during problem solving. For example, it is a common occurrence in mathematics and certain sciences for textbooks to provide a great deal of information on how to perform some calculation or how to apply some principle, but not to provide any information on when such a calculation should be performed or when such a principle should be applied. That is, the problem solver does not understand exactly what it is about the problem that requires an application of the principle.

What might help to make the earlier problem accessible from our representation of the current problem? First, we know that increased similarity between the problems will increase the likelihood of thinking back to the earlier problem.

Second, to the extent that the current problem is represented and processed in a similar way to the past problem, access will be increased (e.g., Lockhart, Lamon, & Gick, 1988; Seifert & Gray, 1990). That is, the representations of the problems may be more similar because they have been processed in similar ways. For example, suppose you were trying to repair some equipment, such as a bicycle, and found that you had made an error in your repair work that needed to be fixed (another problem to solve). You are probably more likely to think of an earlier situation in which this problem was caused by mistaken repair work than a situation in which it arose for some other reason. (Some readers may also notice the relation to the encoding specificity idea discussed in Chapter 7.)

A third means of overcoming the difficulties of access may be of more theoretical importance and practical use. If the problem of access is largely due to content-dependence and lack of understanding of the relevant problem conditions, then abstracting the content and improving this understanding should increase accessibility.

Let us consider two ways in which such content-dependence and understanding may be improved. First, if a problem solver is forced to compare several instances that all have the same underlying abstract structure, the representation may be abstract enough to be accessible by later superficially dissimilar instances. For example, the solution rate (without hints) to the tumor problem increases if subjects are forced to compare multiple instances (see, e.g., Catrambone & Holyoak, 1989; Gick & Holyoak, 1983). In addition, the likelihood of using the convergence solution is largely determined by how appropriately the subjects were able to abstract this idea from their comparison of the instances. The comparison of instances may be important for another reason as well, related to the difficulty of knowing when certain actions should be taken. In many of these situations the hard part of learning is that there may be two actions that are applied in similar situations, but it is difficult for the learner to see the relevant differences in the two situations (i.e., when to do one action and when to do the other). The comparison of instances, in addition to helping clarify the common underlying structure, can also help to point out important contrasts (see Bransford, Franks, Vye, & Sherwood, 1989 for a number of examples of how such contrasts may be used).

Although comparing examples can be quite important in learning, it does have some disadvantages: The learner must see multiple instances, know these instances are all instances of a given problem type, and then compare them. Is there another way to increase the access of just a single instance (as opposed to the generalization over several instances)? Some findings suggest that if the problem solver has a clear understanding of the goal structure in the problem, an explanation of why each action was taken, then such knowledge may be more accessible when solving a later problem (see, e.g., Brown & Kane, 1988). The idea is that if a problem solver tries to explain each step in a problem solution in terms of what the goal is and how this step helps to accomplish the goal, this explanation provides an understanding that is abstracted (at least somewhat) away from the content of the problem. It may also allow the problem solver to adapt the solution for closely related problems, a task that is often difficult for learners (Reed, Dempster, & Ettinger, 1985).

Although such explanations may seem to be a great amount of work, preliminary results indicate that "good" problem solvers tend to be those who explain the steps in examples to themselves and keep close tabs on what they do and do not understand in these explanations (Chi, Bassok, Lewis, Reimann, & Glaser, 1989). For example, suppose you were following a set of instructions on how to repair a malfunction with your bicycle. You may be able to make this repair (if the instructions are complete) even if you do not understand why any particular action is being done. But if you were able to explain why each step was done and what its role was in the repair, you would be more likely to be able to fix some slightly different problem in the future.

In summary, to increase the likelihood of accessing a relevant problem one needs to store the earlier problem on the basis of the underlying structure. When solving a problem, try to understand why each action is being taken. This explanation will help to access earlier problems with similar explanations and provide a useful basis for solving later problems of this type.

Case-Based Reasoning: An AI Approach

Much of the work on problem solving in AI (descended from the Newell and Simon approach discussed earlier) has focused on the idea of solving problems through the application of general principles or heuristics coupled with domain knowledge. Although this work has led to a number of impressive advances, it fails to capture many situations in which people rely on specific earlier problems. Recently, however, an approach called **case-based reasoning** has examined the possibility that much of problem solving can be accomplished by using memory of earlier cases (instances) and adapting them to the current case.

The basic approach was outlined by Roger Schank (who also, with Abelson, introduced the idea of scripts discussed in Chapter 11). He argued (Schank, 1982) that often when we understand what is happening in a situation or choose actions to solve some problem, we do so by remembering some earlier situation or problem that the current one reminds us of, rather than using general knowledge. Knowledge of how a similar problem was solved may be the most relevant knowledge that can be brought to bear during problem solving. Such a procedure may be especially useful when the chain of reasoning is very long or when one's understanding of the domain is incomplete or incorrect. Common examples of such case-based reasoning abound, such as the use of precedents in legal arguments and the pricing of houses by using the price of a recently sold house.

This idea has been incorporated into a large number of different computer simulations (see Hammond, 1989; Kolodner, 1988; Kolodner & Simpson, 1989 for extended discussions). As a very general description, the case-based reasoning paradigm has the following parts:

1. A case is *selected* from memory. The current situation is characterized in some way and this characterization is used to retrieve one or more cases with similar characterizations. The determination of these retrieval cues is an important issue, but most of the current systems use those types of cues that have proven more predictive in the past or those that are central to the understanding of the current case. In some situations multiple cases may be retrieved, but this selection is then followed by a further selection of the case to use for further reasoning.

2. The selected case is *adapted* to the present case. Usually the selected case will be similar to the present case, but not equivalent with respect to all important features. Thus, the system needs to take the solution of the selected case and modify it to be applicable to the current case. Although such adaptation can be very complex, if the selection was a very good one, the modifications that are needed may not be so great.

3. The adapted solution is applied and *evaluated*. Because the system relies on earlier instances, it requires good feedback about the usefulness of the solutions.

4. Memory is *updated*. The new case is stored in memory along with the results of the evaluation. Although most case-based systems also use the knowledge of what case was selected and

how it was modified to determine how best to store this new case (so it can be most useful for helping to solve later cases), the learning process is quite simple compared to many learning systems. Learning is principally the storing of new cases.

The case-based approach has been applied to a large number of very different domains, ranging from dispute negotiations (Kolodner & Simpson, 1989) to recipe generation for Szechwan cooking (Hammond, 1989). For illustrative purposes, let us go over a possible situation in which a person may follow this general series of steps. (A clear exposition of an existing system would require far more space and much background information.)

Suppose a realtor is asked to set a market price for a house that has just come on the market. Several means can be used for price setting, but one bases it on an earlier house sale. Thus, the realtor would characterize the new house using a set of features (age, square feet) and relations (layout, location in town). First, this description would remind the realtor of some other house (or the realtor might have a filing system in which the characteristics thought most important would be used as indexes). Second, the realtor would adjust the price of the new house by its differences with the old house (e.g., extra bathroom, more square feet, worse location). Third, when a price is set the realtor gets feedback. In this situation, feedback might be a house that sells too quickly (the price was too low) or too slowly (the price was too high), or perhaps the ridicule of other realtors. Fourth, the realtor's memory (or filing system) for houses that have been priced would be updated to include this new house. In addition to the characteristics of the house, this case might be indexed by other useful information learned in the course of this pricing, such as what to do when there is a half-finished basement.

Although the idea behind case-based systems may sound quite simple compared to the more search-oriented AI systems, it is important to realize that earlier cases or problems implicitly contain a great deal of information that can be mined to solve later problems. Case-based reasoning takes advantage of this information to guide its problem solving without having to repeat much of what was done in solving earlier problems. Rather than emphasizing representation and search, this more memory-intensive type of problem solving emphasizes access and adaptation. As we will see in the next chapter on expertise, much of the power in problem solving comes from accessing relevant knowledge as opposed to general reasoning skills. Current work is also trying to understand how best to integrate this approach with more traditional AI problem-solving approaches so that a system can have the advantages of each approach.

Summary

In this chapter we presented some fundamental components of problem solving. The problem space view of problem solving as representation and search introduced by Newell and Simon has been the prime organizing framework within problem solving in both psychology and artificial intelligence. Recently, researchers have begun to appreciate the huge influence that representation differences can have on problem solving.

Even with a good representation, however, the vast number of possibilities can make exhaustive search impossible. Much of this chapter can be viewed as different ideas on how to reduce search. Clearly, heuristics are aimed exactly at ways of guiding search so that the more likely possibilities will be considered. Less obviously, perhaps, the work on the use of examples and case-based reasoning provides another way of guiding search. Rather than using general principles and heuristics to help choose the operators, one relies on earlier problem-solving episodes in which a similar problem was solved. Such an episode greatly reduces the search problem by focusing on a solution procedure that has already worked in a related situation. That is, these methods take advantage of a great deal of knowledge about the specific domain to reduce the need to search all possibilities. As we shall see in the next chapter, the use of domain knowledge is crucial in overcoming many problem-solving limitations.

Key Terms

algorithm

case-based reasoning

functional fixedness

heuristic

hill climbing

ill-defined problem

means-ends analysis

problem

problem operators

problem space

problem state

verbal protocols

well-defined problem

working backward

Recommended Readings

The classic account of human problem solving may be found in Newell and Simon (1972). The book is quite intimidating in its scope (and weight), but provides full treatments of problem spaces and their uses. A more general presentation is given in Simon (1978), and Wickelgren (1974) provides an excellent brief account of problems and search, with particular emphasis on mathematics. Hayes (1989) has a more thorough introductory treatment of problem solving. A clear theoretical discussion of verbal protocols and their uses can be found in an article by Ericsson and Simon (1980) or in expanded form in their 1984 book. Duncker (1945) presents a number of interesting demonstrations and thoughts on representation effects and Kotovsky and Fallside (1989) provide a more recent case. Van Lehn (1989) offers an interesting perspective on these and other problem-solving ideas.

The Gick and Holyoak (1980, 1983) papers on the use of earlier related problems have been very influential. The edited volume by Vosniadou and Ortony (1989) contains a number of chapters on this topic. Work on case-based reasoning was originally presented in a very readable book by Schank (1982), but much more detail about particular systems can be found in Hammond (1989) or Kolodner and Simpson (1989). The book edited by Kolodner (1988) consists of a number of conference papers on this topic.

16

EXPERTISE AND CREATIVITY

Chapter Outline

The first rule of discovery is to have brains and good luck. The second rule of discovery is to sit tight and wait until you get a bright idea.

G. Polya, *How to Solve It*

Introduction

Expertise and creativity are fascinating topics because they are cases in which problem-solving ability is pushed beyond its everyday limits. These situations are excellent examples of our themes of constraints and relevance: The problem solver is given incomplete information and must augment it with knowledge, but the potentially relevant knowledge is great. How can these problem solvers tap into the right knowledge and solve problems that most of the rest of us cannot?

In this chapter we take the ideas from the previous chapter on problem solving and apply them to cases of expert and creative problem solving. We begin by examining a variety of research results in expertise and current views of what it means to be an expert and then turn to creativity.

Expertise

Introduction

We have all heard about extraordinary feats of expertise: a chess grandmaster playing blindfolded against a large number of opponents or a mental calculator who can quickly do incredible arithmetic calculations without writing anything down. More mundane examples might include an expert in physics who can easily solve problems that others cannot or an expert diagnostician who can quickly and accurately assess medical problems. How do experts do what they do?

A common view is that experts are expert reasoners with exceptionally good memories. Although it is true, almost by definition, that experts are able to reason well within their domain, the view that they have some general expert reasoning abilities has been cast into doubt by recent research on expertise. Rather than reflecting some general abilities, expertise appears to be heavily domain-dependent. In addition, the emphasis on reasoning has given way to an appreciation of the extraordinary domain knowledge that experts have. We first examine differences between novices and experts in a number of domains in order to clarify the notion of expertise.

Comparing Experts and Novices

The performance of experts and novices has been examined in a wide variety of domains, often using the methods of protocols and simulations. For purposes of exposition we will focus on three areas: chess and mental calculation, semantically rich formal domains (such as physics), and the more perceptually oriented domain of radiology.

Chess and Mental Calculation.   We start with a famous mental calculator, the mathematician A. C. Aitkin (Hunter, 1977). As one example of his expertise, consider what happened when Aitkin was asked the square root of 851. (This is one problem we will not ask you to keep trying until you can get an answer.) After a short interval, he replied, "29.17." Following this, within 15 seconds he answered, "29.17190429." How was he able to do this?

Clearly Professor Aitkin had a remarkable ability, but let us analyze why this is so remarkable. First, most of us face severe memory limitations in performing arithmetic calculations, which is why we insist on using calculators or at least pencil and paper. Second, the task itself is difficult and involves a very long sequence of operations that most of us could not do in our heads.

Aitkin was able to exploit his great experience with and understanding of numbers. He knew a tremendous amount about numbers and could perceive patterns where most of us could not. For instance, he knew all the factors (numbers which, when multiplied together, yield the number in question; the factors for 15 are 3 and 5) of every number up to 1500. When asked to solve a problem with 851, he immediately noted that it is the product of 23 and 37. Aitkin also knew many different ways of calculating and knew which methods were most likely to be useful for specific calculations. The application of his chosen plan was greatly simplified by his ability to work in large steps. Because his general plan freed him from deciding what to do at each step, he was able to concentrate on what he was doing. Some of the complexities of mental computation were avoided by his ability to simply remember many of the intermediate answers, rather than computing them.

Now let's shift to another domain. Why is chess such a hard game for novices? First, the representation of the board information is very complex. For most novices, the representation would need to include each individual piece separately, far beyond what can be kept immediately available. Second, the search space of possible move sequences is very large and most novices do not have any good way to guide this search. A chess expert needs to overcome both of these difficulties.

How do experts represent the board to avoid such memory limitations? Short-term memory is limited in terms of the number of meaningful units or chunks that it can hold at any one time. Experts do not have a superior short-term memory capacity. Rather, experts represent the board positions as groups of chunks that include many more pieces than the chunks that novices use. For example, in one study (Chase & Simon, 1973) a master and novice were shown board positions with 24–26 pieces from the middle of a chess game for five seconds, an example of which is given in Figure 16.1. The board was then covered and subjects were asked to reconstruct the board position on another board. The master chess player was able to place considerably more pieces than the novice (16 versus 4). However, if the board position shown was randomly constructed so that there were unlikely to be any meaningful chess configurations, there were no differences between the novice and expert reconstructions (with both placing between 2 and 3 pieces). This result has been replicated in a variety of other domains, such as the game Go (Reitman, 1976) and electronics (Egan & Schwartz, 1979). Experts appear to chunk the information into larger units and perceive these units very quickly. These chunks are often hierarchically organized so that a master may recognize a whole board configuration.

Chess masters are not searching more than novices, but they are guiding their search much better. They do not consider more moves than chess novices, but the moves they do consider are generally good moves. They can use their perceptions of relevant chunks and their understanding of general principles of chess play to focus on what are likely to be the best possibilities.

Thus the chess and mental calculation experts do not have unusual memories, but rather have learned, for a very specific type of material, how to overcome difficulties imposed by memory limitations and the computational complexity of search.

MIDDLE GAME
Black

White

RANDOM MIDDLE GAME

Figure 16.1   **Example of chess board position used in memory experiments.** *Source*: Chase, W. G., & Simon, H. A. (1973).

Experts and Novices in More Formal Domains.   Some additional points about expertise can be illustrated by comparing novices and experts in a more formal domain, physics. Here are descriptions of how a typical novice and a typical expert might try to solve a physics word problem (adapted from the findings of a number of papers, including Chi, Feltovich, & Glaser, 1981; Larkin, McDermott, Simon, & Simon, 1980; Simon & Simon,

1978). The novice reads the problem carefully, underlining words she believes are important. Novice representations of problems rely heavily on the verbal statement of the problem and the concrete objects presented. Again, the problem solver is faced with too little information and needs to augment it with her knowledge. Unfortunately, her organization in memory of the relevant principles is very slight and does not allow her to understand how the problem might fit into these principles. To solve the problem, then, she must focus only on the information provided and hope for a connection. She first identifies the givens and the unknown. Then she works backward, searching for equations that contain the unknown. These equations often produce other unknowns, and she tries to find equations that contain these new unknowns until she gets one that contains only one unknown. These equations appear to be generated in a somewhat random way except for this constraint of containing the unknown.

The expert is also faced with the difficulty of too little information presented, but her expertise allows her performance to differ from the novice's. First, the expert often pauses before writing and then draws a simple qualitative diagram (Larkin & Simon, 1987 provide some ideas about the general advantages of diagrams). This representation may be added to as the expert elaborates the problem features until a promising avenue of solution is seen. The knowledge organization of the expert differs dramatically from the novice. The principles are richly organized with explanations and associations between principles. The strategy of solution takes advantage of the plan developed from the representation and the organization of knowledge. The plan is successively refined until particular principles can be applied. Equations are then written down, but only in the service of this plan. Thus, she sees a pattern of equations, pause, equations, and so on. Rather than working backward from the goal (the unknown), the expert is proceeding forward from the problem representation.

What are the differences in knowledge that lead to such differences in problem solving? A major difference is in the nature of the knowledge novices and experts have about problem types often called **problem schemata** or problem categories. These are general knowledge structures for understanding, in this case, understanding what type of problem is involved and how to solve it. (Thus problem schemata are similar in structure to the schemata described in Chapter 11.) If novices are given a set of physics problems and asked to categorize them (Chi et al., 1981), they will group those problems together that contain similar physical objects, such as inclined planes or springs. Experts, however, categorize the problems by the laws of physics, such as conservation of momentum or Newton's

Third Law. Examples of the groupings for novices and experts are given in Figure 16.2. Experts can use these categorizations to quickly access the relevant equations for solution. They use their extensive knowledge to augment the incomplete information in appropriate ways. In addition, they do not need to try all the many possible paths from their problem representations. As in chess and mental calculation, great experience with problems within their area of expertise has allowed experts to learn configurations and associated problem-solving procedures. Thus, experts are working forward, using their schemata to direct their search, while novices tend to work backward.

Radiological Expertise. Alan Lesgold and his colleagues (Lesgold, Feltovich, Glaser, & Wang, 1981; Lesgold, Rubinson, Feltovich, Glaser, Klopfer, & Wang, 1988) have been examining differences between expert radiologists and radiology residents in their diagnosis of X-rays. Although one might first guess that these diagnoses are largely dependent on detection, Lesgold and his fellow investigators provide strong evidence that detection is a minor part of the task, which is more properly viewed as problem-solving. Indeed, the description of expert performance in this task closely parallels the descriptions of experts that we have already discussed.

In one set of studies (Lesgold et al., 1981), the task was similar to the one used by researchers investigating chess expertise. The experts and residents were presented with an X-ray for two seconds and then asked to report any abnormalities noticed. They were then shown the film for an unlimited time and asked to think aloud while analyzing it and to dictate a formal report. Experts were more able to quickly detect the patterns in the film and ignore the irrelevant information. These differences in pattern detection were possible because the experts were using a very rich mental representation of the anatomy to allow them to "see" the third dimension. Again, experts were able to augment the incomplete information with their extensive domain knowledge. For example, Lesgold et al. (1988) mention one case in which the residents often discussed an enlarged heart, while the experts correctly attributed the increased heart shadow to irrelevant factors such as poor patient posture and breathing during the X-ray. Experts used these augmented representations to keep track of various constraints, but they were deferring any decision making until the maximal data were available. Thus, these experts maintained a flexible set of options in accord with the data. In addition, like the chess experts, through experience they had developed a large number of perceptual patterns that could be recognized quickly and provide associated hypotheses.

Novices:

Grouping		Explanation	
Problem 7 (23)		Novice 1:	"These deal with blocks on an *incline plane*"

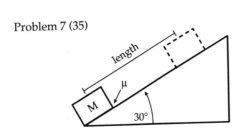

		Novice 5:	"*Inclined plane* problems, coeficient of *friction*"
		Novice 6:	"Blocks on *inclined planes* with angles"

Problem 7 (35)

Experts:

Grouping		Explanation	
Problem 6 (21)		Expert 2:	"*Conservation of Energy*"
		Expert 3:	"*Work-Energy Theorem.* They are all straight-forward problems."
		Expert 4:	"These can be done from energy considerations. Either you should know the *Principle of Conversation of Energy,* or work is lost somewhere."

Problem 7 (35)

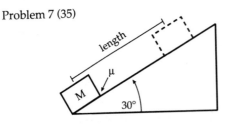

Figure 16.2   **An example of sortings of physics problems made by novices and experts.**
Source: Chi, M. T. H., Feltovich, P. J., & Glaser, R., 1981.

Radiological expertise consists in part of developing these rich sets of configurations or schemata to use in reasoning forward from a recognized pattern. For example, examining a film of a patient with multiple chest tumors, the experts noticed the subtle differences in the haziness between the lungs and used this to diagnose the tumors. Less experienced radiology residents reason backward from possible hypotheses. For instance, an initial hypothesis of congestive heart failure might cause a resident to miss the differences between the two lungs. As residents gain more experience, they begin to form and use these schemata. For a while these schemata are not totally correct and experience is needed to help the residents to refine the schemata. Interestingly, this learning will sometimes lead to a temporary decrease in performance while incorrect schemata are being refined (Lesgold et al., 1988).

Summarizing Expert-Novice Differences. Experts have stored a large number of rich perceptual units with associated procedures. In many situations, experts can use these units to recognize patterns. In more complex cases, experts will use their extensive domain knowledge to elaborate the problem. They are likely to spend considerable time trying to represent the problem qualitatively, often using abstract diagrams to go beyond the simple objects and entities presented in the problem to a deeper representation. The deeper representation will often allow the experts to categorize the problem as a particular type. In some cases, a problem category (a type of schema) will have a standard procedure for solving instances of that type. In other cases, the experts can use the deeper representation and their organization of the domain knowledge to help determine what relevant knowledge to apply. This use will often involve considerable working forward. Although the goal may not be explicitly taken into account, the expert has learned what types of information can be derived from the data and thus are likely to be useful for solving the problem. Another way of thinking about this working forward is that it is largely schema-driven, as the knowledge of the problem category helps guide the experts in their use of the problem representation. Novices tend to use a strategy of working backward from the goal or means-ends analysis. (Gick, 1986 provides a highly readable presentation of these ideas for the interested reader.)

Overall then, experts are using their extensive domain knowledge to help overcome the difficulties of too little information and too many possibilities. Expertise requires a great deal of knowledge to help represent problems, recognize large meaningful patterns, develop categories or problem schemata, and learn associated procedures for solving these problem types.

Developing Expertise

Assuming experts were not born as experts, how do they acquire their expertise? This question is central in current research on problem solving and learning.

Learning to Solve Problems. As the old joke goes: A violinist in New York for a concert gets lost and stops a pedestrian. "Excuse me, sir. How do I get to Carnegie Hall?" the violinist asks. The pedestrian looks at the violin and replies, "Practice." Practice is necessary for gaining expertise. Simon (1980) estimates that a chess master knows well over 50,000 patterns and that it takes at least 10 years to become an expert in any complex domain. Practice is necessary, but not sufficient. Practice helps the problem solver learn the important conditions and actions of the domain and to make many of these actions "automatic."

In the last chapter we spent considerable time explaining how people might use earlier examples in problem solving. One reason for that discussion is that people are generally not very good at learning from the abstract descriptions of principles that are presented along with the illustrating problems. Learning to solve problems appears to require the solution of many problems. How is this problem solving useful for learning?

First, the solution of a number of problems helps to "wean" the learner away from dependence on details of the content. One method for overcoming such content-dependence (to some extent a necessary part of expertise) is to solve problems that vary these contents (see, e.g., Bassok, 1990).

Second, not all types of problem solving are equally effective for promoting learning. For example, means-ends analysis, in which the difference between the current state and the goal is used to guide search (see Chapter 15), is a very effective problem-solving technique. However, John Sweller and his colleagues (e.g., Owen & Sweller, 1985; Sweller, 1988; Sweller & Cooper, 1985) have convincingly demonstrated that the use of means-ends analysis to solve problems can interfere with learning. The argument is worth considering in detail because it helps to bring together a number of points from this chapter and the last chapter. As we have just discussed, expertise is characterized by the use of problem schemata to allow working forward from the givens. To the extent that we want learners to develop this expertise, we need to give them practice in recognizing the problem states and learning which procedures to apply. But means-ends analysis interferes with the learning of this knowledge because it (1) focuses learners on the differences between the goals and the current state (rather than on the current state alone) and (2) requires a considerable use of limited resources in that the problem solver needs to keep track of the current state, the goal state, their relation, the operators, and any intermediate goal set by eliminating a difference earlier. There is little overlap between the activities required to solve problems by means-ends analysis and the problem-solving activities that are required in more schema-driven (working forward) situations. If we want problem solvers to learn to solve problems efficiently in the domain, then we want to help them acquire these schema-driven capabilities. Sweller argues that less directed problem-solving methods may be more effective in helping problem solvers acquire the appropriate schemata. For example, Owen and Sweller (1985) show that the learning of trigonometry problem solving may be enhanced if learners are simply told to calculate as many angles and sides as they can, rather than directed toward calculating a particular quantity. This nondirection allows them to learn the association between particular quantities (e.g., the givens) and the quantities that can be derived from them.

A third point about the effectiveness of practice is that the learner is aided by understanding the goal structure of the problem. The idea that an understanding of the problem promotes transfer is not new (see Katona, 1940), although the arguments supporting this idea were often very vague. The current view is that experts have well-refined problem schemata that allow them to identify the type of problem, provide an explanation of how the parts of the problem are related, and include associated procedures for solving problems. From this view, when learners understand a problem they may be learning various parts of this schema: what features indicate the problem type, what features are irrelevant, how the relevant pieces fit together, and how they relate to the solution.

One Theory of Skill Acquisition. The last decade has seen a resurgence of theories of skill acquisition (e.g., Anderson, 1982, 1987; Polson & Keiras, 1985; Newell & Rosenbloom, 1981; Rosenbloom & Newell, 1987). We consider here one theory that has been particularly influential in psychology, the theory of learning proposed by John Anderson within his ACT* (pronounced "act-star") framework (Anderson, 1982, 1983, 1987). In this view, problem-solving skills progress through three "stages." First, the situation and method for solving problems are encoded as declarative knowledge, usually from instructions and perhaps a worked-out example. (As discussed in Chapter 8, one may distinguish between declarative knowledge, knowledge about a topic, and procedural knowledge, knowledge of how to do some task.) In this stage the problem solver can solve problems by carefully going over the declarative knowledge and figuring out how to apply it to a new problem. That is, the problem solver may have learned the relevant information, but it may not yet be in a form to allow quick, reliable access and application.

In the second stage, as a result of applying this knowledge, knowledge is transferred into a more efficient procedural representation. Anderson uses **productions** to capture this idea of procedural knowledge and has embodied his theory in a computer simulation. Productions are used by many researchers who write computer simulations because productions allow the encoding of procedural knowledge in a simple form. Each production is a simple rule of the general form, "IF certain conditions are true THEN perform some mental or physical action." Each production is constantly checking to see if its particular conditions are met and when they are, its particular actions are performed. Thus, these productions can encode common situation-action pairings, so that they do not need to be recomputed from the declarative representation each time they are needed (reducing the difficulty of the computation). The point of this change from declarative to procedural knowledge is to encode the knowledge so that it is accessed at the relevant time during problem solving.

Third, through further practice, this procedural knowledge is refined and enlarged so that bigger steps may be taken with each application. As we saw in the discussion of expertise, experts can recognize large patterns and have associated procedures for dealing with the situation signaled by these patterns. In addition, experts can combine multiple steps. Anderson captures this expertise by putting together productions so that the conditions can be quite complex (which is equivalent to recognizing a complex pattern), or so that successive steps can be accomplished more quickly.

A simplified example may help to illustrate these three stages. Suppose you are learning to use a word processor and you read the following:

> When you have finished making changes to the file, you will probably want to save it for later editing. To do this, you need to let the word processing program know that you wish to save it in place of the old file (before the changes were made). To do this, first press the F7 key, labeled SAVE, to let the program know that the file is to be saved. You will then be asked whether you wish to replace the old file. To do so, type Y (for "yes") and press the key labeled ENTER.

After reading these sentences, you could go through the steps for saving a file, though you would probably do so slowly, interpreting each sentence. This slow use of the information would be an instance of applying declarative knowledge. Once you have performed this procedure, you may have the information stored in a more efficient way. For instance, you might have something like the following two productions:

P1: If you are working on the word processor
    and the goal is to store the file
THEN press F7.

P2: If you are working on the word processor and
    the goal is to replace the file with a new version and
    you have already pressed F7
THEN press Y and press ENTER.

With further practice these two productions might be combined into a bigger production that would enable you to replace a file:

P3: If you are working on the word processor and
    the goal is to replace the file with a new version
THEN press F7, Y, and ENTER.

This theory provides one set of ideas on how learners may gain knowledge about patterns and their associated actions. It has been used to predict in detail how performance speeds up with practice, as well as the degree of transfer between different tasks (see, e.g., Singley & Anderson, 1989). Although aspects of the theory have recently been questioned (see Carlson, Sullivan, & Schneider, 1989; and a reply by Anderson, 1989), it has been quite influential in emphasizing certain issues about learning and, as we shall see shortly, in providing a theoretical base for instruction.

Teaching Heuristics.   Most current theories of learning focus on how problem solving within a restricted domain may be improved. But what about more general procedures, or heuristics, that can be applied across a wide variety of problems? Can they be taught?

George Polya, a mathematician, pioneered the study of problem-solving heuristics. His book, *How to Solve It*, outlines various heuristic procedures that may be employed to help solve difficult problems. These techniques have been very influential. The argument is that if these heuristics are effectively used by expert problem solvers, teaching them to nonexpert problem solvers may substantially aid their performance. A number of studies have been conducted examining the effects of teaching heuristics on problem-solving performance in a variety of settings (Schoenfeld, 1985, Chapter 6, provides a good review). Surprisingly, teaching heuristics appears to have very little effect on problem-solving performance. That is, these studies generally show little or no effect of such instruction.

Why? Schoenfeld (1985) argues that the heuristics, although perhaps appropriate characterizations of expert problem-solving techniques, are not described in enough detail to guide their application to a problem-solving situation. To illustrate, he takes a reasonable heuristic such as one suggesting it is sometimes useful to consider special cases of an unfamiliar problem. He then shows that this seemingly simple heuristic is really a collection of several substrategies, each of which can apply to different situations and each of which is quite difficult to master by itself. Thus, although the expert may believe he or she is helped by thinking of the heuristic, it is useful only because the expert understands the various substrategies and their applicability. A nonexpert is left with general advice that is almost a cliché, but with no understanding of how to use this general idea to help solve particular problems. As a loose analogy, consider telling a young child at the dinner table to be careful not to spill or break anything. This warning may be useful to older children or adults; they can calm down, pick up delicate dishes with two hands, and so on. But young children do not know *what* to do to be careful and only after breaking something will they (sometimes) realize that they should not have done that particular action.

Does this mean that the teaching of heuristics is a bad idea? No, it only means that the teaching of heuristics described at a general level may be a bad idea. Rather, nonexperts need to be taught how to implement these heuristics so that they can learn the various substrategies and when they are applicable. Schoenfeld has developed instructional methods to teach problem solvers how to understand and analyze problems and these instructional methods appear to show positive effects on later problem solving. For instance, Schoenfeld and Hermann (1982) provided a one-month course in mathematical problem solving. The students were asked to sort a set of 32 problems before they took the course and after they took the course. These sortings were compared to expert sortings and the sortings of comparable students who took a structured programming course instead. Recall that problem categorization by experts is usually done on the basis of the underlying principles, while novices tend to use the surface objects to categorize problems. Schoenfeld and Hermann found that although the two nonexpert groups sorted similarly before their courses (and very differently from the experts), in the second sorting the students who had taken the course on problem solving were sorting much more like the experts, whereas the students who took the structured programming course were still relying on surface objects. Therefore, a course that focuses on understanding and analysis of mathematical problems can have an impact on the categorization of such problems.

Schoenfeld's work and the related work of some other investigators provide some optimism on the teaching of general heuristics. Nonetheless, two cautionary notes are in order. First, although the course covered a variety of mathematical problem types, the generality of the heuristics learned is not clear. Would they be successfully applied to very different types of math problems or to nonmath problems? Second, often the ability to apply a heuristic depends on domain knowledge. Although it may be possible to learn some general heuristics, their successful application will usually require considerable specific knowledge about the domain. For example, the recognition of relevant domain patterns is crucial for expertise and cannot be gotten around by the use of general heuristics. Nonetheless, the careful explicit teaching of heuristics in several domains may make their transfer across domains much easier. Although there may be no substitute for domain experience, the effectiveness of the experience may be increased by such teaching of heuristics.

Computer-Based Tutoring Systems.   Computer systems that help people learn have been in schools since the 1960s. However, they have often consisted of inflexible programmed learning methods and they have not been very widely available. Two major changes have occurred recently that promise systems that may be substantially more useful. First, our understanding of expertise and its development has increased greatly, providing some ideas about what the target skill should be and how people might best learn it. Second, computer capabilities have increased greatly and become very widely available, so that even complex tutoring systems requiring sophisticated computers are not out of the range of many schools.

A variety of tutoring systems are currently being worked on ranging from teaching simple games, to mathematics, to programming. To distinguish them from earlier types of systems and to highlight their use of cognitive analyses, these systems are usually called **intelligent tutoring systems** or intelligent computer-assisted instruction. A good recent overview of a number of these systems is provided in Mandl and Lesgold (1988).

Although the various systems differ greatly, most of them consist of four general components. First, they include a representation of *expert knowledge*. This component captures the target knowledge, that is, what the tutoring system would like the learner to learn. Second, the systems keep a record of the **learner's model**, what knowledge the learner is assumed to have available. This record is kept for each user of the tutoring system and is updated during the learning sessions. The learner's model provides an analysis of what the learner knows and the expert knowledge represents what the learner should eventually know, so the knowledge in the expert component that is not in the learner's model is the knowledge still needed to be learned. (It will also be true that the learner model may contain some misconceptions that need to be corrected as well.) Third, the system needs an *instructional component*, which determines what tutorial strategies will be applied for trying to get the learner's knowledge closer to the expert's. This component must take into account what the learner knows and what the system is trying to teach (i.e., what difference between expert and learner is being worked on). Finally, because the computer needs to interact with the learner, the system needs some type of *interface* or means of communication. Some systems rely on simple displays and typed input, while others use fancy color graphics and input by various pointing devices.

This discussion is rather abstract, so consider a particular tutoring system that will relate to our study of developing expertise. John Anderson has applied his ACT* theory of learning (discussed earlier) by building tutors that incorporate the ideas he thinks are important in learning. Anderson has developed a number of tutors, including ones to teach high school geometry and the programming language LISP (which is the most widely used language for programming in artificial intelligence). The LISP tutor has been used at Carnegie-Mellon University to teach undergraduates since 1984 and has been described and evaluated in a number of publications (e.g., Anderson, 1984; Anderson, Conrad, & Corbett, 1990; Anderson & Skwarecki, 1986). For the level of LISP knowledge being taught, Anderson claims that 500 productions (i.e., condition-action pairs) are needed. These productions represent the expert knowledge of the domain and have been derived through an extensive series of investigations. The student's problem-solving performance is used to infer which productions he or she is likely to have mastered and which ones need to be worked on. The LISP tutor then provides examples that require the use of one of these still-to-be-learned productions. As in his learning theory, Anderson assumes that productions can be learned from declarative knowledge encoded by the learner or by refining earlier productions. The tutor depends entirely on Anderson's expert model and theory of learning for deciding what knowledge is known and what knowledge needs to be taught.

Among the instructional principles used are (1) that almost all instruction occurs by having learners solve problems, an idea discussed as a means of overcoming access difficulties, (2) that feedback needs to be immediate, and (3) that learners should not be allowed to wander too far from the solution path. Although many of Anderson's instructional ideas seem quite reasonable, they are not simply based on intuition but derive from theoretical and empirical motivations. In addition, his approach combines a learning theory with this set of instructional strategies to provide a strong hypothesis about how people can best be taught to learn problem solving within a domain. Although the evaluation of the tutor is still in progress, the preliminary reports are encouraging (Anderson et al., 1990).

Expert Systems

Introduction. **Expert systems** are computer systems that attempt to simulate the reasoning of experts. One of the pioneers in the development of expert systems, Edward Feigenbaum, describes the enterprise as follows: "The goal of an expert system project is to write a program that achieves a high level of performance on problems that are difficult enough to require significant human expertise for their solution" (1983, p. 38). For our purposes, work on expert systems has been valuable for increasing our understanding of expertise.

The research on expert systems began as a scientific study of expertise. Following the protocol-simulation methodology of Newell and Simon, early investigators reasoned that if they could program a computer to provide the same solutions as experts, they had at least a sufficient set of processes for expertise. As the performance of these expert systems improved, however, the commercial potential became clear. Many hundreds of expert systems have been or are being developed for all types of expertise, such as geological decisions, accounting, computer system design, and medical diagnosis. Although many of these systems have not been incorporated into commercial enterprises, a number of them have been and are used often.

Method. The basic idea behind an expert system is to try to simulate the thinking of a particular expert. The developers obtain the cooperation of an expert, hopefully one of the best. A long procedure then begins. The expert is asked for various facts and heuristics (rules of thumb) used in the area. This knowledge is then incorporated into a computer program, often using productions. After quite a bit of this knowledge has been incorporated, the system is evaluated on a series of problems. Invariably the program performs poorly, even on some cases that the expert used to generate the rules. When the expert is confronted with the poor performance of the system, the usual response is something like, "Well, no wonder. Of course you also need to take into account . . ." The expert has not been negligent. As we have discussed, expertise consists of a large number of perceptual patterns and memory-intensive procedures, many of which are not carried out at a conscious level. Nonetheless, the expert can sometimes figure out how she solved a problem by seeing how the stated rules fail to make the same decision the expert might. The new rules and amendments are then added to the system. Frequently, the building of an expert system requires many repeated queries of the expert to clarify and refine these rules as well as to elicit other rules. At the present time, the primary limitation of the work on expert systems is this "knowledge bottleneck"—that is, it is difficult to get knowledge out of an expert and into a system. Current systems usually have knowledge directly programmed into them and do not learn from experience, although this is likely to be a goal of future systems.

The end result of this iterative process is an expert system. The typical expert system consists of two main parts. First, there is the *knowledge base*, the set of rules that have been taken from the expert's suggestions and elicited in the course of the expert's problem-solving performance. Second, there is the *inference method* (often called the inference engine), which decides how to use the knowledge (e.g., whether to reason backward or forward). Most expert systems cover a very specific (and small) domain, but, as we saw, so do human experts. In addition, many expert systems are able to request information to help them make their decisions, such as the results of a lab test or the personal history of a patient.

Results.   What can these systems do? Although it may be a long time before they are able to meet the expectations of those of us who enjoy science fiction books, there have been a number of successes. For example, one system, Meta-Dendral, helped in designing chemistry experiments that led to a publication in the *Journal of the American Chemical Society* (see Feigenbaum, 1983 for a description).

A major area of application of expert systems has been in medicine (see Feigenbaum, 1983; Lundsgaarde, 1987; Shortliffe, Buchanan, & Feigenbaum, 1979 for general reviews). One of the earliest systems, MYCIN (Shortliffe, 1976), helps select antibiotics for bacterial infections through the use of extensive backward reasoning from hypotheses through its approximately 500 rules. Although MYCIN is an older program, later versions have built on it. For example, NEOMYCIN (Clancey & Letsinger, 1984; also see Clancey, 1988) is able to give explanations of why it requested some type of information or how it arrived at a particular conclusion. This explanation capability is crucial for two reasons. First, in many situations people are willing to use an expert system as a consultation program (as one physician might ask the opinion of another), but may be unwilling to simply let it make the decisions. The consulting aspect requires the expert system not only to be able to arrive at a correct conclusion, but also to be able to explain how it did so in a way that the user can understand. Second, if the explanation can be made explicit, it may be used to help teach nonexperts in the domain. For example, Clancey (see 1987 for a recent exposition) has built a tutoring system, GUIDON, to teach some of the expert knowledge contained in NEOMYCIN.

What have we learned from these expert systems? Feigenbaum (1983, 1989) argues that there are two major principles. First, "knowledge is power." As we saw in the work on expertise, domain-specific knowledge is the key. The work on expert systems provides an interesting test of this idea, because the results in developing these systems have generally been that the exact inference method used is not very important. The general reasoning strategy used does not appear to be crucial. The extent and correctness of the knowledge base is what determines the performance of the expert system. Second, much of the knowledge that is important is not simple facts, but rather heuristics—what Feigenbaum calls "judgmental, experiential, uncertain." This knowledge reflects the experts' ability to see complex patterns and to know how these patterns are related to each other and to outcomes.

Summary

In this section we examined expertise and its development. A common theme is the importance of domain knowledge. Experts augment the incomplete information presented in order to get a rich and deep representation of the problem. They also reduce the great computational complexity of some problems by substituting memorized procedures. Anderson's ACT* theory was used as an illustration of ideas on how expertise develops and how these ideas might be incorporated into a tutoring system.

Throughout this chapter and the previous chapter, we have often been focusing on problem solving and expertise in situations in which there is some "correct" (or best) answer. A common question that nonpsychologists have when they hear about problem solving is how it relates to creativity. We examine that question in the next section.

Creativity

Introduction

Almost everyone finds creativity to be an interesting topic. We all have heard wonderful stories about tortured artists whose creative genius drives them mad or inspired scientists who solve, with a single flash of insight, questions that have plagued humankind for many years. What can we say about the cognitive processes of creativity?

As you might guess, creativity is a difficult topic to research. Reasons for this difficulty include disagreements about how to tell whether something is creative and the inability to easily foster creative solutions in a controlled laboratory setting. To discuss this topic, we first look at a couple of cases that we would all view as *not* being creative.

Rigidity in Problem Solving. Consider the following experiment by Luchins (1942; or see Luchins & Luchins, 1950 for some interesting follow-up studies). A subject is told that there are three containers of different sizes that can hold some fluid. There is an unlimited supply of fluid and the subject's job is to pour the fluids between the supply and the containers so as to end up with a specified amount of fluid. For example, as in the second line of Table 16.1 (the first task was used to illustrate the idea to subjects), the containers are of capacity (a) 21 quarts, (b) 127 quarts, and (c) 3 quarts. The goal is to end up with 100 quarts (clearly in container b). How would this be done? An alert subject might notice that $127 - 100$ is 27, which can

Table 16.1   Water jug problems used in Luchins and Luchins (1950).

	The Tasks			
	Containers given (capacity in quarts)			
Problem	**a**	**b**	**c**	**To get**
1	29	3		20 quarts
2	21	127	3	100 "
3	14	163	25	99 "
4	18	43	10	5 "
5	9	42	6	21 "
6	20	59	4	31 "
7	23	49	3	20 "
8	15	39	3	18 "
9	28	76	3	25 "
10	18	48	4	22 "
11	14	36	8	6 "

Source: Luchins, A. S. & Luchins, E. H., 1950.

be gotten by pouring off fluid to fill container a, then pouring it twice to fill container c. That is, the answer can be thought of as b − a − 2c. In fact, problems 2 through 6 can be solved by this same formula. The next two problems, 7 and 8, can be solved by this formula, but can also be solved by a simple formula (a − c for 7 and a + c for 8). Problem 9 cannot be solved by b − a − 2c, but only by a − c. Finally, problems 10 and 11 can be solved by the formula b − a − 2c or by a + c and a − c, respectively.

What is the point of this experiment? Luchins was interested in the "mechanization" of problem-solving procedures. Problems 2 through 6 were used to induce the subject to mechanize the solution procedure. The results (which Luchins collected over the years from many thousands of subjects) are quite striking. Almost three-quarters of the subjects solve problems 7, 8, 10, and 11 by the mechanized procedure (i.e., b − a − 2c) rather than the much more direct solution of a + c or a − c. (Note that other subjects who did not get problems 2 through 6 first almost always used the direct solutions, indicating that it was the first problems that were leading to the application of these more complex procedures.) Even after problem 9, which could not be solved by the b − a − 2c procedure, not many subjects applied the direct solutions.

This phenomenon, called **Einstellung** (German for "attitude"), was used to demonstrate that people will often apply their past experiences directly, to the detriment of simple or more elegant solutions. Clearly, the ability to make use of past experience is necessary to our survival. The point of this demonstration is that we may persevere in applying this past experience in routinized situations even when it is not appropriate.

From this work (and many anecdotes we can all generate), it does appear that sometimes it is useful to approach a problem differently and try to come up with an alternative type of solution. The ability to know when such a change might be profitable and how to accomplish it are important aspects of what most of us think of as creativity.

What Is Creativity?   What does it take to be creative or have a creative solution? Sometimes it seems as if the definition is somewhat circular: Creative solutions are those solutions produced by creative people, and creative people are those people who come up with creative solutions. In fact, we can do a little better than that. For a solution to be creative, it must be both *original* and *relevant*. That is, the solution must be new and it must be a solution, not just some original, irrelevant proposal. For example, a new solution to world hunger might be to jump in the air 20 times, but we would not consider it a creative solution because it will not cure world hunger (or even have the possibility of doing so).

It is important to note that we have defined **creativity** with respect to a *product* or solution, not with respect to the processes that led to the solution. This might seem a little strange, because in a book on cognition we are really interested in the cognitive processes people go through. The question, then, is whether there is something special about the cognitive processes that lead to creative products (as opposed to noncreative products).

The Traditional View

The Idea of Creativity. Although psychologists might argue about what it means to be creative, many nonpsychologists feel quite confident about which of their acquaintances are creative and which ones are not. On a grander scale, most people have strong views that creativity is closely related to imagination, especially involving flashes of insight.

Weisberg (1986) provides details on many illustrations of creativity taken from personal diaries or journals that were kept by creative people. For instance, an important mathematician, Poincaré, described how he had spent weeks working without success on a problem only to have the answer occur to him in a flash while on vacation. Another famous example is the story of how the poet Coleridge wrote the poem *Kubla Khan* from scratch after having it appear to him during (a drug-induced) sleep.

Gestalt psychologists such as Kohler and Wertheimer distinguished "productive" thought, in which novel ideas are generated, from reproductive thought in which the earlier responses are simply applied mechanically, as in the Luchins water jug problem. The Gestalt view of problem solving (and perception) emphasized the importance of the relations among the parts. By this view, understanding the problem, a crucial step toward solving it, requires one to "see" how all the parts fit together to form the whole. Sometimes when one approaches a problem the structuring one gets of the parts is not adequate to solve the problem (perhaps due to the inappropriate influence of past experience). However, an appropriate understanding sometimes comes about through a *spontaneous restructuring* of the problem in which the parts are seen as fitting together in a different way, leading to a new understanding. Although the view is sometimes faulted for vagueness, the central point for our current purpose is that the parts are seen as going together differently, often leading to a feeling of "Eureka!" or "Aha!" Common to many ideas on creativity is this phenomenology of sudden insight.

Stages of Creativity. Several suggestions for the stages one goes through in creativity have been based on introspections or on accounts of how creative people came up with their creative ideas. For example, Wallas (1926) proposed four stages of creative thought. First, there is *preparation*. The problem solver (e.g., scientist, artist) gains knowledge about the area, starts to work on a task, and runs into difficulty. Second, a period of **incubation** occurs in which the problem solver puts the problem aside and does something else, such as Poincaré going on vacation. Third, the solution (or a crucial part of it) occurs in a sudden insight labeled *illumination* (such as the cartoon idea of a light bulb turning on over a character's head). Finally, there is a stage of *verification* in which the insight is checked, because not all insights turn out to be correct. Common to many reports of creativity, as in many people's view, is the idea of a prolonged mental block or obstacle followed by sudden insight.

Despite the plausibility of such a view, a number of points argue against accepting creativity as a fixed set of stages by which novel solutions are produced. First, not all accounts include all the stages and many accounts seem to have some of the stages interleaved. Second, as in memory for anything, these accounts by creative people may contain some distortions. Weisberg (1986) takes several well-known cases and provides strong evidence for alternative accounts that do not support the stage view. As an extreme example, it was later found that Coleridge had a number of earlier drafts of part of *Kubla Khan* written before his alleged insight. In addition, although it is not documented, it seems likely that there are many creative solutions that simply come to the person during problem solving, but whose arrival is not considered unusual enough to record for posterity. Third, and perhaps most important, the stage idea is really at best a description of the *phenomenology* of creative thinking. It is not an explanation of what cognitive processes occur. That is, these stages propose what it "feels like" to go through creative thought, rather than what one is actually doing. This criticism is especially true of the crucial stage of illumination. Even if one assumes the validity of this stage approach, the real question is what leads to illumination (though see Metcalfe & Wiebe, 1987 and Yaniv & Meyer, 1987 for some promising experimental approaches to illumination and incubation).

A More Recent View of Creativity

In the last section we suggested some problems with the traditional analysis of creativity. What might be a more useful approach? We discuss here how creativity might be considered within a general problem-solving framework.

Creativity as Incremental Problem Solving.   What would it mean to argue that creativity is not anything special (i.e., any different from noncreative problem solving)? Clearly, creative products are different from noncreative products (by definition) but the question is: Are creative products produced by cognitive processes that are fundamentally different than the cognitive processes producing noncreative products?

Weisberg (1986) presents a convincing case that creativity occurs through a series of small steps in which earlier ideas are modified and elaborated (e.g., the *Kubla Khan* example mentioned earlier). The incremental nature of creativity occurs as the problem solver runs into obstacles, proposes solutions, runs into further obstacles, and so on, refining and elaborating the earlier solutions. Rather than viewing creative ideas as springing without warning, we should be trying to understand the details of how they develop.

Weber and Dixon (1989) make the same point about the incremental nature of creativity applied to the historical analysis of inventions. They argue that inventions often evolve over long periods of time by the gradual accumulation of the best ideas. To illustrate this point, they describe the historical evolution of a simple hand tool, the sewing needle. Although it may seem a quite simple invention, it is an elegant solution to the problem of having a device that will (1) penetrate the material, (2) convey the thread, and (3) allow the user to pull and push it. Figure 16.3 presents a set of possible precursors to the current butt-eye needle (the eye is in the butt of the needle).

It is important to realize that the artistic creations and scientific

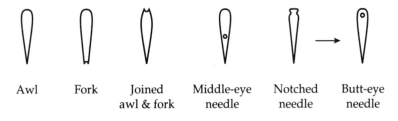

| Awl | Fork | Joined awl & fork | Middle-eye needle | Notched needle | Butt-eye needle |

Figure 16.3   **Possible precursors to the modern button-eyed sewing needle.** *Source*: Weber, R. J., & Dixon, S., 1989.

discoveries are no less important or impressive just because they did not occur by sudden insight. Although some readers may feel that this approach misses some of the essence of the creative process, it allows us to consider the importance of other factors in trying to explain how creativity develops, such as, what is the role of knowledge?

Creativity requires knowledge. Even the traditional view includes in the stage of preparation all the background knowledge that creative people have as necessary for their creative insights. Although one hears stories about people coming to a new problem area and solving problems that have long been agonized over, such occurrences are rare and the few that occur may be due to the person making an analogy to an area in which he or she is expert. In terms of the incremental view, knowledge is also crucial. As in our discussion of expertise, domain knowledge guides search and allows the recognition of patterns that may suggest useful avenues to try.

Creativity as Problem Finding.   Another possibility in the general problem-solving framework is that creative problem solving often involves viewing the problem in a new way. When the problem has been "appropriately" represented, the solution is often clear. Thus, suggestions that creative thinking involves sudden insights (e.g., Wallas, 1926) often bring in the idea that the problem has been re-represented. Creativity training techniques (see, e.g., Gordon, 1961) often try to get the problem solvers to think about the problem in new ways until a solution comes to them.

One suggestion that is generally consistent with these ideas is that real creativity involves not just representing a given problem but "finding" the real problem and representing that. Creative people may not be creative in their solutions but rather creative in their choice of problems. For example, Getzels and Csikszentmihalyi (1976) analyzed how artists painted, starting with the composition. The artists were provided with a table of objects and asked to choose some of the objects, compose a still life, and paint it. The pertinent result is that artists whose paintings were judged to be more original tended to spend more effort choosing objects, sometimes biting into the objects to help make their decision. Perkins (1988) suggests that a hallmark of such problem finding is the extensive exploration of possibilities before committing to an approach.

In fact, such a process has been suggested within the general problem-solving framework for many years (e.g., Newell, Shaw, & Simon, 1964). More recently, Simon (1989) further explains the importance of this problem finding using the term **problem formulation**. The reason for this term is to make clear that such an activity can be viewed as another type of problem solving in which the problem is to decide how best to formulate the problem. Often in trying to solve one problem we need to pose and solve some other problem. Many political issues illustrate this idea, in which there may be some agreed-on situation but multiple formulations of the problem. For example, almost everyone would agree that the degree of homelessness in the United States is shameful, but there would be great disagreement as to what the problem is. How the problem is formulated (is it the lack of adequate welfare, lack of adequate economic incentives, etc.) will have great effects on the type of solutions proposed.

Finally, it should be noted that the incremental and problem-finding views are not mutually exclusive, but rather different in emphasis. Combining these ideas, it may be best to think about creativity as arising from a great deal of refining, elaborating, and reformulating of the problem and its possible solutions. Much problem solving involves reformulating the problem using information gained from failed solution attempts.

Does this view capture the essence of creativity? Simon (1989) argues that it does and reviews how various creative scientific discoveries can be explained in terms of applying some heuristics. Even if this view ends up being shown to be incorrect, its proposal has helped to make explicit some of the research questions that most need answering.

Summary

In this chapter we expanded on two important topics in problem solving. First, we discussed expertise. Experts and novices differ in many ways. Experts use high-level principles to represent and categorize problems and have highly organized knowledge about the relations among the various problem types and principles. They tend to solve problems by working forward from the givens, whereas novices tend to work backward from the goal. These differences all depend on the experts' greater domain knowledge. Although we may learn how to better instruct people on general problem-solving strategies, acquiring extensive domain knowledge will still be crucial for becoming an expert.

Second, we examined creativity. We argued that a traditional view of creativity is inadequate. We then considered viewing creativity as incremental problem solving and problem finding. Although we are clearly far from a full understanding of creativity, our evaluation is that these ideas indicate that much can be learned by considering creativity in the usual problem-solving framework.

Key Terms

creativity

Einstellung

expert system

incubation

intelligent tutoring systems

learner's model

problem formulation

problem schemata

productions

Recommended Readings

Expertise is currently being studied intensively. In addition to the experiments presented here, some useful reviews can be found in Gick (1986) and Reimann and Chi (1989). An edited volume on expertise by Chi, Glaser, and Farr (1988) contains many interesting chapters. These readings include some ideas on the development of expertise as well, but other useful sources are Anderson (1987) and the edited volume by Anderson (1981). Readers interested in heuristics should look at Polya (1945, 1957), Wickelgren (1974), and Schoenfeld (1985). A number of recent books have been published on intelligent tutoring systems, such as the one by Mandl and Lesgold (1988).

Discussions of creative thinking were emphasized by Gestalt psychologists, with Wertheimer's (1945/1982) a very readable and enjoyable book. Weisberg (1986) wrote a clear and interesting short book (with several detailed case studies) arguing against creativity as a special mental activity. Simon (1989) makes a similar argument examining how creativity can be viewed from the traditional human problem-solving framework that he helped develop.

17
REPRISE

We cannot think first and act afterwards. From the moment of birth we are immersed in action, and can only fitfully guide it by taking thought.

Alfred North Whitehead

We have covered quite a variety of topics in considerable detail in this book. In this final section, we wish to briefly provide some further perspective on the field and sum up the points that have served to organize this book.

Trajectory—Current Trends and Future Directions

Cognitive psychology has changed much over the last twenty-five years and is now in an exciting period of progress. In Chapter 2 we presented some ideas on how the field has evolved. In this section we present our views on the progress and directions of the field. We argue that the future will see an increasing integration of both the methods used and the modeling done.

Methods and Measures

Early work on cognition focused on simple tasks and examined straight-forward dependent measures. However, as we began to better appreciate the complexity of the cognitive system, additional methods and measures were included to improve our analyses. We see the future as being particu-larly geared toward increasing integration of methods and measures. Three different senses of integration can be distinguished.

First, the tasks used to study thinking are becoming more complex and integrated into a larger activity. Rather than asking how cognition operates on one simple item, we examine cognition in terms of its role in the whole. To remind you of examples addressed in this book, we can investigate how the perception of depth may emerge from combining information across a large number of individually ambiguous subparts, how the comprehension of a spoken word is influenced by phonological, syntactic, semantic, and pragmatic factors, and how the solution to a problem depends on the earlier problems solved and what was learned from those solutions.

Second, there is diversity and integration of ways of evaluating performance. Rather than examining a single general dependent measure, there is increasingly a focus on trying to account for multiple measures. As we have stressed throughout this book, results are often consistent with a number of interpretations. This underdeterminacy can be partially alleviated by obtaining multiple measures, such as reaction times, errors, and verbal protocols. Finally, even within a single measure, current theories are often trying to account for more aspects of performance such as, in the case of categorization models, both learning and transfer.

Third, there is integration across what have historically been diverse fields. For example, neuropsychological findings from amnesic patients are influencing theories of memory. Studies involving animal learning and conditioning, which had been ignored by many cognitive psychologists as irrelevant, have begun to have an impact in other domains. Models of animal learning have been applied to human categorization with considerable success (e.g., Gluck & Bower, 1988). Finally, there is an increasing trend toward including studies of subjects both very early in their learning, such as children, and very late in their learning, such as experts.

Models

Probably the greatest change in integration has been and will continue to be in modeling. The integration has been both within and between models.

Although it is often useful to try to understand in detail how a particular new task is done, there has been a fundamental change in combining this analysis with other tasks in a more general framework. Increasingly, researchers are seeking principled ways to incorporate new findings into already existing models. This integration prevents the tailoring of assumptions to a single finding and forces one to account for the data with general (across task) assumptions. Again, while the explanation of a single result is greatly underdetermined, this problem is helped by requiring accounts of multiple results. In addition, this integration may lead to unexpected explanations of empirical results (as we illustrated with the SAM model in Chapter 7).

A major change in the modeling is a trend toward more general frameworks, such as the production system architectures or the PDP systems, both of which have been examined in this book. These frameworks have general guiding principles but allow for a diverse set of specific models to be constructed and tested. The analysis of how different assumptions affect the modeling has led to a much better understanding of the important characteristics of models and their limits.

Compared to the complexities of cognition, current theories are incredibly simplified. We cannot expect to come up with the "correct" theory, but rather a useful one—a theory that provides a useful organization of what we know and allows further predictions and extensions to what we do not know.

Furthermore, there will continue to be greater integration of the different model types. That is, while alternative models may be proposed as competitors, there may be means of combining them to exploit their separate insights.

Keeping the World in Mind

Research in cognitive psychology is often guided by analogies or metaphors and over the last twenty-five years or so the computer has served as a useful model of the mind. Computers encode, store, and retrieve information and a great deal of what people do can be considered as information processing. So in some ways people are like computers.

But human beings are also biological organisms that are situated in an environment. Human cognition has evolved in a structured world and the human mind reflects its history. We have argued that progress can be made by asking questions about the functions of cognitive processes based on the idea that intelligence represents a form of adaptation to our environment.

As productive as the computer metaphor continues to be, we attach critical significance to the strategy of "keeping the world in mind." A central point of our book is that *the human mind is NOT a general-purpose computing device.* Instead the human mind embodies a number of commitments or constraints that foster and guide our specific adaptation to this particular world and its possibilities.

It should be clear by now why generalized information processing will not work. In domains ranging from learning and perception to concept formation and problem solving, organisms are confronted with the need to act on the basis of inadequate information. Most often the situation is underdetermined and the resulting ambiguity challenges the organism that would act intelligently. A rat that knows the principles of experimental design would have to design thousands of studies to be sure about why it became ill. Even when a situation can be analyzed in principle, by enumerating the possibilities, in practice, a systematic analysis runs into computational complexity problems. There are just too many possibilities. A general-purpose information processing device, even one orders of magnitude faster than our fastest computers, would be far too stupid to survive in our world. The reason that we *can* act intelligently in our world (to the extent we do) is that the mind embodies certain constraints or guiding principles that represent guesses about what's going to prove significant and useful. These guiding principles are not infallible (again, consider our susceptibility to visual illusions) but they work pretty well.

Our interaction with the world is active—we do not just accumulate experience, we organize, interpret, and theorize about it. Mental representations reflect the goal of establishing correspondences between events in the world and our mental experience. As William James said, mind and world have evolved together and represent something of a mutual fit.

We hope that it is equally clear that to view thought as adaptive does not entail a commitment to the position that cognition is guided by optimality. By the standards of optimality, human cognition can be seen as riddled with false assumptions and failure. This is perhaps most obviously true in the area of decision making where optimality is often readily defined. Here human decision making shows systematic violations of optimality and rationality.

Cognitive psychologists seem to be especially attracted to human error, and for good reason. Human error has the paradoxical quality of revealing the wisdom of the mind. In many cases errors reveal how people are normally capable of success, because errors provide clues to underlying processing principles and strategies.

In short, the study of cognition is not a catalog of errors and shortcomings of the human mind. The impressive thing is that we are capable of intelligent action at all. The brain is a special-purpose computing device that makes bold assumptions about the world, assumptions that for the most part serve us well. From this perspective, cognitive psychologists are in the business of looking beneath the surface of occasional failure to find the keys to successful action.

We end with another quotation:

Errors, like straws upon the surface flow;
He [she] who would search for pearls must dive below.
John Dryden, *All for Love*

GLOSSARY

ACT (Adaptive Control of Thought) theory of memory representation and use, as well as procedural learning. The theory is a combination of a network model for declarative knowledge and a production system model for procedural knowledge.

ad hoc categories categories that are spontaneously created, typically in the service of some goal (e.g., things to take on a camping trip).

affirming the consequent logical error in reasoning; one assumes that if the consequent is true then the premise must be true (that "*P* implies *Q*" and "*Q*" leading to the conclusion "*P*").

algorithm a systematic procedure that is guaranteed to lead to a correct solution to a problem.

algorithmic level level of analysis that describes in a general way what computational steps are needed and what representations are used.

Allais paradox an example of the certainty effect where adding the same amount to two choices reverses the preference.

analog representation a representation that mimics or simulates the structure of its referent in a more or less direct manner. In the case of spatial representations continuous spatial information and spatial relationships might be the relevant structure.

anchoring and adjustment judgment strategy where one starts with some initial estimate or anchor and then adjusts the estimate in light of new information.

anterograde amnesia an inability to learn new information after some trauma.

artificial intelligence the science of writing computer programs to do intelligent things.

atmosphere effect tendency to accept a conclusion as true in reasoning with categorical syllogisms when the quantifiers in the premises and conclusions agree with each other.

auditory theory idea that speech perception derives from the general properties of the auditory system. In contrast to motor theory, auditory theory denies that "speech is special."

automaticity the development of processes that can be run off without the use of attentional resources.

autoshaping refers to a procedure in an operant learning situation where a signal (a key lighting) is paired with the presentation of reward (as in a classical conditioning situation) and the organism "learns" a response (e.g., key pecking, in the case of pigeons) even though none is required.

availability heuristic a judgment strategy in which probability judgments are based on the readiness with which examples are brought to mind.

basic level intermediate level of categorization that appears to be psychologically privileged in that it is the first one learned, shows cross-cultural consistency, and is the natural level at which objects are named.

behaviorism approach to research that focuses on *behavior* as the subject matter of psychology.

biconditional in reasoning it refers to "if and only if." In other words, P implies Q and Q implies P.

blocking refers to the failure to learn about the association between a stimulus and some outcome because of the presence of some other stimulus that already predicts or has been associated with that outcome.

bottleneck model theory of attention where the perceptual system selects one signal (or a small number) from many sources for further perceptual processing.

bounded rationality the idea of taking computational costs and limitations into account to determine what is rational.

case-based reasoning an artificial intelligence approach in which earlier cases (or instances) are retrieved and adapted to help solve the current problem.

categorical perception refers to the observation that continuous variations on a dimension relevant to a phonemic contrast are often perceived in a discrete (all-or-none) rather than a graded manner.

categorical syllogisms class of problems concerned with what conclusions follow from quantified (all, some, none) premises involving categories.

category the set of entities or examples "picked out" by a concept.

certainty effect refers to a tendency for people to violate expected utility in the direction approaching sure gains and avoiding sure losses.

characteristic features attributes that are generally true of a concept, but not always true.

chunking combining several pieces of information into a single unit or code.

chunks units of organized information.

classical conditioning a form of learning in which a hitherto neutral stimulus, the conditioned stimulus (CS), is paired with an unconditioned stimulus (US), regardless of what the animal does.

classical view theory of conceptual structure that argues that concepts are based on defining features.

coarticulation refers to the fact that the articulatory movements for the different sounds for a word overlap one another in time. This means that individual phonetic segments depend on their surrounding context so that there is no single invariant property in speech that corresponds uniquely to a given phonetic segment.

cognitive heuristics reasoning strategies that are easy or natural shortcuts that often work well but sometimes introduce biases and misconceptions.

cognitive psychology the research approach that views intelligent behavior within an information processing framework and which is characterized by a willingness to develop and evaluate ideas about internal mechanisms and procedures that mediate behavior.

cognitive science   refers to the interdisciplinary approach to the study of the mind that includes artificial intelligence, cognitive psychology, linguistics, anthropology, and philosophy.

compensatory response model   theory of classical conditioning that argues that conditioned responses are adaptive and that the conditioned response will either be similar in form or opposite in form to the unconditioned response, depending on what is adaptive.

computational complexity   refers to the observation that many cognitive procedures are impractical because of the time and effort needed to evaluate the very large number of alternative possibilities.

computational level   abstract level of analysis that tells what is being computed and why. In a sense it is a theory of competence.

concept   a mental representation of a category.

conceptual combination   refers to the problem of understanding the meaning of novel concepts derived from combinations of simple concepts (e.g., paper bee).

confirmation bias   tendency to seek out evidence that would support a hypothesis rather than evidence that might disconfirm it.

confounding factor   a factor that varies simultaneously with an independent variable. For example, when a new educational technique is introduced, improvements in learning may arise either because the technique is indeed more effective or because the new technique is novel and different from the usual routine. In this event novelty would be a confounding factor.

conjunction fallacy   tendency to think the conjunction of two events is more likely than one or more of the individual events. It may arise when people use similarity to some prototypic situation rather than probability as the basis of judgment.

connection weights   in PDP models, the weights determining how much the activation of one unit affects the activation of another unit. These weights serve to encode long-term memories.

connectionist models   approach to cognitive modeling that typically views information as a pattern of activation over a network of interconnected cells.

consistent mapping   procedure where the response associated with a stimulus is consistent across trials. This procedure leads to automaticity.

constituents   the parts or components of some unit. Language is characterized by a hierarchy of constituent structures.

constraints   natural assumptions or biases that favor some possibilities over others. For example, rats tend to associate illness with odors and tastes rather than with visual cues.

context effect   the improvement (or decrement) in memory of having information occur with the same (or different) context.

conversational maxims   principles or guidelines for cooperative communication.

conversion hypothesis   idea that some reasoning errors derive from reinterpreting or reversing a premise (e.g., converting "All A's are B's" into the belief that "All B's are A's").

correlation   a measure of the extent to which two variables are related. The relation is not necessarily causal. Correlation coefficients can vary from -1.00

to 1.00 (.00 means the variables are unrelated) and the bigger the absolute correlation (the more it departs from zero, either positively or negatively), the stronger the relation.

creativity   the cognitive activity leading to original and relevant solutions to a problem.

credit assignment   the problem of identifying why some action succeeded or failed so that the learner can perform more successfully in the future.

critical period   period in the development of an organism when it is particularly sensitive to environmental influences. Outside of this critical period, learning may not take place at all.

crosstalk   problem associated with integrating the components of complex stimuli. Crosstalk occurs when a component or constituent of an irrelevant stimulus interferes with or replaces the corresponding component of the relevant stimulus.

CS (conditioned stimulus)   the originally neutral stimulus that is paired with an unconditioned stimulus in conditioning experiments (e.g., bell or tone).

declarative knowledge   knowledge of factual information, including both episodic and semantic information, "knowing that."

deductive reasoning   concerned with which beliefs are licensed or entailed by other beliefs by necessity or logic.

deep structure (underlying representation)   grouping of words that represents the basic meaning of a sentence.

default assumptions   in the absence of specific information slots of schemas may be filled with information that is usually correct; hence it is an assumption made by default.

defining features   attributes that are present in all examples of a concept.

denying the antecedent   reasoning error where people incorrectly interpret "P implies Q" and "not P" as leading to the conclusion "not Q."

dependent variable   the variable measured and recorded by the experimenter.

dichotic listening   listening to two unrelated messages played over headphones. This technique is often used in studies of selective attention.

distributional information   information about word classes that is based on their privileges of occurrence in speech. For example, nouns and adjectives tend to appear after the word *the*, but verbs do not.

dual coding hypothesis   the idea that pictures are remembered better than words because pictures are encoded both verbally and as images.

early selection theory   theory of attention where a signal is selected early in processing and unattended signals are lost and unavailable to the perceiver.

echoic memory   auditory sensory storage buffer.

ecological validity   approach with the ideal of developing theories that operate in realistic everyday situations. Some advocates of this approach would argue that artificial laboratory experiments are sometimes "ecologically invalid" because they fail to capture critical aspects of real-world situations.

Einstellung   the rigid or mechanical application of a solution procedure to a problem.

elimination by aspects   theory of choice behavior that suggests that successive criteria or aspects are considered and any choices not meeting a criterion are eliminated. This process continues until all alternatives but one are eliminated.

empiricism   the idea that knowledge derives from experience.

encoding   the initial processing of a stimulus that leads to a mental representation in memory.

encoding specificity   retrieval depends on the extent to which the retrieval cue matches the information available at encoding.

episodic memory   memory for autobiographical events, including the context (time, place, setting) in which they occurred.

exemplar models   categorization models that assume that classification decisions for new examples are based on their similarity to specific, stored examples rather than similarity to a summary prototype.

expected utility theory   theory that says people should maximize their subjective value or utility which is equal to the subjective value of outcomes multiplied by their probability.

expected value theory   theory that says people should maximize objective value which is equal to the value of outcomes multiplied by their probability of occurrence.

expert system   a computer system that is designed to simulate the reasoning of a particular expert. It consists of a knowledge base (including facts and heuristics) and an inference method for applying this knowledge.

explicit memory   uses of memory requiring the conscious recollection of an experience.

extinction   the weakening of response tendencies when reinforcement is withdrawn.

family resemblance   principle of category organization where members of the category tend to share properties but where there is no property or feature that every member has to have. Family resemblance categories are consistent with the probabilistic view.

fan effects   an explanation for interference effects (from ACT). The more nodes linked to the current node (i.e., the fan), the longer the time to activate these nodes.

feature comparison model   a theory of category verification composed of two stages. The first stage consists of a fast overall comparison, using both characteristic and defining features. If this match is not sufficiently high or low, the defining features are examined.

feature integration theory   theory of attention that suggests conjunctions or combinations of features can only be encoded in a serial manner which requires attention.

features   separable, distinct components that are combined in various ways to create complex entities.

figural effect   observation that it appears more natural in categorical syllogisms to go from the subject of a first premise to the predicate of a second premise in formulating a conclusion than vice versa. This can bias conclusions as a function of the order in which premises are given.

figure-ground   refers to determining which parts of a scene form connected and cohesive objects and which parts are background.

filter theory   theory of attention where the perceptual system selects one signal from many sources for further perceptual analysis.

fixed-action patterns   stereotyped, species-specific behaviors triggered by genetically preprogrammed releasing stimuli.

formants   resonant frequencies of the vocal tract (multiples of the fundamental frequency that are enhanced by the shape of the vocal tract).

frame   structural component of a schema that provides relevant dimensions of information. See also schemata.

framing   phenomenon in decision making where the same information presented in different forms can lead to different decisions.

free recall   a test of memory in which the subjects are asked to reproduce from memory as much of the presented material as possible.

functional fixedness   the tendency to see only the typical use of an object, rather than some new use that might help in solving a problem (i.e., being fixed on its usual function).

gambler's fallacy   tendency to think that prior events can influence outcome of an independent probabilistic event (as when it is "due" to happen).

garden path sentences   sentences like, "The horse raced past the barn fell" where we suddenly realize that we have been constructing the wrong interpretation of the sentence. These sentences make the point that comprehension proceeds "on line" rather than by taking in entire sentences before interpreting them.

geons   features in the form of three-dimensional shapes such as cylinders, cones, and wedges, which are assumed to be the constituents of objects in Biederman's theory of object recognition.

given-new strategy   principle of communication where new information is presented only after a relevant context of old information is provided.

good continuation   refers to the Gestalt principle that contours that vary smoothly along their course tend to be part of the same object.

government and binding theory   Chomsky's recent grammatical theory which aims to reduce differences between languages to variations in a small number of parameters. In this theory there is only one transformation, "move x," where x is a parameter that can vary across languages.

GPS   the General Problem Solver, a computer program developed by Newell, Shaw, and Simon that was capable of solving problems by analyzing them into goals and subgoals and a set of procedures for achieving them.

Gricean principles   conversational maxims such as tell the truth, be informative, be relevant, and be clear.

habituation   a form of learning manifested in reduced response to repeated stimulation.

heuristic   a rule of thumb for problem solving or reasoning, which may lead to a correct answer but is not guaranteed to do so.

hierarchical model   a model of semantic knowledge in which knowledge about objects is stored in a hierarchy or ranking, with instances connected to their superordinates by is-a links.

hill-climbing   a problem-solving heuristic in which one chooses whichever next step brings one closer to the goal.

hindsight bias   inflated estimate *after the fact* for how likely one would have been to know or predict something *before the fact*.

holophrastic speech   refers to a stage in language development where a single word seems to stand for an entire sentence.

homeopathy   belief that causes and effects tend to be similar.

iconic memory   visual sensory storage buffer with large information capacity and brief duration.

ill-defined problem   a problem in which the givens, goals, or means of transforming the conditions are not clearly specified.

illusory correlation   a tendency to see relationships between two variables that are not objectively present in the data.

implementational level   level of analysis where the physical realization of an algorithm or procedure is instantiated.

implicit memory   uses of memory in which some previous experience can affect performance without any conscious recollection of the experience.

imprinting   a learned attachment that is formed at a particular period in life (the critical or sensitive period) and is difficult to reverse.

incidental learning   learning that takes place without any intent to learn. In memory research, it usually involves a test of memory in which subjects are not aware during study that they will be tested for their memory of the material.

incubation   in the traditional view of creativity, the time in which a problem is put aside and the solution is worked upon at an unconscious level.

independent variable   the factor that is varied by the experimenter.

induction   the use of inductive inferences or the process of reasoning from partial knowledge to more general situations. Inductive inferences are not logical truths but they may often be true in experience.

inductive reasoning   concerned with which beliefs support or are supported by other beliefs.

information processing   approach to research that views cognition as involving the encoding, storage, and retrieval of information.

instrumental learning   a form of learning in which a reward is given only if the organism performs the instrumental response (e.g., key peck). What is learned is the relationship between the response and the reinforcer.

intelligent tutoring systems   computer systems that guide a student through the learning of some new information. The tutor keeps track of what the student knows and tries to increase this knowledge until it matches the expert knowledge of the material.

intentional forgetting   an experimental procedure in which subjects are sometimes signaled that they can forget the items presented so far on the list.

interactive activation   assumption typically associated with connectionist models that processing (e.g., in perception) depends on interactive influences at multiple levels of abstraction (e.g., feature, letter, word).

intersection search   in network models, activation spreads down links from the concepts until some connecting path is found (or until it is determined that no appropriate connecting path is likely to be present).

introspectionism   approach to cognition that focuses on the contents of consciousness as the subject matter of psychology.

intuitive physics   naive or intuitive theories about how the world works.

invariants   properties of the proximal (retinal) stimulus pattern that remain unchanged despite various transformations of the distal stimulus or object.

late selection   a theory of attention that suggests that processing limitations arise primarily at late stages of processing where information is being integrated and decisions made.

law of contradiction   one criterion of rationality that states that reasoning processes that operate on the same evidence should not reach contradictory conclusions.

learnability theory   formalism developed to determine under what input conditions a given learning procedure can be expected to succeed at all or within a reasonable time.

learner's model   in intelligent tutoring systems, the representation of what the learner is assumed to know at a given time. It is updated throughout the tutoring sessions.

learning   a relatively permanent change in behavior or knowledge as a result of experience.

learning-performance distinction   refers to the fact that what is learned is not necessarily directly manifest in performance (contrary to some early theories of learning that equate the two).

less-is-more hypothesis   the hypothesis that children's information processing limitations are precisely what allows a child language learner to surpass an adult language learner.

levels of processing   the proposal that different encodings vary in how deeply the material is processed and that deeper processings lead to the material being better remembered. The memory is established as a by-product of the processing.

linear separability   categories are linearly separable if some weighted additive combination of properties can be used to correctly classify examples.

linguistic universals   the set of properties that all languages share. According to Chomsky these properties are innate.

links   in network models, the pointers designating the relation between two nodes, representing which ideas can access which other ideas.

long-term memory   the term referring to the retention of information over long (i.e., more than 30 seconds) periods of time, with a large (unlimited?) capacity. Forgetting from long-term memory is usually thought to be due to retrieval failures caused by interference from other knowledge.

mathematical models   models of cognition that can be cast into mathematical form and which often yield quantitative predictions about behavior.

McCollough effect   an orientation-specific color aftereffect. If one stares at green horizontal bars and red vertical bars, one sees a red afterimage when looking at horizontal bars, and a green afterimage when looking at vertical bars.

McGurk effect   refers to the phenomena when visual information from articulatory movements and the acoustic speech signal are integrated to yield a unitary percept. For example, the articulation of /pa-pa/ coupled with the speech sound /na-na/ produces the percept /ma-ma/.

means-ends analysis   a problem-solving search heuristic in which one compares the current state to the goal state and then chooses the problem operator that will most reduce the difference.

memory decay hypothesis   an idea about the cause of forgetting, in which items that are not recalled or studied for a period of time tend simply to lose strength in memory as a result of an automatic process of decay.

memory span   the number of items (usually digits or words) that a person can immediately repeat back accurately. In adults, a typical memory span would be about seven items.

mental models   knowledge structures that are constructed in the service of understanding and explaining experience. Mental models are constrained by theories about the world rather than empirically derived generalizations.

mental rotation   refers to the task where participants are asked to determine if two objects differ only in rotation. Results from these studies have been used to argue for the existence of analog representations.

metamemory   knowledge about one's own memory and memory abilities, as well as about different memory strategies and their effectiveness for different situations.

method of loci   mnemonic technique for remembering a set of items in order by mentally moving along a familiar path and "dropping off" a to-be-remembered item at each landmark.

minimal attachment   comprehension strategy that favors attaching a new phrase to an old node rather than building up a new phrasal node.

mnemonic devices   strategies or procedures for remembering material, many of which rely on visual imagery.

mnemonists   people who are able to remember large amounts of information.

modularity   view of cognitive organization that suggests that certain cognitive functions operate as special-purpose, isolated mechanisms. Only the outputs of such modules are said to be available to the rest of the cognitive system.

modus ponens   the valid argument structure that says that if P implies Q is true and P is true, then Q must be true.

modus tollens   the valid argument structure that says that if P implies Q is true and Q is false, then P must be false.

morpheme   the smallest significant unit of meaning in language.

motion parallax   a perceptual cue to depth in which as one moves back and forth the images of nearby objects move across the field of vision faster than more distant objects.

motor theory   idea that people perceive speech by virtue of tacit knowledge of how speech is produced and that this knowledge is used to adjust for the lack of invariants in the speech signal.

mutual exclusivity constraint   bias or tendency to expect objects to have only one label.

naive theory   intuitive theories or explanatory structures that people construct to understand their experience. Naive theories are of greatest interest when they conflict with the normatively correct theory.

negative evidence   refers to the observation that language learners rarely receive information about what sentences are *not* grammatical. This is important because many learning procedures require negative evidence in order to succeed.

nodes   in network models, a unit that represents a particular concept or idea.

operant behaviors   responses resulting or followed by a particular effect on the environment.

operant learning or conditioning   a form of learning in which a reward is given only if the organism performs the instrumental response (e.g., key peck). What is learned is the relationship between the response and the reinforcer.

overdetermination of small samples   refers to the fact that when one has many observations on a small sample of cases there will be numerous apparent regularities that arise simply by chance. Consequently, many of these would not generalize to a new sample.

overgeneralization errors   errors that appear to reflect the inappropriate application of a general rule. Whether or not these errors derive from *rules* is a matter of controversy.

partial report technique   procedure for separating memory loss from limited attention by providing a postdisplay signal indicating which part of the display is to be reported.

PDP   also referred to as parallel distributed processing or connectionist models. The models consist of a large number of interconnected units. Concepts are represented as patterns of activations over these units and learning proceeds by changes in the weights of the connections between the units.

phoneme   the smallest significant unit of sound in language.

phonemic restoration effect   a speech illusion that occurs when a nonspeech sound (e.g., a cough) is substituted for a phoneme in a sentence. The listener appears to automatically use the surrounding context to fill in the missing phoneme and listeners are not aware that the phoneme is missing.

phonology   the rules governing the sequence in which phonemes can be arranged.

phrase structure   building blocks or organizational units of sentences that are themselves comprised of words. For example, sentences are naturally broken into a noun phrase and a verb phrase.

picture superiority effect   empirical generalization that pictures are remembered better than words.

placebo effect   change in performance associated with the belief that one is in a treatment condition when in fact one is not. For example, a patient given an inert substance rather than a drug may show improvement.

positive test strategy   tendency to test an implication that will be true if a hypothesis is true.

pragmatic reasoning schemas   reasoning strategies associated with social contracts such as permission and obligation that may or may not be activated in conditional reasoning tasks.

pragmatics   aspects of language that refer to the practical knowledge a language user needs to have in order to communicate effectively.

preference reversals   refers to the inconsistencies between people's choices and the prices or values they place on alternatives.

primacy effect   the superiority in memory for items in the first part of the list compared to items in the middle part of the list.

primary rehearsal   repeating by rote some information without any effort to develop meaningful associations to it. This is an effective way of holding information in short-term memory, but is not very effective for later remembering.

proactive interference memory loss for recently acquired information that is caused by interference from memories acquired earlier.

probabilistic view theory of conceptual structure that argues that concepts are based on characteristic or typical features rather than strict definitions.

probability learning refers to situations where events happen probabilistically, and effective performance depends on learning what these probabilities are.

probability matching refers to a tendency to match the probabilities of events rather than maximize the likelihood of being correct. For example, if one alternative is rewarded 70 percent of the time and the other is rewarded 30 percent of the time, people tend to select the first alternative 70 rather than 100 percent of the time.

problem a person is said to face a problem when he or she has some goal for which no simple direct means is known. Problems consist of a goal, givens, means of transforming conditions, and obstacles.

problem formulation taking an ill-defined problem and determining how to represent the problem. In many situations, the determination of what problem really should be solved is thought to be where much of the creative activity lies.

problem operators in a problem space, the processes that "move" the solver from one state to another state.

problem schema or problem category structured knowledge about a type of problem that allows the problem solver to identify problems of that type, as well as the associated procedures for solving those problems.

problem space the internal representation of the problem, consisting of states and operators.

problem state in a problem space, a state represents the information available to the problem solver in that situation, a "state" of knowledge. The problem solver moves among the states by applying problem operators.

procedural knowledge knowledge about how to do something, "knowing how." Usually thought to be gradually acquired through practice and not easily communicated verbally to others.

productions a simple means of representing knowledge in terms of condition-action pairs: *if* some conditions are met *then* some action is taken. Often used for representing procedural knowledge.

productivity refers to the observation that language is not a closed system in that an unlimited number of sentences can be constructed from a vocabulary and syntax. More generally units at one level of analysis can be combined to create many more units at a higher level of analysis.

propositional representations representations that take the form of abstract languagelike propositions that are not tied to any particular sensory modality.

propositions smallest units of meaning about which one can reasonably assert truth or falsity.

prospect theory theory of decision making that attempts to account for violations of expected utility by assuming that utilities are evaluated relative to a reference point and that subjective probability (which does not correspond in a simple way to objective probability) is integrated with utility to determine choices.

prototype   a mental representation of a category that reflects the central tendency or what is on the average true of a category.

proximity principle   Gestalt principle that suggests that the closer two figures are, the more likely it is that they will be grouped perceptually.

psychological essentialism   belief that things have underlying natures that make them the thing that they are.

rational model   normative model of decision making based on maximizing utility.

recency effect   the superiority in memory (usually in free recall tests) for the items at the end of the list relative to items in the middle of the list.

recursive decomposition   idea that argues that an event at one level of description can be specified more fully at a lower level of description by analyzing the event into components and processes that operate on these components.

reductionism   idea that assumes that the best or correct level of description is the most specific one.

regret theory   theory of decision making that assumes that choices are determined in part by considering how one will feel if different outcomes occur.

reinforcement   an event that can serve to change the likelihood of the behavior that precedes it.

release from PI   an experimental procedure for studying what type of information about the stimulus is being encoded by examining the extent of proactive interference when different types of information are changed.

releasers   particular stimulus patterns that lead to or elicit species-specific behaviors such as fixed action patterns.

repetition priming   the finding that a recent exposure to a stimulus affects its subsequent processing.

representations   internal model linked to external (real-world) objects and events so as to preserve functionally relevant information.

respondent behaviors   responses that are directly elicited by the environment, as in classical conditioning.

retinal disparity   source of depth information associated with stereopsis.

retrieval plan   an organized set of cues to be used in helping to retrieve information.

retroactive interference   memory loss for previously learned information that is caused by interference from recently acquired information.

retrograde amnesia   a loss of memory for events that occurred prior to some trauma.

rigidity constraint   assumption that objects do not change shape while moving. Such an assumption would allow a system to determine shape from motion.

route knowledge   spatial knowledge in the form of the appropriate procedure for navigating from one point to another.

SAM   search of associative memory theory, in which long-term memory consists of a set of interconnected concepts and retrieval is cue-dependent. This theory provides quantitative fits of many data and relates different memory tests.

satisficing   using the criteria of whether an alternative is satisfactory (as opposed to optimal)

savings in relearning   improvement in learning performance for material learned earlier.

schemata   generalized knowledge structures used in understanding. Schemata tell what to expect and what unstated information may nonetheless be inferred as present.

script   a knowledge structure containing information about the sequence of events in routine or stereotypical situations such as going to a restaurant.

segmentation   refers to the problem the language learner faces of determining the correct units or chunks.

self-fulfilling prophecy   refers to the tendency of people to act in such a way as to make what they predicted would happen actually happen. For example, if one expects someone to be hostile, one might behave in a way that brings out unfriendliness.

semantic bootstrapping   refers to the idea that knowledge of semantics helps get the syntactic learning process going.

semantic memory   memory for general knowledge of the world and language. The type of knowledge often found in encyclopedias and dictionaries, but not knowledge about particular events.

semantic relatedness   in the spreading activation model of semantic organization, the organization of memory by the total interconnectedness among concepts.

semantics   the aspect of language dealing with meaning.

serial position effect   the recall of an item in a list depends on where in the list it was presented, with middle items recalled worse than items at the beginning or end.

short-term memory   the term referring to a limited amount of information being retained over a brief period of time. Sometimes thought of as a separate memory store for information before it is transferred to long-term memory or as the activated portion of long-term memory.

simulation models   models of cognition that take the form of computer programs where steps in the program correspond to cognitive processes.

size constancy   refers to the tendency for people to see a given object as being the same size regardless of the size of the retinal image.

slot   component of a frame that is filled in by particular information. In the absence of specific information a slot may have a default value.

smoothness constraint   assumption that the surfaces of objects are smooth relative to their distance from the viewer.

spacing effect   the result that repeated items are better remembered if their repetitions occur apart from each other, rather than being massed or successive.

span of attention   the number of distinct items a person is aware of from a brief presentation of an array of items.

spatial frequency analysis   theory of perception that assumes that object recognition is based on patterns of changes in intensity or contrast associated with an object.

spatial neglect   deficit associated with brain injury where the person acts unaware of objects and events on the neglected side of space and may include neglect of the limbs and body surface.

spotlight metaphor for attention   theory of attention that suggests that attention is like a spotlight in the sense that it is continuous, can be narrowly or broadly focused, and moves continuously from location to location.

spreading activation   a process in network models in which nodes are activated (made available for processing) by their links to other nodes, as if the activation were spreading from node to node through the links.

state-dependent recall   the improvement (or decrement) in recall of information learned when the person's internal state is similar to (or different from) the current state.

stereogram   textures of black and white dots used in studies of stereopsis. A key property of stereograms is that they can be used to study the alignment process as the visual system has to figure out which dots presented to the left eye go with which dots presented to the right eye.

stereopsis   refers to the fact that our two eyes view the visual world from slightly different angles. The difference, retinal disparity, provides depth information.

structural descriptions   theory of object perception based on the idea that recognition is based on comparing images with descriptions that include parts and their spatial relationships to each other.

subset principle   refers to a bias or strategy for language learners to avoid hypothesizing overly general grammars.

sunk costs   framing effect where people continue to engage in unrewarding behavior because of prior investment of resources. Sitting all the way through a terrible movie just because you have paid to get in is an example of sunk costs.

superstitious behavior   refers to a situation where rewards are given independently of an organism's behavior but where nonetheless certain behaviors are "learned" because of their (chance) association with these rewards.

surface structure   the organization of sentences as they are spoken or written.

survey knowledge   spatial knowledge that preserves relevant information about spatial relationships as in a map.

syntactic bootstrapping   refers to the idea that syntactic knowledge helps get the semantic learning process going.

syntax   aspect of language concerned with the way that words combine to form sentences.

systematicity   principle for interpreting analogies where one gives more weight to properties and relations that have corresponding higher order relations.

taxonomic constraint   strategy or bias for assuming that labels refer to objects of the same kind rather than to objects that are contextually or thematically related.

telegraphic speech   stage in language development where inessential words such as articles and pronouns are omitted.

template matching   theory of perception that assumes that object recognition is based on comparing images of objects with stored patterns or templates.

texture gradient   the elements of a textured surface appear to be packed closer and closer away as the surface recedes and therefore texture gradients provide depth information.

transformational grammar   theory of grammar that suggests many forms (surface structures) result from applying a transformation to a base or underlying structure.

transitivity   a criterion of rationality that says if you prefer A to B and B to C then you should prefer A to C. That is, preferences should be transitive.

Turing machine   a simple machine consisting of a tape, a reading device and a table of actions for each state of the machine. Turing proved that such a machine could do any computation that could be performed on a digital computer.

Turing test   a test where a person is communicating over a teletype with either another person or with a computer. If people are unable to tell which is which, then we should agree that computers are intelligent and can think, Turing argued.

type-token distinction   a representation distinction in network models in which the nodes representing general concepts (types) are connected to but distinct from the nodes representing particular instances of that concept (tokens).

typicality   refers to the observation that some examples of a category may be "better" examples or more typical than others. Typical category members have more characteristic features of the category than atypical category members.

typicality effect   in category verification tasks, the finding that typical instances of a category (e.g., robin-bird) are verified more quickly than less typical instances (e.g., penguin-bird).

unusualness heuristic   a general bias or strategy for linking surprising events to unusual preceding stimuli or events.

UR (unconditioned response)   in classical conditioning, the response that is elicited by the unconditioned stimulus without prior training (e.g., air puff to the eye elicits an eyeblink).

US (unconditioned stimulus)   in classical conditioning, the stimulus that elicits the UR and the presentation of which acts as reinforcement.

valid argument   an argument is deductively valid if its conclusion necessarily follows from the premise. The conclusion need not be true in the sense of corresponding to some state of affairs in the world.

verbal protocols   the data of a person talking during some task. Often these protocols are taken during problem solving with the person asked to think aloud while solving the problem.

voice onset time   in speech production the time between the release of air and the beginning of vocal cord vibration. For example, [b] has a shorter voice onset time than [p].

voicing   in phonology, refers to whether or not the production of a consonant is accompanied by the vibration of the vocal chords. For example, [s] is voiceless whereas [z] is voiced.

well-defined problem   a problem in which the goal, givens, and means of transforming the conditions are completely specified.

what system   distinct neuroanatomical system associated with identifying *what* something is.

where system   distinct neuroanatomical system associated with determining *where* something is.

whole object constraint   bias or strategy of assuming that novel words refer to an entire object rather than its parts or properties.

working backward   a problem-solving heuristic that initially focuses on the goal. The solver applies operators to the goal state until it is transformed into one or more of the givens. The solution is then the inverse of each of these operators in the opposite order (i.e., from givens to goal).

working memory   term often used synonymously with "short-term memory," but also used to refer to those functions of short-term memory that are more concerned with its use than with it as a memory store. Often thought of as a mental scratch-pad for manipulating information.

REFERENCES

Ader, R. (1982). Conditioned suppression of humoral immunity in the rat. *Journal of Comparative and Physiological Psychology, 96,* 517–521.

Ader, R., & Cohen, N. (1985). CNS—Immune system interaction: Conditioning phenomena. *The Behavioral and Brain Sciences, 8,* 379–394.

Alcock, J. *Animal behavior* (4th edition). Sunderland, MA: Sinauer Associates.

Allais, M. (1953). Le comportement de phonomme rationnel devant le risque: Critique des postulates et axioms de l'ecole americaine. *Econometrica, 21,* 503–546.

Allport, A. (1989). Visual Attention. In M. I. Posner (Ed.), *Foundation of Cognitive Science.* Cambridge, MA: MIT Press.

Anderson, J. A., Silverstein, J. W., Ritz, S. A., & Jones, R. S. (1977). Distinctive features, categorical perception and probability learning: Some applications of a neural model. *Psychological Review, 84,* 413–451.

Anderson, J. R. (1976). *Language, memory, and thought.* Hillsdale, NJ: Erlbaum.

Anderson, J. R. (1978). Arguments concerning representations for mental imagery. *Psychological Review, 85,* 249–277.

Anderson, J. R. (Ed.) (1981). *Cognitive skills and their acquisition.* Hillsdale, NJ: Erlbaum.

Anderson, J. R. (1982). Acquisition of cognitive skill. *Psychological Review, 89,* 369–406.

Anderson, J. R. (1983). *The architecture of cognition.* Cambridge, MA: Harvard University Press.

Anderson, J. R. (1984). Cognitive psychology and intelligent tutoring. *Proceedings of the Sixth Annual Conference of Cognitive Science Society,* 37–43. Hillsdale, NJ: Erlbaum.

Anderson, J. R. (1987). Skill acquisition: Compilation of weak-method problem solutions. *Psychological Review, 94,* 192–210.

Anderson, J. R. (1989). Practice, working memory, and the ACT* theory of skill acquisition: A comment on Carlson, Sullivan, and Schneider (1989). *Journal of Experimental Psychology: Learning, Memory, and Cognition, 15,* 527–530.

Anderson, J. R. (1990). *The adaptive character of thought.* Hillsdale, NJ: Erlbaum .

Anderson, J. R., & Bower, G. H. (1973). *Human associative memory.* Hillsdale, NJ: Erlbaum.

Anderson, J. R., & Ross, B. H. (1980). Evidence against a semantic-episodic distinction. *Journal of Experimental Psychology: Human Learning and Memory, 6,* 441–466.

Anderson, J. R., & Skwarecki, E. (1986). The automated tutoring of introductory computer programming. *Communications of the ACM, 29,* 842–849.

Anderson, J. R., Conrad, F. G., & Corbett, A. T. (1990). Skill acquisition and the LISP tutor. *Cognitive Science, 13,* 467–505.

Anderson, N. H. (1970). Averaging model applied to the size-weight illusion. *Perception & Psychophysics, 8,* 1–4.

Anderson, R. C., Reynolds, R. C., Schallert, D. L., & Goetz, E. T. (1977). Frameworks for comprehending discourse. *American Education Research Journal, 14,* 367–381.

Arkes, H. R., & Harkness, A. R. (1983). Estimates of contingency between two dichotomous variables. *Journal of Experimental Psychology: General, 112,* 117–135.

Arkes, H. R., Wortmann, R. L., Saville, P. D., & Harkness, A. R. (1981). Hindsight bias among physicians weighing the likelihood of diagnosis. *Journal of Applied Psychology, 66,* 252–254.

Atkinson, R. C. (1975). Mnemotechnics in second-language learning. *American Psychologist, 30,* 821–828.

Atkinson, R. C., & Shiffrin, R. (1968). Human memory: A proposed system and its control processes. In K. Spence & J. Spence (Eds.), *The psychology of learning and motivation* (Vol. 2). New York: Academic Press.

Baars, B. J., & Motley, M. T. (1974). Spoonerisms: Experimental elicitation of human speech errors. *Catalog of Selected Documents in Psychology, 4,* 118. Journal Supplement Abstract Service.

Baars, B. J., Motley, M. T., & MacKay, D. G. (1975). Output editing for lexical status from artificially elicited slips of the tongue. *Journal of Verbal Learning and Verbal Behavior, 14,* 382–391.

Baddeley, A. D. (1978). The trouble with levels: A reexamination of Craik & Lockhart's framework for memory research. *Psychological Review, 85,* 139–152.

Baddeley, A. D. (1983). Working memory. *Philosophical Transactions of the Royal Society London B, 302,* 311–324.

Baddeley, A. D. (1988). The uses of working memory. In P. R. Solomon, G. R. Goethals, C. M. Kelley, & B. R. Stephens (Eds.), *Memory: Interdisciplinary approaches.* New York: Springer-Verlag.

Baddeley, A. D. (1990). *Human memory: Theory and practice.* Needham Heights, MA: Allyn & Bacon.

Baddeley, A. D., & Hitch, G. J. (1974). Working memory. In G. H. Bower (Ed.), *The psychology of learning and motivation* (Vol. 8). New York: Academic Press.

Bahrick, H. P., Bahrick, P. O., & Wittlinger, R. P. (1975). Fifty years of memory for names and faces: A cross-sectional approach. *Journal of Experimental Psychology: General, 104,* 54–75.

Baker, C. L. (1979). Syntactic theory and the projection problem. *Linguistic Inquiry, 10,* 353–581.

Bandura, A. (1982). The psychology of chance encounters and life paths. *American Psychologist, 37,* 747–761.

Bar-Hillel, M., & Fischhoff, B. (1981). When do base rates affect predictions? *Journal of Personality and Social Psychology, 41,* 671–680.

Baron, J. (1988). *Thinking and deciding.* Cambridge, England: Cambridge University Press.

Barsalou, L. W. (1983). Ad hoc categories. *Memory & Cognition, 11*, 211–217.

Barsalou, L. W. (1985). Ideals, central tendency, and frequency of instantiation as determinants of graded structure in categories. *Journal of Experimental Psychology: Learning, Memory, and Cognition, 11*, 629–654.

Barsalou, L. W. (1987). The instability of graded structure: Implications for the nature of concepts. In U. Neisser (Ed.), *Concepts and conceptual development: Ecological and intellectual factors in categorization*. Cambridge, England: Cambridge University Press.

Barsalou, L. W. (1989). Intraconcept similarity and its implications for interconcept similarity. In S. Vosniadon & A. Ortony (Eds.), *Similarity and analogical reasoning*. Cambridge, England: Cambridge University Press.

Barsalou, L. W., & Medin, D. L. (1986). Concepts: Fixed definitions or dynamic context-dependent representations? *Cahiers de Psychologie Cognitive, 6*, 187–202.

Bassok, M. (1990). Transfer of domain-specific problem-solving procedures. *Journal of Experimental Psychology: Learning, Memory, and Cognition, 16*, 522–533.

Bassok, M., & Holyoak, K. J. (1989). Interdomain transfer between isomorphic topics in algebra and physics. *Journal of Experimental Psychology: Learning, Memory, and Cognition, 15*, 153–166.

Bell, D. E. (1982). Regret in decision making under uncertainty. *Operations Research, 30*, 961–981.

Bellezza, F. S. (1984). Reliability of retrieval from semantic memory: Noun meanings. *Bulletin of the Psychonomic Society, 22*, 377–380.

Bellezza, F. S. (1982). *Improve your memory skills*. Englewood Cliffs, NJ: Prentice-Hall.

Bellezza, F. S., & Young, D. R. (1989). Chunking repeated events in memory. *Journal of Experimental Psychology: Learning, Memory, and Cognition, 15*, 990–997.

Bellezza, F. S., Winkler, H. B., & Andrasik, F. (1975). Encoding processes and the spacing effect. *Memory & Cognition, 3*, 451–457.

Berko, J. (1958). The child's learning of English morphology. *Word, 14*, 150–177.

Bernstein, I. L., & Borson, S. (1986). Learned food aversion: A component of anorexia syndromes. *Psychological Review, 93*, 462–472.

Bernstein, I. L. (1978). Learned taste aversions in children receiving chemotherapy. *Science, 200*, 1302–1303.

Bernstein, I. L., Webster, M. M., & Berstein, I. D. (1982). Food aversions in children receiving chemotherapy for cancer. *Cancer, 50*, 2961–2963.

Berwick, R. C. (1986). *The acquisition of syntactic knowledge*. Cambridge, MA: MIT Press.

Bever, T. G. (1970). The cognitive basis for linguistic structures. In J. P. Hayes (Ed.), *Cognition and development of language*. New York: Wiley.

Bever, T. G., & McElree, B. (1988). Empty categories access their antecedents during comprehension. *Linguistic Quarterly, 19*, 34–43.

Biederman, I. (1987). Recognition by components: A theory of human image understanding. *Psychological Review, 94*, 115–147.

Bisiach, E., Perani, D., Vallar, G., & Berti, A. (1986). Unilateral neglect: Personal and extra-personal. *Neuropsychologica, 24*, 759–767.

Bjork, R. A. (1972). Theoretical implications of directed forgetting. In A. W. Melton

& E. Martin (Eds.), *Coding processes in human memory* . Washington, D. C.: V. H. Winston & Sons.

Blakemore, C., & Campbell, F. W. (1969). On the existence of neurons in the human visual system selectively sensitive to the orientation and size of retinal images. *Journal of Physiology, 203,* 237–260.

Bloom, L. (1970). *Language development: Form and function in emerging grammars.* Cambridge, MA: MIT Press.

Bloomfield, L. (1933). *Language.* New York: Holt.

Bock, J. K. (1986). Meaning, sound, and syntax: Lexical priming in sentence production. *Journal of Experimental Psychology: Learning, Memory, and Cognition, 12,* 575–586.

Bolles, R. C. (1970). Species-specific defense reactions and avoidance learning. *Psychological Review, 77,* 32–48.

Boring, E. G. (1950). *A history of experimental psychology.* New York: Appleton-Century-Crofts.

Bourne, L. E., Jr. (1970). Knowing and using concepts. *Psychological Review, 77,* 546–556.

Bourne, L. E., Jr. (1974). An inference model of conceptual rule learning. In R. Solso (Ed.), *Theories in cognitive psychology.* Washington, DC: Erlbaum.

Bower, G. H. (1961). Application of a model to paired-associate learning. *Psychometrika, 26,* 255–280.

Bower, G. H. (1981). Mood and memory. *American Psychologist, 36,* 129–148.

Bower, G. H., & Springston, F. (1970). Pauses as recoding points in letter series. *Journal of Experimental Psychology, 83,* 421–430.

Bower, G. H., Black, J. B., & Turner, T. F. (1979). Scripts in memory for text. *Cognitive Psychology, 11,* 177–220.

Bower, G. H., Clark, M. C., Lesgold, A. M., & Winzenz, D. (1969). Hierarchical retrieval schemes in recall of categorized word lists. *Journal of Verbal Learning and Verbal Behavior, 8,* 323–343.

Bowerman, M. C. (1982). Reorganizational processes in lexical and syntactic development. In E. Wanner & L. Gleitman (Eds.), *Language acquisition: The state of the art.* Cambridge, England: Cambridge University Press.

Bowlby, J. (1969). *Attachment* (Vol. 1). New York: Basic Books.

Braine, M. D. S., Reiser, B. J., & Rumain, B. (1984). Some empirical justification for a theory of natural propositional logic. In G. Bower (Ed.), *The psychology of learning and motivation* (Vol. 18). Orlando, FL: Academic Press.

Bransford, J. D., & Johnson, M. K. (1972). Contextual prerequisites for understanding: Some investigations of comprehension and recall. *Journal of Verbal Learning and Verbal Behavior, 11,* 717–726.

Bransford, J. D., Barclay, J. R., & Franks, J. J. (1972). Sentence memory: A constructive versus interpretive approach. *Cognitive Psychology, 3,* 193–200.

Bransford, J. D., Franks, J. J., Vye, N. J., & Sherwood, R. D. (1989). New approaches to instruction: Because wisdom can't be told. In S. Vosniadou & A. Ortony (Eds.), *Similarity and analogical reasoning.* Cambridge, England: Cambridge University Press.

Braunstein, M. L., & Andersen, G. J. (1986). Testing the rigidity assumption: A reply to Ullman. *Perception, 15,* 641–644.

Bresnan, J. (1978). A realistic transformational grammar. In M. Hall, J. Bresnan, &

G. Miller (Eds.), *Linguistic theory and psychological reality*. Cambridge, MA: MIT Press.

Brewer, W. F. (1977). Memory for the pragmatic implications of sentences. *Memory & Cognition, 5*, 673–678.

Brewer, W. F., & Pani, J. R. (1983). The structure of human memory. In G. H. Bower (Ed.), *The psychology of learning and motivation: Advances in research and theory* (Vol. 17). New York: Academic Press.

Broadbent, D. E. (1958). *Perception and communication*. London: Pergamon Press.

Broerse, J., & Crassini, B. (1984). Investigations of perception and imagery using CAEs: The role of experimental design and psychophysical method. *Perception & Psychophysics, 35*, 155–164.

Brooks, L. R. (1968). Spatial and verbal components of the act of recall. *Canadian Journal of Psychology, 22*, 349–368.

Brooks, L. R. (1978). Nonanalytic concept formation and memory for instances. In E. Rosch & B. B. Lloyd (Eds.), *Cognition and categorization*. New York: Wiley.

Brooks, L. R. (1987). Decentralized control of categorization: The role of prior processing episodes. In U. Neisser (Ed.), *Concepts and conceptual development: Ecological and intellectual factors in categorization*. Cambridge, England: Cambridge University Press.

Brown, A. L. (1989). Analogical learning and transfer: What develops? In S. Vosniadou & A. Ortony (Eds.), *Similarity and analogical reasoning*. Cambridge, England: Cambridge University Press.

Brown, A. L., & Day, J. D. (1983). Macrorules for summarizing text: The development of expertise. *Journal of Verbal Learning and Verbal Behavior, 22*, 1–14.

Brown, A. L., & Kane, M. J. (1988). Preschool children can learn to transfer: Learning to learn and learning from example. *Cognitive Psychology, 20*, 493–523.

Brown, A. L., Bransford, J. D., Ferrara, R. A., & Campione, J. C. (1983). Learning, remembering, and understanding. In J. H. Flavell & E. M. Markman (Eds.), *Handbook of child psychology. Cognitive development* (4th ed., Vol. 3). New York: Wiley.

Brown, C. M. (1984). Computer vision and natural constraints. *Science, 224*, 1299–1305.

Brown, P. L., & Jenkins, H. M. (1968). Autoshaping the pigeon's key peck. *Journal of the Experimental Analysis of Behavior, 11*, 1–8.

Brown, R. (1973). *A first language: The early stages*. Cambridge, MA: Harvard University Press.

Brown, R., & Hanlon, C. (1970). Derivational complexity and the order of acquisition in speech. In R. Brown (Ed.), *Psycholinguistics*. New York: Free Press.

Brunswik, E. (1939). Probability as a determiner of rat behavior. *Journal of Experimental Psychology, 25*, 175–197.

Burtt, H. E. (1941). An experimental study of early childhood memory: Final report. *The Journal of Genetic Psychology, 58*, 435–439.

Butters, N. (1979). Amnesic disorders. In K. Heilman & E. Valenstein (Eds.), *Clinical neuropsychology*. New York: Oxford University Press.

Butters, N. (1984). Alcoholic Korsakoff's Syndrome: An update. *Seminars in Neurology, 4*, 226–244.

Butters, N., & Cermak, L. S. (1986). A case study of the forgetting of autobiographical knowledge: Implications for the study of retrograde amnesia. In D. C. Rubin (Ed.), *Autobiographical memory*. Cambridge, England: Cambridge University Press.

Byrne, R. W. (1982). Geographical knowledge and orientation. In A. W. Ellis (Ed.), *Normality and pathology in cognitive functions*. New York: Academic Press.

Capaldi, E. J. (1967). A sequential hypothesis of instrumental learning. In K. W. Spence & J. T. Spence (Eds.), *The psychology of learning and motivation* (Vol. 1). New York: Academic Press.

Carey, S. (1982). Semantic development, state of the art. In E. Wanner & L. R. Gleitman (Eds.), *Language acquisition: The state of the art*. Cambridge, England: Cambridge University Press.

Carey, S. (1985). *Conceptual change in childhood*. Cambridge, MA: MIT Press.

Carey, S. (1988). Conceptual differences between children and adults. *Mind & Language, 3*, 167–181.

Carlson, R. A., Sullivan, M. A., & Schneider, W. (1989). Practice and working memory effects in building procedural skill. *Journal of Experimental Psychology: Learning, Memory, and Cognition, 15*, 517–526.

Catrambone, R., & Holyoak, K. J. (1989). Overcoming contextual limitations on problem-solving transfer. *Journal of Experimental Psychology: Learning, Memory, and Cognition, 15*, 1147–1156.

Cattell, J. M. (1885). The time it takes to see and name objects. *Mind, 11*, 63–65.

Cavanagh, P., & Leclerc, Y. G. (1989). Shape from shadows. *Journal of Experimental Psychology: Human Perception and Performance, 15*, 3–27.

Cave, K. R., & Wolfe, J. M. (1990). Modeling the role of parallel processing in visual search. *Cognitive Psychology, 22*, 225–271.

Chambers, D., & Reisberg, D. (1985). Can mental images be ambiguous? *Journal of Experimental Psychology: Human Perception and Performance, 11*, 317–328.

Chapman, L. J., & Chapman, J. P. (1959). Atmospheric effect reexamined. *Journal of Experimental Psychology, 58*, 220–226.

Charniak, E. (1973). Jack and Janet in search of a theory of knowledge. *IJCAI Proceedings*, 337–343.

Charniak, E., & McDermott, D. (1985). *Introduction to artificial intelligence*. Reading, MA: Addison-Wesley.

Chase, W. G., & Ericsson, K. A. (1981). Skilled memory. In J. R. Anderson (Ed.), *Cognitive skills and their acquisition*. Hillsdale, NJ: Erlbaum.

Chase, W. G., & Simon, H. A. (1973). The mind's eye in chess. In W. G. Chase (Ed.), *Visual information processing*. New York: Academic Press.

Chedru, F. (1976). Space representation in unilateral spatial neglect. *Journal of Neurology, Neurosurgery and Psychiatry, 39*, 1057–1061.

Cheng, P. W. (1985). Restructuring versus automaticity: Alternative accounts of skill acquisition. *Psychological Review, 92*, 414–423.

Cheng, P. W., & Holyoak, K. J. (1985). Pragmatic reasoning schemas. *Cognitive Psychology, 17*, 391–416.

Cheng, P. W., & Holyoak, K. J. (1989). On the natural selection of reasoning theories. *Cognition, 33*, 285–313.

Cheng, P. W., Holyoak, K. J., Nisbett, R. E., & Oliver, L. M. (1986). Pragmatic versus syntactic approaches to training deductive reasoning. *Cognitive Psychology, 18,* 293–328.

Cherniak, C. (1986). *Minimal rationality.* Cambridge, MA: MIT Press.

Cherry, E. C. (1953). Some experiments on the recognition of speech with one and with two ears. *Journal of the Acoustical Society of America, 25,* 975–979.

Chi, M. T. H., Bassok, M., Lewis, M. W., Reimann, P., & Glaser, R. (1989). Self-explanations: How students study and use examples in learning to solve problems. *Cognitive Science, 13,* 145–182.

Chi, M. T. H., Feltovich, P. J., & Glaser, R. (1981). Categorization and representation of physics problems by experts and novices. *Cognitive Science, 5,* 121–152.

Chi, M. T. H., Glaser, R., & Farr, M. J. (Eds.) (1988). *The nature of expertise.* Hillsdale, NJ: Erlbaum.

Chomsky, C. (1969). *The acquisition of syntax in children from 5 to 10.* Cambridge, MA: MIT Press.

Chomsky, N. (1957). *Syntactic structures.* The Hague, Netherlands: Mouton.

Chomsky, N. (1959). Review of Skinner's *Verbal behavior. Language, 35,* 26–58.

Chomsky, N. (1965). *Aspects of the theory of syntax.* Cambridge, MA: MIT Press.

Chomsky, N. (1975). *Reflections on language.* New York: Random House.

Chomsky, N. (1980). *Rules and representations.* New York: Columbia University Press.

Chomsky, N. (1981). *Lectures on government and binding.* Dordrecht, Netherlands: Foris.

Chomsky, N., & Halle, M. (1968). *The sound pattern of English.* New York: Harper & Row.

Christensen-Szalanski, J. J. J., & Bushyhead, J. B. (1981). Physicians' use of probabilistic information in a real clinical setting. *Journal of Experimental Psychology: Human Perception and Performance, 7,* 928–935.

Clancey, W. J. (1987). *Knowledge-based tutoring: The GUIDON program.* Cambridge, MA: MIT Press.

Clancey, W. J. (1988). Acquiring, representing, and evaluating a competence model of diagnostic strategy. In M. T. H. Chi, R. Glaser, & M. J. Farr (Eds.), *The nature of expertise.* Hillsdale, NJ: Erlbaum.

Clancey, W. J., & Letsinger, R. (1984). NEOMYCIN: Reconfiguring a rule-based expert system for application to teaching. In W. J. Clancey & E. H. Shortliffe (Eds.), *Readings in medical artificial intelligence: The first decade.* Reading, MA: Addison-Wesley.

Clark, H. H., & Clark, E. V. (1977). *Psychology and language.* New York: Harcourt Brace Jovanovich.

Clark, H. H., & Schaefer, E. F. (1987a). Collaborating on contributions to conversation. *Language and Cognitive Processes, 2,* 19–41.

Clark, H. H., & Schaefer, E. F. (1987b). Concealing one's meaning from overhearers. *Journal of Memory and Language, 26,* 209–225.

Cohen, L. J. (1981). Can human irrationality be experimentally demonstrated? *Behavioral and Brain Sciences, 4,* 317–370.

Cohen, N. J. (1984). Preserved learning capacity in amnesia: Evidence for multiple memory systems. In L. Squire & N. Butters (Eds.), *Neuropsychology of memory .* New York: Guilford Press.

Cohen, N. J., & Eichenbaum, H. (In manuscript). *Memory, amnesia, and the hippocampal system.* Cambridge, MA: MIT Press.

Cohen, N. J., & Squire, L. R. (1980). Preserved learning and retention of pattern-analyzing skill in amnesia: Dissociation of knowing how and knowing that. *Science, 210,* 207–210.

Cohen, N. J., & Squire, L. R. (1981). Retrograde amnesia and remote memory impairment. *Neuropsychologia, 19,* 337–356.

Cohen-Levine, S., Banich, M. T., & Koch-Weser, M. P. (1988). Face recognition: A general or a specific right hemisphere capacity? *Brain and Cognition, 8,* 303–325.

Collins, A. M., & Loftus, E. F. (1975). A spreading-activation theory of semantic processing. *Psychological Review, 82,* 407–428.

Collins, A., & Michalski, R. (1989). The logic of plausible reasoning: A core theory. *Cognitive Science, 13,* 1–49.

Collins, A. M., & Quillian, M. R. (1969). Retrieval time from semantic memory. *Journal of Verbal Learning and Verbal Behavior, 8,* 240–247.

Collins, A. M., & Quillian, M. R. (1972). Experiments on semantic memory and language comprehension. In L. W. Gregg (Ed.), *Cognition in learning and memory.* New York: Wiley.

Conrad, R. (1964). Acoustic confusion in immediate memory. *British Journal of Psychology, 55,* 75–84.

Cooper, L. A. (1975). Mental rotation of random two-dimensional shapes. *Cognitive Psychology, 7,* 120–143.

Cooper, L. A. (1976). Demonstration of a mental analog of an external rotation. *Perception & Psychophysics, 19,* 296–302.

Cooper, L. A., & Shepard, R. N. (1973). The time required to prepare for a rotated stimulus. *Memory & Cognition, 1,* 246–250.

Cooper, L. A., & Shepard, R. N. (1978). Transformations on representations of objects in space. In E. C. Carterette & M. P. Friedman (Eds.), *Handbook of Perception* (Vol. 8). New York: Academic Press.

Cooper, W. E., & Paccia-Cooper, J. (1980). *Syntax and speech.* Cambridge, MA: Harvard University Press.

Corkin, S., Sullivan, E. V., Twitchell, T. E., & Grove, E. (1981). The amnesic patient H. M.: Clinical observations and test performance 28 years after operation. *Society for Neuroscience Abstracts, 7,* 235.

Cosmides, L. (1989). The logic of social exchange: Has natural selection shaped how humans reason? Studies with the Wason selection task. *Cognition, 31,* 187–276.

Cover, T. M., & Hart, P. E. (1967). Nearest neighbor pattern classification. *IEEE Trans Inform. Theory.* Vol. IT-B, 21–27.

Craik, F. I. M., & Lockhart, R. S. (1972). Levels of processing: A framework for memory research. *Journal of Verbal Learning and Verbal Behavior, 11,* 671–684.

Craik, F. I. M., & Tulving, E. (1975). Depth of processing and the retention of words in episodic memory. *Journal of Experimental Psychology: General, 104,* 268–294.

Crowder, R. G. (1982). Decay of auditory memory in vowel discrimination. *Journal of Experimental Psychology: Learning, Memory, and Cognition, 8,* 153–162.

Crowder, R. G., & Morton, J. (1969). Precategorical acoustic storage (PAS). *Perception & Psychophysics, 5,* 365–373.

Crowell, C. R., Hinson, R. E., & Siegel, S. (1981). The role of conditional drug responses in tolerance to the hypothermic effects of ethanol. *Psychopharmacology, 73,* 51–54.

Dafters, R., Hetherington, M., & McCartney, H. (1983). Blocking and sensory preconditioning effects in morphine analgesic tolerance: Support for a Pavlovian conditioning model of drug tolerance. *Quarterly Journal of Experimental Psychology, 35B,* 1–11.

Dannemiller, J. L. (1989). Computational approaches to color constancy: Adaptive and ontogenetic considerations. *Psychological Review, 96,* 255–266.

Darby, C. L., & Riopelle, A. J. (1959). Observational learning in the rhesus monkey. *Journal of Comparative and Physiological Psychology, 52,* 94–98.

Dawes, R. M. (1988). *Rational choice in an uncertain world.* San Diego, CA: Harcourt Brace Jovanovich.

Dawes, R. M., & Corrigan, B. (1974). Linear models in decision making. *Psychological Bulletin, 81,* 95–106.

Dell, F. (1980). *Generative phonology.* Cambridge, England: Cambridge University Press.

Dell, G. S. (1986). A spreading activation theory of retrieval in sentence production. *Psychological Review, 93,* 283–321.

Dell, G. S. (1988). The retrieval of phonological forms in production: Tests of predictions from a connectionist model. *Journal of Memory and Language, 27,* 124–142.

Dell, G. S., & Reich, P. A. (1981). Stages in sentence production: An analysis of speech error data. *Journal of Verbal Learning and Verbal Behavior, 20,* 611–629.

Deutsch, J. A., & Deutsch, D. (1963). Attention: Some theoretical considerations. *Psychological Review, 70,* 80–90.

Devine, P. G. (1989). Stereotypes and prejudice: Their automatic and controlled components. *Journal of Personality and Social Psychology, 56,* 5–18.

di Sessa, A. A. (1982). Unlearning Aristotelian physics: A case study of knowledge-based learning. *Cognitive Science, 6,* 37–75.

Diamond, R., & Carey, S. (1986). Why faces are and are not special: An effect of expertise. *Journal of Experimental Psychology: General, 15,* 107–117.

Dickinson, A., Shanks, D., & Evenden, J. (1984). Judgment of act-outcome contingency: The role of selective attribution. *Quarterly Journal of Experimental Psychology, 36A(1),* 29–50.

Diehl, R. L., & Kluender, K. R. (1987). On the categorization of speech sounds. In S. Harnad (Ed.), *Categorical perception.* Cambridge, England: Cambridge University Press.

Domjan, M., & Burkhard, B. (1986). *The principles of learning and behavior.* Monterey, CA: Brooks/Cole.

Driver, J., & Baylis, G. C. (1989). Movement and visual attention: The spotlight metaphor breaks down. *Journal of Experimental Psychology: Human Perception and Performance, 15,* 448–456.

Dulany, D. E., Carlson, R. A., & Dewey, G. I. (1984). A case of syntactical learning and judgment: How conscious and how abstract? *Journal of Experimental Psychology: General, 113,* 541–555.

Dulany, D. E., Carlson, R. A., & Dewey, G. I. (1985). On consciousness and judgment: A reply to Reber, Allen, and Regan. *Journal of Experimental Psychology: General, 114,* 25–32.

Duncan J. (1984). Selective attention and the organization of visual information. *Journal of Experimental Psychology: General, 113,* 501–517.

Duncan, J., & Humphreys, G. W. (1989). Visual search and stimulus similarity. *Psychological Review, 96,* 433–458.

Duncker, K. (1945). On problem solving. *Psychological Monographs, 58:*5, Whole No. 270.

Ebbinghaus, H. (1885). *Uber das gedachtnis.* Leipzig: Duncker and Humbolt.

Eddy, D. M. (1982). Probabilistic reasoning in clinical medicine: Problems and opportunities. In D. Kahneman, P. Slovic, & A. Tversky (Eds.), *Judgment under uncertainty: Heuristics and biases.* Cambridge, England: Cambridge University Press.

Edwards, W., Lindman, H., & Savage, L. J. (1963). Bayesian statistical inferences for psychological research. *Psychological Review, 70,* 193–242.

Egan, D., & Schwartz, B. (1979). Chunking in recall of symbolic drawings. *Memory & Cognition, 7,* 149–158.

Eich, J. E. (1980). The cue-dependent nature of state-dependent retrieval. *Memory & Cognition, 8,* 157–173.

Eich, J. E., & Metcalfe, J. (1989). Mood dependent memory for internal versus external events. *Journal of Experimental Psychology: Learning, Memory, and Cognition, 15,* 443–455.

Eimas, P. D. (1975). Auditory and phonetic coding of the cues for speech: Discrimination of the r-l distinction by young infants. *Perception & Psychophysics, 18,* 341–357.

Eimas, P. D., Siqueland, E. R., Jusczyk, P. W., & Vigorito, J. (1971). Speech perception in infants. *Science, 171,* 303–306.

Einhorn, H. J., & Hogarth, R. M. (1978). Confidence in judgment: Persistence of the illusion of validity. *Psychological Review, 85,* 395–416.

Einhorn, H. J., & Hogarth, R. M. (1981). Behavioral decision theory: Processes of judgment and choice. *Annual Review of Psychology, 32,* 53–88.

Einhorn, H. J., & Hogarth, R. M. (1986). Judging probable cause. *Psychological Bulletin, 99,* 3–19.

Einstein, G. O., & McDaniel, M. A. (1987). Distinctiveness and the mnemonic benefits of bizarre imagery. In M. A. McDaniel & M. Pressley (Eds.), *Imagery and related mnemonic processes: Theories, individual differences and applications.* New York: Springer-Verlag.

Ellis, A. W., & Young, A. M. (1988). *Human cognitive neuropsychology.* Hillsdale, NJ: Erlbaum.

Ellman, T. (1989). Explanation-based learning: A survey of programs and perspectives. *Computing Surveys, 21,* 163–221.

Erickson, J. R. (1974). A set analysis theory of behavior in formal syllogistic reasoning tasks. In R. Solso (Ed.), *Loyola Symposium on Cognition, Vol. 2.* Hillsdale, NJ: Erlbaum.

Ericsson, K. A., & Simon, H. A. (1980). Verbal reports as data. *Psychological Review, 87*, 215–251.

Ericsson, K. A., & Simon, H. A. (1984). *Protocol analysis: Verbal reports as data.* Cambridge, MA: MIT Press.

Eriksen, C. W., & St. James, J. D. (1986). Visual attention within and around the field of focal attention: A zoom lens model. *Perception & Psychophysics, 40*, 225–240.

Estes, W. K. (1955a). Statistical theory of distributional phenomena in learning. *Psychological Review, 62*, 369–377.

Estes, W. K. (1955b). Statistical theory of spontaneous recovery and regression. *Psychological Review, 62*, 145–154.

Estes, W. K. (1964). Probability learning. In A. W. Melton (Ed.), *Categories of human learning.* New York: Academic Press.

Estes, W. K. (1969). Reinforcement in human learning. In J. Tapp (Ed.), *Reinforcement and behavior.* New York: Academic Press.

Estes, W. K. (1973). Phonemic coding and rehearsal in short-term memory for letter strings. *Journal of Verbal Learning and Verbal Behavior, 12*, 350–372.

Estes, W. K. (1976). Structural aspects of associative models for memory. In C. F. Cofer (Ed.), *The structure of human memory.* San Francisco: W. H. Freeman.

Estes, W. K., (1986). Array models for category learning. *Cognitive Psychology, 18*, 500–549.

Evans, J. St. B. T. (1977). Linguistic factors in reasoning. *Quarterly Journal of Experimental Psychology, 29*, 297–306.

Evans, J. St. B. T. (1982). *The psychology of deductive reasoning.* London: Routledge and Kegan Paul.

Evans, J. St. B. T. (1983). Selective processes in reasoning. In J. St. B. T. Evans (Ed.), *Thinking and Reasoning.* London: Routledge and Kegan Paul.

Evans, J. St. B. T., & Lynch, J. S. (1973). Matching bias in the selection task. *British Journal of Psychology, 64*, 391–397.

Falkenhainer, B., Forbus, K. D., & Gentner, D. (1990). The structure-mapping engine. *Artificial Intelligence, 41*, 1–63.

Farah, M. J. (1988). Is visual imagery really visual? Overlooked evidence from neuropsychology. *Psychological Review, 95*, 307–317.

Farah, M. J., Hammond, K. M., Levine, D. N., & Calvanio, R. (1988). Visual and spatial mental imagery: Dissociable systems of representation. *Cognitive Psychology, 20*, 439–462.

Farah, M. J., Peronnet, F., Gonon, M. A., & Giard, M. G. (1988). Electrophysiological evidence for a shared representational medium for visual images and visual percepts. *Journal of Experimental Psychology: General, 117*, 248–257.

Feigenbaum, E. A. (1983). Knowledge engineering: The applied side. In J. E. Hayes & D. Michie (Eds.), *Intelligent systems.* West Sussex: Ellis Horwood Limited.

Feigenbaum, E. A. (1989). What hath Simon wrought? In D. Klahr & K. Kotovsky (Eds.), *Complex information processing: The impact of Herbert A. Simon.* Hillsdale, NJ: Erlbaum.

Feldman, H., Goldin-Meadow, S., & Gleitman, L. R. (1978). Beyond Herodotus: The creation of language by linguistically deprived deaf children. In

A. Lock (Ed.), *Action, symbol, and gesture: The emergence of language*. New York: Academic Press.

Fernald, A. (1984). The perceptual and affective salience of mother's speech to infants. In L. Feagans, C. Garvey, & R. Golinkoff (Eds.), *The origins and growth of communication*. New Brunswick, New Jersey: Ablex.

Fernandez, A., & Glenberg, A. M. (1985). Changing environmental context does not reliably affect memory. *Memory & Cognition, 13*, 333–345.

Ferster, C. S., & Skinner, B. F. (1957). *Schedules of reinforcement*. New York: Appleton-Century-Crofts.

Finke, R. A. (1985). Theories relating mental imagery to perception. *Psychological Bulletin, 98*, 236–259.

Finke, R. A., Pinker, S., & Farah, M. J. (1989). Reinterpreting visual patterns in mental imagery. *Cognitive Science, 13*, 51–78.

Finke, R., & Schmidt, M. J. (1977). Orientation-specific color after-effects following imagination. *Journal of Experimental Psychology: Human Perception and Performance, 13*, 599–606.

Fischhoff, B. (1982). For those condemned to study the past: Heuristics and biases in hindsight. In D. Kahneman, P. Slovic, and A. Tversky (Eds.), *Judgment under uncertainty: Heuristics and biases*. Cambridge, England: Cambridge University Press.

Fischhoff, B. (1988). Judgement and decision making. In R. J. Sternberg and E. E. Smith (Eds.), *The psychology of human thought*. Cambridge, England: Cambridge University Press.

Fischhoff, B., Slovic, P., & Lichtenstein, S. (1979). Subjective sensitivity analysis. *Organizational Behavior and Human Performance, 23*, 339–359.

Fisher, R. P., & Craik, F. I. M. (1977). Interaction between encoding and retrieval operations in cued recall. *Journal of Experimental Psychology: Human Learning and Memory, 3*, 701–711.

Flaherty, C. F., & Becker, H. C. (1984). Influence of conditioned stimulus context on hyperglycemic conditioned responses. *Physiology & Behavior, 33*, 587–593.

Flann, N. S., & Dietterich, T. G. (1989). A study of explanation-based methods for inductive learning. *Machine Learning, 4*, 187–226.

Flannagan, M. J., Fried, L. S., & Holyoak, K. J. (1986). Distributional expectations and the induction of category structure. *Journal of Experimental Psychology: Learning, Memory, and Cognition, 12*, 241–256.

Fodor, J. A. (1981) *Representations*. Cambridge, MA: MIT Press.

Fodor, J. A. (1983). *The modularity of mind*. Cambridge, MA: MIT Press.

Fodor, J. A., & Pylyshyn, Z. W. (1981). How direct is visual perception? Some reflections on Gibson's "ecological approach." *Cognition, 9*, 139–196.

Fodor, J. A., Bever, T. G., & Garrett, M. F. (1974). *The psychology of language*. New York: McGraw-Hill.

Forster, K. I., & Olbrei, I. (1973). Semantic heuristics and syntactic analysis. *Cognition, 2*, 319–347.

Frazer, J. G. (1959). *The new golden bough*. New York: Criterion Books.

Frazier, L. (1979). *On comprehending sentences: Syntactic parsing strategies*. Bloomington, IN: Indiana University Linguistics Club.

Fried, L. S., & Holyoak, K. J. (1984). Induction of category distributions: A framework for classification learning. *Journal of Experimental Psychology: Learning, Memory, and Cognition, 10,* 234–257.

Fromkin, V. A. (1971). The nonanomalous nature of anomalous utterances. *Language, 47,* 27–52.

Fujisaki, H., & Kawashima, T. (1970). Some experiments on speech perception and a model for the perceptual mechanism. *Annual Report of the Engineering Institute* (University of Tokyo), *29,* 207–219.

Gabrieli, J. D. E., Cohen, N. J., & Corkin, S. (1988). The impaired learning of semantic knowledge following bilateral medial temporal-lobe resection. *Brain and Cognition, 7,* 157–177.

Gadzar, G., Klein, E., Pullum, G., & Sag, I. (1985). *Generalized phrase structure grammar.* Cambridge, MA: Harvard University Press.

Galotti, K. M., Baron, J., & Subina, J. P. (1986). Individual differences in syllogistic reasoning: Deduction rules or mental models? *Journal of Experimental Psychology: General, 115,* 16–25.

Garcia, J., Hawkins, W. G., & Rusiniak, K. W. (1974). Behavioral regulation of the Milieu interne in man and rat. *Science, 85,* 824–831.

Garrett, M. F. (1975). The analysis of sentence production. In G. H. Bower (Ed.), *The psychology of learning and motivation* (Vol. 9). New York: Academic Press.

Garrett, M. F. (1976). Levels of processing in sentence production. In B. Butterworth (Ed.), *Language production* (Vol. 1). London: Academic Press.

Garrett, M. F. (1990). Sentence processing. In D. N. Osherson, & H. Lasnik (Eds.), *Language: An invitation to cognitive science.* Cambridge, MA: MIT Press.

Gati, I., & Tversky, A. (1984). Weighting common and distinctive features in perceptual and conceptual judgments. *Cognitive Psychology, 16,* 341–370.

Gelman, S. A., & Markman, E. M. (1986). Categories and induction in young children. *Cognition, 23,* 183–209.

Gentner, D. (1983). Structure-mapping: A theoretical framework for analogy. *Cognitive Science, 1,* 155–170.

Gentner, D. (1989). The mechanisms of analogical reasoning. In S. Vosniadou & A. Ortony (Eds.), *Similarity and analogical reasoning.* Cambridge, England: Cambridge University Press.

Gentner, D., & Collins, A. (1981). Studies of inference from lack of knowledge. *Memory & Cognition, 9,* 434–443.

Gentner, D., & Landers, R. (1985). Analogical reminding: A good match is hard to find. *Proceedings of the International Conference on Systems, Man, and Cybernetics.* Tucson, AZ.

Gentner, D., & Stevens, A. L. (Eds.). (1983). *Mental models.* Hillsdale, NJ: Erlbaum.

Gettys, C. F., Manning, C., Mehle, T., & Fisher, S. (1980). *Hypothesis generation: A final report of three years of research.* (Report No. TR-15-10-80). Decision Processes Laboratory, Dept. of Psychology, University of Oklahoma, Norman, OK.

Getzels, J., & Czikszentmihalyi, M. (1976). *The creative vision: A longitudinal study of problem finding in art.* New York: John Wiley.

Gibbon, J., & Balsam, P. (1981). Spreading association in time. In C. M. Locurto,

H. S. Terrace, & J. Gibbon (Eds.), *Autoshaping and conditioning theory*. New York: Academic Press.

Gibson, E. J. (1987). Introductory essay: What does infant perception tell us about theories of perception? *Journal of Experimental Psychology: Human Perception and Performance, 13*, 515–523.

Gibson, J. J. (1950). *The perception of the visual world*. Boston: Houghton Mifflin.

Gibson, J. J. (1966). *The senses considered as perceptual systems*. Boston: Houghton Mifflin.

Gibson, J. J. (1979). *The ecological approach to visual perception*. Boston: Houghton Mifflin.

Gick, M. L. (1986). Problem-solving strategies. *Educational Psychologist, 21*, 99–120.

Gick, M. L., & Holyoak, K. J. (1980). Analogical problem solving. *Cognitive Psychology, 12*, 306–355.

Gick, M. L., & Holyoak, K. J. (1983). Schema induction and analogical transfer. *Cognitive Psychology, 15*, 1–38.

Gick, M. L., & Holyoak, K. J. (1987). The cognitive basis of knowledge transfer. In S. M. Cormier & J. D. Hagman (Eds.), *Transfer of learning: Contemporary research and applications*. Orlando, FL: Academic Press.

Gigerenzer, G., Hell, W., & Blank, H. (1988). Presentation and content: The use of base rates as a continuous variable. *Journal of Experimental Psychology: General, 14*, 513–525.

Gillund, G., & Shiffrin, R. M. (1984). A retrieval model for both recognition and recall. *Psychological Review, 91*, 1–67.

Gleitman, L. R., & Wanner, E. (1982). Language acquisition: The state of the state of the art. In E. Wanner & L. Gleitman (Eds.), *Language acquisition: The state of the art*. Cambridge, England: Cambridge University Press.

Gleitman, L. R., Gleitman, H., Landau, B., & Wanner, E. (1988). Where learning begins: Initial representations for language learning. In F. J. Newmeyer (Ed.), *Linguistics: The Cambridge survey*. Cambridge, England: Cambridge University Press.

Glenberg, A. M. (1976). Monotonic and nonmonotonic lag effects in paired-associate and recognition memory. *Journal of Verbal Learning and Verbal Behavior, 15*, 1–16.

Glenberg, A. M. (1979). Component-levels theory of the effect of spacing of repetitions on recall and recognition. *Memory & Cognition, 7*, 95–112.

Glenberg, A. M., Bradley, M. M., Kraus, T. A., & Renzaglia, G. J. (1983). Studies of the long-term recency effect: Support for a contextually guided retrieval hypothesis. *Journal of Experimental Psychology: Learning, Memory, and Cognition, 9*, 231–255.

Glisky, E. L., Schacter, D. L., & Tulving, E. (1986). Learning and retention of computer-related vocabulary in amnesic patients: Method of vanishing cues. *Journal of Clinical and Experimental Neuropsychology, 8*, 292–312.

Gluck, M. A., & Bower, G. H., (1988). From conditioning to category learning: An adaptive network model. *Journal of Experimental Psychology: General, 117*, 227–247.

Glucksberg, S., & Danks, J. (1968). Effects of discriminative labels and of nonsense labels upon availability of novel function. *Journal of Verbal Learning and Verbal Behavior, 7*, 72–76.

Glushko, R. J. (1979). The organization and activation of orthographic knowledge in reading aloud. *Journal of Experimental Psychology: Human Perception and Performance, 5,* 674–691.

Godden, D. R., & Baddeley, A. D. (1975). Context-dependent memory in two natural environments: On land and underwater. *British Journal of Psychology, 66,* 325–331.

Gold, E. M. (1967). Language identification in the limit. *Information and Control, 10,* 447–478.

Golding, E. (1981). The effect of past experience on problem solving. Paper presented at the Annual Conference of the British Psychological Society, Surrey University.

Goldstein, E. B. (1980). *Sensation and perception.* Belmont, CA: Wadsworth.

Goodman, N. (1972). Seven strictures on similarity. In N. Goodman (Ed.), *Problems and projects.* New York: Bobbs-Merrill.

Goodman, N. (1985). *Fact, fiction, and forecast.* Indianapolis, IN: Bobbs-Merrill.

Gordon, W. J. J. (1961). *Synectics.* New York: Harper & Row.

Graf, P., & Schacter, D. L. (1985). Implicit and explicit memory for new associations in normal and amnesic subjects. *Journal of Experimental Psychology: Learning, Memory, and Cognition, 11,* 501–518.

Graf, P., Squire, L. R., & Mandler, G. (1984). The information that amnesic patients do not forget. *Journal of Experimental Psychology: Learning, Memory, and Cognition, 10,* 164–178.

Grant, D. A., Hake, H. W., & Hornseth, J. P. (1951). Acquisition and extinction of a verbal conditioned response with differing percentages of reinforcement. *Journal of Experimental Psychology, 42,* 1–5.

Greene, R. L. (1989). Spacing effects in memory: Evidence for a two-process account. *Journal of Experimental Psychology: Learning, Memory, and Cognition, 15,* 371–377.

Grether, D. M., & Plott, C. R. (1979). Economic theory of choice and the preference reversal phenomenon. *American Economic Review, 69,* 623–638.

Grice, H. P. (1975). Logic and conversation. In P. Cole and J. L. Morgan (Eds.), *Syntax and semantics III: Speech acts.* New York: Seminar Press.

Griggs, R. A., & Cox, J. R. (1982). The elusive thematic materials effect in Wason's selection task. *British Journal of Psychology, 73,* 407–420.

Grimshaw, J. (1981). Form, function, and the language acquisition device. In C. L. Baker & J. J. McCarthy (Eds.), *The logical problem of language acquisition.* Cambridge, MA: MIT Press.

Grimson, W. E. L., & Lozano-Perez, T. (1984). Model-based recognition and localization from sparse data. *International Journal of Robotics Research. 3,* 3–35.

Halle, M. (1990). Phonology. In D. N. Osherson & H. Lasnik (Eds.), *Language: An invitation to cognitive science* (Vol. 1). Cambridge, MA: MIT Press.

Halpern, A. R. (1986). Memory for tune titles after organized or unorganized presentation. *American Journal of Psychology, 99,* 57–70.

Hamilton, D. L. (1976). Cognitive biases in the perception of social groups. In J. S. Carroll & J. W. Payne (Eds.), *Cognition and social behavior.* Hillsdale, NJ: Erlbaum.

Hamilton, W. J., & Orians, G. H. (1965). Evolution of brood parasitism in altricial birds. *Condor, 67,* 361–382.

Hammond, K. J. (1989). *Case-based planning: Viewing planning as a memory task.* San Diego, CA: Academic Press.

Hampton, J. A. (1987). Inheritance of attributes in natural concept conjunctions. *Memory & Cognition, 15,* 55–71.

Harley, T. (1984). A critique of top-down independent levels models of speech production: Evidence from non-plan-internal speech errors. *Cognitive Science, 8,* 191–219.

Harmon, G. (1986). *Change in view.* Cambridge, MA: MIT Press.

Harnad, S. (Ed.) *Categorical Perception.* Cambridge, England: Cambridge University Press.

Haviland, S. E., & Clark, H. H. (1974). What's new? Acquiring new information as a process in comprehension. *Journal of Verbal Learning and Verbal Behavior, 13,* 512–521.

Hawkins, R. D., & Bower, G. H. (Eds.). (1989). *Computational models of learning in simple neural systems. The psychology of learning and motivation* (Vol. 23). San Diego, CA: Academic Press.

Hayes, J. R. (1989). *The complete problem solver* (second edition). Hillsdale, NJ: Erlbaum.

Haygood, R. C., & Bourne, L. E., Jr. (1978). Attribute-and-rule-learning aspects of conceptual behavior. *Psychological Review, 72,* 175–195.

Heckhausen, H., & Beckmann, J. (1990). Intentional action and action slips. *Psychological Review, 97,* 36–48.

Heider, F. (1958). *The psychology of interpersonal relations.* New York: Wiley.

Hellige, J. B., & Michimata, C. (1989). Categorization versus distance: Hemispheric differences for processing spatial information. *Memory & Cognition, 17,* 770–776.

Henle, M. (1962). On the relation between logic and thinking. *Psychological Review, 69,* 366–378.

Hetherington, P. A., & Seidenberg, M. S. (1989). Is there "catastrophic interference" in connectionist networks? In *Proceedings of the 11th annual conference of the cognitive science society,* 26–33. Hillsdale, NJ: Erlbaum.

Hildreth, E. C. (1984a). Computations underlying the measurement of visual motion. *Artificial Intelligence, 23,* 309–354.

Hildreth, E. C. (1984b). The computation of the velocity field. *Proceedings of the Royal Society of London, 221,* 189–220.

Hildreth, E. C., & Ullman, S. (1989). The computational study of vision. In M. I. Posner, (Ed.), *Foundations of cognitive science.* Cambridge, MA: MIT Press.

Hilton, D. J., & Slugoski, B. R. (1986). Knowledge-based causal attribution: The abnormal conditions focus model. *Psychological Review, 93,* 75–88.

Hintzman, D. L. (1976). Repetition and memory. In G. H. Bower (Ed.) *The psychology of learning and motivation* (Vol. 11). New York: Academic Press.

Hintzman, D. L. (1984). Episodic versus semantic memory: A distinction whose time has come—and gone? *Behavioral and Brain Sciences, 7,* 240–241.

Hintzman, D. L. (1986). "Schema abstraction" in a multiple-trace memory model. *Psychological Review, 93,* 411–428.

Hintzman, D. L. (1988). Judgments of frequency and recognition memory in a multiple-trace memory model. *Psychological Review, 95,* 528–551.

Hirsh-Pasek, K., Golinkoff, R., Fletcher, A., DeGaspeo-Beaubien, F., & Cauley, F. (1985). In the beginning: one word speakers comprehend word order. Paper presented at *Boston Language Conference*, October 1985.

Hirst, W., Spelke, E. S., Reaves, C. C., Caharack, G., & Neisser, U. (1980). Dividing attention without alternation or automaticity. *Journal of Experimental Psychology: General, 109*, 98–117.

Hirtle, S. C., & Jonides, J. (1985). Evidence of hierarchies in cognitive maps. *Memory & Cognition, 13*, 208–217.

Hockett, C. F. (1963). The problem of universals in language. In J. H. Greenberg (Ed.), *Universals of language*. Cambridge, MA: MIT Press.

Hoffman, H. W., & Ratner, A. M. (1983). A reinforcement model of imprinting: Implications for socialization in monkeys and men. *Psychological Review, 80*, 527–544.

Hogarth, R. M. (1981). Beyond discrete biases: Functional and dysfunctional aspects of judgmental heuristics. *Psychological Bulletin, 90*, 197–217.

Holding, D. H. (1985). *The psychology of chess skill*. Hillsdale, NJ: Erlbaum.

Holland, J. H., Holyoak, K. J., Nisbett, R. E., & Thagard, P. R. (1986). *Induction*. Cambridge, MA: MIT Press.

Holland, P. C. (1984). Origins of behavior in Pavlovian conditioning. In G. H. Bower (Ed.), *The psychology of learning and motivation* (Vol. 18). Orlando, FL: Academic Press.

Holyoak, K. J., Koh, K., & Nisbett, R. E. (1989). A theory of conditioning: Inductive learning with rule-based default hierarchies. *Psychological Review, 96*, 315–340.

Holyoak, K. J., & Glass, A. L. (1975). The role of contradictions and counter-examples in the rejection of false sentences. *Journal of Verbal Learning and Verbal Behavior, 14*, 215–239.

Holyoak, K. J., & Koh, K. (1987). Surface and structural similarity in analogical transfer. *Memory & Cognition, 15*, 332–340.

Holyoak, K. J., & Thagard, P. (1989). Analogical mapping by constraint satisfaction. *Cognitive Science, 13*, 295–355.

Homa, D. (1984). On the nature of categories. In G. H. Bower (Ed.), *The psychology of learning and motivation* (Vol. 18). Orlando, FL: Academic Press.

Homa, D., & Vosburgh, R. (1976). Category breadth and the abstraction of prototypical information. *Journal of Experimental Psychology: Human Learning and Memory, 2*, 322–330.

Howard, J., & Rothbart, M. (1980). Social categorization and memory for ingroup and outgroup behavior. *Journal of Personality and Social Psychology, 38*, 301–310.

Humphreys, L. G. (1939). Acquisition and extinction of verbal expectations in a situation analogous to conditioning. *Journal of Experimental Psychology, 25*, 294–301.

Hunt, E. B. (1975). *Artificial intelligence*. New York: Academic Press.

Hunt, E. B., & Hovland, C. I. (1960). Order of consideration of different types of concepts. *Journal of Experimental Psychology, 59*, 220–225.

Hunter, I. M. L. (1966/1972). Mental calculation. In P. N. Johnson-Laird & P. C. Wason (Eds.), *Thinking: Readings in cognitive science*. Cambridge, England: Cambridge University Press.

Hyde, T. S., & Jenkins, J. J. (1969). The differential effects of incidental tasks on the organization of recall of a list of highly associated words. *Journal of Experimental Psychology, 82*, 472–481.

Intons-Peterson, M. J. (1983). Imagery paradigms: How vulnerable are they to experimenters' expectancies? *Journal of Experimental Psychology: Human Perception and Performance, 9*, 394–412.

Intons-Peterson, M. J., & White, A. R. (1981). Experimenter naivete and imagined judgments. *Journal of Experimental Psychology: Human Perception and Performance, 11*, 317–328.

Jacoby, L. L., & Dallas, M. (1981). On the relationship between autobiographical memory and perceptual learning. *Journal of Experimental Psychology: General, 110*, 306–340.

Jacoby, L. L., Kelley, C. M., & Dywan, J. (1989). Memory attribution. In H. L. Roediger and F. I. M. Craik (Eds.), *Varieties of memory and consciousness: Essays in honor of Endel Tulving*. Hillsdale, NJ: Erlbaum.

Jacoby, L. L., Woloshyn, V., & Kelley, C. M. (1989). Becoming famous without being recognized: Unconscious influences of memory produced by dividing attention. *Journal of Experimental Psychology: General, 118*, 115–125.

James, W. (1890). *Principles of psychology* (Vol. 1). New York: Holt.

Jarvella, R. J. (1971). Syntactic processing of connected speech. *Journal of Verbal Learning and Verbal Behavior, 10*, 409–416.

Jenkins, J. G., & Dallenbach, K. M. (1924). Oblivescence during sleep and waking. *American Journal of Psychology, 35*, 605–612.

Johnson, J. S., & Newport, E. L. (1989). Critical period effect in second language learning: The influence of maturational state on the acquisition of English as a second language. *Cognitive Psychology, 21*, 60–99.

Johnson, W. A., & Dark, V. A. (1986). Selective attention. *Annual Review of Psychology, 37*, 43–75.

Johnson-Laird, P. N. (1983). *Mental models: Towards a cognitive science of language, inference, and consciousness*. Cambridge, MA: Harvard University Press.

Johnson-Laird, P. N. (1988). *The computer and the mind*. Cambridge, MA: Harvard University Press.

Johnson-Laird, P. N., & Bara, B. G. (1984). Syllogistic inference. *Cognition, 16*, 1–61.

Johnson-Laird, P. N., & Byrne, R. M. J. (1991). *Deduction*. Hove, Sussex: Erlbaum.

Johnson-Laird, P. N., & Steedman, M. (1978). The psychology of syllogisms. *Cognitive Psychology, 10*, 64–99.

Johnson-Laird, P. N., Byrne, R. M. J., & Schaken, W. (1990). Propositional reasoning by model. Unpublished manuscript.

Johnson-Laird, P. N., Byrne, R. M. J., & Tabossi, P. (1989). Reasoning by model: The case of multiple quantification. *Psychological Review, 96*, 658–673.

Johnson-Laird, P. N., Legrenzi, P., & Legrenzi, M. (1972). Reasoning and a sense of reality. *British Journal of Psychology, 63*, 395–400.

Jolicoeur, P. (1985). The time to name disoriented natural objects. *Memory & Cognition, 13*, 289–303.

Jones, E. E., & Nisbett, R. E. (1972). The actor and the observer: Divergent perceptions of the causes of behavior. In E. E. Jones, D. E. Kanouse, H. H. Kelly, R. E. Nisbett, S. Valins, & B. Weiner (Eds.), *Attribution: Perceiving the causes of behavior*. Morristown, NJ: General Learning Press.

Jones, G. V. (1990). Misremembering a common object: When left is not right. *Memory & Cognition, 18*, 174–182.

Just, M. A., & Carpenter, P. A. (1976). Eye fixations and cognitive processes. *Cognitive Psychology, 8*, 441–480.

Kahneman, D. (1973). *Attention and effort.* Englewood Cliffs, NJ: Prentice-Hall.

Kahneman, D., & Miller, D. T. (1986). Norm theory: Comparing reality to its alternatives. *Psychological Review, 93*, 136–153.

Kahneman, D., & Treisman, A. M. (1984). Changing views of attention and automaticity. In R. Parasuraman & D. R. Davies (Eds.), *Varieties of Attention.* New York: Academic Press.

Kahneman, D., & Tversky, A. (1979). Prospect therory: An analysis of decisions under risk. *Econometrica, 97*, 263–291.

Kahneman, D., Slovic, P., & Tversky, A. (1982). *Judgment under uncertainty: Heuristics and biases.* Cambridge, England: Cambridge University Press.

Kaiser, M. K., McCloskey, M., & Proffitt, D. R. (1986). Development of intuitive theories of motion: Curvilinear motion in the absence of external forces. *Developmental Psychology, 22*, 1–5.

Kamin, L. J. (1969). Predictability, surprise, attention and conditioning. In B. A. Campbell & P. M. Church (Eds.), *Punishment and aversive behavior.* New York: Appleton-Century-Crofts.

Kandel, E. R. (1976). *Cellular basis of behavior: An introduction to behavioral neurobiology.* San Francisco: W. H. Freeman.

Kandel, E. R., & Schwartz, J. H. (1982). Molecular biology of learning: Modulation of transmitter release. *Science, 218*, 433–443.

Kaplan, C. A., & Simon, H. A. (1990). In search of insight. *Cognitive Psychology, 22*, 374–419.

Katona, G. (1940). *Organizing and memorizing.* New York: Columbia University Press.

Keenan, J. M. (1986). Development of microstructure processes in children's reading comprehension: Effect of number of different arguments. *Journal of Experimental Psychology: Learning, Memory, and Cognition, 12*, 614–622.

Keenan, J. M., Baillet, S. D., & Brown, P. (1984). The effects of causal cohesion on comprehension and memory. *Journal of Verbal Learning and Verbal Behavior, 23*, 115–126.

Keil, F. C. (1979). *Semantic and conceptual development: An ontological perspective.* Cambridge, MA: Harvard University Press.

Keil, F. C. (1981). Constraints on knowledge and cognitive development. *Psychological Review, 88*, 199–227.

Keil, F. C. (1986). The acquisition of natural kind and artifact terms. In W. Demopoulos & A. Marras (Eds.), *Language learning and concept acquisition.* Norwood, NJ: Ablex.

Keil, F. C. (1987). Conceptual development and category structure. In U. Neisser (Ed.), *Concepts and conceptual development: Ecological and intellectual factors in categorization.* Cambridge, England: Cambridge University Press.

Keil, F. C., & Kelly, M. H. (1987). Developmental changes in category structure. In S. Harnad (Ed.), *Categorical perception.* Cambridge, England: Cambridge University Press.

Kellman, P. J., & Spelke, E. S. (1983). Perception of partly occluded objects in infancy. *Cognitive Psychology, 15,* 483–528.

Kellman, P. J., Gleitman, H., & Spelke, E. S. (1987). Object and observer motion in the perception of objects by infants. *Journal of Experimental Psychology: Human Perception and Performance, 13,* 586–593.

Kelly, H. H., and Michela, J. (1988). Attribution theory and research. *Annual Review of Psychology, 31,* 457–501.

Kemler-Nelson, D. G. (1984). The effect of intention on what concepts are acquired. *Journal of Verbal Learning and Verbal Behavior, 23,* 734–759.

Kendall, R. E. (1975). *The role of diagnosis in psychiatry.* Oxford, England: Blackwell Scientific.

Kerr, N. H. (1983). The role of vision in "visual imagery" experiments: Evidence from the congenitally blind. *Journal of Experimental Psychology: General, 112,* 265–277.

Kibler, D., & Aha, D. W. (1987). Learning representative exemplars of concepts: An initial case study. In *Proceedings of the Fourth International Workshop on Machine Learning* (pp. 24–30). Irvine, CA: Morgan Kaufmann.

Kidd, J. B. (1970). The utilization of subjective probabilities in production planning. *Acta Psychologica, 34,* 338–347.

Kintsch, W. (1988). The role of knowledge in discourse comprehension: A construction-integration model. *Psychological Review, 95,* 163–182.

Kintsch, W., & van Dijk (1978). Toward a model of text comprehension and production. *Psychological Review, 85,* 363–394.

Klaczynski, P. A., Gelfund, H., & Reese, H. W. (1989). Transfer of conditional reasoning: Effects of explanations and initial problem types. *Memory & Cognition, 17,* 208–220.

Klatt, D. H. (1976). Linguistic uses of segmental duration in English: Acoustic and perceptual evidence. *Journal of the Acoustical Society of America, 59,* 1208–1221.

Klaus, M. H., & Kennell, J. H. (1976). *Mother-infant bonding.* St. Louis, MO: Mosby.

Klausmeier, H. J., & Sipple, T. S. (1980). *Learning and teaching concepts.* New York: Academic Press.

Klayman, J. (1984). Learning from feedback in probabilistic environments. *Acta Psychologica, 56,* 81–92.

Klayman, J. (1988). Cue discovery in probabilistic environments. *Journal of Experimental Psychology: Learning, Memory, and Cognition, 14,* 317–330.

Klayman, J., & Ha, Y-W. (1987). Confirmation, disconfirmation, and information in hypothesis testing. *Psychological Review, 94,* 211–228.

Kolers, P. A. (1975). Specificity of operations in sentence recognition. *Cognitive Psychology, 7,* 289–306.

Kolodner, J. L. (1984). *Retrieval and organizational structures in conceptual memory: A computer model.* Hillsdale, NJ: Erlbaum.

Kolodner, J. L. (Ed.) (1988). *Proceedings of the DARPA Case-Based Reasoning Workshop.* San Mateo, CA: Morgan Kaufmann.

Kolodner, J. L., & Kolodner, R. (1987). Using experience in clinical problem solving: Introduction and framework. *IEEE Transactions on Systems, Man, and Cybernetics.*

Kolodner, J. L., & Simpson, R. L. (1989). The MEDIATOR: Analysis of an early case-based problem solver. *Cognitive Science, 13*, 507–549.

Kosslyn, S. M. (1973). Scanning visual images: Some structural implications. *Perception & Psychophysics, 14*, 90–94.

Kosslyn, S. M. (1975). Information representation in visual images. *Cognitive Psychology, 7*, 341–370.

Kosslyn, S. M. (1976). Can imagery be distinguished from other forms of internal representation? Evidence from studies of information retrieval times. *Memory & Cognition, 4*, 291–297.

Kosslyn, S. M. (1983). *Ghosts in the mind's machine: Creating and using images in the brain.* New York: Horizon.

Kosslyn, S. M. (1987). Seeing and imagining in the cerebral hemispheres: A computational approach. *Psychological Review, 94*, 148–175.

Kosslyn, S. M., & Pomerantz, J. R. (1977). Imagery, propositions, and the form of internal representations. *Cognitive Psychology, 9*, 52–76.

Kosslyn, S. M., & Shwartz, S. P. (1977). A simulation of visual imagery. *Cognitive Science, 1*, 265–295.

Kosslyn, S. M., Ball, T. M., & Reiser, B. J. (1978). Visual images preserve metric spatial information: Evidence from studies of image scanning. *Journal of Experimental Psychology: Human Perception and Performance, 4*, 47–60.

Kotovsky, K., & Fallside, D. (1989). Representation and transfer in problem solving. In D. Klahr & K. Kotovsky (Eds.), *Complex information processing: The contributions of Herbert A. Simon.* Hillsdale, NJ: Erlbaum.

Kotovsky, K., & Simon, H. A. (1990). What makes some problems really hard: Explorations in the problem space of difficulty. *Cognitive Psychology, 22*, 143–183.

Kotovsky, K., Hayes, J. R., & Simon, H. A. (1985). Why are some problems hard? Evidence from Tower of Hanoi. *Cognitive Psychology, 17*, 248–294.

Krasner, L., & Ullman, L.P. (Eds.) (1965). *Research in behavior modification: New developments and implications.* New York: Holt.

Kristofferson, M. (1972). When item recognition and visual search functions are similar. *Perception & Psychophysics, 12*, 379–384.

Kruschke, J. K. (1990). A connectionist model of category learning. Unpublished doctoral dissertation, University of California at Berkeley.

Kuczaj, S. A. (1977). The acquisition of regular and irregular past tense form. *Journal of Verbal Learning and Verbal Behavior, 16*, 589–600.

Kuhl, P. K. (1987). Perception of speech and sound in early infancy. In P. Salapatek & L. B. Cohen (Eds.), *Handbook of infant perception* (Vol. 2). New York: Academic Press.

Kuhl, P. K. (1990). Toward a new theory of the development of speech perception. *Proceedings of the International Conference on Spoken Language Processing* (Vol. 2). Kobe, Japan: Acoustical Society of Japan.

Kuhl, P. K., & Meltzoff, A. N. (1982). The bimodal perception of speech in infancy. *Science, 218*, 1138–1141.

Kuhl, P. K., & Miller, J. D. (1978). Speech perception by the chinchilla: Identification functions for syntactic VOT stimuli. *Journal of the Acoustical Society of America, 63*, 905–917.

Kuhn, D. (1989). Children and adults as intuitive scientists. *Psychological Review*, *96*, 674–689.

Kunreuther, H., Ginsberg, R., Miller, L., Sagi, P., Slovic, P., Borkan, B., & Katz, N. (1978). *Disaster insurance protection: Public policy lessons*. New York: Wiley.

Labov, W. (1973). The boundaries of words and their meanings. In C. J. N. Bailey & R. W. Shiny (Eds.), *New ways of analyzing variation in English* (Vol. 1). Washington, DC: Georgetown University Press.

Lachter, J., & Bever, T. G. (1988). The relation between linguistic structure and associative theories of language learning—A constructive critique of some connectionist learning models. *Cognition*, *28*, 195–247.

Ladefoged, P., & Broadbent, D. (1957). Information conveyed by vowels. *Journal of the Acoustical Society of America*, *19*, 98–104.

Lakoff, G., & Johnson, M. (1980). *Metaphors we live by*. Chicago, IL: University of Chicago Press.

Landau, B., & Gleitman, L. R. (1985). *Language and experience: Evidence from the blind child*. Cambridge, MA: Harvard University Press.

Landauer, T. K., & Freedman, J. L. (1968). Information retrieval from long-term memory: Category size and recognition time. *Journal of Verbal Learning and Verbal Behavior*, *1968*, *7*, 291–295.

Langer, E. J., & Abelson, R. P. (1974). A patient by any other name: Clinical group differences in labeling bias. *Journal of Consulting and Clinical Psychology*, *42*, 4–9.

Larkin, J. H., & Simon, H. A. (1987). Why a diagram is (sometimes) worth 10,000 words. *Cognitive Science*, *11*, 65–100.

Larkin, J. H., McDermott, J., Simon, D. P., & Simon, H. A. (1980). Models of competence in solving physics problems. *Cognitive Science*, *4*, 317–345.

Lerner, M. J., & Miller, D. T. (1978). Just world research and the attribution process: Looking back and ahead. *Psychological Bulletin*, *85*, 1030–1051.

Lesgold, A. M., Feltovich, P. J., Glaser, R., & Wang, Y. (1981). The acquisition of perceptual diagnostic skill in radiology. Technical report #PDS-1, Pittsburgh: University of Pittsburgh, LRDC.

Lesgold, A. M., Rubinson, H., Feltovich, P., Glaser, R., Klopfer, D., & Wang, Y. (1988). Expertise in a complex skill: Diagnosing x-ray pictures. In M. Chi, R. Glaser, & M. Farr (Eds.), *The nature of expertise*. Hillsdale, NJ: Erlbaum.

Lettvin, J. Y., Maturana, H. R., McCulloch, W. S., & Pitts, W. H. (1959). What the frog's eye tells the frog's brain. *Proceedings of the IRE*, *47*, 1940–1951.

Leventhal, H., Meyer, D., and Nerenz, D. (1980). The common sense representation of illness danger. In S. Rachman (Ed.), *Medical psychology* (Vol. 2). New York: Pergamon Press.

Levine, M. (1971). Hypothesis theory and nonlearning despite ideal S-R reinforcement contingencies. *Psychological Review*, *78*, 130–140.

Lewis, C. H., & Anderson, J. R. (1976). Interference with real world knowledge. *Cognitive Psychology*, *8*, 311–335.

Lewis, D. K. (1973). *Counterfactuals*. Cambridge, MA: Harvard University Press.

Liberman, A. M., & Mattingly, I. G. (1985). The motor theory of speech perception revised. *Cognition*, *21*, 1–36.

Liberman, A. M., Cooper, F. S., Shankweiler, D. P., & Studdert-Kennedy, M. (1967). Perception of the speech code. *Psychological Review*, *74*, 431–461.

Lichtenstein, S., & Slovic, P. (1973). Response-induced reversals of preference in gambling: An extended replication in Las Vegas. *Journal of Experimental Psychology, 101,* 16–20.

Lichtenstein, S., Fischhoff, B., & Phillips, B. (1982). Calibration of probabilities: The state of the art to 1980. In D. Kahneman, P. Slovic, & A. Tversky (Eds.), *Judgment under uncertainty: Heuristics and biases.* Cambridge, England: Cambridge University Press.

Light. L. L., & Carter-Sobell, L. (1970). Effects of changed semantic context on recognition memory. *Journal of Verbal Learning and Verbal Behavior, 9,* 1–11.

Linville, P. W., Fischer, G. W., & Salovey, P. (1989). Perceived distributions of the characteristics of in-group and out-group members: Empirical evidence and a computer simulation. *Journal of Personality & Social Psychology, 57,* 165–188.

Linville, P. W., Salovey, P., & Fisher, G. W. (1986). Stereotype and perceived distribution of social characteristics: An application to ingroup-outgroup perception. In J. Dovidiot & S. L. Gaertner (Eds.), *Prejudice, discrimination and racism.* New York: Academic Press.

Lisker, L., & Abramson, A. S. (1970). The voicing dimension: Some experiments in comparative phonetics. *Proceedings of the Sixth International Congress of Phonetic Sciences.* Prague: Academia.

Livingstone, M., & Hubel, D. (1988). Segregation of form, color, movement, and depth: Anatomy, physiology, and perception. *Science, 240,* 740–750.

Lockhart, R. S., Lamon, M., & Gick, M. L. (1988). Conceptual transfer in simple insight problems. *Memory & Cognition, 16,* 36–44.

Locksley, A., Borgida, E., Brekke, N., & Hepburn, C. (1980). Sex stereotypes and social judgment. *Journal of Personality and Social Psychology, 39,* 821–831.

Loftus, E. F., & Loftus, G. R. (1980). On the permanence of stored information in the human brain. *American Psychologist, 35,* 409–420.

Loftus, E. F., & Palmer, J. C. (1974). Reconstruction of automobile destruction: An example of the interaction between language and memory. *Journal of Verbal Learning and Verbal Behavior, 13,* 585–589.

Logan, G. D. (1988). Toward an instance theory of automatization. *Psychological Review, 95,* 492–527.

Loomes, G. (1987). Testing for regret and disappointment in choice under uncertainty. *Economic Journal, 97,* 118–129.

Loomes, G., & Sugden, R. (1982). Regret theory: An alternative theory of rational choice under uncertainty. *Economic Journal, 92,* 805–824.

Lorayne, H., & Lucas, J. (1974). *The memory book.* New York: Ballantine Books.

Luchins, A. S. (1942). Mechanization in problem solving. *Psychological Monographs, 54,* No. 248.

Luchins, A. S., & Luchins, E. H. (1950). New experimental attempts at preventing mechanization in problem solving. *The Journal of General Psychology, 42,* 279–297.

Lundsgaarde, H. P. (1987). Evaluating medical expert systems. *Social Science and Medicine, 24,* 805–819.

Luria, A. R. (1968). *The mind of a mnemonist.* New York: Basic Books.

MacKay, D. G. (1970). Spoonerisms: The structure of errors in the serial order of speech. *Neuropsychologica, 8,* 323–350.

MacKay, D. G. (1972). The structure of words and syllables: Evidence from errors in speech. *Cognitive Psychology, 3,* 210–227.

MacKay, D. G. (1982). The problems of flexibility, fluency, and speed-accuracy trade-off in skilled behavior. *Psychological Review, 89,* 483–506.

MacQueen, G. M., & Siegel, S. (1989). Conditional immunomodulation following training with cyclophosphamide. *Behavioral Neuroscience, 103,* 638–647.

MacQueen, G. M., Siegel, S., & Landry, J. O. (1990). Acquisition and extinction of conditional immunoenhancement following training with cyclophosphamide. *Psychobiology, 18,* 287–292.

Madigan, S. A. (1969). Intraserial repetition and coding processes in free recall. *Journal of Verbal Learning and Verbal Behavior, 8,* 828–835.

Malt, B. C., & Smith, E. E. (1983). Correlated properties in natural categories. *Journal of Verbal Learning and Verbal Behavior, 23,* 250–269.

Mandl, H., & Lesgold, A. M. (1988). *Learning issues for intelligent tutoring systems.* New York: Springer-Verlag.

Manis, M., Dovalina, I., Avis, N. E., & Cardoze, S. (1980). Base rates can affect individual predictions. *Journal of Personality and Social Psychology, 38,* 287–298.

Manktelow, K. I., & Evans, J. St. B. T. (1979). Facilitation of reasoning by realism: Effect or non-effect? *British Journal of Psychology, 73,* 407–420.

Mann, V. A., & Repp, B. H. (1980). Influence of vocalic context on perception of the [S]–[s] distinction. *Perception & Psychophysics, 28,* 213–228.

Maratsos, M. (1982). The child's construction of grammatical categories. In E. Wanner & L. R. Gleitman (Eds.), *Language acquisition: The state of the art.* Cambridge, MA: Cambridge University Press.

Maratsos, M., & Chalkley, M. A. (1981). The internal structure of children's syntax: The ontogenesis and representation of syntactic categories. In K. Nelson (Ed.), *Children's language* (Vol. 2). New York: Gardner Press.

Marcus, S. L., & Rips, L. J. (1979). Conditional reasoning. *Journal of Verbal Learning and Verbal Behavior, 18,* 199–224.

Markman, E. M. (1989). *Categorization and naming in children: Problems of induction.* Cambridge, MA: MIT Press.

Markman, E. M., & Hutchinson, J. E. (1984). Children's sensitivity to constraints on word meaning: Taxonomic vs. thematic relations. *Cognitive Psychology, 16,* 1–27.

Markman, E. M., & Wachtel, G. R. (1988). Children's use of mutual exclusivity to constrain the meaning of words. *Cognitive Psychology, 20,* 121–157.

Markovits, H. (1989). Conditional reasoning, representation and empirical evidence on a concrete task. *Quarterly Journal of Experimental Psychology, 40,* 483–495.

Markovits, H., & Nantel, G. (1989). The belief-bias effect in the production and evaluation of logical conclusions. *Memory & Cognition, 17,* 11–17.

Marler, P. (1970). A comparative approach to vocal learning: Song development in white-crowned sparrows. *Journal of Comparative and Physiological Psychology, Monograph 71,* No. 2, Part 2.

Marler, P., & Peters, S. (1977). Selective learning in a sparrow. *Science, 198,* 519–521.

Marler, P., & Peters, S. (1988). The role of song phonology and syntax in vocal learning preferences in the song sparrow, Melospiza melodia. *Ethology, 77,* 125–149.

Marler, P., & Sherman, V. (1983). Song structure without auditory feedback: Emendations of the auditory template hypothesis. *The Journal of Neuroscience, 3,* 517–531.

Marr, D. (1982). *Vision.* San Francisco: W. H. Freeman.

Marr, D., & Poggio, T. (1976). Cooperative computation of stereo disparity. *Science, 194,* 283–287.

Martin, E. (1975). Generation-recognition theory and the encoding specificity principle. *Psychological Review, 82,* 150–153.

Martin, R. C., & Caramazza, A. (1980). Classification in well-defined and ill-defined categories: Evidence for common processing strategies. *Journal of Experimental Psychology: General, 109,* 320–353.

Massaro, D. W. (1987). *Speech perception by ear and eye: A paradigm for psychological inquiry.* Hillsdale, NJ: Erlbaum.

Massaro, D. W. (1988). Some criticisms of connectionist models of human performance. *Journal of Memory and Language, 27,* 213–234.

Massaro, D. W. (1989). Testing between the TRACE Model and the Fuzzy Logical Model of Speech Perception. *Cognitive Psychology, 21,* 398–421.

Massaro, D. W., & Cohen, M. M. (1983). Evaluation and integration of visual and auditory information in speech perception. *Journal of Experimental Psychology: Human Perception and Performance, 9,* 753–771.

Massaro, D. W., & Friedman, D. (1990). Models of integration given multiple sources of information. *Psychological Review, 97,* 225–252.

McClelland, J. L., & Elman, J. L. (1986). The TRACE model of speech perception. *Cognitive Psychology, 18,* 1–86.

McClelland, J. L., & Rumelhart, D. E. (1981). An interactive activation model of context effects in letter perception, Part 1. An account of basic findings. *Psychological Review, 88,* 375–407.

McClelland, J. L., & Rumelhart, D. E. (1986a). A distributed model of human learning and memory. In J. L. McClelland & D. E. Rumelhart (Eds.), *Parallel distributed processing: Explorations in the microstructure of cognition. Volume 2: Psychological and biological models.* Cambridge, MA: MIT Press.

McClelland, J. L., & Rumelhart, D. E. (1986b). Amnesia and distributed memory. In J. L. McClelland & D. E. Rumelhart (Eds.), *Parallel distributed processing: Explorations in the microstructure of cognition. Volume 2: Psychological and biological models.* Cambridge, MA: MIT Press.

McClelland, J. L., & Rumelhart, D. E. (Eds.). (1986c). *Parallel distributed processing: Explorations in the microstructure of cognition. Volume 2: Psychological and biological models.* Cambridge, MA: MIT Press.

McClelland, J. L., Rumelhart, D. E., & Hinton, G. E. (1986). The appeal of parallel distributed processing. In D. E. Rumelhart & J. L. McClelland (Eds.), *Parallel distributed processing: Explorations in the microstructure of cognition. Volume 1: Foundations.* Cambridge, MA: MIT Press.

McCloskey, M. (1983). Intuitive physics. *Scientific American, 248* (4), 122–130.

McCloskey, M., & Cohen, N. J. (1989). Catastrophic interference in connectionist networks: The sequential learning problem. In G. H. Bower (Ed.), *The psy-*

chology of learning and motivation: Advances in research and theory (Vol. 24). New York: Academic Press.

McCloskey, M., & Glucksberg, S. (1978). Natural categories: Well-defined or fuzzy sets? *Memory & Cognition, 6*, 462–472.

McCloskey, M., & Glucksberg, S. (1979). Decision processes in verifying category membership statements: Implications for models of semantic memory. *Cognitive Psychology, 11*, 1–37.

McDaniel, M. A., & Pressley, M. (eds.) (1987). *Imagery and related mnemonic processes: Theories, individual differences, and applications.* New York: Springer-Verlag.

McGeoch, J. A. (1942). *The psychology of human learning.* New York: Longmans, Green.

McGurk, H., & MacDonald, J. (1976). Hearing lips and seeing voices. *Nature, 264*, 746–748.

McKenzie, B. E., Tootell, H. S., & Day, R. H. (1980). Development of size constancy during the 1st year of human infancy. *Developmental Psychology, 16*, 163–174.

McKoon, G., & Ratcliff, R. (1986). Inferences about predictable events. *Journal of Experimental Psychology: Learning, Memory, and Cognition, 12*, 82–91.

McKoon, G., Ratcliff, R., & Dell, G. (1986). A critical evaluation of the semantic/episodic distinction. *Journal of Experimental Psychology: Learning, Memory, and Cognition, 12*, 295–306.

McNamara, T. P. (1986). Mental representations of spatial relations. *Cognitive Psychology, 18*, 87–121.

McNamara, T. P., & Miller, D. L. (1989). Attributes of theories of meaning. *Psychological Bulletin, 106*, 355–376.

McNeil, B. J., Pauker, S. G., Cox, H. C., Jr., & Tversky, A. (1982). On the elicitation of preferences for alternative therapies. *New England Journal of Medicine, 306*, 1259–1262.

Medin, D. L., & Edelson, S. E. (1988). Problem structure and the use of base-rate information from experience. *Journal of Experimental Psychology: General, 117*, 68–85.

Medin, D. L. & Florian, J. E. (in press). Abstraction and selective coding in exemplar-based models of categorization. In A. M. Healy, S. F. Kosslyn, and R. M. Shiffrin, (Eds.), *Essays in honor of William K. Estes, (Vol. 2).* Hillsdale, NJ: Erlbaum.

Medin, D. L., & Ortony, A. (1989). Psychological essentialism. In S. Vosniadou & A. Ortony (Eds.), *Similarity and analogical reasoning.* Cambridge, England: Cambridge University Press.

Medin, D. L., & Ross, B. H. (1989). The specific character of abstract thought: Categorization, problem-solving, and induction. In R. J. Sternberg (Ed.), *Advances in the psychology of human intelligence* (Vol. 5). Hillsdale, NJ: Erlbaum.

Medin, D. L., & Schaffer, M. M. (1978). A context theory of classification learning. *Psychological Review, 85*, 207–238.

Medin, D. L., & Schwanenflugel, P. J. (1981). Linear separability in classification learning. *Journal of Experimental Psychology: Human Learning and Memory, 7*, 355–368.

Medin, D. L., & Shoben, E. J. (1988). Context and structure in conceptual combination. *Cognitive Psychology, 20*, 158–190.

Medin, D. L., & Smith, E. E. (1984). Concepts and concept formation. In M. R. Rosenzweig & L. W. Porter (Eds.), *Annual Review of Psychology, 35,* 113–138.

Medin, D. L., & Thau, D. H. (in press) Theories, constraints, and cognition. In H. Pick & P. VandenBroek, (Eds.) *The Study of Cognition: Conceptual and Methodological Issues.*

Medin, D. L., & Wattenmaker, W. D. (1987). Category cohesiveness, theories, and cognitive archeology. In U. Neisser (Ed.), *Concepts and conceptual development: The ecological and intellectual factors in categories.* Cambridge, England: Cambridge University Press.

Medin, D. L., Wattenmaker, W. D., & Michalski, R. S. (1987). Constraints and preferences in inductive learning: An experimental study of human and machine performance. *Cognitive Science, 11,* 299–339.

Medin, D. L., Altom, M. W., Edelson, S. M., & Freko, D. (1982). Correlated symptoms and simulated medical classification. *Journal of Experimental Psychology: Learning, Memory, and Cognition, 8,* 37–50.

Meehl, P. E. (1954). *Clinical vs. statistical prediction: A theoretical analysis and review of the evidence.* Minneapolis: University of Minnesota Press.

Melton, A. W. (1970). The situation with respect to the spacing of repetitions and memory. *Journal of Verbal Learning and Verbal Behavior, 9,* 596–606.

Mervis, C. B., & Rosch, E. (1981). Categorization of natural objects. In M. R. Rosenzweig & L. W. Porter (Eds.), *Annual Review of Psychology, 32,* 89–115.

Metcalfe, J., & Wiebe, D. (1987). Intuition in insight and noninsight problem solving. *Memory & Cognition, 15,* 238–246.

Meyer, D. E., & Schvaneveldt, R. W. (1971). Facilitation in recognizing pairs of words: Evidence of a dependence between retrieval operations. *Journal of Experimental Psychology, 90,* 227–234.

Meyer, D. E., Osman, A. M., Irwin, D. E., & Yantis, S. (1988). Modern mental chronometry. *Biological Psychology, 26,* 3–67.

Meyer, D., Leventhal, H., & Gutmann, M. (1985). Common-sense models of illness: The example of hypertension. *Health Psychology, 4,* 115–135.

Michalski, R. S. (1983). A theory and methodology of inductive learning. *Artificial Intelligence, 20,* 111–161.

Michotte, A. (1963). *The perception of causality.* London: Methuen.

Miller, G. A. (1956). The magical number seven plus or minus two: Some limits on our capacity for processing information. *Psychological Review, 63,* 81–97.

Miller, G. A. (1962). Some psychological studies of grammar. *American Psychologist, 17,* 748–762.

Miller, G. A. (1981). *Language and speech.* San Francisco: W. H. Freeman.

Miller, G. A., & Nicely, P. (1955). An analysis of perceptual confusions among some English consonants. *Journal of the Acoustical Society of America, 27,* 338–352.

Miller, J. L. (1990). Speech perception. In D. N. Osherson & H. Lasnik (Eds.), *Language: An invitation to cognitive science* (Vol. 1). Cambridge, MA: MIT Press.

Miller, J. L., & Jusczyk, P. W. (1989). Neurobiological bases of speech perception. *Cognition, 13,* 111–137.

Milner, B. (1965). Visually-guided maze learning in man: Effects of bilateral hippocampal, bilateral frontal, and unilateral cerebral lesions. *Neuropsychologia, 3,* 317–338.

Milner, B. (1966). Amnesia following operation on the temporal lobes. In. C. W. M. Whitty & O. L. Zangwill (Eds.), *Amnesia*. London: Butterworths.

Minsky, M. L. (1975). A framework for representing knowledge. In P. H. Winston (Ed.), *The psychology of computer vision*. New York: McGraw-Hill.

Minsky, M. L., & Papert, S. A. (1988). *Perceptrons*. Cambridge, MA.: MIT Press.

Mitchell, D. B., & Richman, C. L. (1980). Confirmed reservations: Mental travel. *Journal of Experimental Psychology: Human Perception and Performance, 6,* 58–66.

Moray, N. (1959). Attention in dichotic listening: Affective cues and the influence of instructions. *Quarterly Journal of Experimental Psychology, 11,* 56–60.

Morey, L. C., & McNamara, T. P. (1987). On definitions, diagnosis, and DSM-III, *Journal of Abnormal Psychology, 96,* 283–285.

Morgan, J. L. (1986). *From simple input to complex grammar*. Cambridge, MA: MIT Press.

Motley, M. T., Baars, B. J., & Camden, C. T. (1982). Syntactic criteria in pre-articulatory editing: Evidence from laboratory-induced slips of the tongue. *Journal of Psycholinguistic Research, 5,* 503–522.

Murphy, A. H., & Winkler, R. C. (1977). Can weather forecasters formulate reliable probability forecasts of weather and temperature? *National Weather Digest, 2,* 2–9.

Murphy, G. L. (1988). Comprehending complex concepts. *Cognitive Science, 12,* 529–562.

Murphy, G. L., & Medin, D. L. (1985). The role of theories in conceptual coherence. *Psychological Review, 92,* 289–316.

Murphy, G. L., & Smith, E. E. (1982). Basic-level superiority in picture categorization. *Journal of Verbal Learning and Verbal Behavior, 21,* 1–20.

Murphy, G. L., & Wisniewski, E. J. (1989). Categorizing objects in isolation and in scenes: What a superordinate is good for. *Journal of Experimental Psychology: Learning , Memory, and Cognition, 15,* 572–586.

Myers, B. P. (1987). Mother-infant bondings: A critical period. In M. H. Bornstein (Ed.), *Sensitive periods in development: Interdisciplinary perspective*. Hillsdale, NJ: Erlbaum.

Mynatt, C. R., Doherty, M. E., & Tweney, R. D. (1977). Confirmation bias in a simulated research environment: An experimental study of scientific inference. *Quarterly Journal of Experimental Psychology, 29,* 85–95.

Nakayama, K. (1985). Biological image motion processing: A review. *Vision Research, 25,* 625–660.

Navon, D. (1984). Resources—a theoretical stone soup? *Psychological Review, 91,* 216–234.

Neisser, U. (1967). *Cognitive Psychology*. Englewood Cliffs, N.J.: Prentice-Hall.

Neisser, U. (1982). Memory: What are the important questions? In U. Neisser (Ed.), *Memory Observed*. San Francisco: W. H. Freeman.

Neisser, U., & Weene, P. (1962). Hierarchies in concept attainment. *Journal of Experimental Psychology, 64,* 640–645.

Nelson, K. (1973). Structure and strategy in learning to talk. *Monographs for the Society of Research in Child Development, 38* (Serial No. 149).

Nelson, T. O., Fehling, M. R., & Moore-Glascock, J. (1979). The nature of semantic savings for items forgotten from long-term memory. *Journal of Experimental Psychology: General, 108,* 225–250.

Newell, A. (1980). Reasoning, problem solving and decision processes: The problem space as a fundamental category. In R. Nickerson (Ed.), *Attention and performance VIII.* Hillsdale, NJ: Erlbaum.

Newell, A., & Rosenbloom, P. (1981). Mechanisms of skill acquisition and the law of practice. In J. R. Anderson (Ed.), *Cognitive skills and their acquisition.* Hillsdale, NJ: Erlbaum.

Newell, A., & Simon, H. A. (1972). *Human problem solving.* Englewood Cliffs, NJ: Prentice-Hall.

Newell, A., Shaw, J. C., & Simon, H. A. (1959). A report on a general problem-solving program. *Proceedings of the International Conferences on Information Processing,* 256–265. New York: UNESCO.

Newell, A., Shaw, J. C., & Simon, H. A. (1962). The process of creative thinking. In H. E. Gruber, G. Terrell, & M. Wertheimer (Eds.), *Contemporary approaches to creative thinking.* New York: Atherton Press.

Newport, E. L. (1984). Constraints on learning: Studies in the acquisition of American sign language. *Papers and Reports on Child Language Development, 23,* 1–22.

Newport, E. L. (1988). Constraints on learning and their role in language acquisition: Studies of the acquisition of American sign language. *Language Sciences, 10,* 147–172.

Newport, E. L. (1990). Maturational constraints on language learning. *Cognitive Science, 14,* 11–28.

Newport, E. L., Gleitman, H., & Gleitman, L. (1977). Mother, I'd rather do it myself: Some effects and noneffects of maternal speech style. In C. E. Snow & C. A. Ferguson (Eds.), *Talking to children: Language input and acquisition.* Cambridge, England: Cambridge University Press.

Nickerson, R. S., & Adams, M. J. (1979). Long-term memory for a common object. *Cognitive Psychology, 11,* 287–307.

Nisbett, R. E., Krantz, D. H., Jepson, D., & Kunda, Z. (1983). The use of statistical heuristics in everyday inductive reasoning. *Psychological Review, 90,* 339–363.

Nissen, M. J. (1985). Accessing features and objects: Is location special? In M. I. Posner & O. S. Marin (Eds.), *Attention and performance XI.* Hillsdale, NJ: Erlbaum.

Norman, D. A. (1968). Toward a theory of memory and attention. *Psychological Review, 75,* 522–536.

Norman, D. A. (1981). Categorization of action slips. *Psychological Review, 88,* 1–15.

Nosofsky, R. M. (1988a). Exemplar-based accounts of relations between classification, recognition, and typicality. *Journal of Experimental Psychology: Learning, Memory, and Cognition, 14,* 700–708.

Nosofsky, R. M. (1988b). Similarity, frequency, and category representations. *Journal of Experimental Psychology: Learning, Memory, and Cognition, 14,* 54–65.

Nosofsky, R. M. (1991). Tests of an exemplar model for relating perceptual classification and recognition in memory. *Journal of Experimental Psychology: Human Perception and Performance, 17,* 3–27.

Nosofsky, R. M. (in press). Exemplars, prototypes, and similarity rules. In A. F.

Healy, S. M. Kosslyn, & R. M. Shiffrin (Eds.), *Essays in honor of W. K. Estes (Vol. 1).* Hillsdale, NJ: Erlbaum.

Nosofsky, R. M., Clark, S. E., & Shin, J. H. (1989). Rules and exemplars in categorization, identification, and recognition. *Journal of Experimental Psychology: Learning, Memory, and Cognition, 15,* 282–304.

Novick, L. R. (1988). Analogical transfer, problem similarity, and expertise. *Journal of Experimental Psychology: Learning, Memory, and Cognition, 14,* 510–520.

Nussbaum, J. (1979). Children's conceptions of the Earth as a cosmic body: a cross age study. *Science Education, 63,* 83–93.

O'keefe, J., & Nadel, L. (1978). *The hippocampus as a cognitive map.* Oxford: Clarendon Press.

Oakhill, J. V., & Johnson-Laird, P. N. (1985). Rationality, memory and the search for counterexamples. *Cognition, 20,* 79–94.

Obal, F. (1966). The fundamentals of the central nervous system of vegetative homeostatis. *Acta Physiologica Academiae Scientiarum Hungaricae, 30,* 15–29.

Oden, G. C. (1987). Concept, knowledge, and thought. In M. R. Rosenzweig & L. W. Porter (Eds.), *Annual Review of Psychology, 38,* 203–227.

Oden, G. C., & Massaro, D. W. (1978). Integration of featural information in speech perception. *Psychological Review, 85,* 172–191.

Ortony, A., Vondruska, R. J., Foss, M. A., & Jones, L. E. (1985). Salience, similies, and the asymmetry of similarity. *Journal of Memory and Language, 24,* 569–594.

Osherson, D. N., & Lasnik, H. (Eds.) (1990). *Language: An Introduction to Cognitive Science* (Vol 1). Cambridge, MA: MIT Press.

Osherson, D. N., Smith, E. E., & Shafir, E. B. (1986). Some origins of belief. *Cognition, 24,* 197–224.

Osherson, D. N., Smith, E. E., Wilkie, O., Lopez, A., & Shafir, E. B. (1990). Category-based induction. *Psychological Review, 97,* 185–200.

Osherson, D. N., Stob, M., & Weinstein, S. (1986). *Systems that learn.* Cambridge, MA: MIT Press.

Osterhout, L., & Swinney, D. (in press). On the role of the simplicity heuristic in language processing: Evidence from structural and inferential processing. *Journal of Psycholinguistic Research.*

Owen, E., & Sweller, J. (1985). What do students learn while solving mathematics problems? *Journal of Educational Psychology, 77,* 272–284.

Paivio, A. (1971). *Imagery and verbal processes.* New York: Holt, Rinehart and Winston.

Palmer, S. E. (1975). Visual perception and world knowledge. In D. A. Norman & D. E. Rumelhart (Eds.), *Explorations in cognition.* San Francisco: W. H. Freeman.

Palmer, S. E. (1977). Hierarchical structure in perceptual recognition. *Cognitive Psychology, 9,* 441–474.

Palmer, S. E. (1978). Fundamental aspects of cognitive representation. In E. Rosch & B. Lloyd (Eds.), *Cognition and categorization.* Hillsdale, NJ: Erlbaum.

Palmer, S. E., & Kimchi, R. (1986). The information processing approach to cognition. In T. Knapp & L. Robertson (Ed.), *Approaches to cognition.* Hillsdale, NJ: Erlbaum.

Pashler, H. (1989). Dissociations and dependencies between speed and accuracy:

Evidence for a two-component theory of divided attention in simple tasks. *Cognitive Psychology, 21,* 469–514.

Payne, J. W. (1976). Task complexity and contingent processing in decision making: An information search and protocol analysis. *Organizational Behavior and Human Performance, 16,* 366–387.

Payne, J. W. (1982). Contingent decision behavior. *Psychological Bulletin, 92,* 382–402.

Payne, J. W., Bettman, J. R., & Johnson, E. J. (1988). Adaptive strategy selection in decision making. *Journal of Experimental Psychology: Learning, Memory, and Cognition, 14,* 534–552.

Penfield, W. (1959). The interpretive cortex. *Science, 129,* 1719–1725.

Pennebaker, J. W., & Epstein, D. (1983). Implicit psychophysiology: Effects of common beliefs and idiosyncratic physiological responses on symptom reporting. *Journal of Personality, 51,* 468–496.

Pennington, N., & Hastie, R. (1988). Explanation-based decision making: Effects of memory structure on judgment. *Journal of Experimental Psychology: Learning, Memory, and Cognition, 14,* 521–533.

Perkins, D. N. (1989). Creativity and the quest for mechanism. In R. J. Sternberg & E. E. Smith (Eds.), *The psychology of human thought.* Cambridge, England: Cambridge University Press.

Peterson, L. R., & Peterson, M. J. (1959). Short-term retention of individual verbal items. *Journal of Experimental Psychology, 58,* 193–198.

Peterson, M. J., Meagher, R. B., Jr., Chait, H., & Gilliee, S. (1973). The abstraction and generalization of dot patterns. *Cognitive Psychology, 4,* 378–398.

Pinker, S. (1984a). Visual cognition: An introduction. *Cognition, 18,* 1–63.

Pinker, S. (1984b). *Language learnability and language development.* Cambridge, MA: Harvard University Press.

Pinker, S. (1989). *Learnability and cognition: The acquisition of argument structure.* Cambridge, MA: MIT Press.

Pinker, S. (1990). Language acquisition. In D. N. Osherson & H. Lasnik (Eds.), *Language : An invitation to cognitive science* (Vol. 1). Cambridge, MA: MIT Press.

Pinker, S., & Prince, A. (1988). On language and connectionism: Analysis of a parallel distributed processing model of language acquisition. *Cognition, 28,* 73–193.

Pisoni, D. B. (1973). Auditory and phonetic memory codes in the discrimination of consonants and vowels. *Perception & Psychophysics, 13,* 253–260.

Poggio, T. (1984). Vision by man and machine. *Scientific American, 62–63,* 107–116.

Poggio, T., Torre, V., & Koch, C. (1985). Computational vision and regularization theory. *Nature, 317,* 314–319.

Pollack, I., & Pickett, J. M. (1964). Intelligibility of excerpts from fluent speech: Auditory vs. structural context. *Journal of Verbal Learning and Verbal Behavior, 3,* 79–84.

Polson, P. G., & Kieras, D. E. (1985). A quantitative model of the learning and performance of text-editing knowledge. *Proceedings of the CHI '85 Conference on Human Factors in Computing Systems,* 207–212. New York: ACM.

Polya, G. (1945). *How to solve it.* Princeton, NJ: Princeton University Press.

Polya, G. (1957). *How to solve it: A new aspect of mathematical method* (2nd ed.). Princeton, NJ: Princeton University Press.

Posner, M. I. (1988). Structures and functions of selective attention. In T. Boll & B. K. Bryant (Eds.). *Clinical neuropsychology and brain function.* Washington, D. C.: American Psychological Association.

Postman, L., & Phillips, L. W. (1965). Short-term temporal changes in free recall. *Quarterly Journal of Experimental Psychology, 17,* 132–138.

Presson, C. C., DeLange, N., & Hazelrigg, M. D. (1989). Orientation specificity in spatial memory: What makes a path different from a map of the path? *Journal of Experimental Psychology: Learning, Memory, and Cognition, 15,* 887–897.

Provine, R. R. (1986). Yawning as a stereotyped action pattern and releasing stimulus. *Ethology, 72,* 109–122.

Putnam, H. (1960). Minds and machines. In S. Hook (Ed.), *Dimensions of mind.* New York: New York University Press.

Pylyshyn, Z. W. (1973). What the mind's eye tells the mind's brain: A critique of mental imagery. *Psychological Bulletin, 80,* 1–24.

Pylyshyn, Z. W. (1978). Imagery and artificial intelligence. In C. W. Savage (Ed.), *Minneapolis studies in the philosophy of science* (Vol. 9). Minneapolis, MN: University of Minneapolis Press.

Pylyshyn, Z. W. (1979). The rate of "mental rotation" of images: A test of the holistic analogue hypothesis. *Memory & Cognition, 7,* 19–28.

Pylyshyn, Z. W. (1981). The imagery debate: Analogue media versus tacit knowledge. *Psychological Review, 88,* 16–45.

Quillian, M. R. (1968). Semantic memory. In M. Minsky (Ed.), *Semantic information processing.* Cambridge, MA: MIT Press.

Quine, W. V. O. (1961). *Word and object.* Cambridge, MA: MIT Press.

Raaijmakers, J. G., & Shiffrin, R. M. (1981). Search of associative memory. *Psychological Review, 88,* 93–134.

Rajamoney, S., & DeJong, G. (1987). The classification, detection, and handling of imperfect theory problems. In *Proceedings of the Tenth International Joint Conference on Artificial Intelligence,* 205–207. Milan, Italy.

Ratcliff, R. (1990). Connectionist models of recognition memory: Constraints imposed by learning and forgetting functions. *Psychological Review, 97,* 285–308.

Ratcliff, R., & McKoon, G. (1981). Does activation really spread? *Psychological Review, 88,* 454–462.

Ratcliff, R., & McKoon, G. (1989). Similarity information versus relational information: Differences in the time course of retrieval. *Cognitive Psychology, 21,* 139–155.

Rattermann, M. J., & Gentner, D. (1987). Analogy and similarity: Determinants of accessibility and inferential soundness. *Proceedings of the Ninth Annual Meeting of the Cognitive Science Society,* 23–34. Hillsdale, NJ: Erlbaum.

Rayner, K., Carlson, M., & Frazier, L. (1983). The interaction of syntax and semantics during sentence processing: Eye movements in the analysis of semantically-biased sentences. *Journal of Verbal Learning and Verbal Behavior, 22,* 358–374.

Reason, J. (1979). Action not as planned. In G. Underwood & R. Stevens (Eds.), *Aspect of consciousness*. London: Academic Press.

Reason, J., & Mycielska, K. (1982). *Absentminded? The psychology of mental lapses and everyday errors*. Englewood Cliffs, NJ: Prentice-Hall.

Reber, A. S. (1989). Implicit learning and tacit knowledge. *Journal of Experimental Psychology: General, 118,* 219–235.

Reber, A. S., Allen, R., & Regan, S. (1985). Syntactic learning and judgment, still unconscious and still abstract: Comment on Dulany, Carlson, and Dewey. *Journal of Experimental Psychology: General, 114,* 17–24.

Reber, A. S., Kassin, S. M., Lewis, S., & Cantor, G. W. (1980). On the relationship between implicit and explicit modes in the learning of a complex rule structure. *Journal of Experimental Psychology: General, 114,* 492–502.

Redd, W. H., Jacobson, P. B., Die-Trill, M., & Dermatis, H. (1987). Cognitive/attention distraction in the control of conditioned nausea in pediatric cancer patients receiving chemotherapy. *Journal of Consulting and Clinical Psychology, 55,* 391–395.

Reder, L. M. (1979). The role of elaborations in memory for prose. *Cognitive Psychology, 11,* 221–234.

Reder, L. M. (1982). Plausibility judgments versus fact retrieval: Efficient strategies for question-answering. *Psychological Review, 89,* 250–280.

Reder, L. M., & Ross, B. H. (1983). Integrated knowledge in different tasks: The role of retrieval strategy on fan effects. *Journal of Experimental Psychology: Learning, Memory, and Cognition, 9,* 55–72.

Reed, S. K. (1974). Structural descriptions and the limitations of visual images. *Memory & Cognition, 2,* 329–336.

Reed, S. K., Dempster, A., & Ettinger, M. (1985). Usefulness of analogous solutions for solving algebra word problems. *Journal of Experimental Psychology: Learning, Memory, and Cognition, 11,* 106–125.

Reicher, G. M. (1969). Perceptual recognition as a function of meaningfulness of stimulus material. *Journal of Experimental Psychology, 81,* 274–280.

Reimann, P., & Chi, M. T. H. (1989). Human expertise. In K. J. Gilhooly (Ed.), *Human and machine problem solving*. London, England: Plenum Publishing Corporation.

Reitman, J. S. (1976). Skilled perception in Go: Deducing memory structures from inter-response times. *Cognitive Psychology, 8,* 336–356.

Reitman, W. (1965). *Cognition and thought*. New York: Wiley.

Remez, R. E. (1987). Neural models of speech perception: A case history. In S. Harnad (Ed.), *Categorical perception*. Cambridge, England: Cambridge University Press.

Rescorla, L. (1980). Overextensions in early language development. *Journal of Child Language, 7,* 321–335.

Rescorla, R. A. (1967). Pavlovian conditioning and its proper control procedures. *Psychological Review, 74,* 71–80.

Rescorla, R. A. (1988). Pavlovian conditioning: It's not what you think it is. *American Psychologist, 45,* 151–160.

Rescorla, R. A., & Wagner, A. R. (1982). A theory of Pavlovian conditioning: Variations in the effectiveness of reinforcement and nonreinforcement. In A. H.

Black & W. F. Prokasy (Eds.), *Classical conditioning II: Current theory and research*. New York: Appleton-Century-Crofts.

Reznick, J. S., & Richman, C. L. (1976). Effects of class complexity, class frequency, and preexperimental bias on rule learning. *Journal of Experimental Psychology: Human Learning and Memory, 2,* 774–782.

Richardson, J. T. E. (1980). *Mental imagery and human memory*. New York: St. Martin's.

Richardson-Klavehn, A., & Bjork, R. A. (1988). Measures of memory. *Annual Review of Psychology, 39,* 475–543.

Rips, L. J. (1975). Inductive judgments about natural categories. *Journal of Verbal Learning and Verbal Behavior, 14,* 665–681.

Rips, L. J. (1983). Cognitive processes in propositional reasoning. *Psychological Review, 90,* 38–71.

Rips, L. J. (1986). Mental muddles. In M. Brand & R. M. Harnish (Eds.), *Representation of knowledge and belief*. Tucson, AZ: University of Arizona Press.

Rips, L. J. (1988). Reasoning. In R. J. Sternberg & E. E. Smith (Eds.), *The psychology of human thought*. Cambridge: Cambridge University Press.

Rips, L. J. (1989). Similarity, typicality, and categorization. In S. Vosniadou & A. Ortony (Eds.), *Similarity and analogical reasoning*. Cambridge, England: Cambridge University Press.

Rips, L. J. (1990). Reasoning. In M. R. Rosenzweig & L. W. Porter (Eds.), *Annual Review of Psychology, 41,* 321–353.

Rips, L. J., Shoben, E. J., & Smith, E. E. (1973). Semantic distance and verification of semantic relations. *Journal of Verbal Learning and Verbal Behavior, 12,* 1–20.

Roberts, W. A. (1972). Free recall of word lists varying in length and rate of presentation: A test of total-time hypotheses. *Journal of Experimental Psychology, 92,* 365–372.

Roediger, H. L. (1990). Implicit memory: Retention without remembering. *American Psychologist, 45,* 1043–1056.

Roediger, H. L., & Blaxton, T. A. (1987). Effects of varying modality, surface features, and retention interval on priming in word-fragment completion. *Memory & Cognition, 15,* 379–388.

Roediger, H. L., Srinivas, K., & Weldon, M. S. (1989). Dissociations between implicit measures of retention. In S. Lewandowsky, J. C. Dunn, & K. Kirsner (Eds.), *Implicit memory: Theoretical issues*. Hillsdale, NJ: Erlbaum.

Rosch, E., & Lloyd, B. B. (Eds.) (1978). *Cognition and categorization*. New York: Wiley.

Rosch, E., & Mervis, C. B. (1975). Family resemblances: Studies in the internal structure of categories. *Cognitive Psychology, 7,* 573–605.

Rosch, E., Mervis, C. G., Gray, W. D., Johnson, D. M., & Bayes Braem, P. (1976). Basic objects in natural categories. *Cognitive Psychology, 8,* 382–439.

Rosenbloom, P., & Newell, A. (1987). Learning by chunking: A production system model of practice. In D. Klahr, P. Langley, & R. Neches (Eds.), *Production system models of learning and development*. Cambridge, MA: MIT Press.

Rosenthal, R. (1967). Covert communication in the psychological experiment. *Psychological Bulletin, 67,* 356–367.

Ross, B. H. (1984). Remindings and their effects in learning a cognitive skill. *Cognitive Psychology, 16,* 371–416.

Ross, B. H. (1987). This is like that: The use of earlier problems and the separation of similarity effects. *Journal of Experimental Psychology: Learning, Memory, and Cognition, 13,* 629–639.

Ross, B. H. (1989). Distinguishing types of superficial similarities: Different effects on the access and use of earlier problems. *Journal of Experimental Psychology: Learning, Memory, and Cognition, 15,* 456–468.

Ross, L. (1977). The intuitive psychologist and his shortcomings: Distortions in the attribution process. In L. Berkowitz (Ed.), *Advances in Experimental Social Psychology* (Vol. 10). New York: Academic Press.

Ross, L., Lepper, M. R., & Hubbard, M. (1975). Perseverance in self-perception and social perception: Biased attributional processes in the debriefing paradigm. *Journal of Personality and Social Psychology, 32,* 880–892.

Roth, E. M., & Shoben, E. J. (1983). The effect of context on the structure of categories. *Cognitive Psychology, 15,* 346–378.

Rozin, P., & Kalat, J. W. (1971). Specific hungers and poison avoidance as adaptive specializations of learning. *Psychological Review, 78,* 459–486.

Rozin, P., Millman, L., & Numeroff, C. (1986). Operations of the laws of sympathetic magic in disgust and other domains. *Journal of Personality and Social Psychology, 50,* 703–712.

Rumelhart, D. E., & McClelland, J. L. (1982). An interactive activation model of context effects in letter perception, Part. 2. The contextural enhancement effect and some tests and extensions of the model. *Psychological Review, 89,* 60–94.

Rumelhart, D. E., & McClelland, J. L. (1986a). On learning the past tenses of English verbs. In J. L. McClelland & D. E. Rumelhart (Eds.). *Parallel distributed processing. Explorations in the microstructure of cognition. Vol. 2: Psychological and biological models.* Cambridge, MA: Bradford Books/MIT Press.

Rumelhart, D. E., & McClelland, J. L. (Eds.). (1986b). *Parallel distributed processing. Explorations in the microstructure of cognition. Vol. 1: Foundations.* Cambridge, MA: MIT Press.

Rumelhart, D. E., & Norman, D. A. (1978). Accretion, tuning, and restructuring: Three modes of learning. In J. W. Cotton & R. Klatzky (Eds.), *Semantic factors in cognition.* Hillsdale, NJ: Erlbaum.

Rumelhart, D. E., & Ortony, A. (1977). The representation of knowledge in memory. In R. C. Anderson, R. J. Spiro, & W. E. Montague (Eds.), *Schooling and the acquisition of knowledge.* Hillsdale, NJ: Erlbaum.

Rumelhart, D. E., & Zipser, D. (1985). Feature discovery by competitive learning. *Cognitive Science, 19,* 75–112.

Rumelhart, D. E., Hinton, G. E., & Williams, R. J. (1986). Learning internal representations by error propagation. In D. E. Rumelhart & J. L. McClelland (Eds.), *Parallel distributed processing: Explorations in the microstructure of cognition* (Vol. 1). Cambridge, MA: MIT Press.

Rumelhart, D. E., Smolensky, P., McClelland, J. L., & Hinton, G. E. (1986). Schemata and sequential thought processes in PDP models. In J. L. McClelland & D. E. Rumelhart (Eds.), *Parallel distributed processing: explorations in the microstructure of cognition* (Vol. 2). Cambridge, MA: MIT Press.

Russo, J. E., Johnson, E. J., & Stephens, D. L. (1989). The validity of verbal protocols. *Memory & Cognition, 17,* 759–769.

Ryan, C. (1983). Reassessing the automaticity-control distinction: Item recognition as a paradigm case. *Psychological Review, 90,* 171–178.

Sachs, J. D. S. (1967). Recognition memory for syntactic and semantic aspects of connected discourse. *Perception & Psychophysics, 2,* 437–442.

Sanders, G. S., & Simmons, W. L. (1983). Use of hypnosis to enhance eyewitness accuracy: Does it work? *Journal of Applied Psychology, 68,* 70–77.

Schacter, D. L. (1987). Implicit memory: History and current status. *Journal of Experimental Psychology: Learning, Memory, and Cognition, 13,* 510–518.

Schacter, D. L. (1989). Memory. In M. Posner (Ed.), *Foundations of cognitive science.* Cambridge, MA: Bradford Books.

Schank, R. C., & Abelson, R. (1977). *Scripts, plans, goals and understanding.* Hillsdale, NJ: Erlbaum.

Schank, R. C. (1982). *Dynamic memory.* Cambridge, England: Cambridge University Press.

Schank, R. C., Collins, G. C., & Hunter, L. E. (1986). Transcending inductive category formation in learning. *The Behavioral and Brain Sciences, 9,* 639–686.

Schneider, W., & Detweiler, M. (1987). A connectionist/control architecture for working memory. In G. H. Bower (Ed.), *The psychology of learning & motivation* (Vol 21). New York: Academic Press.

Schneider, W., & Fisk, A. D. (1984). Automatic category search and its transfer. *Journal of Experimental Psychology: Learning, Memory, and Cognition, 10,* 1–15.

Schneider, W., & Shiffrin, R. M. (1977). Controlled and automatic human information processing: 1. Detection, search, and attention. *Psychological Review, 84,* 1–66.

Schober, M. F., & Clark, H. H. (1989). Understanding by addressees and overhearers. *Cognitive Psychology, 21,* 211–232.

Schoenfeld, A. H. (1985). *Mathematical problem solving.* Orlando, FL: Academic Press.

Schoenfeld, A. H., & Herrmann, D. J. (1982). Problem perception and knowledge structure in expert and novice mathematical problem solvers. *Journal of Experimental Psychology: Learning, Memory, and Cognition, 8,* 484–494.

Schooler, J. W., & Engstler-Schooler, T. Y. (1990). Verbal overshadowing of visual memories: Some things are better off left unsaid. *Cognitive Psychology, 22,* 36–71.

Schwartz, B. J., & Sperling, G. (1983). Nonrigid 3-D percepts from 2-D representation of rigid objects. *Investigative Ophthalmology and Visual Science, 24* (3, Supplement), 239.

Searle, J. R. (1969). *Speech acts.* Cambridge, England: Cambridge University Press.

Searle, J. R. (1975). Indirect speech acts. In P. Cole & J. L. Morgan (Eds.), *Syntax and semantics* (Vol. 3). New York: Seminar Press.

Segal, S. J., & Fusella, V. (1970). Influence of imaged pictures and sounds on detection of visual and auditory signals. *Journal of Experimental Psychology, 83,* 458–464.

Seidenberg, M. S., & McClelland, J. L. (1989). A distributed, developmental model of word recognition and naming. *Psychological Review, 96,* 523–568.

Seifert, C. M., & Gray, K. C. (1990). Representational issues in analogical transfer. *Proceedings of the twelfth annual conference of the Cognitive Science Society,* 30–37. Hillsdale, NJ: Erlbaum.

Selfridge, O. G. (1955). Pattern recognition and modern computers. *Proceedings of the Western Joint Computer Conference.* New York: IEEE.

Shaklee, H., & Mims, M. (1982). Sources of error in judging event covariation: Effects of memory demands. *Journal of Experimental Psychology: Human Learning and Memory, 8,* 208–224.

Shaklee, H., & Tucker, D. (1980). A rule analysis of judgements of covariation between events. *Memory & Cognition, 8,* 459–467.

Shanks, D. R. (1986). Selective attribution and the judgment of causality. *Learning & Motivation, 17,* 311–334.

Shanks, D. R. (1989). Selectional processes in causality judgments. *Memory & Cognition, 17,* 27–34.

Shanks, D. R., & Dickerson, A. (1988). The role of selective attribution in causality judgment. In D. J. Hilton (Ed.), *Contemporary science and natural explanation.* Brighton, England: Harvester Press Limited.

Shapiro, K. L., Jacobs, W. J., & LoLordo, V. M. (1980). Stimulus-reinforcer interactions in Pavlovian conditioning of pigeons: Implications for selective associations. *Animal Learning & Behavior, 8,* 586–594.

Shattuck-Hufnagel, S. (1979). Speech errors as evidence for a serial ordering mechanism in sentence production. In W. E. Cooper & E.C.T. Walker (Eds.), *Sentence processing: Psycholinguistic studies presented to Merrill Garrett.* Hillsdale, NJ: Erlbaum.

Shepard, R. N. (1967). Recognition memory for words, sentences, and pictures. *Journal of Verbal Learning and Verbal Behavior, 6,* 156–163.

Shepard, R. N. (1972). Psychological representation of speech sounds. In E. E. David & P. B. Denes (Eds.), *Human communication: A unified view.* New York: McGraw-Hill.

Shepard, R. N. (1981). Psychophysical complementarity. In M. Kubovy & J. R. Pomerantz (Eds.), *Perceptual organization.* Hillsdale, NJ: Erlbaum.

Shepard, R. N. (1984). Ecological constraints on internal representation: Resonant kinematics of perceiving, imaging, thinking, and dreaming. *Psychological Review, 91,* 417–447.

Shepard, R. N. (1987). Toward a universal law of generalization for psychological science. *Science, 237,* 1317–1323.

Shepard, R. N., & Cooper, L. A. (1982). *Mental images and their transformations.* Cambridge, MA: MIT Press.

Shepard, R. N., & Metzler, J. (1971). Mental rotation of three-dimensional objects. *Science, 171,* 701–703.

Shepard, R. N., & Podgorny, P. (1978). Cognitive processes that resemble perceptual processes. In W. K. Estes (Ed.), *Handbook of learning and cognitive processes* (Vol. 5). Hillsdale, NJ: Erlbaum.

Sherry, D. F., & Schacter, D. L. (1987). The evolution of multiple memory systems. *Psychological Review, 94,* 439–454.

Shiffrin, R. M. (1988). Attention. In R. C. Atkinson, R. J. Herrinstein, G. Lindzey, & R. D. Luce (Eds.), *Stevens' Handbook of Experimental Psychology* (Vol. 2). New York: Wiley.

Shiffrin, R. M., & Schneider, W. (1977). Controlled and automatic human information processing: 2. Perceptual learning, automatic attending, and a general theory. *Psychological Review, 84,* 127–190.

Shiffrin, R. M., Dumais, S. T., & Schneider, W. (1981). Characteristics of automatism. In J. Long & A. Baddeley (Eds.), *Attention and performance, IX.* Hillsdale, NJ: Erlbaum.

Shimp, C. P. (1975). Perspectives on the behavioral unit: Choice behavior in animals. In W. K. Estes (Ed.), *Handbook of learning and cognitive processes* (Vol. 2). Hillsdale, NJ: Erlbaum.

Shipley, E. F., Smith, C. S., & Gleitman, L. R. (1969). A study in the acquisition of language: Free responses to commands. *Language, 45,* 322–342.

Shortliffe, E. H. (1976). *Computer-based medical consultations: MYCIN,* New York: Elsevier.

Shortliffe, E. H., Buchanan, B. G., & Feigenbaum, E. A. (1979). Knowledge engineering for medical decision-making: A review of computer-based clinical decision aids. In *Proceedings of the IEEE, 67,* 1207–1244.

Shweder, R. A. (1977). Likeness and likelihood in everyday thought: Magical thinking in judgments about personality. *Current Anthropology, 18,* 637–638.

Siegel, S. (1977a). Morphine tolerance acquisition as an associative process. *Journal of Experimental Psychology: Animal Behavior Processes, 3,* 1–13.

Siegel, S. (1977b). A Pavlovian conditioning analysis of morphine tolerance (and opiate dependence). In N. A. Krasnegor (Ed.), *Behavioral tolerance: Research and treatment implications.* National Institute for Drug Abuse, Monograph No. 18.

Siegel, S. (1989). Pharmacological conditioning and drug effects. In M. W. Emmett-Oglesby & A. J. Goudie (Eds.), *Tolerance and sensitization to psychoactive drugs.* Clifton, NJ: Human Press.

Simon, D. P., & Simon, H. A. (1978). Individual differences in solving physics problems. In R. Siegler (Ed.), *Children's thinking: What develops?* Hillsdale, NJ: Erlbaum.

Simon, H. A. (1957). *Models of man: Social and rational.* New York: Wiley.

Simon, H. A. (1973). The structure of ill-structured problems. *Artificial Intelligence, 4,* 181–201.

Simon, H. A. (1978). Information processing theory of human problem solving. In W. K. Estes (Ed.), *Handbook of learning and cognitive processes* (Vol. 5). Hillsdale, NJ: Erlbaum.

Simon, H. A. (1980). Problem solving and education. In D. T. Tuma & F. Reif (Eds.), *Problem solving and education: Issues in teaching and learning.* Hillsdale, NJ: Erlbaum.

Simon, H. A. (1989). The scientist as problem solver. In D. Klahr & K. Kotovsky (Eds.), *Complex information processing: The impact of Herbert A. Simon.* Hillsdale, NJ: Erlbaum.

Singer, M., & Ferreira, F. (1983). Inferring consequences in story comprehension. *Journal of Verbal Learning and Verbal Behavior, 22,* 437–448.

Singleton, J. L., & Newport, E. L. (unpublished manuscript). When learners surpass their models: The acquisition of American Sign Language from impoverished input.

Singley, M. K., & Anderson, J. R. (1989). *The transfer of cognitive skill*. Cambridge, MA: Harvard University Press.

Skinner, B. F. (1938). *The behavior of organisms*. New York: Appleton-Century-Crofts.

Skinner, B. F. (1950). Are theories of learning necessary? *Psychological Review, 57,* 193–216.

Skinner, B. F. (1957). *Verbal behavior*. Englewood Cliffs, NJ: Prentice-Hall.

Slobin, D. (1966). Grammatical transformation and sentence comprehension in childhood and adulthood. *Journal of Verbal Learning and Verbal Behavior, 5,* 219–277.

Slovic, P., & Lichtenstein, S. (1968). The relative importance of probabilities and payoffs in risk taking. *Journal of Experimental Psychology Monograph Supplement, 78* (3 pt 2).

Smedslund, J. (1963). The concept of correlation in adults. *Scandinavian Journal of Psychology, 4,* 165–173.

Smith, E. E. (1978). Theories of semantic memory. In W. K. Estes (Ed.), *Handbook of learning and cognitive processes* (Vol. 6). Hillsdale, NJ: Erlbaum.

Smith, E. E., & Medin, D. L. (1981). *Categories and concepts*. Cambridge, MA: Harvard University Press.

Smith, E. E., & Osherson, D. N. (1984). Conceptual combination with prototype concepts. *Cognitive Science, 8,* 337–361.

Smith, E. E., Shoben, E. J., & Rips, L. J. (1974). Structure and process in semantic memory: A featural model for semantic decisions. *Psychological Review, 81,* 214–241.

Smith, E. E., Osherson, D. N., Rips, L. J., & Keane, M. (1988). Combining prototypes: A selective modification model. *Cognitive Science, 12,* 485–527.

Smith, L. B. (1989). A model of perceptual classification in children and adults. *Psychological Review, 96,* 125–144.

Smith, S. M. (1979). Remembering in and out of context. *Journal of Experimental Psychology: Human Learning and Memory, 5,* 460–471.

Smith, S. M. (1986). Environmental context-dependent recognition memory using a short-term memory task for input. *Memory & Cognition, 14,* 347–354.

Smith, S. M., & Rothkopf, E. Z. (1984). Contextual enrichment and distribution of practice in the classroom. *Cognition and Instruction, 1,* 341–358.

Smith, S. M., Glenberg, A., & Bjork, R. A. (1978). Environmental context and human memory. *Memory & Cognition, 6,* 342–353.

Snyder, M., Tanke, E. D., & Berscheid, E. (1977). Social perception and interpersonal behavior: On the self-fulfilling nature of social stereotypes. *Journal of Personality and Social Psychology, 35,* 656–666.

Sokal, R. R. (1974). Classification: Purposes, principles, progress, prospects. *Science, 185,* 1115–1123.

Sokolov, E. M. (1963). Higher nervous functions: The orienting reflex. *Annual Review of Physiology, 25,* 545–580.

Solomon, R. L. (1977). An opponent-process theory of acquired motivation: The affective dynamics of addiction. In J. D. Maser & M. E. P. Seligman (Eds.), *Psychopathology: Experimental models*. San Francisco: W. H. Freeman.

Solomon, R. L., & Corbit, J. D. (1974). An opponent-process theory of motivation: I. The temporal dynamics of affect. *Psychological Review, 81,* 119–145.

Spelke, E. S. (1990). Principles of object perception. *Cognitive Science, 14,* 29–56.

Spelke, E. S., von Hofsten, C., & Kestenbaum, R. (1989). Object perception in infancy: Interaction of spatial and kinetic information for object boundaries. *Developmental Psychology, 25,* 185–196.

Sperling, G. (1960). The information available in brief visual presentations. *Psychological Monographs, 74* (Whole number 498).

Spilich, G. J., Vesonder, G. T., Chiesi, H. L., & Voss, J. F. (1979). Text processing of domain-related information for individuals with high and low domain knowledge. *Journal of Verbal Learning and Verbal Behavior, 18,* 275–290.

Squire, L. R. (1982). Comparisons between forms of amnesia: Some deficits are unique to Korsakoff's syndrome. *Journal of Experimental Psychology: Learning, Memory, and Cognition, 8,* 560–571.

Srull, T. K., & Wyer, R. S. (1979). The role of category accessibility in the interpretation of information about persons: Some determinants and applications. *Journal of Personality and Social Psychology, 37,* 1660–1672.

Standing, L. (1973). Learning 10,000 pictures. *Quarterly Journal of Experimental Psychology, 25,* 207–222.

Stanfill, C., & Waltz, D. (1986). Toward memory-based reasoning. *Communications of the ACM, 29,* 1213–1228.

Stein, B. S., & Bransford, J. D. (1979). Constraints on effective elaboration: Effects of precision and subject generation. *Journal of Verbal Learning and Verbal Behavior, 18,* 769–777.

Stemberger, J. P. (1982). The lexicon in a model of language production. Unpublished doctoral dissertation, University of California, San Diego.

Sternberg, R. J. (1982). Natural, unnatural, and supernatural concepts. *Cognitive Psychology, 14,* 451–488.

Sternberg, S. (1966). High-speed scanning in human memory. *Science, 153,* 652–654.

Stevens, A., & Coupe, P. (1978). Distortions in judged spatial relations. *Cognitive Psychology, 10,* 422–437.

Streeter, L. A. (1978). Acoustic determinants of phrase-boundary perception. *Journal of the Acoustical Society of America, 64,* 1582–1592.

Studdert-Kennedy, M. (1976). Speech perception. In N. J. Lass (Ed.), *Contemporary issues in experimental phonetics.* Springfield, IL: Charles C. Thomas.

Sutherland, N. S. (1968). Outlines of a theory of visual pattern recognition in animals and man. *Proceedings of the Royal Society, 171,* 297–317.

Sutton, R. S., & Barto, A. G. (1981). Toward a modern theory of adaptive networks: Expectation and prediction. *Psychological Review, 88,* 135–170.

Sweller, J. (1988). Cognitive load during problem solving: Effects on learning. *Cognitive Science, 12,* 257–286.

Sweller, J., & Cooper, G. A. (1985). The use of worked examples as a substitute for problem solving in learning algebra. *Cognition and Instruction, 2,* 59–89.

Swinney, D. (1979). Lexical access during sentence comprehension. (Re) consideration of context effects. *Journal of Verbal Learning and Verbal Behavior, 18,* 645–659.

Swinney, D., & Osterhout, L. (1990). Inference generation during auditory language comprehension. In A. Graesser & G. H. Bower (Eds.), *The psychol-*

ogy of learning and motivation: Inference context-comprehension (Vol. 25). New York: Academic Press.

Tajfel, H. (1981). *Human groups and social catgeories: Studies in social psychology.* Cambridge, England: Cambridge University Press.

Tajfel, H., & Wilkes, A. L. (1963). Classification and quantitative judgment. *British Journal of Psychology, 54,* 101–114.

Tanaka, J. W., & Taylor, M. (1991). Object categories and expertise: Is the basic level in the eye of the beholder? *Cognitive Psychology, 23,* 457–482.

Taylor, S. E. (1981). A categorization approach to stereotyping. In D. L. Hamilton (Ed.), *Cognitive processes in stereotyping and intergroup behavior.* Hillsdale, NJ: Erlbaum.

Taylor, S. E., Fiske, S. T., Etcoff, N. L., & Ruderman, A. J. (1978). Categorical and contextual bases of person memory and stereotyping. *Journal of Personality and Social Psychology, 36,* 778–793.

Tenpenny, P. L., & Shoben, E. J. (1992). Component processes and the utility of the conceptually-driven/data-driven distinction. *Journal of Experimental Psychology: Learning, Memory, and Cognition, 18,* in press.

Testa, T. J. (1974). Causal relationships and the acquisition of avoidance responses. *Psychological Review, 81,* 491–505.

Tetewsky, S. J., & Sternberg, R. J. (1986). Conceptual and lexical determinants of nonentrenched thinking. *Journal of Memory and Language, 25,* 202–225.

Thaler, R. H. (1980). Toward a positive theory of consumer choice. *Journal of Economic Behavior and Organization, 1,* 39–60.

Thorndyke, P., & Hayes-Roth, B. (1982). Differences in spatial knowledge acquired from maps and navigation. *Cognitive Psychology, 14,* 560–589.

Tinklepaugh, O. L. (1928). An experimental study of representational factors in monkeys. *Journal of Comparative Psychology, 8,* 197–236.

Tinklepaugh, O. L. (1932). Multiple delayed reaction with chimpanzees and monkeys. *Journal of Comparative Psychology, 13,* 207–243.

Tipper, S. P., Brehaut, J. C., & Driver, J. (1990). Selection of moving and static objects for the control of spatially directed action. *Journal of Experimental Psychology: Human Perception and Performance, 16,* 492–504.

Todd, J. T. (1985). The perception of structure from motion: Is projective correspondence of moving elements a necessary condition? *Journal of Experimental Psychology: Human Perception and Performance, 11,* 689–710.

Todd, J. T., & Reichel, F. D. (1989). Ordinal structure in the visual perception and cognition of smoothly curved surfaces. *Psychological Review, 96,* 643–657.

Townsend, J. T. (1971). A note on the identifiability of parallel and serial processes. *Perception & Psychophysics, 10,* 161–163.

Trabasso, T., Van den Broek, P., & Suh, S. Y. (1989). Logical necessity and transitivity of causal relations in stories. *Discourse Processes, 12,* 1–25.

Treisman, A. (1960). Contextual cues in selective listening. *Quarterly Journal of Experimental Psychology, 12,* 242–248.

Treisman, A. (1964). Effect of irrelevant material on the efficiency of selective listening. *American Journal of Psychology, 77,* 533–546.

Treisman, A. (1988). Features and objects: The fourteenth Bartlett memorial lecture. *Quarterly Journal of Experimental Psychology, 40A,* 201–237.

Treisman, A., & Gelade, G. (1980). A feature integration theory of attention. *Cognitive Psychology, 12*, 97–136.

Treisman, A., & Sato, S. (1990). Conjunction search revisited. *Journal of Experimental Psychology: Human Perception and Performance, 16*, 459–478.

Tulving, E. (1972). Episodic and semantic memory. In E. Tulving & W. Donaldson (Eds.), *Organization of memory*. New York: Academic Press.

Tulving, E. (1983). *Elements of episodic memory*. New York: Oxford University Press.

Tulving, E. (1985). How many memory systems are there? *American Psychologist, 40*, 385–398.

Tulving, E., & Thomson, D. M. (1973). Encoding specificity and retrieval processes in episodic memory. *Psychological Review, 80*, 352–373.

Tulving, E., Schacter, D. L., & Stark, H. A. (1982). Priming effects in word-fragment completion are independent of recognition memory. *Journal of Experimental Psychology: Learning, Memory, and Cognition, 8*, 336–342.

Turing, A. (1936). On computable numbers, with an application to the Entscheidungs problem. *Proceedings of the London Mathematical Society, 42*, 230–265.

Turing, A. (1958). Computing machinery and intelligence. *Mind, 59*, 433–460.

Tversky, A. (1972). Elimination by aspects: A theory of choice. *Psychological Review, 79*, 281–299.

Tversky, A. (1977). Features of similarity. *Psychological Review, 84*, 327–352.

Tversky, A., & Kahneman, D. (1974). Judgment under uncertainty: Heuristics and biases. *Science , 185*, 1124–1131.

Tversky, A., & Kahneman, D. (1981). The framing of decisions and the psychology of choice. *Science, 211*, 453–458.

Tversky, A., & Kahneman, D. (1983). Extensional versus intuitive reasoning: The conjunction fallacy in probability judgment. *Psychological Review, 90*, 293–315.

Tversky, A., Sattath, S., & Slovic, P. (1988). Contingent weighting in judgment and choice. *Psychological Review, 95*, 371–384.

Tversky, B. (1981). Distortions in memory for maps. *Cognitive Psychology, 13*, 407–433.

Tversky, B., & Hemenway, K. (1984). Objects, parts, and categories. *Journal of Experimental Psychology: General, 113*, 169–193.

Tweney, R. D., Doherty, M. E., & Mynatt, C. R. (Eds.). (1981). *On scientific thinking*. New York: Columbia University Press.

Ullman, S. (1979). *The interpretation of visual motion*. Cambridge, MA: MIT Press.

Ullman, S. (1989). Aligning pictorial descriptions: An approach to object recognition. *Cognition, 32*, 193–254.

Ungerleider, L. G., & Mishkin, M. (1982). Two cortical visual systems. In D. J. Ingle, M. A. Goodale, & R. J. W. Mansfield (Eds.), *Analysis of visual behavior*. Cambridge, MA: MIT Press.

van Dijk, T. A., & Kintsch, W. (1983). *Strategy of discourse comprehension*. New York: Academic Press.

VanEssen, D. C. (1985). Functional organization of primate visual cortex. In A. Peters & E. G. Jones (Eds.), *Cerebral cortex: 3*. New York: Plenum.

VanLehn, K. (1989). Problem solving and cognitive skill acquisition. In M. Posner (Ed.), *Foundations of cognitive science*. Cambridge, MA: MIT Press.

Vokey, J. R., & Brooks, L. R. (in press). Taming the clever unconscious: Analogic and abstractive strategies in artificial grammar learning. *Cognition*.

Von Neumann, J., & Morgenstern, O. (1944). *Theory of games and economic behavior*. New York: Wiley.

Vosniadou, S., & Ortony, A. (Eds.) (1989). *Similarity and analogical reasoning*. Cambridge, England: Cambridge University Press.

Vosniadou, S., & Brewer, W. F. (1987). Theories of knowledge restructuring in development. *Review of Educational Research, 57*, 51–56.

Voss, J. F., & Post, T. A. (1988). On the solving of ill-structured problems. In M. T. H. Chi, R. Glaser, & M. J. Farr (Eds.), *The nature of expertise*. Hillsdale, NJ: Erlbaum.

Wallace, B. (1984). Apparent equivalence between perception and imagery in the production of various visual illusions. *Memory & Cognition, 12*, 156–162.

Wallace, R. A. (1973). *The ecology and evolution of animal behavior*. Pacific Palisades, CA: Goodyear.

Wallas, G. (1926). *The art of thought*. New York: Harcourt Brace Jovanovich.

Wanner, E., & Maratsos, M. (1978). An ATN approach to comprehension. In M. Halle, J. Bresnan, & G. A. Miller (Eds.), *Linguistic theory and psychological reality*. Cambridge, MA: MIT Press.

Ward, W. C., & Jenkins, H. M. (1965). The display of information and the judgement of contingency. *Canadian Journal of Psychology, 19*, 231–241.

Warren, R. M. (1970). Perceptual restoration of missing speech sounds. *Science, 167*, 392–393.

Warren, R. M., & Warren, R. P. (1970). Auditory illusions and confusions. *Scientific American, 223*, 30–36.

Wason, P. C. (1960). On the failure to eliminate hypotheses in a conceptual task. *Quarterly Journal of Experimental Psychology, 12*, 129–140.

Wason, P. C., & Evans, J. St. B. T. (1975). Dual processes in reasoning. *Cognition, 3*, 141–154.

Wason, P. C., & Green, D. W. (1984). Reasoning and mental representation. *Quarterly Journal of Experimental Psychology, 36A*, 597–610.

Wason, P. C., & Johnson-Laird, P. N. (1972). *Psychology of reasoning: Structure and content*. London: Batsford.

Wasow, T. (1989). Grammatical theory. In M. I. Posner (Ed.), *Foundations of cognitive science*. Cambridge, MA: MIT Press.

Wasserman, E. A., & Neunaber, D. J. (1986). College student's responding to and rating of contingency relations: The role of temporal contiguity. *Journal of the Experimental Analysis of Behavior, 46*, 15–35.

Watanabe, S. (1969). *Knowing and guessing: A formal and quantitative study*. New York: Wiley.

Watkins, M. J. (1975). Inhibition in recall with extralist "cues." *Journal of Verbal Learning and Verbal Behavior, 14*, 294–303.

Wattenmaker, W. D., Nakamura, G. V., & Medin, D. L. (1988). Relationships between similarity-based and explanation-based categorization. In D. Hilton (Ed.), *Contemporary science and natural explanation: Commonsense conceptions of casuality*. Brighton, England: Harvester Press.

Weaver, P. A., & Dickinson, D. K. (1982). Scratching below the surface structure: Exploring the usefulness of story grammars. *Discourse Processes, 5*, 225–243.

Weber, R. J., & Dixon, S. (1989). Invention and gain analysis. *Cognitive Psychology*, *21*, 283–302.

Weir, R. H. (1966). Some questions on the child's learning of phonology. In F. Smith & G. A. Miller (Eds.), *The genesis of language*. Cambridge, MA: MIT Press.

Weisberg, R. W. (1986). *Creativity: Genius and other myths*. New York: W. H. Freeman.

Weisberg, R. W., & Suls, J. (1973). An information processing model of Duncker's candle problem. *Cognitive Psychology*, *4*, 255–276.

Weldon, M. S., & Roediger, H. L. (1987). Altering retrieval demands reverses the picture superiority effect. *Memory & Cognition*, *15*, 269–280.

Wertheimer, M. (1945/1982). *Productive thinking*. Chicago: The University of Chicago Press.

Wexler, K., & Culicover, P. (1980). *Formal principles of language acquisition*. Cambridge, MA: MIT Press.

Wickelgren, W. A. (1969). Context-sensitive coding, associative memory, and serial order in (speech) behavior. *Psychological Review*, *76*, 1–15.

Wickelgren, W. A. (1974). *How to solve problems: Elements of a theory of problems and problem solving*. San Francisco: W. H. Freeman.

Wickens, C. D. (1980). The structure of attentional resources. In R. S. Nickerson (Ed.), *Attention and performance VIII*, Hillsdale, NJ: Erlbaum.

Wickens, C. D. (1984). Processing resources in attention. In R. Parassurment & D. R. Davies (Eds.), *Varieties of attention*. Orlando, FL: Academic Press.

Wickens, D. D. (1972). Characteristics of word encoding. In A. W. Melton & E. Martin (Eds.), *Coding processes in human memory*. Washington, DC: V. H. Winston & Sons.

Williams, D. R., & Williams, H. (1969). Automaintenance in the pigeon: Sustained pecking despite contingent non-reinforcement. *Journal of the Experimental Analysis of Behavior*, *12*, 511–520.

Winograd, T. (1972). *Understanding natural language*. New York: Academic Press.

Winston, P. J. (1980). Learning and reasoning by analogy. *Communications of the Association for Computing Machinery*, *23*, 689–703.

Woodworth, R. S., & Sells, S. B. (1935). An atmosphere effect in formal syllogistic reasoning. *Journal of Experimental Psychology*, *18*, 451–460.

Yaniv, I., & Meyer, D. E. (1987). Activation and metacognition of inaccessible stored information: Potential bases for incubation effects in problem solving. *Journal of Experimental Psychology: Learning, Memory, and Cognition*, *13*, 187–205.

Yeni-Komshian, G. H., & Soli, S. D. (1981). Recognition of vowels from information in fricatives: Perceptual evidence of fricative-vowel coarticulation. *Journal of the Acoustical Society of America*, *70*, 966–975.

Yin, R. K. (1969). Looking at upside-down faces. *Journal of Experimental Psychology*, *81*, 141–145.

Yonas, A. (1979). Attached and cast shadows. In C. F. Nodine & D. F. Fisher (Eds.), *Perception and pictorial representation*. New York: Praeger.

Zaragoza, M. S., & McCloskey, M. (1989). Misleading postevent information and the memory impairment hypothesis: Comment on Belli and reply to Tversky and Tuchin. *Journal of Experimental Psychology: General*, *118*, 92–99.

Zeki, S. M. (1978). Functional specialization of the visual cortex of the rhesus monkey. *Nature*, *274*, 423–428.

COPYRIGHTS AND ACKNOWLEDGMENTS

Fig. 1.1   From *Perceptual organization* by Kubovy/Pomerantz. Copyright © 1981 by Lawrence Erlbaum Associates, Inc. Reprinted by permission.

Figs. 2.1, 2.2   From *Parallel distributed processing, 2. Psychological and Biological Models*, by D. E. Rumelhart, J. L. McClelland and the PDP Research Group, etc. Cambridge, MA: MIT Press, Bradford Books.

Fig. 2.3   From *Approaches to Cognition*, by T. Knapp & L. Robertson, eds. Copyright © 1986 by Lawrence Erlbaum Associates, Inc. Reprinted by permission.

Fig. 2.4   "Ecological constraints on internal representation: Resonant Kinematics of Perceiving, Imagining, Thinking and Dreaming" from *Psychological Review, 91*, 417–447. Copyright © 1984 by the American Psychological Association. Reprinted by permission.

Fig. 3.1   "Behavioral Regulation of the Milieu Interne in Man and Rat" by J. Garcia, in *Science* September 6, 1974, Volume 185. Reprinted by permission.

Fig. 3.4   "Acquisition and extinction of a verbal conditioned response with differing percentages of reinforcement" by D. A. Grant, H. W. Hake and J. P. Hornseth, in *Journal of Experimental Psychology*, 1951, 42, 1–5.

Fig. 4.2   From *Perception and Communication*, by D. E. Broadbent, (1958, Pergammon). By permission of Oxford University Press.

Fig. 4.4   Daniel Kahneman, *Attention and Effort*, © 1973, p. 10. Reprinted by permission of Prentice-Hall, Inc., Englewood Cliffs, NJ.

Figs. 4.5, 4.6, 4.7   From "Controlled and Automatic Human Information Processing: 1. Detection, Search and Attention" by W. Schneider and R. Shiffrin, 1977, *Psychological Review*, 84. Copyright 1977 by the American Psychological Association. Reprinted by the permission of the publisher.

Fig. 5.2   Adapted from "Attached and cast shadows" by A. Yonas in C. F. Nodine and D. F. Fisher (eds.) *Perception and Pictorial Representation*. Copyright 1979 by Praeger Publishers. Reprinted by permission of Greenwood Publishing Group, Inc., Westport, CT.

Fig. 5.6   From "Principles of object perception" by E. S. Spelke, *Cognitive Science, 14*, 29–56. Reprinted by permission of Ablex Publishing Corporation.

Fig. 5.7   Gibson, James J. *The Perception of the Visual World*. Copyright © 1977, 1951 by Houghton Mifflin Company. Used with permission.

Fig. 5.8   Hochberg, J. *Perception*, 2nd ed., Englewood Cliffs, NJ: Prentice-Hall, 1978. Reprinted with permission of the author.

Figs. 5.9, 5.10   From *The Structure of Human Memory* by Charles N. Cofer. Copyright © 1976 by W. H. Freeman and Company. Reprinted by permission.

Fig. 10.4 "On learning the past tenses of English verbs" in *Parallel Distributed Processing: Explorations in the Microstructure of Cognition, Vol. 2* by J. L. McClelland, D. E. Rumelhart & the PDP Research Group. Cambridge, Mass.: Bradford Books, MIT Press.

Fig. 11.1 "Children's conceptions of the Earth as a cosmic body: A cross age study" by J. Nussbaum, 1979. *Science Education, 63*, 83–93. Reprinted by permission of John Wiley & Sons, Inc.

Figs. 11.2, 11.3 "Development of intuitive theories of motion: Curvilinear motion in the absence of external forces" by M. K. Kaiser, M. McCloskey, & D. R. Proffitt. *Developmental Psychology, 22*, 67–71. Reprinted by permission of the publisher.

Fig. 12.3 "Features of similarity" by A. Tversky, *Psychological Review, 84*, 327–352. Reprinted by permission of the publisher.

Fig. 12.5 "Implicit learning and tacit knowledge" by A. S. Reber. *Journal of Experimental Psychology: General, 118*, 219–235.

Fig. 13.1 "Prospect theory: An analysis of decision under risk" by D. Kahneman & A. Tversky. *Econometrica, 47*, 1979, 263–291. Reprinted by permission of The Econometric Society.

Fig. 13.2 "Physicians' use of probabilistic information in a real clinical setting" by J. J. J. Christensen-Szalanski & J. B. Bushyhead. *Journal of Experimental Psychology: Human Perception and Performance, 7*, 928–935. Reprinted by permission of the publisher.

Fig. 14.2 "Structure-mapping: A theoretical framework for analogy" by D. Gentner. *Cognitive Science, 1*, 155–170. Reprinted by permission of Ablex Publishing Corporation.

Fig. 15.2 "Representation and transfer in problem solving" by K. Kotovsky & D. Fallside in *Complex information processing: The contributions of Herbert A. Simon* by D. Klahr & K. Kotovsky (eds.), Hillsdale, NJ: Lawrence Erlbaum Associates, Inc.

Fig. 15.3 From *How to Solve Problems: Elements of a Theory of Problems and Problem Solving* by Wayne A. Wickelgren. Copyright © 1974 by W. H. Freeman and Company. Reprinted by permission.

Fig. 16.1 "The mind's eye in chess" by W. G. Chase & H. A. Simon. In W. G. Chase (ed.) *Visual information processing*. Reprinted by permission of Academic Press.

Fig. 16.2 "Categorization and representation of physics problems by experts and novices" by M. T. H. Chi, P. J. Fletovich, and R. Glaser. *Cognitive Science, 5*, 121–152.

Fig. 16.3 "Invention and gain analysis" by R. J. Weber and S. Dixon in *Cognitive Psychology, 21*, 283–302. Reprinted by permission of the publisher and the author.

Chapter opening quotations by Herman von Helmholtz on page 146 from *Treatise on Physiological Objects* edited by J. P. C. Southall, 1925, III. © 1925, Optical Society of America.

Excerpts on pages 171–172 from B. Milner (1966), "Amnesia following operation on the temporal lobes" in C. W. M. Whitty & O. L. Zangwill (Eds.), *Amnesia*, Butterworth-Heinemann. Reproduced by permission of the publisher.

Excerpts on pages 471–472 from "Schema induction and analogical transfer" from *Cognitive Psychology* by M. L. Gick and K. J. Holyoak, © 1983, Academic Press.

AUTHOR INDEX

Subject Index

B 3
C 4
D 5
E 6
F 7
G 8
H 9
I 0
J